THE FUTURE OF LITERARY THEORY

EDITED BY
RALPH COHEN

ROUTLEDGE • NEW YORK & LONDON

Published in 1989 by

Routledge
An imprint of Routledge, Chapman and Hall, Inc.
29 West 35 Street
New York, NY 10001

Published in Great Britain by

Routledge
11 New Fetter Lane
London EC4P 4EE

Library of Congress Cataloging in Publication Data

The Future of literary theory / edited by Ralph Cohen.
    p.   cm.
  ISBN 0-415-90077-8; ISBN 0-415-90078-6 (pbk.)
    1. Criticism. 2. Literature—History and criticism—Theory, etc.
  I. Cohen, Ralph, 1917–
  PN441.F8   1989
  801'.95—dc19   88-31880
                                                                                    CIP

British Library Cataloguing in Publication Data

The Future of literary theory
    1. Literature. Criticism
    I. Cohen, Ralph, 1917–
    801'.95
    ISBN 0-415-90077-8
        0-415-90078-6 (pbk.)

Contents

Introduction

Ralph Cohen

In reading and rereading these original essays prepared for this anthology, I find myself witnessing a process of transformation. It is as though the concept of "theory" as model building, as hypotheses about meaning, as governed by "evidence," "observation," and tested by "validity" was being converted into new concepts of the self, of evidence, of meaning of model building, of validity. It is as though one were watching the transformation of a caterpillar into a butterfly. Each form of theory writing has its own shape and function and yet is related to earlier forms.

Why this collection? Because we are in the midst of rapid changes in the practice of literary theory and we need to understand why received views of formalism, of literary history, of literary language, of readers, writers, and canons have come to be questioned, revised or replaced. Because we need to examine why and how the writing of theory is undergoing revision. Because the very process of literary change needs to be examined in order to realize which components of past theories are continued and which are abandoned. Because the writing of theory can be enjoyed aesthetically as well as cognitively as its structure changes.

The essays in this collection are densely interrelated. No short introduction can deal adequately with the issues they raise. I wish, therefore, to confine my remarks to the rationale of a literary change which these essays imply. I make this choice because many literary theorists, when they discuss change, rely on scientific models of paradigm change or cultural models of epistemic change or political models of social change, rather than on models appropriate to what takes place in literary theory and practice. Hans Robert Jauss points out in his essay that changes in literary theory can result from lacunae in previous theories, from proposing new perspectives for current theories, from asking new questions.

The contributors to this collection discuss present and incipient directions of theory in terms not always recognizable in the usual models. I have chosen four types of theory change to explain the directions theory is taking: I. Political Movements and the Revision of Literary Theory; II.

Incorporating Deconstructive Practices, Abandoning Deconstructive Ends; III. Non-Literary Disciplines and the Extension of Literary Theory; IV. Seeking the New, Redefining the Old, and the Pleasures of Theory Writing.

I. Political Movements and the Revision of Literary Theory

It is self-evident that feminist theorists and black theorists are part of large political and cultural movements whose agenda demands equality in the marketplace, in social space, in the political arena, in educational institutions. Feminist and black literary theories are thus oppositional to received theories that support, directly or indirectly, the status quo in literary studies. These theorists are powered by resentment against exclusion, against a literary tradition that has disregarded or been ignorant of alternative traditions. When theorists from such groups or those supportive of them enter the academy and theorize about writing, they write in opposition to established theory and its procedures of exclusion. They redefine literary "theory" by relating it to new ends. Thus, for a black critic like Henry Louis Gates, Jr. literary theory must recognize and validate a black vernacular tradition and generalizations about it.

> We must redefine "theory" itself from within our own black cultures, refusing to grant the racist premise that theory is something that white people do, so that we are doomed to imitate our white colleagues, like reverse black minstrel critics done up in white face. We are all heirs to critical theory, but we black critics are heir to the black vernacular critical tradition as well. Our task now is to invent and employ our own critical theory, to assume our own propositions, and to stand within the academy as politically responsive parts of a social and cultural African-American whole.

The feminist critics, too, seek to redefine literary theory so that it provides a body of generalizations about gender differences and their literary consequences, making theory responsive to gender and cultural differences between male and female readers and writers. Gates's essay and the feminist essays explain that formalist literary theory as a "meaning" model conceals the social and political functions of theory and overlooks the differences in tradition that characterize black and white, male and female readers and writers.

Their redefinition of theory proceeds not merely by a change of aim, but also by addition of components such as autobiography, anecdotes of exploitation or oppression, discussions of gender and of cultural differences. Such a revised concept places at the forefront of its argument the impact of theory upon social and political attitudes, though it does not deny that theory needs to generalize properly and study particular works. Cultural critics in general seek to make readers self-conscious of the ideology that writing imposes upon them. In this respect, feminist and black literary theorists often align themselves with Marxist and Marxist revisionary historians to trace and describe procedures of class conflict and exploitation. Some feminist theorists also align themselves with psychoanalysts, especially Lacan, to offer new theories of the self.

The reader will, upon reading the essays of Catharine Stimpson, Sandra Gilbert and Susan Gubar, and Elaine Showalter, readily recognize how complex, balanced and heuristic they are in their social and literary analyses. For these essays, despite agreements upon gender difference, chart disagreements about methods, about the nature of a feminist tradition, about differences among women. I quote from Catharine Stimpson's essay which describes the range of feminist theorizing:

> Some of the strongest feminist criticism shows how far "inside" one, or more, of the boundaries of power many women writers are; how much might divide them from a reader, female or male, who is "outside" those boundaries. In the 1970s, despite Woolf's doubts, Charlotte Brontë was a magnetic figure for feminist critics; the fictive autobiography of Jane Eyre an arche-narrative. Yet, in the 1970s Marxist feminist critics revealed the ideological assumptions about class in *Shirley*. In the 1980s, Third World critics have spoken on *Jane Eyre* as a "cult text" that underwrites the "axiomatics" of imperialism. Why must Bertha die if Plain Jane is to live?
>
> Showing that some women have had some power helps to erode the representation of all women as powerless, which a brand of feminist theory has mistakenly proposed. Fidelity to complexity respects women's lives. In addition, presenting the differences among women helps to erode the attraction of falsely universal descriptions of women and sexual difference. The commonality of the female becomes nothing more, nothing less, than an accident of birth, a chromosomal draw. This, in turn, can erode the general attraction of the falsely universal. These moves are the promise of a critical method I call "herterogeneity." Herterogeneity is the marking of differences among women, for themselves and as a way of recognizing and living generously with all but homicidal difference/s—among tongues and texts; tribes and territories; totems and some taboos.

The social and political nature of these theories should be acknowledged as academic manifestations of much larger non-academic movements that struggle to realign the economic, sexual, and racial places of women and minorities in society. But although contributors primarily address a university audience, they still aim to change how readers read, think, and write. It is not a matter of changing individuals, but of making them conscious of the groups to which they belong and to teach them to read oppositionally texts that support the prejudices of an exclusionary society.

But the fact that most of the feminist and black critics are themselves institutionally based delimits both their vocabulary and their contribution to the larger non-academic audiences they wish to change. This represents a paradox that has not yet been resolved; it remains a problem for the future of theory. This paradox is nowhere more obvious than in the university classroom where students are confronted by different literary perspectives and vocabularies. In such an environment, oppositional critics often find themselves welcomed into mainstream departments and find that some of their oppositional vocabulary is appropriated by theorists who do not see themselves as oppositional. The university tends to modify as well as to clarify the nature of oppositions as can be seen in Gates's view of the function of the black theorist in the 1980s.

> My task—as I see it—is to help to guarantee that Black and so-called Third World literature is taught to Black and Third-World (and white) students by Black and Third World and white professors in heretofore white mainstream departments of literature and to train university graduate and undergraduate students to think, to read, and even to *write* clearly, helping them to expose false uses of language, fraudulent claims and muddled arguments, propaganda and vicious lies, from all of which our people have suffered just as surely as we have from an economic order in which we were zeroes and a metaphysical order in which we were absences. These are the "values" that should be transmitted through black critical theory.

The function of the black critic in the academy, according to Gates, is not the function of a white critical theorist like Gerald Graff—no matter how much opposition they may share. Graff sees the university as an arena of conflict and of efforts toward conflict accommodation. The academy hosts teachers who oppose the teaching of theory altogether as well as those who practice it. To those who oppose it (because they believe it to be irrelevant to reading pleasure or to analyzing the inimitable character of literary texts) Graff correctly insists on the theoretical implications of such resistances.

> Whatever a teacher says about a literary work, or leaves unsaid, presupposes a theory—of what literature is or can be, of which literary works are worth teaching and why, of how these works should be read and which of their aspects are most worth being noticed and pointed out.

And this resistance to theory, to enacting a change in formulations or practices is also found among art historians. Rosalind Krauss notes this resistance in her discussion of art historians:

Art historians are shy of theory, rarely enunciating the ones they must undoubtedly have in order to be able to work at all. Theories of historical change. Theories of continuity. Theories of representation. Theories of the role of form. Theories of referentiality. Theories of function. And most important, theories of verification. For art history is proud of its roots in the German soil of *Wissenschaft*, even before that of *Geschichte*.

The teachers who hold these entrenched positions approve, as many oppositional theorists do, the policy of plural perspectives in the classroom. But the isolation of different perspectives also isolates the possibility of change. In combatting this view, Graff advocates a teaching procedure in which conflicting theories are neither mediated nor ignored but made "part of what education is about." And in this view he has a strong ally in Alasdair MacIntyre who argues for the recognition and exposure of conflicts that now characterize the study and teaching of the humanities:

> a contemporary humanistic education cannot avoid being an initiation into those conflicts, conflicts in which each of us cannot but be partisan and which our partisanship is so integral to our stance as scholars and teachers that we owe it to our colleagues and to our students as well as to ourselves to identify ourselves within the academy in terms of it.[1]

What Graff and MacIntyre ask for is teaching that carefully lays out the argument of a position together with the rationale for holding it. The procedure would be a demonstration of how critical and theoretical thinking can proceed without denying that other examples of critical thinking are possible as a result of different ends. No matter how careful one is to propound a particular position, one is, in this procedure, faced with an impasse: two irreconcilable and unmediatory positions.

The idea of change here is in the theory of teaching, not in the theory of literature. Although the procedure is to permit oppositional critics to develop their theories with care, it does as much for the teaching of entrenched criticism. Such a position, however useful as a teaching procedure, leaves unexplored the obvious fact that literary theories do change. It seems, therefore, that a conflict model neglects to inquire into construction of theories or perspectives. As forms of writing these possess components such as aims, methods, vocabularies, images, arguments that are not all in conflict. Indeed, for conflict to exist there must be some aspects both wish to achieve despite differences in methods or discourses.

Christopher Butler, however, suggests that changes with regard to the theories of the self, for example, are the result of significant groups of people talking about human identity in one way rather than another: "We will create the self of the reader by the vocabularies we devise to describe him or her, and not attempt to discover it by attempting to adjudicate between two models." But can we avoid asking how new vocabularies are devised? This surely is a problem for the future of literary theory, though one possible solution is offered by Elaine Showalter in defining connections between feminist and Afro-American theories usually opposed to one another.

> Both feminist and Afro-American criticism have brought together personal, intellectual, and political issues in our confrontations with the Western literary tradition. We have both followed traditional patterns in the institutionalization of critical movements, from our beginnings in a separatist cultural aesthetics, born out of participation in a protest movement; to a middle stage of professionalized focus on a specific text-milieu in an alliance with academic literary theory; to an expanded and pluralistic critical field of expertise on sexual or racial difference. Along with gay and postColonial critics, we share many critical metaphors, theories, and dilemmas, such as the notion of a double-voiced discourse; the imagery of the veil, the mask, or the closet; and the problem of autonomy versus mimicry and civil disobedience.

II. Incorporating Deconstructive Practices, Abandoning Deconstructive Ends

There can be no doubt that the essays by Hillis Miller and Geoffrey Hartman and Jonathan Culler describe deconstructive theory in decline. Hillis Miller, a leader of this movement, writes that Paul de Man thought "that *the* task of criticism in the coming years could be a kind of imperialistic appropriation of all literature by the method of rhetorical reading often called 'deconstruction'." But he adds that not only has the task not been carried out with much systematic rigor since 1979, but "there has been a shift away from an interest in 'reading', to various forms of hermeneutic interpretation, which means a focus on the relation of language to something else, God, nature, society, history, the self, something presumed to be outside language. There has been, by one of those (perhaps inexplicable, certainly 'overdetermined') displacements of interest, a tremendous increase in the appeal of psychologistic and sociological theories of literature, such as Lacanian feminism, Marxism, Foucaultianism."

It is Hillis Miller's contention that "the study of literature has a great deal to do with history, society, and the self, but that this relation is not a matter of thematic reflection within literature of these extralinguistic forces and facts, but rather a matter of the way the study of literature offers perhaps the best opportunity to identify the nature of language as it may have effects on what de Man calls 'the materiality of history'.

Here 'reading', in the sense of rhetorical analysis of the most vigilant and patient sort, is indispensable. How else are we going to know just what a given text is and says, what it can do?"

Yet many of the articles in this volume do just that—insist on close and careful reading of texts. I have quoted Gates above, and close reading can be found in Gilbert and Gubar's analysis of "Khubla Khan" as well as in the essays by Graff and Christopher Butler. Hillis Miller quotes from an essay by Jonathan Culler on "The Future of Criticism" and indicates his agreement with its statements:

> The struggle against the debilitating effects of mass culture must take place on a different front: by teaching critical thinking, perhaps by analyzing the ideological status and structures of mass media productions and exposing the interests at work in their functioning. Arguments about what literary works and what historical knowledge to require will only distract attention from the pressing problem of how to insure that schools encourage intellectual creativity, teach critical thinking, close reading, analysis of narrative structures and semiotic mechanisms.[2]

This statement, when compared with the feminist's arguments and those of Gates, makes very apparent the shift in theoretical priorities that has taken place. What Culler brackets as a distraction—"Arguments about what literary works and what historical knowledge to require will only distract attention from the pressing problem . . . "—is essential for making a change in theory according to Gates and the feminist contributors to this collection. The creation of a feminist tradition or black tradition in literature requires bibliographical search in pursuit of appropriate texts. It is not a matter that can be made ancillary to a revised theory; rather it makes such theory possible. For theories rest upon the range of texts to which they refer. As Alastair Fowler puts it, "In the last resort, literary theory is only as comprehensive and as penetrating as the reading it is based on."

Hillis Miller writes that our "fundamental task, the new rationale of the humanities, is to teach reading and the effective writing that can only come from or accompany a sophisticated ability to read." This legacy of deconstruction is incorporated into theories that have aims which resist deconstructive views of language and humanism. The theoretical changes such theories introduce do not discard deconstruction as a whole. If we consider Jonathan Culler's listing of the contributions Paul de Man has made to literary theory and criticism, we realize that some of these have been incorporated into theories that abandon de Man's attitudes to grammar, rhetoric, and language. Even when theorists incorporate his views of reading, they add to them the hypothesis that value assumptions govern readings. Reading involves the values that one wishes to test or discover or confirm. Particular readings are connected with values that are confronted by others who oppose them. Reading can even reveal values that were unanticipated.

Martha Nussbaum, in a detailed study of Henry James's *The Ambassadors* based on its structure and its ethical implications, argues that Derrida and other theorists have failed to deal with an obvious fact about literature: "It speaks *about us*, about our lives and choices and emotions, about our social existence and the totality of our connections." Her argument is that literary theory needs ethical theory to clarify "what it is that works of literature offer to our sense of life" and to raise ethical questions pertinent to the values the text offers but does not explore. On the other hand, the study of a novel like *The Ambassadors* makes important contributions to ethical theory by enriching our understanding of the question, "How Should One Live?" A literary theory that deals profoundly with ethical questions

> gestures toward the limits of ethical consciousness, making us aware of the deep elements in our ethical life that in their violence or intensity lead us outside of the ethical attitude altogether, outside of the quest for balanced vision and perfect rightness. It can include or at least indicate, the silence into which its own responsive prose has no entry.

What is taking place in Nussbaum's essay is a perception of literary theory that would lead to a reconceptualization of knowledge, a study of the structure and artistry of "major" literary texts as explorations of feelings, thoughts, and actions in ethical contexts. And literary theory would operate in conjunction with systematic ethical texts to control and expand the inquiry. In this respect it might indeed analyze the structure of formal ethical texts to assess the formulations of ethical issues in the two different kinds of texts.

III. Non-Literary Disciplines and the Extension of Literary Theory

It needs to be stated, and this collection makes it clear, that literary theory or its components, have affected and altered conceptions of disciplines from psychoanalysis to history, sociology, anthropology and art history. Roy Schafer, for example, argues that different psychoanalytic schools are governed by different perspectives that control the evidence and the results:

> each perspective seems to bring about somewhat different types of phenomena, with theory-specific implications, that can be taken to indicate change for the better. This is why debate between schools of analysis over their relative effectiveness are never resolved and may be unresolvable, even if still worth debating.

And his discussion of the analyst and analysand, like the analysis of the structure of a text from a particular perspective of the reader, leads him to suggest that the analyst is no neutral observer; rather, he can create evidence by his analysis. He modifies this, however, by remarking that the "ideal analyst is well prepared to defer having arrived at the sense of any answer at all."

Schafer himself points to a number of correspondences between theoretical literary premises and those in his psychoanalytical views: just as the literary reader co-authors a text so that the analyst may be considered a co-author of the analysand's text; "Among these features that are shared by psychoanalytic and other readings are the mixture of conventionalized and individual narrative and interpretive approaches and the *therapeutic consequences of the work*"; "critical interpreters of an art work have their own scholarly and technical obligations" just as analysts fulfill their obligations "by trying conscientiously to help bring about good results."

My point here is that literary theory has helped shape some current views of psychoanalytical theory, and that it is one-sided to assume that literary theory is the parasite that feeds upon psychoanalytic theory. The case is often otherwise—that what is selected from psychoanalysis is what was and is available in literary theory.

The extensive role that literary theory plays in the analysis of historical writing has been argued by Hayden White in numerous books and articles.

> It is because historical discourse utilizes structures of meaning-production found in their purest forms in literary fictions that modern literary theory, and especially those versions of it oriented towards tropological conceptions of language, discourse, and textuality, is immediately relevant to contemporary theory of historical writing.

White points out that theorists of historical discourse cannot ignore literary theorists' new conceptions of language, speech, and textuality because these have "reproblematized an area of inquiry which, in historical theory at least, had for too long been treated as having nothing problematical about it." The new views of language in literary theory are far from definitive, involving disagreements about the indeterminacy of language, the nature of its acculturation, the interaction between grammar and rhetoric, the distinction between literary and non-literary language.

But insofar as literary theory is a discourse about discourses, it inevitably analyses the discourses of history and is, therefore, a theory of history as well as of literature. In White's terms, "modern literary theory must of necessity be a theory of history, historical consciousness, historical discourse, and historical writing." The different components of literary theory extend like a web through different disciplines, become a guide to interpretation, a source for correspondence, a basis for analysis. Thus Schafer can draw the concept of indeterminacy from a Derridean theory and the concept of co-authorship from a phenomenological theory.

The interaction of disciplines is implicit in the very title of Schafer's "The Sense of an Answer: Ambiguities of Interpretation in Clinical and Applied Psychoanalysis," since it refers to Kermode's *The Sense of an Ending: Studies in the Theory of Fiction;* implicit as well in the theory of perspectivism that presupposes unmediatory alternatives. It is explicit in Schafer's argument about the correspondences between text and reader and between analyst and analysand in constructing the latter's narrative. What this implies is that versions of literary theory have entered the discourse of psychoanalysis and that psychoanalytic writing can be considered a form of discourse for which literary theory provides the tools for analysis.

What does the future of literary theory look like to other non-literary theorists? To Martha Nussbaum, it offers procedures for the ethical analysis of major literary structures. It intersects with the texts of major philosophical works on ethics and tests them, questions them, and considers their claims in terms of careful structural analysis of particular works. Nussbaum thus offers a limited and specific version of interdisciplinarity directed at basic ethical questions about how we can best live. But she is cognizant of the limited audience for such inquiries, especially to those outside the academy. She asks, "Can any possible practical goal be achieved by subtle precise writing about books that most people in public life do not read anyway?" "Well," she replies, "what can we do but try?"

For Hayden White, literary theory that inquires into and generalizes assumptions about language is indeed a theory of history as well. For him, literary theory occupies a central role in the study of historical writing and poses no problem in relating popular accounts of events to sophisticated explanations. The analysis of discourses based on theories of discourse removes for him the highly problematic relation that literary theorists find in dealing, for example, with fictions of the Civil War and historical accounts of it. In this respect the historian challenges the literary theorists of language and narrative to reconsider questions about narrative and its components, about the interrelation of form to the content of narratives, about the inevitable assumptions or ideologies that underlie writing. Even when a crucial change occurs in a society, such as the shift from orality to literacy, beginning readers possess assumptions about knowledge that intervene in their reading. Brian Stock writes that

> if we are to reason consistently, we have to give up the notion that we
> are ever in direct contact with a reality that is totally independent of
> what goes on in our minds, even though the existence of that reality

is not called into doubt. Beginning readers do not read in the absence
of prior knowledge; even non-literates experiencing literate culture for
the first time come to the written word with their own agendas.

What relation literary theory has to the human mind and which aspects
of theory are persistent in response to writing is a problem of change
that merits future inquiry. To what extent must cultural change include
cultural continuity?

There is, therefore, for these theorists, no question of the impact of
literary theory upon theorizing in other disciplines, even though some
members of a discipline resist the application of literary theory to their
practices. In contrast to such resistances, Arthur Danto's conception of
literary theory reconceives it as the paradigm of the human sciences.
His hypothesis is that "texts, as literary artifacts, are projections and
extensions of the unifying structures of a self or a life. The principles,
whatever they are, that enable us to tell and follow stories, to construct
and read poetry, are the principles that bind lives into unities, that give
us the sense of chapters ending and of new ones beginning. The future
of criticism lies in making these principles explicit."

For Danto, the future opens the possibility of a change in the status
and conception of literary theory. The concept of unities in life and
literature is one of connections, not necessarily of coherence and he talks
of "history *Zusammenhangs*"—historical connections—of Foucault and
the textual connections of Derrida: "even if texts do not hold together
the way Derrida supposes they do . . . the scope of textual theory is
collectively widened and a redistribution of the map of learning is in
order." Literary criticism and theory, in Danto's conception, should lead
us to reexamine discontinuities, ruptures, gaps in terms of our comprehension of them. For although one grants these disruptions, they are
comprehended as forming some type of connection. The answers, for
Danto, as to what these connections or unities might be, lie within the
domains of criticism and theory.

IV. Seeking the New, Redefining the Old and the Pleasures of Theory Writing

Danto's request for principles that would establish literary criticism
and theory as studies in their own right is met in several essays in this
collection. Wolfgang Iser, for example, in "Towards a Literary Anthropology" not only asks new questions but provides answers to them. He
in no way denies the cultural impact of present criticism and theory, but
provides a framework that subordinates them to studies of fictions and
the imagination.

No one will deny the indexical value of literature both for history and society, but what emerges almost incidentally from this fact is the question *why* such a mirror as literature should exist, and how it enables us to find things out. Since literature as a medium has been with us more or less since the beginning of recorded time, its presence must presumably meet certain anthropological needs. What are these needs, and what does this medium reveal to us about our own anthropological make-up?

The needs that literature fulfills in the production of fictions is the need for human beings to extend themselves. The procedures of extension involve complicated interactions between fictions and imagination. Iser argues that those are not identical and that the individuality of different works arise from the variety of functions exemplified in the varied interrelations.

The objectives of such a theory are not merely to indicate the deficiencies of a culture, but to bring out desires, needs, and necessities that rightfully belong to it. This theory makes it possible, according to Iser, to have access to the possibilities of the unconscious in dreams. And it will make it possible for readers to achieve self-enlightenment. Literary anthropology

> may achieve a self-enlightenment of the human being—not to be brought about by the erstwhile encyclopedic accumulation of knowledge considered to be a prerequisite for education, but by elucidating our unconscious guidelines, thereby triggering a chronic process of reflexion which will no longer seek its fulfillment in some kind of ideal. Rather, this process will enable us to see through the attitudes offered to us, if not imposed on us by our everyday world.

The aim of seeing through attitudes offered us is a component of cultural theories discussed above, but the context in which they are discussed has been altered. The diagnosis of human conditions and a reappraisal of human faculties are aims that could be shared by the theoretical changes advocated by Stock and Danto. The changes lead to inquiries about how the imagination affects the construction of literature and literary theories. The impact of culture, the theoretical procedures that incorporate legacies while altering their function, the realization of how texts intersect with and thus alter each other are all present in the essays of this volume. Remapping humanistic knowledge through literary theory seems a recurrent theme. The future of literary theory, however, holds different possibilities for different critics.

Alastair Fowler and Jean-Marie Schaeffer, for example, contribute a new theory of genre, older versions of which are often dismissed by poststructuralist critics. Fowler writes:

Until now, genre theory has largely consisted of empirical listing of generic repertoires, or (more superficially still) of structuralism's aprioristic dichotomies. These preliminaries behind, it should now be possible to investigate how the features of generic repertoires are related functionally. Accepting that genres exist as cultural objects, we can go on to ask how they work. How, for example, does the diction of seventeenth century georgic, with its metaphorical generality ('finny drove'; 'scaly flocks'), relate to the kind's impulse of descriptive specificity?

Fowler's essay provides new perspectives upon the functioning of genres as cultural objects. But the theoretical change he proposes may prove far more radical than matters of function. He writes, "It might be no bad thing, in fact, for literary theory as a whole to be reformulated in terms of genre, rather as mathematics was in large part reformulated, earlier this century, in terms of set theory." The theoretical change in genre theory that he envisions is one that undertakes to explain the multiple changes that genres undergo: "In actual literature, such categories as historical kinds, modes and constructional types seem to overlap, change and change places in more fluid ways than most theorists have cared to admit."

Gregory Ulmer's personal essay can be understood in one sense as a genre study on the Foucauldian model. The change in theory he describes is the result of the new "nexus of history, politics, language, thought and technology in the last decade of this millenium." In structuring his essay ("mystory") in personal terms, he seeks a new perspective on theory. "Mystory is theory performed in the dimension of anecdotes." And he declares that "through mystory theory fits television." Other essays in this collection do not address the verbal component in films or television, though the theory of mixed media will certainly demand analysis in the future.

One further direction for the future lies in the analysis of the very language and structure of theories. For the components of theory and their combination may reveal unanticipated connections with regard to language, feeling and the themes of existence. Literary theory, by unmasking itself, may then appear more clearly as a necessary and desirable human act. The autobiographical statement of Hélène Cixous can serve as an example of a new way of composing theory, of revealing how writing became intertwined with herself and the other, how it was part of her body, her family, her culture, her ethnic identity, her gender, her sense of alienation and her awareness of mysteries beyond language.

> My writing was born in Algeria out of a lost country of the dead father and the foreign mother. Each of these traits which may seem to be chance or mischance became the causes and opportunities of my writing.

I have had the luck to have foreignness, exile, war, the phantom memory of peace, mourning and pain as the place and time of my birth. At the age of three I knew, among the flowers and their scents, that one could kill for a name, for a difference. And I knew that uprooting existed. But also good uprooting. I should give you a date as well, 1940 for instance. I saw that human roots know no borders and that under the earth, at the very bottom of the ladder of the world, the heart was beating.

My first others were the Arabs, the scarabaei, the French, the Germans. My first familiars were the hens, the rabbits, the Arabs, the Germans, etc.

And the tongue that was singing in my ears? It was languages: Spanish, Arabic, German, French. Everything on this earth comes from far off, even what is very near. I listened to all the languages. I sang in German. I also cackled with the hens. I lost myself often within the city of my birth. It was a veiled woman: it was a signifier. It was ORAN. I had everything:

OR-AN	-	HORS EN	-	ORAN-JE
(Golden-year)		(Outside-in)		(Oran-I: Orange)

The first of my treasures was the name of my native city which was Oran. It was my first lesson. I heard the name Oran and through Oran I entered the secret of language. My "sortie" occurred through entrance. I discovered that my city meant *fruit* through the simple addition of me. *Oran-je—Orange*. I discovered that the word held all the mystery of fruit. I will let you unravel to infinity the composition, decomposition of this name. Then I lost Oran. Then I recovered it, white, gold and dust for eternity in my memory and I never went back. In order to keep it. It became my writing. Like my father. It became a magic door opening onto the other world.

If I am asked why her essay begins this anthology, I reply that Cixous, novelist and dramatist and critic, writes theory out of a lyric sense of the place writing has in her life and how, despite the fact that writing can create for her a paradise or hell, it makes survival possible. Theory is for her a personal and public commitment to ethical and literary values. How better to begin a collection of essays on what literary theory can or ought to be?

Notes

1. "The Humanities and the Conflicts of and with Traditions," *Interpreting the Humanities*, II, Woodrow Wilson National Fellowship Foundation, 1986, p. 31.

2. The published version of this passage appears in *The Current in Criticism*, ed. Clayton Koelb and Virgil Lokke, Purdue University Press, 1987, pp. 31–32. The last sentence in this version reads as follows: "Argument about what literary works and what historical knowledge to require will only distract attention from the pressing problem of how to insure that schools encourage intellectual activity by teaching critical thinking, close reading, and the analysis of narrative structures and semiotic mechanisms."

1

From the Scene of the Unconscious to the Scene of History

Hélène Cixous

Everything I am going to say here is what I would truly have said to myself. Which will not mean that it will be "true" for everyone. For when it is a question of writing, it is always a question of, and can only be a question of, truth. I say *truth* and I am not saying knowledge and I am not saying consciousness. It is a question of unknown truths. Writing makes its way in the darkness of these truths. One doesn't know. One *goes*. I follow, eyes closed, what I feel. Feeling does not mislead.

It is in wanting to know that one is often deceived. I presage: then I seek to translate into words what is being written in fevers, in heartbeats, in luminous songs. I wonder what it is called.

I am not someone who loves darkness: I am in it. Through living it and traversing it and transposing it into words, it seems to me that it clears up, or simply that it becomes more welcoming to me.

I feel an affinity with all those who do not deny the existence of mysteries that beat in the breast of the world. What I do not understand, I respect.

I love the imminence of light. Its promise.

I will tell you the story of a path. Let me ask your forgiveness for saying "I": up to the present I have never said "I" in this manner. I speak of others. Allow me that, in saying "I," I may be speaking also of others. "I" is many other travelers whom I know and meet, just as Hofmannsthal, in "The Voyager," meets poets from the past, who are ever present.

In the beginning there was for me and there is for me *Paradise Lost* This paradise had a name, Algeria, which I experienced in the present

---

Translated by Deborah W. Carpenter

and which I discerned, through infantile prophecy and the anticipation of all my senses, to be already the country of memory. I feared, without knowing it, the disappearance of the maternal body.

My writing was born in Algeria out of a lost country of the dead father and the foreign mother. Each of these traits which may seem to be chance or mischance became the causes and opportunities of my writing.

I have had the luck to have foreignness, exile, war, the phantom memory of peace, mourning and pain as the place and time of my birth. At the age of three I knew, among the flowers and their scents, that one could kill for a name, for a difference. And I knew that uprooting existed. But also good uprooting. I should give you a date as well, 1940 for instance. I saw that human roots know no borders and that under the earth, at the very bottom of the ladder of the world, the heart was beating.

My first others were the Arabs, the scarabaei, the French, the Germans. My first familiars were the hens, the rabbits, the Arabs, the Germans, etc.

And the tongue that was singing in my ears? It was languages: Spanish, Arabic, German, French. Everything on this earth comes from far off, even what is very near. I listened to all the languages. I sang in German. I also cackled with the hens. I lost myself often within the city of my birth. It was a veiled woman: it was a signifier. It was ORAN. I had everything:

OR-AN	—	HORS EN	—	ORAN-JE
(Golden-year)		(Outside-in)		(Oran-I: Orange)

The first of my treasures was the name of my native city which was Oran. It was my first lesson. I had heard the name Oran and through Oran I entered the secret of language. My "sortie" occurred through entrance. I discovered that my city meant *fruit* through the simple addition of me. *Oran-je—Orange.* I discovered that the word held all the mystery of fruit. I will let you unravel to infinity the composition, decomposition of this name. Then I lost Oran. Then I recovered it, white, gold, and dust for eternity in my memory and I never went back. In order to keep it. It became my writing. Like my father. It became a magic door opening onto the other world.

Before the Father

You have before your eyes a rare and previous text by Clarice Lispector:

Sunday, Before Sleep

On Sundays, the family used to go to the quay of the port to watch for the ships. They leaned against the low wall, and if the father were still alive he would perhaps still have before his eyes the oily water, in such a way he stared at the oily water. The daughters worried obscurely, they called him to see something better: look at the ships, papa!, they instructed him worried. When it got dark, the illuminated city turned into a great metropolis with high and swiveling stools in each bar. The youngest daughter wanted to sit on one of the stools, the father found it amusing. And this was gay. (. . .) That was when she knew bar *ovomaltine*, never before such a great luxury in a tall glass, heightened more by the foam, the high and uncertain stool, *the top of the world.* Everyone waiting. (. . .) Also the astonished distrust that *ovomaltine* would be good, the one who isn't worth anything is me. (. . .) But all of that was surrounded by the father, and she was well within this small world in which walking hand in hand was the family. (. . .) Before falling asleep, in bed, in the darkness. Out of the window, on the white wall: the gigantic and fluctuating shadow of the boughs, as if of an enormous tree, which in truth did not exist in the patio, there only existed a meager bush; or the shadow of the moon. Sunday was always that immense night that engendered all of the other Sundays and engendered cargo ships and engendered oily water and engendered milk with foam and engendered the moon and engendered the giant shadow of a little tree.

Domingo, antes de dormir

Aos domingos a família ia ao cais do porto espiar os navios. Debruçavam-se na murada, e se o pai vivesse talvez ainda tivesse diante dos olhos a água oleosa, de tal modo ele fixava a água oleosa. As filhas se inquietavam obscuramente, chamavam-no para ver coisa melhor: olhe os navios, papai!, ensinavam-lhe elas inquietas. Quando escurecia, a cidade iluminada se tornava uma grande metrópole com banquinhos altos e giratórios em cada bar. A filha menor quis se sentar num dos bancos, o pai achou graça. E isso era alegre. (. . .) Foi quando conheceu *ovomaltine* de bar, nunca antes tal grosso luxo em copo alto, mais alteado pela espuma, o banco alto e incerto, *the top of the world.* Todos esperando. (. . .) Tambem a desconfiança assustada de que *ovomaltine* é bom, quem nao presta sou eu. (. . .) Mas tudo isso era rodeado pelo pai, e ela estava bem dentro dessa pequena-terra na qual caminhar de mão dada era a família. (. . .) Antes de adormecer, na cama, no escuro. Pela janela, no muro branco: a sombra gigantesca e flutuante dos ramos, como se de uma árvora enorme, que na verdade náo existia no pátio, só existia um magro arbusto; ou era sombra da lua. Domingo foi sempre aquela noite imensa que gerou todos os outros domingo e gerou navios cargueiros e gerou água oleosa e gerou leite com espuma e gerou a lua e gerou a sombra gigantesca de uma árvore pequena.

—Clarice Lispector[1]

---

[1] "Domingo, Antes de dormir," in *Para não esquecer* (SãoPaulo: Alicia, 1978).

I've included the Brazilian text because it presents itself immediately in a graphically more readable form. It's an admirable little text that narrates a Sunday. "Sunday was always that immense night that engendered all of the other Sundays and engendered cargo ships and engendered oily water and engendered milk with foam and engendered the moon and engendered the giant shadow of a little tree." In Brazilian "tree" is feminine, thus the text finishes on the note of "a little (she) tree." And this is what Sunday was, *domingo*, day of the master, day of the father. I'm displacing: the father was "always that immense night that engendered all of the other Sundays . . . and engendered the giant shadow of a 'little tree,' " whose other name was Clarice Lispector. Without engaging in a more precise analysis of this text, I want simply to suggest something both essential and banal: it is that *one begins to want to write in the presence of the father*, before the symbolic father, before the absent father—it's not a question of the real father—before the dead, ideal father, in order to please him, or, as the text puts it, in order to have the extraordinary experience of the "ovomaltine de bar"; in the Brazilian text *ovomaltine* is written in italics in a remarkable way, for here again is an oran-name. It's the mysterious thing with the foreign name that opens the path to pleasure. Before the father, in order to please him, one goes to a place from which to make the discovery of America, from which *to say the extraordinary words*. The key to the secret word "ovomaltine," or again to "the top of the world," is in His possession.

Upon reading this little text, some years ago, I rejoiced and was filled with wonder because it was like the poetic summary of my first text, called *Dedans*.[2] *Dedans* was necessarily written within the father, in seeking him right up to death and *revenant* (coming back, ghostly). There is something simple and mysterious in the origin of a writing: "I" am in the father I carry within me, he haunts me, I live him. There is a rapport between the father and language, the father and the "symbolic."

And the mother? She is music, she is there, behind, the force that breathes, the mother who obviously for all French writing is the sea, *la mer*. In my language we have the good fortune to be able to say that the mother is the sea, this makes up a part of our imaginations, it tells us something. In the English language the mother says m'other, my other.

The mother sings, the father dictates. I can take that for myself, but I can also give it Tsvetaeva, the great Russian poetess. (Read "My mother and music," one of her prose texts.)

One begins thus by wanting to conquer, to win love. Then—Enter death. The outside. All is lost. Everything is to be regained. I believe

---

[2] Trans. *Inside* (New York: Schocken Books, 1986).

that one can only begin to advance along the path of discovery, of discovery of writing or of something else, from the point of mourning or in the reparation of mourning. In the beginning the gesture of writing is linked to the experience of disappearance, to the feeling of having lost the key to the world, of having thrown it away. Having suddenly acquired the precious sense of the rare, the mortal, and having to regain, urgently, the entrance, the breath, having to keep the trace. We have to do the apprenticeship of Mortality.

Language as a Country

When I wrote *Dedans* it was in a certain sense inside and outside of the tomb of my father, or of every man, or, as Shakespeare would say, of neither man nor woman[3], in resistance to loss. My father my mother my country, they all lose, my language plays my father loss my mother sea my fathers my tongues. All is lost except words. This is experience as a child knows it: words are our doors towards all the other worlds. At a certain moment for the person who has lost everything, whether that means, moreover, a being or a country, language is what becomes the country. One enters the country of words. This is what has been done by all the contemporary Russian poets in an explicit manner. There is the other country, a marvelous country: one enters it through the love of language. It is a country where the poets live, those whom Kafka calls the "watchers" and whom Clarice Lispector would call the "secret agents"; the people who have in common the saving of the almost imperceptible keys to the world of survival. In this country the spatial terrestial geographic frontiers and also the time frontiers are erased: from century to century, the inhabitants communicate and transmit. This is the work of all those who teach and transmit and all those who practice an art. There everything is exile and nothing is exile. A *Correspondance à trois*[4] is formed, into thousands.

The great struggle has begun: the struggle of love and of death.

Those who love also engage themselves to die, those who love "fall" in love. Love reminds us of death. One of us will see the other die. In either case, me. Perhaps knowing that we are mortals and saving each minute, consecrating it to life, is the task that animates certain writings. For me, joining the party of life is itself my political party. There are people who are in the party of death in writing as in politics; this is something of which we speak very little, though it is essential. I go to

---

[3] *Hamlet*.
[4] *Correspondance à trois: Rilke, Pasternak, Tsvetaïeva* (Paris: Gallimard, 1983).

the side of those who have a drive toward redemption, protection, reanimation, reincarnation. One must protect the living and the dead. For it is possible to kill the dead, too, one can bury them, erase them to infinity. One must manage, through writing—through working at any equivalent of writing—to "give a hand to what one has lost," as Clarice Lispector would say.

And so it is a question of living and surviving. Writing follows life like its shadow, extends it, hears it, engraves it. It is a question of living to the end without losing sight of life for a minute, which is immense *work*.

I think of those who have tried to live life to its extremities, to the last hour. I think of Kafka. I think of magnificent works like the *Journal* of Etty Hillesum. This is a journal of life that was written by a young Jewish woman, twenty-seven years old, who lived in Amsterdam. She was like an older sister of Anne Frank. The journal was kept up all the way to the brink of Auschwitz where she died in 1943. It's an account which struggles from hour to hour to save, in the enclosure which becomes more and more narrow, more and more monstrous, the vestiges of life, until, when there is no more earth, the sky remains, then less and less sky, until finally no more sky at all. But she is living out an extreme force. And furthermore, this book contains another message which is for me a great happiness: Etty Hillesum read Rilke while sitting on a trash can in a tiny corner of the Jewish Consul, which had as a mission the expedition of the Jews to the oven. It was really a circle of the *Inferno*. She read Rilke in this world where the people hastened to not die, not die, to kill, she wrote this. It is what one can best hope for poetry: that it will serve in the face of death. Etty read Rilke right up to death. Rilke saved her, but she saved Rilke.

It is this living between poetry and death, with poetry and life, that allows us to know in an immediate sense that we are *in the process of living*, in the process of using a part of Creation, a part of the living thing that has been allotted and measured out to us. Living as if before birth or death, each day a first day and a last day. Joy and trembling. This is what writing serves as for me: it's a small trembling light in the darkness of the path. One writes from death toward death in life. One also writes between Hell and Paradise, because sometimes it is hell, sometimes paradise. Sometimes one screams and sometimes one sings. If I speak of hell and of paradise, it is because these are two essential motifs of our imaginations, our destiny and all writing.

Hell, Paradise. In the beginnings there is hell.

It seems to me that the story of writing always begins with hell. Just like the story of a life. First with the hell of the ego, with this primitive primordial chaos that is ours, these darknesses in which we struggle when we are young and from which we also construct ourselves. On emerging from this hell, be it simply the hell of the unconscious or a real hell, there is paradise. But what is Paradise? Hell is much easier to describe and depict, since we know it from Dante. Hell is incomprehension, it is dreadful mystery, and also the demonic or demoniac feeling of being nothing, controlling nothing, of being in the unformed, tiny, before the immense. And also of being bad and sometimes even evil. Our wickedness is one of vertiginous themes that opens the space of writing.

One writes in order to emerge from this hell in the direction of the hidden day. One writes toward what will prove at last to be the present. That's what paradise is, managing to live in the present. Acceptance of the present that occurs, in its mystery, in its fragility. It means accepting our lack of mastery, knowing that the present passes, but that this is good because it passes presently; it means knowing how to pass from anguish to astonishment and how to make the incomprehensible a source of wonder, it means loving the night, no longer dreading it, treating it like a star-flecked day. But that is work, difficult work, which, when we are still very young, we cannot even think of. It's the great work of living the instant, it requires a great rapidity of soul and at the same time a great slowness. That's why it occurred to me to say: "paradise is hell." It is not rest, but restlessness, the incessant effort to be there, confrontation with the exhausting richness of "there is," of "*Es gibt.*" At a certain moment one can hope to reach the point of writing not in order to mourn the past, but to become a prophet of the present. At that moment one has *paradise to do*, one does it. It is not given to us. We risk losing it, we regain it without cease.

The Dangers of Paradise

And it is thus that in paradise one runs into danger, because paradise is a balcony onto the hells of the world. In paradise one risks something which is discreetly called "forgetting." There again writing is entirely called for. One must not forget. Writing is in the end only an *anti-oubli*. It is in one's interest to write in order to both feel the passing of, and not forget that there is, hell. Writing is (should be) the act of reminding oneself of what is, in this very instant, of remembering what has never existed, remembering what could disappear, what could be put off limits, killed, scorned, remembering the far off, minimal things, turtles, ants, grandmothers, the good, first and burning passion, women, nomadic peoples, peoples who are exiled little by little, flights of wild ducks. We who are rich and free we are all the prisoners of liberty, we are prisoners in full liberty. Liberty blinds us, imprisons us.

Writing is perhaps the way to remember all those who have fought, who fight to save the human grain, the grass, the sky, the beauty of what is true or rather the truth of things, all kinds of beauty, it is the creation of a recognition-work; it is exploring and recognizing the tiny and the great, the fulgurant atrocity of apartheid, the tearing tenderness of the liberated prisoner for those who remain in prison, it is the taste of an Indian sweet. I will cite an anecdote which I find sublime: it concerns the great Russian poetess Akhmatova, dead in 1961, who went through all the setting in place of the Soviet century and whose first husband, a poet, was shot, the second husband dying in deportation, the son spending almost all his life in deportation. She used to stand in line outside the prisons of Leningrad, and one day (she recounts this): she is in line, the people have numbers, suddenly a faceless woman turns back toward her because the woman with no face in front of her tells her: Akhmatova, the great poetess, is standing behind you. And the facelss woman asks: could you know how to describe this? Akhmatova responded: yes. She did a little of what Etty Hillesum did with Rilke. Yes, she could know how to describe the indescribable, she would know how to give the gift of recognition to these people who had become faceless as a result of the greatest misery, the one which makes us into strangers to ourselves. I love the fact that she dared to say that and that she did it for everyone in giving the name, the right, the cry, to pain. Just as Etty Hillesum repeated: the sky is not yet rationed, I am happy.

The Writer is One of the Rich

Writing, in any case, when it is done from the bottom of the heart, is paradise even in hell. Writing always means being saved in a certain way. The writer is a rich person. This is for me the problem of being a writer. It is a paradoxical richness, both necessary and dangerous. For richness deprives us of the treasures of poverty. The poor have the treasures of those who have practically nothing. It is the source of marvelous tragic desires we don't have when we are rich. We have known this poverty, although we wouldn't even know it as true poverty. We have known it as children when we were outside poverty and outside richness, in the time when everything was dear, inaccessible, precious, much higher up than us. Could we go back to the time from "before the lobster?" I'm borrowing this metaphor from Clarice Lispector who said on writing a text about a very poor, almost inexistent little woman who has never in her life eaten more than bits of sausage sandwich: "but I have eaten lobster, how am I going to go about understanding this?" This is our problem. I also have eaten lobster, I was eighteen years old and, thank god, had an attack of indigestion.

How to write about those who do not write? We should present ourselves this problem. How was Clarice Lispector able to speak of Macabea, as she called her little character? How to grant oneself the project of writing about the Khmers? This is a question that has come back endlessly to me under its thousand different faces for the last twenty years. And it's only very recently that I've begun to offer it a response. It's a question of letting them speak, the Macabeas, the Khmers. But how does one let them speak? How to avoid putting my tongue before their tongue? I've found something which moreover has been granted to me: it's the theater that helps me let them speak. How to come to the theater, how to make changes of scene, a change of genre, when one "is" a fiction writer?

For me this is the end of an apprenticeship. I was not born a writer of drama. I believe this to be the case for many writers. There is a certain path of development to follow: it's the path of the self, one must develop in the self outside the self. In the theater one can only manage with a self that has almost evaporated, that has transformed itself into space. It's a self that has come to be reconciled with the difficulties of the world. But it is not given, it must be formed. It seems to me that there is an entire span of time, the time of the ego, which one must go through. One must become acquainted with this self, make a descent into the agitated secret of this self, into its tempests, one must cover this complex route with its meanderings into the chambers of the unconscious, in order to then emerge from me towards the other. The ideal: less and less of me and more and more of you. This cannot be a conscious aim. The meaning of this journey comes after it's over, but the itinerary is inevitable.

First of all *dedans*, the place where one makes acquaintance with mythologies, where one learns the secrets of narratives by way of dreams, where one collides with drives, which Freud called our Titans. One must go see what is taking place in reality, what is repressed, what prevents us from living or from thinking and which is always on an epic scale, though these are unformed and dangerous epics. One must go back to the origins, work on the mystery of origins, for this is how one comes to work on the mysteries of the end. Going to work on the question of *where?*, *where from?* in order to work next on *next*. And thus one can hope someday to arrive at the point of fulfillment where the ego will hold fast, will consent to erase itself and to make room, to become, not the hero of the scene, but the scene itself: the site, the occasion of the other.

Here is one of the most beautiful stories in the world: it is a story which so to speak does not exist. It enticed me to the point where I wrote a book on this story-that-does-not-exist, and I think that it continues to not exist in my book: *Limonade tout était si infini. Limonade es war alles so grenzenlos* is a sentence of Kafka's.[5] This is thus a story of Kafka. One day Kafka met someone who became one of his closest friends, Oscar Baum. Oscar Baum was blind: as a child he had lost his sight in an accident. Oscar Baum recounts how he met Kafka: he saw him. He *saw* him lean toward him. As if Oscar Baum could see someone lean very low to greet him. A greeting which happens also to be very much the Khmer greeting. And how was Oscar Baum able to see someone he could not see leaning over him? *By miracle.* Because Kafka had long hair, and, in bowing so low a litle wisp of his hair brushed against Oscar Baum's forehead. This is how Oscar Baum knew that Kafka had bowed low before him. He saw it. This is the scene itself of delicacy with regard to the other. Because Kafka behaved in this scene with the same regard for blind Oscar Baum as if Oscar Basum had been able to see, because he did not inscribe the blindness of Oscar Baum, he granted him sight, the duration of a greeting. And a God wanted Baum to be made aware of this; it's unique, Oscar Baum saw, in his blindness, Kafka bow to him.

Coming to the delicacy of Kafka is not given to everyone, it is only on the horizon of what one can hope for. But it is when one has been able to reach the moment of opening oneself completely to the other that the scene of the other, which is more specifically the scene of History, will be able to take place in a very vast way. I don't say I have reached this by myself. I have had many lessons from others.

Wendung[6]

The first lesson I received was that there was the *unhoped for other.* In my writing that took several turns. The first turn was the encounter with Clarice Lispector. Two people came to speak to me in 1977 of a writer named Clarice Lispector. I had never heard of her. *Editions des femmes* was preparing a book of hers. I glanced at some fragments of texts, I was dazzled, I took it to be a wonderful accident. And then as I went on in the text I discovered an immense writer, the equivalent for me of Kafka, with something more: this was a woman, writing as a woman. I discovered Kafka and it was a woman. This was at a time when I had written a lot and had read a lot and I was feeling a little lonely in literature. And then out of the blue I met this woman. It was unexpected. This

---

[5] This isn't a sentence from Kafka—the writer. It is a sentence from Franz, the man, no longer writing books, agonizing, writing only rapid and sublime messages of life, life-phrases, flashes of eternity. It is a last sentence. Perhaps the last. Its purity, its symbolic and yet concrete strength, its density, make it one of the most beautiful poems in the world. Yet it was not a poem. Only a sigh. And also the portrait of Regret.

[6] I have borrowed this title from Rilke's superb text.

gave me Clarice Lispector but also many other Clarice Lispectors. She was my contemporary. She was there and I didn't know it! If she could exist then it meant that still others existed. I was in the situation of the explorer who says to herself: there are at least ten Americas. And then I regained the hope of waiting, I could wait infinitely. It is as Mandelstam has sung: when one knows that a bottle with the poet's letter has been thrown into the sea, when one knows that one day a hand was out-stretched, then something will arrive, one will come upon the other and others will arrive. This law of meeting and sublime friendship has re-mained with me. Since then I have always hoped for unknowns to happen onto. Between times I have discovered some but there are still others. And that has reminded me that *there is promise*. From the moment that there has been, there will be, there is the other somewhere. This is essential to know.

And History?

After the other writing, the other thought, there are all the others and in particular the ones most difficult to reach and most immediately pres-ent, the peoples. And History? Terrible question that has haunted me without cease. It has long resonated for me as the echo of a fault. I didn't feel guilty but I was, or at least I wasn't guilty but I felt guilty, etc. I formulated and then dismissed my shame: you write when someone dies. My path is escorted by the phantoms of peoples, the whole span of my texts, they are there. At given moments I was haunted by Vietnam then by Greece then by Iran. My texts are filled with these peoples who suffered, who fell or pulled themselves up. Which History is mine? Of whose History am I the witness? How to unite History and text? I don't know which History is mine. Perhaps as a Jew it is Jewish History, but I haven't really known which one or how? I first came up with the answer of a particular period in time, and I defined myself as Jewoman, in a single word because it was simpler and truer that way. One cannot not speak of the scandals of an epoch. One cannot not espouse a cause. One cannot not be summoned by an obligation of fidelity.

It happens that at a certain moment of my life I found myself in the midst of women's History. That is not where I was when I began to write in 1966. In 1968 there was the explosion of women's History but I wasn't in it. Then at a certain moment I couldn't not be in it. It was impossible for me not to take it into account; to refrain from speaking of it was impossible for me morally and politically and thus I found myself in it and proceeded as far as I could go.

But in the domain of women nothing can be theorized. No science can say anything about it. The only thing one can say is that writing can, not tell or theorize it, but play with it or sing it. To hold discourse on it is to be overtaken by theoretical reduction. When one talks woman to you, you must *respond* and respond as if to an accusation. At the same time, I have always answered to the least ill effect for myself, all the while knowing and accepting that this is accompanied by a loss of eternity, of the undefined, of the limitless.

Being a woman cannot be demonstrated, it must be felt, it must make itself felt, it is the experience of a pleasure. But one cannot give proof of it, "one cannot prove the existence of what is more true," and, as Clarice Lispector would say, "skillfulness is believing, believing while crying." I believe that some believe and some live and others don't. I also believe that between those who live and feel, and those who do not feel, do not live, *there is no passage.* Except love. Those who live can lay hands on those who do not live and love them enough to make them understand, but this is an individual enterprise and one which requires a great deal of time.

Yes I am woman, I am in a rapport of fidelity to origins, to near relations. I am mother, daughter, I cannot stop myself from being woman. I say this as Sihanouk in my play says: I cannot stop myself from being Cambodia. This is not something which one escapes. And from one fidelity to another there is a good deal of understanding, as between difference and difference, as foreigners muster together, as from one sentiment of difference to another one can reach an understanding even in a foreign language. Thus, from difference to difference, I have come to something which may seem very different from what I have done up to the present: to the scene of theater, to the scene of History.

I have always thought that History could only be treated poetically in texts (unless one is a historian), that it had to be sung, that it should be an epic like the Iliad. History with its human face: Destiny. But does the epic still have its citizen's rights today? In the Theater, yes. The epic still exists there, it is a place where what one might call "legend" still exists.

Enter the Others

It is in the theater that I had my second meeting, and this meeting was multiple. The theater is the most marvelous place for someone who writes: it is really the *immediate* site of desire of the other, of desire of all the others. The great theoretician of the nô, Zeami, comes to mind. He lived in fourteenth-century Japan. His Book teaches all the secrets of this art made from the art of the text, the body's art, and the art of living. The *art of the spectator* makes up a part of the art of nô. The art of being a spectator. Of doing good to the spectator too. There are entire chapters of Zeami that detail very precisely, in the Japanese way, the work of the troupe, the actor, the director on the spectator. It is a labor of attention and reception. He says to you: according to the state of the spectators, which you will feel immediately, something is going to happen, and the nô will be played differently. If it is a little late at night for example, you must be more lively and fresh, you must wake the people up, even change the text, and we discover thus that the nô implies the audience in a very intense manner: in truth, the public is at work. That's what theater is: the desire of all the others. It's the desire of all the characters, the audience's desire, the actors' desire, the director's desire, it's the desire of the others that are us. And to get there, one must reach this state of *"démoïsation,"* this state of without me, of depossession of the self, that will make possible the *possession* of the author by the characters. This is the overwhelming experience the author has. While writing the play *L'Histoire terrible mais inachevée de Norodom Sihanouk, roi du Cambodge,* I was suddenly invaded by a whole people, very specific persons whom I didn't know in the least and who became my relatives for eternity. I ascertained then that this is exactly what happens to the actor. The true actor is someone whose ego is reserved and humble enough for the other to be able to invade and occupy him; he makes room for the other in an unheard of manner.

The Birth of Characters

Here is the way characters come to me. First, they are born. They are born through the chest. The heart is swollen. They are at first no more than a phrase, a sign, a smile, this is truly how they introduce themselves. And three lines later, there they are suddenly whole, upright, in the midst of destiny, in the midst of their story, with their worries, their hopes, their ways of conceiving the world. They then become my near relations, my supplemental family. One might think that they would return to the imagination from which they came. Not at all. They stay and mingle with us, they become ancient living realities, who, their own lives finished, retire—forever—in our memories.

This survival we owe to the actors. The life which they have given to a character is something no one can take back. It is like maternal love, absolutely given. But a character who is unloved, unadopted by his maternal defender, actor-actress, will, in front of the audience as before the gods, return to limbo. Actors are mothers. And the mothers are good or bad as usual. Some defend their children through love, and others through pride, as in the judgment of Solomon. One immediately recognizes the character who has been defended by love; for he becomes the world's child, he goes to the audience smiling, with trust, an innocent step, for he loves the whole world.

The first character of *L'Histoire Terrible* to emerge from my heart was King Suramarit. Dead and very much alive and altogether remarkable for his extreme vitality. He was the first, and I knew immediately that he would always be there, the most enduring, the most faithful, the most immortal, the most vast, and, in short, I loved and needed him.

Afterwards came the reactions, my own and those of others. Mine? I thought: here is the ferryman, the father and contemporary of the dead and the living, the guardian, the nurse, true king of the Theater, the one who suspends the combat between the spirit of legend and the spirit of realism upon his entrance on the stage.

And the one who responds to our most ancient desire: the wish to cross through to death, wholly alive.

Others thought: "I recognize him! It's King Hamlet, the father of Hamlet!" I had never thought of that! But I had thought: "There is my father again, it's really him and there's nothing unusual about that." Wasn't he already created, *revenant*, the first character of my texts of fiction, the hero of *Dedans*?

He comes back now to help me open the book of theater. The dead in flesh and blood, this was my childhood dream as I fought against the misery of the poor unclothed bones. The theater makes our most archaic desires come true.

Good and Evil

In the theater, the author takes no sides but that of the Theater (or God or human Truth). And human truth is: goodness, wickedness. Under the eye of the Theater everyone has equal odds.

There are odious characters in my play. Hate exalts them. What do I know of hate? What worried and trusting love has made me suffer and discover. Like everyone.

In reality I wouldn't have been able to bear to meet these hateful ones. But in truth, I let them enjoy their rage as they emerged from me.

Cruelty; the theater is always cruelly magnificent or cruel, paroxysmally. It gives us the chance to meet cruelty, which is a part of existence. One must have courage to see it. And to show it: that is the actor's mission.

Tender cruelty of the actor to himself, in going so far behind himself, before himself, across the jungles of being to search for the character and bring him back from the night of life, to the stage. Letting himself be possessed by the other, as if his body were engaged in an immense and dizzying errancy in search of its own person, and eventually of its other name. What terrified joy when he finds himself, other! The author also takes this path: I regain my trembling voyage in the actors' journeys.

Acrobats, the actors jump across the gap left by the ego. Such a detachment from the self in order to rejoin the other, to whom one lends oneself entirely, is in itself a form of sainthood. The actor is always somewhat saint, partly woman: he must give life through withdrawing himself. Besides this, everything is woman in the theater: the producer is woman, bringer-into-the-world of characters *and* actors.

Is the author Hélène Cixous going to boast of her sainthood? No. For the author loses a self but multiplies into twenty characters, heady consolation. It's the actor who is a saint, who exchanges himself often with one character. That is really the loss of one life and the undergoing of another. And it is the director who offers the world to the characters and erases himself into pure space.

Men and Women

I have never dared create a real male character in fiction. Why? Because I write with the body, and I am a woman, and a man is a man, and I know nothing of his *jouissance.* And a man without body and without pleasure, I can't do that. So what about men in drama?

The theater is not the scene of sexual pleasure. Romeo and Juliet love each other but do not make love. They sing love. In the theater it's the heart that sings, the breast that opens up, one sees the heart rend. The human heart has no sex. The heart feels in the same way in a man's breast as in a woman's. That does not mean that characters are demicreatures who stop at the belt. No, our creatures lack nothing, not penises, not breasts, not kidneys, not bellies. But I don't have to write all that. The actor, the actress give us the whole body that we don't have to invent. And everything is lived and everything is true. This is the present that theater makes to the author: incarnation. It permits the male author to create women who will not be feigned, and the woman author is granted the chance to create perfectly constituted men!

Time in Theater: Urgency

The discovery of theatrical time is essential for someone who, like me, has written fiction during a long period of time. My texts are tapestries, and they weave themselves in a horizontal manner: what is given to these texts is the chance to take their time to make sense, and sometimes to send meaning quite far off in an afterthought. The Book has all its time and even eternity. The reader can drop the book, come back to it, close it forever, read it in one night or in a year, there is an absolute liberty which is also a limit, in the reading of the text.

In the theater, impossible. Drama writes itself out in a "vertical" manner. Enter Hamlet: and you don't have a minute, you have ten seconds, thirty seconds for everything to write itself out and make itself understood. The theater is impatience. The theater shouts: Hurry! Hurry. Shakespeare's plays are so great because they are carried away by impatience. Cleopatra is impatience incarnated.

Instead of beginnings that never cease to begin and that always seek to begin, which is the proper "pace" of the text, "Fire!" is the gait of the theater. Occasionally when I was still a pupil, I didn't enter like thunder because I was still trailing on the side of fiction. I began too far off, behind the curtain. But theatrical time takes place *in front of* and in the narrow space of the stage which is almost "zen" it is so economical. *Time is also space.*

Writing done for the theater should be "zen." It should be a violent condensation. One must lose neither time nor attention. No detours. No scenery, no set. Let space be nude. Stages with scenery are stages that lose attention, they are stages of trompe l'oeil and thus of dummy intelligence, where one begins looking over there whereas it is happening here. The look of the spectator should go straight to the actor's heart. And each sentence should permit one to go to the actor's heart.

The theater is an eternal yet extremely mortal genre. Those who live it know that it is *going to end.* One lives its life its death immediately. Passion and ethics come from this. The author also must accept his mortality, more than ever, in several ways. First, the author encounters his limits: he is not God, he is only a demi-god. That means that he writes a demi-oeuvre. He writes something and then he awaits his other as a soul awaits its body. He waits for the other part of the theater to come to him, the part that will be given by the actors. The author's proprietary instincts are inhibited, which is a good thing. On the other hand the instinct for friendship is developed.

And then, one also learns to write *a book of four verses.* I think this is the dream of every author: "One day I will write the book of four verses." One day, the final day, I will write a book of three words. Certain theater lines contain an entire book, it's an extraordinary art. An asceticism: from a whole book I have only kept three breaths: It is of an oriental modesty.

The Voyage in Orient

I am going to respond to a question that has been put to me a thousand times: why did I write a play about Cambodia?: Why should Cambodia be in my writing and why do I speak not of "women" but of Cambodians? I had already answered a thousand times in as serious as possible a manner. Then suddenly an answer came to me, the last one and the one which I had not thought of. It is called "Orian." Has the mystery of genders taken hold of me? Here I am still in *or* ("gold," "now"), in the Orient, in a somewhat enriched Oran. Why Asia, why the Orient? Because it is not me, because it is me, because it is the world different from myself that teaches me myself, my difference, that makes me feel my/its difference. And also because Asia is religious in its soul, because one greets others by joining both hands together, because it gathers back together, because it conserves and it kills, because it is poor and it is rich, because it is black next to the white non-color, because it is our pre-history and our present past. Because there are masks: in Asia they believe in masks, in the visage-soul, in the other, because women continue to move in Asia with the slow grace of rivers, because they continue. It's a reality that exists in billions. Because there is so much death and thus so much life.

Before writing a play on Cambodia, I had heard from the poets who are most dear to me that "life is oriental," this is what Clarice Lispector says, what Herman Hesse and what Hofmannsthal say. They have always known that life is oriental. It is slow, and it composes itself like a bouquet of flowers, which is a useless and necessary art. And then in Asia they are hungry. Lacking hunger, "after the lobster," that is a danger for our society. And in Asia the fruit and grain from which everything else begins, including love, writing, and theater, are revered.

Why Cambodia? Out of concern for what is precarious. Precarious is what can be retained and obtained by prayer. These last reflections I dedicate to the Cambodians in the camps. They are precarious, they live in precarious huts of straw and bamboo that are true houses of love and dance, that are under the gun and before death, in exile, that are masterpieces of lightness and fidelity. I dedicate them to these Cambodians we saw in the camps of refugees and resisters, who fight there for an art and a culture menaced with extinction, where the Khmer children who were born in the camps and have never known anything but the fences of the camp, learn eternal dance.

And then there is a man I met in the camps, and who ever since comes back to me, his name is Pierre, he is an old man, he is a saint. He resembles a grasshopper *(sauterelle)*. Grasshopper in Brazilian is *Esperanca*. Languages are inspired. A grasshopper is like hope or hope is like a grasshopper, these are very fine things that one confuses with nature, because they are transparent and green and one sees the green of nature through them. And they are almost invisible but still very alive. This saint who for five or six years now has taken care of the Cambodians in the camps, who every day finds other tears to mingle with their tears, he is hope. For that matter, it was his word. It's the first time that I have heard someone say this word and with so many tears and so much beauty. He himself is so tenuous so precarious. He stares and abundantly gives many tears of love. He gives the word hope the tiny bit of flesh that he has on his bones. He saves this word the way the dancers save the dance. Perhaps this is another name for writing, this name Espérance. With this name, it carries us further than ourselves.

2

"Figuring the nature of the times deceased": Literary Theory and Historical Writing

Hayden White

In a recent essay, Jacques Barzun characterized himself as "a student of history . . . formerly engaged in the strange ritual of teaching it" and then added, parenthetically, "strange, because, properly, it can only be read.[1]

By "history," of course, Barzun did not mean the actual events, structures and processes of the past, but rather the accumulated learning of his profession. In this brief aside, however, Barzun reminds us of some truths that modern historical theory has tended regularly to forget: namely, that the "history" which is the subject of all this learning is accessible only by way of language, that our experience of history is indissociable from our discourse about it, that this discourse must be written before it can be digested as "history," and that this experience, therefore, can be as various as the different kinds of discourse met with in the history of writing itself.

On this view, "history" is not only an object we can study and our study of it, but is also and even primarily a certain kind of relationship to "the past" mediated by a distinctive kind of written discourse. It is the fact that historical discourse is actualized in its culturally significant form as a specific kind of writing that licenses us to consider the relevance of literary theory to both the theory and the practice of historiography.

Before proceeding to a discussion of the relevance of literary theory to historical writing, however, a few remarks about historical discourse and the kind of knowledge it deals in must be made. First, historical discourse is possible only on the presumption of the existence of "the past" as something about which it is possible to speak meaningfully. This is why historians do not normally concern themselves with the metaphysical question of whether the past *really* exists or the epistemological question of whether, if it does exist, we can *really* know it. The existence of the past is a necessary presupposition of historical discourse, and the fact that we can actually write histories is a sufficient proof that we can know it.

But, secondly, historical discourse, unlike scientific discourse, does not presuppose that our knowledge of history derives from a distinctive method for studying the kinds of things that happen to be "past" rather than "present." The events, persons, structures, and processes of the past can be taken as objects of study by any and all of the disciplines of the human and social sciences, and indeed, even by many of the physical sciences. To be sure, it is only insofar as they *are* past or are effectively so treated that such entities can be studied historically; but it is not their pastness that makes them historical. They become historical only in the extent to which they are represented as subjects of a specifically historical kind of writing. Barzun is right in saying that history "can only be read," but it can only be read if it is first written. And it is because history must be written before it can be read (or, for that matter, before it can be spoken, sung, danced, acted, or even filmed), that literary theory has a relevance, not only to historiography, but also and especially to philosophy of history.

This characterization of historical discourse does *not* imply that past events, persons, institutions, and processes never really existed. It does *not* imply that we cannot have more or less precise information about these past entities. And it does *not* imply that we cannot transform this information into knowledge by application of the various methods developed by the different disciplines comprising the "science" of an age or culture. It is intended, rather, to highlight the fact that information about the past is not in itself a specifically *historical* kind of information and that any knowledge based on this kind of information is not in itself a specifically *historical* kind of knowledge. Such information might better be called "archival," inasmuch as it can serve as the object of any discipline simply by being taken as a subject of that discipline's distinctive discursive practices. So, too, it is only by being made into the subject of historical discourse that our information about and knowledge of the past can be said to be "historical."

Historical discourse does not, then, produce new information about the past, since the possession of both old and new information about the past is a precondition of the composition of such a discourse. Nor can it be said to provide new knowledge about the past insofar as knowledge is conceived to be a product of a distinctive method of inquiry.[2] What historical discourse produces are *interpretations* of whatever information about and knowledge of the past the historian commands. These interpretations can take a number of forms, ranging from simple chronicle or lists of facts all the way over to highly abstract "philosophies of history," but what they all have in common is their treatment of a narrative mode of representation as fundamental to the grasping of their referents as distinctively "historical" phenomena. Adapting a famous phrase of Croce's to our purposes, we may say that where there is no narrative, there is no distinctively historical discourse.[3]

I realize that in characterizing historical discourse as interpretation and historical interpretation as narrativization, I am taking a position in a debate over the nature of historical knowledge that sets "narrative" in opposition to "theory" in the manner of an opposition between a thought that remains for the most part "literary" and even "mythical" and one that is or aspires to be scientific.[4] But it must be stressed that we are here considering the question, not of the methods of research that should be used to investigate the past, but rather that of historical *writing*, the kind of discourses actually produced by historians over the course of history's long career as a discipline. And the fact is that narrative has always been and continues to be the predominant mode of historical writing. The principal problem for any theory of historical writing, then, is not that of the possibility or impossibility of a scientific approach to the study of the past, but rather that of explaining the persistence of narrative in historiography. A theory of historical *discourse* must address the question of the function of narrativity in the production of the historical text.

We must begin, then, with the undeniable historical fact that distinctively historical discourses typically produce narrative interpretations of their subject matter. The translation of these discourses into a written form produces a distinctive object, the historiographical text, which in turn can serve as the subject of a philosophical or critical reflection. Whence the distinctions, conventional in modern historical theory, between past reality, which is the historian's object of study; historiography, which is the historian's object of study; historiography, which is the historian's written discourse about this object; and philosopy of history, which is the study of the possible relations obtaining between this object and this discourse. These distinctions must be borne in mind if we are to comprehend the different kinds of relevance that modern literary theory bears to both the practice and the theory of historical writing.

I

Current literary theory has both a direct and an indirect relevance to the understanding of historical writing. It is *direct* insofar as literary theory has elaborated, on the basis of modern language theory, some general theories of discourse which can be used to analyze historical writing and to identify its specifically "literary" (i.e., poetic and rhetorical) aspects. In the substitution of the notion of discursive structure for the older, nineteenth-century notion of "style," considered to be the secret of "fine writing," modern literary theory provides new conceptions of literariness itself. These new conceptions of literariness permit a fine discrimination of the relation between the form and the content of the historical discourse than was formerly possible on the basis of the idea that facts constituted the "body" of the historical discourse and style its more or less attractive, but by no means essential, "clothing."[5] It is now possible to recognize that in realistic, no less than in imaginary discourse, language is both a form and a content and that this linguistic content must be counted among the other kinds of contents (factual, conceptual, and generic) that make up the total content of the discourse as a whole. This recognition liberates historiographical criticism from fidelity to an impossible literalism and permits the analyst of historical discourse to perceive the extent to which it *constructs* its subject matter in the very process of *speaking about it*. The notion of the content of linguistic form scumbles the distinction between literal and figurative discourses and authorizes a search for and analysis of the function of the figurative elements in historiographical, no less than in fictional, prose.

The relevance of modern literary theory to historical writing is *indirect* insofar as the conceptions of language, speech, writing, discourse, and textuality that inform it provide insights into some problems traditionally posed by *philosophy of history*, such as the classification of the genres of historical discourse, the relation of a historical representation to its referents, the epistemological status of historical explanations, and the relation of the interpretative to the descriptive and explanatory aspects of the historian's discourse. Modern literary theory illuminates all of these problems by directing attention to what is most obvious about historical discourse but has not been systematically taken account of until recently, namely, that every history is first and foremost a verbal artifact, a product of a special kind of language-use. And this suggests that, if historical discourse is to be comprehended as productive of a distinctive kind of knowledge, it must first be analyzed as a structure of language.

It is remarkable that philosophers of history should have taken so long to recognize the importance of language for the understanding of historical discourse, especially since modern philosophy in general has made language a central object of interest in its examination of other departments of science. This lapse was in part due to the fact that modern historians themselves have tended to treat their own language as an unproblematical, transparent medium for both the representation of past events and the expression of their thought about these events. But it was also due to the fact that the philosophers who took historical discourse as a specific object of analysis tended to believe in the possibility of dissociating the factual and conceptual content of a discourse from its "literary" and linguistic form for purposes of assessing its truth-value and the nature of its relationship to reality. Thus, for example, recent philosophers of history have typically treated narrative less as verbal structure than as a kind of explanation by storytelling and regarded the story told in a given history as a structure of argumentative concepts, the relations among the parts of which were logical (specifically syllogistic) rather than linguistic in nature. All this implied that the content of a historical discourse could be extracted from its linguistic form, served up in a condensed paraphrase purged of all figurative and tropological elements, and subjected to tests of logical consistency as an argument and of predicative adequacy as a body of fact. But this was to ignore the one "content" without which a historical discourse could never come into existence at all: language.

During the very period in which this argument model predominated among analysts of historical discourse, philosophers such as W. V. O. Quine, John Searle, Nelson Goodman, and Richard Rorty were showing the difficulty of distinguishing *what* was said from *how* it was said even in the discourses of the physical sciences, let alone in such a non-formalized discourse as history.[6] Their work confirmed what had been a founding presupposition of modern linguistics, namely, that language is never a set of empty "forms" waiting to be filled with a factual and conceptual "content" or attached to pre-existent referents in the world, but is itself in the world as one "thing" among others and is already freighted with figurative, tropological, and generic contents before it is actualized in any given utterance. All this implied that the very distinctions between imaginative and realistic writing and between fictional and factual discourse, on the basis of which historiographical writing had been analyzed since its disengagement from rhetoric in the early nineteenth century,[7] had to be reassessed and reconceptualized.

In fact, the most cursory examination of the language of actual historical writings would have revealed that the content of the historiographical discourse is indistinguishable from its discursive form. That this is so is confirmed by the fact that classic historiographical works have continued to be valued for their "literary" qualities long after their information has become outdated and their explanations have been consigned to the status of commonplaces of the cultural moment in which they were written. It is true that, in speaking of the "literary" nature of such historiographical classics as those written by Herodotus, Tacitus, Francesco Guicciardini, Edward Gibbon, Jules Michelet, Alexis de Tocqueville, Jacob Burckhardt, Theodor Mommsen, Johan Huizinga, Lucien

Febvre, or Richard Henry Tawney, we may often have in mind their status as models of "interpretative" thought as well as their status as exemplars of a felicitous writing style. But by designating their work as "literary" we do not so much remove it from the domain of knowledge-production as simply indicate the extent to which literature itself must be considered to inhabit that domain insofar as it, too, provides us with similar models of interpretative thought. Literary discourse may differ from historical discourse by virtue of its primary referents, conceived as "imaginary" rather than "real" events, but the two kinds of discourse are more similar than different in virtue of the fact that both operate language in such a way that any clear distinction between their discursive form and their interpretative content remains impossible.

It is for reasons such as these that we must reject, revise, or augment the older mimetic and model theories of historical discourse. A history is, as F. R. Ankersmit puts it, less like a picture intended to resemble the objects of which it speaks or a model "tied to the past by certain translation rules," than "a complex linguistic structure specifically built for the purpose of *showing* a part of the past."[8] On this view, historical discourse is not to be likened to a picture that permits us to see more clearly an object which would otherwise remain vague and imprecisely apprehended. Nor is it a representation of an explanatory procedure intended finally to provide a definitive *answer* to the problem of "what really happened" in some given domain of the past. On the contrary, to use a formulation popularized by E. H. Gombrich in his studies of Western pictorial realism, historical discourse is less a *matching* of an image or a model with some extrinsic "reality" than a *making* of a verbal image, a discursive "thing" which interferes with our perception of its putative referent even while fixing our attention on and illuminating it.[9]

Paul Ricoeur has argued that historiographical text is related to its referent in the way that the vehicle of a metaphor is related to its tenor. In his view, a historical discourse is a kind of extended metaphor—the traditional definition of allegory—and must be seen, therefore, as belonging to the order of figurative, as well as to those of literal and technical, speech.[10] This is why historical discourse, like literary discourse or figurative language in general, typically appears to be, as Ankersmit puts it, "dense and opaque" rather than thin and transparent, and resists both paraphrase and analysis by logical concepts alone.[11] Like poetic discourse as characterized by Roman Jakobson, historical discourse is "intensional," i.e., is systemically intra- as well as extra-referential. This intensionality endows the historical discourse with a quality of "thingi-ness" similar to that of the poetic utterance, and this is why any attempt to comprehend how historical discourse works to produce a knowledge-effect must be based, not on an epistemological analysis of the relation of the "mind" of the historian to a past "world," but rather on a scientific study of the relation of the things produced by and in language to the other kinds of things that comprise the common reality. In short, historical discourse should not be considered primarily as a special case of the "workings of our minds" in its efforts to know reality or to describe it, but rather as a special kind of language use which, like metaphoric speech, symbolic language, and allegorical representation, always means more than it literally says, says something other than what it seems to mean, and reveals something about the world only at the cost of concealing something else.

It is the metaphoric nature of the great classics of historiography that explains why none of them has ever "wrapped up" a historical problem definitively, but has always rather "opened up" a prospect on the past that inspires more study. It is this fact that authorizes us to classify historical discourse primarily as interpretation, rather than as explanation or description, and above all as a kind of writing which, instead of pacifying our will to know, stimulates us to ever more research, ever more discourse, ever more writing. As Ankersmit puts it:

> The great books in the field of the history of historiography, the works of Ranke, de Tocqueville, Burckhardt, Huizinga, Meinecke or Braudel, do not put an end to a historical debate, do not give us the feeling that we now finally know how things actually were in the past and that clarity has ultimately been achieved. On the contrary: these books have proved to be the most powerful stimulators of the production of *more* writing—their effect is thus to estrange us from the past, instead of placing it upon a kind of pedestal in a historiographical museum so that we can inspect it from all possible perspectives.[12]

None of this implies that we should not discriminate between the activity of historical research (historians' study of an archive containing information about the past) and that of historical writing (historians' composition of a discourse and the translation of it into a written form). In the research phase of their work, historians are concerned to discover the truth about the past and to recover information either forgotten, suppressed, or obscured, and, of course, to make of it whatever sense they can. But between this research phase, which is really quite indistinguishable from that of a journalist or a detective, and the completion of a written history, a number of important transformative operations must be performed in which the figurative aspect of the historian's thought is intensified rather than diminished.

In the passage from a study of an archive to the composition of a discourse to its translation into a written form, historians must employ the same strategies of linguistic figuration used by imaginative writers to endow their discourses with the kind of latent, secondary, or connotative meanings that will require that their works not only be *received* as messages but *read* as symbolic structures.[13] The latent, secondary, or connotative meaning contained in the historical discourse *is* its interpretation of the events that make up its manifest content. The kind of interpretation typically produced by the historical discourse is that which endows what would otherwise remain only a chronologically ordered series of events with the formal coherency of the kind of plot structures met with in narrative fiction. This endowment of a chronicle of events with a plot structure, which I call the operation of emplotment, is carried out by discursive techniques that are more tropological than logical in nature.

If this is so, then logical analysis must be augmented by tropological analysis if we are to have the analytical categories necessary for an understanding of how historical discourse produces its characteristic knowledge-effects. If, when viewed from the perspective of the logician, the typical historical discourse must be seen as having the structure of an enthymeme rather than that of a true syllogism, it is because turns more tropical than logical preside over both its endowment of a series of events with the structural coherency of a plot form *and* its endowment of a set of facts with whatever meaning it is supposed to possess. Indeed, it is only by troping, rather than by logical deduction, that any given set of the kinds of past events we would wish to call "historical" can be (first) *represented* as having the order of a chronicle; (secondly) *transformed* by emplotment into a story with identifiable beginning, middle, and end phases; and (thirdly) *constituted* as the subject of whatever formal arguments may be adduced to establish their "meaning"—cognitive, ethical, or aesthetic, as the case may be. These three tropological abductions occur in the composition of every historical discourse, even those which, as in modern structuralist historiography, eschew storytelling and try to limit themselves to statistical analyses of institutions and long-term, effectively synchronic, ecological and ethnological processes.

Why characterize these abductions as tropological?

Because, first, while events may occur in time, the chronological codes used to order them into specific temporal units are culture-specific, not natural; and, moreover, must be filled with their specific contents by the historian if he or she is to constitute them as *phases* of a continuous process of historical development. The constitution of a chronicle as a set of events that can provide the elements of a story is an operation more poetic than scientific in nature. The events may be "given," but their functions as elements of a story are imposed upon them—and are imposed by discursive techniques more tropological than logical in nature.

Secondly, the transformation of a chronicle of events into a story (or congeries of stories) requires a choice among the many kinds of plot structures provided by the cultural tradition of the historian. And while convention may limit this choice to the range of types of plot structures deemed suitable for the representation of the types of events being dealt with, this choice is at least relatively free. There is no necessity, logical or natural, governing the decision to emplot a given sequence of events as a tragedy rather than as a comedy or romance. Are there intrinsically tragic events, or does it depend upon the perspective from which they are viewed? To emplot real events as a story of a specific kind (or as a mixture of stories of specific kinds) is to trope those events. This is because stories are not lived; there is no such thing as a "real" story. Stories are told or written, not found. And as for the notion of a "true" *story*, this is virtually a contradiction in terms. *All* stories are fictions. Which means, of course, that they can be "true" only in a metaphorical sense and in the sense in which a figure of speech can be true. Is this true enough?

And, thirdly, whatever argument a historian may explicitly advance to explain the meaning of the events contained in the chronicle will be as much about the plot used to fashion the chronicle into a particular kind of story as it will be about the events themselves. This means that the argument of a historical discourse is ultimately a second-order fiction, a fiction of a fiction or a fiction of fiction-making, which bears the same relationship to the plot that the plot bears to the chronicle. Typically, the "explanation" will be the story with the events left out and only its conceptual content ("facts" on the one side and plot "connectives" on the other) offered up as the material for logical (or, more technically, nomological-deductive) handling.

Structuralist historical discourse achieves the effect of producing a "scientific" account more by the tropological move of disemplotting previously emplotted sets of historical events than by the provision of anything like the kind of understanding of history that the physical sciences provide for the understanding of nature. Paul Ricoeur has shown, in his recent *Time and Narrative,* how the *Annales* school of historians were required first to build narrative discursive structures into their accounts of the past, in order to permit them to pass for specifically *historical* accounts, prior to depriving them of this narrativity in order to pass them off as "scientific" analyses.[14] In historiographical reflection, it would appear, a scientific handling of historical materials is rendered possible only on the basis of a tropological swerve neither more nor, it should be added, less justifiable on cognitive grounds than that which renders possible a "literary" handling of these same materials.

Historical studies have never had a Copernican Revolution similar to that which founded the physical sciences. It is only the prestige of the physical sciences themselves, based on their success in providing modern mankind with a control over nature only previously dreamed of, that inspires the effort to apply their principles of description, analysis, and explanation to history. But until such a Copernican Revolution occurs, historical studies will remain a field of inquiry in which the choice of a method for investigating the past and of a mode of discourse for writing about it will remain free, rather than constrained. In historiography, discourse has always been, and is likely to remain, rule-inventive as well as rule-governed. In any scientific discipline, you can make new rules only by troping, swerving from, old ones, but in historiography you can apply the old rules only by tropological tactics. This does not imply that traditional historiography is inherently untruthful, only that its truths are of two kinds: factual on the one hand, figurative on the other.

II

Tropology is not, of course, *a* theory of language, but rather a more or less systematized cluster of notions about figurative language deriving from neo-classical rhetorics.[15] It thus provides a perspective on language from which to analyze the elements, levels, and combinatorial procedures of non-formalized, and especially pragmatic, discourses.[16] Tropology centers attention on the "turns" in a discourse: turns from one level of generalization to another, from one phase of a sequence to another, from a description to an analysis or the reverse, from a figure to a ground or from an event to its context, from the conventions of one genre to another within a single discourse, and so on. Such turns *may be* governed by formal rules of logical exposition, mathematical projection, statistical inference, generic or oratorical conventions (of storytelling, legal disputation, political debate, and so on), but most often, they consist of violations of such rules.[17] In complex discourses such as those met with in historiograpy or indeed any of the human sciences, the rules of discourse formation are not fixed. Unlike the transitions of a formalized discourse, which are governed by explicit rules of selection and combination, the turns of any given non-formalized discourse and the order of their occurrence are not predictable in advance of their actualization in a specific utterance. This is why efforts to construct a logic or even a grammar of narrative have failed. But the turns can be identified, classified as types, and generic patterns of their typical orders of occurrence in specific discourses established.

The classification of the tropes of language, speech, and discourse remains an uncompleted (and in principle uncompletable) project of figurative linguistics, semiotics, neo-rhetoric, and deconstructive criticism. However, the four general types of tropes identified by neo-classical rhetorical theory appear to be basic: metaphor (based on the principle of similitude), metonymy (based on that of contiguity), synecdoche (based on the identification of parts of a thing as belonging to a whole), and irony (based on opposition).[18] Considered as the basic structures of figuration, these four tropes provide us with categories for identifying the modes of linking an order of words to an order of thoughts (e.g., "apple" with "temptation") on the paradigmatic axis of an utterance and of one phase of a discourse with preceding and succeeding phrases (e.g., "transitional" paragraphs or chapters) on the syntagmatic axis. The dominance of one mode of associating words and thoughts with one another across an entire discourse allows us to characterize the structure of the discourse as a whole in tropological terms. The tropological structures of metaphor, metonymy, synecdoche, and irony (and what I take—following Northop Frye—to be their corresponding plot types: Romance, Tragedy, Comedy, and Satire), provide us with a much more refined classification of the kinds of historical discourses than that based on the conventional distinction between "linear" and "cyclical" representations of historical processes.[19] They also allow us to see more clearly the ways in which historical discourse resembles and indeed converges with fictional narrative, both in the strategies it uses to endow events with meanings and in the kinds of truth in which it deals.

But, it might very well be asked, so what? As Arnaldo Momigliano puts it: "Why should it concern me if a historian prefers to present the part for the whole rather than the whole for the part? After all, I do not care if a historian has chosen to write in an epic style or to introduce speeches (*discorsi*) into his narration. I have no reason to prefer synecdochic historians to ironic ones or vice versa."[20] In Momigliano's view, the only requirements of historians are that they discover the truth, present new facts, and offer new interpretations of the facts. "To be sure," he concedes, "in order to be called historians, they have to turn (*volgere*) their research into some form of story. But their stories have to be true stories.[21] Only the truth of the facts and, presumably, the plausibility of interpretations count; the linguistic form and generic mode in which these are presented, the diction and the rhetoric of the discourse, are of no import.

But it does matter whether events are presented as parts of a whole (with a meaning not apprehendable in any of the parts taken individually), after the manner of a Platonic realist, or a whole is presented as nothing but the sum of its several constituent parts, after the manner of a nominalist. It matters to the kind of truth that one can expect to derive from a study of any given set of events. And I am confident that even Professor Momigliano would admit that the choice of a farcical style for the representation of some kinds of historical events would constitute, not only a lapse in taste, but also a distortion of the truth about them. So, too, for an ironic mode of representation. A mode of representation such as irony is a *content* of the discourse in which it is used, not merely a form—as anyone who has had ironic remarks directed at them will know all too well. When I speak to or about someone or something in an ironic mode, I am doing more than clothing my observations in a witty style. I am saying about them something more and other than I seem to be asserting on the literal level of my speech. So it is with historical discourse cast in a predominantly ironic mode, and so it is with the other modes of utterance I may employ to speak about anything whatsoever.

The same kind of response can be made to historians and philosophers of history who reject rhetorical analysis of historical texts on the grounds that they divert us from the more serious issues with which a politically committed or socially engaged criticism should be concerned. In a recent essay, Gene Bell-Villada, a historically self-conscious critic of Latin American literature, writes:

> Meanwhile, in the face of a domestic sociopolitical panorama that begins to look vaguely "Latin American," plus certain South American "friendly regimes" that behave more and more Nazi-like, the only response that the U.S. "critical establishment" can come up with is its elaborate paraliterary schemes, its wars on referentiality and its preachments that "History is Fiction, Trope and Discourse." The families of several thousand Salvadoran death-squad victims may entertain other thoughts about history.[22]

I have no doubt that the families alluded to in this passage do indeed have "other thoughts about history" than that it consists of "Fiction, Trope and Discourse"—if they bother to think about "history" at all. They would be as foolish as Professor Bell-Villada apparently thinks I am if they even "entertained" such thoughts. But that is really not the point at issue. The "history" we are discussing is that which takes shape in language, emotion, thought, and discourse in the attempt to make sense of the kind of experiences those families have endured. In the case he cites, these are first and foremost political experiences, and one of the ways of making sense of such experiences is to think about them "historically." But such thought is all the more likely to be tropical, discursive, and fictional (in the sense of "imaginary") in the extent to which it is politically engaged or ideologically motivated. There is no position "above the battle," not even the Marxist one, that is not similarly tropical, discursive, and fictional. A failure of historical consciousness occurs when one forgets that "history," in the sense both of events and accounts of events, does not just happen but is *made*. Moreover, it should be added, it is made on both sides of the barricades, and just as effectively by one side as by the other.

Bell-Villada knows this perfectly well, as his own remarks on the sense of history that pervades the work of the modern Latin American writers makes clear. Would he wish to say that their works do not teach us about real history because they are fictions? Or that, being fictions *about history*, they are devoid of tropisms and discursivity? Are their novels less true for being fictional? Are they less fictional for being historical? Could any history be as true as these novels without availing itself of the kind of poetic tropes found in the work of Mario Vargas Llosa, Alejo Carpentier, José Donoso, and Julio Cortázar?

III

I have offered elsehwere some arguments in support of the positions outlined above and demonstrations, in the form of extensive explications of specific historiographical texts, of their possible utility for understanding what is involved in the composition of a historical discourse.[23] I will not try here to recapitulate the details of these arguments for want of space, but it may be helpful to have summarized some of the kinds of objections raised by critics of the positions advanced here. The general objections are four.

The *first* objection to the theory is that it seems to commit us to linguistic determinism or, what amounts to the same thing in the minds of some critics, linguistic relativism. On this theory, it is argued, the historian appears to be a prisoner of the linguistic mode in which he initially describes or chartacterizes his object of study: he can only see what his language permits him to conceptualize. This circumstance appears to set limits on what can be learned in the process of investigating the evidence and does not take account of the fact that historians undeniably do change their perceptions of things in the course of their research and revise their conceptions of the meanings of these things on reflection on the evidence.

A similar argument, advanced on the same general grounds, is raised with respect to the historian's finished written account of his findings. The tropological theory of historical discourse appears to obscure the fact that a historical work is a *report* of facts discovered in research, of the historian's beliefs about the truth of these facts, and of the best argument he can envisage regarding the causes, meaning, significance, or import of these truths for the comprehension of the domain of occurrences that he has studied. In suggesting that the connections among the various elements, levels, and dimensions of the discourse in which the argument is set forth are tropological, rather than logical or rationally deliberative, historical discourse is deprived of its claims to truthfulness and relegated to the fanciful domain of fiction. These two arguments are often united and expressed more concisely in the declaration that the theory makes of historiography little more than rhetorical exercise and thereby undermines history's claim to provide truths about and knowledge of its objects of study.

The *second* general objection is directed against the theory of the tropological nature of language and its implications for the theory of historical discourse. The tropological theory of language appears to dissolve the distinction between figurative and literal speech, making the latter into a special case of the former. The theory views literal language as a set of figurative usages which happen to have been regularized and established *as literal speech* by convention alone. What is literal in one moment of a language community's development can therefore become figurative at another moment and vice versa, so that the meaning of a given discourse can change with any change in the rules for determining what counts as literal speech and what counts only as metaphor. This seems to vest the authority to determine the meanings of discourses, not in the intentions of their authors or in what the texts written by them manifestly say, but in readers or reading communities, who are permitted to make of them whatever they wish or whatever the current conventions governing the distinction between literal and figurative speech permit. Thus, it seems that, on the tropological theory of language, we could no longer appeal to "the facts" in order to justify or to criticize any given interpretation of reality. What could count as a fact would be infinitely revisable, as the notion of what counted as a literal statement and what counted as a metaphorical one changed. In sum, the tropological theory of language and of discourse strikes at the very conception of factuality, and especially at historians' claims regarding the factual truthfulness, not only of their statements about particular events, but of their discourse as a whole. If a factual statement is not only a singular existential proposition cast in literal language, but such a proposition *plus* the implied conventions for determining what shall count as literal and what as figurative in that proposition, then such statements can no longer be taken at their face value. Like printed money, they can only be cashed in at the going rate of their value in literalist specie. Since this rate of exchange is always in flux, one can never know where one stands in relation to the "facts of reality." The tropological theory of language, then, threatens history's centuries' long claim to deal in facts and therewith its status as an empirical discipline.

The *third* general objection to the tropological theory of language and discourse in its relation to historical discourse turns upon its implications regarding the nature of the objects studied by historians. The theory seems to imply that these objects are not found in the real world (even if this real world is a past one), but are, rather, constructions of language, spectral and unreal objects, poetically or rhetorically "invented" and having their existence only in books. The theory, in a word, stresses the poetic (self-referring), conative (affective), and above all metalinguistic (codifying) functions of historical discourse at the expense of its referential (predicative), phatic (communicative), and expressive (authorial) functions.[24] Since a historical discourse is intended to be *primarily* referential, expressive (of its author's rational thought about its referents) and communicative, the tropological theory of discourse improperly treats the history as if it were only a fiction. Thereby, the "reality" of its referents is denied, being replaced by what Roland Barthes disparagingly called "the reality-effect,"[25] a purely rhetorical construction. But since the objects of historical study are (or were) real objects and historians intend to make precise references to them and truthful statements about them, the elision of the distinction between the referential function and the other functions of discourse brings under question the existence of reality itself and the very possibility of a specifically "realistic" representation of it.

If the tropological theory of language and discourse seems to undermine the historian's claim to deal in facts about particular real objects, it is even more threatening to the claim to deal in facts of a more general, collective, or processual nature. This is especially the case with respect to the notion that the tale told by the narrative historian is a "true" rather than an "invented" story. "True" is here understood as conforming to "what really happened" wherein "what really happened" is considered to have been a form of human life, individual or collective, having the outline and structure of a story. Tropological theory, in suggesting that a story can only be a construction of language and a fact of discourse, appears to undermine the legitimacy of the claims to truthfulness of the traditional mode of historical discourse, the narrative. Thus, while seeming to dissolve the scientific historian's claims to scientificity, the tropological theory of the historical discourse also dissolves the traditional narrative historian's claim to have provided a story that is true rather than imaginary.

Finally, a *fourth* objection to the use of a tropological theory of language for the analysis of historical discourse turns upon the question of its implications for the epistemic status of the historiographical critic's own discourse. If all discourse is fictive, figurative, imaginative, poetico-rhetorical, if it invents its subjects rather than finds them in the real world, if it is only to be taken figuratively, and so on, as the tropological theory seems to suggest, then is this not true also of the discourse of the tropologist? How can the tropological critic take his own discourse seriously or expect others to do so? Is not tropology itself a fiction, and whatever statements made on its basis nothing but fictions of the fictions it purports to find everywhere? In short, the tropological theory of language appears to make a cognitively responsible criticism impossible, and as such undermines the activity of criticism itself.

IV

These objections will appear more or less compelling in the degree to which one has confidence in the conventional distinctions between literal and figurative speech, referential and non-referential discourse, factual and fictional prose, the content and the form of a given type of discourse, and so on. Where that confidence is strong, the alternative formulations of the distinctions offered by modern language and literary theory will appear unnecessary and their utility for the understanding of historical discourse inconsequential. It should be stressed, however, that tropological theories of discourse do not so much dissolve these distinctions as reconceptualize them. Whereas traditional critical theory views the literal and figurative, fictional and factual, referential and intensional dimensions of language as opposed, and even mutually exclusive alternatives for all *serious* discourse, modern language and literary theory tends to view them as the poles of a linguistic continuum between which speech must move in the articulation of any discourse whatsoever, serious or frivolous. Insofar as this movement within discourse is itself tropological in nature, we need a tropological theory to guide analysis of it.

As for the objections themselves, the following replies can be made:

First, there is nothing in tropological theory implying linguistic determinism or relativism. Tropology is a theory of discourse, not of mind or consciousness. Although it assumes that figuration cannot be avoided in discourse, the theory, far from implying linguistic determinism, seeks to provide the knowledge necessary for a free choice among different strategies of figuration. Nor does it suggest, after the manner of Benjamin Lee Whorf, that perception is determined by language and that the truthfulness of a discourse is relative to the language in which it is written. As a theory of discourse, tropology has much to say about representation, but nothing to say about perception.

Secondly, tropology does not deny the existence of extra-discursive entities or our capacity to refer to and represent them in speech. It does not suggest that "everything" is language, speech, discourse, or text, only that linguistic referentiality and representation are much more complicated matters than the older, literalist notions of language and discourse made out. Tropology stresses the metalinguistic over the referential function of discourse because it is concerned more with codes than with whatever contingent messages can be transmitted by specific uses of them. Insofar as codes are themselves message-contents in their own right, it expands the notion of message itself and alerts us to the performance, as well as the communicative, aspect of discourse.

Thirdly, the thesis that all discourse is tropological in structure does indeed suggest that this is true also of the tropologist's own discourse. But this only implies that tropological analysis must be elaborated in full consciousness of its own figurative aspect. Far from implying that tropological analysis is a frivolous game, tropological theory implies rather that we should rethink the distinction between serious and playful discourse itself. When tropological critics analyze the tropological structure of a text, they are speaking about *facts*—facts of language, discourse, and textuality—even if they are speaking in a language that they know to be as much figurative as literal. They are *referring* to things they perceive or believe that they perceive in the text, even if they are referring as much in the indirect way of figurative speech as in the direct way of literalist speech. Is their discourse to be taken "seriously," then, as "really meaning" what it says? Of course it is, but only insofar as "seriousness" is not equated with a narrow literal-mindedness, "meaning" is not equated with only literal meaning, and "really" is not understood as foreclosing the possibility that figurative speech can be as truthful in its own way as literal speech.

Fourth, then, tropological theory does not collapse the difference between fact and fiction, but redefines the relations between them within any given discourse. If there is no such thing as "raw facts," but only events under different descriptions, then factuality becomes a matter of the descriptive protocols used to transform events into facts. Figurative descriptions of real events are not less "factual" than literalist descriptions, they are only factual—or, as I would put it, "factological"—in a different way. Tropological theory implies that we must not confuse "facts" with "events." Events happen, facts are constituted by linguistic description. The mode of language used to constitute facts may be formalized and rule-governed, as in scientific and traditional discourses; it may be relatively free, as in every "modernist" literary discourse; or it may be a combination of formalized and free discursive practices. In the second and third cases, tropology offers a better prospect for a theory of discursive invention than either logical or grammatical models of discursivity. And since historiography has for the most part been and is likely to remain a combination of rule-governed and free discursive practice, tropology has an especial relevance to the effort to understand it.

Tropology is especially useful for the analysis of narrative historiography, because narrative history is a mode of discourse in which the relations between what a given culture regards as literal truths and the figurative truths expressed in its characteristic fictions, the kinds of stories it tells about itself and about others, can be tested. In historical narratives, the dominant plot forms utilized by a culture to "imagine" the different kinds of meaning (tragic, comic, epic, farcical, etc.) that a distinctively human form of life *might have* are tested against the information and knowledge that specific forms of human life *have had* in the past. In the process, not only are past forms of human life endowed with the kinds of meaning met with in the forms of fiction produced by a given culture, but the degrees of "truthfulness" and "realism" of these forms of fiction to the facts of historical reality and our knowledge of it can be measured. This relationship between historical interpretation and literary representation applies not only to their mutual interest in generic plot structures, but also to the narrative mode of discourse which they mutually share.

V

It is because historical discourse utilizes structures of meaning-production found in their purest forms in literary fictions that modern literary theory, and especially those versions of it oriented towards tropological conceptions of language, discourse, and textuality, is immediately relevant to contemporary theory of historical writing. It bears directly on one of the most important debates in contemporary historical theory: that of the epistemic status of narrativity.

This debate arises against the background of a forty-year discussion, begun in the 1940s, among philosophers and historians, over the issue of history's possible status as a science.[26] The question of narrative was addressed in this discussion, but primarily in terms of its suitability to the aim and purposes of scientific discourse. One side in this debate held that if historical studies were to be transformed into a science, the narrative mode of discourse, being manifestly "literary" in nature, was inessential to the study and writing of history. The other side considered narrative to be, not only a mode of discourse, but also and most importantly a specific mode of explanation. While narrative explanation differed from the mode of (nomological-deductive) explanation prevailing in the physical sciences, it was not to be considered inferior to it, was especially suited to the representation of historical as against natural events, and could therefore be used with perfect propriety for the explication of specifically historical events. This particular debate came to an end sometime during the 1970s, in the way one would expect a philosophical debate to end, in a compromise. It was decided by general consensus that narrative was properly used in historiography for some purposes but not for others.

But no sooner had the matter been seemingly resolved than it was reopened by the explosion on the critical scene of another argument that had been building in another quarter and which had to do with the implicit "content" of narrative discourse in general. While the older dispute had focused on the relation of narrative discourse to scientific knowledge, the newer one stressed the relationship of narrative to myth and ideology. Thus, for example, Barthes argued that narrativity itself was the effective content of "modern myth" (by which he meant "ideology"). Julia Kristeva (following Louis Althusser) indicted narrativity as the instrument by which society produced the self-oppressing, compliant "subject" out of the originally autonomous "individual." Jacques Derrida cited narrative as the privileged "genre of the law." Jean-François Lyotard attributed the "postmodernist condition" to the breakdown of a "narrative knowledge" purely "customary" in nature. And, most recently, Sande Cohen represented narrative consciousness as the incarnation of a purely "reactive" and "disintellective" mode of thinking and the principal impediment to "critical" and "theoretical" thought in the human sciences.[27] At the same time, however, defenders of narrativity were not wanting. Certain leading historians, such as Laurence Stone, Dominick LaCapra, James Henretta, and Bernard Bailyn, have recently stressed the desirability, if not the necessity, of narrative as an antidote to the disaffection of lay readers put off by the abstractness and lack of intimacy of "technical" historiography. Some redoubtable *Annalistes*, most prominently Emmanuel Leroy Ladurie and Jacques Le Goff, have not only come around to admitting the desirability of narrative for the representation of certain kinds of historical phenomena, but have actually committed overt acts of historiographical narrativity. Among literary theorists, Fredric Jameson has attempted to re-energize Marxism by stressing its status, less as a science than as a "master narrative" of history that could provide both an understanding of the past and the grounds necessary for the hope of transcending the "alienating necessities" of a history lived as a story of class oppression. And finally, from the quarter of philosophical hermeneutics, Paul Ricoeur, in what amounts to the most comprehensive attempt to synthesize modern Western thought about history, *Time and Narrative*, has set forth a veritable metaphysics of narrativity and defense of its adequacy, not only to historical representation, but also to the representation of the fundamental "structures of temporality.[28]

Obviously something other than a question of "literary form" was involved in this debate. Except for those professional historians who regarded it as a cosmetic for a knowledge too dreary to be taken straight by a lay audience, narrative was being treated as much more than a medium for transmitting messages that might just as well be conveyed by other discursive techniques. On the contrary, narrative was being treated as if it were a message in its own right, a message with its own referent and a meaning quite other than that which it appears only to "contain." For example, Jameson speaks of narrative as "a central instance of the human mind and a mode of thinking fully as legitimate as that of abstract thought."[29] Lyotard and Alasdair MacIntyre, though from diametrically opposed ideological perspectives, cite the social function of narrative as a mainstay of any effective "legitimation" of knowledge and ethico-political authority.[30] And Ricoeur maintains that narrative, far from being only a form, is the manifestation in language of a distinctively human experience of temporality.[31] All this in opposition to the idea, advanced by the hostile deconstructors of narrativity, such as Barthes, Kristeva, Derrida, and Cohen, that narrative is the still undissolved residue of mythic consciousness in modern thought. In a word, far from being considered only a form, narrative is increasingly being recognized as a discursive mode whose content *is* its form.

Now, from the standpoint of traditional literary theory, the notion that the form of a discourse might be one its contents would have to be treated as either a paradox or a mystery. From the perspective provided by tropological theory, however, there would be nothing paradoxical or mysterious at all about such a notion. This content of a form of discourse would be linguistic in nature and would consist of the structure of its dominant trope, the trope that serves as the paradigm in language for the representation of things as parts of identifiable wholes. On this view of the matter, narrative can be characterized as a kind of discourse in which synecdoche functions as the dominant trope for "grasping together" (Greek: *synecdoche;* Latin: *subintellectio,* the *parts* of a totality apprehended as being dispersed across a temporal series into a *whole* in the mode of *identification.*[32] This mode of discourse can be differentiated from those in which the parts of an apparent whole are related to one another by resemblance (metaphor), contiguity (metonymy), or opposition (irony or catachresis). There is nothing particularly metaphysical about the representation of discrete things, whether these be individual persons, social institutions, or sets of events, as unities whose aspects are identifiable as attributes of the wholes of which they are part. We do this in ordinary speech (whatever that may be) all the time. We do it in philosophical language when, after the manner of Aristotle, Leibniz, Hegel, William James, Alfred North Whitehead, and John Dewey, we wish to indicate and reflect upon those aspects of reality that appear to be organic rather than mechanistic in their structure and mode of development and articulation. We do it in historical language when we wish to speak about continuities, transitions, and integrations. And we do it in literary language when we wish to write narrative novels, poems, or plays.

Viewed from this perspective, narrative is not so much either a distortion of that "reality" given to us in perception (Barthes's "myth") or an epiphanic manifestation of a metaphysical ground of being (Ricoeur's "structures of temporality"), but the appearance in discursive form of one of the tropological possibilities of language use. Viewing the matter this way, we can begin to appreciate the extent to which programs undertaken either to expunge narrativity from "serious" discourse or to elevate it to the status of an expression of Being, or Time, or Historicity, are equally misguided. Narrative is a cultural universal because language is a human universal. We can no more expunge it from discourse than we can legislate discourse itself out of existence. Narrative may be the very soul of myth, but this is because myth is a form of linguistic discourse, not because narrative is inherently mythical. And the same can be said of the relation of narrative to literary fiction. Some literary fictions are cast in a narrative mode, but this does not mean that all narratives are literary fictions. What it means is that both mythic and literary narratives are linguistic figurations.

So, too, for the relation of narrative to historical (and, by extension, all "realistic") discourses. A historical representation can be cast in the mode of a narrative because the tropological nature of language provides that possibility. Therefore, it is absurd to suppose that, *because* a historical discourse is cast in the mode of a narrative, it must be mythical, fictional, substantially imaginary, or otherwise "unrealistic" in what it tells us about the world. To suppose this is to indulge in the kind of thinking that results in belief in contagious magic or guilt by association. If myth, literary fiction, and traditional historiography utilize the narrative mode of discourse, this is because they are all forms of language-use. This in itself tells us nothing about their truthfulness—and even less about their "realism" inasmuch as this notion is always culturally determinate and varies from culture to culture. Anyway, does anyone seriously believe that myth and literary fiction do *not* refer to the real world, tell truths about it, and provide useful knowledge of it?

The question of the relation between narrative and history has received especial attention in recent literary theory because it is central to a crucial problem of literary history, that of the relation of literary modernism to literary realism. The transition from realism to modernism appears to many interpreters to have entailed the repudiation of both the form of the narrative and any interest in the representation of "historical reality."[33] To Marxist interpreters especially, the one repudiation appears to have been a function of the other. Thus, the argument runs, the realism of the classical nineteenth-century novel was a result of the discovery that "social reality" was "historical" in nature. The discovery of the historical nature of social reality was the discovery that "society" was not only, or even primarily, tradition, consensus, and continuity, but also conflict, revolution, and change. The realistic novel was the necessary expression in literature of this discovery, not only because it took "historical reality" as its "content," but also because it developed the inherently "dialectical" capability of narrative form for the representation of any reality specifically "historical" in nature. The abandonment of normal narrativity by modernist writers, therefore, was the expression on the level of form of the rejection of "historical reality" on the level of content. And since fascism was based on a similar rejection of historical reality and a flight into purely "formalist" political solutions for "real" social contradictions, modernism could be seen as the expression in literature of fascism in politics.[34]

Now, this debate within modern literary theory over the nature of literary modernism—a debate that has been extended to comprise postmodernism as well—recapitulates many of the arguments of an earlier debate in the human sciences precipitated by the so-called "crisis of *historicism*."[35] This crisis was manifested in a general despair of ever attaining to that "objective science of history" sought in the nineteenth century as an antidote to ideology in social and political thought. It was marked by the onset in the human sciences of moral and epistemological relativism, critical pluralism, and methodological eclecticism. In many respects, the crisis was caused by the very success of traditional, Rankean historical studies in mapping the political, social, and cultural diversity, not only of human history in general, but of those ethical values, aesthetic ideals, and cognitive structures that supposedly made human nature qualitatively different from its "animal" counterparts. Historical knowledge appeared to confirm the idea that, if culture distinguished human beings from animals, the forms of culture were infinitely variable and both knowledge and values were culture-specific rather than "universal." Moreover, it appeared that historical knowledge itself, far from being the key to the comprehension of human nature, might be only a particular prejudice of modern Western civilization. Whence the need felt for new sciences of society and culture that would be genuinely universalistic in scope and orientation, utterly free of any link to the values of any specific culture, and programmatically ahistorical in their approach to the study of social and cultural phenomena.

Neo-positivism and structuralism were the forms assumed by the envisioned new sciences. These were offered as alternatives to a superannuated "historicism" in the human sciences in general and to traditional historical studies in particular. At issue in historical studies specifically was the possibility of an approach to the study of history shorn of the illusions of nineteenth-century "realism" in all its forms, literary, phil-osophical, social scientific, and historiographical alike.

In many respects, then, contemporary debates within the human sci-ences over the relation of traditional historiography to its "scientific" alternatives resemble current debates within the field of literary studies over the relation of literary realism to literary modernism—and not ac-cidentally, since what is at issue in both is the question of the adequacy of a given form of discourse, the narrative, to the representation of a given content, "historical reality." If the two debates seem seldom to converge or fuse, it is because each of them tends to take for granted as an *explanans* what the other treats as an *explanandum*.

Thus, for example, the debate within literary studies over modernism unfolds under the aegis of a notion, shared by modernists and anti-modernists alike, that "history" provides a neutral ground of "facts" that can be appealed to for the characterization of what modernism is really all about, what its true social or cultural significance consists of, and what its ideological function *really* is. This is especially the case when Marxist critics, secure in the conviction that Marxism *is* the science of history promised by the nineteenth century, purport to disclose the true ideological content and historical significance of modernism considered as a period style. Similarly, the debate within historical theory over the status of traditional narrative history proceeds on the assumption, shared by anti- and pro-narrativists alike, that narrative is a form of "literary" discourse, that literature deals in "imaginary" rather than "real" events, and that, therefore, historical studies must either purge themselves of narrative or use it only to make the "details" of historical reality "inter-esting" to an otherwise distracted readership. The literary critics appeal to history as an unproblematical body of facts for the solution of problems in literary theory, while the historical theorists appeal to what they conceive to be an unproblematical notion of the relation of "literature" to "reality" to site the question of narrative's function in historical dis-course. So it goes in most theoretical discussions: any given field of knowledge must presuppose the adequacy of the practices of at least one other field in order to get on with its business.

But modern literary theory provides a perspective on historical writing more comprehensive than those envisioned by participants in the debate over the nature of narrative discourse, on the one side, and those engaged in the debate over the nature of historical knowledge, on the other. Historical discourse (as against historical inquiry) is a special case of discourse in general. Consequently, theorists of historical discourse can-not afford to ignore the general theories of discourse that have been developed within modern literary theory, on the basis of new concep-tions of language, speech, and textuality which permit reformulations of the traditional notions of literality, reference, authorship, audience, and codes. Not because modern literary theory provides definitive answers to the questions raised by these new conceptions of language, speech, and textuality, but rather because, on the contrary, it has reproblematized an area of inquiry which, in historical theory at least, had for too long been treated as having nothing problematical about it.

In an essay published in *Communications* in 1972, Barthes suggested that the kind of interdisciplinary work demanded by the modern human sciences required, not so much the use of a number of established disciplines for the analysis of a traditionally defined object of study as rather the invention of a new object which would not belong to *any* particular established discipline.[36] Barthes proffered "the text" in its modern, linguistic-semiotic conceptualization as such an object. If we follow out the implications of this suggestion, we can begin to grasp the significance of modern literary theory for the understanding of what is involved in our own efforts to theorize historical writing. One of the most important implications is that we will no longer be able to regard the historiographical text as an unproblematical, neutral container of a content supposedly given in its entirety by a "reality" that lies beyond its confines. We do not have to go as far as Barthes was willing to go at that time in dividing "text" into the two possibilities of the "readerly" and the "writerly" and then holding that the former was only a special, disguised case of the latter—especially inasmuch as the heuristic utility of the notion of "text" derives from its function as designating a new problem for research rather than serving as a solution to an old one. We might wish, however, to explore the extent to which historical writing serves as the privileged site of the "readerly" text and provides a paradigm of all putatively "realistic" discourses.

Barthes himself suggested as much in an eassy entitled "The Discourse of History" (1970). Here he points out how contemporary scientific historiography has given up the quest for "the real" in favor of the more modest, and ultimately more "realistic" task of simply rendering history "intelligible." At that point in the development of his own theories of discursivity, Barthes thought that this entailed the abandonment of "narrative structure." He thought that because narrative had been "developed with the cauldron of fiction (in myths and the first epics)," it was *therefore* inherently unsuited to serve as "the sign and the proof of reality" in any discourse whatsoever.[37]

In Barthes's view, modern scientific history, by which he meant the structuralist historiography of the *Annales* type, resembled literary modernism by virtue of its interest in the "intelligible" rather than the "real." But if this is the case, it follows that "structuralist" history is no more "realistic" than traditional history. Moreover, if it is a question of the "intelligible" rather than the "real," narrative is just as effective a discursive instrumentality for producing it as the dissertative mode favored by every scientific historiography.

However, Barthes's suggestion of the resemblances between structuralist history and literary modernism does have implications for our understanding of what is involved in their apparent, shared hostility to narrative discourse. I say "apparent," because it is now possible to recognize that literary modernism did not so much reject narrativity, historicity, or even "realism," as rather explore the limits of their peculiarly nineteenth-century forms and expose the mutual complicity of these forms in the dominant discursive practices of high bourgeois culture. In the process, literary modernism revealed new or forgotten potentialities of narrative discourse itself, potentialities for rendering "intelligible" the specifically modern experiences of time, historicial consciousness, and social reality. Literary modernism did not repudiate narrative discourse, but discovered in it a content, linguistic and tropological, adequate to the representation of dimensions of historical life only implicitly perceived in nineteenth-century realism, both literary and historical. The adequacy of the "content of the form" of literary modernism to the representation of both the form *and* the content of the kind of historical life we wish to call "modern" argues for the relevance of literary modernism to a modern historical discourse.

It also argues, I would suggest, for the relevance of modern literary theory to our understanding of the issues being debated amongst theorists of historical thought, research, and writing. Not only because modern literary theory is in many respects fashioned out of the necessity of making sense of literary modernism, determining its historical specificity and significance as a cultural movement, and devising a critical practice adequate to its object of study. But also and primarily because modern literary theory must of necessity be a theory of history, historical consciousness, historical discourse, and historical writing.

3

Historical Worlds, Literary History

Brian Stock

I begin this essay with a personal reflection. I am honored to participate in a discussion of the present direction of literary theory. But my appearance in such a volume strikes me as being somewhat anomalous. My unease results from two rather different states of affairs. It comes about from the fact that I am a medievalist. It also arises from my methods, which are both historical and literary, and which are considered unorthodox by some of my colleagues.

I turn to the question of method shortly. Let me first address the issue of marginality as it relates to the field of medieval studies. Am I exaggerating? To some it may seem so. Our universities are well served by courses in medieval life and thought. Graduate programs have never been more popular. But this is a narrow band of academic culture. If one looks elsewhere, one sees another picture.

Especially if one takes the long view. Compare the situation of the medievalist today to his or her role in society a century ago. No one would deny that the medievalist appears more and more an outsider, even at times a stranger, to what successive periods of fashion have called the contemporary. I think of academic subjects like linguistics, sociology, and anthropology, which all began life in the university curriculum with a medieval component, as well as more practical fields like law, which, in the time of Maitland, was inseparable from a consideration of medieval traditions.[1] Among the founders of sociology, Max Weber, Georg Simmel, and Ernst Troeltsch were all acquainted with the fundamentals of medieval history. I recall only one major anthropologist in our time who began his work with a background in medieval studies, the late Victor Turner.

I hasten to add that the breakdown of contact with the roots of modern culture, as well as its historiography, in the Middle Ages is more apparent than real. What has happened is that the period between antiquity and the Renaissance has become both near and far at once. Allow me to explain.

The Middle Ages are no longer part of operative cultural memory, as they were in the days when medieval latinity still made up a part of the educational system. The medieval period of history, together with its cultural associations, has disappeared from everyday consciousness. This vanishing act has made it difficult to understand how aspects of "the medieval" can still influence our outlook. For instance, in a neighboring and modernizing culture, we learn of crowds of young people who follow the Imam Khomeni and are apparently eager for martyrdom. We suspend our powers of historical analogy and label the whole affair "irrational." We do not recall the Children's Crusade of 1212 or the economic and social changes that led up to it. We comfort ourselves with the idea that the negative element in medieval popular culture is definitively in the past. The existence of a "holy war" is just one sign among others that a certain style of medievalism is alive and well. It is also evidence that the symbols that influence thought and action are not always publicly accessible.

The Middle Ages, then, are near, even if they have been pushed into a literary unconscious. But they are also far. The period is now distant enough from contemporary culture that it is best viewed through the lens of anthropology. I am not referring to the uniting of methods of history and anthropology which was proposed many years ago by E. E. Evans-Pritchard, and which has benefited both disciplines. Rather, I have in mind that the Middle Ages has now joined the ranks of "other cultures." Medieval men and women are not as different from us as the Tikopia or the Azande. Nor are they as remote from our experience as archaic societies like the Mayans. But, like classical Greece or ancient Israel, they have become a society known to us principally through texts (or through artifacts decipherable as texts). If one leaves aside academic traditions and the human archives found by chance in isolated corners of Europe, it would be fair to suggest that the last effective link between the modern world and the Middle Ages was in the Catholic Church. When Latin was abandoned, that link was broken. Above all, one lost touch with liturgical memory, which had for centuries provided a bond of continuity between the communities of the living and the dead. One can regret the change, or try to recapture a lost sensibility through scholarly revivals (as did the Romantics, thereby helping to invent the modern study of the Middle Ages and to create a new audience for its art and literature). But these are efforts at historic nostalgia. Whether we like it or not, a phase of human development is now sufficiently alien in its pastness that we have no choice but to recognize it as such.

The acceptance of otherness is a starting point. But we must also bear in mind, as I suggest, that the distinctiveness of the Middle Ages arises from within western culture, not outside it. Where then do the operative boundaries lie? E. R. Curtius claimed that, for the purposes of literary history, the entire period between 1050 and 1750 exhibited a certain "unity of structure."[2] But this unity need not be understood only as referring to the teaching of rhetoric or the filiation of great minds. There is also continuity in the economic and social spheres. This was the thesis of Marc Bloch and Lucien Febvre, the founders of *Annales*, and of Fernand Braudel, who continued and institutionalized their program. As far as I am aware, Curtius made no use of their work; and, within the French school, there has been little or no acknowledgment of the German antecedents of *Annales*, who were active during Curtius's youth and undoubtedly influenced his outlook.[3] In view of the common background, which, between the wars, was overlooked primarily on political grounds, it is not surprising to find that Curtius's notion of a unity of structure is similar to Braudel's much discussed idea of *la longue durée*.

Annales is the mainstream of thinking about *mentalité* in our time. But *Annales* is best described as a great river with many tributaries, and all of these have not led in positive directions. It is not often enough pointed out that the success of *Annales* weakened the study of cultural history through overemphasis on economic factors, and, by taking its econometric models from the present, it inadvertently widened the gap separating the medieval and modern consciousness. While illuminating macrosociological aspects of *mentalité*, *Annales* dealt a serious blow to literary history by demoting such issues as intentions, individuality, and periodization. It also struck a blow at Marxist approaches to the sociology of literature by effectively replacing causality with types of functionalism. The theories of *mentalité* (I stress the plural) developed in the *Annales* tradition are less convincing as explanations than as records of adjuncts of material change. Until Michel Foucault, other approaches within *Annales* were not taken seriously. Many of the lessons learned patiently in two centuries of German philology and hermeneutics were forgotten, or, during the heyday of structuralism, deliberately abandoned.

Worse, as far as culture was concerned, continuity was stressed at the expense of productive conflict. Here again, the *Annales* tradition dovetailed curiously with German thinking, whose chief students of the Latin Middle Ages between the wars, Erich Auerbach, E.R. Curtius, and Leo Spitzer, came up with different versions of the same narrative of continuity, theirs taking the form of the passing away of Romance language unity. What this narrative could not account for was epochal change within the Latin West. The credibility gap widened as one approached A.D. 1050. There was general recognition that what took place was not just a mutant of the economy, nor was it just another medieval revival of classical studies. The age of Anselm, Abelard, and St. Bernard was something new. But new in what? What precisely was the "modernity" of which so many of the period's leading intellectuals spoke? Within the continuity thesis, there were many explanations.

One thinks of ideas about individuality, or that of the "renaissance of the twelfth century." However useful such notions were, they failed to capitalize on the sense of discontinuity which so many men and women in high Middle Ages felt and talked about.

One reason why the inner life of the age remained elusive was that the models of interpretation were largely oriented around separate disciplines. What was needed was an approach which transcended this limitation and attempted to account for literary and historical change at once. My contribution to the discussion was to suggest that we work at a more modest level than the disciplines of high culture, then or now, and to look, not so much at the content of ideas, but rather at the means of communication by which they were transmitted from one age to the next. In this perspective, the eleventh and twelfth centuries emerged as the period in which the West definitively consolidated a textual reference system for culture. Literate revolutions had occurred before: the Middle Ages were preceded by Israel, Greece, and Islam, and further back in time by India and China. But, just as these civilizations differed from each other in their uses of literacy, so they turned out to differ fundamentally from the medieval West. Furthermore, what took place in the Middle Ages was not a simple replacement of oral by written tradition, although this was what it was in part and that was how it was perceived at the time. Instead, there was a realignment of oral discourse within a real or implicit system of meaning involving texts, readings, interpretations, and audiences. Literacy, that is, the ability to read and write Latin, was not widespread, and this must not be forgotten. But numbers mattered less than the change in thinking that literacy stood for. The medieval non-literate was somewhat like the amateur in the world of computers. He was affected in subtle ways by a technology he did not fully understand. In the later Middle Ages, writing gradually emerged as the dominant form of cultural representation. The changes eventually touched the lives of everyone, literate and non-literate.

Literacy implies "literature." One of the questions that can be asked of my approach is what I mean by literarture and literary history. There is a simple and a complicated answer, which I take in order.

Put simply, if literacy creates literatures, then a literature is anything that can be written down (including much that is not written down during the Middle Ages owing to the conventions of oral discourse). Such literatures all have the qualities of narrative and discourse; they all tell stories about the past, and these stories are structured representations. As Natalie Davis has phrased it, there is a narrative even in the archives. Literary history therefore is not one but many; it is the histories of these literatures. The question is not whether a literature is "popular" or "learned," although that may be relevant, or whether the issue of genre is legitimate, since, in these terms, it is almost always a signpost to shifting psychological dispositions. The main concern of the student of *mentalité* is a recognition of the broadness and complexity of the field, from which no textualized monuments can be automatically excluded.

Some may be tempted to remark that what I am proposing is both obvious and unworkable. But what else does one do in a period like the Middle Ages in which there are few genuinely privileged texts and many works which, for other than purely literary purposes, have important stories to tell? Hugh of St. Victor observed sometime in the 1120s that there are as many *artes* as there are bodies of material to substantiate them.[4] He did not suggest, and I do not, that all literary history is the same. But an account of privileged writings, in Hugh's case the Bible and the pagan classics, does not rule out others. His persperctive is the right one for approaching the genesis of new modes of thought in the Middle Ages. It is right because we are dealing with a literary phenomenon, not an economic or social development in disguise; and because its history is therefore an ethical matter, as medieval hermeneutics makes abundantly clear.[5] What the Middle Ages lacks is a notion common to ancient and post-Renaissance criticism to the effect that everything which pertains to literature is highly literate. In this respect the study of its Latin and vernacular writings has a good deal to teach the informed contemporary reader.

One can put these issues another way. It is fashionable nowadays in the humanities to assert that our knowledge of the outside world is always mediated. For literates the chief form of mediation is the text. The next stage of the argument is a kind of solipsism, in which it is proposed that we know nothing but what we make of the text. We therefore know everything about what is unimportant, the mediating instrument, and nothing about what is important, knowledge outside what we read. Through deconstruction and pragmatics, many students have turned in frustration to bald alternatives—respectively, that the text can tell us nothing or that it can tell us everything. One answer to this type of skepticism has arisen in a new anti-intellectualism, which implies that theory is useless in literary studies. What is needed is a return to old-fashioned explications involving a lot of empirical facts and only empirical knots to tie them together. But there is another possibility. We can combine the subjectivity of the literary with the objectivity of the historical and thereby achieve an interpretive strategy which is literary and historical at once. This demands that we retain the positive achievements of structuralism, in particular the notion that a text is anything written and a good many things that are not; and more importantly, it demands that we return to some of the principles of the golden age of historical writing in the nineteenth century, an age which began with Jacob Burckhardt and came to a close in such works as Johan Huizinga's *Herfsttij der Middeleeuwen* (1919) and Ernst Kantorowicz's *Kaiser Friedrich der Zweite* (1931).[6]

It is not by accident that I have chosen as my examples two medievalists. Burckhardt too began life as a medievalist, and the debate over Burckhardt has largely consisted of differences of opinion over the meaning of the Middle Ages. In simplified terms the central question was, and is, whether the Middle Ages includes what we customarily call the Renaissance. The large literature on Burckhardt is paralleled by an equally great volume of studies devoted to Max Weber. While the two are rarely if ever compared, the revisionists to the "Protestant ethic" thesis have included a healthy number of medievalists, who have stressed that "capitalism," however we define it, was well established in the West before the fourteenth century. One may think what one wishes of the Middle Ages, and one may feel, as I do, that the contemporary medievalist is a mere shadow of his former self; but there is no doubt that the medieval past, along with classical antiquity, has played a major role, perhaps, through symbolic inversion, *the* major role, in creating the modern consciousness of the past. It has functioned as an historical memory for an entire civilization, and, like all memory, it has recorded many things which we prefer not to have recalled. When history was less a university discipline, and the historian less embarrassed to be creating what Sir Richard Southern calls "a work of art,"[7] it was easier to see the role of earlier periods in creating one's understanding of the present or the immediate past. The university curriculum suppresses the humanist ideal in the name of professionalism or the ideals of scientific historical research. As a result, our imaginative links with the past move into an historical unconscious.

I raised the possibility earlier of a more complicated answer to the problem of literacy and literary history. This involves a further consideration of subjectivity and objectivity. Before proceeding to this issue, it would be best if I clarified what I mean by these loaded terms.

When we take up the question of literacy and society, there are obviously two dimensions to what we are talking about. One dimension is part of the external world: in order to become literate, we have to make sense out of written characters, either letters or ideographs. These characters do not just exist in our minds, even though they may be the by-product of arbitrary connections between sound and mental events. Like numbers, they have both a cardinal and an ordinal sense, and, like numbers, they partially create meaning from the outside. Although they have a mental existence, their existence does not depend on their being mental.

If we move from letters to texts, the same relations hold. Recent psychological research has reaffirmed Augustine's view that a text acts upon the mind in the way that a blueprint works for an architect.[8] It is a skeletal structure or an ordered set of clues. In this sense it has an objective existence. The finished design, on the other hand, is a product of the understander's mind: it interrelates perception, intentionality, and representation. It stands in a subjective relationship to the objectively existing written characters in the outside world. We may put this another way by saying that, as far as literateness is concerned, objective and subjective mean outside and inside the mind. The products of thought also attain a kind of objectivity, as Kant observed. But this is another matter. In framing the problem in black and white terms I have for the moment ruled out many relationships crucial to the growing field of pragmatics. I have done so because it is important to establish at the outset of any inquiry into new forms of consciousness that objectivity is not just an aspect of subjectivity, an easily manageable and reducible perspective on a reality we can never know. W. V. O. Quine has remarked that about ninety-nine percent of what a scientist does is subjective. Here I am concerned with the other one percent. For, in the reading process, one can make a similar case. The creation of the text is largely the work of the reading subject. But the brain cannot, and we should not, dispense with the notion of external signs.

The growth of literacy in the medieval West, then, is *both* a literary and an historical problem, not, as some would see it, a problem in historical rhetoric or literary history alone. And it is literary history because it is first history in the sense that, with the shift from oral to written culture, linguistic events are perceived as textualized facts. This is evident if one observes, as I did, the relationship in the Middle Ages between written communication and the interpretive models which arose from and helped to shape medieval life and thought.

Two issues stand out here in particular importance.[9] First, what happens when texts are introduced into formerly non-literate groups? There is a long prehistory to this problem: it lies at the root of *mentalité*, as well as theories of cognitive development from Lévi-Bruhl to Lévi-Strauss. The two sides in the debate have usually asked, using preconceptions as their point of departure, whether it is, as Marx suggested, material forces which influence beliefs, attitudes, and actions, or whether, as Max Weber responded, the forces might have acted at least some of the time the other way. My approach is not to concentrate on the dramatic beginnings or ends of the process, that is, depending on one's ideology, on matter or mind, but on the intervening or mediating stages of development, which have not been given adequate attention. At the risk of overgeneralizing, I would see a reiteration of a pattern. As individuals learn to read, or have texts read to them, they invent or intend models through which to act and to interpret their actions. Worlds are projected, then lived: having been lived, they are projected, modified, and lived again. The constructive and reconstructive patterns amount to a type of literary history, but this must be understood literally as a combination of conceptual schemes and experienced narratives for which texts are merely switching-stations. This type of analysis is especially helpful with medieval literary and historical materials. The necessity of a textual reference system for action was normal for a society discovering literacy, and often led to the projection of literary models where there was little or no evidence to back them up: false genealogies, imaginative historical reconstructions, and above all highly creative uses for forgery.[10] For, in falsifying a text, the forger nonetheless created the ordered set of relations in all texts. These could be used for dishonest profit, but they could also serve as schemata for what were believed to be righteous, even divinely inspired plans.

A relation emerged, I found, between texts and what I have called textual communities: it was a reversal of what we normally think happens in the realm of theory and practice; that is, it resulted not in a set of conceptualized processes but in processualized concepts. Moreover, the tentative solution to this problem naturally led to a second issue. If texts were the operative units influencing medieval micro-societies, what did the individuals in these communities mean when they spoke of "texts"? Where did texts rest on the admittedly hazy boundary separating language and ontology? As it turned out, at the same time as textual communities emerged in large numbers, a theoretical debate was also undertaken on this very question. It centered on the nature of the eucharist, the ceremony of consecration of the bread and wine during the mass. The basic issue was how, by analogy with a text, something which was changing could be permanent, or, put differently, how something inwardly eternal could be outwardly subject to time. The solution—if one can call it that—involved a rebirth of hermeneutics, for what the participants ended up talking about was not relations between things but relations between texts. What resulted from this long, complex debate was not an acceptable definition of a text, or of reality, but the humbling recognition that, in a literate society, there is no way to bypass textual mediators between experience and expression. It is no accident that so much of later medieval philosophy was devoted to the question of language, things, and thoughts. It is no accident that the problem was not solved then, and is not solved today.

I have drawn upon two examples from my research in order to illustrate what, in my view, is a central issue in *mentalité*. The process is close to what Nelson Goodman calls "worldmaking," the symbolic procedures by which minds construct universes of meaning out of worlds already known and bring these constructions to bear on their thoughts and actions.[11] What I have rejected in the earlier theory of *mentalité* is not the priority of economic and social over cultural forces but the idea that there are any priorities at all. For, if we are to reason consistently, we have to give up the notion that we are ever in direct contact with a reality that is totally independent of what goes on in our minds, even though the existence of that reality is not called into doubt. Beginning readers do not read in the absence of prior knowledge; even non-literates experiencing literate culture for the first time come to the written word with their own agendas.

The view I am espousing goes back to Kant and Hume, but it amounts to a textual rather than a philosophical reinstatement of subjectivity.[12] And its insights can be used in two ways. One is to demythologize the medieval worldview of itself, which was based on the notion of an aboriginal reality independent of our own minds and hence on a version of what Alfred Tarski has called the correspondence theory of truth.[13] At the very moment this view was in its heyday, the mid-thirteenth century, it was already being undermined. The major force at work was not heresy, a rival philosophy, or internal opposition in theology, although all of these existed and have been singled out by historians as causes of the breakup of monolithic realism in medieval thought: it was rather a more subtle revolution brought about by writers, readers, and audiences. What happened in the medieval world was so mundane and predictable that it hardly needs documentation. As the activities of reading and writing grew, so did the varieties of interpretation. A realm of subjective cognition gradually took shape which had as its basis the humanist ideal of the thinking subject as opposed to the object of thought. This type of individualism, even when it acted transindividually, seriously undermined the concept of a single, stable external reality because the inherited idea of the real was now denied by the fluctuating forms of consciousness by which the real was brought into being. Every person who read, listened, debated, and thought could potentially arrive at somewhat different conclusions about what a text meant. And this meant, *in potentia,* that all texts had either an arbitrary meaning or no meaning at all—a point wryly noted by Ockham. The birth of readership is often assumed to be a Reformation phenomenon, which had to await the arrival of the printed book. But to view the changes from this vantage point is to see only the end of a long process which begins around the eleventh century. It would be a more accurate reflection of the historical record to propose that subjective hermeneutics, once they were implanted in western thinking, could only grow in one direction. Ironically, the result of this development was the controverting of the culture in which they were born.

The first lesson, then, is deconstructive, or, more precisely, destructive: it is to show that what has been taken to be the "medieval world-picture" is not a picture at all—even the metaphor, I suspect, is more suitable for the Renaissance—but a generalization based upon syntheses which were falling apart the moment they were brought into being. But there is another, more positive role for this sort of research. This is the reconstruction of the ways in which the medievals made their worlds and the manner in which these perceptual and cognitive structures, once invented, lived narrative lives of their own, influencing a wide variety of activities. For, if we replace the notion of an external reality to which all subjective thought refers with the more useful conception of objective and subjective worlds as schemata of thought, then a central role is assignable to the reading process and to literary history. Such an approach has greater validity for the medievals than for ourselves. Owing to the literary nature of all education, their mental worlds were not only made of previous constructions, as all mental worlds are, but, in the absence of what we would call science, statistics, or experimentation, they were made of previous *literary* worlds. In any literate culture, and especially in a culture discovering literacy, these worlds are by-products of the reading process. They are the active recreations of a tradition which is no longer identifiable with transmission by word of mouth but by sacred texts, written laws, and literature. This history is not only literary history, but is always involved in literary history.

So far in this essay I have been focusing on one dimension of the problem of medieval communications, namely literacy. I now wish to discuss reading, which is a related area of interest. Before doing so, it may be useful to distinguish between "literacy" and "reading" as conceptual tools. Although they are obviously parts of a whole, the difference between them is important in the understanding of ideas and society.

The issues can be conveniently approached by recalling a major weakness in classical theories of social psychology, which arose from the intellectual clumsiness with which they tried to bridge the individual and the collective. The goal was an account of the transindividual; in order to achieve it, the particular aspects of historical experience were uninterpreted, misinterpreted, or simply left to speak for themselves. Although they differ in much else, an avoidance of individuality is common to Marxist, Weberian, and Durkheimian notions of ideas and society, as well as to their various contemporary offshoots. Structuralism and post-structuralism are in part expressions of frustration at the failure of older sociologies to offer a definitive solution to the problem. But it is here that a theory of communication which distinguishes between literacy and reading can be of value. For the view from the vantage point of literacy begins with the collective. The point of departure of reading is the individual. If we adequately describe relations between the two, we have effectively bridged the gap.

The essential difference can be put as follows. There are a number of aspects of the problem of literacy which have to be considered in individual terms, beginning with the standard test of being able to sign one's name. Nonetheless, the study of literacy is primarily an avenue into the field of collective mentality. This is because a concept like literacy has no meaning outside the society which defines its terms of reference. In the notion of reading just the opposite state of affairs obtains. We may speak of the reading habits of a society, but we are using a metaphor to describe the activities of individuals. For everyone reads with his or her set of eyes. To speak of literacy is therefore to shift the discussion towards the societal; to speak of reading is to shift it towards the individual. The ideal is to work from the two focal points of communication at once.

If we orient the inquiry in this manner, a number of literary and historical questions naturally come to mind.

The first concerns reading itself.[14] We have to ask what is meant by reading. This involves a minute investigation of terms like *ráedan* and *legere* as well as the larger relations between perception and cognition. We have to determine whether there were differences between ancient and medieval culture, and, more importantly, between the three major religions of the medieval West, Judaism, Christianity, and Islam. Another set of questions can be asked about internal matters. How did reading transmit oral versus written messages? How was the text recreated and conditioned by readers and listeners? Did it matter whether they were high or low born, or whether they were literate or non-literate? Again, how did reading practices impinge upon modes of interpretation and explanation? Is it accidental that a new era of silent reading in the West in the twelfth century coincides with the appearance of Hugh of St. Victor's *Didascalicon*, in which, for the first time, reading and hermeneutics are viewed as a single issue? Finally, we have to ask how the shift from word to text affected the mechanization of culture, the creation of a cultural marketplace, and the prerogatives which Foucault identified as epistemic sources of power.

A second set of issues concerns the manner in which reading, silently or aloud, relates to inner mental processes. In general, during the eleventh, twelfth, and thirteenth centuries, reading was the most potent single force bringing about the rediscovery of the inner life of men and women. One of the first signs of this was a renewed interest in auto-biography, which is visible in the actual life histories of men like Abelard and Guibert of Nogent, but which also surfaces in saints' lives, chronicles, and poetry. Subjectivity and personal experiences were re-evalued along with a whole range of distinctions involving the internal and the external. There was also an interest in abstraction, in intentionality, and in forms of religious experience involving combinations of inner commitment and outer expression, such as conversion, confession, and the examination of conscience. Mental states were isolated in secular contexts; there arose a new literature of dreams, visions, and the emotional life. The notion of interiority found its way into more academic pursuits. In historical writing, for instance, there was a growing awareness of an inner logic, meaning, or mystery to outer actions, an intentional pattern which was often concealed by the apparent randomness of events. In scientific thinking the dominant metaphor was *homo microcosmos*, man as a mi-crocosm of the natural forces at work in the universe. And the notion of interiority lies behind the medieval and contemporary debate on individualism.

These may be called aspects of consciousness based upon reading, and they worked in harmony with memory. The growth of reading habits extended the range of what William James called short-term and long-term memory. For, as storage passed from reliance on the human mind alone to a combination of mind with external archives, the accessing and processing of information became easier, more democratic, and decid-edly functional. The scholastic system, Abelard proposed, was more accurate and objective than classroom exercises based on verbal inter-change and personal recollection. Reading also favored the increase in range of two other sorts of recall, personally experienced events and symbolically representable knowledge. Through the exercise of memory, now augmented by written versions of past events, medieval authors helped to invent a complex remembrance of things past, imparting to experience a historical and phenomenal flavor which distinguished it from perception, thought, or imagination. This episodic or narrative recollection was part of a more protean development, the extension of semantic memory.[15] Through the lexicalization and legibility of language, the generic or categorical memories by which individuals clarified, in-terrelated, and characterized objects and events were greatly enhanced. Historic nostalgia is a common theme in medieval writing, as is the interaction of the individual and collective aspects of memory.

As the variety of conscious activity increased, so did interest in the private life. From the eleventh century a number of roles involving public and private knowledge began to undergo change and in some cases to reverse the patterns of the early Middle Ages. In the largely oral society of the "first feudal age," private experience was largely left unrecorded. What had value for society was publicly displayed and frequently immemorialized in ritual. After 1050, by contrast, public routines and rituals acquired value chiefly as they related to the meaningful structures of inner experience. Externalities, now recognized as such, became meaningless, as numerous heretics and reformers noted in their criticism of the Church. The model for this new emphasis on private experience was reading, either individual reading in the case of prayer, devotions, and poetry, or public reading, as in the case of preaching and recited literature. One possible laboratory for examining this transformation is the idea of penance, which, in the Middle Ages, is both a sacrament and a group of rites, symbolic activities, and patterns of thought in secular culture. As one passes from the public penance of the later ancient world and the early Middle Ages to the largely private penitential system of the later Middle Ages, one also proceeds from an age of public to one of private reading. The arbiter of experience, here as elsewhere, is the interior mental event, which is analyzed in conjunction with texts, reading, and audiences. This interiority is also one of the starting points for rule-based ethical and social theory, which, Max Weber argued, distinguishes western from eastern institutional development.

One way of looking at these patterns of inner and outer activity is to call them narratives. As I have noted, with the rise of literacy, we see the emergence of textual communities for interrelating thought and action among interpretive groups. We also observe different levels of understanding of story and discourse. In medievel terms, the latter refers mainly to a separation of the sequence of events themselves from their representation in an oral or a written form. The growth of readers, listeners, and a public in the later Middle Ages chiefly affected the nature of discourse, which, as an autonomous structure obeying the rules of intertextuality, began to play a large role in relating ideas and society. One of the major lines of development in this complicated history arises from the manner in which the conceiving and playing out of narrative roles acted as an instrument for the introduction of moral and ethical notions into everyday life. There were many ways in which this took place: in preaching, in hagiography, in art and architecture, in liturgy, and in mass rituals like the pilgrimage. The common factor in these experiences was the endowing of life with a narrative pattern, which, whether conceptualized or dramatically enacted, related behavior to a script which was assumed to have acquired aesthetic coherence and moral value. Ethical rightness provided a rationale for action; through narrative design, stories were viewed as structures embodying principles of rationality. These principles could be extracted from the stories, codified and discussed separately, as scholastic hermeneutics emphasized. But the rise of new relations between the individual and society in the

Middle Ages was inseparable from the rules, metaphors, and histories inherent in the narratives themselves.

The final chapter in an inquiry of the type I have roughly outlined is a re-examination of tradition, not only of its content, but more particularly its literary history, its relationship to writers, readers, and publics. Tradition is perhaps the most poorly understood of our basic concepts for dealing with culture. Divergent notions in Marxist and non-Marxist critical theory have not clarified the picture,[16] and, in the field of religion, Protestants and Catholics, to mention only two religious groups, appear to be willing to engage in an ecumenical dialogue but not as yet to embrace a common approach to cultural language.[17] Since the later nineteenth century, tradition has also been something of an anomaly in theories of modernization and rationalization.[18]

The question of tradition is inseparable from the transition from oral to written culture and from the emergence of a society of readers. In the West, this passage begins as early as the New Testament, whose authors, it has been convincingly shown, shared technics of oral teaching and memorization with contemporary rabbinic schools.[19] In Christianity, the formative stage of the idea of *traditio* or $\pi\alpha\rho\acute{\alpha}\delta\sigma\sigma\iota\varsigma$ reaches its culmination in the well-known reflections of Irenaeus of Lyons. A second phase is initiated in the ninth century, and develops its range of interests in the late eleventh-century biblical theology of Anselm of Laon. But the issues are by this time too complex to be identified with a single figure, school, or manner of thinking. What is shared by all medieval accounts of early Christianity is a sufficient distance from the original events that all discussion effectively concerns the problems of texts and interpretations. Divine intercessions apart, meaning can only be acquired from reading, or rather from readings. What is in fact reading becomes identified with the process of thinking. The basic positions in hermeneutics appear— text-orientation and reader-orientation. The principles evolved in theological debate gradually feed into poetry, prose, and the consideration of social issues. Tradition, or opposition to a certain idea of tradition, becomes a mainspring of change: the reconstruction of tradition by means of what is largely literary history is the foundation on which medieval culture is built. The objective uses of tradition are easy to tabulate, and include the authors, schools, churches, and ideologies through which a *translatio studii* is brought about. The subjective uses of tradition are more varied and less easy to categorize. At one extreme one finds the endowing of language with a seminal and totalistic force which leads eventually to nominalism. But there is a more balanced approach to language and culture. It appears as early as Augustine, it expands its horizons during the Middle Ages, and it reappears much later in such writers as Vico and Dilthey.

4

Perceptive Equilibrium: Literary Theory and Ethical Theory

Martha Nussbaum

> Mrs. Newsome's dress was never in any degree 'cut down',
> and she never wore round her throat a broad red velvet band:
> if she had, moreover, would it ever have served so to carry
> on and complicate, as he now almost felt, his vision?[1]

Speaking to Little Bilham about Chad Newsome's surprising development, Strether describes his own viewpoint and his interest:

> I'm speaking—in connexion with her—of his manners and morals, his
> character and life. I'm speaking of him as a person to deal with and
> talk with and live with—speaking of him as a social animal. (170)

The speech of literary theory, especially in recent years, has not often shared Strether's concerns and connections. I believe that it has an impoverished future without them. I imagine, instead, a future in which our talk about literature will return, increasingly, to a concern with the practical—to the ethical and social questions that give literature its high importance in our lives. A future in which these interests, like Strether's here, will find themselves connected to an interest in Mme. de Vionnet—in, that is, those emotions and desires that do not reside harmoniously within the domain of ethical judgment. In which a literary-philosophical inquiry, with something like Strether's "candour of fancy" (30) and his "conscientious wonder" (28), will ask what literary works express about these matters—express in virtue of their "content," but also, and inseparably, in virtue of their forms and structures, their ways of describing: since those ways are "at all times" (as Strether "philosophized") "the very conditions of perception, the terms of thought" (202). In short: a future in which literary theory (while not forgetting its many other pursuits) will also join with ethical theory in pursuit of the question, "How should one live?"

Join, I mean, not as didactic moralist but as both devious ally and subversive critic. For we notice that Strether's answer contrasts his own fuller perception of Chad with the narrow moralizing vision of Woollett Massachusetts. And before the assault of Strether's crowded perceptions those of us who are drawn to systematic ethical theorizing will be likely to feel, as he does, that "an inexorable tide of light seems to have floated us into our perhaps still queerer knowledge"(293).

The Absence of the Ethical

Recent literary theory has taken a keen interest in philosophy. In fact, it is hard to distinguish it from philosophy, either by the nature of its questions or by the names to which it turns for illumination. Questions about realism, relativism, and subjectivism; about skepticism and justification; about the nature of language—these are now common ground between the two professions. And in pursuit of these questions literary theory discusses and teaches not only the work of philosophers who write directly about literary matters (such as Nietzsche, Heidegger, Hans-Georg Gadamer, Stanley Cavell, Nelson Goodman, Hilary Putnam), but also the ideas of many (for example W.V.O. Quine, Paul Feyerabend, S.A. Kripke, Thomas Kuhn, Jürgen Habermas) who do not. (These lists, intentionally eclectic, show, too, the diversity of the philosophical styles and methods that have influenced the current literary scene.) Indeed, with several prominent contemporary figures—above all Jacques Derrida and Richard Rorty—there is no clear answer to the question, to which profession do they belong? The question, indeed, loses its interest, since the professions share so many issues, and since differences about method are internal to each group, rather than divided simply along disciplinary lines.

But when we turn from epistemology to ethics, the situation is very different. This is a rich and wonderful time in moral philosophy.[2] One cannot find for generations—since the time of John Stuart Mill, if not earlier—an era in which there has been so much excellent, adventurous, and varied work on the central ethical and political questions of human life. Questions about justice, about well-being and social distribution, about moral realism and relativism, about the nature of rationality, about the concept of the person, about the emotions and desires, about the role of luck in human life—all these and others are debated from many sides with considerable excitement and even urgency. These philosophical debates have frequently become interdisciplinary, touching as they do upon human issues that are central to more than one field of study. On the emotions, for example, moral philosophers have a lively dialogue with psychologists; on moral relativism, with cultural anthropologists;

on rationality and well-being, with economists. One would certainly expect that literature and theory about literature would play a role in these debates. For literature offers us insight on all of these questions, and in a way that is inextricable from literary forms. So one would expect that the people whose profession it is to think in general about literature and its forms would speak to these issues and join in these public debates.

This, we know, has not happened. Literary criticism dealing with particular texts and authors continues, of course, to speak about the ethical and social concerns that are central to those authors. But even this sort of concern has been constrained by pressure of the current thought that to discuss a text's ethical or social content is somehow to neglect "textuality," the complex relationships of that text with other texts; and of the related, though more extreme, thought that texts do not refer to human life at all, but only to other texts and to themselves.[3] And if one turns from criticism to more general and theoretical writing about literature, the ethical vanishes more or less altogether. One way we perceive this is by considering the philosophical references. Philosophers' names constantly appear. But the names of the leading moral and political philosophers of our day—of John Rawls, Bernard Williams, Thomas Nagel, Derek Parfit, Amartya Sen, Gerald Cohen, Thomas Scanlon, and still others—and also the names of the great moral philosophers of the past—of Mill, Bentham, Henry Sidgwick, Rousseau, of the ethical sides of Plato, Aristotle, Hume, and Kant—do not appear, more or less, at all. (This is strikingly true even of those recent moral philosophers, such as Bernard Williams, Hilary Putnam, and Iris Murdoch, who have criticized systematic ethical theory in ways that lead them to ally themselves with literature.) These writers about ethics are not studied in literary theory programs, as their epistemological and metaphysical companions are; those among them (past and present) who write on both ethics and epistemology are studied one-sidedly. In short, these diverse and excellent analyses of human social experience are usually not taken to have any interesting bearing on the activity of the theorist.

Literary theory could neglect moral philosophy and still show a keen interest in the ethical—though I shall later offer, tentatively, some reasons why a turn to philosophy can offer valuable illumination here. But in the midst of all this busy concern with other types of philosophy, the absence of moral philosophy seems a significant sign. And in fact it signals a further striking absence: the absence, from literary theory, of the organizing questions of moral philosophy, and of moral philosophy's sense of urgency about these questions. The sense that we are social beings puzzling out, in times of great moral difficulty, what might be, for us, the best way to live—this sense of practical importance, which animates contemporary ethical theory and has always animated much of great literature, is absent from the writings of many of our leading literary theorists. One can have no clearer single measure of this absence than to have the experience of reading Jacques Derrida's *Épérons*[4] after reading Nietzsche. Once one has worked through and been suitably (I think) impressed by Derrida's perceptive and witty analysis of Nietzsche's style, one feels, at the end of all the urbanity, an empty longing amounting to a hunger, a longing for the sense of difficulty and risk and practical urgency that are inseparable from Zarathustra's dance. A longing for some acknowledgment of the fact that Nietzsche saw a crisis at hand for Europe, for all of human life; that he thought it mattered deeply whether one lived as a Christian or in some other as yet unspecified way; and that he dedicated his career to imagining that way. Nietzsche's work is profoundly critical of existing ethical theory, clearly; but it is, *inter alia*, a response to the original Socratic question, "How should one live?" Derrida does not touch on that question. "Of all that is written," says Zarathustra, "I love only what a man has written with his blood."[5] After reading Derrida, and not Derrida alone, I feel a certain hunger for blood. For, that is, writing about literature that talks of human lives and choices as if they matter to us all.[6]

This is, after all, the spirit in which great literature has been and is written and read. We do approach literature for play and for delight, for the exhilaration of following the dance of form and unraveling webs of textual connection. (Though even here I would not be quick to grant that there is any coherence to an account of aesthetic pleasure that abstracts altogether from our practical human interests and desires.) But one of the things that makes literature something deeper and more central for us than a complex game, deeper even than those games, for example chess and tennis, that move us to wonder by their complex beauty, is that it speaks like Strether. It speaks *about us*, about our lives and choices and emotions, about our social existence and the totality of our connections.[7] As Aristotle observed, it is deep, and conducive to our inquiry about how to live, because it does not simply (as history does) record that this or that event happened; it searches for patterns of possibility—of choice, and circumstance, and the interaction between choice and circumstance—that turn up in human lives with such a persistence that they must be regarded as *our* possibilities. And so our interest in literature becomes (like Strether's in Chad) cognitive: an interest in finding out (by seeing and feeling and otherwise perceiving) what possibilities (and tragic impossibilities) life offers to us, what hopes and fears for ourselves it underwrites or subverts.[8]

To explain how literary theory lost this practical dimension would be a long story. This story would include the influence of Kant's aesthetics; of early twentieth-century formalism; of the New Criticism. It would include the influence of several prevailing trends in ethical theory as well—above all that of Kantianism and of Utilitarianism, ethical views that in their different ways were so inhospitable to any possible relation with imaginative literature that dialogue was cut off from the side of ethics as well.[9] It would include, too, a critical look at some writing about literature that did, during this long period, keep ethical concerns in view. For much of this writing has understandably given ethical writing about literature a bad name, by its neglect of literary form and its reductive moralizing manner. It has been easy enough to feel that ethical writing must do violence to the literary work. Of course it should have been obvious that to concentrate on form to the neglect of the work's sense of life and choice is not a solution, only violence of a different sort. It should have been recognized that neither sort of violence is required: that we grasp the practical content of a literary text adequately only when we attentively study the forms in which it is embodied and expressed; and that, in turn, we have not correctly described the literary form of, say, a James novel if we have not asked what sense of life it expresses. But, with certain striking exceptions,[10] this was on the whole not acknowledged; and we can see the historical reasons why.

One important task for a future literary theory, as I see it, will be to write out this history in detail. I shall not attempt that task here. I shall instead begin on a different part of the enterprise that I imagine. By bringing one example forward in a certain amount of detail, I shall try to illustrate this idea of a literary theory that works together with ethical theory, sketching out some of the concerns this theory might have; and I shall suggest ways in which a dialogue with moral philosophers might help us develop them. It will be no surprise by this point in the argument that I shall talk about James's *The Ambassadors*, which I take to be a major work in moral philosophy—talking about what it is to be assailed by a perception, about how the character of Mrs. Newsome's gown points to a deficiency in some accounts of ethical rationality that even now influence our daily lives.

Reflective Equilibrium

But before we can begin to talk of Strether we need some story, however sketchy and incomplete, about the enterprise in which I propose to join literary theory with ethical theory.[11] For some enterprises, and some descriptions of this one, will demote one or the other party to the partnership. The very difficulty of discovering a non-prejudicial description of the task of ethical inquiry will itself illuminate our problem; and the concealed prejudices in prominent contemporary philosophical descriptions of the task will begin to show us what moral philosophy has lost through the absence of a dialogue with literary thought.

I have said that the question with which my projected literary-ethical inquiry begins is the question, "How should one live?"[12] This choice of starting point is significant. This question does not (like the Kantian question, "What is my moral duty?") assume that there is a sphere of "moral" values that can be separated off from all the other practical values that figure in a human life. Nor does it assume, as does the utilitarian's focus on the question, "How shall I maximize utility?" that the value of all choices and actions is to be assessed in terms of a certain sort of consequence that they tend to promote. It does not assume the denial of these claims either. So far it is neutral, leaving them for investigation inside the inquiry. The point is to state the opening question in a general and inclusive way, excluding at the start no major story about the good life for human beings.

The inquiry asks, then, what it is for a human being to live well. This investigation as I imagine it, is both empirical and practical. Empirical, in that it is based upon and responsible to actual human experience; it aims to elicit an "intelligent report," as James puts it, of that experience— that is, of "our apprehension and our measure of what happens to us as social beings."[13] (It is not, as Kant thought, *a priori*.) Practical in that it is conducted by people who are themselves involved in acting and choosing and who see the inquiry as having a bearing on their own practical ends. They do not inquire in a "pure" or detached manner, asking what the truth about ethical value might be as if they were asking for a description of some separately existing Platonic reality. They are looking for something in human life, something, in fact, that they themselves are going to try to bring about in their lives. What they are asking is not, what is the good "out there," but, what can we best live by, and live together as social beings? Their results are constrained, and appropriately constrained, by their hopes and fears for themselves, their sense of value, what they think they can live with. This does not mean that inquiry cannot substantially modify their antecedent conception of their "target," specifying goals that were vague before and even convincing them to revise in substantial ways their conception of their goal. But their end is practice, not just theory. And inquiry is valuable because it contributes to practice in two ways: by promoting individual clarification and self-understanding, and by moving individuals towards communal attunement.[14] By now this view of procedure should be recognizable as Aristotle's; it has been endorsed and used by later thinkers, such as Henry Sidgwick and, recently and influentially, by John Rawls, in *A*

Theory of Justice.[15] It has a good deal in common with Henry James's remarks about his purpose as a novelist.

The central procedural idea is that we work through the major alternative views about the good life, holding them up, in each case, against our own experience and our intuitions. The first step will be to get a perspicuous description of these alternatives (though we should bear in mind that these descriptions will already contain an element of evaluation and response). Prominent among these views will be views embodied in texts of many kinds, both recent and older. Next we notice and clearly describe the conflicts and tensions among the views that we find. Where there is inconsistency or irreconcilable tension—and where this tension corresponds to something that we notice in our own experience and thought (individually or communally) we aim to revise the overall picture so as to bring it into harmony with itself, preserving, as Aristotle says, "the greatest number and the most basic" of the original judgments and perceptions. There is no rule about how to do this.[16] Individuals simply ask what looks deepest, what they can least live without—guided by their sense of life, and by their standing interest in consistency and in community. That is, they want to arrive at a view that is internally coherent, and also at one that is broadly shared and sharable. (Thus frequently they will move away from a personal claim, even when narrow consistency does not require it, in order to find one on which more of them can agree.) Nothing else is non-negotiable, not even the precise interpretation of these regulative principles themselves. The procedure is holistic:[17] it holds nothing unrevisable, but seeks for coherence and "fit" in the system as a whole.

So far, notice, we have said nothing about what faculties of the person (intellect, imagination, emotion) we trust, or trust most, inside the procedure; nothing, again, about which judgments we would tend to trust more than others; and nothing very concrete about how, and in what result, the procedure comes to an end. This is appropriate, since norms of good (or rational) judgment and appropriate sorting—of the intelligent "reading" of life—are themselves up for debate inside the procedure. But in preparing the way for Henry James's contribution (which I believe to be closely related to Aristotle's), I want to describe a prominent and influential version of the Aristotelian procedure that does add at this point some further (and very un-Aristotelian) specifications. What is interesting for us is that these are added as if they were about as non-controversial as anything could possibly be; and indeed, within the tradition of modern moral philosophy, this is pretty well true. In *A Theory of Justice*, then, describing the task of moral theory, John Rawls adopts a procedure that he traces explicitly to Aristotle; but he makes three significant additions to the general outline I have reported.[18] First, Rawls gives a name to the desired end of the procedure: it is "reflective equilibrium." This is the condition at which we arrive when we have gone through the procedure; the name suggests balance, an absence of inconsistency or tension, and the dominance of intellectual judgment. Second, he provides an account of "considered judgment" that tells us which judgments to trust and mistrust during the procedure. (He seems to assume from the start that we are using only standing judgments of varying degrees of concreteness, and not immersed situational perceptions.)[19] Mistrusted will be "those judgments made with hesitation, or in which we have little confidence. Similarly, those given when we are upset or frightened, or when we stand to gain one way or another can be left aside."[20] This is taken to give us the conditions "in which our moral capacities are most likely to be displayed without distortion."[21] Finally, Rawls later adds five constraints that must be met by any ethical theory that will even be seriously considered during the procedure of scrutiny. These conditions are that its principles should be *general* in form and *universal* in application; that they should be *public* and available to all; that they should impose a general ordering on conflicting claims; and that these principles should be regarded as final and conclusive— "the final court of appeal in practical reasoning." In short, "if we think in terms of the fully general theory which has principles for all the virtues, then such a theory specifies the totality of relevant considerations and their appropriate weights, and its requirements are decisive."[22]

I have said that Rawls regards these requirements, including the final five, as relatively uncontroversial. And so, indeed, they have been, in contemporary debates about his (otherwise controversial) theory. Strether's relation to them is no simple one, as we shall see; much of our work on his story will consist in articulating this (sometimes tragic) relation. And in general we might expect that ethical thought that begins from literature—which, if it shares anything at all, would seem to share a commitment to the ethical relevance of particularity and to the epistemological value of feeling—would not find these limits at all trivial or uncontroversial. Should we indeed aim at a condition of balance or equilibrium? Should this equilibrium indeed be "reflective"—that is, presumably, (as Rawls uses the word) a condition that is detached from powerful feeling and from particular situational immersion? Should we in fact exclude our bewilderment and our hesitation from the deliberative process? Should we automatically mistrust the information given us by our fear, or grief, or love? (For being in love would surely count as a case of "being upset.") Should we in fact go for theories that embody generality and universality—rather than saying, with Aristotle, that "the discrimination lies in perception"?[23] Do we believe that a general (rather than a particular) ordering *can* be imposed, and imposed in advance, upon conflicting claims? Above all, do we feel that a general system of principles can and should be a court of last appeal in practical reasoning, determining standards all in advance of life itself? In these conditions we begin to sense the austere presence of Mrs. Newsome, "all fine cold thought," impervious to surprise, idealistic and exceptionless in her justice.

Straightness and Surprise

'That's just her difficulty—that she doesn't admit surprises. It's a fact that, I think, describes and represents her; and it falls in with what I tell you—that she's all, as I've called it, fine cold thought. She had, to her own mind, worked the whole thing out in advance, and worked it out for me as well as for herself. Whenever she has done that, you see, there's no room left; no margin, as it were, for any alteration. She's filled as full, packed as tight, as she'll hold, and if you wish to get anything more or different either out or in—'

'You've got to make over altogether the woman herself?'

'What it comes to,' said Strether, 'is that you've got morally and intellectually to get rid of her.' (317)

James's richly comic portrait of Mrs. Newsome lies at the center of his story of Strether's adventure. Present vividly in her absence, she articulates, by contrast, Strether's moral movement; he begins as her ambassador, the agent of her antecedently fixed moral purpose: he ends as a child "toddling" alone, a diver in depths, a hearer of strange and crowded voices, a floater upon inexorable tides of light. To understand Strether's struggle we must understand *her*—and with a certain sympathy: asking how, for example, her refusal of surprise "falls in" with the fact that she is all fine cold thought, asking, too, why her vision of life appeals to our friend and stirs, as it continually does, his moral imagination.

We notice first and most obviously her moralism, her preoccupation with questions of moral right and wrong, with criticism of offense, with judgment upon vice. "Essentially all moral pressure" (292), as Strether describes her, she motivates his own obsession with discipline and punishment, his determination "always, where Lambert Strether was concerned, to know the worst" (213). Indeed he is attracted to her, perhaps, just because of "his old tradition, the one he had been brought up on and which even so many years of life had but little worn away; the notion that the state of the wrongdoer, or at least this person's happiness, presented some special difficulty" (337). It is no accident that her principles are, for him, embodied in the dream figure of a judging mother who "loom(s) at him larger than life" until "he already felt her come down on him, already burned, under her reprobation, with the blush of guilt . . . He saw himself, under her direction, recommitted to Woollett as juvenile offenders are committed to reformatories" (207–8).[24] To her obsession with the priority of moral right, which fills, it seems, the entirety of her exalted consciousness (the presence of moral pressure is "almost identical with her own presence" [292]), we may add rigorism in her conception of principles. Everything in her world must be "straight" (Strether, later, calls her "the whole moral and intellectual being or block"); and her rules of right admit of no softening in the light of the present circumstance, the individual case. "She was the only woman he had known, even at Woollett, as to whom his conviction was positive that to lie was beyond her art": she "refused to human commerce that mitigation of rigor" (57). Strether links his thought of her with the idea of an exceptionless justice that dwells outside "in the hard light" (174). This moral rigorism, together with the ubiquity of moral assessment, permits her two attitudes only, when confronted with a new occurrence: approval, or disapproval. "From the moment they're not delighted," Strether says of her and her new Ambassador Sarah, "they can only be—well what I admit she was" (303).

If universal and general principles of right take precedence over (and indeed swallow up) all other elements of life, there are three aspects of human experience that Mrs. Newsome especially dislikes and avoids: emotion, passivity, and the perception of particularity. These items are connected in an interesting and, in a certain sense, profoundly appealing way. Strether describes her as a person who "won't be touched" (317); when he imagines her his eyes "might have been fixing some particularly large iceberg in a cool blue northern sea" (318); and, as we have seen, he refers to her, in her "tightly packed" fullness, as a "block." Her emotional coldness is seen by him, in these images, as an aspect of her larger impassivity, her resistance to any modification by worldly circumstance. This is why her being all "fine cold thought" "falls in" so well with her resistance to surprises. Solid and purely active as she is (essentially all *pressure* without response), life cannot leave a mark on her. It is not *permitted* to enter in, or to pull anything out. She is, Strether muses, the sort of meal that can be "served cold" (represented by an ambassador) "without its really losing anything" (316) of its essential flavor—so little does its character consist in responsiveness to what is at hand.

This connection between absence of emotion and absence of passivity is made long before on behalf of Woollett as a whole, then Strether tells Maria Gostrey, "Woollett isn't sure it ought to enjoy. If it were, it would" (9). The first half of this remark is frequently quoted by critics; the second is, I think, even more significant. For it informs us that Woollett conceives of everything valuable in life as activity that can be morally willed. If it *were* sure that enjoyment was its duty, it would set itself to do that duty, it would simply will itself to enjoy. The oddness of this idea reminds us that some of the valuable things in life have more to do with passivity and responsiveness than with active willing; and their connection with "ought" is therefore to be viewed with deep suspicion.

What all this comes to is that the people of Woollett cannot, will not, live in the present moment, confronting the things that life brings their way in all their newness and particularity. They come to a situation determined that it should not touch them, holding their general and rather abstract principles fixed and firm. These principles, the court of last appeal in practical reason, even govern what they may *see* and consider relevant in the new. Particularity of vision brings surprise, surprise passivity and a loss of moral control. Chad is therefore "the youth," Mme. de Vionnet "the Person"; it is already clear beforehand what principles will govern Woollett's dealings with them. Any more personal encounter is made impossible by the nature of the view itself. It comes to what Strether, speaking for the Woollett in himself, calls "the obsession of the other thing": "I'm always considering something else; something else, I mean, than the thing of the moment" (11). And this tendency, which strikes Strether with perplexity and even with "terror," is Mrs. Newsome's fineness and her exaltation.

For Mrs. Newsome is "exalted." Behind her coldness and her blocklike hardness, Strether permits us to understand the deep sense of dignity that motivates her assault upon life. "Pure and by the vulgar estimate 'cold,' " she is not, he reflects, coarse or hard, but, rather, "deep devoted delicate sensitive noble" (201). We see her underlying motivation nowhere more revealingly than in the one verbatim quotation we are given:

> Sarah's answer came so straight, so 'pat', as might have been said, that he felt on the instant its origin. 'She has confided to my judgment and my tenderness the expression of her personal sense of everything, and the assertion of her personal dignity.'
> They were the very words of the lady of Woollett—he would have known them in a thousand; her parting charge to her child. (295)

This surprises us at first; for we may have been encouraged by some of Strether's remarks to think of this woman as a hard insensitive being, whose utterances would be icy imperatives. Her words, which we are told to see as exemplary, suggest, I think, a more complex understanding. We have here the expression of a keen sense of human dignity—of an idea of our worth as agents that is the basis of Kantian morality (and through this of Rawls's Kantianism). It is the idea that we do not need to go through the world as the plaything of its forces, living "from hand to mouth," merely "floating" with its currents. We are dignified moral beings; and it is in virtue of our moral powers of will and judgment that we can *be* dignified, making rather than being made, agents rather than victims or dependents. Strether recognizes Mrs. Newsome by the assertion of her dignity; and he knows that what the vulgar see as coldness is really a kind of nobility. What this comes to, I think, is that he sees her moralism as based on an idea of the dignity of agency. To the noble and autonomous moral agent, nature has, and should have, no power to jolt or to surprise, and also no power to inspire delight and passionate wonder. Such an agent will seem cold to the vulgar; but any other relation to the world surrenders dignity, inviting violation or at least seduction.

Such an agent will treat others with an equal respect, attending to their own dignity as moral beings. For Mrs. Newsome, we remember, would never wear her dress cut down, encouraging Strether to perceive her as a surprisingly particular physical being and so to surrender his own dignity before her. (In her actual black ruched dress she reminds him of Queen Elizabeth, virginal out of a commitment to autonomy, preserver of the dignity of a nation [29].) What seems like insensibility in the women of Woollett is, from their point of view, the high determination to treat each other person as an autonomous moral will, relating to them through the moral faculties and judging them with a stringency that shows respect for their freedom. Any note of tenderness would compromise this moral relation. When Strether yields to the gentle voice of Marie de Vionnet, the Woollett in him observes, "She really had tones to make justice weep" (164).

It is because Mrs. Newsome is no mere caricature, but a brilliantly comic rendering of some of the deepest and most appealing features of Kantian morality, that the novel has the balance and power that it does. We see the Kantian attitude as one that gives us a special dignity and exaltation; we see it, too, as a deep part of our culture. We see that the women of Woollett, unlike Marie de Vionnet in her love of an irreplaceable particular person, are able to triumph over life and to avoid becoming its victims. But that's just it: they triumph over life, they don't *live*. What is absent from the speech of the lady of Woollett? Particularity; the names of Chad and of Strether; the injunction to look and see; a sense of personal vulnerability; a fear of loss. Strether says that no trivial alteration will make this woman admit surprises, and we feel that he is correct. But is there another way to be rational and moral, a way that is more hospitable to life?

Strether begins the novel with a question. (The first sentence is: "Strether's first question, when he reached the hotel, was about his friend.") That's already a departure. From the beginning we sense in him a curiosity about the actual situation before him, an openness and a lack of self-sufficiency, that make him a dubious ambassador of Mrs. Newsome's will. In the style of Woollett, the interrogative, we feel, must play a small role. Strether is still closely linked, at this point, to his past, but: "He was burdened, poor Strether—it had better be confessed at the outset—with the oddity of a double consciousness. There was detachment in his zeal and curiosity in his indifference" (2). In his moral purpose as ambassador is an independence of purpose; in his lack of interested engagement with the new is an eager desire to *see* it. His initial steps into the new world that confronts him are marked by a child's fresh delight in seeing and an undirected openness to the new concrete thing. He has "the idlest eye" (21) for the sights and sounds of the garden; the "smallest things so arrested and amused him" (23). He finds himself "given over to uncontrolled perceptions"—among them the perception of Maria Gostrey's complicating neckband; and he takes this surprising piece of red velvet as "a starting-point for fresh backward, fresh forward, fresh lateral flights" (20). His relation to his situation is dominated, above all, by the sense of freshness and susceptibility to adventure; and he sees this susceptibility as connected with a new sharpness of perception:

> Nothing could have been odder than Strether's sense of himself as at that moment launched in something of which the sense would be quite disconnected from the sense of his past and which was literally beginning there and then. It had begun in fact already, . . . begun with a sharper survey of the elements of Appearance than he had for a long time been moved to make. (5)

This sense that life is an adventure, and that part of its joy precisely is the confrontation with the new—this is a sense of life already far removed from that of Woollett, where dignity is preserved by keeping down the new, acknowledging it only insofar as it exemplifies some law whose sense is already understood. Mrs. Newsome is about as far removed from the childlike as a human being can be. (In comparing her to Queen Elizabeth—who never even mothered children and seems to the reader of history to have been always adult, always self-sufficient—Strether depicts her as heroically untouched by any horrible or wonderful aspect of life.) But Strether, as he embarks on his adventure, becomes no longer a controlling adult; he is a child learning to "toddle" (201), eyes wide open, vulnerable, wondering at each new thing.

In his growing awareness of the world we discover the three elements of judgment that Mrs. Newsome above all avoids, significantly linked in his affirmation as they were in her denial. Most emphasized in the text is Strether's willingness to be passive, surrendering the invulnerable agency of the Kantian self. He speaks of "letting go" (209), of "taking things as they come" (49), of living "from hand to mouth" (173); perceptions bear in or "press" (165) upon him, acting on him rather than being made or impressed upon the world. He even feels himself to be like a person who has "been tripped up and had a fall" (165), so sharply does life make itself felt. But passivity is more often joyous. A sharp "assault of images," in Gloriani's garden, makes him have "the consciousness of opening . . . for the happy instant, all the windows of his mind, of letting this rather grey interior drink in for once the sun of a clime not marked in his old geography" (116). In the novel's continual emphasis on this feature, we are made to feel that it is somehow a key to all the rest: that a willingness to surrender invulnerability, to take up a posture of agency that is porous and susceptible of influence, is of the highest importance in getting an accurate perception of particular things in the world.

For Strether's vision of particularity involves a willingness to be incomplete, to be surprised by the new, to see that and how our "actual adventure" (105) transcends our "personal experience." And so, by being able to grant the incompleteness of past experience, which he calls "this last queer quantity" (105), Strether allows himself to emerge as (in Maria's words) a person for whom "nothing . . . will ever come to the same thing as anything else" (41). Part of this vision of the particular lies in his sharp concrete perceptions of particular objects and people; part, too, in a new willingness to see a composite situation as so connected together, so complex in its relations, that as a whole it is like no other. Just as Maria's neckband is permitted to complicate his vision, so in general new elements constitute new relations. "All voices had grown thicker and meant more things; they crowded on him as he moved about—it was the way they sounded together that wouldn't let him be still" (298).

And this vision of particularity is shaped (as Woollett's view could not be) by the responsive activity of the emotions and the imagination, working closely together. From the beginning, Strether is surprised by "how much there had been in him of response" (3); and Maria correctly observes, "No one feels so much as you. No—not any one" (248).

All of this comes together in the sense of happy though perplexed immersion in the adventure of living[25] that makes it possible for Strether to make such simple statements as, "The Sunday of the new week was a wonderful day" (114)—a chapter opening that could never have been written by the lady of Woollett; in the way, too, that he is with people, "looking kindly from one to the other and wondering at many things" (132); in the hesitation with which he searches for names (28), gropes after the right description for the strange things that confront him. Hesitation and bewilderment are a part of his sense of life, *and* part of its accuracy:

> 'It isn't playing the game to turn on the uncanny. All one's energy goes to facing it, to tracking it. One wants, confound it, don't you see?' he confessed with a queer face—'one wants to enjoy anything so rare. Call

> it then life'—he puzzled it out—'call it poor dear old life simply that
> springs the surprise. Nothing alters the fact that the surprise is para-
> lyzing, or at any rate engrossing—all, practically, hang it, that one sees,
> that one *can* see.' (100)

The life of perception feels perplexed, difficult, unsafe. (Strether's
sentences here have the awkwardness and riskiness of which he speaks.)
But this life also seems to Strether—and to us—to be richer, fuller of
enjoyment, fuller too of whatever is worth calling knowledge of the
world.

Strether's consciousness finds vivid metaphors to express this new
moral attitude—images of improvisatory game-playing (5); of complex
connectedness and the absence of Woollett "straightness"; of childhood,
of flying; above all, images of water, and of water and light together—
signaling that illumination is now seen as inseparable from a risky passivity before the physical being of things. (To Sarah's protest against his
new view, he replies that he can hardly help the way he has come to
see: "an inexorable tide of light seems to have floated us into our perhaps
still queerer knowledge" [293].) We notice, too, how he and Maria Gostrey, in conversation about what they have seen, will arrive at a new
perception and, struck by it as if by finding themselves suddenly in a
place where they have never been and to which they have not realized
they were going, exclaim, "So there we are,"—or, "Then there we are"
(255, 258, 370). (The novel, which began with a question, ends on just
such a moment of surprised arrival.)

In the new norm of perception, unlike the norm of Woollett, there is
a bewildering problem about authority. For if the ethical norm consists
not in obeying certain antecedently established general rules, but in
improvising resourcefully in response to the new perceived thing, then
it is always going to remain unclear, in the case of any particular choice
or vision, whether it is or is not correctly done. This does not mean that
there are no criteria and anything goes. But it does mean that the standard
will ultimately be nothing harder or clearer than the conformity of this
choice or description to those of agents on whom we can rely for competent judgment—just as, in Aristotle's very similar view, the norm of
good perception is the judgment of a certain type of person, the person
of practical wisdom.[26] In this very way, when Strether wonders whether
he has not "only been silly," his recourse can only be to think of the
company he keeps:

> He glanced at such a contingency, but it failed to hold him long when
> once he had reflected that he would have been silly, in this case, with
> Maria Gostrey and Little Bilham, with Madame de Vionnet and little
> Jeanne, with Lambert Strether, in fine and above all with Chad New-
> some himself. Wouldn't it be found to have made more for reality to
> be silly with these persons than sane with Sarah and Jim? (220)

And we ourselves, in asking how right Strether is, can only do the same—wondering, for example about whether Chad Newsome's judgment is, after all, such a very fine thing, and wondering about the part of Lambert Strether's imagination that holds Chad in such great esteem. There is no sure guarantee, either for the judge or for our judgment about him. As Aristotle says in just this context, "The discrimination lies in perception."

This is an ethical norm to rival the norms of Woollett.[27] It deserves to be taken seriously as a picture of rationality and correct choice. And insofar as it captures our imagination and answers to our sense of life, it calls into question those elements of the pictures of judgment and agency in our moral theories that are motivated by the concerns of Woollett and resemble Woollett in their structure. Holding Strether up against Rawls's idea of considered judgment and his constraints upon admissible theories, we want to object that feelings may after all in many cases be an invaluable guide to correct judgment; that general and universal formulations may be inadequate to the complexity of particular situations; that immersed particular judgments may have a moral value that reflective and general judgments cannot capture. We want to suggest that bewilderment and hesitation may actually be marks of fine attention. As Strether summarizes the matter, "There's all the indescribable—what one gets only on the spot" (247)—and all of this appears to be omitted from the data that lead to reflective equilibrium. Indeed, his experience suggests a rival story about the end of the ethical process itself. There is still a search for equilibrium here, as Strether tries to make it all "hang beautifully together" (276). But his equilibrium, dealing, as it does, with impressions, emotions, and, in general, with particulars, had better be called by a different name. We would do better, perhaps, to call it "perceptive equilibrium": an equilibrium in which concrete perceptions "hang beautifully together," both with one another and with the agent's general principles; an equilibrium that is always ready to reconstitute itself in response to the new.

Can we view this new norm as simply an extension of the old one— so that we *supplement* Rawls's general theories with the immersed judgments of experience? This idea has been persuasively argued, with reference to Aristotle and Rawls's Aristotelianism, in some very interesting recent writing by Henry Richardson, who coins the name "extended reflective equilibrium" to designate the end of an ethical procedure that takes in all of this.[28] Strether had, we recall, a different view about Mrs. Newsome—that one cannot touch her, put any of life into her, fully packed as she is; that it's fundamental to her entire being and her basic motivation not to *be* touched by the immersed perceptions of life. (We supported this in our analysis of her Kantian conception of agency: for we said that it was fundamental to her whole project not to be passive towards the world.) So what one must do, if one chooses to value perceiving, is to get rid of "the whole moral and intellectual being or block." (To put it differently, you cannot add Maria Gostrey's red velvet band to Mrs. Newsome's ruche: she would not wear such a garment, she would view it as a desecration of her dignity.) This does not mean that the way of perceiving cannot make use of rules and universal principles; plainly it does, and it would be an important part of an extended inquiry into Strether's standards to ask how and when.[29] But it cannot use them in the way and for the reasons that Mrs. Newsome would recommend; and it must give a central place to elements of judgment that she would, for consistency and dignity, insist on leaving out.

What prepares Strether to see this way? Why, among all those who come out from America to Paris, does he alone "come out" in fact,[30] opening himself to the influences of perception? We are given several clues. One, certainly, is his low sense of his own dignity. So far is he from asserting it that he permits himself to be treated, persistently, as an agent of the purposes of others. His name (in the Woollett Revue) is "on the green cover, where he had put it for Mrs. Newsome" (50); and his willingness to serve as her ambassador shows a not altogether robust sense of Kantian autonomy. It is an unsettling thought, and one on which James insists,[31] that this very weakness in him (from the point of view of our interest in our dignity) may be a necessary preparation for this other sort of strength.

But James points even more insistently to another sort of preparation. For from the beginning Strether has a deep connection with literature. An editor and writer himself, he has a serious love of all the arts, but especially of the literary art, and the novel above all. The imagination of the reader and the writer are shown as abilities that have prepared him to see and to respond in a non-Kantian way. His concern with novels is an old one; and Paris recalls it to him, reminding him of the "lemon-colored volumes" he brought back from Europe and of "the sharp initiation they represented" (52). These volumes have been sitting "stale," "soiled," even unbound, in Woollett—but their memory "throbs again" for him in Paris until his conscience reacts with alarm, "amusing itself for the forty-eight hours by forbidding him the purchase of a book" (52).

It does no good: for the early love of stories floods back, animating his desire to wait and see, his tendency to attend to new people and events with the novelist's "vision kindly adjusted,"[32] a loving non-judgmental attention to their particularity. References to his favorite authors grow increasingly dense until, floating finally in the current of new sights and sounds, he notices that "it was the way of nine tenths of his current impressions to act as recalls of things imagined—of some fine firm concentrated heroine of an old story, something he had heard, read, something that, had he a hand for drama, he might himself have written"

(175). And writing too (narrative, however, and not dramatic)[33] expresses increasingly his determination not to fall short, not to miss anything that is there to be seen and cared for: "When anything new struck him as coming up, or anything already noted as reappearing, he always immediately wrote, as if for fear that if he didn't he would miss something" (153). It is the narrative character of his letters (quite different, we must suppose, from her own) that so alarms Mrs. Newsome. Writing this way, seeing this way, he is no longer her ambassador. His style gives him away.

Here James shows us that there is a complicity between the consciousness of the reader (and the writer) of stories and the consciousness, the morality, of perception. For stories cultivate our ability to see and care for particulars, not as representatives of a law, but as what they themselves are: to respond vigorously with senses and emotions before the new; to care deeply about chance happenings in the world, rather than to fortify ourselves against them; to wait for the outcome, and to be bewildered—to wait and float and be actively passive. We are so accustomed to the novel that we tend to forget how morally controversial a form it has been in the eyes of various sorts of religious and secular moralisms. (Even as I write this, fundamentalist parents in the state of Tennessee are seeking a ban on stories that freely exercise the imagination, holding that the law laid down in the Bible is truth enough.) Questionable with very good reason: for the novel acknowledges a wonder before worldly sensuous particulars that Mrs. Newsome would never feel or approve; and they attach a dangerous importance to outcomes that lie beyond the control of the moral will. By showing us the novel's world (more or less) through Strether's eyes, indeed by making it next to impossible to distinguish those eyes from the author's eyes—and by showing us at the same time how different the story would look (or the events and people would, as a non-story, look) to the women of Woollett— by letting us know enough of what they see to discover that they do not perceive and could not describe the same reality—James makes a case for the moral significance of the novelist's (and the reader's) "sense of life," for the vigilant and responsive imagination that cares for everyone in the situation and refuses the injunction of Woollett to "simplify" for the sake of purity and safety. The very sentences are Strether's, straining towards perceptual rightness in the midst of wonderful puzzling mysteries.[34] The sentences of Woollett are crisp, "straight," and, as Strether says, "pat." And the fullness, the density, of the narrative style is itself the fitting expression of a certain sort of moral imagination. Indeed, James recalls to us that even the novel, with all its richness, can actually express but a fraction of the crowded consciousness of someone who is really making an effort to *see*. For at one point he remarks, "If we should go into all that occupied our friend in the watches of the night we should have to mend our pen; but an instance or two may mark for us the vividness with which he could remember" (83). The novel has its own simplifications—but it is the genre, among the available forms of writing—that most appropriately exemplifies what James calls the "projected morality."[35]

Perception and Method

We begin to see two opposing conceptions of practical reason, together with some of the motivations for and consequences of each. The morality of perception is put before us in a textual form that fittingly expresses its claim upon our imaginations. What now would be the next step in the proposed interchange between literary and ethical theory? Here nothing can be said in depth; but I can sketch out some of the pieces that I think this larger project might include.

First, I believe, we would need, in pursuing our goals of understanding and attunement, to get a much richer and deeper understanding of the Kantian conception and of its modern continuations (Rawls's above all). This novel is Strether's story. Mrs. Newsome does not do full justice to the power of Kant's arguments in the way that Strether does justice to his own way (and to Aristotle's related conception). If we are correct about the close relationship between content and form this is no accident. No narrative dealing in empirical particulars *could* see Kant's conception in a fully sympathetic way. This does not mean that there isn't a special interest, too, in seeing just what sort of character in a story (in our lives) a thoroughgoing Kantian would be: for this certainly helps us see how Kant matches (or fails to) our own active sense of life. But we would want to look at the arguments of Kantian philosophers directly and seriously in their own right; otherwise this inquiry could too easily get corrupted, get used to treating complex philosophical positions as straw men. The same applies to other leading ethical conceptions with which Strether's perception might fruitfully be contrasted—above all, the morality of classical Utilitarianism.[36]

Having started on this sort of investigation, we would now, I think, want to look very carefully at the different elements of Strether's conception (and their relatives in the contrasting conceptions) asking how they are connected and interrelated, how each one is supported and defended. How the perception of particularity is connected with an openness to surprise; how both are connected with a commitment to the cognitive guidance of feeling. Of particular importance here will be to ask what role rules and universal principles *can* and should play inside the morality of perception, and in general what sort of systematic theoretical approach to practice would be compatible with Strether's insights. This needs to be carefully considered, if we want to defend this conception as normative, especially for our public life. I imagine that by confronting Strether (and his philosophical relatives) with challenges from the Kantian and Utilitarian positions we will arrive at a deeper understanding of this position, and of the connection all the positions have with our own sympathies.

At this point many fruitful and interesting projects suggest themselves. We need to pursue in much greater depth and detail the stylistic portion of my argument, saying a great deal more, in connection with many more authors and many different genres and styles, about the practical and human expressive content of structural choices at all levels of specificity. And we would want to look at philosophical authors as makers of stylistic choices, asking what ethical commitments their own literary choices express. (I suspect that we will often discover that some of these choices are not supported by the argument in the "content" of the work, and that some may even be in tension with the content—as when an article about the crucial cognitive role of the emotions is written in a style that seems to assume that the intellect is the only part of the reader worth addressing. It is not clear that there are no good reasons for this discrepancy; but we need to ask hard questions about it.)

We would also want to turn to our own lives, both private and public, examining the conceptions of rationality (of the person, etc.) that we discover there, and asking how all this fits with what we have so far puzzled out. It would be an especially useful exercise, for example, to work through the contemporary economic literature on rationality, in which there is much pertinent debate about commensurability, about ordering, about universality, and to see what elements of Strether's "position" are incorporated in these debates; to ask, too, what workable social science could be built on what Strether offers us. Many other related projects can be imagined.

Throughout this open-ended inquiry, we will need to maintain as much self-consciousness as possible about our own methods and our implicit ends, asking what evaluative content they themselves express. Perceptive equilibrium is not the same end as reflective equilibrium; it does not use the same judgments or the same faculties. This does not mean that there can be no objectivity in the ethical inquiry; it does not mean that all choices of method are subjective.[37] But it does mean that procedures themselves are value-laden, and thus part and parcel of the holistic enterprise they organize; replaceable, like any other part, to the end of deeper and more inclusive attunement. So we must examine them at each stage, asking whether they are capable of doing full justice to everything that our sense of life wants to include.

Perception and Love

At this point, however, we are brought back again to *The Ambassadors*. For we have given, so far, too simple a story about Strether's imagination.[38] And part of the longer story of perceptive equilibrium is surely to discover the ways in which James's novel itself complicates our admiration for Strether, causing us to see that the perception of life may not have, in the end, an equilibrium—that the keen sight of the writer and reader of life is in a standing tension with the "sight" of passion. We have thought of Strether as yielding to the impressions of life as they unfold themselves before him—as allowing himself to be seduced. We must now think, also, of his inability to see, and later to accept, the sexual love of Chad and Marie de Vionnet; his inability to see Maria Gostrey's deepening feeling for him; his failure to examine and to acknowledge his own complicated feelings for Marie de Vionnet, and his jealousy of Chad. We must think of his blush of shame, when he realizes how he had concealed from himself their intimacy, "dressed the possibility in vagueness, as a little girl might have dressed her doll" (334). He too has simplified life; and by refusing himself feelings and ways of living that he could not reconcile with his personal demand for perceptual clarity and unselfish general concern, he has prevented himself, in the end, from perceiving a crucial fact about the situation around him. (" 'It's beautiful,' he said to Miss Barrace, 'the way you all can simplify when you will.' But she gave it to him back. 'It's nothing to the way *you* will when you must' " [200].) When he does confront Marie de Vionnet in his newly gained knowledge, he cannot achieve, in this one case, a particular perception; she becomes, distanced by his own inner refusal of passion, a mere abstraction. "It was actually moreover as if he didn't think of her at all, as if he could think of nothing but the passion, mature, abysmal, pitiful, she represented, and the possibilities she betrayed" (345). From her wonderful variegated self she becomes, for him, merely "a creature so exploited," "a maid servant crying for her young man." Distant watcher, pitying judge, he is in the end, in his way, the ambassador of Woollett; for his sharp eye will not turn aside in tenderness before the intimacy of others, and his spirit will not moderate its ubiquitous demand for rightness and for judgment. He too resists; he too refuses to allow his vision to be complicated by the band of broad red velvet.

And now we see, too, that the earlier remark about Strether's "double consciousness" can have another reading. There *is* a curious "detachment in his zeal"—in his zeal to see there is a detachment from strong emotion. And in his "indifference"—his perceiver's impartiality, the equipoise of the body drawn strongly to no extreme—there is an almost voyeuristic "curiosity," the curiosity of the uninvolved gaze.

And this incompleteness in Strether is unmistakably linked to his interest in literature: for we are shown repeatedly that the stance of the reader and writer of life is a stance that achieves a certain clarity of vision at the expense of a certain emotional depth; one that forgoes, or even scorns, immersion in the darker, messier passions, one that "reduces" them all to a simplified generic story, read with only a reader's interest (to what Strether calls "the convenient terms of Victor Hugo" [175]). The outing during which Strether makes his upsetting discovery has been seen by him, up until that moment, as if it were the exploration of a Lambinet painting that he remembers: his life, to that point, "continued in the picture . . . and had meanwhile not once overstepped the oblong gilt frame" (325). Even the loving couple in their boat can be held in the "picture" (or the story, since the picture has, for Strether, a marked narrative quality)—so long as he doesn't have to acknowledge them as the very individuals he cares about and has to deal with in his own personal life, so long as he doesn't have to acknowledge his own personal feelings of jealousy and longing. Then the story is no longer just a story, then it is a threat to equilibrium.

James reminds us here that before a work of art we are detached perceivers, free to explore all fine perceptions, but liberated (or cut off) from the tumultuous perceptions of personal passion, freed also—as we enjoy its delicious half-expected surprises—from the hard jolting shocks of the real surprise that mark our actual personal relations. Reading is a preparation for a life that is lived at one remove from life, a life that gains fineness and clarity by warding off certain risks and dangers. Is this good, or is it bad? When Strether sits, later, in Maria Gostrey's dining room, he reflects: "To sit there was, as he had told his hostess before, to see life reflected for the time in ideally kept pewter; which was somehow becoming, improving to life, so that one's eyes were held and comforted" (365).[39] Art does not simply perceive life; it also comforts us by keeping us at a distance from life's violence and arbitrariness. (For even when its content deals with violent passion, our own relation to it is not violent; the terms of Victor Hugo are indeed so much more "convenient" than those of our own loves and jealousies and fears and angers.) The novelist stands apart from some of the confusing complexity of the human scene; he owes his clarity to that "improving" absence of immersion. And yet, doesn't this make him, as a human being, somehow incomplete, somehow lacking in humanity? Reassuring Strether, who fears that Waymarsh may talk about him behind his back, Maria says, " 'For what do you take people, that they're able to say words about anything, able remorselessly to analyze? There are not many like you and me' " (26). The novelist is a third; as readers we follow. Is this, in fact, a good or full way to live?

Do we put such problems down to Strether's own idiosyncrasy, or are they the faults of the morality of perception? One of his reflections is, I think, significant. What he dislikes about the revealed intimacy is that it was, before, concealed: it went on between two people apart from perception and description. "Intimacy, at such a point, was *like* that— and what in the world else would one have wished it to be like? It was all very well for him to feel the pity of its being so much like lying" (334). What Strether senses is that what he calls the "deep deep truth" of sexual love is at odds with the morality of perception, in two ways. It asks for privacy, for others to avert their gaze; and on the inside it asks that focus be averted from all else that is outside. Lovers see, at such times, only one another; and it is not really deep if they *can* carefully see around and about them. That vision excludes general attention and care, at least at that moment. And this intimacy is a part of the world that demands *not* to be in the eyes of the perceiving, recording novelist— at least not in all of its particularity. But to the person who is dedicated to perceiving (to novel-writing), that looks like a bad way to be; bad both because it impedes the subject's moral vision of the whole and because, it asks not to be included as objects in that vision. To be sure, these ruminations emerge from Strether's loneliness. But he is convinced that loneliness is the condition of luminous perception; and his fear of intimacy is at the same time a fear for his moral being.

We need to take this seriously. Perception as a morality enjoins trust in responsive feeling; but its feelings are the feelings of the friend. (Strether's first question was about his friend; and the novelist's vision of him is a vision "*kindly* adjusted.") There is reason to suppose that the exclusivity and intensity of personal love would in fact impede the just and general responsiveness that these gentler feelings assist. And if they impede that, they impede the perceiver's contribution to our moral project, to our communal effort to arrive at perceptive equilibrium. But the recognition that there is a view of the world from passion's point of view, and that this view is closed to the perceiver, shows us that perception is, even by its own lights, incomplete. The perceiver as perceiver cannot see it all; to get the whole he must at times stop being the sort of person who cares for wholeness. As a perceiver he is morally admirable, both wonderful and quite lovable. Yet just that commitment that Maria loves (not just admires, but loves) in Strether, just that is the reason why he not only cannot love her, but cannot in any way understand or see her love or any love. She "can't resist" him when he tells her the reasons for his refusal; this is their comedy and their tragedy. Maria's "all comically, all tragically" (370) is a response to the moral impossibility of human love. For so long as our eyes are open, we are wonderful and lovable and finely responsive; but when we immerse ourselves in the most powerful responses, entering silence closing our eyes, are we then capable at all of asking questions about our friends, of thinking of the good of the community? And if we are not capable of this, are we worthy of the deepest feelings and commitments of others? James once wrote about his mother that, swallowed up in her intense love of her husband and family, she had nothing "acutely to offer."[40] Does any lover do better? Without this depth life seems incomplete and perception itself seems blind; but it cannot itself be ordered inside the equilibrium of perception or seen by its fine-tuned vision of the complete life.

This complicates still further our idea of what might be, the practical goal of ethical inquiry. It would be simple if Strether's perceptive equilibrium were simply undercut, shown not to be a high human goal. But perceptive equilibrium is loved and affirmed, "all comically, all tragically," at the novel's end. It is what makes him fine and lovable, even while it is what makes him incapable of love. It would be simple, again, if we were shown a way in which Strether's incompleteness could be completed and filled up, by love, in some harmonious manner. (A way in which the novelist could have an intimate personal life and still see for us all.) Neither of these easy exits is offered us. And if there is for us any prospect held out for a life that combines fine perception with the silence and the hidden vision of love, it would only be in a condition that is not itself "equilibrium" at all, but an unsteady oscillation between blindness and openness, exclusivity and general concern, fine reading of life and the immersion of love.

Here we find another way in which the novel can make a contribution to ethical theory. So far it has (or this one novel has) shown the way from a narrow Kantian understanding of the question, "How should one live?" to a wider and richer understanding. Now it asks us to see the limits of that ethical question itself. It gestures towards the limits of ethical consciousness, making us aware of the deep elements in our ethical life that in their violence or intensity lead us outside of the ethical attitude altogether, outside of the quest for balanced vision and perfect rightness. It can include, or at least indicate, the silence into which its own responsive prose has no entry.

Literary theory and Ethical theory

I have imagined a literary theory that works in conversation with ethical theory. I have imagined this partnership as a practical one, in which we search for images of life by which we might possibly live together, and ask what conceptions and images best match the full range of our perceptions and convictions, as we work towards "perceptive equilibrium." (And now we have, too, the thought that the goal might not be equilibrium at all, but a dynamic tension between two possibly irreconcilable visions.) I have imagined that literary theory will make a creative and rather radical contribution to this enterprise—as we see from the fact that its very end and its methods have been called into question by Strether's achievement, and his tragedy.

Why, however, *should* literary theory engage itself with ethical theory here? For we might acknowledge the practical dimension of literature and insist on restoring that dimension to theoretical writing, without taking the further step proposed here. Why can't the literary theorist simply say about Henry James what it is lucid and helpful to say, without studying and teaching Kant and Aristotle, Bentham and Rawls, and drawing these figures into the account he or she gives of James's novels? This question arises all the more since major figures of past theory with whom I implicitly link my proposal—F.R. Leavis, say, and Lionel Trilling—seems to have been perfectly able to speak of the ethical content of literature and the ethical expressiveness of literary forms, without bringing moral philosophy into the picture.

The explicit and deep study of ethical theory will, first of all, clarify to us just what it is that works of literature offer to our sense of life. We grasp by contrasting; we sense what something *is* by bounding it off against something different. If it should prove true that novels share certain ethical commitments (to particularity, to the moral relevance of surprise) just in virtue of their form, we will grasp these shared commitments better by seeing on what grounds some philosophers have denied or refused them. We grasp the force of James's account of perception more clearly when we see how it goes against norms of considered judgment that prevail in almost all of the Western ethical tradition. And we have to do this by reading the philosophers in a serious way, not, as I say, by using them polemically, as straw men. Our understanding is enhanced in a different way when we encounter inside philosophy several friends of perception and of literary insight, whose explicit arguments against much of the prevailing tradition clarify for us the elements of Strether's accomplishment. (I think here, in different ways, of Aristotle, of Iris Murdoch, of Bernard Williams—and, also, of William James.)[41] And if we look more closely now at the examples of Leavis and Trilling, I think we will discover that they do not go against these claims. For Leavis's denigration of the late novels of James[42] is, I believe, superficial in a way that most of his work is not, precisely *because* he does not make these reflective philosophical contrasts and so demarcate for himself what it is that James is opposing and putting forward. Trilling's wide and deep knowledge of political and ethical and psychological thought, though displayed with understated grace and elegance, does, I think, consistently inform his most memorable and characteristic writings—not least his essays on James in *The Liberal Tradition*.[43]

Then too, ethical theory, just because of its systematic and inclusive disciplinary character, can contribute to our understanding of a literary work by raising questions that this work may or may not explicitly ask itself, concerning the relationship of its ethical views to other issues on which we have to make up our mind—issues about social structure, about economic distribution, about the self and personal identity. My imagined theoretical dialogue will, for example, lead us to ask what political structures are compatible with Strether's moral norm, whether in opting for that norm we would have to forgo some or all of our democratic traditions. We will have understood James more deeply if we can answer this question. And the answer will emerge not only out of a deeper reflection about novels such as *The Ambassadors* and *The Princess Casamassima*, but also out of a more general reflection about the connections between a conception of personal rationality and a political conception.

These are some reasons why literary theory needs ethical theory. (And this close connection with theory would be one way of distinguishing literary theory, should we want to, from good criticism—to which it should always remain almost inseparably close.) On the other side a similar and equally strong argument can be made. It is reasonably clear by now what that argument is: that literary theory can improve the self-understanding of ethical theory by confronting it with a distinctive conception or conceptions of various aspects of human ethical life, realized in a form that is the most appropriate one for their expression. Insofar as great literature has moved and engaged the hearts and minds of its readers, it has established already its claim to be taken seriously when we work through the alternative conceptions.

These alternatives could be described and investigated by the ethical theorist; sometimes they are. But this too often results in a criticism that simply mines the work for a set of propositional claims—rather than, what I am calling for, an investigation of that which is expressed and "claimed" by the shape of the sentences themselves, by images and cadences and pauses themselves, by the forms of the traditional genres, by narrativity, themselves. It seems unlikely that this richer ethical task can be carried out by someone who is not in the habit of attending to these things.

But why should we *care* about describing literary alternatives to ethical theory? Suppose there is a task in (or side by side of) ethical theory that literary people are best equipped to perform: why should anyone want to take on that task, rather than some other one of the many interesting tasks that literary theory might and does perform? If moral philosophers (or political theorists or economists) have gotten themselves into difficulty, why should we bail them out? Here I come back to my idea of the practical goal of ethical inquiry—which involves self-understanding and communal attunement. These goals matter. Each of us is not only a professional, but a human being who is trying to live well; and not simply a human being, but also a citizen of some town, some country, above all a world of human beings, in which attunement and understanding are extremely urgent matters. Now certainly we can promote these goals in indefinitely many ways, apart from our professional lives: by raising children, by engaging in some form of political action, by using our money generously, by seeing and conversing and feeling. And yet, when a person happens to have a professional activity that is or becomes relevant to major ends of human life—how exhilarating that activity then is, and how deep, I think, the obligations it then imposes.

All around us other intellectual disciplines are shaping the private and public life of our culture, telling us how to imagine or think about ourselves. Economic theory forges conceptions of human rationality that govern public policy decisions, decisions about the distribution of food, about social well-being. Legal theorists and jurists search for understanding of basic rights (for example, the right to privacy) and the role that they play in our lives with one another. Psychology and anthropology describe our emotional lives, our experience of gender, our forms of communal interaction. Moral philosophy attempts to arbitrate disputes concerning medical care, abortion, basic freedoms. Literary theory has been too silent too long in these debates. And yet it has a distinctive speaking role to play—a first part of which might be to confront reigning models of political and economic rationality with the consciousness of Strether. Silence, in these matters, is a kind of capitulation. If these alternatives are not brought forward and described, we will go on being governed from day to day by conceptions of rationality that seem impoverished next to the ones we know well and care about in novels that we love. Worse, most people will not perceive, and therefore not really have, the choice among conceptions. The hungry will be fed (or not fed) according to some idea of the person; patients will be treated; laws and policies will be made—all according to some conception or conceptions of human personhood and human rationality. If we do not take a hand in these choices, they will be made by default without us.

I propose an apparently thankless task. Is there any reason at all to suppose that entrenched conceptions (of rationality, of value) that currently govern our daily lives through their reception in economic theory and public policy will be modified by contact with Lambert Strether, or that the holders of these conceptions will pay any attention at all to Henry James and related authors at any time? Can any possible practicable goal be achieved by subtle precise writing about books that most people in public life do not read anyway? Those of us who are Americans might also ask: can *any* writing that is Strether's, that is responsive and delicate and committed to perception, impose itself upon the form of our American culture, concerning which we sometimes have good reason to think (as Strether of Mrs. Newsome) that it "won't *be* touched," that it can only come to a question of dislodging "the whole moral and intellectual being or block" that looms up before us, with its strange combination of utilitarianism and religious moralism, like some particularly large blue iceberg in a cool blue northern sea. (The same question may of course be asked about the practical value of ethical theory itself, with whose collaboration we propose to "touch" her—though theory's colder hand may less quickly be felt as a threatening assault.)

Well, what can we do but try? Some major choices affecting our lives—say, Supreme Court decisions—are made in effect by one or two complex reflective processes in the minds of one or two reading, thinking, feeling beings. An eloquent piece of writing (say, about James on the moral value of privacy) might possibly alter the course of that reflection. Do we know such things before attempting? James once wrote that the task of the literary imagination, face to face with social obtuseness and general failure of perception, would be:

> to *create* the record, in default of any other enjoyment of it; to imagine, in a word, the honourable, the producible case. What better example than this of the high and the helpful public and, as it were, civic use of the imagination?[44]

We could aim, for a future, at that degree of love. (Though bewildered, increasingly, about the nature of that love and its relation to other loves, to life itself.) His plain gravestone, in the Cambridge Cemetery, on an open bright hill (where one can sit and read all morning alone in the still sun, vaguely hearing children's voices reflected up, as it were, from the school below) bears the inscription: "Henry James, novelist, citizen of two countries, interpreter of his generation on both sides of the sea." So—as Strether observes—there we are.[45]

5

The State of the Art of Criticism

Geoffrey H. Hartman

Contemporary literary analysis exposes, once more, the ambiguity of language; and it does so not to impugn words and induce new schemes for a "real character," a more stable and truthful language-structure, but to heighten our awareness of the complex resource already in place. "Where the old Rhetoric," I.A. Richards writes in his *Philosophy of Rhetoric*, "treated ambiguity as a fault in the language, and hoped to confine or eliminate it, the new Rhetoric sees it as an inevitable consequence of the powers of language . . . " Ambiguity, at least in art, confirms these "powers," and suggests that modes of reading which assert the possibility of literal or unmediated expression are terrible simplifications.

These simplifications, however, enter a vicious cycle reactive to freer modes of reading. While it is liberating to celebrate ambiguity as indeterminacy, the very ease of doing so exacerbates the fever of fundamentalism that chronically ravages the body politic. The polemics of the situation do not work for the critical spirit unless we can make a case on behalf of the negative energy of intellect all around us. "The mind of man," Christopher Smart wrote, "cannot bear a tedious accumulation of nothings without effect." So we may ask ourselves: Is Derrida's "atheology" perhaps the equivalent of a negative theology? Are we in

---

This essay was written in May 1986. One thinks one is writing for the future and that two or three years should not matter. But I already see, from this point in time, that the essay reflects too exclusive a concern with fundamentalism and its challenge to freedom of interpretation. Had I been asked to write this essay now, the emphasis would have included other than religious kinds of positivity. The quest to make theory politically accountable—always a difficult, sometimes a repressive factor in the intellectual life—is approaching the 1930s in intensity. In that era Left and Right, and other warring dichotomies, fortified a dangerous habit of stereotyping which I.A. Richards focused on, long before deconstruction. During the last six months an extremely hostile questioning of deconstruction (after the disclosure of Paul de Man's articles of 1940–42 in the collaborationist Belgian newspaper *Le Soir*) have troubled me with a sense that in the literary humanities too, not just in religion or the political religions, the quest for moral and intellectual fundamentals reinstates itself with a surprising righteousness. At this point, then, while I stand behind my essay, I am less certain that literary theory has a future. We may have to produce not only (as I indicate) a better sociology of literature; we may also have to overcome the suspicion that theory is but an exercise in ideology, or the opium of intellectuals who wish to evade political commitments and hard judgments.

the presence of a "negative classicism," as André Malraux defined the unconventional strength of modernist painting? Should we accept a philosophy of history like that of the Saint-Simonians who took comfort in the fact that after each skeptical age there would arise an organic and myth-filled age? Do we credit Michel Foucault's insight, developed above all in his *History of Sexuality*, that all our liberated talk about repression and censorship is merely a way of extending and intensifying the directorial powers of church and state that now penetrate via our own "critical" claims into the innermost recesses of a private sphere they were intended to guard? Can even art escape being propaganda?[1]

I take it for granted that we remain in an age of criticism, but one traversed by a return to religious faith, to clear commitments and often to fundamentalist kinds of faith. Now it is hard to get one's historical bearings on the frequency of these cycles: T.S. Eliot announced in 1929 his return to religion and conservative politics; the same year Walter Lippmann published *A Preface to Morals*, analyzing the dissolution of the ancestral order and suggesting that neither modernism nor fundamentalism could lead to that "religion of the spirit" appropriate to a "Great Society." We know too well, also, that fascism expressed apocalyptic traits and a fervor of adhesion that have typically characterized the more fanatic religions. So that the evidences of a return from the 1960s on to either cultic or conventional religion need not surprise.

Whatever reasons for contemporary reactions to "Whirl is King" (Aristophanes), the problems that affect literary and cultural criticism remain the same as in other eras. I will single out the problem of doing interpretations at a time when texts seem to be overly porous, that is, so ambiguous or variable in the history of attributed meanings that the cry is heard, why should we study literature? A time too when, obversely, the import of texts is decided by authority, with the aid of the idea that there is one meaning, often defined as "literal."

We can turn once more to Richards for a modern focus on this dilemma. He asks criticism to foster an "intellectual tradition" that "tells us . . . how *literally* to read a passage."[2] If he had said: how not to read literally, the emphasis would have fallen on the interpretive complexity of art. Yet a modern prejudice, linked to the change of hermeneutics into criticism, makes him put his statement the other way. He is, of course, a realist rather than a fundamentalist, one who admires that stubborn and commendable streak in us which links literature to life, not only to more literature. Like Wallace Stevens, he too keeps "coming back and coming back / To the real: to the hotel instead of the hymns / That fall upon it out of the wind." Yet by the end of the paragraph what is deplored is not the loss of reality but the loss of interpretive flexibility. This is where theory comes in, as a supplement to the recovery of a skill. Our age,

Richards suggests, is "losing its skill in interpretation" and "begins the reflective inquiry which may lead to a theory by which the skill may be regained—this time as a less vulnerable and more deeply grounded, because more consciously recognized, endowment."

Richards also posits a time near the beginning of modern English when we actually "read aright." He connects the adroitness of later 16th- and much 17th-century writing to social and religious causes that coincide with the flourishing of English: the wide circulation of sermons as well as plays, letters as well as poetry, controversy as well as fiction and translation.[3] By the end of this period, certainly, the very prose Richards himself writes, as well as the genre of essayistic criticism, has been created.

But we have little evidence of how the literature of that period was interpreted (*Rezeptionsqeschichte* not having been invented); what evidence there is belongs to the history of taste and does not take the form of sustained analysis. Certain prefaces and some self-commentating sermons or works, like those of Donne, seem to constitute an exception, but is that enough to make up for the lack of a global view of 17th-century culture or a better grasp of the way art reflects on itself and its text-milieu? These questions point to what has in fact developed since Richards: 1) reader-reception theory; 2) a new historicism that wishes to ascertain the "episteme" (Foucault) of a culture by appreciating all its signifying *and* repressive practices, not only canonized works; and 3) a more general awareness of how cultures augment their fictions through interpretation and obversely their interpretive discourse through fiction. (Frank Kermode's subtitle to *The Genesis of Secrecy*, "The Interpretation of Narrative," could as easily read "The Narrative of Interpretation.") Together the three tendencies expand the definition of what literature is, redeem the isolation of belles-lettres, and shift attention to unfreedoms of speech challenged by forceful though oblique or marginalized cultural practices. A further movement, puzzling and influential deconstruction, is a critique of all canonical or new-historical schemes that put a bit of weight behind interesting allegories, turning them once more into comprehensive symbols or paradigms.

I am trying to inch forward from Richards to the contemporary scene by constructing a historical narrative that avoids progressive claims. The loss of interpretive skill that Richards responds to, whatever its ultimate cause, is still with us. It obliges us to expand our view of the history of criticism, and to see that we cannot start it around 1700. What we call criticism is only the tip of the iceberg compared to the vast commentary-tradition stretching back to Midrash and Patristic exegesis, and beyond that to Alexandria, Philo, and the sopherim. The age of criticism is a distinctive though very late development. Yet one can hold to Richards's distinction between skill and theory, as between nature (i.e., vulnerable endowment) and its conscious reinforcement (i.e., a more thoroughly grounded, immunized endowment). Together with the utopian premise that attaches to Richards's notion of educability, there emerges a pragmatic caution that projects the skill to be grounded not as something given or gained once and for all but as a second nature, a habit of the flexible and reflective intelligence. Even though Richards uses one period as a touchstone for his conception of interpretive mobility, his attitude toward that skill is anti-foundationalist. The literal for him always stands in relation to other modes of reading, and the critical spirit itself is clearly more than an auxiliary and subordinated gift.

It is here that I sense a real difference between our present work, which remains close to Richards, and that of others in Eliot's generation or the American New Criticism. As promoters of modernism, the New Critics brought contemporary literature into the university and linked it to what they called "the tradition." It was a pedagogically progressive yet culturally conservative movement. The New Critics were also surprisingly conservative in their attitude toward the critical spirit. Like Eliot, they stressed its capital importance in the work of creation but remained wary of its freelance and sometimes autonomous character. They overlooked, as it were, Oscar Wilde's deflation of the artist. "I am always amused," he wrote, "by the silly vanity of those writers and artists of our day who seem to imagine that the primary function of the critic is to chatter about their second-rate work." In the Eliot tradition the critical spirit was considered dangerous, corrosive, too self-conscious, when left to its own recognizance. It was safer leaking from art as irony, paradox, or ambiguity. Uneasy about the creative potential in criticism, Eliot remarked in 1956: "These last thirty years have been, I think, a brilliant period in literary criticism in both Britain and America. It may even come to seem, in retrospect, too brilliant." What might he have said of the next thirty years?

The emphasis has shifted from integrating high modernist art into the canon, to the work of reading that helped to establish the canon and can therefore also modify it. Our picture of the literary universe is no longer that of great, autonomous, quasi-Scriptural books clustered at the center, attracting into their orbit satellite and epigonal works of Interpretation. That picture can never be entirely effaced; it has, let us say, a Ptolemaic value. But our concept of what is creative projects today a more eccentric, or decentered map. It is not only that social movements, gathering momentum in the 1960s have overturned hierarchy, patriarchy, academy, monogamy, in the realm of letters. That is the surface, I think, of a tidal change that began when structuralism, joining anthropological and linguistic findings, reformed Western concepts of creativity by rationalizing episodic compilations, from folklore to South American myths. Using binary opposition as a structural principle, Lévi-Strauss explained how meaning was made and remade: how cultures dealt with contradictions in their belief-systems. So primary creation and secondary interpretation lost their rigid boundaries; though to expand the canon does not mean the proportional representation of every ethnic group but an acknowledgment (that must stand the test of time) of the devoted work of commentators and critics. The significant new work of art is gathered in, if at all, by them: we no longer maintain the image of the perfect work or objectified mind over there, and the consumer or interpreter desirous of communion with that brilliant object over here.

In these matters Richards was in advance of Eliot, or more democratic and experimental. *Practical Criticism* (1929) showed that art was not all that available even to acculturated students; that education had to undo both mental simplification and cultural prejudice; and that especially in a competitive modern era, where consumables replace the more difficult experience of art, the culture had to find a way of "endowing" criticism. It may seem like a small thing, but despite recent complaints about bringing criticism into the university and so over-institutionalizing it (as if each year the university were aborting Edmund Wilsons and Kenneth Burkes), to write and read critical texts with the same care that we give to literature—to bring, as it were, even the literature of criticism into the canon—is an achievement we are still working on.

Most of us, I have found, do not think criticism very productive, or read it with much pleasure. It has too many undeveloped allusions and ricochets. Within the casual flow of critical words there is a charged and overdetermined quality. Like pastoral, criticism seems always to glance at greater matters, and Richards's prose is a case in point. It evades fixed terminologies and never seems indebted to a central discipline. Yet it is steeped in the vocabulary of the social sciences. This absence of one fixed doctrine is crucial; it explains both the suggestiveness of criticism and the fact that there is this sort of writing able to avoid dogmatic resting points and explicitly systematized argument.

It is quite possible, then, even necessary, to subject critical prose to explication. The first who did so in a sustained manner, who took it to have a texture, was John Crowe Ransom in *The New Criticism*, the title lending its name to the movement he discussed. Other New-Critical practitioners applied close reading exclusively to fiction, and insisted with Eliot that "you cannot fuse creation with criticism as you can fuse criticism with creation." Our recent, more acute awareness of intertextuality, which has lessened the a priori ranking of fiction over commentary and enabled us to see the mediated and redacted nature of all texts, even when a named author originates them, is making us more medieval and midrashic in studying criticism as a creative yet text-dependent activity.

Take Richards's opening once more: "Intellectual tradition tells us . . . how *literally* to read a passage." It sets up a shifting series of ideas. Is Richards raising the issue of what might restrain interpretation (the chapter is entitled "The Bridle of Pegasus"), or what might liberate it? Is he calling for the rediscovery of hermeneutics as a discipline, but within a non-religious, that is, primarily intellectual frame? That is the direction Heidegger will go, with the difficult aim to depragmatize meaning and to explore (if not explain) why we cannot speak "being" at the present time, like a Scripture does or a few great poets. Is not "intellectual tradition," however, an oxymoron, since traditions are notoriously resistant to rationalization? Does "intellectual" then, intend "secular"—in which case the critic would be seeking an alternative tradition to the one that sustained the religious if unstable society of 17th-century England? The subject-phrase that opens the paragraph is impersonal, evoking like Eliot does an authoritative guide.

We are on a train that must switch from one rail to another, yet our journey takes us along both. It is essential (1) to explore the antagonism of theory and tradition, which Richards accommodates by the notion of "intellectual tradition." It is also essential (2) to explore the question of critical style, that is, how to read *criticism* aright, which leads us to acknowledge a conflict between the essayistic mode and descriptive poetics.

Yet we can relate (2) to (1). The growth of a science of literature that looks down on the familiar essay replays the antagonism of theory to tradition. Essayistic criticism is held to be merely impressionistic or epigonic (parasitic) by scientific critics. It is accused of using the resources of figuration in a lax or self-contaminating way. From it, consequently, no rules can be derived for reading aright the auxiliary prose that exists to help us read literature aright. "Figurative language," a typical statement runs, "is a stereotype of 'essayistic' criticism. It is a symptom of its epigonic character: 'essayistic' criticism imitates the semantics of its object language because it is unable to develop its own descriptive language; therefore, it cannot rise above the level of paraphrase or parody" (Lubomir Dolezel).

Practically speaking, the contradiction between descriptive modes and essayistic ones is less formidable than it appears. For however inventive of categories and technical words the science of literature may be, it relies—like literature itself—on the critical essay to integrate and familiarize its terms. Is it not, in fact, a sin against literary science to forget that the social and pedagogical prose we use in most discussions originates in the essayistic criticism of the latter half of the seventeenth century and the beginning of the eighteenth? That prose was inspired by the protodemocratic ideal of the "honnête homme" or gentleman, and it has remained almost totally stable as an ethos and a style from the time of *Tatler* and *Spectator* to that of the *New York Review of Books*. Indeed, the return to technical poetics is often a protest, one of several, against the demi-intimacies of this style that pretends to a conversational equality of author and reader and subdues class distinctions as well as the signs and trappings of expertise. Even Hans-Georg Gadamer is tempted to put his key concept of a "fusion of horizons" under its aegis. *Horizontverschmelzung,* he claims, is "the full realization of conversation, in which something is expressed that is not only mine or my author's, but common."

In addition to a science of literature, or integral to it, we need a sociology. Important as the conversational imperative was in forming a communicative prose, it drifted into a bad gentility promoting chit-chat or causerie even in professional circles. While not bad in itself, since one can only praise what James Boswell described as "gaiety of conversation and civility of manners," the habit was unfortunate in the way it censored both enthusiasm and the scientific spirit. Its decorum tyrannized over large tracts of French and English letters.[4] Richards's insistence on theory is clearly a provocation to the genteel and amateur tradition: it calls for research, protocols, professionalism, empirically tested principles. The title of his first book, *Principles of Literary Criticism* (1924), gains resonance against the background of the parodic Jane Austen opening of R.H. Tawney's *The Acquisitive Society* (1920): "It is a commonplace that the characteristic virtue of Englishmen is their power of sustained practical activity, and their characteristic vice a reluctance to test the quality of that activity by reference to principles. They are incurious as to theory . . . " Richards lifted a Cloud of Unknowing from the humanities at the risk of admitting scientific and artisinal ideals. *Chariots of Fire* (1981), the Hugh Hudson film about life at Cambridge in the 1920s, renders the situation against which the emphasis on theory protested.

There surely is an "ordeal of civility" (J. Cuddihy) which the founders of the "sciences humaines"—Marx, Freud, Lévi-Strauss—and their followers had to undergo. The genteel tradition of learning was also, moreover, a gentile tradition; to jump forward a little, when Harold Bloom used Buber's "I and Thou" as a framework for Shelley's mythmaking, or Gershom Scholem's understanding of Kaballa to argue for his theory of misreading, the jittery dovecotes of English studies did not coo with pleasure. An eloquent article denouncing Bloom and one of his colleagues, entitled "The Hermeneutical Mafia: After Strange Gods at Yale," not only alludes to one of Eliot's most Christian books but makes it clear that something not quite gentlemanly was going on in the Old School.

Essayistic criticism, in short, is not always part of the tradition but fights an internal battle by fashioning an iconoclastic style. When we read Coleridge on "the modern Anglo-Gallican style," which he despised because it was without "the hooks and eyes of intellectual meaning, never oppressing the mind by any after-recollection," do we not suspect that it was to redress such attenuation that Jacques Derrida—*enfin*—appeared?

A neglected aspect of the ordeal of civility concerns women. Though the conversational ideal is attached to the "gentleman," in France it is also perpetuated by the salons. The civilizing power of women over men was, in any case, a chivalrous cliché that came into the Renaissance via legends and books of courtesy. The cliché intimated also the other side of woman: her seductive potential that could lead men to break out of the bonds of conventional behavior. For Virginia Woolf the issue posed itself in terms of the domestication of women; and in that domestication, in the tying down of the wildness, in confining her to the role of consort, mother, housekeeper, the conversational ideal played its part. It was not gossip (often subversive) but social chit-chat that kept the emotions in check, albeit at the cost of trivializing overt relationships.

Woolf's short stories, *Monday or Tuesday* (published in 1921, augmented and republished after her death) show that kind of conversation eating into woman's soul. She even seems to cooperate with it: the Mrs. Dalloway figures in Woolf's fiction are as reticent about their true feelings as the men. So "Together and Apart" depicts the impasse of small talk as it unseals yet soon freezes a momentary affection. Words are frigid, they fail to betray (in the sense both of express and give away) persons who must hunt and haunt each other by these wary, destabilizing tokens. Alongside this Jamesian theme another prevails at the level of near-caricature: tags of poetry and gilded phrases rise up in the female soul— even identifying themselves as that soul—to create a prose poem that counterpoints an asthenic causerie. This rape by revery, by golden speech ("Thinking thus, the branch of some tree in front of her became soaked and steeped in her admiration for the people of the house; dripped gold; or stood sentinel"), is as disconcerting as the more prosaic impositions of society. Each stream of thought, color it gold or gray, is composed of clichés and keeps language within an airless realm of signifiers. Sasha Lasham, we read, "was glad she was with Bertram, who could be trusted, even out of doors, to talk without stopping . . . he chattered on about his tour in Devonshire, about inns and landladies, about Eddie and Freddie, about cows and night travelling, about creams and stars, about continental railways and Bradshaw, catching cod, catching cold, influenza, rheumatism and Keats . . . " For woman's soul, "by nature un-mated, a widow bird," this distancing of the outdoors by pseudo-intimate talk at once preserves virginity and disastrously confirms its violation. "At that moment, in some back street or public house, the usual terrible sexless, inarticulate voice rang out; a shriek, a cry. And the widow bird startled, flew away . . . " ("A Summing Up").[5]

At this point I wish to propose a historical generalization. If the history of commentary spans more than two millenia, then the period René Wellek describes as "Modern Criticism" is dominated by closure and premature synthesis. From about 1660 to 1950 (I chose dates that should be modified by a knowledge of national traditions) a neoclassical decorum triumphed, despite traumatic breaks and perhaps because of them. Even when art was adventurous, criticism remained reactionary. It requires, of course, more than the pop sociology I can offer to indicate how many factors conspired to produce that loss or limitation of interpretive skill which is Richards's point of departure.

The closure characterizing that period involves an ethos of language refinement that goes back in England to Charles the Second and the "Augustan" age, and is still notable in Richards's mentor, C.K. Ogden, who published Bentham's incisive attack on legal fictions and wrote a tract against "word-magic" entitled *Debabelization* (the occasion was the Basic English project, which Richards too supported). Sacred hermeneutics are marginalized; there is a general weakening of multivocal diction and a consensus in favor of plain or common speech and whatever genres and formal unities could be derived from Aristotle. The "limitary tone of English thought," as Emerson called it, is formed.

There is nothing original in identifying such a period of closure. Nor in suggesting that a fear of enthusiasm, which leaves its stamp on Swift's greatness, is the scarlet thread that runs through an age in which a *via media* decorum spread to all matters in hopes of damping the fires of controversy and preventing a recurrence of bloody schisms. Mikhail Bakhtin, taking Continental rather than English literature as his text, sees a similar period characterized by the attempt to repress vernacular energies and popular—especially mocking and so potentially revolutionary—speech. My sense is that this period continues much longer in criticism than in art, and with fewer exceptions.

So decisive, in any case, is the disintoxication of prose and the suspicion of visionary poetry beyond Spenser, Shakespeare, and Milton, that Somerset Maugham can assert of the King James Bible that it has been harmful to English prose. "The Bible is an oriental book. Its alien imagery has nothing to do with us. Those hyperboles, those luscious metaphors, are foreign to our genius." The latter consisted, according to Maugham, in plain speech. "Blunt Englishmen twisted their tongues to speak like Hebrew prophets." He does not see how he passes from bluntness to refinement, as he concludes: "To write good prose is an affair of good manners . . . good prose should resemble the conversation of a well-bred man." Though written in the late 1930s, these lines might have been redacted in Will's Coffee House where the Tatler held forth in the first decade of the 18th century.

I am under no illusion that in pursuing the question of style, and pitting theory against gentility, I have resolved the larger issue of the relation of theory to tradition. My purpose was to suggest that in this area too we do not know we are talking in prose. I would now like to consider the influential movement of deconstruction, to see how it stands to the lines of thought I have followed: the question of critical style, and the antagonism of theory to tradition.

"La chose est oblique," Derrida writes at the end of *Glas.* Obliquity affects the thing, that is every effort to describe what is the case, every historical reconstruction, every representation of reality. The problematics of reading with which modern criticism is concerned, and the ambiguity or distortedness of signs (even as we pass from partial criticism to holistic theory) cannot offer more than the pattern of a rigorous subversion of idealistic, bourgeois, pseudoclassical assumptions—in short, of tradition as error. Hegel's key notion that mind reveals and grasps itself as a "labor of the negative" is set to a harsher music. Yet "labor" in Marxist thought denotes not a temporal, quasi-religious waiting in patience, but an actual if alienated force in social relations, and a negated value in economics.

The recovery of that negated value in the history of criticism—so negated that it can reappear only as a "negative" value—is what attracts us to the strongest and most theoretical thinkers of the present era: Walter Benjamin, Martin Heidegger, Theodor Adorno, Maurice Blanchot, Jacques Derrida, Paul de Man. We recognize that the negative form of their intellectual energy *is* an energy—that it can inspire, and without promising an edifying or progressive result. When we recall how parsimonious Eliot is about precisely this critical energy, and how much talk surrounds us concerning human powers being laid waste by the options, distractions, stimulus-flooding, alienating tempo, and endless semiosis of modern life, then we realize how difficult it has been to make that negated energy work *for* rather than *against* us. Indeed, Freud's classic analysis of the discontent in civilized life predicts that we cannot reach the stage where labor puts on a purely human face. It is doomed to produce collective relations that are a form of slavery as well as of love, and modes of leisure that drift toward passivity and nirvana-like regression.

It is fascinating that the problem of "economy" is raised by Eliot always in an aesthetic rather than a sociopolitical context. His critique of *Hamlet,* and his formula of the "objective correlative," repeat in another form his view on William Blake. The artist who lacks an authorized worldview has to expend too much of his energy in creating rather than adapting one. This anxiety about the energy required to meet the challenge of modernity is not a factor in Georg Lukács, for example; for him there are untapped resources in the repressed working-class ethos, and the very tearing of the veil energizes, because it reveals something real, material, and labor-related rather than spiritual-ghostly.

At the same time this conversion of the negative into revolutionary energies can lead to coercive and totalitarian demands. An example is Ernst Jünger's *The Worker* (*Der Arbeiter*), a long, articulate tract of political philosophy published the year before Hitler came to power. Jünger attacks the arts as an intolerable luxury, the last refuge of bourgeois stability and fetishized traditions. He castigates their lack of productive power and predicts the development of great weapons of destruction to counterbalance this hoarding of cultural goods. He demands, in fact, a radical lightening of the baggage foisted on us by culture and education ("eine Gepäckserleichterung . . . die man sich gar nicht gründlich und umfassend genug vorstellen kann"). In words that are unbearably ominous today, because they express so openly the totalitarian coercion, Jünger asks for a complete mobilization ("totale Mobilmachung") whose task it is to "turn life into energy, as it manifests itself in business, technology and communications through the whirring of wheels, or on the battlefield as fire-power and mobility."

The disconcerting agility with which totalitarianisms of the Right and the Left compete for the worker's soul, the way clichés like fetishism and totality are appropriated by both sides, yields a first perspective on the problematic "purity" of deconstruction. There is an awareness that to reverse values or oppositions is not enough, that it is only the beginning of an inquiry to disclose the mutuality of such oppositions, and a verbal vertigo as frightening as the vacuity it displaces. But there is also a question about the character of the intellectual and transformative energy claimed by revolutionary thinkers. Does that energy escape messianic or visionary sources of hope, the same often denounced as being at the root of our incapacity to live simply and humanely?

When de Man says, paraphrasing Walter Benjamin, "It is not at all certain that language is human" (or words to that effect), he cannot be going back to the thesis that language has a divine origin, since foundationalism is strenuously resisted by deconstruction. It is precisely language with its peculiar deferrals of meaning that undermines the metaphysical positing of origin or end. Nor is it likely that the statement is a naive agnostic reflex. As one of those gnomic utterances by which de Man unsettles us, it reintroduces a worry about the nonhuman or transcendent impulse in language. That had previously troubled the question of the invention (origin) of words; now it returns as a question concerning the inventions (products) of language. For however practical and expressive our linguistic abilities are, they stand in a distancing, even renunciatory relation to phenomenal reality. Thinking and naming (un-naming), language and the labor of the negative, converge. One often senses an alliance between deconstruction's interminable analysis of texts (sometimes in the form of a "plurisy" of verbal play that "dies in its own too much"), and the negative counsels of a theology that renounces worldly values and especially a possessiveness regarding the divine names. Deconstruction is still engaged in identifying and removing anthropomorphism from thought. It says no more, no less, than that language has no "proper" meaning, and so must, yet cannot, be appropriated.

What keeps deconstruction mysterious is only the opaqueness of its social or political motive. It seems to enact an intellectual scruple that serves no one. It therefore leaves itself open to the charge that it does not care to change things, that it is content to tease language and mind by its paradoxes and paranomasia. According to its detractors, it is at most a powerful critique of academic pretensions; and did we not know already, with their idol Nietzsche, that university culture is a mode of professional deformation, a *Gelehrtenkultur?* In view of the purity of deconstruction (which may be paradoxically related to its sense of the impurity or overdetermined character of writing and politics) it is consoling to remember critics of the 1920s and 1930s who debated the fate of language and reading in modern society.

Yet deconstruction, for its part, also emphasizes reading. (That emphasis, in fact, helped its acceptance in America.) Now, however, ad hoc concepts adopted by the New Critics to motivate their concentration on reading ("organic unity," "heresy of paraphrase," "intentional fallacy") are given a fully negative development. Theories of impersonality, of intertextuality, of an "inmixing of the Other," model the text as a field of forces in which writers inscribe their experience. The new model entails a questioning of masterful author, all-stabilizing ego, and incarnate word. A linguistic or semiotic critique arises of how language is prematurely synthesized and appropriated. Also how words take their revenge: Derrida's analysis of *pharmakon* in Plato shows that it means undecidably poison and cure, and that this in-difference affects the entire system.

In terms of reading, the handling of ambiguity is a very sensitive matter. Art, in some sense, speaks beyond the doubt and irony it subsumes, just as every ideology-critique is indebted not only to what it criticizes (which could produce political stalemate and leave everything, as before, open to schemes of violence) but to a unitive mythology represented by Northrop Frye as an infectious principle of structure. How is ambiguity to be contained? From the 1930s (especially after William Empson) and into the 1950s, the disclosure of ambiguity was often accompanied by a theory of archetypes, generally indebted to Jung and Kerenyi, that grounds polysemy as a positive value. There was a tendency to link myth and archetype to, in particular, Romantic art, as if that explained the residual magic of all literature, its recuperative and unifying qualities in an enlightened age. Movements like deconstruction not only revise this view of Romanticism by showing the latter's dialectical and ironic style—even when most "symbolic"—but keep an analytic eye on the otherness, rather than supposed therapeutic intimacy, of symbol and archetype. The post-Flaubertian nausea of Roland Barthes, when he senses a cliché, is also a reaction to *masked* otherness, to the insidious violence of stereotypes in both conservative and emancipatory thought. If "it is not at all certain that language is human" one reason is that these stereotypes are easily given the spurious (often politically motivated) authority of archetypes.

At every point, then, deconstruction prefers to develop the notion of critique as impasse. Take the question of discursive style: is deconstruction scientific or essayistic? We can reply that it belongs to the sphere of the essay, because deconstructive reading no longer aims to establish a master-code but undoes every totalizing perspective. Yet it also belongs, in spirit, to the science of literature. We certainly have cause to place deconstruction on the side of theory, since its largest effort is to see Western tradition as a totality, one that has erroneously promoted the closure of the commentary process by reifying canon and book. Taking a page from Georg Lukács, we could argue that deconstruction's totalizing view "distorts into purity" a tradition that envelops us, and which we cannot criticize from the outside—the more so as "outside" "inside" presupposes a dichotomy deconstruction views with suspicion. It cannot be classified disjunctively as a philosophy *or* as a type of literary analysis. It is clearly both; and while it implies a theory of reading, that theory seems to be effective only as a set of practices, of actual readings, which revise and so revive texts in an "intellectual" tradition stretching from Plato to and beyond Mallarmé.

I sometimes feel that deconstruction itself is the impasse. The name stresses analysis, and *Abbau* rather than *Aufbau* in the wake of the grand spiritual narratives, the dialectical structures which *Geisteswissenschaft* built up after Hegel. Wilhelm Dilthey is the grand old man of those grand narratives, though Gadamer is a worthy successor. Theory for both Dilthey and Gadamer articulates the inner form of tradition, which is held to be its truth rather than untruth; and theory cannot triumphally replace, only manifest, a rich historical evolution. To make of theory a critical rather than totalizing instrument—or totalizing in the service of criticism—motivates the extra-skillful structuralism *(avant la lettre)* of Northrop Frye, which integrates William Blake's at once visionary and radical Protestantism. Perhaps the best one can do is to "place" deconstruction, and to show that it is not a foreign import but connects with English developments that had glimpsed the impasse of theory and tradition.

For this, curiously, we must return to Coleridge, and chapter 13 (an unlucky chapter) of his literary autobiography. That he wrote a literary biography is remarkable in itself and suggests the text-haunted character of his imagination. He adopts, in chapter 13, a "Constructive Philosophy" which tries to break from the entanglement of texts by identifying the role of imagination in the (mainly Fichtean) dialectic by which otherness is derived from ego. About to tie himself into a knot, he interrupts the chapter by inserting a letter from a prudent friend, advising him that this kind of talk is neither intelligible nor sellable. Coleridge then jumps to the famous definition of imagination (primary and secondary) every schoolboy can learn by heart. The characteristic virtue of Englishmen, their practical instinct, wins out; and Coleridge's autobiography has to compose itself of two rather than three types of discourse: a narrative of the readings that have determined him, together with (instead of the masterful paradigm of Constructive Philosophy) passages of practical criticism that disclose the unifying power in imagination—a unity which neither his life nor his philosophy could demonstrate.

Now Constructive Philosophy is a term applied to the work of Schiller, Fichte and Schelling (today called identity-philosophy) that culminates in Hegel's effort to overcome the formalism of Kant. Prior to Derrida it received its strongest antithetical response in Heidegger, and the Frankfurt school (Theodor Adorno, Max Horkheimer, Walter Benjamin, Herbert Marcuse). Derrida moves away from the possibility of identity to a radical notion of difference that seeks to avoid any foundational or resolving concept. Difference is not difference in contrast to identity, as if we could base it on the experience of a self-identical thing. So *deconstruction* is a fitting name, if we recall that Schelling, while respecting the contradictions that open up in thought when it tries to recover "repressed sources" ("versiegte Quellen"), defines *construction* as the resolving of contradictions ("Aufhebung der Gegensätze"). Deconstruction is a twig that twitches for the "versiegte Quellen" of suppressed or sublimated contradiction in every system or text.

Indeed, it shies even from "interpretation" because interpretation-theory (hermeneutics) is traditionally engaged in a textual or conceptual harmonizing of contradictions. The neutral, even flat resonance of "reading" suits it better; and though reading means more than reading—though reading, in deconstruction, is raised to a second power—there is no suggestion that logical or grammatical or rhetorical forms can be moved to a higher plane when they clash with one another. The conflict of systematized modes of analysis is valued, even when it leads to an impasse in the construction of a single, unified meaning. That language works in this manner, always imperfect from a mechanical or totalizing perspective, that it must, in fact, use error (some call it tradition) as its energy, is what makes it so remarkable an instrument.

I have to end sometime, so let it be with two observations. One concerns the surprising anti-hermeneutic stance of deconstruction. It not only directs the notion of allegory against allegoresis but refuses to harmonize the text with itself or think of literary works as having a yummy, mysterious inside—a depth-dimension that would bestow existential pathos on inner division and ambivalence. The removal of this myth of depth also shows itself as a suspicion of psychologism, naive intentionalism and essentialist views like the "Proper Meaning Superstition" Richards analyzes in his *Philosophy of Rhetoric*. Its play with the words of a text, at the same time, which is often—in Derrida—as consistent and extravagant as that of the midrashic rabbis, sets up an impasse in which an ancient interpretive skill is recovered yet cannot be grounded by either faith or theory. Like clowns or jongleurs, deconstructionist critics repeat the same act with language, obliging us to think of its negative, dismantling, as well as promissory, aspects.

My last observation concerns the "metaphysical pathos" many have nevertheless felt in deconstruction. It is, more precisely, a methodological pathos: a mourning over the self-invalidating nature of all methodologies. Only a desire for rigor, in the form often of a near-Pascalian hatred of egotism (the source of delusion and moral fallibility), remains. In an era where literary studies claim to be autonomous yet have absorbed the often minute and pugilistic intensity of religious kinds of exegesis, it is all too easy to put secular hopes on literature rather than Scripture. The working-out of this confusion—foreseen by Matthew Arnold—preoccupies most literary thinkers at present, and partially explains the puristic demeanor of deconstruction, which can become merely hygienic and mechanical. The larger issue here is in what sense we can lay claim to a Scripture, whether in the form of the Bible, or a secular canon (a national, privileged corpus of writings) or even to something special defined as literature in distinction to what is not literary. But when it scrupulously points to the reversibility of hierarchical constructs or to foreclosures in the commentary-process; when it challenges, by close reading, assumptions about the unity of the work of art or discloses the drive in every type of discourse for unmediated expression, a drive that includes mimetic as well as mystical residues, indeed everything associated with the dew still clinging to the words "origin," "presence," "being"—then deconstruction is not a symptom of lack of conviction but a sane and sustained response to ersatz religions.

6

The Function of Literary Theory at the Present Time

J. Hillis Miller

Not long ago Paul de Man could cheerfully say, with how much or how little of irony is impossible to know, that *the* task of criticism in the coming years would be a kind of imperialistic appropriation of all of literature by the method of rhetorical reading often called "deconstruction." "But there is absolutely no reason why analyses of the kind suggested here for Proust," said de Man, "would not be applicable, with proper modifications of technique, to Milton or to Dante or to Hölderlin. This will in fact be the test of literary criticism in the coming years."[1] It can hardly be said that this task has been carried out in the years since 1979 with much systematic rigor. This is true in spite of the widespread influence of "deconstruction," in spite of the many books and essays written about it, and in spite of the brilliant work of younger critics influenced by de Man. But there has been more talk about deconstruction, as a "theory" or as a "method," attempts to applaud it or to deplore it, than there has been an attempt to do it, to show that it is "applicable" to Milton or to Dante or to Hölderlin, or to Anthony Trollope and to Virginia Woolf.

In fact there has been a massive shift of focus in literary study since 1979 away from the "intrinsic," rhetorical study of literature toward study of the "extrinsic" relations of literature, its placement within psychological, historical, or sociological contexts. To put this another way, there has been a shift away from an interest in "reading," which means a focus on language as such, its nature and powers, to various forms of hermeneutic interpretation, which means a focus on the relation of language to something else, God, nature, society, history, the self, something presumed to be outside language. There has been, by one of those (perhaps inexplicable, certainly "overdetermined") displacements of interest, a tremendous increase in the appeal of psychologistic and sociological theories of literature such as Lacanian feminism, Marxism, Foucauldianism. This has been accompanied by a widespread return to old-fashioned biographical, thematic, and literary historical methods that antedate the New Criticism. Work based on such methods is often blithely carried on as if the New Criticism, not to speak of more recent rhetorical methods, had never existed. This geological slippage or drift is as much visible on the "right" as on the "left." It is as much present in the nostalgias of a Walter Jackson Bate for a time before the New Criticism, as he sees it, disastrously narrowed the range of literary study[2] as in the disdain and impatience of young Marxists and Foucauldians for a study of literature cut off (so they say) from history and politics. It is as if a great sigh of relief were rising up from all across the land. The era of "deconstruction" is over. It has had its day, and we can return with a clear conscience to the warmer, more human work of writing about power, history, ideology, the "institution" of the study of literature, the class struggle, the oppression of women, and the real lives of men and women in society as they exist in themselves and as they are "reflected" in literature. We can ask again pragmatic questions about the uses of literature in human life and in society. We can return, that is, to what the study of literature has always tended to be when it is not accompanied by serious reflection on the specificity of literature as a mode of language. Paul de Man or Jacques Derrida make such extravagant demands on the mere act of reading a poem, a novel, or a philosophical text that it makes one tired just to think of it. Surely reading cannot be all that difficult! Or require such self-consciousness, such hesitations. Surely no one can be expected to master the intricate rigor of the deconstructive way of reading and apply it habitually. We need to get on with it. Taking seriously what deconstruction says about the language of literature or about language as such might cause an indefinite delay or postponement of our desire to turn our attention to the relations of literature to history, to society, to the self. De Man has, in what is already a classic essay on the topic, "The Resistance to Theory,"[3] analyzed the reasons for this impatience, this collective desire to repress, to evade the difficulties of seeing literature clearly and thinking out rigorously its nature as a specific use of language. It is proof of what de Man says in the essay that the essay itself was rejected for inclusion in a volume sponsored by the Modern Language Association of America on the relations of literary study to other disciplines. Apparently de Man's theory of the resistance to theory met considerable resistance.

The shift away from the rhetorical study of literature is often accompanied by a false account of what is actually said about the extrinsic relations of literature by de Man, Derrida, or their colleagues. These critics are said to be concerned only with language and to cut language off from the real world of history and of living men and women. Deconstruction is lumped with other outmoded, "sterile," and "elite" "formalisms." It is opposed to the newer sociological methods which are pragmatically engaged in the real world outside language. All honor to the motivations which underlie this shift, the noble desire for social justice, for the improvement of the situation of women and minorities, for a clear understanding of the ideological presuppositions which invisibly manipulate us, of which the shift in commitment I am describing is surely a conspicuous example. And all honor to the impatience with the actual hard work of reading, the nagging sense that reading may be cut off from the real obligations of life, the desire to make the study of literature somehow count, have effects of power in society and in history. It is hard to imagine wholeheartedly admiring the man or woman who does not have some kind of passion for social justice and is willing to work for it.

The question is what this has to do with the study of literature. It is in defining that liaison that the difficulties and disagreements begin. My contention is that the study of literature has a great deal to do with history, society, the self, but that this relation is not a matter of thematic reflection within literature of these extra-linguistic forces and facts, but rather a matter of the way the study of literature offers perhaps the best opportunities to identify the nature of language as it may have effects on what de Man calls "the materiality of history." Here "reading," in the sense of a rhetorical analysis of the most vigilant and patient sort, is indispensable. How else are we going to know just what a given text is and says, what it can do? This can never be taken for granted beforehand, not even after that text has been overlaid by generations of commentary.

Since "reading" in this sense is indispensable to any responsible concern for the relations of literature to what is outside it, it would be a catastrophe for the study of literature if the insights of deconstruction, along with those of the New Criticism and of such critics as William Empson and Kenneth Burke, were to be forgotten or were to be relegated to an overpassed stage in some imagined historical "development," so that they no longer need to be taken seriously in the actual, present-day work of literary study. I should go so far as to say that, to paraphrase de Man, "the task of literary criticism in the coming years" will be mediation between the rhetorical study of literature, of which "deconstruction" is by far the most rigorous in recent times, and the now so irresistibly attractive study of the extrinsic relations of literature. Or rather, since, as Thomas Keenen reminds me, the word *mediation* is part of the vocabulary of dialectical thinking and suggests always the possibility of some synthesis or *Aufhebung,* usually at the expense of one or the other parties, it would be better to say "confrontation" or "encounter" or "negotiation of the non-negotiable," since, it may be, the rhetorical study of literature or the "literariness" in any piece of language as soon as it is taken as a text is the encounter with that thing articulated within language which is altogether irreducible or explicable by historical, sociological, or psychological methods of interpretation. Even "encounter" or "confrontation" is misleading, since that thing of which I speak can never be seen face-to-face, only indirectly, as in those traces or tracks of the passage of a cosmic particle in a bubble chamber. In any case, without the rhetorical study of literature, focused on language, its laws, what it is, and what it can do, particularly on the role of figurative language in interfering with the straightforward working of grammar and logic, as the parasitical virus interferes with the working of the host cell, we can have no hope of understanding just what the role of literature might be in society, in history, and in individual human life.

In our anxiety to make the study of literature count we are always in danger of misplacing that role, of claiming too much for literature, for example, as a political or historical force, or of thinking of the teaching of literature as too explicitly political. No one can doubt that literature is performative, that it makes things happen, that it is a way of doing things with words, and no one can doubt that the teaching of literature always has a political component, perhaps most when I am most silent about its political implications, ignorant of them or indifferent to them. It is not so much that the performative effects of literature, for better or for worse, are overestimated, as that they are often located in the wrong place. Sociological theories of literature which reduce it to being a mere "reflection" of dominant ideologies in fact tend to limit its role to that of passive mirroring, a kind of unconscious anamorphosis of the real currents of power. Study of literature would then tell readers something they could probably learn better elsewhere, by direct study of historical documents, for example. De Man, on the other hand, goes so far as to say that "textual allegories on this level of rhetorical complexity (he is speaking of Jean-Jacques Rousseau's *Social Contract*) generate history" (AR 277). In order to understand how it might be the case that a certain kind of language would make what we call history happen it is necessary first to understand what it means, in the case of a given text, to speak of it as a textual allegory with a high level of rhetorical complexity. It is necessary, that is, to *read* the *Social Contract* or whatever other text is our concern, no easy matter, nor one that happens as often as one would like, before going on to studying with confidence those extrinsic relations. To put this another way, those extrinsic relations themselves are intrinsic to the text. The distinction between intrinsic and extrinsic, like most such binary oppositions, turns out to be false and misleading. Those apparently "extrinsic" relations themselves require a rhetorical analysis, for example a clear understanding of the various figures of speech always necessary in one form or another to talk about the relation of a work of literature to its "context": "reflection," which is metaphor; "context," which is metonymy; "ideology," which is anamorphosis, and so on.

It is in fact not the case that the work of de Man or Derrida is entirely "intrinsic," entirely concerned with language as such, limited to language in rarefied isolation from the extralinguistic. There is a fully elaborated theory of the historical, psychological, and ethical relations of literature already present, for example, in de Man's *Allegories of Reading*. Work he was doing in the last two or three years of his life was increasingly focused on such questions, no doubt as one more example of that almost universal shift to politics, history, and society which marks the specificity of the current moment in literary study. No doubt this present essay is yet another example of that. In that essay I mentioned earlier entitled "The Resistance to Theory," for example, de Man has this to say about the contribution of a rhetorical study of literature to social, political, and historical understanding:

> It would be unfortunate, for example, to confuse the materiality of the signifier with the materiality of what it signifies. This may seem obvious enough on the level of sight and sound, but is less so with regard to the more general phenomenality of space, time or especially of the self: no one in his right mind will try to grow grapes by the luminosity of the word "day," but it is very difficult not to conceive the pattern of one's past and future existence as in accordance with temporal and spatial schemes that belong to fictional narratives and not to the world. This does not mean that fictional narratives are not part of the world and of reality; their impact upon the world may well be all too strong for comfort. What we call ideology is precisely the confusion of linguistic with natural reality, of reference with phenomenalism. It follows that, more than any other mode of inquiry, including economics, the linguistics of literariness is a powerful and indispensable tool in the unmasking of ideological aberrations, as well as a determining factor in accounting for their occurrence. Those who reproach literary theory for being oblivious to social and historical (that is to say ideological) reality are merely stating their fear at having their own ideological mystifications exposed by the tool they are trying to discredit. They are, in short, very poor readers of Marx's *German Ideology*. (RT 11)

One may wish to argue with this or to say that de Man has got the relation of the study of language and literature to politics all wrong, but only in bad faith could one say he does not explicitly account for the political and historical implications of his theory of language and his theory of what he calls "literariness." Or rather it would be better to speak of what he has written not as abstract theory but as praxis, since almost all of his work centers on the reading of some text or other, for example the series of essays on different works by Rousseau in *Allegories of Reading.* Or rather, to refine still further, what he has written, like all good literary study, is neither pure theory nor pure praxis, "practical criticism," nor yet a mixture of the two or something between the two, but a mode of interpretive language which is beyond the false and misleading opposition. One might call it "exemplification," but that would leave open the question, "exemplification of just what?" The answer must be that each good example of reading is an exemplification of other examples, according to a strange logic of synecdoche in a situation like literary study in which there exists no possibility of totalization or the establishment, once and for all, of an all-encompassing general theory. If, in any case, one of the simultaneously practical and theoretical dimensions of Paul de Man's work is a scrupulous accounting for the referential, historical, social, and political effects of literature, the same thing can just as decisively be demonstrated for Jacques Derrida, who has all along included consideration of the institutional, political, and social implications of his work, for example in *Positions,* or, more recently, in an interview entitled "Deconstruction in America."[4]

That the opponents of the rhetorical study of literature from both sides of the political spectrum continue to misrepresent it as ahistorical and apolitical may indicate the importance of what is in question here. The stakes, one can see, are enormous, both for literary study as such and for the function of literary study in society as it is now and as it is likely to be in the coming years. The stakes are enormous, that is, in continuing to think out the implications of a rhetorical study of literature for our political and ethical life.

No one can doubt that radical changes have been occurring in American society and in the relation of universities to society, therefore, in the social function of the study of literature and of literary theory. Perhaps most conspicuous of those changes going on at this moment is the new permeability of the university to invasion by industrial research. More and more research in the university is being funded not by the federal government and not by endowment funds but by grants and contracts from private industry. This seems to me the major change occurring at this moment. Though it may seem so distant from what we do in the humanities as to be irrelevant, I think this is in fact not the case. These new forms of "cooperative research" are associated with other forms of permeability, other forms of the invasion of the borders of the university. These are altering in fundamental ways the function of humanistic study in society.

The consensus on the function of the humanities in American life lasted until about the time I went to college in 1944. That consensus was largely the product of the humanism of Matthew Arnold as it was embodied in the curriculum of American colleges and universities. That curriculum was oriented primarily toward preparing white anglo-saxon middle-class males for professions: law, medicine, teaching, public service, business, the protestant ministry, and toward preparing white anglo-saxon middle-class women to be better wives, mothers, hostesses, and community servants. The idea was that you went off for four years to a protected and sequestered place, often protected and sequestered from the "opposite sex," and there assimilated the humanistic values by reading Plato, Shakespeare, Robert Browning, and so on, in preparation for entering society. The consensus about humanistic study saw it as primarily thematic and stylistic. Courses in the humanities were in aid of the assimilation of the best that has been thought and said in our Western tradition from the Bible and the Greeks on down. Such courses also provided models of style mostly taken from Victorian prose. In the required Freshman course I had at Oberlin College in 1944 we read Arnold, Newman, Mill, Huxley, and the Lang, Leaf, and Meyers translation of the Iliad. There was a general consensus on the canon a student of literature should read. It was primarily English: Chaucer, Shakespeare, Milton, Pope, Wordsworth, Tennyson, Arnold, T.S. Eliot, not a woman among them, and foreign works were usually read in translation, as is still the case in innumerable courses in "masterpieces of Western literature" across the United States today. This meant a general assumption of the translatability of works in that canon that happen to have been written in Latin, Greek, or Italian. In spite of lip service paid to "language requirements" and to the desirability of being able to read French, German, or Latin, the consensus I am describing depending fundamentally on the assumption that the great masterpieces in any language can and have been translated without significant loss into English. It is no wonder that those "language requirements" gradually eroded, since the necessity of reading Homer or Dante or Dostoevsky or Baudelaire or Nietzsche "in the original" was by no means generally recognized.

At that very moment, though I certainly did not know it, this consensus was breaking down. *Understanding Poetry* was already being tried out in a gingerly fashion in certain advanced classes in English at Oberlin, and the same thing was happening all across the country. The New Criticism was, as Walter Jackson Bate in the essay mentioned earlier here astutely recognizes, a major blow at the consensus. As soon as you start assuming that anyone can read a poem, that no special knowledge or membership in a particular class with a particular education is necessary, and as soon as you shift, however benignly, from attention to *what* is said, the thematic content, to *how* it is said, to tone, style, figures of speech, devices of presentation, it is the beginning of the end for that consensus. Sooner or later some teachers or students will see that the how contaminates and undermines the what. The long-term effect of the New Criticism, that is, was far different, perhaps exactly the opposite, of the conservative intentions of its founders. The birth of American deconstruction out of Paul de Man's participation in Reuben Brower's "Hum 6" course at Harvard might be taken as an allegory of that process.[5]

A second blow at the consensus was struck by the introduction of the discipline of comparative literature into the curriculum of American colleges and universities. However benignly intended and conservative in its intent, this move led ultimately to a recognition of an essential untranslatability from one language to another. This means, as Bate sees clearly, a breaking of the authority and domination of Departments of English, a gradual recognition of why it is one must study foreign languages: not to come back from them into English but to stay in them, to go native, one might say. From the point of view of that old Arnoldian consensus about the humanities both the New Criticism and the development of comparative literature were subversive. They were ultimately lethal invasions, destructive parasites within the host organism, generated by the organism itself.

To these two internal self-generated attacks on the old consensus about the humanities may be added social changes outside the university: the new assumption that all Americans ought to have a higher education; the rise of great public universities; the shift to a notion that women too should be educated for professional work (a change of incalculable importance); the gradual realization that the United States is a multilingual not a monolingual country; technological developments like television; jet planes that bring European scholars here in a few hours; extremely rapid translation of European "theoretical" works, so that they often appear in English first—in short, the general internationalization of humanistic study.

The result of all this crossing of borders has been a breakdown or dissolution of that old consensus. I do not think it can be reconstructed by fiat. At most, or at worst, a beguiling but ultimately repressive simulacrum can be reimposed in its place, as is in some quarters being attempted now. This is in fact perhaps the greatest danger to the humanities at the moment. By "repressive" I mean for example forcing a Latino or Thai in Los Angeles, a Puerto Rican in New York, an inner-city black in either city to read only *King Lear, Great Expectations,* and other works from the old canon, and to read them for a "content" and according to theological assumptions that are prescribed beforehand. This is what Joseph Conrad called "The Suppression of Savage Customs," which, as you remember, turned into "Exterminate all the brutes." The Latino, Thai, black, or Puerto Rican is assumed to be a "brute" until she or he can be turned as much as possible into that white middle-class male for whom the canon was intended. The dissolution of the consensus about humanistic study, a dissolution in which both internal and external factors have, as I have said, cooperated, has meant an irrevocable breakdown of the canon, a breakdown of the assumption of translatability, and, finally, a breakdown of the assumption that humanistic education is primarily aesthetic (has to do with pleasure) and thematic (has to do with values).

What I mean by the shaking of the canon should not be misunderstood. I do not mean we should no longer read Sophocles, Dante, Shakespeare, Milton, Wordsworth, and the rest. Surely it is good that they still be read. But they are read differently now, partly as a result of new ways of reading which have shown that they are far more problematic than perhaps they once seemed, far less the secure and stable repositories of the values and ideas of our cultural tradition than some defenders of the canon still seem to think they are. Canonical works now can be seen as especially concentrated forms of universal features of language, the tendency of figurative language, for example, to subvert straightforward grammatical or logical meaning. In addition, canonical works are read differently now because they are read in a different context, by students brought up on television, cinema, and popular music, for example, or in courses in which they are set side by side with noncanonical works. The ideology of the traditional canon involves both the exclusion of noncanonical works and strong presuppositions about how the canonical works are to be read. The shaking of the canon is accomplished by the rejection of both these forms of delimitation.

What rationale for the study of the humanities should be put in the place of the old consensus? I think there can be only one answer. Preservation, conversation, the keeping of the archives, the whole work of memory, remembering, and memorialization: yes, this remains an indispensable task of humanistic study. But our past is remembered differently now and some different things are now recalled into memory, for example, black literature and history or the history of women and writing by women. Memory and the storing and interpretation of what is remembered is not a passive but a vital and passionate act, an act each generation does anew and differently as it appropriates history for its own purposes. One of the important effects of the new modes of literary theory has been to redefine what it is that is worth remembering and what procedures of recovery and reinterpretation should be followed to make sure we remember what we want to remember.

Along with that perennial task of humanistic study, however, study of the humanities, in the present context of our multilingual, multiracial society, a society whose cultural traditions, for better or worse, are primarily shaped by the mass media, must become again focused on another traditional task, the teaching of *reading*. Courses in the literature departments should become primarily training in reading and writing, the reading of great works of literature, yes, but with a much broader notion of the canon, and along with that training in reading all the signs: paintings, movies, television, the newspaper, historical data, the data of material culture. An educated people these days, an informed electorate, is a people who can read, who can read all the signs, no easy thing to learn.[6]

Our fundamental task, the new rationale for the humanities, is to teach reading and the effective writing that can only come from or accompany a sophisticated ability to read. This transformation of the task of teachers in the humanities has come partly from radical changes in our society itself, and therefore from changes in the role of the universities and colleges that are a major institution within that society, and partly from accompanying internal changes in the disciplines themselves. The most conspicuous of the latter, especially in literary study, is the new centrality of theory. The future of literary theory is immense (to paraphrase Matthew Arnold) because it is the fundamental tool of both the tasks of humanistic study in the coming years as I have defined them: the work of archival remembering and the work of the teaching of critical reading as the primary means of combating that disastrous confusion of linguistic with material reality, one name for which is "ideology."

7

Historia Calamitatum et Fortunarum Mearum or: A Paradigm Shift in Literary Study

Hans Robert Jauss

Since the 1960s the study of literature has undergone a paradigm shift for which the journal *New Literary History* in particular has served as a platform of theoretical debate. Modern literary science has abandoned the old paths of historical-positivistic philology and now concerns itself both theoretically and practically with the understanding and interpretation of literature. Historically this involves the application of its past experience to the shaping of the present while currently it involves the forms of communication which contact with works of art makes possible in the life of society. Ralph Cohen, the founder of *NLH* has ventured with his latest project once more into an area that offers new challenges to his colleagues. The theoretical debate will now cross the limits hitherto taken for granted, i.e., research into literature of the historical past and the present, and press on toward a prefiguration of its future! I am certainly not the only one whom this bold intention confronts with a double dilemma: Since the literary historian as historian is only a prophet looking backwards, how can he write about the future of literary theory (and thus become a prophet looking forward) without ceasing to be a scholar? And how can he transform his subjective experiences into objective expectations and prognoses without violating a basic rule of the scientific community, once formulated as follows: "A scientist should never attempt to judge his own contributions, whether significant or not, but especially when not"?

Faced with this dilemma I have requested permission to write neither about the *past* of literary theory (about which so much has been said so often!) nor about its *future* (which cannot yet be told), but rather about

Translated by Rodger C. Norton

its *past future*. In saying this I am thinking of a segment of the history of scholarship in which I personally took part as an eyewitness and an active subject as well as a passive object. To write such a history from the aspect of this "past future" requires a renunciation of the Aristotelian teleology of beginning, middle, and end, and hence of the logic of a necessary development—a logic that is apparent only because it is gained retrospectively. Further, it requires that one include things intended and unintended, fulfilled and unfulfilled, in short, that one reintroduce into the past the openness of the future. This means nothing less than the narration of a history in the discontinuity of its experience, with a constant cleavage between purpose and result, as a German proverb states: "because, firstly, things are going to change, and secondly, not in the way you think they will."

Therefore I have written a segment of scholarly history as a *historia calamitatum et fortunarum mearum*,[1] in order to depict the most recent paradigm shift in literary studies from my personal perspective and from the experiences of my group, the former Heidelberg assistants who later became members of the "Constance School." This history of our "past future" might be of interest to the non-German reader in two respects. On one hand, it is a record of the experiences—the expected and unexpected events, the hopes and disappointments, the successes and failures—of the first generation of scholars after the second World War who attempted to renew the study of literature. On the other, it may serve as an example to the next generation, who, in regard to the future of literary theory, may learn from this account how difficult and laden with chance is a reform carried out against institutional resistance (and this applies, I am sure, not only to Germany!). An event cannot simply be planned and brought about. As we all know, this holds true not only for politics and history but also the history of scholarship and not least for the "paradigm shift in literary study."

After these preparatory remarks, I shall now willingly employ my license, and consider myself no longer the object but rather the subject of a segment of the history of literary scholarship of the post-war epoch. I shall begin my retrospective at the point of time when the individual research of my earlier career was drawn into a process which—as could not yet be envisioned *in actu*—has led in the last three decades to a

---

[1] The following text was originally written in reply to a request of the Deutsche Forschungsgemeinschaft (German Research Association) in 1983 and was published in *Forschung in der Bundesrepublik Deutschland: Beispiele, Kritik, Vorschläge (Research in the Federal Republic of Germany: Examples, Criticisms, Suggestions)*, ed. Christoph Schneider (Weinheim, 1983), pp. 121–34. The request was not for an objective report on the state of present research in my discipline and its prospects for the future, but for a piece of scholarly autobiography that would trace the process of seeking and finding, in order to furnish examples of the initiation, methodology and impact of research.

"paradigm shift' from the traditional philologies to a general literary study. During the reconstruction of the German universities, the modern philologies, following the example of the classical, soon became rigidified again into methodologically secured, conventionalized fields of study. After the excesses of the nationalistic histories of literature and the humanities during the Hitler period, they returned to the same safe haven, showing no concern for a new legitimation of the traditional literary and aesthetic education that would have been demanded at the so-called "Zero Hour." They relied on the tried and true paradigms of neopositivist historicism or formalist text analysis. In the time-honored histories of the national literatures they saw the unquestionably valid framework for an unlimited accumulation of historical knowledge, just as they saw in the work-immanent interpretation of the classics the selfless ethos of the philologist removed from all political and social controversy. They were blind to theory because they believed that, for the prevailing philological practice, all theoretical decisions had long since been made. Was it not true that the older generation of dissertation directors had attained eminence without ever having to justify their work theoretically? So it went without saying that in the 1950s the philological paradigm of historical and aesthetic education in other countries—especially in the United States and France—began to surrender its social function, while education became more and more a question of technological and sociological training. Non-historical methods such as logical positivism, empirical social research, and structural linguistics established an ideal of scientific rigor, measured by which the historical-philological method had to seem, in the public mind, to be unserious, trapped in subjectivism, removed from society, and thus behind the times.

When I ask myself today what was really my deeper, half-subconscious reason for seeking new concepts of research, I see it above all in the discredit into which my discipline had fallen and which, even in Germany in the 1960s, could not be overlooked, but also in the necessity of having to defend the scientific and social relevance of my discipline against the new "savior sciences." In my dissertation (on the works of Marcel Proust) and in my habilitation treatise (on animal literature in the Middle Ages) I had already followed a theoretical line of questioning in my interpretations. The first work dealt with the phenomenological problem of temporality and remembrance in the modern novel, and the second with the hermeneutic problem of the strangeness and dissimilarity of a different concept of the nature of man. Yet, methodological reflection was not a criterion that qualified me for my first teaching position (1959, at Münster). I did not become more deeply involved in a debate about theory until a concern for opening new research possibilities prompted me to demonstrate the disputed capacity of my discipline to deal with theory. Therefore, the three main objects of my research in the ensuing period all reflected an apologetic strategy: the apologia for medieval literature, beginning with a compendium entitled *Grundriss der romanischen Literaturen des Mittelalter's (Outline of Romance Literatures of the Middle Ages)*, since 1961; the apologia for literary history, which should rest upon a new foundation, the so-called "Rezeptionsasthetik" as enunciated in my inaugural lecture at the University of Constance in 1967 and published as *Literaturgeschichte als Provokation (Literary History as a Challenge to Literary Theory)*; and finally (since 1972) the apologia for aesthetic experience, which grew out of my involvement in an interdisciplinary research group ("Poetics and Hermeneutics") founded in 1963.

But it is not by chance that the "apologia" in the Christian occident has been especially valued by theologians as a weapon of the *ecclesia militans* that was particularly suited to protect the purity of a dogma and which therefore had also usually been applied in intellectual history not for but against progressive knowledge. If the above-mentioned research programs did, indeed, enjoy an unexpected and internationally recognized success that has lasted to the present day, this may be due to the fact that the apologia for historical understanding and aesthetic experience could, paradoxically, be addressed to two hostile camps at the same time: the dogmatism of the outdated historical-philological method on the one hand, and, on the other, the anti-historicism of the prevailing structuralist theories. Yet, this provocation would certainly have soon evaporated if it had not been based on a program which, with the new questions that it posed, opened up new tasks and areas for literary research.

I deliberately speak of "new questions" rather than of "research lacunae." The idea of turning toward a new type of investigation of the Middle Ages with the intent of seeking the model character of this epoch in its alterity and historical remoteness, and, second, toward a literary history of the reader in order to counter the disrepute of the old literary history, and, third, toward an aesthetic theory derived from the experiencing of literature and art, was in no way the product of assiduous work by a philologist. It did not involve working through mountains of secondary material to arrive at the most recent state of research, in order finally to be rewarded perhaps by the finding of an undiscovered lacuna. If, from these briefly sketched beginnings in the last two decades there have indeed come new directions of research, the success of which is now apostrophized—somewhat prematurely to be sure—as a "change of paradigm" in literary study, then my role as the subject of this piece of history of our discipline is to be found mainly in the initiative I took to propose and justify a reversal of direction in the interrogative process, which then could be tested with the help of friends and students and further developed in the face of constant outside criticism. That this initiative was able to convince others can be credited to me only in a smaller part, but otherwise can be explained by the fact that the situation was favorable, that it exposed a latent need and seemed to promise that which a reorientation of questioning in academic research apparently always brings: a new approach that saves time and labor. For such reorientation permits us to shorten the approach through the ever larger accumulation of previous findings by making them accessible again from a different point of view. It enables us to reduce a discouraging complexity of unbounded knowledge and widely differing procedures or— stated more simply to save expenses. I shall return later to explain the favorable circumstances of the incipient university reform at that time. Let me first posit the reasons for my criticism of the idea that the best chances for successful scholarship lie in the seeking and finding of gaps in existing research.

What one generally calls a "research lacuna" is, when we look more closely, a metaphor that is no longer transparent. It implies an accumulative conception of academic research and suggests the image of a mosaic-like completion and perfection of knowledge as if it were only a matter of searching out a blank space on the map of research in order to gain, along with the new object sought, a new paradigm of scholarly effort. This would then strip the hitherto prevailing paradigm of its validity, *vulgo*, "falsify" it or at least make it a borderline case, in order, finally, to relegate it to the museum of the history of science.

This conception was contradicted particularly by Thomas S. Kuhn when, in his well-known book, he set up the model of a discontinous process of scientific history in opposition to the non-linear progress of a knowledge that can be rendered false again and again. In this discontinous process, scientific revolutions unfold in such a way that what is new in the historical transformation of closed interpretative systems must assert itself eventually because it cannot spontaneously take the place of the old. I have thus far used Kuhn's model but must add that in my opinion it underestimates the function of question and answer in the preparation, assertion, and legitimation of the new. Kuhn himself uses question and answer merely in the reduced form of the riddle and its promised solution, which, he says is characteristic of a phase of normalized science. Accordingly, the scientist's activity is in essence a task of precise definition within the no longer questioned framework of the prevailing paradigm, which guarantees the sure presence of a solution, determines in advance which of the facts can yield informative results, and thereby eliminates the danger of wasting time on insoluble questions. For Kuhn, therefore, that which is new can only appear from outside through the unexpected occurrence of an anomaly that does not fit into the recognized paradigm, demands an explanation from premises not yet known, and thereby introduces a change of paradigm. But how does one arrive at the perception of an anomaly that was already in existence before it was first perceived? If it was the hitherto valid paradigm, which let only the expectable be observed and anomalies be overlooked, how can an anomaly then suddenly be noticed after all and become relevant as the origin of new knowledge? Here the metaphor of an unexpected event, falling as it were from heaven, obviously conceals the hermeneutically evident circumstance that an assumedly objective observation presupposes the initiatory basis of an (often already forgotten) anticipatory question. One must change the line of questioning before one can see something in a different way or discover something new. An excellent example seems to be that offered by modern science (although I cannot judge its broader applicability) in the story of the discovery of the double-helix, which introduced the paradigm shift in molecular biology: "The key to [Linus Pauling's] success was his reliance on the simple laws of structural chemistry. The alpha-helix had not been found by only staring at X-ray pictures; the essential trick, instead, was to ask which atoms like to sit next to each other."[2]

The new thing which can open up a field of research hitherto unseen or neglected and can reorient the scholar's work, does not need to be a *terra incognita* as far as method is concerned. It can come from a new perspective on that which is old, long since known, and yet overlooked. In my case, the "anomaly" which in Kuhn's model should introduce a change of paradigm, was a simple question that had not been posed for a long time. In literary history, the reader had of course always been involved—as addressee of the author; as a party of mediation between the work and its effect; as a receiving, selecting, and rejecting subject in the formation of tradition. Yet, the history of the arts, since the beginning of their scientific consideration at the time of Renaissance Humanism, was so matter-of-factly understood to be the history of works and their authors that the question of the third party, the reader or public, was not expressly posed or was relegated to the "unscientific" field of rhetoric. The posing of this question today, in view of the crisis of my discipline and of the university institution—ultimately a crisis of historical education—opened a view toward the possibility of renewing

---

[2] James D. Watson, *The Double Helix* (New York: Atheneum, 1968), p. 50. For the history of the functioning of question and answer, see my account in "Aesthetische Erfahrung und literarische Hermeneutik," chapter II A (Frankfurt: Suhrkamp, 1982), published as *Aesthetic Experience and Literary Hermeneutics* (Minneapolis: Univ. of Minnesota Press, 1982).

literary history, exhausted and mired in positivism, by giving it the task of seeking a new understanding of the history of literature as a communicative process between all three parties. Thus was opened an unexpectedly broad field of study—the hitherto scorned or forgotten evidence of the response to literature by generations of its readers and interpreters, the value of which was brought to light for the very first time by the history of the reception and the effect of works that has flourished since that time. The continued success of this new paradigm—which has now so firmly established itself within the most varied scholarly movements that the preparation of the documents dealing with reception has become a kind of obligatory task in literary-historical research—gives abundant proof of what I have stated about the economy principle in the research process. Formerly the doctoral candidates in philology were confronted, when addressing any work of world literature, by a mountain of previous interpretations, often numbering in the hundreds. These were supposed to be surpassed by a new interpretation, of an originality that was more and more difficult to attain, indeed, impossible except perhaps for a genius. But now the candidates could start immediately on a scarcely cultivated field and gain new knowledge that sprang from a different insight into the presumably exhausted subject and spared them the difficulty of having to accomplish a miracle of subjective interpretation.

This may suffice as an example of the initiation of successful research in my discipline. Certain questions remain: To what degree can my case be generalized beyond the hermeneutic discipline? Can there be derived from it a maxim to the effect that the chances of successful research and meaningful progress also in other areas do not lie in the discovery of lacunae in any safely conventionalized scholarship, but rather in the recognition of a possible and hitherto scarcely used direction of questioning, which certainly cannot always be justified so simply and in advance by an obvious deficiency as in the case of the reception theory of the Constance School?

I should now like to turn to the question whether and how the initiatives for such research were aided or hindered in their corporative and interdisciplinary development by the university institutions. For that, the three undertakings alluded to above might serve as examples, in three different respects, for the general development of the last two decades. The first, which developed on the basis of the old "Ordinarien-" or senior-professor system, was put into jeopardy by the reorganization of the university, and stagnated for many years. The second profited at first from university reform in a newly founded institution, but then almost fell victim to the restrictive higher education policy and could only with great effort maintain itself by means of the private commitment of its participants. The third has flourished up to the present, perhaps only because it was formed by a free co-optation of competent scholars from different disciplines, and because it expanded and, thanks to two grants, was able to work and publish independently of university institutions and of the obligation to produce reports and successful results that would have been imposed by the official research agencies.

The *Grundriss der romanischen Literaturen des Mittelalters (GRLMA) (Outline of Romance Literatures of the Middle Ages)* was conceived amid difficulties typical of the situation after World War II. It was the first attempt—initiated by Erich Köhler and me in 1959, struggled over at professional meetings, and joined by an international group of medievalists—that sought to overcome the isolation of German medieval scholarship, which had been compromised during the Hitler period. The purpose was to bring together scholars of all Latin nations, from the most varied academic directions and ideological camps, for mutual research dedicated to the concept of modernized medieval study, for which new tools—the complete documentation and typological-historical determination of all texts within the communicative system of literary genres (a five-digit total!)—first had to be prepared. The optimism underlying and sustaining this project became apparent to me, quite understandably, only when I could look back at its increasing problems and unfulfillable goals, at its various adaptations to new research desiderata and its surprisingly slow progress. In two decades only four of the planned thirteen volumes (with additional documentary half-volumes) have been completed, and another decade will presumably be needed in order to finish the work, which is already in the hands of a second generation of editors and collaborators. Of course, such delays are not rare in humanistic scholarship, especially in that of an editorial and lexical nature, and the German Research Association has in this case not made its long-term investment of aid in vain. Even with its present results, the *GRLMA* has completely fulfilled the promise of its title and created a lasting tool for medieval research in several disciplines, and thus has certainly helped Romance studies in Germany to regain international prestige. Yet, considered in the frame of a general history of science, this makes the question all the more interesting: Why was this research—so thoroughly innovative in its conception—not able to fulfill the expectations of its founders despite such Herculean efforts?

From my viewpoint, the difficulties of this undertaking can be traced primarily to four reasons. Firstly: The double goal of a completely documented summation of previous research and the testing of new lines of investigation produced a vicious circle. Secondly: New research was difficult to carry out with older, already prominent scholars; it required a younger group of active collaborators. Thirdly: The double crisis of the university as an institution and of the legitimacy of historical-philological education exposed this long-term project to considerable hindrance and jeopardy. Fourthly: Even the most complete guidelines and models cannot properly direct the work of cooperative research; its coordination demands the regular dialogue of concurrent research colloquia.

The guiding concept of the *GRLMA* was bound to offend traditional philology. The new compendium was intended to succeed the paradigm of tradition-oriented research. Medieval literature was no longer to be interpreted as a connecting link between antique and modern, but rather to be comprehended in its own historical world as the model of a culture that was exemplary in its very strangeness, and to be discovered through a new approach—the horizon of expectations or "Sitz im Leben" (place in everyday life)—and through studying the history of the function of literary genres. To make its innovations, this demanding program presupposed a knowledge of the repertory of texts and genres, which the collaborators had to provide, together with new data appropriate to the conception involved. But the collaborators were not yet prepared for the double task of producing a complete textual repertory in conformance with the canonical demands of neopositivistic philology and of evaluating this repertory according to the hermeneutic, social-historical demands of the modern concept. We also could not choose the collaborators freely, according to their scholarly competence and interest in a renewal of medieval study. In the ideologically precarious situation of the post-war period, the German founders of the program found it necessary first to win over their most prominent professional colleagues from France, Italy, and Spain in order, with their authority, to have any hope of beginning the project with an international personnel. Also involved was a sharing of the editorial tasks, for which an equitable participation (not to mention prestige) of nations and scholarly movements was of primary concern. So began the long history of our calamities, the documentation of which has filled an entire office wall with loose-leaf files.

After the first, easy successes of our research diplomacy, the leading scholars in our field proved, with one admirable exception—Jean Frappier of Paris—to be pronounced individualists who, to be sure, had gladly lent their names to the undertaking and had suggested possible co-workers, but who had no serious intention of making their research part of the common endeavor or of carrying out its concept of forming and leading research groups. In the worst such case, the leading representative of a national philology, who for years had left every letter unanswered, surprised us with a monumental treatment of the research area entrusted to him—which, however, without a word to us, he had written for a rival publisher. So the work load for most volumes fell back upon the innocent shoulders of the German chief editors, who had the endless chore of replacing lost collaborators (which today number more than half of the original seventy), winning over the new ones and orienting them, and dealing with dilatory or incompetent colleagues, whose work finally had to be taken over by our own editorial staff, in addition to their original tasks. Furthermore, all of this had to be done under the pressure of having the success of the project dependent upon first publication of our own volumes as models of the work to be done. To make our discomfort complete, the crisis of the traditional university, in all the countries involved, gradually began to erupt during this same phase of our work. This furnished a welcome alibi for the dilatory collaborators, but it also made additional claims upon us, since we neither wanted to nor could stand aside in the battle over the new structure of a democratic university. Since this battle made public the crisis of historical education, and since the relevance of the study of medieval literature in particular was under attack by the technocrats of the so-called "Curriculum Reform," our undertaking was unexpectedly deprived of its hitherto unquestioned legitimacy. The significance of medieval studies, together with present-day concerns of research and pedagogy, had to be rejustified and fought for in all governing bodies.

The excessive demands put on my generation of academics during these years is certainly well enough known. Yet, I should explain here briefly why the criticism of the "research privilege" enjoyed by the "Ordinarien" (senior professors) could only draw a weary smile from us. Rapid achievement of our project's goals, which by their very nature required leadership and active participation within a particular research area, would alone have required a full day's work. But in addition we found ourselves overburdened in our three-fold role as researchers, as teachers with increased duties, and as "Institut"-directors with new and time-consuming obligations demanded for the "Reform." It was truly a Sisyphean task, for which even the partial sharing of the load by an editorial assistant furnished by the German Research Association could do little to compensate. If I had to begin such an undertaking again, I would insist that the institution first assure the necessary free time for research; I would also organize beforehand a more homogeneous team, consisting of my own students and of scholars who would be prepared for genuine cooperation and willing to invest their own research in the common endeavor, and finally I would create a dialogic basis for this mutual labor in the form of accompanying research colloquia. My successor, Hans Ulrich Gumbrecht, has proven the inestimable value of such organization. With it he was successful in giving new form to the volume devoted to the historiography of the Middle Ages. He made good use of the opportunity to form a new research group by giving it an interdisciplinary composition and by winning over scholars from neighboring fields for collaboration or consultation. Thus, in a number of highly regarded colloquia which the group itself published,[3] a new concept was developed that gave the *GRLMA* a connection with the "Nouvelle Histoire," which at present enjoys an excellent reputation. Of no small value is also the fact that thereby a new phase of international communication was begun, bringing a productive discourse between all collaborators, which their predecessors had hoped for, but, because of the above-mentioned difficulties, had not been able to achieve.

My initiative to begin the necessary revitalization of literary history by researching the reception of literature was not a solitary decision, born at the writing desk. It was part of the reform experiment at the University of Constance (founded in 1966), and I participated in it as a member of the first group of professors to be called there. The initiative had its origin in discussions with the social sciences, which at first played the leading role, and it was made institutionally practicable in the newly founded university. Its basic idea was to transform the old autonomy of the "Institut" (department) into the cooperative structure of "Units of Teaching and Research," thus creating the first so-called "Fachbereiche" of the German university system, and to try interdisciplinarity as a guiding principle on all levels (as seen in the interfaculty committees for research, teaching, training of junior personnel, and examination. This concept permitted us actually to do what elsewhere remained a nice, but empty, formula, namely, to develop teaching out of research and then to transfer the stages and results of theory development into new study models. The idea conceived by five professors in the fields of English, German, Latin, Romance, and Slavic languages to create a "Fachbereiche" called "Literaturwissenschaft" (Literary Studies)—could be best realized here. These men were Wolfgang Iser, Wolfgáng Preisendanz, Manfred Fuhrmann, myself, and Jurij Striedter. All of us gladly surrendered the privileges of

---

[3] *Literatur und Gesellschaft des Spätmittelalters* (*Literature and Society of the Late Middle Ages*). Supplemental volume of the *GRLMA*, ed. H. U. Gumbrecht (Heidelberg, 1980). A second, companion volume on problems of the reception of medieval literature is in preparation.

departmental chairmanship for this project and—having been called to the University of Constance at the same time, thanks to the wise policies of the founding rector, Gerhard Hess—organized ourselves into a research group. At this time there was no institutional model for this group's concept of general literary study, either inside or outside the country. Its aim was to transfer the traditional curriculum of the national philologies into the new interdisciplinary unit of general literary study based on development of theory, not merely on comparative consideration of literature. Thus a demand was created for philological-historical praxis to be opened to new lines of investigation, which other research groups abroad—the Formalists in Russia, the Structuralists in Prague, the New Critics in the United States, the Nouvelle Critique in France—had long ago begun and worked out in systematic fashion and which now had to be developed by the Germans in their effort to recover lost ground. This effort has produced, among other achievements, editions of the writings of Russian Formalism, of Prague Structuralism as well as Russian semiotics, which the contributions of University of Constance slavists and linguists have made accessible to Western scholarship again or, in part, for the first time.

The further development of this group, which soon came to be called the Constance School, can be briefly traced. Its aesthetic and historical theory, completely oriented at first on problems of reception or effect, has evolved more and more into a theory of literary communication. In the same measure as the scope of its research reached beyond autonomous art and modern literature into literary tradition outside the humanistic concept of the work of art, more and more questions arose that classical aesthetics and literary hermeneutics had neglected. Foremost for me was the question concerning the experience of art, or what could be called aesthetic praxis, which underlies all manifestations of art as productive activity *(poiesis)*, receptive activity *(aisthesis)*, and communicative activity *(katharsis)*. From this it followed that the analysis of the implied reader had to be supplemented by the analysis of the historical reader, and the reconstruction of the immanent horizon of expectations, which the work implies or anticipates, had to be supplemented by the reconstruction of the social horizon of experience, which the reader supplies or brings from his or her own historical "Lebenswelt" (life world). The classical dichotomy of fiction and reality resolved into the dialectical relationship of theme and horizon: Literary fiction was henceforth to be interpreted as horizon of historical reality, and the real world as horizon of fictive worlds. The dogma of the self-referentiality of the poetic text was once again reduced to an historically limited validity, to the epoch of aestheticism. The problems of understanding far-removed or strange literary worlds and of the dialogic character of aesthetic communication moved more and more into the foreground of research interest.

Proceeding from this position, reform models for a study of literature were developed that were intended to be useful both for the education of a new type of teacher of literature for the secondary school, as well as for those professions that originated in the environment of the old and the new cultural media. The Constance School's ideas for reform of outdated philological-literary education aroused much attention both in professional circles and in the public and political arena. They were much discussed, were adopted to a large extent by more recently founded institutions, and were "exported" by literary specialists of the younger generation in Constance who had subsequently taken teaching positions at other universities. Meanwhile, the hopes that were held for the Constance study model found the least fulfillment in our own state of Baden-Württemberg. After being tested and put in finished form, our model was rejected by the Ministry of Culture for the remarkable reason that it unfortunately did not conform to the requirements of the traditional examination system—which, ironically, our program at its founding had been commanded to reform! During the ensuing controversy over our study model, the shelves on a second wall of my office became filled with files containing the drafts of its preliminary phase, the records of the numerous efforts, through concessions and reformulations, to save it from the ministerial bureaucracy's attempt to equalize all innovations, and finally the bad compromises in the new state examination regulations, which also had been rejected repeatedly by higher-ups.

This is a chapter out of the history of the so-called "Gebremste Reform" ("Stalled Reform"),[4] at the conclusion of which the only remaining question was why, after a decade of the most dedicated and strenuous efforts, the present form of the university emerged—a form that no one, regardless of where one stood, could have wanted to be this way. As far as the Constance program is concerned, the rejection of its study model was followed by a "Proposed Structural Plan" from the Ministry of Culture, which was presented to the university rectors of Baden-Württemberg on December 14, 1976. Here a sudden burst of Swabian thrift called not only for the "thinning-out" of the social science fields but also the elimination of the literary and linguistic offerings of the University of Constance. Although this sellout of official educational policy was prevented, the dubious fact remains that the

---

[4] A reference to *Gebremste Reform—Ein Kapitel deutscher Hoschschulgeschichte: Universität Konstanz 1966–1976* (*Stalled Reform—A Chapter in the History of the German University: University of Constance 1966–1967*), ed. H. R. Jauss & H. Nesselhauf (Constance, 1977).

decision against the literary studies program was obviously arrived at by purely arithmetic means without consideration of, and scarcely with knowledge of, the international prestige that made the Constance School different from the seminars of the other universities of Baden-Württemberg, which were evidently deemed more worthy of preservation. By this time, to cite only one piece of evidence, many of the program papers and publications of the Constance School had already been translated into other languages,[5] and evidence of their influence was already being seen in the strong influx of students, doctoral candidates, and young scholars from universities outside the Swabian province.

This review of events makes it clear that my group would have done better not to follow the Humboldtian principle of the Constance Reform, namely that of developing teaching out of research. It would not have been affected by a restrictive university policy that was interested only in educational efficiency if, from the beginning, it had regarded its teaching duties as a routine task and withdrawn for its research into a "special research unit." Nevertheless, I doubt that its research, if done in isolation and freedom, would have been so effective. In saying that, I am not thinking solely of the productive urge to test new research through instructional dialogue, but also of the opportunity, rendered more difficult in a research organization, of repeatedly recognizing and training new students. The Constance literary study group really became a "School," which was able to survive nearly twenty years of all sorts of external problems, only because it produced and incorporated within itself during this time a second (actually even a third) generation that opened new areas of research in both the development and application of theory (especially in the sociology of literature, the peripheral fields of legal history and anthropology, cultural semiotics, and the empirical analysis of communication media).

---

[5] My inaugural lecture at Constance, "Literaturgeschichte als Provokation" (1967) [Translator's note: Published under the same title in Edition Suhrkamp 418 (Frankfurt, 1970); Engl. version: *Towards an Aesthetic of Reception*, trans. Timothy Bahti, intro. Paul de Man (Minneapolis: Univ. of Minnesota Press, 1982)] has been translated into fifteen languages; and W. Iser's "Appelstruktur der Texte" (1970) has appeared in eight languages. [Translator's note: This essay was published in English as "Indeterminacy and the Reader's Response in Prose Fiction," in *Aspects of Narrative*, ed. J. Hillis Miller (New York, 1971).] Translations of my book *Ästhetische Erfahrung und literarische Hermeneutik* (1977) are scheduled to appear very soon in English, Italian, Spanish, and Rumanian. [Translator's note: This has since been published in English as *Aesthetic Experience and Literary Hermeneutics*, trans. M. Shaw, Univ. of Minnesota Press, 1982.] W. Iser's *Der Akt des Lesens* (1976) has appeared in complete or partial editions in English, Japanese, French, Korean, Portuguese, and Hungarian. [Translator's note: This has since been published as *The Act of Reading: A Theory of Aesthetic Response* (Baltimore: Johns Hopkins Press, 1978).]

There were many individuals in the group who had fulfilled the habilitation requirement for university positions but made their services available for a lengthy period because of the current lack of teaching opportunities—to their misfortune but to the great benefit of the continuity of the School. Thanks to their presence, the program was able, after the summer of 1979, to develop an organization that provides for the testing of new research concerning instructional dialogue on the next level above ordinary subject matter training, and that also permits the integration of guests from abroad as the work progresses. This is the post-graduate program "Theory of Literature and Communication," which has a large enrollment in its basic courses, its interdisciplinary seminars and research colloquia, perhaps not the least because other universities still lack such a program (the description of which is available from the "Fachgruppe Literaturwissenschaft der Universität Konstanz"). It is scarcely surprising that this flourishing post-graduate program, which regularly has thirty to fifty participants, mostly doctoral candidates from our own university or from abroad, is supported solely by the voluntary commitment of the local docents and visiting docents of related fields. The Ministry of Science approved it under the customary official condition here "that it must not cost anything," that is, that none of our own budgetary resources or positions be used and that the subsequently increased teaching obligations be taken care of similarly (except for a slight lessening of loads in the case of interdisciplinary functions). Our own university gives full support to this program insofar as its modest resources permit. Yet there are limits to what it can effectively contribute because, firstly, our research falls outside the general guidelines (which on the whole pertain to empirical research that does not have to employ the dialogic method); secondly, there is no hope of getting the additional positions that are actually needed; and finally, the individuals finishing their habilitation are forced to leave the university because of the lack of middle-level positions.

Is this the way things must be and must remain?

The most pleasurable scholarly undertaking for me in the last two decades has been the research group "Poetics and Hermeneutics," founded in 1963. It was actively involved in the re-examination of the old "Geisteswissenschaften" and their redefinition as hermeneutic disciplines, and has, in the process, endured unscathed all the attacks and compromises of university reform and counter-reform. My pleasure can be best characterized by the observation that the administrative records of this enterprise, on a third wall of my office, require only one file, which easily holds all the drafts, programs of meetings, and funding requests for twenty years, while beside it the published results of our labor fills the rest of the shelf with twelve volumes totaling almost 6000 pages. The success of this research group, whose series of publications is so notable in the professional world that it has been compared with the publications of the Warburg Library in the 1930s, can be explained by various innovations in its working methods and organization: basically interdisciplinary orientation, shared leadership, open planning, scholarly investigations that transcend individual fields, dialogic deliberations with subsequent elaboration of the findings, and augmentation of the personnel through co-optation. Of course, I do not claim that these points, taken individually, were innovations. They became so only in their totality, and indeed only because the group up to now has established no formal set of procedures and was able to develop *in actu* its unwritten rules. Its activity was supported by a consensus that permitted it to form a community accustomed to discussion, constantly confronted by guests with a different expertise, and permitted it also, through the principle of co-optation, to guarantee continuity and renewal at the same time.

The initiatory group consisted of Hans Blumenberg, Clemens Heselhaus, and myself (all in Giessen at that time), also Wolfgang Iser (then in Würzburg). In the grouping of the disciplines according to specialities, the combination of philosophy, poetic praxis, and hermeneutic reflection proved to be a rich source of experience that could be profitably drawn upon again and again in the discussion of historical, aesthetic, linguistic, and soon also theological, anthropological, and sociological problems. Procedures were developed that provided for colloquia at nearly regular two-year intervals, for which usually a full week of oral exchange was set aside. The two-year preparatory period allowed the group to study scholarly material that was submitted and distributed in advance so that the discussion could be carried on with knowledge of all the contributions. The avoidance of lectures and *ad hoc* discussion sessions (from whose caprice the ordinary conferences often suffer) has become an absolute rule. Instead, the written contributions to be introduced for debate can be briefly presented from the viewpoint of the chairman introducing the debate, can be confronted from other perspectives and, through questioning, be brought into connection with the broader problem. Of equal importance, we have discovered, are the subsequent elaborations of the discussion results in the form of statements and supplementary reports chosen by the editors from the minutes of the colloquia and requested *post festum* from the participants. In contrast with other comparable research projects, the work of this group is not bound to the fulfillment of a long-term plan. It merely has a number of projects under discussion that are feasible but not yet closely defined. At the end of a colloquium it usually decides only the general topic of the next and thus preserves for itself the very valuable freedom to make a later, more timely, choice of subjects that also take up problems shown by the present deliberations to be especially worthy of discussion.[6] The organizational structure is as simple as possible: the preparation, leadership, and editing of the proceedings of the colloquia are delegated in turn usually to two members who relieve each other in their pen-wielding chores. The group of regular members, from about ten disciplines, invite to each colloquium enough guests with competence in the particular topic to have a total of no more than twenty-five participants in each discussion.

I cannot venture to answer the question whether the research group "Poetics and Hermeneutics" is not just a new "example of outstanding research," sought for by the German Research Association, but also a paradigm to be recommended in the present situation to other teams of researchers, since the personal and professional combination that has made it successful cannot simply be imitated. I can only imagine that it would be useful to compare the working methods of our group and their benefits for research with those of other types of institutes of advanced studies, and then to consider what the augurs of the governments and of the grant foundations can do to encourage interdisciplinary research that uses the "dialogic method," which up to now, I must regretfully admit, has obviously flourished best in Germany only when carried on outside the university and free of government control.

Videant iuniores . . .

---

[6] Titles of the series "Poetik und Hermeneutik": I. Nachahmung und Illusion (Imitation and Illusion); II Immanente Ästhetick—Ästhetische Reflexion: Lyrik als Paradigma der Moderne (Immanent Aesthetics—Aesthetic Reflection: Lyric as Paradigm of the Modern); III. Die nicht mehr schönen Künste. Grenzphänomene des Ästhetischen (The no longer Fine Arts: Boundary Phenomena of the Aesthetic); IV. Terror und Spiel: Probleme der Mythenrezeption (Terror and Play: Problems of Myth Reception); V. Geschichte—Ereignis und Erzählung (History: Occurrence and Narration); VI. Positionen der Negativität (Positions of Negativity); VII. Das Komische (The Comical); VIII. Identität (Identity); IX. Text und Applikation: Theologie, Jurisprudenz und Literaturwissenschaft im hermeneutischen Gespräch (Text and Application: Theology, Jurisprudence and Literary Studies in Hermeneutic Discourse); X. Funktion des Fiktiven (Functions of the Fictive); XI. Das Gespräch (Discourse); XII. Epochenschwelle und Epochenbewüsstsein (Threshold and Consciousness of Epochs) [München: Fink-Verlag].

8

Woolf's Room, Our Project: The Building of Feminist Criticism

Catharine R. Stimpson

This essay is an assay, a descriptive weighing of feminist criticism, and an "I say," a practitioner's account of its controlled and uncontrolled substances. My text is Virginia Woolf's *A Room of One's Own*, which she began in 1928.[1] Woolf's room has become a project that draftily houses us. In her power, failures, and perplexities, she is a major architect and designer of feminist criticism.

In 1928, Virginia Woolf was forty-six years old. In two years, she had published two major novels: *To the Lighthouse* and *Orlando*. Her body had become the presence photographs now commemorate: the sculptured bones; the huge, liquid eyes that at once delve into and elude another's gaze. In the fall, she accepted an invitation to give two lectures at Cambridge University, for her a haunted site. She admired the women of Cambridge, but pitied them their poverty and destinies, to become "schoolmistresses in shoals." She noted, ironically, "I blandly told them to drink wine & have a room of their own."[2] Her husband, Leonard, accompanied her to one lecture; her lover, Vita Sackville-West, to the other. Woolf was an equal opportunity companion.

In 1929, Woolf issued her revised lectures. She delighted in producing. She once noted, "I mean its the writing not the being read that excites me" (D III, 200). Yet, she feared the consumption of her toil. Predictably, she was anxious about potential responses to *A Room*. The terms of this anxiety are symptoms of a larger cultural malaise as well. In the 1920s, Woolf could observe and absorb the effects of the dismantling of feminism as a political movement and the robing of modern heterosexuality as a social norm.[3] In 1928, she and Leonard were possible witnesses at the obscenity trial of Radclyffe Hall's polemic against homophobia, *The Well of Loneliness*. Indeed, *A Room* sardonically, if fleetingly, refers to Sir William Joynson Hicks, the Home Secretary who prosecuted and persecuted Hall and her publisher. Woolf worried that readers, especially men, would find *A Room* too strident, its author too identified with women. She asked if her tone was not too "shrill" and "feminine." She warned herself that she would be "attacked as a feminist and hinted at for a sapphist."

Woolf, though, was logophilic, logging in the forests of language. Ultimately, faith in her text defeated fear. Her diary notes that she wrote it with "ardour & conviction" (D III, 262). The public's reception justified that faith. Though she continued to brood about male anger, she cheerfully recorded her sales figures. Although money, and the approval it signifies, calmed her qualms, her diary still records the internalization of dominant sexual ideologies. When she writes of *A Room*'s success, she mentions the stimulus of her marriage. Before publication, her anxiety about being read as a writer was inseparable from anxiety about being read as a lesbian. After publication, relief at being read as a successful writer was inseparable from relief at being a successful woman, that is, married.

Woolf's swerving, dancing, fleeing sets of maneuvers between homosexuality and heterosexuality prefigure three centers of gravity in feminist criticism. The first is women's interests. To be a feminist critic is to react to and act for women and, at the very least, their place and space in culture. The second center is heterosexual interests. The sexual preference of many feminist critics is heterosexual. So are their professional settings, their classrooms and libraries. The third center is male dominance. Men still regulate many of those sexual practices, classrooms, and libraries. Moreover, every feminist critic must come to terms, if not to grief, with traditional philosophical and cultural schemes, which men have constructed and then, like so many Mr. Goodwrenches, patched up.

Feminist criticism seeks a method that places the first two centers in creative oscillation, in theory, for theory, in practice, for practice, and cuts off the pull of the third. Serving actual women and visions of new sexualities, feminist criticism refuses to serve male domination. At its worthiest, feminist criticism analyzes sexism, not as an isolated system, but as a synecdoche for other hierarchies. Sexism is their partner and a part that stands for the whole mean mess. Because of this, the feminist look at sex and gender is a perspective that permits us to gaze at·everything.[4] The feminist overhaul of sex and gender is an activity that can permit us to overhaul everything.

Obviously, restlessness and suspicion are the preludes for such perspectives, this activity. Feminist criticism is neither a cheerleader for things as they are, nor the Quaalude of discourse. *A Room* is an agitating series of gestures that forbids complacency, security, and premature intellectual closure. Its quick shifts in tone—from sardonic to blandishing, pragmatic to fanciful, tough-minded to tantalizing, declamatory to nuanced—tug at any stable relationship between narrator and reader.

Skillfully, Woolf uses the darts of style to project a theory that must stimulate, appeal to, and justify discontent. However, in part because her stylistic choices have a clear theoretical and rhetorical purpose, *A Room* remains within the margins of literature. It swims towards, but never dives into, what Rosalind Krauss has called "paraliterary space":

> the space of debate, quotation, partisanship, betrayal, reconciliation; but . . . not the space of unity, coherence, or resolution that we think of as constituting the work of literature . . .

Woolf retains the Play with her drama; the Author with her voices; the Argument with her criticism.[5]

The Author slyly begins by paraphrasing another's voice, that of a member of the audience that her Primary Narrator is about to address as a Lecturer. This Mr. Bennett-like voice from the crowd is demanding some reliable association between any lecturer's subject and the announced title. "But, you may say, we asked you to speak about women and fiction—what has that got to do with a room of one's own?" (p.3). The Author further appears to diminish the Lecturer's authority through presenting her as a wee thing. She has not sought out the podium. On the contrary, she has politely responded to a request to talk about women and fiction.

However, Woolf, the Author, is parodying the cultural passivity that Western culture has assigned to women and that *A Room* will lacerate. Within a paragraph, the Primary Narrator/Lecturer will confidently seize on a radical methodology. Refusing to hand over a product, a "nugget of pure truth," she will instead describe an intellectual process, an approach to truths. She will foreground means, not end. Significantly, her process is to tell a story, to invent. Lies, she declares proudly, will "flow" from her lips. Fiction will wrap around, and wrap up, history and criticism. As Woolf blurs the cognitive domains of fiction and fact, she implies that statements about history and criticism are just that, statements. Because they are cultural erections, they can come down as blithely, or as dogmatically, as they went up. Because of power of political structures over culture, a statement is often what the state has meant.

Woolf's manipulations of the narrative voice also simultaneously destabilize and restabilize the text. The Primary Narrator's identity is mobile, fluid, expansive, indifferent to an audience's wish to pin a person to a name. During her tale, she encounters and then, becomes, a series of Marys. " . . . call me Mary Beton, Mary Seton, Mary Carmichael or by any name you please" (p. 5). These Marys do have their meaning. Mostly unmarried, they are also figures in an old English ballad.[6] Woolf is proclaiming and claiming, entertaining and entering, a genre that she will later feminize.

The story of *A Room* is "about" the Narrator/Lecturer preparing her talk "about" women and fiction, itself a quest for women's genres. Slyly, Woolf calls on the pastoral for the first episode in that adventure. Waiting to lunch at an Oxbridge men's college, like Kings or Trinity, the Narrator is fishing on a river bank. This is not the landscape of "The Waste Land," which Eliot, a friend of the Woolfs, had published six years earlier. For the feminist, nature is lusciously poetic; fruitful. Male culture is arid; barren. As the Narrator strolls towards her party, across a "grass plot," among buildings, the guardians of male culture—a choleric Beadle, a librarian who looks like an angel of death—block her way. The librarian keeps her from seeing holograph manuscripts by Milton, a father of modern English culture, and by Thackeray, the grandfather of Woolf's own stepsister. Literarily, the Narrator is disinherited.

However, lunch is lovely, a luxury, an idyll. In contrast, dinner at an Oxbridge women's college, Girton, perhaps, is sparse: gravy soup, grey meat, dry biscuits, tattered cheese. Lunch has been the stage set for wonderful company and talk. Dinner is a grungy setting. Afterwards, a tutor, Mary Seton, will tell the Narrator about the arduous founding of the college in the nineteenth-century. Woolf was no Marxist, but *A Room*'s juxtaposition of a winey lunch and a watery dinner, and of the histories of the colleges in which they are cooked, acerbically dramatizes the importance of money to education and public culture. So doing, Woolf anticipates the revelation of the material contexts of writing of Marxist feminist critics.

The Narrator next speaks from London, the center of the British Empire, which has employed many of the best and the brightest of male Oxbridge graduates. She is doing research for "Women and Fiction" in the British Museum. Meditating again on the power of wealth, she thinks of her aunt, Mary Beton, whose legacy of 500 pounds a year has given the Narrator the freedom to write, to think about money in the British Museum. Like Mary Wollstonecraft, Woolf connects economic dependence and psychological autonomy; economic dependence and subservience. As a result, the money matters more to the Narrator in her daily life than the political right to vote. Moreover, the legacy has passed from one woman to another. Small though it might seem, compared to the assets of aristocrats and financiers, the gift of one woman to another is empowering, not crippling.

Despite its resources, the Museum frustrates the Narrator. She is an active reader, but the pages on its shelves tell her nothing about "Women" or nothing but tripe. Again like Wollstonecraft, in *A Vindication of the Rights of Woman*, the Narrator is appalled and disgusted by the libraries about women. She leads, and provides material for, the feminist inquiry into women as readers and the constitutive power of gender in reading.[7]

In love with textuality, but not with her culture's preferred texts, the Narrator goes home. She will spend much of the rest of *A Room* in her own library. Women, Woolf implies, will rewrite those preferred texts only when they are within their own spaces. During the next two days, the Narrator reads some more—first a first novel, *Life's Adventure*, by a woman, Mary Carmichael. Reveling in starting point after starting point, the Narrator, in an apostrophe, directly addresses the third Mary and dwells on her first sentence, "Chloe liked Olivia" (pp. 86–88). The Narrator is happily responding to new cultural relationships: between woman as writer and woman as subject, and, within the fiction that emerges, between women as friends. Creating the Narrator, Woolf is herself establishing such relationships: between Woolf as writer and her Narrator/Lecturer as subject, and, within *A Room*, her fiction, between the Narrator/Lecturer and Mary Carmichael.

Later feminist critics have praised the Woolf/Carmichael redemption of women's literary friendships. However, the verb, "to like," is less erotically charged than the verb "to love" or "to desire." As Cora Kaplan has shown, Wollstonecraft's feminist theory reflects her retreat from links between women and passion, in part because the ideology she was rejecting had restricted women to the sphere of the passions. Woolf shrinks from links between women and lesbianism, in part because the ideology she was half-accepting kept women to the sphere of heterosexual passions. If Wollstonecraft denies sexuality because she feared reinforcing a powerful construction of women's nature, Woolf denies lesbian sexuality because she feared the power of a burgeoning construction of women's nature.

The next day, after *Life's Adventure*, the Narrator rummages through some male culture: a novel by Mr. A; some criticism by Mr. B., both worthy boobies. Their stuff is honest, but egocentric. The narrative "I," like the male actor in history, is a phallic tower that overshadows and blots out the reality that surrounds it. In contrast, Woolf's narrative "I," which may serve as a model for the female actor in the future, is a sinuous observer who insinuates herself into reality. Indeed, the Narrator merges, near the end of *A Room*, with an earlier character, the Fernham scholar Mary Beton. Woolf writes, "Here, then, Mary Beton ceases to speak" (p. 109).

Woolf cannot end her tale with a sentence about women's silence. She returns to her first scene: the Narrator/Lecturer responding to an interlocuter. Psychologically, the Narrator has dramatized a process of alternation between fused and individual identities. Now a single ego, she begins to banter with her audience. She mocks the genre of the public speech. "Here I would stop," she jokes, "but the pressure of convention decrees that every speech must end with a peroration" (p.

114). However, the lecturer is too committed to her subject, and to her audience, to close with a silvery and negating laugh. In 1662, in *Female Orations*, Margaret Cavendish bravely took the same male-dominated form and pulled it apart so that it might speak from and for women. The Narrator/Lecturer tries a similar transformation. She gives her audience, and Woolf's reader, an inspiriting, uplifting peroration in which she imagines newly born women writers who will redeem all those other women whom history has stifled, suffocated, and gagged: " . . . she would come if we worked for her . . . so to work, even in poverty and obscurity, is worth while" (p. 118).

Obviously, this play has a point, this narrative something about which to natter. Woolf has designed a general theory of women, gender, and culture. As Wollstonecraft had done in the late eighteenth century, as Simone de Beauvoir was to do in *The Second Sex* in the mid-twentieth century, as all feminist critics now do, Woolf analyzes women as cultural victims who have suffered from a double whammy. Her invention of Judith Shakespeare, William's sister, the tragic heroine of a short story within the Narrator/Lecturer's quest tale, is a brilliant parable of female deprivation. First, women have been kept from producing culture, from being representors. If they have wanted to do so, two ghosts have inhibited them: "Milton's bogey," and Margaret Cavendish, almost his exact contemporary, the "crazy" Duchess of Newcastle, an aristocratic bag lady, a second " . . . bogey to frighten clever girls with" (p. 65). Both figures masculinize cultural authority and stir up female anxiety if women grasp that baton. Milton personifies the male author; the Duchess the fate of the woman who dares to be like him. Woolf's metaphor is apt, progressive, and crafty. A bogey is scary, but the province of the bogey is the nursery, not the study. Like Mrs. Ramsay, with her son James in *To The Lighthouse*, we can dissipate bogeys with reason, confidence, and love.

The second whammy is that the representations of women that culture does permit are, at best, distortions. Woolf suggests that people must serve as the primary witnesses of their own experience. If they do not, ideology will bear false witness. Although *A Room* lacks the invigorating detail of later feminist accounts of "male" representations, like Kate Millett's *Sexual Politics* in 1970, Woolf deftly satirizes the pictures Englishmen have made and hung of Englishwomen. Leaking from the emotional poles of fear and sentimentality, these images now stick on the rhetorical poles of insult and gush.

Woolf's satire is neither an emotional nor a rhetorical pole. Rather, her games, her parodies, are a median strip between an anger against men that she feels, and fears, and a sweet concern for men that she fears, and does not feel. *A Room* runs between two Victorian ways: the enraged laughter of Bertha Mason and the loving smile of the Angel in the Home. Contemporary feminist criticism distances itself from Woolf's repression of anger as firmly as Woolf distances herself from Charlotte Brontë's expression of it. In the early 1970s, two exemplary texts—Adrienne Rich's poem "The Phenomenology of Anger" and Hélène Cixous's prose poem "The Laugh of the Medusa"—created images of women who could not really speak until they gave voice and vent to rage.

Since *Sexual Politics* in 1970, the study of the patterns of the representation of women has increased in sophistication. In the early 1970s, such work tended either towards a sociological focus on "stereotypes" and "images," which the machinery of socialization would imprint on little girls and boys, or towards a Jungian focus on "archetypes," which the collective unconscious would pass through to little girls and boys.[8] Then, in the 1970s, feminist critics began to employ, and to mix variously, three methodological tools: structuralism and semiotics, as their guide to large-scale sign systems; revisionary psychoanalysis, as their guide to the relationship of language to the unconscious; and Marxist theory, as their guide to ideology. If these tools can be awkward together, each helps to supplement the earlier catalogues of "women in culture" with "gynesis," the exploration of "the feminine," a signifier that both men and women can trade in our symbolic contracts.[9]

Woolf blames "patriarchal society" for women's deprivation. When she focuses on patriarchy as a psychological structure, as an organization of desire and feeling, she presents men as greedy for validation and self-esteem. Without them, men cannot control others, at home or abroad; cannot stick up colonial empires. Men need women to feed their psychic appetites. If Freud argues that civilization demands the repression of the instincts, Woolf counter-argues that an uncivilized civilization demands the repression of women. Without the Existential vocabulary of de Beauvoir, Woolf also predicts the dialectics of gender domination of *The Second Sex*. In 1938, in *Three Guineas*, Woolf explicitly adapts a rude Oedipal theory to explain why so many men deny the identity of others in order to assert their own; why so many fathers amputate the limbs of wives, daughters, sons, and servants in order to build up prosthetic phall/i. The logic of *A Room* is more metaphorical. Woman are the enhancing mirror into which men must gaze, but never step behind. Women are men's addiction. Without woman, " . . . man may die, like the . . . fiend deprived of his cocaine" (p. 36).

Woolf cannot dwell with deprivation alone. Feminizing an ethic of heroism, she asserts that women have defeated the patriarchy's efforts to rule their creativity as well as procreativity. Woman have been neither blinded, deafened, nor silenced. Indeed, their place outside of male culture, their alienation, has given them a critical viewpoint; their constricted passages a perspective; their artlessness an art. Such a sense of hope, of trust in women's possibilities, has buoyed up feminist criticism. In 1974, Alice Walker's poignant essay, "In Search of Our Mothers' Gardens," was to apply Woolf's insights to black women. Walker was generous. *A Room* has the racism that infiltrates feminist criticism. In a treacherous paragraph, immediately after the parable of Judith Shakespeare, Woolf's Narrator is flipping through images that express men's need to appropriate people, places, and things. Distinguishing women from men, she generalizes:

> It is one of the great advantages of being a woman that one can pass even a very fine negress without wishing to make an Englishwoman of her. (p. 52)

Carelessly, cruelly, the sentence ruptures "woman" from "Negress," granting "woman" subjectivity and "negress," no matter how fine, mere objecthood.

Far less distastefully, Woolf suggests three strategies for mapping women's creativity that have influenced women's studies. First, at the same time as the *Annales* school in France was establishing modern social history, she calls for a women's history based on the kind of sources social history was to use: dietary customs, house plans, "parish registers and account book" (p. 47). Next, she outlines a more specifically literary history, at least for white Englishwomen. So doing, she is an early practitioner of what Elaine Showalter was, in the 1970s, to call "gynocritics," the study of the styles, genres, values, relationships, and intertextualities of women writers. Woolf's originary figure is neither a mystic nor a queen, but Aphra Behn, the first professional woman writer in English. Her exemplary genre is neither the letter nor the diary, but the novel, the form that provided women with an income. Once again, Woolf, the daughter of Wollstonecraft, fuses economic independence and the textualized female imagination.

In 1985, Sandra M. Gilbert and Susan Gubar codified a women's literary tradition in English in their massive Norton anthology.[10] Not surprisingly, their "Preface" opens with a quotation from *A Room*. Like Woolf, Gilbert and Gubar have had their trashings and thrashings. The least plausible, most hostile voices make two unrelated claims: 1) That no one can separate out women writers as a group, that "women writers" is a silly, empty category; and 2) That someone can separate out women writers as a group, but that Gilbert and Gubar have transmogrified every woman writer into a feminist. More sensitive voices also make two, more connected claims: 1) That Gilbert and Gubar have left out too many women of color; too many citizens of Commonwealth countries; and too many experimental writers;[11] 2) That the anthology, nevertheless, as a Norton anthology, re-establishes the theory of the canon. A female canon is worse than a male, because feminist criticism was to disarm the canon's brag that a few, select texts have a mandate from art and history.

Since the 1970s, the study of women writers has expanded wonderfully, especially work with women of color; colonized women; lesbians; and, to a degree, ethnic women. *A Room* does not foresee the diversity of women writers, feminist critical approaches, and literary histories. Virginia Woolf looks back at Aphra Behn. However, Doris Lessing, gazing back at Virginia Woolf and Olive Schreiner, doubts the validity of a women's tradition. Alice Walker helps to recover Zora Neale Hurston. Adrienne Rich looks across at Audre Lorde and back at Anne Bradstreet and Emily Dickinson. Feminist criticism has had to polish lenses other than those of gender to sight its subject: lenses of race, class, nationality, age, religion, sexuality, community culture. For example, does a writer hear an oral tradition or not?

No feminist critic can gloss over the conflicts these lines of sight engage. For women writers are more than women. They belong to many "writing communities" at once.[12] The citizens of one may suspect and hate the citizens of another. Woolf realized the causes of some differences among women. Mary Carmichael wears " . . . the shoddy old fetters of class on her feet" (p. 92). However, unable to foresee the diversity of women writers, Woolf could not imagine a feminist critic's mind full with the task of tracing the networks and stresses this diversity sets up. Among the virtues of the Norton anthology is that it reminds such a critic that s/he must eventually choose some texts over others to present to a reader, in classrooms and elsewhere. Because our critique of the canon and our catalogue of women writers are still incomplete; because the differences among women are so volatile and difficult, feminist critics have not always said how they will make such choices and why. They cannot defer much longer.

Finally, Woolf's third strategy for the mapping of women's creativity is to ask for a re-interpretation, a de-coding, of despised women and marginal utterances. She writes:

> When . . . one reads of a witch being ducked, of a woman possessed by devils, of wise woman selling herbs, or even of a very remarkable man who had a mother, then I think we are on the track of a lost novelist, a suppressed poet, of some mute and inglorious Jane Austen. (pp. 50–51)

Each of these figures—the witch, the possessed (madwoman or hysteric), the healer, the mother—is central to feminist criticism as an emblem of a woman struggling to speak in one sublimated vocality or another. Moreover, the Narrator/Lecturer goes on, the unsigned text might be by a woman. She ventures to guess " . . . that Anon, who wrote so many poems without signing them, was often a woman" (p. 51).

In A Room, the dissolution of the self in anonymity is painful. The self ought to be present in the signature. Embedded in Woolf's distress is a liberal, humanistic commitment to the individual. Not only should an author be associated with her, or his, work; name with act. Neither law, nor custom, nor the opinions of others should fetter the self. Each of us is most authentic when free; most free when authentic. Such beliefs are consistent with an endorsement of the conscious human subject, its capacity to use language to reach meaning, and some historical narratives. Such beliefs also sustain the feminist critic who wishes to subvert the patriarchs who have obliterated, ridiculed, and condemned woman as subject and to redeem her.

Such critics work from many positions, within many genres. Read, for example, a poem that seems to allude to A Room. A woman painting a room of her own. She has red paint.[13] She fantasizes that her room is going to look dangerous, explosive, infernal, or, even worse, vulgar. Then, in a series of flashes, she associates her paint with that on Greek vases, and the vases, the amphora, with her uterus and ovaries. Sardonically, she mourns, "Ours is a red land, sour/with blood it has not shed . . . " Reduced to blood and the womb, women have then been read as such. Yet, the speaker is painting her room, controlling the "red." The poet is writing, controlling what will be "read." This permits the final line: "Why not a red room?" The question asserts a will to language, the recreation of a trope. It calls out the troops against a standard reading of a trope, but not against standard interpretations of the operations of a trope.

Logically, however, Woolf's commitments are inconsistent with Woolf's style, with that blurring of fact and fiction. Her irony, metaphors, and shifts in narrative voice call into question the coherence of the human subject; the possibility of solid truths that language might boost, even if language does slip, slide, congeal, and freeze, like putty in an O-ring; and our trust in representational acts as anything more than a series of signifying practices. Because of its inventiveness, A Room foreshadows a strain of post-modernism[14]; because of its self-division, a conflict within feminist criticism about post-modernism.

Let me defame through condensation. Several alternatives collide together in this contested zone in feminist criticism. Critic A can defend "traditional" notions of self, discourse, and meaning. She can, more or less, rely on realism. She can comfort herself with the fact that most feminists in practical politics implicitly agree with her. Critic B can valorize the holes and fissures in the discourse of the powerful because the feminine rises from them. Sibyl's voice spirals up from her cave; from dark cracks in ancient boulders. Critic B brews poetry with radical feminist and lesbian politics. Critic C can absorb herself in post-structural theory and shrug off political questions. To her skeptics, she embodies what might happen to feminist theory if academics seize and carry it away from feminist activity. Critic D, who hears the voices of some of the smartest feminist critics, can reconcile elements from post-modernisms and feminisms.[15] Like feminism, post-modernism trusts differences; like feminism, post-modernism distrusts hierarchies. Even more rigorously than most sorts of feminism, post-modernism prosecutes ideological and representational codes. Unhappily, unlike all feminisms, post-modernism often seems to forget actual women—their breath and bone, grit and grandeur—in its infatuation with the "crisis of the subject" and the "feminine" as a pre-Oedipal discursive mode.[16]

Think of Woolf in her reading chair with papers from these critics. She might respect the seriousness of a Critic A; handle passion of a Critic B delicately. Woolf reflects that passion in *Three Guineas*. If a Critic C were to forget the common reader, Woolf's gift for mockery might flash about. If a Critic D were doing intellectually risky things, in agile and deceptively simple language, Woolf might begin to take notes. She might ask of them all what was best for women, and for women and writing, at the present moment.

For much of *A Room* is a practical guide to what women need in order to work productively, excitingly. Woolf's most quoted prescription is for the virtuous room, a place of solitude and privacy, less luxurious than a mansion, less crowded than a tenement, and those five hundred pounds a year, enough to pay the rent on a nice room and stock its shelves. Yet, she is aware of other needs as well. Psychologically, her writers must have patience and stamina. Emotionally, like all writers and artists, her women should get validation and support from others close to them. Socially, her women must be educated. Woolf suspects the myth of the untutored genius, of either sex, of any class. For genius at once soars beyond and absorbs tradition. Emily Dickinson is herself and Protestant hymns. Only systematic education, from a school, from a parent, can teach tradition. Despite Woolf's influence, some academic feminists, like many radical feminists outside of the academy, believe that if women were to speak, they would speak beautifully and truthfully. Feminizing a Romantic delight in the primitive and a Rousseauistic delight in the pre-social, such a notion applauds the apparently spontaneous text: the letter, the journal, the diary. So, too, did Woolf, but not because she thought they proved the existence of untutored genius.

Finally, Woolf's writers, in the present, need new themes. A modernist, she feared nodding repetitions. Tentatively, but not tremulously, *A Room* suggests what these new subjects might be: first, women's lives, the Chloes and Olivias, their friendship, their laboratories, and next, our common life, inseparable from the domesticity, the washlines and kitchens, where women have lived so long and hard. Paradoxically, the everyday will provide the raw material of innovation. Like Woolf, feminist theory and criticism have recuperated the value of the daily here and now. Breaking into and irrevocably altering established cultures, the writing of the everyday will, for Critic A, reveal women's historical experiences; for Critic B, an essential female experience; for Critic C, the promise of feminist post-modernism. As Teresa De Lauretis proposes:

> feminism defines itself as a political instance, not merely a sexual politics but a politics of experience, of everyday life, which later then in turn enters the public sphere of expression and creative practice, displacing aesthetic hierarchies and generic categories, and which thus establishes the semiotic ground for a different production of reference and meaning.[17]

Despite its ardent flair, the prophetic leaps and historical grounding from which these leaps are made, problems hold up and gird *A Room*. They distress and baffle feminist criticism still. Saying what "feminism" means to "feminist criticism" is simpler than saying what "woman" does. Feminism offers an analysis of history and culture that foregrounds gender, its structures and inequities; a collective enterprise that foregrounds women's resistance to inequities; and Utopian visions of a different, and better, future that enables and ennobles that resistance. Six decades or so after *A Room*, three decades or so after *The Second Sex*, "woman" and "women" furnish feminist criticism with analytical material; members of that collective enterprise; and the jig and saw of puzzles.

The specific puzzle that *A Room* represents, but never resolves, is whether "woman" refers to a genus, which nature constructs, or to a characterological genre, which societies and culture construct. Since binary oppositions place "woman" with and against "man," such a query links up with those concerning sexual difference itself. At once charmingly seductive and teasingly elusive, Woolf declines to say if she refuses to speculate about the causes of sexual difference because she might incriminate herself; because she fears the wilds of uncertainty; because no one really knows; or because no one will ever "really know." Taking refuge in conceit, the Narrator gambols:

> But these are difficult questions which lie in the twilight of the future.
> I must leave them, if only because they stimulate me to wander from
> my subject into trackless forests where I shall be lost and, very likely,
> devoured by wild beasts. (pp. 80–81)

Woolf's glissandos about sexual difference echo through a famous,
packed passage about the *womanliness* of the woman writer in which the
synergistic association of undecidability and nature occurs. Genderizing
grammar, these long paragraphs isolate a "man's sentence," which Samuel Johnson and Edward Gibbon wrote, and a female sentence, which
Jane Austen and Emily Brontë dared to pioneer. If such a fundamental
unit of grammar is inflected, as female or male, surely rhetoric and genre
might be inflected, too. Surely, the building block shapes the building,
be it arcade or dome. For some, Woolf's female sentence dissents from
and criticizes male dominance. It " . . . has its basis not in biology, but
rather in cultural fearlessness . . . . "[18] True, but only partly true. For *A
Room* further naturalizes, not only undecidability, but women's writing.
The Narrator muses: "The book has somehow to be adapted to the body,
and at a venture one would say that women's books should be shorter,
more concentrated, than those of men . . . " (p. 81). *This* fencing sentence
both extends nineteenth-century theories of sexual difference and points
toward late twentieth-century theories of "writing from the body" and
"écriture féminine." *These* female textualities promise to be polymorphous, polydimensional, polysemous. They will help women, no longer
the Pretty Polly Parrots of the patriarchy, to disrupt and escape from
unilateral, unilinear linguistic armaments.

In part to explain her genderizing of grammar, Woolf throws away a
seed of a sentence that feminist criticism has planted and nurtured: "For
we think back through our mothers if we are women" (p. 79). Woolf's
subject and predicate fuse two domains that patriarchs have severed:
the first is male, public, productive, and rational; the second female,
domestic, reproductive, and arational. The immediate context seems to
limit "mothers" to literary predecessors. Woolf's mothers seem to be
Aphra Behn and Jane Austen rather than Julia Duckworth Stephen.
However, feminist critics have responded to the entirety of *A Room*. They
have also swung along with the return to the figure of the mother that
feminist theory made in the mid-1970s. Their inquiries have become a
matrix of overlapping, overlipping questions.

Some questions, the more positivistic, ask about the appearance of
cultural representations of the mother. Others concern the meaning of
that figure, "The Mother Tongue." Is there a Mother Tongue that licks

us into speech? If so, where would new grammarians find that speech? As Julia Kristeva suggests, in avant-garde texts? As Mary Daly urges, in the Journals of radical feminists? Still other questions, which psychoanalysis has forged, seek the influence of the maternal presence in the creation of culture. Does the son's need to rip himself away from the mother, a self-conscious repetition of the cutting of the umbilical cord, lead to the father's culture? How does the cultural daughter mediate between the father's language and the mother's language? Does she have, as Margaret Homans discovers in nineteenth-century women writers, two languages? That of the father and of the mother.[19]

As feminist criticism has matured, it has begun to extend its female genealogy from twin sets, sisters, and mother/daughter dyads to grandmothers, stepmothers, aunts, and cousins. Yet, Woolf also warns against too exclusive an interest in women. The same text that praises women's lives, that oracularly murmurs of female sentences, declares, sternly indifferent to the priggish demands of internal consistency: " . . . it is fatal for anyone who writes to think of their sex. It is fatal to be a man or woman pure and simple . . ." (p. 108). The woman writer's model is no longer the good mother, but the androgyne, "woman-manly or man-womanly" (p. 108). The woman writer must be capaciously interested in everything but membership in an interest group. Forbidden to focus too compulsively on her own sex, the woman writer must avoid the polemic on behalf of her sex, the feminist text. Strictly judged, *A Room* might fail Woolf's own test for real literature, for "poetry." Implicitly, Woolf is setting up a series of equivalences, each a unit that balances both genders: the creative mind; the good marriage; and, perhaps, the ballot box after female suffrage. Explicitly, if Woolf has invented Judith Shakespeare as the heroine of loss, she casts William Shakespeare as the hero of gender integration. He rebukes Milton, the cultural patriarch.[20]

Woolf's theoretical contradictions when she writes about the "woman question," spaciously defined, have their reflecting image in her life in 1928: in love with, perhaps in bed with, Vita Sackville-West; in love with, certainly at home with, Leonard Woolf. In cultural criticism, in psychosexual practice, Woolf stands simultaneously outside, beside, and inside the borders of heterosexuality and of her sex. These borders are as fluid, as subject to redrawing, as those of counties and countries. Woolf's stance, then, occupies many places; her position many points.

This multiplicity can be a metonymy for the cultural situation of women and, more precisely, of feminist critics. For one woman belongs to many classes at once. No class has the same relationship to political or cultural power. That, obviously, is why there are many classes. Despite male dominance, female tokens drop into the turnstiles of society and rush down the fast tracks on the other side. Queen Elizabeth I knew classical languages and gave state speeches. *A Room*'s Narrator feels alienated when she walks down Whitehall. In *Three Guineas*, despairing of society, Woolf will imaginatively transform alienation into a political group, the perpetually marginal Society of Outsiders. She will separate herself from Wollstonecraft and the feminist theory that justifies women's place inside society and, most important for Wollstonecraft, inside reason and discourse. Nevertheless, *A Room*'s Narrator is a daughter of the British Empire. The generous aunt who leaves her a legacy dies in a fall from a horse in Bombay.

Some of the strongest feminist criticism shows how far "inside" one, or more, of the boundaries of power many women writers are; how much might divide them from a reader, female or male, who is "outside" those boundaries. In the 1970s, despite Woolf's doubts, Charlotte Brontë was a magnetic figure for feminist critics; the fictive autobiography of Jane Eyre an arche-narrative. Yet, in the 1970s, Marxist feminist critics revealed the ideological assumptions about class in *Shirley*. In the 1980s, Third World critics have spoken of *Jane Eyre* as a "cult text" that underwrites the "axiomatics" of imperialism. Why must Bertha die if Plain Jane is to live?[21]

Showing that some women have had some power helps to erode the representation of all women as powerless, which a brand of feminist theory has mistakenly proposed. Fidelity to complexity respects women's lives. In addition, presenting the differences among women helps to erode the attraction of falsely universal descriptions of women and sexual difference. The commonality of the female becomes nothing more, nothing less, than an accident of birth, a chromosomal draw. This, in turn, can erode the general attraction of the falsely universal. These moves are the promise of a critical method I call "herterogeneity." Herterogeneity is the marking of differences among women, for themselves and as a way of recognizing and living generously with all but homicidal difference/s—among tongues and texts; tribes and territories; totems and some taboos.[22] Less globally, because feminist criticism is supple enough to mesh with other tools, from bibliographical notations to theoretical hermeneutics, it opens up criticism itself to the push and play of several languages.

The explorations of feminist criticism begin with the experiences of women and the functions of sexual difference. Herterogeneity goes on to sight the differences among women that body and community, place and history, have bred, and, often, inbred. Dwelling with these distinctions instructs women and women in the disabilities of monolithic thinking about "woman" binary thinking about the duality of "woman"/ "man." In such instruction is, if not salvation, at least a salutation of the Other, others, and othernesses. Is there no room for this?

9

The Mirror and the Vamp:
Reflections on Feminist Criticism

Sandra M. Gilbert and *Susan Gubar*

What is the place of feminist criticism in the history of ideas? Five centuries ago Christine de Pizan declared that a utopian city of ladies was to be founded on the "field of letters"; some two hundred years later Mary Astell invited women to retreat into an intellectual community where they could partake of the hitherto forbidden fruits of knowledge; and still more recently Virginia Woolf proposed to establish "a new college, a poor college," a "Society of Outsiders" in which women excluded from male centers of learning could have not only rooms but institutions of their own.[1] Have the dreams of these thinkers been realized with the rise of feminist criticism over the past two decades? And if so, ought feminist criticism to be seen as a theoretical school separate from (if equal to) other intellectual movements? In other words, should feminist literary analyses be viewed as products of, or ruptures with, what has heretofore been defined as our critical heritage? As our title is meant to suggest, we suspect that feminist criticism, as it is now practiced on both sides of the Atlantic, is very much a product of the central intellectual currents that have shaped modern western thought even while we also believe that such criticism inevitably seeks to disrupt the very traditions that have formed it.

When, more than thirty years ago, M.H. Abrams published *The Mirror and the Lamp*, his influential study of the development of romantic ideology and iconography, he focused on the contrast between the mimetic and the expressive impulses, between the classical concept of the artist as one who holds a mirror up to nature and the romantic idea of the artist as a lamp lit from within by the spontaneous overflow of powerfully luminous feelings. Reviewing and discussing the aesthetics of figures from Plato and Longinus to Wordsworth, Coleridge, and Shelley, Abrams did not, of course, mention any feminist thinkers nor would any discussion of female-authored writing have seemed relevant to his enterprise.[2] Yet we will argue that the categories he established usefully

---

This essay is dedicated to M. H. Abrams with admiration and affection.

illuminate the intellectual assumptions and strategies of most contemporary feminist theorists and, further, that feminist modes of inquiry may themselves reveal new aspects of the material he was examining.

The mirror: for a number of feminist critics, Abrams's symbol of art as mimetic representation becomes a space in which to capture the shifting historical images of gendered reality. Whether tese thinkers critique misogynistic characterizations of women, recover and reevaluate lost writers, or celebrate male- or female-authored characters as positive role models, they implicitly define the function of criticism at the present time as the mirroring—the transcription—of a knowable history constituted by real authors, real readers, and objectively verifiable cultural conditions. Often, working from the assumption that literature "is a reflection of objects and events,"[3] they use texts to explore social and psychological contexts, pointing to ways in which neglected or only partially understood works function to document a neglected or misinterpreted cultural history. In addition, as they reconceptualize the past, they question received modes of periodization and evaluation, but they do not, as a rule, challenge the concepts of reality which underlie the very activities of periodization and evaluation.

The lamp: for other feminist critics, Abrams's emblem of the artist's subjectivity and inspiration has taken on a gender but retained its romantic energy. In the works of these thinkers, the self-generated brilliance of the heroic poet can be said to serve as a paradigm for the critic's expressive autonomy as well as for rebelliously anti-rational and anti-hierarchical impulses that have been repressed but not erased by patriarchal culture. But because such impulses are associated with the alienated, the dispossessed, and the marginalized—all of which can be represented by "the feminine"—Abrams's lamp, figuratively speaking, metamorphoses at the hands of these critics into a vamp, both a fatal seductress and a ferociously "Undead" figure who haunts the nightwood of the collective unconscious. Whether they seek to liberate the power of the feminine from the constraints of patriarchal discourse, strive to reverse or dissolve the binary oppositions of culture/nature, man/woman, mind/body, and day/night, or struggle to annihilate the hegemony of the "phallocentric" subject and the "phallologocentrism" of the very idea of history, these theorists implicitly define the function of criticism at the present time as a defiantly inspired and demonically sensual attack on—indeed, a seduction and betrayal of—patriarchal systems of thought.

Thus the categories classic and romantic ultimately, though perhaps paradoxically, can be said to subsume two very different strains of the feminist thought which supposedly wishes to locate itself outside such received structures. Even if writers like Christine de Pizan, Mary Astell, and Virginia Woolf dreamed of female intellectual communities situated far from the madding crowd of philosopher-kings, their descendants would seem to have had to take their places in the great chain of being that is the history of ideas.

To hold a mirror up to the nature of culture is, of course, primarily an empiricist project, and, perhaps for that reason, it is an activity which has been principally undertaken by American and English feminist literary critics. As Elaine Showalter has pointed out in an important essay entitled "Toward a Feminist Poetics," the two modes of feminist criticism—"critique" and "gynocriticism"—that we are identifying with Abrams's classical and rationalist "mirror" developed sequentially but continue to be of equally compelling interest to scholars who study the works of both male and female authors.[4] According to Showalter, those who opt for the mode of "critique" tend to focus on the problems of "woman as the consumer of male-produced literature"[5] and therefore to castigate men as troubling mates who define women, in Katherine Rogers's phrase, as troublesome helpmates.[6] Thus, following Judith Fetterley's vision of male-authored classics as texts which require female readers to "identify against themselves," a number of feminist critics struggle to learn what Susan Shibanoff calls "the art of reading as a woman," an art which would allow them to perceive, in Fetterley's words, the patriarchal "designs" of masculinist texts.[7] But, we would add, advocates of the methodology of "critique" often also reproach women writers—both precursors and contemporaries—for their complicity in male-defined ideologies or for their victimization by such ideologies.

While critics from Marilyn French to Linda Bamber are, for instance, disturbed by Shakespeare's depiction of woman as the dark lady who is an incarnation of otherness, thinkers from Lee Edwards to Suzanne Juhasz and Denise Levertov have been distressed, respectively, by George Eliot's hostility to her heroines' ambitions, by Marianne Moore's ladylike decorum, and by Sylvia Plath's and Anne Sexton's apparently self-indulgent rhetoric of suicide.[8] At the same time, however, a number of "critiques" of male-authored literature function as vindications of men of letters. Carolyn Heilbrun traces healing images of androgyny in a range of texts by men as well as women; Nina Auerbach finds a powerful female community in Henry James's *The Bostonians* and empowering images of demonic women in late nineteenth-century texts by such male artists as Algernon Charles Swinburne and H. Rider Haggard; and Suzette Henke and Bonnie Kime Scott praise James Joyce's literary depictions of the feminine.[9]

According to Showalter, too, those who opt for the mode of "gynocriticism" are concerned with the issue of "woman as the producer of textual meaning, with the history, themes, genres, and structures of literature by woman," and therefore they tend to recuperate and reevaluate the achievements of literary women through the ages.[10] Thus, from Ellen Moers's *Literary Women* and Patricia Meyer Spacks's *The Female Imagination*, which were the first critical attempts to define a female literary tradition, to Showalter's *A Literature of Their Own*, which traces the evolution of British women's fiction through the three stages that she defines as "Feminine, Feminist, Female," and our own *The Madwoman in the Attic*, which studies the strategies developed by nineteenth-century English and American women to cope with their "anxiety of authorship," feminist critics have explored the psycho-dynamics of female creativity.[11] More recently, from Barbara Christian's *Black Women Novelists*, which traces "the development of a tradition" from 1892 to 1976, to Rachel Blau DuPlessis's *Writing beyond the Ending*, which examines an array of narrative strategies deployed by twentieth-century female writers to "delegitimate" (female) romance and (male) quest plots, to numerous analyses of individual women of letters, feminist critics have examined the impact of women's history on women's literary history, as well as the metaphors, themes, and forms employed by women writers.[12]

Obviously both the modes of "critique" and of "gynocriticism" are grounded in the assumption not only that literature is shaped by and reflects social conditions but also that criticism is an activity which, through the interpretation of texts, can analyze and alter such conditions. Thus, whether she holds a mirror up to masculinist or feminist works, the feminist critic who employs the strategies Showalter describes is fundamentally a rationalist: she believes that, through careful argumentation and scrupulous documentation, she can persuade readers of both sexes to change the sexual politics represented by the sexual poetics she studies. A realist, she works with (and usually within) established structures—the institutional structure of the academy as well as the intellectual structures signified by such words as "author," "history," "canon," "genre," "nationality," "class," and "race." For her, the meaning of meaning, while it may be complex, multiple, or even contradictory, is and must be decipherable as part of a militant project of cultural renovation.

To ignore the significance and signature of the author, this critic feels, would be to perpetuate patriarchy's traditional erasure of female reality. Thus, whether her approach is marxist, psychoanalytic, or phenomenological, she wishes to relate texts to their biographical contexts in order, on the one hand, to demonstrate how individual women of letters have triumphed over difficult circumstances or, on the other hand, to show

how social pressures have inhibited or deformed female creativity. To deny the possibility that history can be known and interpreted, she thinks, would be either to acquiesce in patriarchal constructions of a false past or to forfeit the future that might be invented through re-imaginings of the past. Thus, whether she seeks to excavate forgotten texts, to alter received methods of periodization, or to trace alternative literary genealogies, she assembles both literary and sociocultural documents in order to reflect in new ways on the relationship between tradition and the individual talent.

To overlook both the politics and the inevitability of canon formation, she believes, would be naively utopian, since the realities of textbooks, syllabi, anthologies, and publishers' lists cannot be evaded. Thus she struggles to devise a canon of her own which would, at the very least, complement and supplement the library of mostly male-authored classics that she has inherited. To fail to confront the conventions and constrictions of genre categories would be, she considers, to disregard both the significance of genre hierarchies and the effect of those hierarchies on the relationship between genre and gender. Thus she attempts to revalue certain genres in which women have frequently worked and to explain why other genres may have seemed alien to the female imagination. Finally, to neglect the pressures of nationality, class, and race, she claims, would be to deny the material conditions that have often divided or united women. Thus, whether her subject is colonial America, working-class Victorian London, or Harlem in the 1920s, she tries to integrate the life of the author not just with newly found patterns of history, a reformed canon, and reevaluated genres but also with those ethnic and racial elements that shape and differentiate female experiences.

Because these projects are all, in one way or another, political, they sometimes have the faults of their virtues. For the critic who rereads the words of the text in order to change the text of the world, the mirror of description can become a tool of prescription as ideology blurs evaluation. To be sure, American and English feminist criticism originated in a recognition that such supposedly neutral interpretive and evaluative strategies as those employed by the New Critics were marked by hidden ideological assumptions about the centrality of male experience and the inevitability of patriarchal hierarchies. At least initially, therefore, it was necessary for feminists to argue that, since all critical acts are in some sense political, women readers should resist masculinist ideologies together with their evaluative consequences and devise specifically female-centered modes of interpretation and evaluation.

But from Cheri Register in 1975 to Lillian Faderman in 1981, the urgent need to provide women with "positive role models" has influenced some

critics to praise or blame authors solely on the basis of their characterizations of women. "To earn feminist approval," wrote Register, "literature must perform one or more of the following functions: (1) serve
as a forum for women; (2) help to achieve cultural androgyny; (3) provide
role-models; (4) promote sisterhood; and (5) augment consciousness-
raising."[13] Specifically focusing on role models, Faderman attacked Radclyffe Hall's *The Well of Loneliness* as "bathetic" because this "popular
rendition of 'congenital inversion' further morbidified the most natural
impulses and healthy views."[14] More recently, a number of feminist
critics have even more radically interrogated traditional evaluative criteria, deciding that, as Lillian Robinson puts it, "We need to understand
whether the claim is being made that many of the newly recovered or
validated texts by women meet existing criteria or, on the other hand,
that those criteria themselves intrinsically exclude or tend to exclude
women and hence should be modified or replaced.[15]

The attempt by some feminist Americanists to counter the exclusion
of women from the canon of the so-called American Renaissance is a
particularly dramatic example of this politically motivated repudiation
of received evaluative criteria. While Nina Baym, the author of *Woman's Fiction*, one of the earliest studies of the domestic novel as a part
of an alternative American tradition, carefully qualified her readings of
works by such writers as E.D.E.N. Southworth, Susan Warner, and
Maria Cummins with the confession that "although I have found much
to interest me in these books, I have not unearthed a forgotten Jane
Austen or George Eliot, or hit upon even one novel that I would propose to set alongside *The Scarlet Letter*," others in the field have not been
so moderate.[16] On the lecture circuits, at least one feminist scholar of
American literature—Annette Kolodny—has advised audiences to close
their Melville and open their Warner, insisting that if students and
teachers would stop reading Hawthorne, Emerson, Thoreau, and Melville for five years and devote themselves instead to such exemplary
products of women's culture as Warner's *Wide, Wide World* and Cummins's *The Lamplighter*, they would change their minds not only about
nineteenth-century America but also about what constitutes literary
greatness.

A well-known essay by Jane P. Tompkins most vividly epitomizes
the potential problems implicit in Kolodny's politically charged advice.
Discussing *Uncle Tom's Cabin* as a paradigmatic "popular domestic novel
of the nineteenth century," Tompkins declares that this genre "represents a monumental effort to reorganize culture from the woman's point
of view . . . [a] body of work . . . remarkable for its intellectual complexity, ambition and resourcefulness." Yet on the next page of her essay she concedes "that the work of the sentimental writers is complex

and significant in ways *other than* those which characterize the established masterpieces," asking "the reader to set aside some familiar categories for evaluating fiction—stylistic intricacy, psychological subtlety, epistemological complexity . . . "[17] With what criteria, however, would critics like Kolodny and Tompkins replace these categories? How clear are the mirrors that they hold up to nineteenth-century American fiction?

It is, of course, true that, as Nina Baym puts it, the canon shaped by critics from F.O. Mathiessen, Perry Miller, and Henry Nash Smith to Lionel Trilling and Leslie Fiedler is informed by a male ideology of heroic individualism.[18] Yet the canon with which such critics as Kolodny and Tompkins counter the traditional American Pleiade is often based on an equally strong—if different—ideology, an ideology which defines excellence as the inscription of communal, conventionally female virtues like maternal nurturance, sisterly supportiveness, pious purity, and emotional expressiveness. In their own way, therefore, the feminist successors of the male Americanists who first defined the contours of our literature are undertaking acts of evaluation that are as ideologically bound as those for which they criticize their masculinist precursors. Equally to the point, the ideology that these feminists espouse is itself more suspect than they concede, since it can be and has been argued that the work of the sentimental novelists actually perpetuates the concept of separate sexual spheres which privatized and subordinated women throughout the nineteenth century.[19]

Of course, some feminist critics struggle to get beyond the issue of ideology by addressing themselves to questions of genre. Tompkins, for example, proposes that we evaluate *Uncle Tom's Cabin* not as a novel but as a jeremiad. As a novel, she concedes, the book lacks psychological subtlety and epistemological complexity, but as a jeremiad, she finds, it is rhetorically coherent, intricate, and effective. Does the need to switch generic labels, however, along with the need to privilege a different feminine ideology, imply a kind of special pleading? Certainly such moves would seem to suggest the feminist critic's tacit agreement that women writers cannot be judged by the same standards that we would apply to male artists and therefore perpetuates the patriarchal assumption that women are not equal to men. Paradoxically, moreover, these gestures have the effect of creating an alternative "feminine" canon that would exclude female-authored texts which can be judged excellent by supposedly masculinist standards—for instance, such psychologically subtle and epistemologically complex works as Elizabeth Drew Stoddard's *The Morgesons*, Elizabeth Stuart Phelps Ward's *The Story of Avis*, and the poems of Emily Dickinson.

Just as disturbing, if certain genres, different standards, and particular values are defined by feminists as inevitably and appropriately feminine, the politicized recovery of the past might well lead to political prescriptions for the future, with women writers being praised as "positive role models" if they produce texts that fit certain preconceived patterns and dismissed as "male-identified" if they write other kinds of works. Finally, if some of the developments in nineteenth-century American studies point to directions in which, say, feminist students of the Renaissance or the eighteenth-century have begun to move, then there is a danger that feminist political desire might tend to falsify aspects of reality as much as masculinist ideology has. For when the mirror of description becomes a tool of prescription, its surface clouds so that—because, as Blake put it, "the eye altering alters all"—the critic can perceive in it only what she wants to see.

If desire becomes a problematic (but peripheral) issue for the mirror critics, it is both a source of power and a subject of analysis for the group we are calling vamp critics. Of course, those critics in France, England, and America who practice the arts of the vamp have a number of projects. To disentangle the "feminine" from patriarchal constraints, they call for an *écriture féminine* or *parler femme* that would inscribe the body of female desire in, as Mary Jacobus puts it, "a language freed from the Freudian notion of castration, by which female difference is defined as lack rather than Otherness.[20] To confront the hierarchical binary oppositions out of which, they believe, patriarchal culture has been constituted, they seek, first, to excavate subordinated or repressed terms (the body, the pre-Oedipal, nature, woman, night), arguing, with Julia Kristeva's *Revolution in Poetic Language*, that beneath or behind symbolic language one can discern the "space" of the "semiotic *chora*," a space that is "Indifferent to language, enigmatic, and feminine . . . rhythmic, unfettered, irreducible to its intelligible verbal translation . . . musical, anterior to judgment but restrained by a single guarantee: syntax.[21] Then, to annihilate binaries altogether, they seek to bestow upon the subordinated or repressed term the gift of endlessly fluid fluency and multiplicity, declaring, with Luce Irigaray's *This Sex Which Is Not One*, that woman "is indefinitely other in herself . . . One would have to listen with another ear, as if hearing *an 'other meaning' always in the process of weaving itself, of embracing itself with words, but also of getting rid of words in order not to become fixed, congealed in them.*"[22] Finally, in the words of Toril Moi, to enable "feminist criticism to escape from a disabling author-centered empiricism," they argue that "female writing" is not what some critics, as Peggy Kamuf puts it, "quite banally understan[d]" as "works signed by biologically determined females of the species.[23]

Because these critics compose treatises that are, as Catherine Clément tells Hélène Cixous in a dialogue at the end of *The Newly Born Woman*, "halfway between theory and fiction" and because they continually reiterate a creative, Coleridgean "I AM" based on the authority of their own subjectivity, they have, of course, significant affinities with the poets whose aesthetic of the lamp Abrams discusses.[24] But the satanic seductiveness and darkened energy of their discourse aligns them more firmly with vamps—both *femme fatales* and vampires—than with lamps. Sensual and playful in its deployment of conceits, puns, and neologisms, the language of such theorists as Cixous and Irigaray is also marked by its persistent references to the erotic, to *jouissance*, and to the primary and secondary characteristics of the female body.

But if their styles are often as organic and orgasmic as their preoccupations, these feminists tend, in addition, to stage and engage in flirtatious encounters with male thinkers from Plato and Descartes to Sigmund Freud, Jacques Lacan, and Jacques Derrida. Vamping the masters of male intellectual history, they prove that what Jane Gallop calls "the daughter's seduction" is both exhilarating and imperiling because, as they resurrect the repressed figures of, say, the sorceress and the hysteric, they threaten that the unleashed female desires of these *femmes* will be *fatale* to the culture that the fathers have begotten: "When 'the Repressed' of their cultures and their society come back," writes Cixous, "it is an explosive return, which is *absolutely* shattering, staggering, overturning, with a force never let loose before, on the scale of the most tremendous repressions . . . "[25] Even while their vamping has an apocalyptic goal, however, these writers are also notably vampiric. Recovering the "Undead" repressed pre-Oedipal female self that, they claim, has been staked and beheaded throughout history, they suck the blood of male theory, thieving a language they wish to destroy. Dreaming of illicit night flights or of upside-down categories, they evoke the "black bat airs" that surround Dracula and his female acolytes. And like Dracula, who crosses the channel to England in the hold of the bad ship *Demeter*, they would enter and transform culture riding in the vessel of the Great Mother.

Clearly both the modes and the manners of the vamp arise from a set of assumptions about literature, society, and criticism very different from but just as urgent as those that inform the theories of the rational, empirical Anglo-American mirror critic. More radical and romantic than her counterpart, the vamp critic also believes that literature reflects and refracts social conditions but, unlike the proponents of "critique" and "gynocriticism," she does not suppose that the interpretation of literary texts is the primary politically transformative activity in which the critic ought to engage. Frankly substituting prescription for description, she is hortatory and visionary, elaborating utopian imaginings of the future rather than documenting analyses of a dystopic past. Frankly ex-centric, she works outside established structures, refusing to accept what she sees as the hegemonic categories represented by the words "author," "history," "canon," "genre," "nationality," "class," and "race." For her, the meaning of meaning is "always already" fictive and any attempt to decipher the boundless indeterminacy of language necessarily replicates and is complicitous with patriarchal modes of control.

To believe in "the author as the transcendental signifier of his or her text" is, the vamp critic thinks, to acquiesce in a hierarchical concept of authority which subjects what ought to be the "free play of signification" to a monolithic intentionality.[26] Thus, whether she reads a text by a man as if it were written by a woman or analyzes a text by a woman in order to "disentangle"—not "decipher"—complexities and contradictions through which the "feminine" manifests itself, she sees the critical use of biography as a yielding to a phallocratic "metaphysics of presence."[27] From this mistrust of a metaphysics of presence, she believes, it follows that to imagine history as knowable and narratable in the ordinary, empirical sense is to elaborate a set of naive stories about persons, places, and things that mirror the very phallocentric assumptions against which she is struggling. Thus, whether she meditates, as Irigaray does, on the history of ideas, whether with Catherine Clément she broods on the figures of the sorceress and the hysteric in texts from the fifteenth-century *Malleus Maleficarum* to Freud's *Dora*, or whether, like Cixous, she reconstructs the Medusa as radiant and laughing, she seeks to write a mystic anti-history of what is not and never has been, in the belief that "History is always in several places at once, there are always several histories under way."[28]

To participate in the process of canon formation, she feels, would be to be contaminated by a patriarchal and humanistic system in which monuments of unaging intellect function despotically to establish an oppressive, normative model of "greatness."[29] Thus, refusing to construct even a canon of acceptable "feminine" writing, she produces what are often essentially meta-critical meditations on the cultural processes of signification. To attend to generic conventions, she feels, would limit the free play of the critical imagination. Thus she often reads psychoanalytic case histories as if they were fictions and novels as if they were philosophical treatises, while herself frequently producing texts which— like Cixous's writing "halfway between theory and fiction"—rebelliously cross generic boundaries. Finally, although she sometimes defines herself as a marxist and expresses concern about "material conditions," she tends—with Kristeva—to blur the distinctions between all marginalized groups because, she believes, all have been subordinated by the same hierarchical social structures or—with Cixous and Irigaray—to ignore such categories because she sees "woman" as a transcultural, transhistorical construct. Thus, whether her subject is Chinese women, Shakespeare's Cleopatra, Lewis Carroll's Alice, or Bernini's madonnas, she focuses on the multiple forces of the text in order to annihilate the authority of both author and history and to liberate the lost libidinal energies of the feminine.[30]

Delectably sensual and transgressive as some of the writing of the vamp critics has been, it, too, has the faults of its virtues. The vamp is glamorous, an actress in a kind of guerrilla theater, but the drama of seduction and betrayal that she enacts in her foray against patriarchal structures may end up being as seductively treacherous to women as to men. Certainly, if paradoxically, the French concepts of *écriture féminine* and *parler femme* are as prescriptive as the American notion of "positive role models." For what if not every female imagination is captivated by dreams of literary *jouissance*, of writing in white ink, of linguistic weaving and unweaving, of volcanic eruption and choric pulsion? Equally to the point, why should texts by so-called "biologically determined females of the species" be dismissed as unfeminine if they are not marked by these characteristics? And why should works by biologically determined males of the species be celebrated as "inscriptions of the feminine" if they do have these characteristics? By the prescriptive standards of these critics, Jane Austen and George Eliot would be considered unhealthily repressed and "male-identified," while James Joyce and Georges Bataille would appear triumphantly liberated and "feminine."[31] For Austin and Eliot seem to be working within conventional structures, using ordinary language, and editorializing against the economy of pleasure, while Joyce and Bataille seem to be subversively revising inherited structures, boldly repudiating patriarchal pieties, and yielding with commendable polymorphous perversity to an economy of *jouissance*. Yet, as we have argued elsewhere, Austen and Eliot placed themselves in many ways in a consciously female literary tradition both by enacting resistance to male literary and social authority and by affiliating themselves with female precursors and contemporaries, while modernist men like Joyce and Bataille consistently devised and exploited complex experimental strategies precisely to ward off a newly intense threat of the feminine.[32]

Besides defining a cultural inheritance of the feminine which has been articulated primarily through forays into male-authored texts, forays that ignore precisely the contradictions to which they recommend we attend, the vamp critics seem oddly unaware of their own romantic origins. From William Blake in England and Walt Whitman in America to Arthur

Rimbaud and André Breton in France, romantic and surrealist poets have overturned hierarchical binaries (*The Marriage of Heaven and Hell*), celebrated the pleasures of the erotic as against the repressions of the neurotic ("Children of Adam" and "Calamus" poems), reveled in imaginings of excess, irrationality, and intoxication ("Le bateau ivre"), and praised the dreamlike energies of the feminine ("L'Union libre"). More specifically, as Abrams notes, the romantic aesthetic that informs the works of these poets is based on a dedication to the organic rather than the mechanical, to imagination rather than reason, to the spontaneity of nature rather than the artifice of culture, to the visionary dream state of night rather than the conscious constraints of day, to the liberation of energy rather than the conservation of decorum. Thus, though thinkers like Cixous and Irigaray seem to be claiming that their theories are historically unprecedented and though many of their acolytes unquestioningly accept this claim, they do have precursors, and precursors whose uses of the strategy of *"renversement"* are often as associated with masculinism as those of Joyce and Bataille. For, as a number of critics have observed, even those romantics whose ideology could be seen as proto-feminist depend on a concept of the hero or the poet-priest who speaks with the divine authority of the "phallologocentric," Coleridgean "I AM."

But if it is possible to situate the vamp critics not only in a tradition of authors but in a tradition of authorial authority based on the assertive subjectivity of the speaking subject, what happens to Toril Moi's declaration that Cixous enables "feminist criticism to escape from a disabling author-centered empiricism . . . ?"[33] More generally, what happens to the vamp's commitment to, in Moi's phrase, "the free play of the signifier" as opposed to "the author as the transcendental signified of his or her text?"[34] Here we must, at last, confront the major difference between mirror and vamp critics: where mirror critics believe in the real existence of an entity called an author—a being shaped by and capable of shaping culture—the vamp critics frequently consider that, as Nelly Furman insists, "literature is not a representation of experience" and that therefore "from a feminist viewpoint the question is not whether a literary work has been written by a woman and reflects her experience of life, or how it compares to other works by women . . . ."[35] Indeed, with Peggy Kamuf, these critics believe that "To affix a signature" to a text is to ascribe "a determinate intentionality" to the work and thereby to "contain an unlimited textual system, install a measure of protection between this boundlessness and one's own power to know, to be this power and to know that one is this power.[36]

Of course the empiricist response to such romantic and ostensibly revolutionary claims would be twofold. First, hardly anyone since the rise of "New Criticism" and the fall of the "intentional fallacy" has ever conflated the authorial signature with any notion of "determinate intentionality." Second, if texts are absolutely boundless, authority—as in Barthes's works—inexorably floats free of what Adrienne Rich calls the "absorbed, drudging" writer and lands in the mind of the critic, who can become as coercive and capricious as authors are said to be.[37] Thus, while the vamp school implicitly espouses the "uncertainties, mysteries, and doubts" Keats associated with "negative capability," their hermeneutic practices ultimately fall into the narcissistic mode that Keats defined as Wordsworth's "egotistical sublime." For if the text is mysteriously boundless and unknowable, it contains no signification to which the reader must defer, and anything—uttered by the critic—goes. But that French theorists like Cixous and Irigaray, as well as Anglo-American thinkers like Moi, Furman, and Kamuf, appropriate for themselves such solipsistic authority reminds us again of the boundless ambition of the vamp, whose intellectual striptease ultimately displays not the recalcitrant autonomy of the world of the text but the naked brilliance of the text of her desire.

To be sure, any self-respecting vamp would note that, in critiquing her strategies as we have here, we are ignoring the nature of linguistic/aesthetic constructs and specifically the ways in which such constructs are constituted not by authors but by "the free play of the signifier." Different as they are, Kristeva's theory that "Art—this semiotization of the symbolic—. . . represents the flow of *jouissance* into language," Irigaray's vision of the woman "ceaselessly embracing words and yet casting them off to avoid becoming fixed, immobilized," and Barthes's sense that "writing ceaselessly posits meaning ceaselessly to evaporate it" share a belief that a text always is and must be a place where the signifier playfully, even insouciantly, detaches itself from the signified.[38] Yet what is this free-playing signifier and on what playground does it romp? What forces shape both its "semiotic pulsions" and its fluid symbolizations? In other words, how does a "free-playing signifier" meet "a material condition"?

More seriously, if texts are ontologically "boundless," how can one identify the marks of material reality in them, much less make the claim—asserted in their various ways by both mirror and vamp critics—that the history of material reality is phallocratic and phallologocentric? As Leon Roudiez observes, Kristeva herself does not deny "all intentionality or [refuse] to give a role to the conscious person who writes the work; rather [she emphasizes] that consciousness is far from dominating the process, and that the writing subject is a complex, heterogeneous force."[39] For a logical consequence of the Barthesean "death of the author" advocated by such theorists as Moi, Furman, and Kamuf would be the kind of metahistorical "death of history" that sometimes seems to be propounded by Hayden White and others who argue for the fictionality of all historical schema.[40] Yet neither mirror nor vamp critics subscribe to such a view precisely because both schools do take as an axiomatic starting point the long historical reality of patriarchal culture. Even from the point of view of the vamp, then, it would appear that, if we are to resist such a culture, we must concede not only its autonomous and intransigent existence but the inscription of that existence in texts which are really—if multiply—decipherable.

How, then, might we draw upon the mimetic strength of the mirror and the expressive fervor of the vamp in order to move past the conflicts over description and prescription, definition and evaluation that divide these equally committed feminist camps? To begin with, we might pay closer attention to the eerie, indeed uncanny, relationship between the two groups. Decorous and rational, the mirror critic would seem to be a far more law-abiding citizen than the vamp. Yet, like a dark double, the vamp acts out the desire for apocalyptic revolution against law and order that lurks on the other side of the mirror. At the same time, the vamp's rage depends on evidence collected by and in mirrors. Therefore, though there is on the surface no marriage of true minds between these two methodologically and theoretically opposed feminists, their shared revisionary project means that, uneasy as their relationship is, in the words of Luce Irigaray, "one doesn't stir without the other.[41] More, such a paradoxical union of opposites means that neither term of this binary need annihilate the other. Where in *The Madwoman in the Attic* we traced a nineteenth-century plot that required the sacrifice of the desirous female rebel to insure the survival of her more respectable double, the history of ideas in which we are placing all these critics does not, happily, lead to such a denouement.

Indeed, when the feminist critic looks into the mirror of the texts, she may well find there the vamp, the alien self that she both is and is not. Perhaps, finally, for this reason, Freud's notion of the uncanny provides a model for a criticism that would link classical mimetic analysis with romantic expressivity. Noting the etymological connection between *"das Heimliche"* and "its opposite *das unheimliche,"* Freud argues, after all, that the "uncanny is in reality nothing new or foreign, but something familiar and old-established in the mind that has been estranged only by the process of repression"—it is, in other words, either the familiar other or the unfamiliar self.[42] At the center of his essay on the subject, for

example, there is a moment of revelation when the familiar is defamil-
iarized as the otherness of the secret self disrupts the apparently sealed
and coherent surface of "reality":

> I was sitting alone in my *wagon-lit* compartment when a more than
> usually violent jerk of the train swung back the door of the adjoining
> washing-cabinet, and an elderly gentleman in a dressing gown and a
> traveling cap came in. I assumed that he had been about to leave the
> washing-cabinet which divides the two compartments, and had taken
> the wrong direction and come into my compartment by mistake. Jump-
> ing up with the intention of putting him right, I at once realized to my
> dismay that the intruder was nothing but my own reflection in the
> looking-glass of the open door. I can still recollect that I thoroughly
> disliked his appearance. . . . Is it not possible, though, that [my] dislike
> of [him] was a vestigial trace of that older reaction which feels the double
> to be something uncanny?[43]

Though Irigaray has specifically reproached Freud for his valorization
of the scopophilic male gaze, arguing in a discussion of "The Uncanny"
that for Freud and other men "woman's sexuality is no doubt the most
basic form of the *unheimlich*" and herself associating the feminine not
with vision but with touch, it seems to us that the persistent feminist
metaphor of re-vision, along with the recurrent appearance in female-
authored writing, of mirrors in which two are seen as one or one is seen
as two, suggest that women's enterprise in patriarchal culture might be
precisely the excavation and confrontation of the Uncanny.[44] For certainly, at least in *das Unheimliche*, the Uncanny is that which the supposedly rational and phallic gaze can neither control nor possess. And
thus it might be said to represent those aspects of the self and the world,
the reader and the text, which suddenly, in a moment of disruption,
manifest themselves, as Wallace Stevens once put it, "more truly and
more strange."

If mirror and vamp critics could unite in seeking both the truth and
the strangeness of female- and male-authored literary works, such terms
as "author," "history," "canon," "genre," "nationality," "class," and
"race" might take on new and rich meanings. All these categories would
still exist in the ways the mirror critics claim they do, but their multiple
and conflicting energies might be released, as the vamps would have
them be. If we could, for instance, respond to the problems posed by
these terms from the alienated perspective of the critic who emphasizes
the complex processes of signification, if we could admit and analyze
the contradictory pressures inscribed in any text, perhaps we would free
ourselves from, on the one hand, the formulaic evaluative strategies of

the mirror critics and, on the other hand, the ahistoricisms and imprecisions of the vamp critics. If we could abandon prescription and acknowledge the paradoxical possibility that male- or female-authored texts may actually be strengthened by their distillations of politically "incorrect" cultural contexts, we might be free to reinscribe both the masculine and the feminine in a new way.

How, further, might mirrors describe without prescribing yet retain the phenomenological force of desire and dread associated with the vamp? A number of women writers have, in fact, tried to solve this problem. Most simply, Virginia Woolf declared in *A Room of One's Own* that women should reject the magnifying mirror of male greatness recommended by patriarchal gentlemen in favor of a mirror which would give men a more realistic view of themselves, a view which might disturbingly embody female responses to male gestures:

> Women have served all these centuries as looking-glasses possessing the magic and delicious power of reflecting the figure of man at twice its natural size. . . . if [woman] begins to tell the truth, the figure in the looking-glass shrinks; his fitness for life is diminished. . . . The looking-glass vision is of supreme importance because it charges the vitality; it stimulates the nervous system. Take it away and man may die, like the drug fiend deprived of his cocaine.[45]

Her advice in a sense summarizes the strategies of feminist "critique" and rebellious vamping at their most effective. More passionately, such poets as Mary Elizabeth Coleridge and Judith Wright describe encounters with the alienated female self trapped in the mirror, encounters which function as exemplary instances of a kind of "gynocriticism" very different from that practiced by some of the mirror thinkers we have been describing but similar in a number of ways to techniques used by vamps.

In "The Other Side of a Mirror," Coleridge's speaker conjures up a vision of "a woman, wild / With more than womanly despair," a woman who has "no voice to speak her dread" but nevertheless forces her interlocutor to whisper, "I am she!"[46] In "Naked Girl and Mirror," Wright's speaker contemplates a reflection of her body but protests, "This is not I" and, even when the "dark brimming eyes" of the body command her to "—be me," she concludes that "Your lovers shall learn better, and bitterly too,/if their arrogance dares to think I am part of you."[47] Using the metaphor of the mirror to objectify splittings in the self, both poets allow alien and unsettling images of the female body and soul to emerge from the other side of conventional reality and both thereby confront precisely the otherness within the experiential self—the defamiliarization of the familiar—that Freud associated with the Uncanny. It is, perhaps, this problematizing otherness that many American and English feminist critics evade, ignore, or reject. But, as we have seen, it is just this otherness that the more romantically inclined French and francophilic critics perhaps excessively fetishize. We would argue, though, that if desire and dread could retain the hope of objectivity but nevertheless focus on their own lineaments, the mirror might become an arena in which the passions of the vamp can be usefully enacted.

But the male-authored text can also be seen from the combined perspectives of mirror and vamp critics in such a way that both male and female readers find themselves there "more truly and more strange." If we turn, for example, to such a romantic touchstone as "Kubla Khan"— by Mary Elizabeth Coleridge's great uncle—first exploring it as a mirror critic would and then as a vamp might, we will see that each interpretation in some sense needs the other in order to enrich the poem. In addition, we will see that a feminist analysis of this text's uncanny dreamwork might illuminate aspects of the romantic imagination that Abrams did not touch upon but which imply unexpected connections between the birth of feminism and the rise of romanticism while also raising interesting questions about women's place in the aesthetic revolution of the early nineteenth century. "Kubla Khan," as we shall show, particularly lends itself to this sort of analysis because of its explicit sexualization of the dreaming poet's concerns about creativity. But of course those concerns permeate most of the works produced by Coleridge and his contemporaries, so that this supposedly incomplete and elliptical text can be taken as a paradigmatic romantic utterance.

If we begin by approaching "Kubla Khan" as a mirror critic might, we would probably view the poem as a product of the tensions between four figures: the godlike patriarch Kubla, the demonic male poet "with flashing eyes and floating hair," the abandoned "woman wailing for her demon lover," and the muse-like "damsel with a dulcimer." After pointing out that the two women in the poem are, in one way or another, subordinated—one wailing for her lost lover, the other functioning as an inspirational muse for the male poet—the mirror critic would emphasize both the transcendent authority of Kubla as originatory artificer and of the romantic poet as "holy" and wholly artificer of the poem as a "miracle of rare device." In addition, she would note that the female landscape of caverns and chasms is here "girdled round" with constraining walls and towers, even while it is threatened by the phallic force of a ceaselessly erupting (male) fountain. Finally, she would express distress at the demonic poet's desire to appropriate and incorporate female fruit (honeydew) and maternal fluid (the milk of paradise).

Where the mirror critic would castigate Coleridge for these moves, however, the vamp might celebrate him, for she would most likely produce a very different reading of "Kubla Khan." From her point of view, the whole poem could arguably be viewed as a subversive immersion in and enactment of "the feminine." Setting himself against Kubla's icy patriarchal authority and distancing himself from the horrors of the phallic fountain, the poet imagines "ancestral voices prophesying war" against the rationality that would girdle an untrammeled landscape round with confining walls and towers. For her, the fragmented, sometimes incoherent night thoughts of the dreaming poet would seem to articulate a rebelliously fluid identification with the impassioned desire of the wailing woman or the visionary primacy of the damsel with her dulcimer, a female whose racial foreignness (as an Abyssinian maid) would figure his own striving toward otherness. Finally, she would argue that, in his wish to himself become a sorcerer—a kind of male witch with "flashing eyes and floating hair" around whom culture would have to weave a restraining circle—and in his passion for the female honeydew and milk of paradise, the speaker aligns himself with the vamp's own valorization of sorceress and hysteric, of choric pulsions and silences, of disruptive cries and whispers.

How might we negotiate between, on the one hand, the mirror critic's mimetic castigation and, on the other hand, the vamp's expressive celebration? How can we draw upon the strengths as well as the tensions implicit in the interpretive stances of these two schools? We would propose that "Kubla Khan" can be read as an uncannily anxious vision of female sexuality and male belatedness. More, we would suggest that the romantic "chasm" between male and female which traverses the text splits its effects while deepening its historical meaning. For, while the ideology that would no doubt inspire and inform the mirror critic's negative assessment of "Kubla Khan" might be grounded in an accurate grasp of the text's desire to appropriate and enclose "the feminine," the vamp's appreciative evaluation of the poem, though very likely based on a misreading of its secret anxieties, would surely be more to the point.

What the ostensibly slumbering poet of "Kubla Khan" dreams, after all, is a revisionary version of the family romance. In the classic Oedipal plot, the son, defiant of but daunted by the apparent omnipotence of the father and desirous of the mother, seeks to achieve a potency of his own, but in Coleridge's romance the father, though powerful, has lost his omnipotence while the mother, though still desirable, is far more daunting than Freud's version of Jocasta. As paradigmatic progenitor,

Kubla erects the walls of culture—his "stately pleasure dome"—above the primal female caverns and "fertile ground" through which runs "Alph," the sacred river whose name suggests both Alpheus, the Miltonic source of song, and Alpha or Aleph, the originatory letter of the alphabet. Yet despite the Khan's apparent omnipotence, his domain is haunted by the image of a "woman wailing for her demon lover," and the fragility of his "pleasure dome" is emphasized by its proximity to those caverns that are twice said to be "measureless to man."

From the point of view of the poem's speaker, moreover, Kubla's kingdom is rocked by the quasi-sexual violence of an almost overwhelming primal scene, for from the "deep romantic chasm" the panting earth forces out a phallic "mighty fountain" which flows "in tumult" through "the caverns measureless to man." Such a scene might at first appear to emblematize the ruler's unparalleled patriarchal virility. Yet, as the poet observes, "this tumult" of "dancing rocks" and high-flung water is associated not just with the generation of the sacred river but also with "Ancestral voices prophesying war," suggesting that, on the one hand, the landscape of Xanadu figures a fall into history, with its inevitable Oedipal warfare between fathers and sons, and that, on the other hand, this *paysage moralisé* symbolizes a sexuality which is itself a kind of warfare.

But if Kubla's oxymoronic "miracle of rare device"—his "sunny pleasure dome with caves of ice"—is fragile even when it is under the control of the legendary patriarch, it is an artifact whose magic is altogether unavailable to the poem's dreaming speaker. Significantly, though the muselike "damsel with a dulcimer" has appeared to him in a vision, singing of a patriarchal Miltonic mountain "where Abassin Kings their issue guard," he can only *wish* to "revive within me/Her symphony and song," and only *dream* that he would then "build that dome in air."[48] But surely the speaker's belatedness in regard to both the damsel and Kubla might be said to reflect Coleridge's own belatedness in regard to such precursors as the Milton of "Lycidas" and *Paradise Lost* or the Shakespeare of *The Tempest*, whose Prospero has commanded "cloud-capp'd towers" and "gorgeous palaces" which are all "melted into air, into thin air."[49]

It would seem, however, that the chasm in culture which divides the poem's speaker from Kubla and which separates Coleridge from his literary forefathers is specifically associated with the uncanny appearance of all "the feminine" elements that would have been celebrated by the vamp critics—the measureless caverns, the wailing woman, the muselike damsel, even the unattainable nourishment of Paradise. Thus the mirror critics' identifications of misogyny in the text might appear to be justified. Yet precisely the intensity with which Coleridge transcribes not, as the vamp critics might believe, his wishful fantasies about the feminine, and not, as the mirror critics might imagine, his appropriation of female fecundity, but, rather, his anxiety about sexuality gives the poem its fabled resonance. In addition, the entranced accuracy with which he connects sexual anxiety both with his own sense of historical belatedness and with his speaker's inability to reconstruct Kubla's originatory "miracle" in air, much less on earth, gives the work its power.

A parable about the fracturing of culture, "Kubla Khan" presents itself as a wistful fragment that the romantic poet would shore against the ruin of his imagination, and thus it depends upon strategies that would be deployed by many of Coleridge's romantic contemporaries as well as his Victorian and modernist heirs. For some of them, too, the *unheimlich* chasm in culture would be associated with the female body, with what Freud called the *"heim* [home] of all human beings . . . the place where everyone dwelt once upon a time and in the beginning"[50] But Coleridge's dream-vision is almost unique in the detail with which it proleptically glosses Freud's assertion that "whenever a man dreams of a place or a country and says to himself, still in the dream, 'this place is familiar to me, I have been there before,' we may interpret the place as being his mother's genitals or her body."[51] At the same time, however, Coleridge's poem is representative in its demonstration that, when the chasm of romanticism opened culture to the revolutionary and anti-rational forces associated with nature, with imagination, with unconsciousness, and with spontaneity—that is, to all the terms that had been repressed by what vamp critics would define as patriarchal binaries—male artists felt not only oppressed by the burden of the past but threatened by what was analogically "the feminine" in themselves.

Thus, "Kubla Khan" dramatizes Coleridge's, and other poets', struggles with what Abrams calls "the fateful concept that artistic creation is primarily an unwilled and unconscious process of mind"—a quasi-feminine yielding to uncontrollable forces—even while, as it demonstrates the poet's skill at composing measures about "caverns measureless to man," the poem allows Coleridge at least to establish himself as what Abrams calls "the master of the fragment."[52] Finally, therefore, the relationship of such qualified and anxious mastery to the uncanny otherness of "the feminine" suggests that Harold Bloom's theory of romanticism as primarily an aesthetic defense against the strong son's belatedness to his literary fathers needs to be supplemented by an awareness that such belatedness is made more horrifying by the poet's fear of feminization or of engulfment by the unfathomable forces of the feminine.[53]

For women writers, the romantic chasm in culture seems to have had two contradictory consequences. To begin with the hard-won authority through which the romantic man of letters sought to control and confine the disruptive processes that energized his art tended, as Margaret Homans and others have pointed out, to define women as muses, as *femmes fatales*, as earth mothers, and as brides of nature—but never as speakers of the potent Coleridgean "I AM."[54] It is arguably for this reason that in the era traditionally called "the romantic period"—the years bracketed by the publication of *Lyrical Ballads* in 1798 and the passage of the First Reform Bill in 1832—there was such a striking discrepancy between male and female literary production. For indeed, given the received chronology of romanticism, it is possible to decide that women did not have a romantic period at all; at least, there are no female poets in this age who are equivalent to Blake, Wordsworth, Coleridge, Byron, Shelley, and Keats.[55] At the same time, however, the reversal of conventional hierarchies that fostered the emergence of revolutionary forces analogically associated with the feminine clearly started a chain reaction that was to lead to the feminist movement of the mid-nineteenth century.

After all, as early as 1792, Mary Wollstonecraft moved directly from a *Vindication of the Rights of Man* that was profoundly influenced by her commitment to the ideals that inspired the French Revolution to her more famous *Vindication of the Rights of Woman*. As, throughout the rest of her career, she struggled to define and defend those rights, moreover, she alternated between just the two modes of feminist discourse represented by the mirror and vamp schools we have been discussing here. On the one hand, in her polemical *Vindication* she spoke in a rational, neo-classical manner, with censorious energy, about the misogynistic images of women that reflected and perpetuated the sexual inequities of her society. On the other hand, both in her life and her fictions, she expressed a broodingly romantic determination to defy patriarchal edicts by confronting the madness in her self and her world. In this last regard, moreover, Wollstonecraft's self-analyses were representative rather than eccentric, for, as Irene Tayler and Gina Luria have insightfully observed, "as the novel evolved through the decade from Wollstonecraft to Austen, what emerged was woman's version of the shift from mirror to lamp, her analogue to the poetry of the male Romantic poets, insofar as both are defined by their intense concern for self-exploration and self-determination."[56]

No doubt even more influenced by the romantic movement's revolutionary energies, Wollstonecraft's and Austen's descendants developed and extended both mimetic and expressive strategies. From Mary Shelley and Charlotte and Emily Brontë in England to Emily Dickinson in America, post-romantic women writers revived and revised the energies of romanticism for their own, implicitly feminist ends, critiquing culture's confinement of women while passionately articulating their own Byronic "hunger, rebellion, rage."[57] In doing so, along with such nineteenth-century polemicists as Caroline Norton, Margaret Fuller, and Florence Nightingale, they provided a link between Coleridge's visionary company and the revisionary company of contemporary feminist thinkers. Thus, in its defamiliarization of the familiar, its confrontation with the uncanny feminine, "Kubla Khan" records a male dream to which both mirror and vamp critics must attend, because it is, in a sense, a founding myth of the culture which actually gave birth to the intellectual tradition in which, as we have argued here, both feminist schools participate.

Might it happen, though, that even if we defamiliarize the familiar in the ways we have suggested, the very nature of institutional structures—particularly the structures of the academy—would force us, mirrors and vamps alike, into situations of cooptation that would familiarize just the unfamiliar that we propose exploring? More particularly, by placing feminist criticism in the context of a predominantly patriarchal history of ideas, are we implying that such criticism can or should be aligned with traditions that have almost always been oppressive to women? How, after all, can feminist theory be continuous with the modes of thought it seeks to disrupt? These are, of course, vexed and vexing questions which have significant professional as well as intellectual implications. For if feminist critics have been assimilated into both the academy and the history of ideas, they would seem to be in danger of replicating what Gerald Graff has called "the now-familiar paradox of the institutionalized revolutionary."[58] Feminism's problem might then be that, as Virginia Woolf feared in *Three Guineas*, if women enter the public sphere they simply acquiesce in masculinist activities, but if they remain privatized they forego the opportunity to transform patriarchal hierarchies.[59]

We want to speculate that a way out of this apparent double bind may be found, yet again, in Freud's meditation on the uncanny. "The uncanny effect," he wrote there, "is often and easily produced by effacing the distinction between imagination and reality, such as when something that we have hitherto regarded as imaginary appears before us in reality."[60] For Christine de Pizan, Mary Astell, and even Virginia Woolf, the community of feminist scholars that we have here classified as mirror and vamp critics was still essentially a utopian imagining. But now that city of ladies has appeared before us in reality, a reality which must inevitably be uncannily transformed by this surfacing of the repressed.

Perhaps ultimately, then, the "chasm" between the categories of imagination and reality, like the great divide between the concepts "masculine" and "feminine" or the rift between mirror and vamp critics, can only be negotiated if, as in a quotation from W. B. Yeats that Abrams used as an epigraph for his *The Mirror and the Lamp*, "the soul . . . become[s] its own betrayer, its own deliverer, the one activity, the mirror turn lamp."[61] Perhaps, as we betray ourselves into new positions and as we deliver ourselves into history, our feminist critical dialogue, uncannily echoing, though in so far largely unfamiliar terms, the familiar debate that Abrams documents, will represent as profound a cultural shift as the intellectual and political revolutions which accompanied the move from classicism to romanticism. But in order to foster such a cultural metamorphosis, we must understand its historical roots, since the future can only be reinvented if we reinterpret the past. That feminist criticism can be defined through metaphors similar to, if different from, those which govern other forms of critical discourse means that we can enter into precisely the dialogues that will allow us to see in a new light an image of the shifting cultural heritage we are continually seeking to change.

10

Literary Genres and Textual Genericity

Jean-Marie Schaeffer

> "Who hastens has understood; one should dwell upon any-
> thing; one would soon find that the clearest discourses are
> woven from obscure terms."
>
> Paul Valéry,
> Monsieur Teste.

Everyone agrees that the question of literary genres is fairly tangled.
We can distinguish three factors that conspire to this result. The first is
due to the recent history, romantic and post-romantic, of generic theories
and of the status these theories have granted generic categories. The
second results from the difficulty of defining the status of the textual
classes that are supposed to form genres. The third results from a specificity of generic names, the fact that they are partly self-referential and
consequently contribute to the institution of the historical reality they
claim to describe. I propose here to take the measure of these difficulties
and to indicate a few ways out. The theory of genres that will be outlined
implicitly will be much less ambitious than the ones that are generally
recognized. I hope what is lost in theoretical force will be at least partly
counterbalanced by a greater descriptive exactness.

Genre as the Explanatory Principle of Literature

The way in which literary studies have used the notion "literary genre"
since the 19th century is closer to magic thought than to rational investigation. In magic thought the word creates the thing. That is exactly
what has happened with the notion of "literary genre"; the very fact of
using the term has led us to think we ought to find a corresponding

Translated by Alice Otis

entity which would be added to the texts and would be the cause of their relationship. In other words, most 19th and 20th-century generic theories would have us believe that literary reality is bicephalous: on the one hand we would have the texts, on the other the genres. These two notions are accepted as autonomous literary entities that are then to be related, the genres serving to interpret the texts.

This conception is recent; it was unknown before Romanticism and what ensued, that is, the systems of objective idealism (Schelling or Hegel) and the evolutionist literary theory (represented in France by Ferdinand Brunetière).[1] Generic names and generic questions existed before Romanticism, to be sure. But they were inserted into a problematic and an epistemology irreducible to the causal model advanced since that time.

Thus in the classical era generic notions were essentially conceived as criteria serving to judge the conformity of a work to a norm, or rather to a set of rules. In such a descriptive-normative conception, the question of conformity or deviation of *a* given text in relation to a set of rules gains the advantage over the problem of relations between *the* texts and the genre(s). A given genre, tragedy for example, is in reality a definition functioning as the yardstick by which individual works are measured and valorized. The drive to classify is not, indeed, totally absent, but it always comes second, a simple consequence of the fact that several texts are confronted with one norm; it is never the essential object that presides in the elaboration of generic reflection. We can find an indication of it in the fact that intergeneric classification remains purely enumerative; even if the classical era accepts a hierarchy among the main genres (epic, drama, comedy) and the lesser genres (ode, elegy, sonnet, fable, etc.), this hierarchy is purely axiological and does not lead to a global logical structuration or to a system. It stands to reason that the idea according to which the genres would be the prime mover of literature capable of being used as the *explanation* for the existence of individual texts, is beyond the horizon of classical thought; genre is not an explanatory notion but a criterion of critical discrimination.

The functioning of generic definitions as critical criteria is tied closely to the general conception of literature that was maintained in the classical age: it is conceived essentially as the field of attempts, ever repeating,

---

[1] Brunetière's evolutionism is of Darwinian inspiration. Therefore it is a theory of the natural cycle and the struggle among the various genres. Brunetière, of course, shares the historicism inherent in all 19th-century generic theories, since he identifies the history of literature with a natural evolution subject to an intrinsic necessity. As was already the case with the romantics, the individual work that is significant in a given genre becomes the fundamental literary unity. See F. Brunetière, "La doctrine evolutive et L'Histoire de la Littérature" dans *Etudes critiques sur l'histoire de la littérature française*, 6th series (Paris: Hachette, 4th ed., 1922).

of the imitation of ideal models. That the models are ancient is only a contingent trait, since it is not shared by all classical poetics; but that poetry is the field of imitation and emulation is an idea that the defenders of the Ancients and those of the Moderns shared alike. The generic theory, then, is indissociable from a problematic of imitation, not so much of exemplary texts as of stable rules abstracted from such texts. This means that it is basically pragmatic, directed toward poetic activity to come; all of the descriptions can be translated into prescriptive propositions. Contrary to a received idea, the classical theories, even when they admit the paradigmatic value of the Ancients, are therefore always turned toward the future, what is of consequence to them is the normative value of the generic models for subsequent literary activity.

A radical change in conception occurred toward the end of the 18th century; henceforth literary theory would no longer be conceived as a descriptive and/or normative activity but as a speculative, interpretive undertaking. A new object saw the light of day: literature as an autonomous historical entity. The objective of the generic theory was to interpret the existence and intrinsic organization of this new object: why and how does literature exist? Pressured by this question, genres were transformed into the causal principle of the existence of literary texts. If there are literary texts, if these texts have the properties that they have, and if they follow one another historically as they do, it is because genres exist that constitute their essence, their foundation, their principle of inherent causality. Genres were no longer norms, abstracted from exemplary texts; they were coextensive with literature as the organic unity of the texts. From this time on, as I have said, literary reality was bicephalous. Whence the rise of the question of the categorical and ontological status of genres, as well as that of their embodiment in the texts.

Just as it is interpretive, the generic theory of the 19th century is turned entirely toward the past; its birth is also the birth of the history of literature. It was followed by a split between interpretative and generic (meaning "objective" and "neutral") literary history and criticism, evaluative and limited to the immanence of the individual work.[2] This distinction was unknown in the classical era, for which the theory of genres was pre-eminently where criticism and evaluation were carried out.

---

[2] Friedrich Schlegel, Jena theorist of romanticism, thus was one of the fathers of both the history of literature and of immanent criticism. It goes without saying that I do not share the conception defended in a number of recent studies, inspired by the ideas of Jacques Derrida, which support the unsurpassable character of romantic questioning, redefining it to a deconstructivist perspective as the irreducibility of textuality to any structural identity. For an illustration of this conception see J. Derrida himself, as well as Ph. Lacoue-Labarthe and J.-L. Nancy in *Glyph 7*: "The Strasbourg Colloquium," Johns Hopkins University Press, 1980.

We can express things differently; with the romantic revolution we entered an era of essentialist generic theories, that is, theories that claimed to explain the existence and essential characteristics of literature through generic definitions. These essentialist theories are subdivided into two groups, according to the epistemological obedience of the definition they give for the relation between genres and texts.

For a Platonist, the genre is to the individual text what the idea is to the phenomenal object—its timeless model, its *eidos*. Genre not only "is" but, for that matter, it alone "is"; the empirical texts are only realizations more or less in accordance with this abstract essence. In more contemporary terms it could be said that the genre is "a matrix of textual competence," or more traditionally that it is the "foundation" of a textual class. In the 19th century this conception was notably defended by Goethe, who distinguished between historical and theoretical genres—"natural forms" of poetry and timeless essences being realized more or less perfectly in actual texts.[3] In the 20th century, it is found first in the generic theories drawing their inspiration, consciously or unconsciously, from phenomenology; founded on the thesis of a *Wesensschau*, of an eidetic generic vision, it is prevalent mainly in monographs devoted to the individual genres. The phenomenological conception, on the other hand, lends itself with difficulty to the establishment of global generic systems, since it does not postulate a necessary relationship among the varied ideal essences corresponding to given genres. In order to establish global generic systems, while remaining within Platonic epistemology, the "structuralist" model is indispensable; the generic system, then, is identified with a matrix of universal competence from which would be derived the different individual genres (opposed according to mutually exclusive traits) as well as the texts realizing them empirically.

The "structuralist" model very quickly runs into the problem of the relationship between its theoretical generic categories and the historically accepted genres. If we do not want to postulate a perfect independence between the two domains (I shall try to show farther on that such a postulate, apart from the fact that it is scarcely plausible, resolves nothing, since the essential problems of the generic question concern its logical status), we are obliged to abandon Platonic epistemology for a historicist variant of neo-Aristotelianism.

According to classical Aristotelian epistemology, the genres are internal to the texts; a genre is the set of texts implementing the same internal finality. This conception is expressed from the very first sentence of the *Poetics*, which proposes to treat of the poetic art "and its

---

[3] See *Noten und abhandlungen zu besserem Verstandnis des westöstlichen Divans*, in Johann Wolfgang Goethe, *Sämtliche Werke*, volume 3 (Zurich: Artemis Verlag, 1977), pp. 480–481.

kinds (*eide*, aspects, forms), each considered in its own essence (*dunamis*)."[4] But in Aristotle this crypto-organic model doesn't lead to a generic theory in the modern sense of the term, because it lacks the evolutionist constituent (and the concomitant idea of literature conceived as an autonomous historical organism). It was only with romantic historicism that the organicist conception could really flower; the genre became the causal force explaining literary evolution.[5] The thesis that literature exists as an *autonomous* historical continuity is inseparable from the postulate that a proper causality, of the generic order, exists at the foundation of this reality. The genre thus becomes the *ratio cognoscendi* and the *ratio essendi* of literature.

Hegel is unquestionably the most prestigious representative of this neo-Aristotelian epistemology; the texts, conceived according to their literary essence, realize the genres historically, and the evolution of literature is the organic development of its generic determinations. All of the historical or systematic generic theories, and God knows they are legion, can be reduced to this Hegelian archetype.

The difference that exists between the Aristotelian theory and the neo-Aristotelian theories of the romantics or Hegel is simple to grasp. What is "missing" in Aristotle is the idea that generic notions are the *ratio essendi* of texts in their historical interrelations. Furthermore, its organicism of the interior *dunamis* is partly neutralized by the idea that the existence of texts, like that of all artifacts, is referable to the human *techne*, and so to a finality that remains external to them. Also, the generic dynamic does not come into play between a summation of textual objects

---

[4] See Aristotle, *La poétique*, 47 a, trans. Dupont-Roc et Lallot (Paris: Editions du Seuil: 1980), pp. 32–33. The fact that Aristotle speaks of the *eidos* of texts and not of their *genos* indeed shows that he is concerned not so much with the problem of classes of texts as with the definition of their internal form. Or, to put it differently, his approach is not genetic but definitional; his organicism intervenes solely at the level of the immanent structure of the texts (the reciprocal agreement of the parts and the whole).

[5] See G. Willems, *Das Konzept der Literarischen Gattung* (Tübingen: Max Niemeyer Verlag, 1981), on the Aristotelian prehistory of organicism and its flowering in 19th-century aesthetics, notably in the Hegelian F. Th. Vischer. To be sure, Aristotle speaks of the "growth" of tragedy and says that it stopped when it "attained its proper nature (*physis*)" (*Poetics*, 49 a 9–15). But I think that even this strongly organicist affirmation does not imply the idea of an evolution in the modern sense of the term; it refers to the passage from potentiality to actuality. Tragedy is really tragedy only once it is consonant with its nature; once it has attained this state, all growth stops. The actualization of tragedy stretches into historical time because poets did not from the outset realize works consistent with its nature, but this actualization is not the evolution of tragedy. Furthermore, the *Physics* determines "having attained its proper nature" as signifying "having attained the form which corresponds to the definition" (*La Physique*, 193 a 36, cited by Dupont–Roc et Lallot, p. 171), which indeed shows that the Aristotelian approach always remains fundamentally definitional. Simplifying a little, it can be said that in Hegelian historicism tragedy is the historical totality of its becoming, whereas with Aristotle, as long as there is growth there is still no real tragedy.

and their condition of existence as the historical organism. It does not even concern the genesis of individual texts; it is referable solely to the reciprocal agreement of the various elements within a given text. In romantic and Hegelian organicism, on the other hand, the finality is that of a transtextual teleology, inherent in the historical evolution of a textual series and being realized genetically in and through the individual texts. It is the internal generic finality, and not a certain number of intentional human acts corresponding to a *techne,* which constitutes the *ratio essendi* of literary history.

The essentialist theories, whether Platonic or neo-Aristotelian, seem unacceptable to me, because they imply a reification of the notion of "genre." This reification takes two forms. On the one hand we witness an abusive simplification of the logical status of the relations between texts and genres, relations that are reduced to the model of inclusion or "belonging to." On the other hand, the essentialist theories fail to recognize that generic names are not confined to describing generic "reality," but that, in part, they also institute it. I should like to analyze these two points now.

The Logical Status of Generic Classifications

It could be tempting to dismiss the foregoing considerations in their entirety by maintaining that the question of generic classifications can be rendered independent of all essentialism; one could maintain that to obtain that result you only have to confer the simple function of a meta-textual logical structuration on the classification. In other words, we would leave in abeyance the genetic and evolutive question in order to construct purely synchronic classes established according to mutually exclusive criteria chosen freely by the theoretician in order to guarantee the logical coherence of his classification. These classes, then, do not claim to furnish an essentialist definition of texts, but a simple theoretical grid permitting manipulation of the texts according to structurally pertinent categories.

The solution encounters several problems, nevertheless. The first results from the fact that the number of criteria according to which any two texts can be regrouped is indeterminate; if I choose my properties judiciously, nothing forbids me to introduce any text into any class. But, when we speak of a generic theory, of course we are talking about a theory that is based on generic distinctions that have been recognized during literary history.[6] Unfortunately, we shall see that historically

---

[6] In this connection see Tzvetan Todorov, *Les Genres du discours* (Paris: Editions du Seuil, 1978), p. 48.

allowed genres radically under-determine the texts they regroup. A purely structural classification, then, has no reason to coincide, even in its general outlines, with historically accepted genres.

A second objection seems to me yet more decisive. The "structuralist" conception shares with essentialist theories the same overly simplistic view of the logical status of generic classifications. This status, in fact, is far from being clear. We are currently using the notion of genre in several very different contexts. Thus we speak of the genre of Menippean satire or of classical tragedy; in other words, we employ the term as the name serving to identify a class of texts. But we also use the term in a predicative function. Then it designates a characteristic attributed to an individual text: *Don Quixote* is a novel; "The Cicada and the Ant" is a fable. For the most part we assume that this predicative relation is the simple translation of a relation of inclusion: *Don Quixote* is a part of the novelistic genre. In other words, we pass from a relation that includes several texts in the same class to a relation that attributes the same quality to the objects. Finally, we sometimes happen to speak of ancient genres, theatrical genres, and simply of genres; in that case we are stating predications bearing on a set composed of several textual classes. Placing these classes in a relation of reciprocal exclusion, we implicitly suppose that they obey the same logic and so can form a system.

Properly understood, each of the four uses can render us services, but we get lost in an inextricable confusion if we admit that the term "generic" possesses the same status and/or functions in the same way in all cases. That is, however, what most generic theories presuppose; taking the relation of inclusion of a text in "its" genre as the methodological crux, they make it the universal pattern of the study of genericity.

The privilege granted the relation of inclusion stems from the fact that the generic classification is generally copied closely from the classification of animal or vegetal organisms. Such a classification proceeds by lateral equivalences and vertical inclusions: every dog is reducible to an exemplar of the canine species, which in its turn is integrated into the mammalian class, etc. In the same way, a given ode is thought to be reducible to the genre "ode," which in its turn would be a sub-genre of lyric poetry, etc.

However, the classification of texts by inclusion in a generic definition to which each of their number would *de jure* be reducible (one fable would be to another fable what one dog is to another dog), creates many problems. In the first place, we can note that while in the classification of a given animal in the dog species, the temporal vector does not intervene, it is omnipresent in the generic classification. Generic morphology, even in the most stable genres, such as the fable, for example, is always relatively open. The difference between the two domains is easily explained: the recurrence of zoological resemblances is referable to a causal, genetic continuity; but no mechanism of that sort exists in the evolution of a literary genre. The logic of the textual tradition is always a logic of discontinuity, and there is no "genetic" bond, except in a metaphoric sense (and this genre of metaphors should be mistrusted), between two texts. Of course, we often say that one text engenders another, but I must admit, however, that I have never yet been able to witness the corresponding parturition process.

The crux of the problem lies in the difficulty, if not the impossibility, of superimposing a pure, logical classification of genres on their essentially historical status. At least we cannot do it if we want the generic theory to keep an explicative import. In this perspective, generic classification cannot, in fact, neutralize the effective historical dynamics that institute the classes it studies, without, at the same time, neutralizing its own effective literary foundation, which is textual genericity.

To phrase the paradox differently, the generic class is an extensional historical class that does not allow a univocal intensional definition. The passage from extension to comprehension, from texts to generic properties, is never reversible; we cannot infer from the intentional definition of a textual class to one of the texts in the class. In fact, when we pass from the question of class as an extensional category to the question concerning the judgment of the inclusion of a text to the class, we are inclined to justify the latter by an intensional definition, applicable, all things being equal in other respects, to each member of the class. But the effective genericity of a text is not reducible to its status as a singularized member of a class whose definition in comprehension could be presupposed; it must be referred to the precise function that the member has performed in *the historical constitution* of the class. In order to understand the generic function of a text "c," we must examine the generic tradition as it was at the time "c," and not as we see it now, at the time of retrospective classification—let us say for example at time "f." In other words, we cannot examine it in the name of the logic of inclusion. When we seek to elucidate the relationship of the *Aeneid* to the epic, the question we ask ourselves is not that of its belonging to the class as it may be defined once the *Aeneid* is a part of it, but that of its shaping force, the shaping force that is precisely one of the reasons the class such as we know it today possesses one appearance rather than another.

Owing to the fact of the temporal constitution of generic classes, the logic of inclusion possesses a radically ambiguous status. To say that text "c" belongs to genre "x" makes sense only if the proposition is stated from the viewpoint of a subsequent state "f" in the given textual tradition; at the level of its own temporality, text "c," far from belonging to genre "x" as it will be defined in "f," is, at least *de jure*, a questioning of generic state "b," and so partially determines what the genre will be in "f." Every text, inasmuch as it is grasped in its genesis, is always logically either posterior or anterior to a given generic classification: posterior to the generic norm in relation to which it is going to be made up, anterior to the generic norm of which it will constitute a new, original element. Far from being definable with the aid of the genre, it is the individual text that decides, in part, what a contingent ulterior generic definition will be. It follows that generic classification, inevitably retrospective, can never have a genetic or interpretive function; the properties that it retains annul the temporal constitutional logic of the class.

The absence of the obligatory recurrence of stringently identical traits, which we find in numerous genres, is linked to this temporal dynamic. Whereas the set of dogs shares certain recurrent (genetic) characteristics that are both necessary and sufficient to identify a given animal as belonging or not belonging to the species, the evolution of numerous literary genres does not disclose such characteristics. The different texts that we integrate into a genre are often linked by simple "family resemblances" in Wittgenstein's sense: they do not all necessarily share the same recurrent characteristic or characteristics, but a given text shares some characteristics with some of its "congeners," some other characteristics with other "congeners." Thus a text p shares the bundle of traits A with texts q and r; q in turn shares traits B (different from A) with s, which, furthermore, shares part of traits A with q and r; r in turn, in addition to the A traits that it shares with p, shares other traits C with it and with s, etc.

In other words, a genre is far from forming a univocal class; it is formed of several networks of partial resemblances that, through a process of overlapping, form the literary genre in its historical variability. Therefore the intensional generic definition of retrospective classifications inevitably neutralizes this variability. We cannot get out of this by saying that generic classification refers to prototypes, since the very notion of prototype already implies a neutralization of the temporal dimension. But neither does that mean that generic definitions are necessarily additive or cumulative. Whence a dilemma: either the theorist wants a powerful theory, and in this case the generic definition as it is derived from the logic of inclusion is much too strong for the set of all texts (of its corpus) considered one by one; or conversely, he decides to adopt a low profile and to retain only the features shared hypothetically by all members of the class, and in this case he will arrive at a definition too weak in relation to any subset of texts (of its corpus) considered by itself. The description in comprehension, therefore, always leads to the formation of an ideal type. In itself this is not an objection to the definitional classification, on condition that the "ideal type" is considered as a retrospective abstraction and not as the causal model of the genesis of the textual series.

But I think we ought to go farther. If we tend so often to consider the ideal type as the interpretive model, that is no doubt partly due to the very form of the definitional judgment, which leads us astray. The following is the most current formulation of this judgment:

(1)"(a) is a novel."

This formulation is unfortunate because it places "a" in the position of *definiendum* and "novel" in predicate position, in the position of *definiens*. To postulate such a relation is, to begin with, to postulate too univocal a relation between the generic name and the text that bears it. We shall see that the generic nomination possesses the most varied communicational statuses, irreducible to that of a simple descriptive judgment. Or, to put it differently, it is an integral part of the pragmatic constitution of the text and so adds something to it. Furthermore, the definitional form itself implies perverse effects; it presupposes that we can know what the text is with the help of the notion "novel," whereas in the vast majority of cases, and in spite of all we can say on the subject of the horizon of expectation, it is the opposite that takes place. We know more about the text than we know about the genre, even if we are theorists of the genre. In fact our knowledge goes from texts to genres much more than from genres to texts. The proposition then would more correctly be:

(2)"a novel = for example (a)."

This expression is less unfortunate because it places the genre in the position of *definiendum* and the text in the position of *definiens*. Furthermore, the indefinite article indicates that the relation of text to genre is not strictly definitional but is on the order of the relationship of an exemplar to a purely extensional class; it does not presuppose strict definitional identity of all exemplars entering the class.

We can describe the situation differently: generic names do not possess a sufficient and necessary definition. They function rather as proper nouns, that is to say their reference is first in relation to their definition.[7] A certain generic name is associated with a given text, and for that reason is associated with certain properties of the text in question. The concept associated with the name does not determine the reference but has the status of an *a posteriori* encyclopedic knowledge concerning the reference. The reiteration of this procedure on an indefinite number of texts associated with the same name delivers the generic class to us. Therefore we have access to the letter through an open encyclopedic knowledge and not through a true definition. The fact that a text is an exemplar of an extensional generic class does not imply that it is accessible through a strict general definition.

In order to know genres, we apply ourselves to texts; we cannot do the reverse, except by exposing ourselves to bitter disappointments. The real *definiens* is always the text, the *definiendum*, always provisional, being the genre. The genre is a class whose extension is open and whose intension is always provisional and partial. It is provisional because no immutable criterion decides whether a new text belongs to a given genre. We shall see that this relation of inclusion calls for a decisional aspect irreducible to any definitional determinism. It is partial because it does not account for the complexity and diversity of the factors that cause a given text to become inserted in a given generic tradition.

We see why a classificatory approach to the generic question, if it is not used with much circumspection, risks being only of quite relative pertinence. On the one hand, the extension of the class is never described adequately by the definition whose value is purely heuristic. On the other hand, therefore, it stands to reason that *a fortiori* the definition cannot be considered an explanation of the genesis of the class or of its functional status. Now most generic theories intend to be interpretive; their definitions claim to deliver the principle of the constitution of the class. Whence the inevitable return of essentialism, since we admit implicitly that the definition delivers to us the rules of textual generation that, if historical circumstances allow, will produce a given textual class

---

[7] W.V.O. Quine, studying classifications by similarity (not based on genetic characteristics) of natural species, has shown the impossibility of defining a class by similarity (see W.V.O. Quine, *Ontological Relativity and Other Essays* [New York: Columbia University Press, 1969].) As to the theory of signification that I am defending here, it is "extensionalist" and ties in with the theory of direct reference set forth by Hilary Putnam in "The Meaning of Meaning," *Minnesota Studies in the Philosophy of Science*, 7, 1975, pp. 131–93. Of course it is necessary to distinguish between the Logic of the exemplarity of literary genres and the theory of prototypic specimens holding in the field of natural species. The difference is due both to the temporal logic that intervenes in the constitution of the generic class and to the partly decisional character of generic nomination, not only at the moment of initial christening (which is a triviality), but at the time of each reiteration.

according to purely internal determinations that are logically, if not historically, presupposed by the individual texts.

We can add still another difficulty. According to the logic of inclusion, genres form mutually exclusive classes; therefore, when we study genericity at the level of individual texts, we notice that a text is very often situated at the intersection of several different generic traditions, and thus it cannot be defined by the traits that refer it to a unique class. What the romantics called "the mixing of genres" is simply the fact of the multi-generic character that is the attribute of a great number of texts, at least in high literature. I shall come back to it briefly farther on.

The preceding considerations imply neither a condemnation of classification nor a rejection of the structural method in the domain of generic studies. They merely show that generic concepts are "soft" concepts, not "hard" ones; their limits are definitionally fuzzy and I believe it is fruitless to cherish the dream of a global generic system formed of mutually exclusive classes, unless one prefers the charm of a system to its descriptive or interpretive import. These limits are also those of value for the study of textual genericity; but as the latter limits itself to an historical reconstruction and inductive research of different generic systems, there is much less risk of definitional essentialism in it. Let me add that, contrary to appearances, the analysis of textual genericity— that is to say the study of generic mechanisms—may be more interesting from a structural viewpoint than the study of genres as classificatory sets, at least if the structural approach is understood as a study of textual mechanisms.

Names of Genres, Genres, and Generic Theories

Generic theories, whether they are historicist or "structuralist," tend to start from the postulate that generic notions are theoretical categories by birth. This overlooks the fact that those notions are generic *names* in the first place and that the function of these names is far from being purely metaliterary. In reality, generic terms are at least partially pragmatic; they do not solely describe literary phenomena, they also enter into their constitution. By that I mean that generic nomination always possesses a self-referential aspect, because it implies a decisional constituent; the term "epic" refers to all the texts that the literary institution, at a given epoch or through the ages, accepts as "epics." This decisional constituent occurs even in what are customarily called "fixed forms"; thus when Gerard Manley Hopkins replaced the quatrains of the sonnet with tercets he changed a "definitional" aspect of the genre. He could just as well have introduced a different name to term his poems; he did not do so, and this decision not only affected the pragmatic status of his own poems, but it also rearranged the "laws" of the sonnet at the same time, transforming the rule of two quatrains into an optional rule. Generic definitions and the criteria they retain sanction decisional strategies, at least in part. Generic names, then, do not explain literary history; they are a specific constituent of it—the study of relationships between texts and genres must be preceded by the study of relationships between texts and genre names.

It is necessary, therefore, to start from the fact that the existence of a genre is first of all that of a sort of proper name coupled to a text. This generic designation can be the deed of either the writer, the critics, or the theorists. In the first case the designation can be termed indigenous, whereas the two latter operations are exotic. If the distinction between indigenous theories and exotic theories is important at the level of the analysis of textual genericity, it loses a large part of its pertinence at the level of the long-lived history of generic names, a history that generally leads to a mixing of indigenous and exotic denominations. But the bare fact that indigenous generic theories exist obviously confirms the idea that generic names are also pragmatic categories with a highly self-referential component; a text not only applies certain generic rules, but it also very often christens itself as belonging to a specific genre.

This self-identification obeys complex strategies. Thus the fact that a text assumes a certain generic denomination by no means implies that the rules actually applied by it are reducible to those associated with the chosen generic name until then. To take a case of particularly patent disagreement, Stendhal, in his Preface to *La Chartreuse de Parme*, calls his work a "novella," a thoroughly heterodox generic self-nomination in relation to the accepted use of the term and one that had little success, since we consider the text to be a novel.[8] Furthermore, generic designation generally refers the text to a single generic norm, whereas at the level of its effective genericity it is often at the intersection of several norms. The study of relations between generic designation and effective genericity, therefore, throws a light on the relations between the textual status and the pragmatic status of the literary work. . . .

The omnipresence of evaluation factors in generic theories is remarked not only within the description of a given genre but also in the classification of different genres. To the hierarchy of works within a genre corresponds a hierarchy among the various genres. The case of novelistic literature is particularly revealing; most of the classicist generic classifications, like the speculative theories of the 19th century (if we except

---

[8] Perhaps the motivation for the denomination comes from the fact that Stendhal borrowed the subject matter of his work from a brief Italian account that could possibly pass for a sort of historical novella. In other words, his generic self-nomination does not refer to his text but to his source.

the Jena romantics), give it only a marginal position. In Hegel this leads to the paradoxical result that the most important form of contemporary literature is discussed in a single paragraph—not as a specific genre, moreover, but as a prosaic derivative of the epic, whereas the latter, nonexistent in the epoch in which Hegel wrote, is analyzed for more than a hundred pages.

Sometimes a classicist wishes to salvage certain works that circulate under the "novel" denomination; he then attempts the impossible in order to draw the "manifestations" of genre toward some other genre accepted as canonical. Thus in 1675 Rapin, inspired by Horace, granted the satyr a canonical place following the epic, tragedy, and comedy. But the term, which in Horace designated the *satyr-play*, in Rapin designates the *satire* in the sense of Juvenal's satires. Whereas Horace defined the genre both modally (representation) and thematically (mixture of tragedy and comedy), Rapin defined it in a purely thematic way. At the same time, he ushered in "the Don Quixote Novel" and "the Rabelais satyr,"[9] in other words, narrative works that Horace's principle certainly excluded. But this *quid pro quo* allowed Rapin to introduce some novels he valued into the framework of a canonical genre, when elsewhere he debased the novelistic genre. In the same way, if most German authors of novelistic literature in the 18th century labeled their works "story" (*Geschichte*) and not "novel" (*Roman*), it was, above all, in order to escape the poor public image the term "novel" had in the critical literature of the epoch.

The Rapin example, incidentally, shows the weight of canonical theoretical texts. In some epochs this weight was such that everything was tried in order to reconcile the entire body of genres with the classifications of Horace or Aristotle. In that way, a generic classification often arose from a faulty interpretation of generic distinctions accepted as canonical. This is what happened with Rapin when he identified the satyr-play with satires. With regard to the 19th century, Gérard Genette has shown how the great romantic and Hegelian triad of epic, lyric, and drama, which some contemporary critics continue to consider as designating the three basic generic attitudes, arose little by little from a contamination of the Aristotelian distinction between tragedy and epic by the Platonic theory of the three modalities of expression: the narrative mode, the representative mode, and the mixed mode.[10]

The self-referential and prescriptive aspect of generic theories is closely related to the fact that texts are always under-determined by generic

---

[9] René Rapin, *Réflexions sur la poétique de ce temps et sur les ouvrages des poètes anciens et modernes* (1675) (Geneva: Librairie Droz, 1970), p. 126

[10] See Gérard Genette, *Introduction à l'architexte* (Paris: Editions du Seuil, 1979), reprinted in *Théorie des genres* (Paris: Editions du Seuil, 1986).

names. I have already said that no generic denomination can stand as being both the necessary and the sufficient condition to define a given text. To be more precise, generic names always select some generically pertinent textual traits. That means two things. On the one hand, the traits selected by the name are not necessarily the only ones that are pertinent from the viewpoint of textual genericity, nor the most important (a writer or an editor can have an interest in misleading). On the other hand, generic traits are never the program of the self-generation of the global text. This obviously condemns the essentialist theories that claim to see in the genre the intrinsic causality of the historical evolution of literature and the *ratio essendi* of the texts taken in their individuality. It also explains the paradoxical situation in which these theories find themselves of having to over-determine their generic definitions, practically identifying them with the characteristics of some paradigmatic texts, in order to be able to maintain their essentialist pretension. Also, generic theories of the classical age are epistemologically less incompatible with what I have called textual genericity than are the evolutionist-organicist theories developed since the romantic revolution. In order to understand this, one must remember that the fundamental units of analysis in the classical theories are not so much the texts as a whole as certain precise textual traits functioning as identification signs. With the romantic revolution, on the other hand, it is the text as a closed system that becomes central to the critical undertaking. At the same time, the generic model becomes a global model. There is a close tie between the birth of the idea of the organic autonomy of the work and that of evolutionist-organicist generic theories; only the latter allow disrupting the solipsism of the text (reified as a closed system), through postulating an evolutionary relationship among the different texts or a common relation to a single ideal type. From the moment we drop the idea of the text-organism, there is no longer any reason to keep what was its counterpart, that is to say the organicist-evolutionist theory of genres.

We may draw two conclusions from the preceding set of considerations. The first is that, paradoxically, they legitimate the generic classifications (including the essentialist classifications), since they have brought out their undeniable pragmatic function. The establishment of generic classifications (in any form whatsoever) is a constant fact of literary history, and it would be ridiculous to deny its importance, not only from the pedagogical viewpoint but also from that of the historical construction of literature. The latter, in fact, is always a constructive reading of the written and oral tradition of a given culture. Therefore, it is always a question of flashing the spotlight on the mass of accessible textual documents. This flash of the spotlight is inevitably incomplete and biased (because of the self-referentiality of the generic terms and the under-determination of the texts), but the richness of the distinctions introduced into this amorphous mass is also always an index of the living relation that a given epoch maintains with the literary traditions that precede it, as well as of the ideological importance it grants its own literary practice. Furthermore, in the guise of indigenous theories, generic classifications are intimately bound to textual genericity; the relation between these two aspects of literary texts, if it is sometimes conflictual, is never arbitrary. Insofar as a text enters into social communication, it is generally called on to situate itself with respect to the structure of the accepted literary field of its epoch—to make a place there for itself. In order to do this, it can obviously capitalize on the partially decisional character of generic nomination, which functions as a buffer between textual genericity and accepted generic paradigms.

The second conclusion has already been stated at the end of the preceding section. It is vain to expect a theory of genres to be more rational and systematic than the enumeration of different generic names elaborated in the course of literary history. Furthermore, such a sophisticated theory would be of no use because it would only be the theory of an imaginary object. . . .

Textual Genericity

I should like to conclude with a few remarks devoted to the question of the textual status of genericity. By textual genericity I mean the set of the elements of a text that are referable to a modeling function performed (directly or through the intermediary of explicit norms) by other texts. The function of these reference texts, therefore, is that of a model or norm that the text in question transforms into a rule (or rules) that it applies.[11] The passage from the model or norm to the rule may be conflictual. That is particularly clear in the case of texts that are situated at the intersection of several generic traditions. . . .

For reasons of space, I shall limit myself to the textual aspect in the restricted sense of the term, that is, to the properties of the text through which it is situated in, returns to, or withdraws from one or several established generic traditions.

---

[11] Is it really necessary to stress the fact that this research of pertinent generic traits always remains hypothetical? Model and norm on the one hand, rules on the other, are obviously interdependent terms; a textual trait is generically pertinent only in the horizon of a norm or model; conversely, a model and a norm become visible only insofar as they constitute the horizon of textual rules. Moreover, the reconstruction of the model shares all the limits of the classificatory approach; it is the description of an ideal type. Only the norm—explicit—is directly accessible.

To the degree that the generic relation is always a relation of reduplication and/or variation that a given text has to certain other earlier texts functioning as models or norms, it can be comprised in the field of transtextual relations.[12] But the functionality of the transtextual relation is not always the same. We can roughly distinguish two generic *relations*.

Synthetic Genericity. The text stands directly in relation to a certain number of hypotexts functioning as *models* and from which it will extract its own rules or to which it will oppose its rules. In this generic relation, the text delineates its own hypotextual tradition in intaglio, positively or negatively. Or, to express it differently, the synthetically generic text constructs its own generic lineage (its model). This situation, favorable to the diversity and mobility of generic traditions, is found in a particularly clear manner, in the vast domain of narrative literature, where a multiplicity of local and transient generic models correspond to the various genres, without any presence of explicit norms. A narrative text thus illuminates a more or less vast hypotextual corpus with respect to which it assumes status. In a more general way, synthetic genericity occurs in the non-canonical genres, in epochs in which explicit institutional constraints are growing weaker. In an exemplary way, this is the case in high literature of the contemporary epoch, which knows fewer explicit norms than the classical age.

Analytical Genericity. The text reproduces or deviates from a certain number of explicit norms (or from norms that can be rendered explicit). In this case the transtextual relation is always mediated by a prescription; the text does not refer directly to hypotexts but takes aim at them through the filter of an analytical norm. This relation can be found in genres that are defined by recurrent formal norms—the sonnet for example, and, in a more general way, all of the fixed forms. It is also the case, on a much more constraining plane, in certain canonical genres of the classical age: thus 17th-century French tragedy submitted to prescriptions at the same time thematic, formal (the law of the three unities, among others), and pragmatic (the effect produced should be terror or pity). Among the analytical generic relations must also be numbered hypertextual procedures in the broad sense of the term, brought into play in the parody, the travesty, or the pastiche, for example, whose norms do not prescribe intratextual traits but a certain relation between two texts—the ordered

---

[12] I am borrowing the terms transtextuality, hypertextuality, hypotextuality, and their derivatives from Gérard Genette, *Palimpsestes* (Paris: Editions du Seuil, 1982), an important book to which my reflections of genres owe much. Transtextuality is nothing other than the set of elements putting one text in relation with other texts, whatever the nature of the relation may be. Hypertextuality is the relation that a posterior text (called the hypertext) maintains with an anterior text (called the hypotext), exclusive of commentary relation.

transformation of a hypotext or stylistic imitation.[13] Thus the travesty prescribes a "stylistic transformation with a degrading function"[14] and the pastiche a stylistic imitation.

The status of the text in relation to the generic horizon is not the same in both cases; in the system of analytical genericity it appears as conformity or deviation, whereas in the synthetic system it is conceived instead as either the imitation or the transformation of the model. The two processes obviously can occur parallel to each other in the same text. They remain no less distinct; the norms are prescriptive, explicit (at least potentially), and possess a metatextual status; conversely, the models are "transcriptive" generally silent, and purely hypertextual. Furthermore, the analytical processes, by the mere fact of their institutional status, often give rise to traditions bound to a given historical configuration. At least this is true of composite analytical norms (thematic and formal); the situation is different for the "fixed forms" and above all for those strange genres called parody, travesty, or pastiche. Thus if it is true that some literary epochs are more favorable to parody than others, it is no less true that, to the degree that it is a purely technical process, it is, as it were, of all times. The set of all parodies does not form a historical textual series of the same quality as the *chanson de geste*, the novella, the picaresque novel, etc. We cannot speak of an evolution of parody as we can speak of an evolution of the epic. This shows us that the distinction between the synthetic relation and the analytical relation is not sufficient to describe the different generic dynamics, since it does not take into account the distinction in status existing between genres such as classical tragedy on the one hand, parody on the other.

In order to complete the analysis, the status of *rules* must be examined. We can distinguish between texts that possess constitutive generic rules and those that possess only purely regulative rules. The distinction, which I pick up from John Searle,[15] is the following: a constitutive rule is a rule in the absence of which a discursive act is not recognized in its specificity; a regulative rule performs within a field defined by a constitutive rule that it enriches with contextual constraints. The constitutive rule is necessarily recurrent, whereas the regulative rule, to some extent, is facultative. There are genres that are unquestionably circumscribed by constitutive rules: for example, genres that *imitate* a specific extraliterary discursive practice; this is the case in a fictive diary or a novel in letters. But a genre can also *institute* a specific discursive act; thus the fable is based primarily on a constitutive rule requiring that the narrative

---

[13] See Genette, *Palimpsestes*, pp. 17–88.
[14] Genette, *Palimpsestes*, p. 33.
[15] See John Searle, *Speech Acts* (Cambridge: Cambridge University Press, 1969).

possess an allegorical translation (in the vague sense of the term). Some regulative rules of the Aesopian fable are directly motivated by this constitutive rule; the narrative must present a single (or at the very most double) situation, its length must not be such that it prohibits its univocal translation into a sapiential saying or a given ethic; it accords preference to animal worlds (inasmuch as these spontaneously invite a semantic translation), etc. In other words, some of the essential regulative rules of the fable are motivated directly by the pragmatic status of its discursive apparatus.

The question of the eventual link between the two distinctions I have just proposed seems to be a relevant one. . . . Are constitutive rules the simple textual translation of analytical norms? . . .

We do see that there is a difference in status between rules based on literary norms, that means on explicit poetological prescriptions, and constitutive rules in the proper sense of the term, which originate in fundamental discursive forms, presupposed, instituted, or imitated by the literary field.[16] All constitutive rules give rise to analytical norms but not all analytical norms necessarily give rise to constitutive rules. In the case of analytical norms, it is necessary to distinguish between institutional obligation and discursive necessity. A norm that is obligatory at a given historical epoch is not necessary in the same sense as a norm that serves to identify a specific discursive act. In fact, obligatory norms lead to regulative rules; always imposed by the literary institution, they are never sheltered from a bold stroke introducing a new rule of the game and leading to a change in the literary norm with the acceptation of the same denomination.

I have already recalled that Hopkins's sonnets contravene the norm of the classical sonnet; and still we feel that they are sonnets. Another famous example is that of the elegy, which antiquity had defined by the recurrence of a metrical norm (the distich), whereas in post-antiquity literature this definition gave way little by little to a thematic, purely regulative definition, the recurrent formal norm being abandoned. Let us note as well that the passage from the ancient definition to the modern definition does not imply an exclusion of the prosodic norm; it merely ceases to be a recurrent rule and becomes a trait of synthetic genericity. This explains how the ancient elegy and the modern elegy could continue to be considered a single genre, the change implying a simple weakening of the formal norm and the addition of a content norm. On the other hand, if we wished to define the fable without reference to the obligatory

---

[16] On the subject of the thorny question of relationships between generic rules and discursive forms, see Todorov's comments in "L'origine des genres," *Les Genres*, pp. 44–59.

allegorical interpretation, the change would be much more fundamental; allegorical interpretation refers to a discursive act whose specificity escapes the legislation of literary conventions. Furthermore, it forms an oppositional pair with direct interpretation; we are concerned, in other words, with a term that is inserted into a paradigm. To abandon the allegorical interpretation, therefore, gives rise to direct interpretation— its opposite. At the same time, and this is a rule that holds, generally speaking, for genres defined by contrast, the fable's "other" arises, namely the animal narration (*Roman de Renart*), which no longer possesses a regular allegorical translation. . . .

Another important distinction concerns the level of investment of generic rules. At least three levels can be distinguished: the level of the discursive act (among others the modal level), the thematic level, and the formal level. The more the number of textual levels invested by the rules is elevated, the more the generic series form historically interdependent series. . . . The more the number of textual traits invested by the generic rules is restricted, the less the genre seems to be bound to a given historical conjecture. But the inversion is only partially true. It is unquestionably so for genres depending directly on a constitutive rule, that is, imitating or initiating a specific discursive act whose identity circumscribes the genre. It is also true that some fixed forms, for example, lyrical genres such as the ballad or the sonnet have been integrated in the most diverse literary epochs. But here the identity of name actually conceals a diversity at the level of effective rules. On the one hand, neither ballad nor sonnet has maintained a formal definition strictly identical in all its incarnations. On the other hand, in the case of the ballad, a content norm has ended by supplanting the formal norm. The romantic ballad is defined by its theme more than by its form, which no longer coincides with that of the traditional Romance ballad (limited to three stanzas with refrain). So we cannot speak of a true continuity of the same formal norm through successive historical incarnations; even the "fixed forms" correspond for the most part to several different generic traditions according to epoch and nation. As for thematic traits, the question is scarcely more univocal; if a multiple historical resurgence of satire and elegy, or even the eclogue, is plausible it seems evident, on the other hand, that the destiny of the *chanson de geste* is indissociable from the Christian Middle Ages. It is still no less true that the more the number of levels of the text that are "prestressed" is elevated, the less great is the writer's latitude of maneuver and the more the genre will be inscribed in a field of specific historical constraints. This is the situation we find for the canonical genres of the classical age, accepting analytical norms investing both the thematic field and the formal mold of the texts.

So it seems to be true that the degree of historicity of literary genres is different according to the level(s) on which they define their rules. . . .

The preceding considerations obviously are outrageously schematic and do not claim to circumscribe the field of textual genericity. But I think the formal study of generic phenomena would take a profitable turn undertaking research of textual mechanisms along these lines, if only as a corrective to the biased view of the logic of genres that generic classifications and systems offer us.

11

The Sense of an Answer: Ambiguities of Interpretation in Clinical and Applied Psychoanalysis

Roy Schafer

In writing their versions of structuralist and post-structuralist approaches to epistemology, methodology, language, meaning, truth, blindness, rhetoric, paradox, and power, critical theorists often enter into dialogue with psychoanalysis. They take note of both the bearing of their contributions on psychoanalysis and the uses they have found for interpretive precedents already established by Sigmund Freud and other psychoanalysts. Although these dialogues vary with the critical theory or anti-theory being espoused and the particular writer espousing it, they all throw into question some or all of these psychoanalytic precedents. Unlike these critical theorists, most clinical psychoanalysts (certainly, most American psychoanalysts) continue to ignore these intellectual developments. To understand this differential of interest it is not enough to make due allowance for the difficulty in the way of the psychoanalyst's combining a substantial amount of clinical practice, reflection on that practice, and psychoanalytic scholarship, with close study of the work of critical theorists. By close study I refer to study of this other vast scholarly output, sufficient to help the psychoanalyst understand these interdisciplinary dialogues and perhaps establish a preferred position of his or her own or even dare to join the conversation more intimately than that. For whatever the practical difficulty, it has never been more urgent for analysts to make these interdisciplinary efforts.

It is particularly urgent that analysts confront anew the epistemological and methodological presuppositions that ground, pervade, and control their principles and practice of interpretation; for it has been strongly argued that all interpretation is inherently ambiguous, inconclusive, contestable, internally at odds with itself, blinding or repressive—as well as illuminating, and dependent always on a specific context that is, however, infinitely revisible in scope and criteria of relevance. It is well to remember in this connection that those critical theorists who have generally or specifically questioned the grounds of psychoanalytic interpretation are not so much its enemies as they are scholars who take it seriously. Consequently, psychoanalysts imperil their own discipline when they avoid dealing with what seem now to be inescapable problems of finding things out, knowing them, understanding them, and communicating them—if it makes sense any longer to continue to refer to these activities as different from, and independent of, one another.

Simultaneously, it is incumbent on practicing psychoanalysts to contribute to the interdisciplinary dialogues by writing about the way they do arrive at and convey interpretations—what I call the sense of an answer—and how in general they attend to their daily concerns with remaining competent members of the clinical psychoanalytic community. These contributions are needed to offset a special problem: the interdisciplinary dialogues typically feature close readings of selected fragments of Freud's writings—usually, it seems, his early writings, as though only at the outset was Freud a true Freudian—when it would not be stretching things to say that Freud's writings and the received versions of them put forth by later analysts no longer represent or control the practice of analytic interpretation to the extent that critical theorists often assume. What they assume has the effect of denying psychoanalysis a history and so a future, too; and that denial may be (for the psychoanalyst) in the service of an unconvincing economy, authority, and success of critical discussions of psychoanalysis. Hence the need for psychoanalysts to present modern versions of their work in interdisciplinary contexts.

As I see it, then, my essay requires a prologue written from the standpoint of contemporary psychoanalytic practice, to be followed by a main text that searches for points of connection between this practice and the ongoing dialogues of critical theorists.

In my prologue ("Some Versions of Psychoanalysis") I shall present some workaday examples of clinical and applied psychoanalysis together with some individual comparative commentary on them. A fuller exploration of the common problems of these two types of analytic endeavor will be presented in the main text ("The Sense of an Answer"). It is these common problems that can be used to develop a livelier and broader context for considering psychoanalytic interpretation in relation to contemporary criticism than is now available. The prologue's illustrations will be sketchy. I shall set forth only enough to raise questions for my main text. First, there will be a conventional Freudian interpretation of part of the story of Snow White. After that, two pieces of clinical analysis, one featuring interpretation of some prominent personality characteristics of women whose mothers appear to have been beset by severe narcissistic problems, and the other featuring interpretation of the rhetoric of severely narcissistic men undergoing psychoanalysis. Instead of interpretation of a fairy tale, I could have used psychohistory, psychobiography, analysis of the creative process, or some other familiar application of psychoanalysis; I must hope that, by the end of this essay, the reader will be ready to grant that the fairy tale illustration has been adequate for my purpose.

Some Versions of Psychoanalysis

Snow White. In the familiar version of the story of Snow White, she is sentenced to death by a vain mother-figure who wishes to be the fairest of all. Sentence is pronounced after this sinister stepmother has been told by the mirror on the wall that Snow White is fairer than she. Snow White is depicted as her innocent passive victim. *Interpretation:* This is a defensively disguised presentation of the daughter's positive (cross-gender) and aggressive oedipal aspirations and tribulations. This girl envies her mother's queenly feminine role, attributes, and sexual opportunities. In her wishful reality and by dint of considerable projection, she transforms her mother into a wickedly vain, envious, and vengeful woman who thinks nothing of destroying her own "innocent" flesh-and-blood. The super-narcissistic stepmother is now the split-off bad mother and the punitive maternal superego who, because she is greatly feared as well as loved, is useful to the daughter in strengthening the repression of her rivalrous oedipal wishes. Thereby, both the control of the daughter's aggression and the future of her relationship with the mother whom she also loves and depends on are assured, and the appearance of the daughter's passive innocence is maintained. At the same time it is unconsciously understood by the reader, who cannot but be oedipally guilty to some extent, that Snow White deserves to be punished for her rivalrous and matricidal impulses; there is no fooling the superego, for like Jimmy Durante's nose and like the Shadow, it knows.

Freudian clinicians are familiar with this kind of life-historical narration by patients. Even when they allow, as Freud did, that many mothers do compete enviously and punitively with their daughters, they claim to know, or they confidently expect it to emerge, that in these narratives they are encountering a mixture of reality-tested and imagined object relations that have been given shape and content by the conflict of instinctual drive derivatives and restraining structures. And with respect to the immediate clinical situation, they know (they say) that they are encountering a blend of disclosure, warning, and resistance in the already forming transference. In these cases, and sooner or later, analysts are prepared to uncover (as they say) by interpretation some version of the core unconscious fantasy or storyline of Snow White. They have a sense that they have *the* answer to the question, "What is wrong?"

But this sense of closure is not incontestable, for there is an object-relations analyst, one who more or less follows the lead of Melanie Klein,[1] hovering over the Freudian analyst, saying that that's not it at all; in fact, the Freudian analysis of Snow White is pretty superficial. Really, it's an obvious case of the daughter's projection of the aggression of the Death Instinct. The mother's breast (her apple) is envied by the destructive daughter; envy leads by way of projection to spoiling the good breast (it is a queen with a poisoned apple); and the greedy incorporation of that now bad breast results in the symbolic murder of the daughter by the evil introject. Snow White is a fairytale version of a universal unconscious fantasy that has little or nothing to do with the attitudes and conduct of real mothers. The fantasy's source is in the paranoid-schizoid position of the first months of life. Only trivially, if at all, does it involve actual experience with figures in the external world and only secondarily does it involve the Freudian Oedipus complex of a much later and less deeply anxious phase of development.

To complicate matters further, there is a self-psychological follower of Heinz Kohut[2] pointing out that neither the Freudian nor the Kleinian has been attending adequately to Snow White's experience of her narcissistically disturbed mother. This is the mother who does not or cannot provide that gleam in her eye—of appreciation, admiration, confirmation—that is essential to the daughter's growth of a cohesive self, a self with the impetus and direction provided by vigorous and defined aims. By looking only in the mirror, that is, at her own self, this mother consigns Snow White to the dead, that is, to the realm of those with stunted, fragile, joyless, and inert selves. It is a case of the mother's poisonous lack of empathy and the daughter's arrested development and aimlessness.

What is one to do in this crowd before the analytic mirror? What should I do? Should I pick one line of interpretation, blind myself to the others, and declare that now I have the answer? If I did that, I would be deciding, on some combination of theoretical, temperamental, and professionally opportunistic grounds, to adopt a doctrinaire form of the identity of a Freudian, object-relations, or self-psychological analyst. Should I say instead, "All of the above," and not worry about the intrinsic confusions of eclecticism? There are more than a few psychoanalysts who do that, and they do it in a way that is evidently insecure, just plain flashy, or intimidating in its intellectual omnivorousness and anal-retentiveness—or is it phallic exhibitionism or grandiosity? Perhaps I should just steer clear of applied analysis altogether, and regard it as an inconsequential, inappropriate, inconclusive, and debased form of psychoanalysis. Or perhaps I should (as I have) involve myself in comparative analytic thinking-through of these three systems of thought and maybe others as well? But if I did that, what ground would be left under my feet? Where could I find the authority for my work? How would I know what was real? How defend myself against the criticisms of colleagues? How arrive at the sense of an answer?

For many years I did mainly restrict my interest in any form of applied analysis. I regarded that form of analysis as, at best, a poor relative of clinical analysis and something of a freeloader. Of late, however, my reading and my own clinical and theoretical efforts[3] have led me to realize that I have been avoiding some serious issues that go to the heart of understanding the nature of any kind of psychoanalytic interpretation, and in this essay I am beginning to try to correct the error of my ways.

Do I mean *"any* kind of psychoanalytic interpretation?" Is it also difficult to understand the nature of clinical interpretation, and is the difficulty the same as that I just brought up in connection with Snow White? I think so, and I am going to continue to try to persuade you that this is the case.

Severely narcissistic mothers and their daughters. The narcissistic mothers I have singled out for consideration are those who may be described as malignantly devoted to stunting not only their daughter's development of sturdy self-esteem but their capacity for satisfying relationships with their fathers, siblings, other girls and women, and the male sex in general—in other words, everybody. These mothers are divisive in everything they do. They use for all it is worth the dyadic or symbiotic strategy of divide and conquer. Some of their daughters rebel through promiscuity, eating disorders, addictions, geographical flight, or some combination of these. Others—the ones I am here concerned with—stay and submit. In the main they become "good girls" and remain "good girls" of the latency-age type. They are reticent, easily embarrassed, and sexually and socially naive, inhibited, and easily overstimulated. They are much like Snow White, except perhaps in some scattered, furtive, and rebellious sexual episodes that they themselves don't understand or take responsibility for. To the compassionate observer, they are the innocent victims of their mother's depradations, and the accounts of these depradations come across convincingly as so relentless and heartless that they may provoke even the experienced clinician to wince or choke up on hearing about the horror of it all, which horror includes witnessing the daughters' continuing attempts to idealize or at least defend these mothers.

How may we interpret psychoanalytically the life-historical narratives presented by these daughters? The Freudian view would have us say something like this: these daughters are conflict-ridden with respect to the libidinal and aggressive wishes that enter into their narcissism and object-relatedness; out of anxiety, guilt, and shame they are hiding behind repressions, and they are yielding ambivalently to something between a severe maternal superego and a persecutory introject; they yield by becoming obedient, oedipally sexless latency-type girls as well as, on a deeper level, passive, innocent, preoedipal infants. There is an additional factor that is related to the positive libidinal strivings of these daughters: by living out their own fantasied castration by the phallic mother, they are able to identify with their fathers, whom they see as castrated victims of these mothers, and thereby they are able to adopt a partly gratifying bisexual position in the ostensibly horrible mother-daughter relationship and to cling to it tenaciously.

Or should the accounts of these daughters be interpreted, as earlier I interpreted Snow White, in the object-relational or self-psychological mode? At least in the schematic fashion I have been following, it would not be difficult to develop these alternatives—breasts both poisoned and made poisonous by the daughter's projections, glares rather than gleams in the maternal eye, and so on. How to decide? How to choose or synthesize? How to define oneself as analyst? As a being in the world, or in any world? How to tackle such large theoretical issues? Or whether to.

Can these analysands say anything to help the analyst decide? The conventional psychoanalyst says they can and do; one has only to listen closely to analysands and be guided by what they say. Each school of psychoanalysis claims to be fairest of all in that it presents itself as based on listening that is far more acute, empathic, and rigorous than its rivals' modes of listening. But is it the case that the psychoanalyst simply listens to the analysand? If so, and despite large areas of agreement among themselves, why then do psychoanalysts disagree with one another so often and so strongly? Could it be that each of them is just interpreting the life-historical narratives of analysands in the same way he or she would interpret Snow White, that is, in an applied way and with ready-made interpretations? Could it be that the analyst approaches the analysand as sets of stories to be retold in terms of the storylines provided by preferred analytic theories? These unsettling questions don't go away just because analysts repress or disavow them.

The rhetoric of narcissistic men. These men do not take readily or kindly to the analyst's interventions. They say, "I never thought of that," as though the first order of business is to determine who comes up with the ideas, or, if not that, to announce surprise that anyone else would have something of interest to say about them. Also in response to the analyst's interventions, they say, "That could be," in a tone that suggests that they are going to weigh each puny intervention on a very grand scale of judgment before reacting to it. Often, they repeat the analyst's interpretations some time after they have been made, not only as though they themselves have been the first to think them but as though they should be admired by the analyst for their achievement. They cannot hear or retain what the analyst says if the analyst interrupts, speaks at any length, or develops a point along a line they have not initiated and authorized. They respond to the analyst as something of a bore, reminding one of the definition of a bore as someone who is an expert in your own field. Often these narcissists say, "I don't know what this means" and "I can't figure that one out," and never once do they allow themselves even to think of asking the analyst for guidance or interested participation. In these cases, it seems for a long time that the analyst can aspire to be nothing beyond the status of a minor and intrusive expert.

What is the psychoanalytic meaning of this rhetoric? Do these men feel castrated by their vain, competitive, and controlling fathers? Are they also victimized by their own pathological ego ideal formation, a development that is attributable to the impossibility of their ever satisfying vain fathers who cannot take genuine pride in themselves and who undermine their sons by their ruthless competitiveness? Are these men also repetitively enacting the life-historical story of how they had to develop defensive grandiosity in order to deal with the helplessness and hopelessness they felt in relation to their nebulous, masochistic, and ungiving mothers, the kind of women who are more than likely to be married to men of their father's type? And are they simultaneously enacting their full retreat from their oedipal desires for these mothers who, typically and obviously, are unhappy, isolated, and sexually unfulfilled in their marriages? Are the grandiose aspirations of these men being played out in spectacular feats of rhetorical and other control and controllingness that inevitably reek with anal sadism, and is their anality intensified by submissive wishes to be the castrated recipients of the love of their unreliably involved but idealized fathers? These men's narrations of their childhoods, their dreams and slips and defenses, their struggles with guilt and shame, their responses to Freudian interventions, all are likely to bear out these interpretive conjectures concerning the psychoanalytic import of their rhetoric.

And yet, to indicate only one alternative view of this rhetoric, one could say that, in their rhetoric, these men manifest Kohut's disorders of the self as well as any analysand could: deprived and traumatized by mother and father alike of developmentally crucial empathic mirroring and holding up of attainable ideals; forced into the compensatory construction of grandiose selves; in the analysis, using their power of control to protect their fragile nuclear selves against further traumatization by the analyst who might make interpretations ill-suited to their inner experience and tolerance; anal sadism present as a by-product ("disintegration product") of their disturbance of self and not as a central dynamic; not so much conflicted as deprived, wounded, frightened, and self-protective. On this view, each of these men must use this rhetoric in order to survive with whatever self he can muster and to keep it on hold for that improbable future occasion when it might be safe to let it begin to grow. How well this self-psychological account fits them, how warmly the less damaged of these men will begin to receive it as time goes on, and how amply they will confirm it with more life-historical narratives of the same sort, provided that these interpretations are imparted to them slowly, appropriately, and empathically and that they are allowed to appropriate the interpretations in their own characteristic way for as long as they need to.

Again, we seem to have to confront the necessity of making a difficult choice. With regard to each clinical group, I have been applying the language and logic of different theories to roughly the same or similar descriptive phenomena. In each case, however, it could be said that it is as though I have been interpreting a story in a book or that I have simply been retelling one story in the terms of another. What is clinical here and what is applied? The disturbing questions of knowing and knowledge remain before us in clinical practice as in applied. The sense of an answer eludes us. To get any further, one must, I think, take up questions of first-person speech, statements of intention, and the nature of the psychoanalytic dialogue and its interpretation.

The Sense of an Answer

Does psychoanalysis accept and rely on the authority of first-person speech? Does the pronoun *I* spoken aloud carry special weight in establishing the authentic presence of the speaker? Are the analysand's first-person locutions sufficient or even necessary for purposes of both grounding and verifying the analyst's interpretations? Is it essentially through what the analysand says aloud in the first person that the analyst arrives at the sense of an answer to analytic inquiries? If, in response to an intervention, the analysand says, "That's not what I meant" or "That was not the result that I intended," is the psychoanalyst then required to revise the intervention? Is closure guaranteed by the analysand's assertions?

These questions may seem pointless to those familiar with clinical analytic work, the obvious answer to each of them being "No." The familiars know that, for one thing, speech may be inauthentic in its being deliberately or unconsciously misleading, incomplete, or biased. They also know that a good deal about what is in fact the case according to conventional judgment is communicated nonverbally through expressive movement, silence, and certain forms of acting out, and also communicated obliquely in narratives about others; and they know, too, that any of these other communications may contradict what is being or has been asserted explicitly in the first person by the analysand. Additionally, they accept the conclusion Freud[4] reached in "Constructions in Analysis": an accumulation of indirect responses of various sorts, such as slips, dreams, reminiscences, and transferences, may add up to proof that a reconstruction of early experience is valid even though the analysand has produced no certified memory of that piece of personal history. And finally, not to go on too long about this one issue, those familiar with clinical analysis know that at extreme moments in any one case, or as a rule in certain extreme cases, the analysand may be present in body but psychically absent or incommunicado. Thus, first-person speech is inherently problematic. To a noteworthy though lesser extent, this conclusion also guides ordinary social intercourse, where hearing is not always believing.

And yet it has been said, and it has often been implied, that there is all the difference in the world between clinical and applied psychoanalysis in that, in applied analysis, "there is no patient to talk back." To refer to the patient who talks back is, however, to imply some debatable presuppositions. First, it implies that in doing applied analysis, one can have one's own sweet way with the material at hand because that material is utterly passive and because there are no criteria for verification of applied analytic interpretations, the consequence of these conditions being that if one is clever, one will find it easy and safe to do applied analysis. In contrast, the clinical analyst, confronted by first-person assertions and responses, cannot do both a good job and escape the rigors and deep experiences of clinical work. On this view, applied analysis is more like a flirtation, a rape, or a forced feeding than a total, interactive, and caring relationship. Additionally, reference to the patient who talks back presupposes that clinical interpretation is simply empirical, inductive, objective, and verifiable by known and independent criteria within the psychoanalytic dialogue; in contrast, applied analysis is a derivative and speculative enterprise that is parasitic on the clinically well-grounded theory of psychoanalysis. Thus, in the absence of a patient who can talk back, applied analysis is a monologue, not a dialogue with built-in, scientifically sound verificational feedback. It is lower in the hierarchy of psychoanalytic practice.

In making this case for back-talk, analysts are according a special place to the spoken words of the analysand. They are granting much authority to the analysand's saying yes and no to the confessions, disclosures, rememberings, and shocks of recognition that are delivered with the presumed authenticity of first-person speech. Indeed, analysts do often grant this same authority to their analysands when, in order to make their own argument more persuasive, they quote them; it is common for the analyst to say or write, "As this patient put it so well . . ." and to follow with a quote whose unexamined "eloquence" is intended to put the finishing touches on an argument and establish the sense of an answer. For example, "Now I know that there was poison in mother's kindnesses" or "It is better to be a star in the gutter than an undistinguished workhorse." In each case, the analyst speaks or writes as if "that says it all." Not only is there a sense of *an* answer; this is *the* answer.

Evidently, then, analytic thinking about speech, interpretation, and verification presents inconsistencies or paradoxes. Something vital seems not to have been thought through. The comparisons of clinical and applied analysis that follow are intended to deal with this difficulty, and they will involve some clarification of the theory of psychoanalytic interpretation, the relation of theory to practice in psychoanalysis, and the criteria of proof and truth that are customarily invoked in psychoanalytic work. Although what will be offered adds up only to a small selection of observations, critical remarks, and suggestions, the consequences for our understanding the nature of psychoanalytic interpretation will not always be on a small scale.

For present purposes it will be useful first of all not to take for granted any sharp commonsensical boundary line between clinical and applied analysis. Let us rather assume provisionally that there is only one psychoanalysis and that its practice encounters a variety of problems the nature of which will depend in each instance on the details of the specific content being defined within the specific context being established. The methodological step I am urging requires us to concentrate on sameness rather than difference, congruence rather than divergence, interpretation in general rather than particularized versions of it. This will be a psychoanalytic world without parasites or freeloaders. Taking this methodological step should help us begin to see clearly what clinical analysts have in common with those critics and critical theorists who, in recent years, can be said to have been having a love affair with psychoanalysis. Are these critics and theorists just being reckless romantics, frustrated creative writers, or emotionally deprived academics looking for thrills in applied analytic work, or are they, as I believe, engaged in fundamentally sober, even if often evidently ambivalent, common cause with clinical analysts?

At the beginning of my main text, I questioned the authority of presence in speech. I referred there to misleading as well as communicative aspects of speech, silence, and other nonverbal actions in the analytic situation. At that point, I was already implying a perspective on the analyst at work, namely that he or she takes everything in the analytic situation as a text that requires interpretation or that might, by suitable interventions, be developed to the point where it is enough of a text to yield to a psychoanalytic interpretation. Ordinarily, the analysand's professed intentions, while they must count for something, do not by themselves settle any question of analytic meaning or significance. Like any other text presented to the world, the analysand's text does not remain in his or her control. Once uttered or enacted, it becomes public property in the world of psychoanalysis and part of that world's possible histories. The analysand's declaration of intention is itself very likely to be taken as a text—for example, as defensive rationalization, a false lead, or a gesture of appeasement.

At most then, the analysand is used as a consultant on his or her utterances, and the consultation is itself considered to be further interpretable text. For the most part, this consultation is carried out not under the aspect of privileged opinion or insight; it is carried out by way of the analyst's interpreting the analysand's further free associations. Thus, the analyst treats the analysand in the same manner that many literary critics treat authors, that is, with interest in what they say about the aims of their writing and the methods they have employed, but with an overall attitude of autonomous critical command rather than submission or conventional politeness, and with a readiness to view these explanatory comments as just so much more prose to be both heard as such *and* interpreted.

Now, there is nothing psychoanalytically radical about this view of psychoanalysis as a form of text interpretation. In one respect, I am merely restating an analytic truism. The truism holds that for purposes of developing insight through interpretation, one cannot rely simply or directly on manifest content or what is readily available consciously to the analysand. For instance, one does not interpret, let alone accept at face value, manifest dream content or accept the analysand's direct dream interpretations as conclusive communications about aims and meanings, just as one does not take the manifest wishfulness of a daydream as an unmediated or uncompromised expression of a primal wish. In another respect, I am only restating Freud's criteria for the verification of reconstructions: verification is established by an accumulation of indirect or implicit responses, *the kind of responses that become evidence only upon interpretation, further analytic dialogue, and further interpretation.*

To take clinical analytic work as text interpretation is to establish the analyst as an influential co-author of the analytic text that is being interpreted. The text, in other words, is never fully delivered to the analyst; rather, it evolves out of the analysand's and the analyst's interpenetrating contributions.[5] Increasingly, the two of them inhabit the text of the analysis, and at times it does seem that cohabit would be the best word for it. Cohabitation is what follows from throwing into question manifest content, including manifest avowals of intent and other such "explanations." In the end, the text and its interpretation are not distinguishable. If, as I claim, it is the case that I am restating psychoanalytic truisms, analysts should not find it difficult to grant this much about their work of interpretation, and yet many or most analysts still balk at accepting the ideas of text analysis and co-authorship when they are stated this baldly; for it may seem to them to undermine their sense that *the* answer exists *in* the material and is to be *uncovered*; the latent lies *under* or *behind* the manifest; psychoanalysis is a *depth* psychology; and so on.

To agree that analysts interpret interpenetrated or cohabited texts is to accord to constructivism and its corollary, perspectivism, an essential place in psychoanalysis and to put into permanent question the traditional psychoanalytic claim to the status of an empirical, inductive, objectively observational science. Constructivism and perspectivism are theoretical positions on what one can and should mean by "reality" or on the sense in which we can "know" reality. Constructivism is the position according to which the world we claim to know objectively is not given directly to perception and reason. Rather, reality is constructed according to rules; these rules are usually implicit but ascertainable through critical study, no matter whether they are known to the constructor or not. People follow these rules in observing or making observable whatever it is that they go on to say is in the real world. Broadly viewed, these rules are pretty much the same among members of the same culture and historical period, although the selection, comprehension, and application of the rules are more or less individualized. Hence, the cultural diversity within conformity or conformity within diversity that we generally acknowledge and more or less accept. The result is not reality plain but a perspective on reality or, more exactly, *reality by means of a perspective.*

According to this epistemological position, there is no coherent, sense-making way to approach a text, indeed there is no way to say what the text is that is to be approached, other than by constructing reality by means of a particular perspective and using consistently the language that manifests this perspective. However vulnerable the perspective may be to deconstructive demonstrations of its incompleteness and inconsistencies, and however much it may overlap other perspectives, it is distinguishable from other perspectives by criteria that are accepted by some segment of the critical community. On this basis, Freudian, self-psychological, and object-relational perspectives are taken to be different by most members of the psychoanalytic community.

To present perspective in narrational terms: a perspective is made up of more or less coordinated sets of storylines that allow one to state in a followable way what is being counted as a relevant and significant fact; these sets of storylines also imply the special appropriateness of certain methods of fact-finding and they indicate how best to use these methods; and the narratives they generate also enact the kinds of organization of facts that are to be considered legitimate, important, coherent, and complete.

Instead of the terms constructivism, perspectivism, and narration or storyline, one often encounters words and phrases, such as paradigms, models of the mind, leading metaphors, or just plain theory, being used to grapple with the same issues of knowledge of reality or how to arrive at the sense of an answer.

On the view I am espousing, Freudian theory specifies and authorizes certain technical methods for eliciting and defining certain phenomena and then organizing them serially and hierarchically within increasingly abstract levels of conceptualization and clinical generalization; and Freudian theory requires that all of this be done differently from the way things are done by the analysts of other schools. For the sake of consistency, coherence, and completeness, and for the sake of a sense of Freudian identity, this requirement of difference has to be met. In the case of self-psychological theory, for example, there is plenty of difference from the Freudian: the self-psychological theory has no instinctual drives or primary stages of infantile psychosexuality; it has little or nothing in the way of defense or resistance, internalized object relations, and tripartite psychic structure. The phenomena elicited or defined by means of the self-psychological perspective are dependent on the unique integration and limitation of the technical procedures that it authorizes. Self psychology is rule-governed as is Freudian psychology, but the rules are different enough to establish its identity.

For the most part, I shall be employing in what follows the Freudian perspective on constructing the psychological reality of human beings. More exactly, however—and to establish my general thesis this point cannot be overemphasized—I can remain only within one such perspective, namely, my own version of the Freudian perspective, as that is all I can reasonably claim to have. There are Freudian versions of the Freudian perspective that differ from mine. This heterogeneity explains why at their meetings conventional Freudians continue endlessly to schedule panel discussions and symposia devoted to traditional concepts and problems, such as the meaning or nature of transference and acting out. It also explains why they disagree with one another at clinical conferences and in their evaluations of colleagues and trainees. The conventional Freudian texts vary to some extent from one analyst to the next. Conventional analysts develop more or less different versions of the basic Freudian storylines of infantile psychosexuality, aggression, anxiety, guilt, self-esteem problems, danger situations, maturation, and so on. Consequently, it takes interpretation just to say what is essential to Freudian thought, and no one interpretation is the final one. There is no way to avoid being put in the position of having to confront on demand the extent to which one's assertions are saturated with perspectivism and constructivism.

If it is so that the analyst co-creates analytic data, that analytic observations make sense and attain significance only within a perspective, and that only by the analyst's following, each in his or her own way, some more or less systematized and coherent set of basic storylines, then there can be no successful defense of the traditional Freudian image of the analyst. In this image, the analyst is a straightforward inductive empiricist, an objective and independent clinician who simply observes what analysands set forth and draws the inevitable conclusions. Interpretation, then, is indistinguishable from inevitable conclusion and final closure. That image is one of a number of possible images of the analyst but it is one that is defensible only relatively, that is to say, it is defensible at all only if it is taken to mean that the analyst is probably more objective about the analysand than the analysand's relatives. The traditional image has become a joke. It depends on blindness enforced by anxiety before authority. That image may now be seen to be a naive, precritical, or unreflective representation of the analyst; it may be seen to be a coercively repressive and anti-intellectual representation as well. It is the image one finds easily in the implicitly authoritarian rhetoric of what may now be regarded as the old school of Freudian analysis. More important, however, the image is presented more or less subtly in the polemical presentations made by members of *every* school of analysis. The fairest of them all: analysts who can still tell us confidently in each instance exactly what's what; they seem never to have heard of or taken seriously constructivism and perspectivism, visions or versions of reality, heterogeneity and self-contradiction at home or abroad. They stand for the image that all but some of the youngest analysts have grown up on, and so there is still widespread reluctance among analysts to put this image up in their intellectual attics along with self-preservative instincts, psychic energy, and certain sexist psychoanalytic generalizations that trivialize women in relation to men.[6]

On the basis of the preceding discussions, it would be just as warranted to recommend viewing clinical analysis as a form of applied analysis as to continue viewing applied analysis as parasitic on clinical analysis, for clinical work is thoroughly, even if inconsistently, regulated by theory. Clinical interpretation makes manifest a prescribed perspective; it has its method, its language, and its own preferred sets of storylines. True, psychoanalysts present it as a plain fact that clinical analysis often facilitates personal change for the better, in whatever terms best suit the individual case. As an engaged clinical Freudian I would not contest that presentation. But the further claim is then made or implied that for this reason psychoanalysts occupy some position that privileges them to make and follow their own laws of knowledge and to ignore the history and current states of general theories of interpretation.

In contrast, it is being argued here that clinical analysis is not a thing apart and that nothing specific follows from this presentation of effected personal change. So far from that change being an independent or unambiguous variable, it is part of the initial conception of what analysis is. That is to say, change cannot be used to validate clinical interpretations, for the final account of change, far from being theory-free, is shaped and presented in the terms of the methods, the storylines, and the interpretations of one or another psychoanalytic perspective. Each perspective, theory, or paradigm presents change at least somewhat differently, and owing to its regulative effect on technical practices, each perspective seems to bring about somewhat different types of phenomena, with theory-specific implications, that can be taken to indicate change for the better. This is why debate between schools of analysis over their relative effectiveness are never resolved and may be unresolvable, even if still worth debating.

It is perhaps easier to see how the analysis of very young children may be regarded as a form of applied analysis. In that kind of analytic work, play and other behavior, much of it nonverbal, can be grasped and used analytically only by bringing to bear, on this less-than-ideal type of material, analytic theory that has been much more thoroughly worked out in the analysis of adults.[7] The quality of being applied is also not too difficult to see in analytic approaches such as the old-fashioned Kleinian and the cruder Freudian and self-psychological, in all of which one encounters tedious sameness in the occasions and contents of interpretive intervention, and in the Kleinian case particularly what other analysts regard as an overabundance and excessive depth of theory-dictated interpretation of rather limited amounts of material.

Hardest of all of the cases to see as applied (at any rate, hardest for me) is modern and subtle though still theory-laden Freudian clinical analysis, owing to its *relatively* greater tolerance for prolonged ambiguity and freely wandering association, its *relatively* sustained interest in eliciting rather than imposing fantasy material, its exploring *relatively* more fully spontaneous shifts of subjective experience and memory, and its *relatively* greater interest, however ambivalent, in new theoretical possibilities.

What now can be said of that presumably privileged person, the patient who talks back? A case has already been made for the assertion that talking back does not encounter a passive, yielding, unquestioning analyst. Yes and no, right and wrong, yes but, not quite, that's off the wall, and so on: the analyst can always and does often take these responses by analysands as further analytic material and tries to do so in the thoughtful and artful way that Freud began to outline in his paper on constructions in analysis and that he often illustrated in his case studies and clinical examples. That is to say, the analyst can try to find some analytic interpretive way to assess the relevance and coherence of these responses by analysands and thereby convert them into evidence for the interpretation that has already been made.

For example, a male analysand promptly forgot an interpretation that explained why certain repressions of previous analytic interpretations had been occurring. The interpretation was this: by his forgetting, he was acting out a fantasy of defectiveness. His forgetting this interpretation of his forgetting was transformed by the analyst into further evidence in support of that very interpretation, and at that moment the analyst was transforming it into evidence in the crucial context of the transference; subsequently, the analyst was able to construct the interpretation that the analysand was enacting the fantasy of being castrated into defectiveness by the analyst's cutting interpretations. An analyst with a different perspective might have transformed this forgetting of interpretation into something else. I will presume to speak for Kohut[8] and say that he might have made it into evidence for the traumatizing effect of, first of all, the interpretation of repressive defense and the implication that the defectiveness was only a fantasy, contrary to the subjective experience of the analysand, and, second, the implication that the analyst knows better than the analysand the truth of the analysand's self-experience. All of which, being exceedingly unempathic, must have led to some further fragmentation of the analysand's fragile self and thereby to his inability to retain or retrieve the latest interpretation. Briefly, the analyst's interpretation was more of an assaultive rejection and devaluation than anything else, and the self of the analysand was being iatrogenically traumatized and fragmented.

Another example is that of the analysand who became very angry in response to an interpretation. The analyst used that response, along with other factors, as evidence that the interpretation's correctness was threatening to the patient and that this threat was being warded off by anger. In this instance, however, the anger could have been interpreted differently even if still in keeping with the general Freudian perspective; for it could have been argued that the interpretation was premature or that one of the effects of the previous interpretation had been to lift the repression of anger itself. And the angry response could have been interpreted in still other ways according to other analytic perspectives (e.g., the interpretation was superficial or unempathic, therefore frightening or disappointing, and therefore angering in either case).

My examples are intended to suggest how evidence is created by analysis. Contrary to the empiricist-analyst's view, my view is that evidence is not served up on a platter, nor does it reach out to grab you by the throat. Although it is easy to note back-talk, it is difficult to prove unassailably or reach a firm consensus on just what it is that is being said. Psychoanalytic claims about what is being said and why (insofar as these are distinguishable) are essentially contestable.

Lest it seem that I am presenting the analyst as completely closedminded once he or she has made an interpretation, I must point out that interpretations are often and appropriately offered conjecturally; the analyst delivers them in a way that implies that alternative, supplementary, or revised possibilities of interpretation are still open to consideration. The ideal analyst is well prepared to defer having arrived at the sense of any answer at all.

It is necessary to return now to more direct comparison of applied and clinical analysis in order to deal with another sense in which one can take the statement that only in clinical analysis is there a patient who can talk back. In this other sense, the patient can talk back by showing change for the better, change for the worse, or no change at all, however each is defined in the specific case. For ease of exposition, I shall refer in the following remarks only to change for the better; this discussion should be readily applicable to change for the worse and no change at all without my spelling out those applications.

In connection with talking back by improving, one can argue that after all analysis is a therapy; its goal is to help the analysand improve. In contrast, an art work does not require therapy and the goal of applied analysis is not so much to change the art work for the better as to help its audience understand it and appreciate it better. Properly considered, the art work does not talk back. On this view, if it could talk back, it would have no right to do so, as it is not sick. But this argument is unhelpfully simplistic in that it does not do justice to the process and the results of both therapy and applied analytic projects, and it misconceives the relationship between an art work and its audience.

On the side of therapy, to deal with that first, I have already mentioned that there always has been and probably always will be room for controversy among analysts concerning the changes brought about by analytic therapy. Analysts would generally agree that among the forms of resisting there are flights into health, manic defenses, and transference cures, all of which may create false impressions of resolution of conflict and disappearance of symptoms in a lasting way.[9] The analyst may therefore disagree with the analysand when the latter insists that things have improved greatly as a result of deeper understanding. The analysand's first-person testimony cannot be decisive in this respect.

Furthermore, analysts are likely to differ with one another in the way they apply such concepts as transference cure to a series of suggestive cases where more data are available than the analysand's explicit first-person testimony and also the testimony of the treating analysts. And even in the case where all analysts would agree that there has been change for the better, they could not be expected to be unanimous about the degree of such change, nor would every one of them be likely to describe the change and explain it in precisely the same way, especially if they belong to different schools of analysis. For example, conventional Freudians do not usually accept the benefits of self-psychological treatment as true psychoanalytic results, seeing them rather as the benefits of supportive psychotherapy or as transference cures. On their part, self psychologists are quite ready to redescribe and reexplain the benefits of Freudian analysis in the terms of self psychology; they portray these benefits almost as accidental by-products of good intentions hampered by poor technique based on poor understanding. Furthermore, many of the changes in question are not measurable at all, for how can one measure subtle yet highly important improvements in the patient's quality of life, the patient's vision of reality,[10] and his or her adaptation-enhancing integration of personal life-historical narratives? Upon reflection, therefore, it cannot be convincingly argued that talking back through recovery is a reliable and unambiguous feature of clinical analysis.

Turning now to the side of the art work—say, a poem—one may question the flat assertion that applied analytic interpretation of a poem is not therapy. Following analytic interpretation of the poem (or for that matter following any other competent interpretation of it), the reader may better experience the poem's structural unity, richness of meaning, and potential impact within the perspective provided. For this reason, one may legitimately say that the poem has become more alive and integrated; that it has been rendered available to enter into a more developed relationship with the reader, something more on the order of a mature, mutual, and modifiable relation of whole persons than one that features narcissistic aloofness and inaccessibility, schizoid weirdness, limitation to sexual organs, or something on that more disturbed and disturbing order. It would be arbitrary to insist that in consequence of interpretation only the reader has changed, for it can be argued that the poem changes with the reader as the reader becomes more expert. It is no longer the same poem. There is no determinate text of the poem.

Markings on a page—the last resort of the anti-constructivist—are not the poem: the markings do not by themselves make a statement; they do not demand to be read or understood in only one way; they do not even sound.

On this basis, one may speak of interpretive recuperation or recovery of the poem. This idea is not new to literary criticism. Many of today's critics accept the proposition that a poem exists within the individualized relationship between it and the audience. Although their accounts differ in certain respects, they do agree that in necessarily interpreting in order to read at all, the reader becomes a co-author of the text; and in making this argument, they have supplied the inspiration and background for my earlier argument that the analyst may be considered a co-author of the analysand's text. If, with the help of "applied" psychoanalytic understanding, along with other forms of understanding, the reader of the poem is better prepared to approach it as a particular kind of art work than he or she might have been otherwise; if, in other words, the reader is an integrated and competent member of one or more definable interpretive and narrative[11] communities and on this basis can draw on their conventions and observe their standards, then one might say that, in being psychoanalytically informed, the reader has been helped to bring about change for the better in both parties involved in the relationship. Among these features that are shared by psychoanalytic and other readings are the mixture of conventionalized and individual narrative and interpretive approaches and the *therapeutic consequences of the work.*

Furthermore, the art work may be said to exert therapeutic influence on its critically prepared audience by introducing it to restorative perspectives on reality and restorative opportunities for subjective experience and understanding not previously available to it. Freud learned from Homer, Shakespeare, & Co. just as he made it possible for them to become more than they had ever seemed and for their audience to learn still more from them. Independent cases can be made for Freud's perspectival finding what was there to be discovered in literature, for his having re-created literature in his own image, and for a continuing interpenetration of and tension between both of these, and the same can be said for his contribution to the utterances of analysands.

There are those, however, who might still want to argue for an essential and hierarchical difference in favor of clinical work. They would point out that in clinical analysis talking back by changing for the better is a more important achievement. It is more important in that it concerns human welfare directly. Going further, they might also point out that in clinical analysis, but not in applied analysis, there is professional obligation to bring about this change.

It is, however, not the case that the clinical analyst is obliged to get good results, however those are defined. The clinical analyst fulfills his or her professional obligation by trying conscientiously to help bring about good results. Any feeling of obligation beyond that of making a good effort should generally be viewed as disturbed and disturbing countertransference involving some combination of guilt, overidentification with the patient, rescue fantasies, defensive grandiosity, and so on. And on their part, critical interpreters of an art work have their own scholarly and technical obligations, too, even though the nature and extent of these are always being debated.

As to which kind of recovery is more important, that of a patient or that of an art work, there is no way to adjudicate that issue except in terms of values or ideology that are not intrinsic to the psychoanalytic project. Clinical psychoanalysis does not prescribe the health values that it abides by once it begins by mutual consent; psychoanalysts do not properly exhort the general public to be in analysis. Moreover, one cannot hope to encounter in this realm of judgments of importance, universal agreements one way or another.

Consequently, it is warranted to reject the argument that the patient's talking back through recovery (or through personal disruption or stasis) distinguishes clinical analysis from applied analysis. At the least, it is warranted to reject that argument in its absolute, extreme, and unarticulated form. If we do not let ourselves be coerced by tradition into attending only to differences, if we focus on sameness as well as difference, we can see that clinical and applied analysis have in common co-creation and interpenetration of interpretable texts or of texts-as-interpretation. Clinical and applied analysis emerge as versions of one psychoanalysis, there being no clear-cut parasitic relationship of one to the other. Both amount to the same work carried out under varied conditions. Clinical and applied analysts sink or swim together.

I am stating as my conclusion what earlier I recommended as a provisional assumption that could help us get on with the discussion, and yet, I maintain, I am not back where I started. Although I have not attained the sense of an answer, I have, I think, changed the sense of the questions that have arisen about applied analysis and stirred up some parallel questions about clinical analysis as well. But, of course, readers will not take my word for any of this, for they have been recreating this text from the time they started reading it, and they will have been developing their own sense of an answer to my arguments and perhaps decided that it would have been better if I had formulated other questions and other answers.

12

Towards a Literary Anthropology

Wolfgang Iser

I

Surveying the current state of literary theory in the space of a single essay can only be like taking a snapshot, and hence a great deal is liable to be left out. But perhaps it is best to begin with the fact that, for all the current discontent regarding theory, there is still much interest in methods of interpretation. From New Criticism right through to Deconstruction, this interest remains comparatively constant in spite of shifting preferences. Some methods find favor relatively swiftly, but this does not save them from an equally swift waning of their attraction, as is the case with Deconstruction, whose dominance is already fading in America. Its importance is due not least to its emphasis on textuality—a commitment firmly established by the New Critical practice of interpretation. Herein lies its structural kinship to New Criticism, for both approaches stress close reading—and indeed prominent advocates of Deconstruction have actually described it as the closest of close reading. Scrutinizing the text,then, is their common feature—irrespective of noticeable differences in execution—and so they take the text as something given, to be focused upon from different angles. These, in turn, are conditioned by cultural requirements and hence are subject to change.

One wonders, however, whether this is the only reason for the relegation of once prominent modes of interpretation, in the course of which process literary theory itself has become a tarnished endeavor. Literary theory—at least in the past—was conceived as providing the framework for methods of interpretation, which implies that its prime concern was model-building. It is, however, this constriction to model-building that has caused present-day literary theory to come under increasing fire. The criticism leveled against theory cannot be met either through the innovative claims of the individual methods or through their occasional

For Stanley Cavell

pretensions to universality, for no matter how new or how comprehensive they may be, or claim to be, they all depend ultimately on the existing text for confirmation of their claims.

It is therefore scarcely surprising that talk is now of pluralism or even a new pragmatism. Such talk is based on the conviction that perhaps after Deconstruction there can be no more generally acceptable concepts, so that all different approaches must be allowed free rein and the text—as something naturally given—must be continually related to situational requirements.

There are also trends towards breaking the confines of the literary text and extending insights gained from literature and art to the media at large. Behind this movement is the more or less conscious idea that literature and art are no longer the cultural paradigms that they were, as their function has shifted to the mass media which now truly represent our civilization. Without doubt this is a highly significant change of direction, for it touches on something that the merry-go-round of changing approaches has always left unquestioned—namely, the assumed validity of the literary text as a cultural paradigm. But what at present casts certain doubts on this trend towards expansion is the negative motivation behind its overstepping the old limits. Dissatisfaction is a good driving force, but it cannot provide a foundation for a theory to embrace the heterogeneity of the media in terms of what they signify. Thus it is not enough to make an eclectic transference of literary and artistic methods of criticism to the exploration of the media, but what does make the movement noteworthy is the fact that paradigms turn into such by virtue of their signification.

The body of literary texts is also a sign, the significance of which remains obscured as long as the canonized status of the text is left unquestioned. To mediate between the canonized text and the respective present is no longer the exclusive business of interpretation, in view of the fact that literature as a medium is also indicative of the needs to which it responds. In addressing itself to this issue, literary theory is bound to change direction. Instead of providing a matrix for model-building, it has to explore the sign-function of the medium, thus turning the text into a reflection of the needs in question.

Literature as a mirror, though, is by no means a new discovery and we are well acquainted with the multifarious types of subservience to which literature has been subjected down through the ages. The question, however, which now arises is whether literature—in relation to history or society—reflects something special that neither philosophies of history nor sociological theories are able to capture. No one will deny the indexical value of literature both for history and society, but what emerges almost incidentally from this fact is the question *why* such a mirror as literature should exist, and how it enables us to find things out. Since literature as a medium has been with us more or less since the beginning of recorded time, its presence must presumably meet certain anthropological needs. What are these needs, and what does this medium reveal to us about our own anthropological makeup? These are the questions that would lead to the development of an anthropology of literature. Literary theory would thus take on a new function, for it must be remembered that its now disputed status came about largely through its attempts to establish frameworks in order to counter a merely taste-oriented, impressionistic type of interpretation, and to provide models as a much needed impulse to legitimize literary criticism itself.

In so doing, it was exposed on two flanks to attacks which ultimately undermined its initial success. Insofar as it served to structure frameworks of interpretation, it became more and more an institution for model-building: insofar as it served to legitimize criticism, it tended more and more to draw on other disciplines, thus imposing alien orientations on literature, very often to its disadvantage. This applied above all to frameworks taken from psychoanalysis, Marxism, and social theory in the broader sense. Instead of subjugating the medium to theories successful in other realms of thought or social practice, we must make the medium the starting point if we are to pinpoint the indexical value it appears to possess. A literary theory with this aim will cease merely to provide models of interpretation, and instead will enable us to ask and perhaps to understand why we have this medium, and why we continually renew it. We may be able to draw our answer from studying the anthropological implications of texts, or in other words by developing literary anthropology as a paradigm for research. By using the special nature of this medium to open up insights into our human equipment, we shall make literature an instrument of exploration. Such an approach may even reveal what literature is and does, and at the same time it will automatically rid us of the thorny problem of having to examine what is literary in literature, or what is poetic in poetry.

Current structuralism still torments itself with the unwieldy concepts of "literariness" or "poeticity," without seeming to realize that this is simply the same old problem that plagued classical aesthetics. Our awareness that literature cannot be ontologically defined is a direct offshoot of the problems bequeathed to us by classicism. And so terms like "literary" and "poetic" merely disguise what in fact is the continuation of autonomous art in an age when art can no longer find its own justification within itself. Literature is not self-sufficient, so it could hardly bear its own origin within itself. What it is, is the result of its function. This was already apparent to Edmund Burke, who—although he was by no means a radical—in 1756, while Classicism still flourished, traced the Sublime and Beautiful back to their anthropological roots, thus impairing the "auratic" character of the work of art rather than confirming its classical attributes.[1]

Burke, however, can also be regarded as an exemplary warning against an anthropologically oriented literary theory, for he considered what he had exposed as the conditionality of classical attributes as being constants of human nature. A literary anthropology faces the same danger. The moment it passes off its findings as anthropological constants, or draws its heuristics directly from other anthropologically oriented disciplines—especially psychoanalysis—it will obscure, if not eclipse, the state of affairs to be investigated.

If there were really anthropological constants—and many people believe that there are—then history would be nothing but an illustration of them. Instead, historical situations continually activate human potentials, which issue forth into a history of their own variegated patternings. These cannot be exclusively attributed either to anthropological dispositions or to given circumstances, but they are products of an interaction, have a touch of singularity, and always exceed the conditions from which they emerge. The result of such interactions sheds retrospective light on potentials and on the necessity of their historically conditioned actualizations. Literature appears to modify anthropological dispositions to the extent that their otherwise hidden peculiarities come to light. For this reason it must not be subjected to received notions of cultural anthropology, devoted to investigating the structures of archaic civilizations, but requires a heuristics of its own, which will enable us to answer questions such as: Why do we need fiction?

II

Fictions are inventions enabling man to extend himself—a state of affairs which can be studied from various angles. If we ask what is the point of these inventions, we are confronted with the different uses to which they have been put, and will have to distinguish between the many fictions which pervade our everyday life and the fictionality of literature. Clearly they are not the same, but take on different forms according to their function, thereby implicitly revealing the different needs that they satisfy. The link between fiction and function is not, of course, a new discovery. It has always been to the forefront whenever attempts have been made to purge fiction of the taint of deception. As deception is generally for a specific purpose, even this negative charge is evidence that fiction is defined according to its use. The latter will determine whether judgment is positive or negative, but whichever is the case, it is clear that intention governs function and therefore form.

The process emerges vividly from two significant attempts made in the 19th century by Jeremy Bentham and by Hans Vaihinger to rehabilitate fiction. Bentham *thematized* it by introducing "fictitious entities" into epistemology as the unalterable modality for the given nature of all reality. Vaihinger *systematized* it by extolling fiction as the basis for the constitution of all reality. Bentham believed that he could distinguish between "fictitious entities" and "real entities" on the ground that "real entities" are given, though perceivable only through their mode of existence,[2] which, in turn, is a "fictitious entity," because there can be no factual correspondence to it *in re*. Vaihinger believed that fiction was the "consciously false" which constituted realities but then had to be abstracted from them in order to allow what has been constituted to perform its function.[3] Thus for Vaihinger, virtually everything was fiction, apart from human emotions, which were ultimately necessary as realities in order to prevent the whole world from being hollowed out into a fiction.

What is important for the present context, however, is not the individual statements of Bentham and Vaihinger concerning the use of fiction, but the fact that their respective concepts of its function led to very precise definitions. Historically, this precision is easy to explain, for fiction could only be rehabilitated in opposition to a tradition that left no doubt as to its negative nature—this was particularly true of the empirical tradition—and indeed Vaihinger actually felt it necessary to hold his work back for several decades because he did not think the time was ripe for his particular insights.[4]

Bentham's and Vaihinger's certainty over the use of fiction was conditioned by their attempts to counter the then current trends of thought, and if such certainty has vanished today, we are, as a result, much freer to perceive the variety of fiction's uses. It is no longer restricted to the epistemological confines to which Bentham and Vaihinger had to refer in their effort to rehabilitate it. At that time it could only justify itself as a mode of explanation in epistemological terms, as epistemology held sway in 19th-century philosophy.

But if fiction is seen as a means of explaining, or even as positing realities, then it relapses into that which it had already been in many of its historical and mythological guises—namely, "concord-fiction,"[5] a phenomenon which Bacon regarded as the psychological satisfaction of the human mind in creating certainty where "the nature of things doth deny it."[6] Viewing fiction as "concord-fiction" means identifying it exclusively with its explanatory function, which not only restricts it to a single use but also entails making it into the very object that in fact it is meant to explain. Thus fiction for Bentham is the mode of existence of all reality, while for Vaihinger it is the basis for constituting reality. Even if we do not regard these definitions as "concord-fictions" in the sense of what Frank Kermode calls "complementarities,"[7] fiction—against the background of its philosophical reevaluation—still remains a basis for something outside itself, which it is bound to be if its function is to explain. Indirectly, this means that the nature of the use decides what fiction is, and between fiction and its uses there is an interaction of reciprocal differentiation.

Explanation is therefore no more than a single, though classic instance, which was regarded as being *the* function of fiction, because it initiated a debate that had developed a history of its own.

The more fiction eludes an ontological definition, the more unmistakably it presents itself in terms of its use. If it is no longer confined to an explanatory function, its impact becomes its prominent feature. Impacts, however, can only be made on or within given contexts, which, in turn, condition the respective use fiction is meant to achieve. Thus the field of application is responsible for the differentiation of fiction. No matter what its constitutive presuppositions may be, fiction will always be a mode of exercising an impact, and what is effected will vary according to requirements necessitated by the context in question. As long as fiction is restricted to explanation, it functioned as "concord-fiction," which had to incorporate the inaccessible into otherwise familiar realities. If fiction, however, is conceived as a mode of impacting, the indefinability of our world is inscribed into it, and hence qualifies all its restriction-breaking as pragmatic necessity. Impacting as the pragmatics of fiction never loses sight of its situational function, whereas explanation as the semantics of fiction aims precisely to make its situational necessity disappear. Thus the pragmatic function unfolds the special use of fiction, and the special use determines the individual nature of the fiction.

It has always been assumed that fiction can produce realities. For Vaihinger this was an incontrovertible truth, which led to his formulating the law of "shift of idea."[8] Ideas, he assumed, pass through a transformation of their inherent potential. At first they are realities, because they are taken for the thing itself, though they were originally only devised in order to explain the thing. Once this latter fact is accepted, they change into hypotheses, but still with the insinuation that there is a certain reality which corresponds to them. Finally, these hypotheses reveal themselves to be fictions which—precisely because there is nothing that corresponds to them—condition the constitution of realities. In "truth," however, all realities for Vaihinger are just such fiction, even if their operational success makes them appear to be a reality and may therefore prevent us from realizing that they are fictitious. Wherever and whenever realities are produced, there are fictions involved.

The law of shifting ideas is in fact a continual rearrangement of the attributes of reality, and ultimately such a process can only function on the basis of an assumed distinction between fiction and reality. But discussing fiction on such a basis means taking up what one might call meta-standpoints which presuppose knowledge of this distinction. This tacitly assumed "knowledge" may, in turn, be a fiction, dictated by pragmatic needs, much as one finds in politics. The reality of politics is a striking example of fiction performing a double function. It is at one and the same time something masked and something unmasking: in the former case its claims to reality are challenged, and in the latter it gains reality by its critique, i.e., through that which it unmasks. Its reality then consists in its operative function, which therefore means that it cannot be identical to that which it produces. Consequently it is different from what it does and from what it brings about, and so a clear-cut distinction between fiction and reality is hardly to be upheld. For there is no transcendental stance which would allow us to distribute the predicates of fiction and reality according to a preordained frame of reference. To maintain such a distinction can only be an *asylum ignorantiae,* and therefore the solution which offers itself is to discard the time-honored, but by now frozen opposition of "fiction vs. reality" altogether in view of their interpenetration. Instead, we may perhaps conceive the fictive as a means of overstepping the given, which is bound to cause a transformation of what is.

Whatever the use of fiction may be, everything fictitious is something made, and making entails determinate intentions. Fiction is thus produced under certain conditions that demand consistency and that denote its referential nature. The referentiality is bound up with a discernible objective that fiction is designed to fulfill, and herein lies a major distinction between fiction on the one hand and illusion and convention on the other. Fiction is neither totally deceptive nor totally dependable. It is an "As If" indicating hypothetical presuppositions, which cannot be eclipsed no matter what disguise the fiction may adopt. The "As If" always aims at overshooting what is, and for this reason it has to have a certain direction, adumbrating by its referentiality the function it is meant to fulfill—a function which is conditioned by the context upon which the impact is to be made.

The ability to cause an impact is not totally derived from the use to which fiction is put, so that the question arises as to the extent to which fiction is actually capable of truth. To say that it is would imply that all traditional definitions must either be totally changed or at least so modified that their status is altered. Previous definitions vary according to the nature of the use, and irrespective of whether they are stretched to generalizations or narrowed down to individual cases, in none of its many applications does fiction depart so far from its function that it can be contained within the confines of a single definition—not least because its referentiality will decide on its use and on its form.

In Kantian philosophy the "As If" figures as the quintessence of everything thinkable, and therefore fiction is something to which there is no alternative. This is what makes it feasible for fiction to appear in an infinite variety of contexts, but especially where boundaries have been drawn and need to be crossed. Thus fiction is never more than the thinkable, and so is more comprehensive than any of the contexts that give rise to its function. In this way, and perhaps only in this way, is fiction a truth in our experiential world. It is a truth, however, not to be substantiated by any manner of proof, as its only backing lies in the fact that there is no alternative to fiction; out of this arises its potency.

It is clear from this glimpse of the "truth" of fiction that the latter is to be viewed from different perspectives which may relate to its function or to its necessity. The more pragmatic the viewpoint, the more differentiated will be the various uses: but if the focus falls on the necessity, then the clearer will be the nature of the "truth" as a lack of alternative to fiction. Both aspects are closely linked together. The lack of alternative, however, sheds no light on the multiplicity of uses, just as this multiplicity prevents the extrapolation of any generalized pattern of usage. Through the concurrence of functional use and capability of truth, fiction continually opens up the unforeseeable, and as such it offers a standpoint from which to investigate the anthropological makeup of man.

From all this we may draw a conclusion concerning the way in which fiction is classified. Many current definitions testify to a myopic view imposed not only by tradition and convention, but also by the various pragmatic functions. The idea that it is a deliberate falsehood, as Vaihinger still believed, is just one particularly vivid form of identification which is not fundamentally different from those advanced today by cognitively oriented linguistics.[9] But such reifications of its use do not in fact define fiction. If it allows us to penetrate the impenetrable to which it alone holds the key, then the lack of any alternative to it—as well as the impossibility to derive its nature solely from its function—should be reflected in all the various attempts to describe it. It is true that fiction largely coincides with its use, but that is only a half-truth, for fiction itself does not arise out of the context of its use.

As human beings' extensions of themselves, fictions are "ways of worldmaking,"[10] and literature figures as a paradigmatic instance of this process because it is relieved of the pragmatic dimension so essential to real-life situations. The fictionality of literature is not identical to the result it creates, but is rather a *modus operandi* which manifests itself in distinguishable acts.

III

These acts are marked by the fact that they are boundary-crossings, the concerted action of which sets literature apart from other types of fiction already described.

There are three basic acts: selection, combination, and self-disclosure, which for analytical purposes may be distinguished from one another, but which interact and so compose the underlying pattern of fictionality operative in the literary text. The act of selection makes inroads into extratextual fields of reference, and by disrupting them creates an eventful disorder, in consequence of which both the structure and the semantics of these fields are subjected to certain deformations, with their respective constituents being differently weighted according to the various deletions and additions. Thus each field is reorganized in the text, but its new form includes and indeed depends on its function in our interpreted world. This function now becomes virtual and provides a background against which the new structure may stand out in relief, thus giving focus to an intention underlying the "coherent deformation."[11] Furthermore, the act of selection splits up each field of reference, since the chosen elements can only assume significance through the exclusion of others—this being the precondition for the eventful disorder, the resolution of which demands the assembly of a new meaning.

The act of selection also culls elements from other texts, but the resultant intertextuality should not be thought of merely in terms of blurring distinctions, or simply transcending the text to which reference has been made. The segments alluded to in the passages quoted begin to unfold unforeseeably shifting relationships both with their own context and with the new one in which they have been transplanted. Whatever form these relationships may take, two different types of discourse are always present, and their simultaneity triggers a reciprocal revealing and concealing of their respective contextual references. From this interplay there emerges a semantic instability which is exacerbated by the fact that the two sets of discourse are also contexts for each other, so that each in turn constantly switches from background to foreground, becoming a theme viewed from the standpoint of the other and vice versa. The resultant dynamic oscillation between the two ensures that their old meanings now become potential sources for new ones. The text itself becomes a kind of junction where other texts, norms, and values meet and work upon each other; as a point of intersection its core is virtual, and only when actualized—by the potential recipient—does it explode into its plurivocity.

The structure pinpointed in the act of selection also underlies the act of combination. Here the boundaries that are crossed are intratextual, ranging from lexical meanings to the constellation of characters. Once again the process should not be mistaken for a mere act of transcendence, because the various clusters—whether they be words with outstripped meanings or semantic enclosures broken open by the characters—are inseparably linked together and thus inscribe themselves into one another. Every word becomes dialogic, and every semantic field is doubled by another.

Through this double-voiced discourse every utterance carries something else in its wake, with the act of combination duplicating what is present by that which is absent—a process that often results in the balance being reversed, the present serving only to spotlight the absent. Thus what is said ceases to mean itself, but instead enables what it is not said to become present. The double meaning engendered by the act of combination thereby opens up multifarious connections within the text.

A similar doubling effect comes about through the literary text's disclosure of itself as fiction. This occurs on two different levels: that of the attitude to be imposed on the reader, and that of what the text is meant to represent. If the literary text reveals itself not as discourse, but as "staged discourse," asking only that the world it represents should be taken as if it were a real world, then the recipient must suspend his or her natural attitudes to the thing represented (i.e., the real world). This does not mean that the natural attitude is transcended, for it is still present as a virtualized background against which comparisons may be made and new attitudes may take their shape. If we regard the world of the text as being bracketed off from the world it represents, it follows that that which is within the bracket is separated from the reality in which it had been embedded. Consequently there will be a continual oscillation between the bracketed world and that from which it has been separated. The former, therefore, becomes a medium for revealing what has remained concealed in the empirical world, and whatever may be the relation between the two, it is the "As If world" that brings about the interplay between them.

Thus self-disclosed fictionality as an act of boundary-crossing causes the recipient's natural attitude to be doubled by a new one that is demanded of him or her, while the world of the text is doubled by that from which it has been bracketed off, and whose reverse side is thereby brought to the fore.

The various acts of fictionalizing carry with them whatever has been outstripped, and the resultant doubleness might therefore be defined as the simultaneity of the mutually exclusive. This formula may help us to describe the structure of the fictional component of literature. It also allows for certain distinctions that are pertinent to the literary text, for example setting it off from structures which govern our everyday world but are outstripped by the coexistence of what is mutually incompatible. The coexistence of the mutually exclusive gives rise to a dynamic oscillation resulting in a constant interpenetration of things which are set off from one another without ever losing their difference. The tension ensuing from the attempt to resolve this ineradicable difference creates an aesthetic potential which as a source of meaning can never be substituted by anything else. This does not imply that the fictional component of literature is the actual work of art. What it does imply is that the fictional component makes the work of art possible.

Yet fictionality is only an instrument that channels the necessary flow of fantasy into our everyday world. As an activity of consciousness it taps our imaginary resources, simultaneously shaping them for their employment, and so the interplay between the fictional and the imaginary turns out to be basic to the heuristics of literary anthropology.

But what *is* imaginary? This has always been a thorny problem, even for those philosophers who were traditionally regarded as sceptics and of whom it has been said that their scepticism generally helped to eliminate unanswerable questions as pseudoquestions. What David Hume called synonymously "fancy" and "imagination" he saw as "a kind of magical faculty in the soul, which, tho' it be always most perfect in the greatest geniuses, and is properly what we call a genius, is however inexplicable by the utmost efforts of human understanding."[12] The imaginary defies discursive definition not least because it cannot be isolated but only exists in connection with something else, forming an indivisible alloy.

This can be borne out by important examples. As Hume, Kant, and Wittgenstein demonstrated in their different ways, perception could not take place without a proportion of imagination. Perception functions neither as factual recording nor as pure concoction. Above all it is the continuity and the identity of the object perceived that can only be established by way of an imaginary ingredient, for the actual impression of perception can only come about in relation to non-actual perception. This process has been summed up as follows by P. F. Strawson, referring to Kant:

Insofar as we have supplied anything like an explanation or justification of Kant's apparently technical use of "imagination," we have done so by suggesting that recognition of an enduring object of a certain kind *as* an object of that kind, or as a certain particular object of that kind, involves a certain sort of connection with other nonactual perceptions. It involves other past (and hence nonactual) perceptions, or the thought of other possible (and hence nonactual) perceptions, of the *same* object being somehow alive in the present perception.[13]

There is a similar argument in Wittgenstein. If seeing functions primarily as "seeing as," then the object is identified with the aspect under which it is perceived. Mary Warnock interprets this as follows:

In concentrating on the particular kind of seeing which he [i.e., Wittgenstein] calls seeing an aspect he has done two things. First he has linked at least *this* kind of seeing (or hearing) with knowing or having concepts; and in some cases he has linked it as well with the use of the imagination. Secondly, he has connected the actual use of images with some cases of aspect-seeing and has strongly suggested their use in cases of recognition . . . We may therefore quite legitimately argue that he has raised again the question raised by Hume and Kant as to the role in *all* perception (not just aspect-seeing) of the imagination; and that the connexion between perception and imagination is through the image itself (for the notion of aspects and that of images are, as he says, akin). Whenever seeing and hearing seems to take us beyond the actual immediate object of the sense . . . there it looks as if Wittgenstein . . . has left room for the imagination.[14]

These arguments, advanced in the analytical tradition, counter the suspicion that the imaginary is nothing but a problem of discourse, or that it is simply a prerequisite for a heuristics necessary to literary anthropology. Instead it is evident from both Kant's and Wittgenstein's assessments that the imagination is not a separable faculty, but exists in combination with other faculties and indeed can only operate in conjunction with them if they are to function adequately. This, of course, does not tell us anything about the nature of the interplay, or why the imaginary portion is necessary for the production of a stable perception or impression of the object. It only tells us that these non-actual or aspectual "images" have to precede objects in order for us to perceive them as such.

A quite different philosophical approach leads to a similar conclusion. Jean-Paul Sartre considered the imaginary as an ideational activity, the unfolding of which is due to its being governed by consciousness. This holds true even for the dream, where consciousness is frozen as pure ideation and consequently deprived of its intentionality. Thus for Sartre the dream is the complete realization of a self-contained imaginary, as he puts it, whose total dominance removes all freedom from us.[15]

The same applies to madness and hallucination, but even here a preliminary ideational process is involved during which consciousness loses its freedom, although such images could not exist if consciousness were not present, albeit in a state of paralysis. Madness, hallucination, and dream feature a certain tangibility of the imaginary by swamping the intentionality of consciousness, thus indicating a tilt in the balance between conscious and imaginary components.

In daydreaming the slant given to the interpenetration of the conscious and the imaginary is again different. What we sense as diffuse, discontinuous, or associative strands are qualifying features of an ideational activity in which intentional directions have paled to insignificance. In all these cases, the kaleidoscopically changing relationship between the conscious and the imaginary condition the shifting patterns into which are ideational activity is cast. In fact, the latter arises out of the intimate permeation of the conscious and the imaginary, just as the continuity and identity of the perceived object issue from the interpenetration of actual and imagined non-actual perceptions.

It is evident from the experiences described above that the imaginary cannot possibly be regarded as a *materia prima* that merely has to be processed. On the contrary, it only exists in combinations, i.e., with sight, with consciousness, and hence in forms through which we establish contact with the world. But it is precisely because the imaginary can only be grasped by way of its contextualization that we are tempted to try and define it by isolating it.

If we look at the most significant of these definitions that have sought to capture the imaginary in its history, we will be struck by a phenomenon that has already emerged from the Kant, Wittgenstein, and Sartre examples. The imaginary has long been considered as a tangible manifestation of perfection, and it was assumed that art only allowed man's participation in it. This concept was virulent up to Nietzsche, who regarded art as an urge to transform our phenomenal world to the pitch of perfection. Such ideas radiate a knowledge as to what the imaginary is, but they mark it off in contradistinction to reality, whereas in fact it counters and compensates for reality, thus being conditioned by what it is supposed to transcend. The contrast which is integral to the definition completely ignores the dependence.

The same is true of those concepts that view the imaginary as "otherness." In the traditional invocation of the Muses, this otherness can be grasped as inspiration and invention. It enables something to come into the world that had previously not existed, and so its appearance is able to bring about an impact which could not be deduced from that which already is. In relation to the empirical world, the imaginary as otherness is a sort of holy madness which does not turn away from the world but intervenes in it.

But even when definitions are more rational or analytic, their referentiality remains integral. If the imagination is seen as a faculty, which is the case from Kant to Coleridge, it assumes its shape by presenting itself either as the organizer of interacting conditions of cognition, or as the unending repetition of nature in the human mind.

If the imaginary is equated with the unconscious, then there has to be consciousness in order that the errant offshoots of fantasy can be experienced. And finally if the imaginary is desire, then there has to be what Jacques Lacan calls "mirror stage" which the self projects of itself, because the imaginary is the reverse side of the self which can only be made palpable through a mirror image.

Whether the imaginary potential is viewed as perfection, otherness, the organizing faculty of cognition, unconscious fantasy, or desire, every one of these ontologically oriented definitions shows that it can only be grasped by way of its function and so in relation to contexts, which may be a counter-image to existing realities, a world shaken by inspiration, an organized interplay of cognitive faculties, an explanatory schema for the interpenetration of the conscious and the unconscious, or a deprivation that cries out for expression. None of these historical concepts makes the imaginary into *materia prima* that merely has to be processed, and although all the definitions, being discursive, aim primarily to capture the imaginary as a determinate phenomenon, they also demonstrate clearly that it is viewed in the context which enables it to take effect. For in all the definitions mentioned it has something of the character of an event; it acts as a counter to imperfection; it changes the world in which it appears; it combines the cognitive faculties by interrelating their various functions; it wanders fantastically through the conscious mind; and it overturns the barriers to desire by way of a mirror image. In its eventfulness, the imaginary reveals itself only as a function and never as a substance. It precedes what is, even if it can only show itself through what is.

From this roughly sketched history of the various notions designed to capture the imaginery, there emerges the fact that the latter will take on different forms according to its varied performances in different contexts, and so it may reasonably be assumed that the literary context will again give rise to a different type of manifestation. Hence we may rule out the idea that the imaginary is nothing but a heuristic construct, concocted for the purpose of making a theory of fictionality work. On the contrary, here as elsewhere there is indisputable evidence that such a potential exists.

IV

The history of the concept reveals to what extent the imaginary is given a perspective slant by the contexts within which it manifests itself. It may seem therefore as if the latter were nothing but a setting subservient to the appearance of the imaginary, whereas this supposed subservience in fact conditions the precise manifestation of the imaginary and shapes the *form* of its presence. This holds equally true for the interplay between the imaginary and the fictional, the latter providing the medium for the imaginary to assume a tangible gestalt. It is inherent in the nature of all media that they point to that which they themselves are not. The fictional—as I have outlined elsewhere—is an "As If" construction, which goes beyond itself in order to act as bearer for something else. In so doing, it imposes a perspective upon that which it is not but which it bears. Therefore the imaginary, which is manifested through the medium of fictionality, also has a form which reveals the perspective imposed upon it by the medium. The fictional and the imaginary thus interpenetrate, with the medium giving form to that which it is not, and at the same time ensuring the manifestation of that which it is not by imposing a perspective on it.

We have seen that fictionalizing acts as boundary-crossings should not be taken as a process of transcending, but, rather, of doubling, because whatever has been left behind is dragged along in the wake of the individual acts and remains a potential presence. This is what constitutes the basic doubling structure of fictionality in literature. Moreover this doubling structure is of a more comprehensive nature, for it always repeats an extratextual world within the text, thus establishing a simultaneity between the repeated world and the reason for its repetition, or sometimes even presenting two worlds in coexistence, as evinced by the 1500-year-old tradition of pastoralism.

There is a striking similarity between the doubling structure of fictionality in literature, and those phenomena of perception described by Strawson with reference to Kant. The continuity and identity of the perceived object are established by actual perception being doubled by non-actual, the combination of which generates evidence that the individual object has been properly perceived. On the basis of this experience, literary fictionality appears to be a paradigmatic manifestation of the imaginary. For if the imaginary must always be bound up with something else (e.g., sight and consciousness) in order to be revealed, then its ideal manifestation is in the doubling structure of literary fictionality. If the imaginary can only be presented by way of a medium, then obviously it cannot be totally equated with that medium. It will always be something "other." And if the medium itself is a doubling structure, not only will it link the imaginary to something determinate which it cannot itself be, but at the same time it will reveal that the positions which have been doubled are bound, through this very doubling, to be changed. The positions cease to represent something determinate, and instead they begin to adumbrate something which they themselves are not. In this way both their status and their function undergo a change, simultaneously featuring both their structure and its undoing. In this manner they become a matrix for what might be termed the interplay of constantly shifting "figurations."

It must be pointed out, however, that the manner in which the fictional dominates the imaginary is not the same as that which prevails in acts of perception and consciousness, where the imaginary is functionally related to and therefore absorbed by the respective pragmatic use. The doubling structure of literary fictionality gives presence to the imaginary as a diversified play of transformation which liberates it from all directly pragmatic links. In acts of perception and ideation, sight and awareness must be doubled by the imaginary, while the doubling of literary fictionality is the distinctive medium for the imaginary, whose presence consists precisely in the fact that it enables us to view things differently from what they seem to be.

Now if fictionality is the medium of the imaginary, the question naturally arises as to how we can ultimately distinguish the one from the other. Certainly the medium gives a particular perspective to the mode of manifestation, but the latter could not be described if medium and mediated were identical. If we define fictionality as a doubling which conditions the presence of the imaginary, the doubling itself can only come about because there is a difference between the things doubled. Indeed this difference is the very origin of the doubling, and whatever may be the individual nature of the double state of affairs in literature, the difference itself remains both intangible and ungraspable. It is the hollow space between the world repeated in the text and those fields of reference from which that world is extracted; it is also the space between the discourses, semantic enclosures and lexical connotations of the text, and finally it is the space between the world represented by the "As If" mode and that for which the "As If" mode acts as an analogue enabling conception. Fictionality gives presence to the simultaneity of the mutually exclusive, thus becoming the medium for the imaginary, but the imaginary, as we have seen, cannot be fully equated with the perspective imposed on it by the medium. It manifests itself, rather, as a difference that cannot be deduced from the medium itself. This difference spotlights the imaginary as resistance to conceptualization.

As literature does not allow the imaginary to be absorbed into the pragmatic applications of the real world, it enables us to concentrate our attentions on the nature of our human resources. It is not subjected to any premature definition but is simply present in all its multifarious forms, the exploration of which is a basic objective of literary anthropology. Relieved of all practical constraints, literary fictionality can exploit the imaginary in any number of ways. It can allow its inherent consciousness to be swamped by the imaginary, or it can freeze the imaginary into a purely cerebral configuration. Between these two extremes are innumerable possibilities, and indeed this very freedom of play turns out to be a basic category for capturing the protean potential of the imaginary. Play also structures the interpenetration of the fictional and the imaginary, without determining the relationship which unfolds itself in a veritable welter of games. It simultaneously allows us to reverse the games we play, and thus erase the definite imprint made on the relationship in order to manifest the imaginary differently. As play precedes any control exercised by thinking, the interplay between the conscious and the imaginary highlights the fact that neither exists independently of the other. There are no formal boundaries to this interplay, even though every literary work plays the game in its own particular way. Indeed the game itself becomes a means of making present that which defies definition, while those elements of the imaginary that are to be observed through the literary work can only be mirrored forth by way of the game.

V

If the interplay between the fictional and the imaginary forms the heuristics of a literary anthropology, the question arises as to what objectives such an anthropology is supposed to have. The question might be tackled from a pragmatic, a systematic, and an historical point of view.

Pragmatically such an approach would seek to diagnose human conditions. The text as a cultural object would then become a sign for the mastery of a situation and hence for the clarification of those potentials that must be mobilized if mastery is to be achieved. From this would emerge a physiognomy of history that would detach itself from its political, economic, and social features because, as elements of the prevailing culture, these provide the conditions for the necessary funneling of fantasy into that culture, thereby revealing the reverse side of what thought and social systems have claimed as their overriding validity in the cultural context. This uncovering need not be confined to stressing deficiencies—it may also bring out desires, needs, and necessities which may now take their rightful place by courtesy of fantasy.

In systematic terms, a literary anthropology would allow a reappraisal or even a reopening of an issue apparently long since decided on by the Aristotelian tradition as to the nature of human faculties. The assumed clear distinction between imagination, reason, and the senses, as settled by faculty psychology, crumbles when applied to literature. Literature draws its life from interaction between imaginary, conscious, and perceptual activities, and appears to have no clear basis or origin in any one of these "faculties." If one takes the clear-cut distinctions of faculty psychology as a framework, literature appears to merge them in a protean coalescence. Imaginary, conscious, and perceptual activities constantly inscribe themselves into one another, in consequence of which the "faculties" appear condensed or distorted, transfigured or mirrored, dramatized or subverted.

This implies a certain "family likeness" between literature and dream, which gives rise to the question why basic dream structures recur so insistently in literature. What is repeated, however, never remains precisely the same in the repetition, and literature is not merely a copy of the dream but, rather, facilitates something which is not possible through the dream itself: access without fear to that which is inaccessible.

The "family likeness" may also suggest that dream and literature are not dependent on each other so much as being different manifestations of a common stock. Such a suggestion is supported by the fact that literature reverses the retrogradient movement of the dream into one that is progradient: instead of repeating archaic conflicts, it opens up new possibilities. Literature appears to entertain a transgressive relationship to the dream pattern in the sense that it steps out of what it repeats. Repetition comes to full fruition by exceeding the repeated, otherwise it remains lifeless and sterile. If literature repeats the dream, a doubling is bound to occur, resulting in a change of perception; we are caught up in the dream, and what we live through is made by the repetition into an object of observation. But what can be observed can also be changed, and indeed *is* changed by the very process of observation.

Finally, there is also an historical objective for literary anthropology. Research devoted to literature and the arts in the broadest sense was, as long as bourgeois culture held sway, closely associated with the formation of personality. In the latter half of our century the erosion of the idea of education as well as that of the significance of the individual has had far-reaching repercussions on the inherited canon, whose validity was challenged to such a degree that a total abolition of disciplines concerned with interpreting literature and the arts was considered to be in accordance with current social interests.[17] The study of literature as practiced by the various academic disciplines had its justification in opening up the treasures of a book culture whose benefits they were meant to spread. For the disciplines were committed to developing humanity, and to training human faculties in order to promote the ennobling of man.[18] In view of the fact that these ideas no longer apply, the question arises as to whether an anthropologically oriented study of literature is able to regain some of the importance of literature for our lives in the manner taken for granted by the scholars of yore.

Clearly literary anthropology does not want to provide that kind of education once promised by the study of literature. But instead it may achieve a self-enlightenment of the human being—not to be brought about by the erstwhile encyclopedic accumulation of knowledge considered to be a prerequisite for education, but by elucidating our unconscious guidelines, thereby triggering a chronic process of reflection which will no longer seek its fulfillment in some kind of ideal. Rather, this process will enable us to see through the attitudes offered to us, if not imposed on us by our everyday world. If at first its character will be fundamentally critical, nevertheless it will constantly bring to light our own situational premises, thereby exposing that which constitutes our outlook.

This, however, is a very cautious answer to the question of how literary anthropology might legitimize itself. It is cautious because it conforms to the social and cultural code of our time, which is predominantly critical. This is very evident today in America, where the trend is towards criticism of institutions and of power monopolies. It is to be hoped that there will not be a repetition of the process that took place in Europe in the late 1960s and early 1970s, when literary studies—because they were regarded as a medium for revolutionary institutional change—ceased to be important subject matter altogether. After this historical experience, the heirs of bourgeois culture must now see that the desire to change institutions through literature is nothing but a delusion.

Can literary anthropology ever be more than just another way of transposing the current critical code into an interpretative practice? Perhaps it may form the starting point for a task to be shared by all the interpreting disciplines in the humanities—namely, to work out a theory of culture. In view of the heterogeneity of cultures that the twentieth century has opened up to us, the need for such a theory seems to be particularly impelling. The task would not only endow the interpreting disciplines with a new goal, but would also restore to them the legitimacy that they have lost. Certainly such a theory could not be achieved by literary theory alone, but the study of literature can contribute to an interdisciplinary discussion both by stating problems and by identifying issues. As the product of a particular culture, literature draws life from tensions with and impacts on the cultural context from which it has emerged. It intervenes in its real environment and establishes its uniqueness not least by highlighting its otherness in relation to the situations that have conditioned it. In this manner it adumbrates new regions which it inscribes into the already charted topography of culture. For if what is, is not everything, then what is must be changeable.[19] It is this function of literature in the context of culture that moves the overriding objective of literary anthropology into focus.

Literature is not only the continual recurrence of the world in which we live, but it is also the reflection of what we are. For this reason it has been primarily conceived as mimesis. But no matter what definitions this term has been given in history, mimesis is always a repetition which produces something. Initially mimesis was thought to be the representation of the constituent forms of nature or the perfection of that which nature had left imperfect. Thus mimesis as a repetition is also an overstepping of limits.

How are we to understand this "overstepping"? The Aristotelian tradition claimed that the constitutive forms of nature existed, as did their perfectability through art, and so the two original impulses of the mimetic tradition implied the at least temporary absence of that which was to be represented. From the very beginning, therefore, the inherent tendency underlying the repetitions of art and literature was towards making the absent present. It can be said, then, that the recurrence of particular worlds in the literary text has always taken place on the prior understanding that it is a mode of staging what is not there, or that which is not directly accessible. Why have we created this mode of staging, and why has it accompanied us throughout our history? The answer must certainly be the desire, not to repeat what is, but to gain access to what we otherwise cannot have. We have no access, for example, to the beginning, the end, or the "ground" out of which we are: "Ich bin, aber ich habe mich nicht" ("I am, but I do not have myself").[20] The beginning and the end are extreme paradigms of realities that we can neither experience nor know. But there are also experiences such as identity, love, etc., whose reality is just as incontestable as the fact that we can never known precisely what they are. Evidently, however, we are not prepared to accept the limits of cognition, and so we need images to mirror forth the unknowable. These images are nourished by the ideas and desires that hold us in thrall, but they can have neither permanence nor enduring validity. As a consequence, their content, which gives shape to those inaccessible phenomena arising from and fashioned by the cultural context of the day, will be changeable. The images of that which is withheld from us thus reflect the potential range of the respective cultural reality. This is doubled by what we might call its reverse side, its inaccessible areas. The doubling brought about by literature in turn produces what is characteristic of all doubling: a change of perception. This does not mean that the cultural context changes; it is, however, translated into the dimension of its perceivability. The doubling, therefore, allows us to see ourselves in that within which we are entangled, and in this respect literature is a decisive means of shaping cultural reality. It must be stressed again that literature does not reflect this reality, but mirrors its reverse side, which would otherwise remain hidden by the cultural context itself, and it is the mirroring that conditions literature's formation of cultural reality.[21] By throwing into relief the uncharted regions of the prevailing culture, it changes the map, which is overlaid by the imagery of what remains cognitively unfathomable.

The interplay between the fictional and the imaginary provides the necessary heuristics for such an exploration. Fictionality in its boundary-crossing capacity, is first and foremost an extension of man which, like all operations of consciousness, is nothing but a pointer towards something other than itself. Basically it is void of any content and hence cries out to be filled, and it is into this structured void that the imaginary potential flows, because what is unavailable both to cognition and perception can only be given presence by way of ideation. Without the imaginary, fictionality remains empty, and without fictionality, the imaginary would remain diffuse. Out of their interplay emerges the staging of that which is unavailable to us.

If this staging is indeed a necessary alternative to what we are, the investigation of it would endow literary anthropology with an irrefutable legitimacy. Simultaneously a more far-reaching question would be posed as to why we cannot cease to create such images, even though we are aware of their illusory character, and know that they cannot supply the answers we are so anxious to learn. Historical experience shows that the validity of these imaginary worlds becomes increasingly short-lived if the staging merely features compensation for what has been withheld from us. Clearly the staging itself must not lead to closure, but must remain open-ended, if its spell is not to be broken. This historic observation testifies to the fact that we ourselves are the end and the beginning of these stagings, each of which is nothing but a possibility. What, however, does it mean that we find an insatiable pleasure in making ourselves into our own possibilities, and cannot—in spite of knowing what it is—cease to play the game of our potentials? It is to questions of this kind that literary anthropology has to address itself.

13

The Future of Theory: Saving the Reader

Christopher Butler

Humanism and Antihumanism

The background to my argument lies in the debate concerning the nature of the subject in recent Continental philosophy and theory.[1] It is a debate in which the avant-garde of theory has aimed to dislodge the notions of intention as predominant for interpretation, of the author as origin and authority, of the humanist subject as controlling the discourses a writer "uses," and of the presence of "character" within fiction.

The humanist position had appealed to the notion of an essential humanity. The narratives of history and literature were equally to be seen as the product of the thoughts and actions of natural subjects to whom one could attribute specific "characters" or "personalities," and who, however various and unique, produced acts which could be assessed in a generally negotiable moral language. The authority of this language derived from Kantian arguments concerning its universalizability. It relied on the notions of intention, choice, moral responsibility, and so on, and was thought to be generally negotiable, because, inter alia, it was thought to describe the mental processes of which individuals were capable, whatever the cultural or political contexts of their actions. Within this position, even the critique of society was ultimately focused in relation to the individual, so that even post-Kantian concepts like "alienation" and "reification," and existentialist "bad faith" and "inauthenticity," were interpreted at least partly as entailing the loss or perversion of this central human nature.[2]

The antihumanist attack on this viewpoint sees it as no more than a prescientific philosophical anthropology, interesting maybe as the description of supposedly desirable cultural practices, but not really capable of the claims to universalizability which underwrote it. The humanist attitudes sketched above are thus to be seen as an essentially changing ideological response to specific historical situations. In particular, men do not make history (or narrative) as the humanist would wish; for history when "correctly" analyzed can be seen to be an impersonal process without any subjects. A notion like alienation, according to Louis Althusser, is not an ethical, but an ideological concept, dependent on Hegel, which needs to be superseded by a scientific historical materialism. A knowledge of society cannot be based on our experience as subjects. This more "correct" analysis depends, of course, upon the substitution of another, dialectical master narrative whose nature as philosophical speculation or as economic "science" is far from clear. In particular, it is not obvious that any such "scientific" account is really wholly independent and exclusive of ethical discourse. But the main point remains: even the most resolute of humanist fictions will ultimately tell us, not about the unique human individual, but about the ideological systems operating through him or her. This argument need not be specifically Marxist: it is that way in Althusser, but the work of Claude Lévi-Strauss and Michel Foucault and Jacques Lacan can also be seen as "dethroning the subject" without needing any explicit commitment to a Marxist view of history.

Catherine Belsey, for example, contrasts the positions of Freud and Lacan from this point of view. She tells us that although Freud challenged the Cartesian basis of subjectivity, and so liberal humanism itself, his therapy was quickly used as part of "the bourgeois practice of analysis itself, which reintegrates the individual into society as it is." In depending on the concept of a "fixed unchanging human nature," Freudian analysis has been "the ally of a liberal humanism." The Lacanian "Copernican revolution," however, demonstrates for her as for so many other literary theorists, that "The unconscious is not a repository of biological drives but, like subjectivity, a construct, created in the moment of entry into the symbolic order, produced in the gap between the subject of discourse, the *I* of the *énoncé*, and the subject of the enunciation, the *I* who speaks."[3] And if we agree with Lacan and his followers that this symbolic order is phallogocentric, then the entry into it is crucially different for boys and girls. We can, if we wish, follow Lacan in showing how subordinating gender differences are culturally constructed. We, thus, have a psychological as well as a political attack on the humanist position, which attempts to revise preexisting notions of "human nature."

They can also enter into alliance; indeed the use of a Lacanian position to attack liberal humanism from the Marxist left is typical, since it is also supposed to dissolve the individual subject into the focus of the larger conflicts of ideology.[4]

It is this "larger" context of conflict and incoherence that the Marxist critic wishes to make the focus of attention in critical theory. Thus, Terry Eagleton asserts that "Liberal humanism has dwindled to the impotent conscience of bourgeois society, gentle, sensitive, and ineffectual," because it has an "essentially contradictory" relationship to modern capitalism. It "grossly overestimates" the transformative power of its discourse, because it considers persons in isolation from social context. It is "a suburban moral ideology, limited in practice to largely interpersonal matters," incapable of drawing out the "full implications" of its own position.[5]

The support for this view often enough comes (though not without qualification) from the antihumanist arguments of Althusser, who accuses humanist philosophy of subscribing to the fundamental postulate that there is a "universal essence of man" possessed by each individual, an "empiricism of the subject" conveying an "idealism of the essence." For

> Since experience is, by definition, what subjects have, and subjects are ideological constructs, it is impossible for subjects as such to have genuine knowledge. Any theory (Hobbes, Descartes, Rousseau, Kant . . .) which invokes the category of the subject as if it were epistemologically fundamental (as if subjects *could* arrive at knowledge) is itself ideological, since it takes the subject to be the source of that which is reflected in its "knowledge."[6]

Persons are the functional supports or effects of social processes, and misrecognize themselves in believing in their own autonomy and subjectivity. Althusserian and other Marxist analyses of ideology working through the individual are supposed to free the subject from this self-misrecognition. This is indeed a reasonable thing to do; but it does not necessarily lead to the privileging of a Marxist class analysis, as so many of its proponents seem to believe. For the self constructed by ideology may similarly misrecognize itself in other roles as well, for example those dictated by the current view of sexual differences. The logic of the Althusserian argument can lead us to attempt to free ourselves from more than one kind of misrecognition. It is, as we shall see, a separate question, whether the most *important* of these liberating aims involves an attack on class roles and their stratification as analyzed by Marxists.

In what follows I wish to show that what is basically at issue in this argument as it affects literature, is the status of "liberal humanist" moral concepts, and hence the size and abstraction of our frame of reference for persons, as Eagleton suggested above. I believe that the liberal humanist position remains in contention because underlying any such more extended framework, there is a human subject—however divided and skeptical about his or her own reliability as a "source" of knowledge or self-knowledge—who may be brought to *recognize* his or her class function or Lacanian internal divisions or sexual identity.[7] This is because, as Kate Soper argues, "morality" is not identical with "bourgeois values."

> It is just as implausible to suppose that conscious experience is the mere by-product or 'epiphenomenon' of social structures and economic relations as it is to suppose that the latter have no impact on its formation. Nor is it realistic to treat morality as a form of conspiracy arising with the bourgeois epoch. This is the line adopted by that 'crude marxism' which would have us identify 'morality' with 'bourgeois values' and view the latter as ideologically 'constructed'. But the suggestion that the moral attitudes suited to the maintenance of capitalism are inculcated into individuals by means of ideological 'apparatuses' must be resisted on several grounds. First, it denies the relative autonomy of moral feeling and action, much of which has little direct political consequences and may even be in conflict with the values dictated by the dominant economic rationality of the day; second, it invites us to view morality as a form of extrinsic repression of our 'natural' selves rather than as an intrinsic form of sensibility essential to any form of human coexistence; and third, it fails to recognize that we must be already creatures possessed of a certain distinctive moral sense if we are to respond to the pressures of 'ideology' in the first place.[8]

Her conclusion is that we should not dispense with ethics in favor of "theory," as if it were the "mere reflex" of other, essentially nonmoral processes. I am going to support this view with respect to literary theory, since I believe that the liberating political aims of the attack on humanism are in any case ultimately "moral" rather than "theoretical" ones.

This is because one of the paradoxes of the Marxist view of history as the conflict between classes, of which the individual can be no more than the allegorical representation, is that its teleology seems to look for the establishment of a society in which individuals mysteriously regain a Kantian subjective status. This line of thinking extends from the first chapter of *Das Kapital*.[9] Indeed, a similar hidden Kantian aim may be discerned even in Althusser; for if we play no part as individuals in the formation of the structures that constitute us, what point is there in our engaging ourselves in the attempt to alter them? If individuals don't have any status for the theory, what sense does it make to speak of them as "dominated" by social structures or of "liberating" them from them?[10]

Similarly, an acceptance of the Lacanian position surely gets its point or use from a political or clinical indication of the direction in which we could free ourselves from it. Indeed, from what position does Lacan himself speak? There is a paradox here too, particularly in the Lacanian treatment of the relations between the sexes, which might be thought to encourage women to engage in resistance to the patriarchal phallogocentric order he describes.

> If there is no prediscursive reality to which women (or men) can turn
> in the struggle against a patriarchal ordering of society, then the chal-
> lenge to the phallic status can only be made in language. But this implies
> nothing less than the construction of a different logic.[11]

Lacan thus produces an antihumanist notion of the subject, which still wishes to use the humanist rhetoric of struggle, victimization and loss.

What the moral aims behind even the antihumanist position seem to require then, is the *extension* of ethical discourse to a political dimension. We will see this in our exemplary texts in the following section, and also, briefly, in the feminist arguments they imply, which to my mind successfully politicize those interpersonal relations which have hitherto been secluded in the "personal" realm of the sexual. The aim is thus to reconstruct a reading subject who is not merely the bearer of class re-lations, or of dominant ideologies, or of a contradictory sexual identity, but who is worth saving. For it is one of my predictions concerning the future of theory, that the as yet unperceived interaction, rather than antipathy, between humanist and antihumanist theories will become more important. This essay is an attempt to clarify part of what may be involved.

Two Seductions

The two fictional accounts of seduction which follow show very clearly a tension in our thinking about persons; in particular that between our wish to think of ourselves as autonomous (as acting in accordance with our desires) and not manipulated by others, and, in this situation in particular, the threat that seduction poses to the autonomy of another person, precisely by manipulating them in the service of a sexual desire. (Which often enough in literature looks like that form of "aesthetic con-sumption" on which Henry James, for example, lays so much stress.) This demand, for the autonomy for the self and subservience of the other, reveals deep incoherences in our moral thinking which are parallel to the humanist and antihumanist arguments we have discussed. For the seducer sees himself as "free," and the other is subjected to the ideological structures through which we (as male narrators, usually) desire them. (The simplest and yet most worrying of these is the male gaze. She is seen as "beautiful" and therefore desirable. But her inter-preted beauty thus seen has nothing to do with her autonomy as agent. For we surely have a very limited responsibility for the qualities, rather than the use, of the bodies we inherit.)

The two texts I have chosen reflect, I think, quite different conceptions of human identity, which are broadly humanist and antihumanist. My first example, from John Berger's novel G,[12] "asks" to be interpreted according to liberal existentialist premises (with a humanist Marxism also presupposed) and the second, Donald Barthelme's short story "Alice," is symptomatic of that deconstruction of personal identity which is part of the postmodern aesthetic within which it is written. The implications of this opposition are immense, and in what follows I will concentrate on what seems to me worth most attention in future, because it is attacked by the antihumanist position, which denies any universalizable moral language to describe such relationships. My two texts are also, I believe, truly representative of a deep division within the culture surrounding contemporary experimental fiction; the liberal, which includes John Fowles, Mosley, Muriel Spark, and others, and the postmodern, which includes Walter Abish, Robert Coover, John Hawkes, and Leonard Michaels.

The hero of G is in many respects to be seen as Don Juan. In the passage I consider he seduces a chambermaid, Leonie, whom he has "pursued with notes, with jokes, with whispered conversations, with declarations of love and extravagant compliments" (131). But what Berger emphasizes within this rich man/poor maid context, is the apprehension of each other's individual identity, which is at stake for them, and ultimately for the writer.

> That he [G] had succeeded, that it was indeed she, Leonie, who was standing there, looking with uncertainty at him, was established once and for all in his mind by the most characteristic facts about her: her large fingers, her broad squashed looking nose, the coarse stringy wisps of hair escaping from under her maid's cap, her peasant's unpowdered complexion. (131 ff.)

The "ugliness" of this is presumably intended to suggest that G can escape some of the stereotypes of the male gaze. Leonie, on the other hand, sees G as a man rich enough to fly in an airplane (in 1910), but she, too, is chiefly impressed by his particularity, though, significantly enough, not as body but as agent: "She could distinguish . . . between a man who is begging for favors, or, alternatively, may try to grasp them, and a man who, in face of a particular woman, is compelled to present himself to her as he is. This is some of what she meant when she said to herself: he has come for me" (132). This combination of intimacy and strangeness is central. Leonie "is in danger of mortal sin" (134), and yet has a sense of unreality: "*It was like a dream*" (134). When G touches her, "She had the sensation that wherever his hands went they lifted her and took away some of her weight" (134). Berger turns to metaphor here, the most trickily particularizing of literary modes:

everything that she had been was turned to sand and shelved at the borders of this experience to disappear beneath its waters and become its unseen, mysterious lake bed. To express her experience it would be necessary for us to reconstruct around ourselves her unique language. And this is impossible. Armed with the entire language of literature we are still denied access to her experience. There is only one way of, briefly, entering that experience: to make love to her. (135)

This last comment reflects, I think, one of the most peculiar doctrines of liberal critics like John Bayley; the notion that love is a particular *kind* of intuitive apprehension of the other: "We desire in obedience to the fixed patterns of our sexual imagination, but we fall in love because we are really seeing another person,"[13] Berger is aware that the language of literature can never seize the individuality of the person, yet he wishes to suggest that making love may be an expression of it. It is an act of recognition of the other (as *pour-soi* in terms of language and as *en soi* in terms of the body, in Sartrean terms):

Your image covers the entire surface of his body like another skin. All your appearances surround his penis.

You have never seen yourself like this.

Looking at you, he recognizes you. His recognition cannot be put out. It burns what it recognizes. And by the light of its burning it recognizes more and more until it is so bright that it recognizes as familiar what it has never seen.

He has never seen you naked and now you are (136).

At this point the narrator reflects that "Some say of my writing that it is overburdened with metaphor and simile; that nothing is what it is but is always like something else. This is true, but why is it so? Whatever I perceive or imagine amazes me by its particularity" (136). Since his aim is to convey uniqueness, his metaphors are to be seen as coordinates for description, by "likening aspect with aspect" (137). His awareness of language and its inadequacy is seen as a model for his attempt to describe the experience of the lover going beyond language, as an appreciation of unique qualities.

But lovemaking, even if it has these virtues, is ultimately a means of escape from a larger context. For Leonie later realizes that G will leave her, and Berger attempts to specify a social context for this and the morality it implies:

For Leonie it was not hard to accept. The choices open to her had always been limited; she thought of most of the conditions of living as unchangeable; and so the idea of the extraordinary was central to her life. She was superstitious. (145)

But the analysis goes deeper than this. For the "extraordinary" also happens in an even more general context than this, which Berger describes in introducing the next amorous episode of G's life. The general reflections here on the status of women are strongly paralleled by his views on the way in which they appear in painting,[14] and show how the Marxist position we looked at earlier may be taken. For moral agents are always the bearers of social roles, and human relationships take place within a state of the historical evolution of those roles, as rich or poor, and equally importantly (as feminist criticism has shown) in relation to the body. Thus Berger says that "A man's presence was dependent on the promise of power which he embodied" (149), whereas "To be born woman was to be born within an allotted and confined space, into the keeping of man" (149). A woman is thus split, seeing herself in private as she really is, but also having to be perpetually aware of the way she appears to men:

> A woman had to survey everything she was and everything she did because how she appeared to others, and ultimately how she appeared to men, was of crucial importance for her self-realization. Her own sense of being *in herself* was supplanted by a sense of being appreciated *as herself* by another. Only when she was the content of another's experience did her own life and experience seem meaningful to her. In order to live she has to install herself in another's life. (149 ff.)[15]

Berger thus both denies and affirms class descriptions; for he tries to show how in sexual relations an appreciation of individuality may be achieved; and yet the context in which the encounter takes place denies reciprocity, since it is clearly determined by the class and sexual roles he describes. These compose a narrative order, which expresses an intelligible rationality of sexual motivation and response, and makes an assessment of moral responsibility possible. His novel provides a classic instance, from a Marxist point of view, of the tension between the particularity of character and the generality of "moral," "social," "sexual," and "class" roles in the liberal humanist literary tradition. For G bears not only his social roles but also, for the reader, the conventionally defined "character" of Don Juan. The reader sees him as condemned by the cultural traditions and ideals he exploits, to reenact with variations a given role.

The narrator of Barthelme's story, "Alice," is, on the other hand, a quite different, ironically viewed, "low mimetic" protagonist.[16] The erotic aim of his desire is essentially intermittent and blocked and the narrative of its achievement is independent of the rationalizing commentary provided by Berger.

> I want to fornicate with Alice but it is a doomed project fornicating with
> Alice there are obstacles impediments preclusion estoppels I will exhaust
> them for you what a gas see cruel deprivements SECTION SEVEN
> moral ambiguities SECTION NINETEEN Alice's thighs are like SEC-
> TION TWENTY-ONE . . . (123)

By a teasing reflexivity, he promises us the narrative direction of seduction, but threatens to deprive us of it: "Alice's thighs are like golden
varnished wooden oars, I assume I haven't seen them" (125). Indeed,
the promise (which is one of mere likeness, compare Berger's use of
metaphor) of "SECTION TWENTY-ONE" is deferred and differanced
by the "estoppels" of the text itself. For him, as for Lacan, "desire behaves
in precisely the same way as language; it moves ceaselessly on from
object or from signifier to signifier, and will never find full and present
satisfaction just as meaning can never be seized as full presence."[17] The
male seducer always desires *under a description*, which bears all the signs
of patriarchy. Nevertheless, the antepenultimate paragraph turns out to
be the promised SECTION FORTY-THREE, in which as we were earlier
promised, "the actual intercourse intrudes" and the object of desire is
thus described, up to a point:

> I began chewing Alice's long and heavy breasts first one then the other
> the nipples brighten freshen then I turned her on her stomach and
> rubbed her back first slow then fast first the shoulder then the buttocks
> . . . (130)

This is paid for by the (male) reader immediately, in a reflexive paragraph
which dissipates the narrative into a series of options and questions.
The text breaks out into a multiplicity of possible interruptions which
destroy all those individualizing and rationalizing explanations of motive
and effect on which a conventional story of seduction "ought" to depend.
The narrator is distanced from the object as he is invaded by

> possible attitudes found in books 1) I don't know what's happening to
> me 2) what does it mean 3) seized with the deepest sadness, I know
> not why 4) I am lost, my head whirls, I know not where I am 5) I lose
> my self 6) I ask you, what have I come to? 7) I no longer know where
> I am, what is this country? 8) had I fallen from the skies, I could not
> be more giddy 9) a mixture of pleasure and confusion, that is my state
> 10) where am I, and when will this end? 11) what shall I do? I do not
> know where I am . . . (130 ff.)

Part of his (and our) difficulty is that we are caught in two radically
different narrative modes. One of these is progressive but underdeter-
mined, in which the narrator begins "on West Eleventh Street shot with
lust I speak to Alice." The other, which recurs throughout the story, is

indeterminate and surreal—full of the verbal "noise" of images that keep interfering with one another, as in the conclusion to the story:

> cornflakes people pointing to the sea overboots nasal contact 7 cm prune the audience sense car correctly identify chemical junk blooms of iron wonderful loftiness sentient populations. (131)

The text, thus, finally breaks down into indeterminacy, first of motive and affect, and then of language. We were, in a way, warned that this might be the case at the beginning; and I think that this flow and conflict of discourses within the text may be designed to call into question conventional moral concepts like "regret." For the narrator's son Hans would be "insulted" by the narrator's desire to fornicate with Alice, and "whispers" that he is "faced with a problem in ethics, the system of the axiologists . . . but I am not privy to these systems." This despite "nights of ethics at the New School 'good' and 'bad' as terms with only an emotive meaning" (128). The notion of regret is "battologized" (i.e., needlessly repeated in speaking or writing) in the story:

> that's chaos can you produce chaos? Alice asked certainly I can produce chaos I said I produced chaos she regarded the chaos chaos is handsome and attractive she said and more durable than regret I said and more nourishing than regret she said . . . (123)

A postmodern "open work" like this asks the reader, as Umberto Eco points out, "to place himself deliberately in the midst of an inexhaustible network of relationships." The reader's attempt to preserve a coherent reading position, and thus a coherent identity, is dispersed amongst the competing languages of the text, by which he or she is thus decentered. None of these languages seems to be commanded or controlled by the narrator; indeed in texts like this "an incomplete knowledge of the system is, in fact, an essential part of their formulation." Indeed Eco sees this "tendency toward the ambiguous and the indeterminate" as "a crisis of contemporary civilization."[18] The crisis that it symbolizes is, I think, deeply involved in the conflict between the identities constructed by the humanism and antihumanism we outlined earlier. We can see how this may be if we contrast two sets of interpretative strategies for these texts, which demand quite different roles and identities for the reader, and attempt to construct quite different interpretative communities.

Interpretation and the Reader

Jean-Paul Sartre's *What is Literature?* may be taken to represent an extreme Kantian liberal position, an individualist existentialism against which (even in its Marxist form in the *Critique*) many antihumanists are implicitly reacting.[19] For him, the writer expresses his freedom in addressing the freedom of another, and draws his readers into a Kantian Kingdom of Ends. The text offers "a way out of the 'humanist' dilemma between being for oneself and being for others" for through it we transcend this conflict, so that we "are able finally to recognize ourselves in an object that does not objectify us in the sense of treating us as a 'mere object.' "[20] The text creates a social group which prefigures a socialist harmony, but also demands of the reader a coherent strategy of action.

> The writer has chosen to reveal the world and particularly to reveal men to other men so that they may assume full responsibility before the object which has been made bare. It is assumed that no one is ignorant of the law because there is a code and the law is written down; therefore, you are free to violate it, but you know the risks you run. Similarly, the function of the writer is to act in such a way that nobody can be ignorant of the world and that nobody may say that he is innocent of what it's all about.[21]

Here person confronts person via the text. For if no one is supposed to be able to excuse himself from responsibility, then there also has to be an implicit acceptance of the Kantian generalization argument. We are all assumed to be the "same" in the relevant respects. The nature of the reader with respect to the text is to be an autonomous moral being who treats others as equals. In recognizing the mimetic adequacy of the text to the world, it is accepted, for the purpose of a universalizable moral judgment, that there are no relevant differences between readers. The reader also accepts a position of responsibility, because in reading the text he or she is engaged with the world, in recognizing the likeness of the one to the other.[22]

Thus for Sartre any act of recognition that the generalizations Berger makes concerning sexual and social roles are adequate to fictional events which are sufficiently like those which may occur in our own everyday world, would force us (with the power of law) to accept that we should act appropriately with respect to them, and draw appropriate generalizing moral principles from them. Crudely put, if we accept that the male gaze supplants a woman's apprehension of the way she is in herself (her autonomy), so that she has to "install herself in another's life," then we, as readers emerging from the Kingdom of Ends produced by the text, should not act in the world to cause this "split" in identity. This humanist point of view is one with which many feminist critics would agree, and the desirable consequences of accepting it are a powerful (pragmatic) argument in its favor. For if we accept the Kantian humanist account of autonomy, and believe that the identity of persons should be unified as far as possible, and that deconstructing them in this way (which in the way Berger describes women, provides a nice parallel to the decentering analyses of Althusser and Lacan) is wrong, then we should resist the division of personality that sexual roles may cause, just as we should resist alienation in work. Here the political belief which accepts that persons may be decentered by conflicting ideological demands relies on the humanist moral conception of autonomy.

The mimetic adequacy of the test is, of course, not an unproblematic matter (as the work of Paul de Man and others has shown), and it is particularly so in the light of Berger's metaphors and Barthelme's surrealism. Furthermore, to adopt Sartre's prescription you have, I think, to be able to adopt another person's point of view and to see its coherence or incoherence in two senses: (1) as a plan of action (e.g., seduction, or resistance to male incorporation), so that a social role may at least construct an identity for particular types of action, and (2) to see how the implied principles of action here might agree or conflict with the moral principles involved in obeying the imperative of autonomy respecting autonomy.

Now although a reader convinced by Sartre may wish to derive Kantian rules from the text here, she or he will come up against the difficulty raised earlier by the Marxist argument. This is because the liberal humanist reader accepts that there is a point beyond which circumstances (and notably, social roles) are not allowed to alter cases and prevent the use of the generalization argument. For such a reader, it must always be possible to stand back from any situation and pass judgment on it from "a purely universal and abstract point of view," because "it is in the self and not in moral roles or practices that moral agency has to be located."[23] If it is not possible to stand back in this way, then the reader cannot make a general judgment of persons, but only of particular (past) roles.

For some Marxists indeed, there is always in practical action some aspect of social role and social context which *does* alter the case. Thus, G may be a Sartrean *lover* as he attempts to recognize the autonomy of the other. But he is far from a Sartrean or Kantian *seducer*, for in arriving at the exercise of a lover's virtues he displays (as Berger is careful to tell us) a rich man's lack of concern for the social consequences of his action (Leonie's sense of mortal sin and her broken engagement which Berger later mentions). And so Berger seems to privilege the role of lover, but very quickly recontextualizes even this with his reflections on men and womens' attitudes to the very bodies they bring to sexual relationships. But as I have argued above, even this can be brought to submit to Sartre's principles, if and only if we can be brought to believe in the desirability of a "humanist" autonomy under such circumstances, and refuse to submit to the antihumanist argument, that human nature is such that this autonomy is just not possible in the world as we know it.

I think that it is possible to see how this might work for Berger, but there are obvious difficulties here for the narrator of "Alice," who seems to lack any such coherent role (and to offer no more than a speaking voice to the object of his desire). We can see how this may be if we look at an alternative model for interpretation, which by focusing on language rather than character in the text, tries to construct a very different community of readers, absolved from any concern for a moralizing autonomy. This community is one proposed by Roland Barthes.

In *The Pleasure of the Text* Barthes is concerned in particular with those works which bring to a "crisis" the reader's relation with language, as does Barthelme's story, with its indeterminacy, its "inexhaustible" (and peculiarly indeterminable) network of relationships, and its surrealism. Here we are, as Barthes desiderates, adrift on a sea of semiotic systems. For he wishes us to accept that any writer, once within language is "always on the blind spot of systems, adrift, he is the joker in the pack, a *mana*, a zero degree, the dummy in the bridge game . . . . his place, his (exchange) value, varies according to the movements of history, the tactical blows of the struggle."[24] (Like Lacan, he thus attacks the notion that to enter into language is to enter into a state of individual sovereignty.) Even if one does not accept this *general* thesis concerning the writer in relation to language at all times and places, we can still see its application to the types of text I have exemplified. Thus, Berger adverts to the problematic of metaphor, but attempts to justify his narrator's control of it, whereas Barthelme expresses a psychological confusion which is, ironically enough, numerically ordered, and yet allows conflicting types of discourse to come together in his story, to the point of a hedonistic "chaos," which is "handsome and attractive" and "more durable than regret" and yet "nourishing." His story is symptomatic of the Barthesian/Lacanian lack of command of language (particularly if one takes its surreal elements as expressions of eruptions from the subconscious).[25]

In doing this Barthelme also teases us by resisting one of the panaceas of realism, particularly for an erotic tale of this type; that is, he denies us that pleasure of the text as the "corporeal striptease [of] narrative suspense" which Barthes ridicules by generalizing our desire for narrative coherence and final revelation in sexual terms. This desire, whatever one may think of its application to, say, the nineteenth-century novel as a whole, certainly seems appropriate to the texts we are considering. "The entire excitation takes place in the *hope* of seeing the sexual organ (schoolboy's dream) or in knowing the end of the story (novelistic satisfaction)" (10). This, for Barthes, is mere pleasure (as provided for example by Berger); but Barthelme aims at "bliss." For Barthes defines this in extremely significant terms of the subjecthood of the reader and of moral judgment. For the work of bliss not only brings to a crisis the relationship of the writer/reader to language, but through this allows us to participate

> in the hedonism of all culture . . . and in the destruction of that culture; he enjoys the consistency of this selfhood (that is his pleasure) and seeks its loss (that is his bliss). He is a subject split twice over, doubly perverse. (14)

The subject constructed by the texts Barthes here prefers, within the text and as reader of it, denies the holistic order, not only of realism but of that type of moral judgment that requires a (Kantian) unified self. Subjected to play, the reader is even indifferent to logical contradiction, and indeed the demand for "a psychology of consistency" is "legal terrorism" (3). One is immediately reminded of Sartre's reliance on just such a legal metaphor here, and this may well be part of what Barthes attacks. He goes on to make clear that the result of this isn't just a kind of polymorphously perverse liberal pluralism, a form of intellectual opportunism (though that is part of what game and play imply), but, in his view, a direct attack via the text on the Sartrean community we have described above. For he asserts that

> The pleasure of the text does not prefer one ideology to another. *However:* this impertinence does not proceed from liberalism but from perversion: the text, its reading, are split, what is overcome, split, is the *moral unity* that society demands of every human subject. (31)

And he seems in recommending this, to think that such a subject would have escaped from those discourses of power which combine to decenter the subject and deprive him of authenticity in the antihumanist account we have cited above. For the linguistic creativity and disorientation of the text of bliss, as in Barthelme's surreal lists, evades the language of power, which (as Barthelme says of battologized or repeated regret), is "statutorily a language of repetition." For

> schools, sports, advertising, popular songs, news, all subliminally repeat the same structure, the same meaning, often the same words: the stereotype is a political fact, the major figure of ideology. (40)

One would have to conclude that *G*, as a mere text of pleasure, provides us with just such (Sartrean) stereotypes. It fails to allow the reader to be that perverse and *happily* decentered being who has evaded coercive and stereotyping moral judgments.

The listing of the narrator of Alice's options (and his surreal lists) on the other hand, seem to me to *express* bewilderment, certainly, but also a sense that choices for action could only be made on emotive rather than on the principled grounds expressed by Berger. By this I mean that the position of the narrator in Barthelme's story exemplifies what he could have learned at the New School concerning emotivism in ethics, that is the view that all evaluative and moral judgments are nothing but expressions of preferences, attitudes, or feelings. If this is the case, no rational argument based on principles and rules of the Kantian or any other kind, can secure assent to one course of action rather than another. In acting we merely follow our desires ("shot with lust," for example) and our intuitions, and in reading as Barthes would have us, we aim at a purely selfish hedonism, which is rationalized as a form of self-liberating escape from social restraints. Furthermore, the emotivist will tell us that in judging actions we merely express approval or disapproval. There are no independent criteria we can appeal to in judging what it would be good or right to do. Alastair MacIntyre believes, indeed, that many of the actual practices of "modernity" conform to this model; we act as if emotivism were true.[26]

He also points to two further consequences of emotivism which are surely exemplified by texts like Barthelme's. Firstly, that "emotivism entails the obliteration of any genuine distinction between manipulative and non-manipulative social relations." These figure importantly in any narrative of seduction. Secondly, he comments that "the emotivist self can have no rational history in its *transitions* from one state of moral commitment to another. Inner conflicts are for it necessarily *au fond* the confrontation of one contingent arbitrariness by another. It is a self with no given continuities, save those of the body which is its bearer and of the memory which to the best of its ability gathers in its past."[27]

G has the ability to attempt a continuous, intention-dominated narrative, and the narrator of "Alice" doesn't, which leads me to observe that the emotivist account applies to Barthes's account of bliss and to the dénouement of Barthelme's story, which, is its lack of an ordering that could reflect the rational reflection of a single subject, expresses (admittedly in an exaggerated manner) just that decentering effect of conflicting beliefs that the antihumanist points to. For although the antihumanist theorist concentrates for strategic purposes on the conflicts between rather different types of discourse (of the conscious and the unconscious, of the conflicting social roles enforced by ideology, etc.) the emotional and moral confusion of attitudes in the narrator's list, and the juxtaposition of chaos and surrealism to it, expresses just the *same* type of conflict which may arise in a subject who is unable to arrive at the "humanist" position of a unified character acting in a coherent role.

Thus MacIntyre goes so far as to say that we simply don't know what an agent is doing if we can't order his intentions within an historical context, and that the intelligibility of an action depends on a narrative sequence (in which such intentions can presumably be ordered). Furthermore, he argues that narrative intelligibility and accountability presuppose the concept of a personal identity, and this presumably could not be of the decentered kind.[28] Barthelme's story brilliantly shows, as do other texts, like Coover's "The Babysitter" and *Gerald's Party*, what the world would be like if these assumptions were removed.

MacIntyre's position would, thus, lead us to treat the narrator of "Alice" as a pathological case, out of control of his language (as in many ways a traditional surrealist at least would want to be) and of his intentions. But the suggestion of pathology prejudges the argument in a way I am inclined to resist. For even if the decentered state of consciousness were psychologically real, it is a separate question whether we would prefer to treat persons (and texts) as if they were responsible for what they say.

I am not about to suggest then, that many (postmodernist) experimental works are bad because they neither contain nor imply any coherent moral commentary of the kind we found within G. The first of these options would hope for an authority within narrative which the philosophical conflict I am describing makes impossible. The second option of direct implication is equally unrealistic, if we wish to judge persons rather than simply express our pleasure or dislike at the presentation of (e.g., violent) events. This is because the antimimetic and contradictory presentation of the nature of the protagonist in the text denies such interpretations. To read such a narrative is to *experience* the loss of identity within the extreme antihumanist position in a way that is impossible for us in reading the (coherent) theory of it, which is often used to maneuver the reader into a less moralizing ideological position. (As we have already seen in section one, this maneuver in antihumanist theory may be paradoxically inconsistent, in that it is justified in the end by its attempt to free the reader into accepting a superior morality, which would free him or her from the decentering which the theory posits.) Thus, Berger suggests a way in which the experience of split identity in women may be approached, and a fuller analysis of this, and a means of liberation from it, may be given in feminist theory.

Conversely the account implied by "Alice" could be supported, by attacking the apparently coherent humanism of G (and particularly its appeal to metaphor) with a deconstructive skepticism. But the moral issues raised by this contrast seem to me to be of too great a pragmatic importance for us to allow our interpretations of these texts to collapse into theories concerning the adequacy of language, rather than looking at the subjects their rhetorics construct and the undoubtedly "going concerns" of the two communities which these texts and such interpretations of the subject would create. For even if a skeptical deconstruction of Berger were correct (e.g., by an application of Barthes's *general* theory of language to him), both the pragmatist and the existentialist could combine to argue that if we are to make "real life" interpretations of actions rather than falling into the infinite regress of questioning the ways in which they are described, we have to choose at some point what to believe about the *subject's* relation to language, even if this results in the end in our relying on a useful fiction. But how can we make such a choice?

A Pragmatist Moral?

Our analysis involves competing accounts of the nature of human nature. But these are only relative to one another, because they are, in fact, dependent on the analysis of different underlying historical narratives; of the rise of individualism, of the ideological burden of the individual under capitalism as seen by the Marxist, and of the quasi-mythical progress through the mirror stage into the symbolic order given by Lacan.

The first comment that a pragmatist would have to make about this is skeptical: neither account can claim to be a "true" account of "the nature of human nature," either as represented in fiction or in the reader. This is partly because the truth of the matter is not "out there" written into the nature of things, but depends on our changing descriptions of it. We may wish to go back (MacIntyre) or go forward (Althusser *et al*), but no philosophical account of the self is ultimately going to "win" by achieving epistemological certainty. We are thus looking at the ends served by competing language games.

The future is involved here, because language games supersede one another: "the vocabulary of ancient Athenian politics as against that of Jefferson, the moral vocabulary of St. Paul as against that of Freud, the jargon of Newton versus that of Aristotle, the idiom of Blake rather than that of Dryden." These examples are drawn from Richard Rorty, who continues: "it is difficult to think of the world as making one of these better than another, of the world as deciding between them."[29]

In arguing about types of moral representation which involve systematic vocabularies or language games of this kind then, we are not arguing about their precise descriptive adequacy, but about the moral ends involved in using them to make sense of the life we actually live. One might add too, that the invention of such descriptions of the world is not vulnerable to a superior scientific vocabulary. For the continuing survival value and usefulness of many writers' descriptions seem to far exceed that of those of any contemporaneous underlying scientific or philosophical theory we may find for them. This is because the prestigious success of philosophically supported scientific thinking in securing technological control of aspects of the non-human world "out there" is one which only takes place in the context of these more long-lived beliefs about the self, and not vice versa. We may thus rely on art to provide us with new languages for character and new positions for the reader, and the metaphoricity of these languages is no bar to their usefulness, in telling us for example where to look for the psychoanalytically divided or decentered character (this is, after all, part of the point of many postmodern texts and of surrealism in general).

How then can we choose when objective criteria for choice are not available, and there is no obviously superior form of discourse to appeal to? Cultural changes of the kind involved in the humanist-antihumanist debate are not in fact secured by applying criteria or by principled decision. We cannot simply jump from one position to another, any more than we can simply *decide* to become an atheist or change our spouses, or to adopt a thoroughgoing feminist point of view by a single act of decision according to criteria. To an extent then, the "future of theory" has to wait for that type of cultural change in which significant groups of people find themselves talking about human identity in one way rather than another. We will create the self of the reader by the vocabularies we devise to describe him or her, and not discover it by attempting to adjudicate between two models, for "the human self is created by the use of a vocabulary rather than being adequately or inadequately expressed in a vocabulary."[30]

It is thus irrelevant to be asked to offer conclusive arguments for or against the two descriptive positions I have outlined. We could indeed attempt to show that they are inconsistent or deconstruct themselves. But in doing this, as the Derrideans found in attacking logocentrism, we stay within their vocabularies anyway, and so there are at best limited strategic gains to be made here toward change. The arguments we adopt are essentially directed to the further end of showing that a better form of description is available. But better for what? The arguments we have analyzed are the sites of a contest between entrenched vocabularies. These may seem not to allow us to do what we want. They are confronted by half-formed new ones, which "vaguely promise great things," as indeed the Marxist analysis of the decentered self ultimately does. Barthelme's and other postmodern work as well as their associated critical procedures can thus be best seen as attempts at systematic redescriptions that engage us with a certain kind of decentered irrationality, and thus lead us to look at new aspects of behavior.

The further ends I suggest above are put into play by Leo Bersani, who asks hopefully whether "a psychology of fragmentary and discontinuous desires can be reinstated . . . an Arcadia of polymorphous perversity" (and then looks to Norman O. Brown, Herbert Marcuse, R.D. Laing, and Gilles Deleuze and Félix Guattari to support it).[31] In discussing the theater of Robert Wilson, he uses terms that seem to me to apply to Barthelme and others:

> Ideally, that enjoyment [of their work] would be so intense that audiences would become anxious to make their own personalities designify, to substitute a sensual heterogeneity of being for psychological coherence. Understanding and judgment are irrelevant; we are asked to change our mode of being. (310)

Like Barthes, he asks "that we attempt to resist the appeal of the unity of personality assumed by all humanistic psychologies" (310). And the reasons for this are moral and political:

> An exuberant indefiniteness about our own identity can both preserve the heterogeneity of our desires and rescue us from the totalitarian insistence natural to all desire. (314)

But this Barthesian view of hedonism as inherently antitotalitarian is open to a number of objections even on its own terms. As we have seen, resistance to ideology may require a subject which is not heterogeneous; and indeed as a form of emotivism, it may well be an evasion of any real confrontation with dominant ideologies. It would hardly be in a position to confront the hidden "totalitarian insistence" of G or the narrator of "Alice" in the sexual sphere; and it is certainly a position which is open only to an élite. On the other hand, the hedonist positions of Barthes and Bersani do show a positive rather than merely resistant use for the antihumanist position. In its light we may see Barthelme and other postmodern experimentalists as offering an antihumanist poststructuralist paradigm which attempts to supersede the Marxist humanism of Berger.[32] There is no way to get into such a new vocabulary (and, if Bersani were to be satisfied, a sense of our own new identity), except to live into it. But this may be complacent in assuming the "progressive" features of the new. How could we resist this? Or do we accept the new vocabulary as liberating us to do more things than the old, to which we can always recur? This seems to me to be the right solution, though tainted perhaps with the liberal notions of choice from a larger menu, and I can't coherently defend it.

It follows from what I have said that alternative vocabularies are more like alternative tools than alternative bits of a jigsaw puzzle. What we now need to know, is how far these alternative vocabularies *get in each other's way.* If we use one what do we lose of the other? Is the new one really so revolutionary that it wishes to drive out the other for good? A peculiar challenge arises for us here, in that the conflict I have described is a contemporary one rather than being conveniently laid out for our inspection in the historical past. A theory like Rorty's works well with the benefits of hindsight and a healthy skepticism about any predecessor's final success. But it is complacently inadequate in its account of artistic vocabularies, which he seems to think may simply supersede one another. It is surely not the case, as he suggests, that Yeats invented new tools to take the place of old (e.g., Blakean) ones. For most theorists seem to believe that the language of literature functions differently in this respect from the highly institutionalized and normalized and inherently progressive discourses of science, psychology, and philosophy. What is more, we often invent new artistic tools of this kind without knowing in advance what job they will do. And when it comes to subjecting the language-inventing avant-garde to a theoretical or philosophical critique, we do not see it so much in itself as give it a job to do by putting it into alliance with better entrenched ideological positions. Hence, the connection I have tried to make between antihumanism in philosophy and what I suggest may be its correlate in literature.

We are therefore left I think with two separate spheres for investigation—firstly, of the plausibility of the psychological *descriptions* given by avant-garde literature and its associated decentering theory, and secondly, of the status of the moral language we then use to analyze it. For as I have suggested, it is very difficult, even for antihumanist theory, to escape from long-term Kantian commitments here, along with their assumptions about the desirability of a unified personality, within a social order (often Utopian) that might respect it.[33] It looks as though some form of Kantian liberal doctrine will refuse to be ejected even here, and that the most that the antihumanist can say is that this moral or ethical language tends to distract us from a more important task, that of theorizing the self as it exists within society. (Liberal humanist doctrines may also, of course, *distract* those who are to be saved from seeing themselves in a larger context, as possessed of class position and a potential class solidarity. But such considerations look to a humanist end; they are not so much the sign of theoretical conflicts as recommendations for a merely prudential division of necessary work.)

Humanist moral considerations may, in any case, be justified in the shorter term. For we would treat people differently on Berger's and Barthelme's models, particularly if, in the role of seducer, they appeared to us as Barthesian hedonists, as Derridean existentialists deprived of metaphysical means of support, as the decentered or alienated figures of Lacan and many Marxists, or indeed as liberal humanists. It all depends on what we want to do, as we can easily see if we imagine a position with clear short-term moral aims confronting all these: that of the feminist, who would, I guess, see more to work from in the Berger/ Kantian position than the Barthelme/Barthes one. Indeed, so far as the future of moral criticism of the kind I have tried to resurrect here is concerned, the future of theory may well depend greatly on feminists, who have a very strong interest in using all these theoretical positions towards particular realizable ends. I believe that these are in essence liberal and egalitarian, but that is another story, whose narrative still lies in the future.

14

The Future of Theory in the Teaching of Literature

Gerald Graff

In some ways, the current quarrel over whether to theorize or not to theorize in the teaching of literature rests on a false premise. For any teacher of literature is unavoidably a literary theorist. Whatever a teacher says about a literary work, or leaves unsaid, presupposes a theory—of what literature is or can be, of what literary works are worth teaching and why, of how these works should be read and which of their aspects are most worth being noticed and pointed out. Even the most seemingly intuitive encounter with a literary text (or any other text) is, as we have learned to say, already theory-laden. There is no such thing as "just reading" a text, transparently, in a noncontextual vacuum, for there is no reading that does not bring to bear a certain context, interpret from a certain angle or set of interests, and thus throw one set of questions into relief while leaving others unasked.

To put it another way, one lesson of recent theory is that texts do not fully interpret themselves. Any particular reading experience is determined not only by the text in question, but also by the choice of interests the reader brings to the text before reading it. It is no easy matter, frequently, to determine where the meaning of the text ends and the reader's share begins, and one of the more hotly contested issues among recent theorists is whether it is possible to make such a distinction at all.[1] Recent theorists agree, however, that it is not just *what* we read but *how* we read it that strongly conditions the results of our reading—and therefore the results of our teaching as well. For if texts do not fully interpret themselves, they do not teach themselves either. How they are taught will depend on theoretical choices.

The very decision to teach literature at all as a school and college subject was a significant theoretical choice. Until the 1870s in the United States, and even later in England, most educators assumed that the English and American classics—as opposed to the ancient Greek and Latin ones—did not need to be taught in formal classes, for they would naturally be read and discussed in the home, or in the town and college

literary and debating societies which still flourished beyond the turn of
the century. It was only after the eclipse of the classical curriculum that
the idea of teaching the native literature in formal courses ceased to be
controversial and came to seem obvious common sense. It is possible to
imagine a very different past had the educators who initially divided
the world of learning into departments chosen to subsume "language
and literature" under philosophy, ethics, or history instead of making
it an autonomous entity. Whatever the justification of the division of
subject matter they did adopt, we should recognize that the division
constituted a theoretical choice which has had far-reaching consequences.

1

   The question, then, is not *whether* literature teachers should or should
not be theorists, but what theory or theories they will follow. This is a
point which has been frequently made of late, but how well it has been
heard is another matter. One still encounters the widespread belief that
teaching students to read literature is primarily a matter of inculcating
a technical skill. Reading is still thought of as an experience which operates ideally at a direct, pretheoretical level, and is therefore a purer,
more humanistic experience when complicated as little as possible by
alien considerations of theory. First we learn to read, according to this
widely accepted model, and then subsequently—if we are so inclined—
we can go on to theorize our experiences of reading. At best theory is
seen as an optional interest, something added to the essentials of literary
experience and, thus, properly reserved for the advanced student who
has already learned how to read. At worst, theory is felt to be an offense
to tradition and to humanism in the Matthew Arnold sense, something
that intrudes between literary texts and their readers.
   This notion that "theory" and "humanism" are naturally at odds,
however, is belied by the history of the academic professionalization of
literary studies. My recent look into this history leads me to conclude
that the current eruption of literary theory is not a purely novel and
unprecedented event, but the latest revival of an old and recurrent impulse which at one time commanded the allegiance of many traditionalists themselves.[2] The current theory movement is only the latest and
most intransigent of a succession of calls for theory, calls that first began
with the displacement of the classical curriculum by the modern languages, and that became a motif in humanistic reform thinking long
before the word became associated with a radical challenge to humanism.
In speculating about "the future of literary theory," it is useful to con-
template its past.

The cry for theory has been a persistent response to the chronic discrepancy between the Arnoldian humanist pretentions of academic literary studies and their actual professional practices. The contradiction between the ideals of Arnoldian humanism and what happened to those ideals when institutionalized in the university inspired a demand for theory at the very outset. To cite only one early example, in 1908 Irving Babbitt complained that "the modern languages have had so much practical success in supplanting Greek and Latin that they have hardly felt the need as yet of justifying themselves theoretically."[3] Babbitt and his fellow New Humanists were attacking that poverty of "general ideas" which they saw as the cause and consequence of the aimlessly accumulative positivism that typified most of the new philological and historical research.

This early appeal to theory in reaction to the fact-worship of the research ideal was subsequently appropriated by the first-generation of New Critics, who proceeded to supplement the New Humanists' critique with an analytic methodology and to reconcile it with the modernist literary taste which the Humanists had scorned. Though they are nowadays praised or damned as anti-theoretical empirics, the New Critics actually regarded themselves as defenders of theory. In 1938, for example, John Crowe Ransom observed that theory "always determines criticism, and never more than when it is unconscious. The reputed condition of no-theory in the critic's mind is illusory."[4] It is no accident that one of the most influential of New Critical texts bore the title *Theory of Literature*, or that its authors, René Wellek and Austin Warren, argued in the book that "literary theory, an *organon* of methods, is the great need of literary scholarship today."[5]

Wellek and Warren's conception of "literary theory" was certainly very remote from those which prevail today. Yet it anticipated a considerable part of the agenda of recent theory—e.g., the "mode of existence" of a literary text, the relation of intention to literary meaning, the nature of literary value, the problem of literary reference and truth, and the relations of "intrinsic" and "extrinsic" criticism. Recent theorists have questioned whether theory should be conceived as an "organon of methods" or as a rigorous critique of all pretensions to method, they have doubted whether literature has any isolable "mode of existence" apart from its various contexts, and they have challenged the distinction between the intrinsic and the extrinsic. Yet many of the issues disputed in recent theory continue to be those defined in *Theory of Literature*.

Then, too, most of the first-generation New Critics were not merely explicators, as they are sometimes remembered today, but social critics armed with sweepingly general theories of the function of literature in a civilization they diagnosed as overrun by science and industrialism.

Even in its most narrowly explicative exercises, New Critical analysis tended to treat literary texts as allegories concerned with such larger questions as the alleged dissociation of sensibility, the decline of tradition, or the war between science and poetic imagination. New Critical interpretive methodology was linked with social and pedagogical projects ranging on the political spectrum from the agrarian program of Ransom and Tate to the radicalism of Kenneth Burke. It was only as the New Criticism became institutionalized in college curricula and pedagogy after World War II that its method of "close reading" became detached from the theoretical and cultural programs which had originally inspired the method with larger purposes.[6]

But in succumbing to this separation of theory from practice, the New Criticism only retraced a pattern that had been played out earlier by the research scholarship against which it had reacted. At its entry into the university, that research scholarship had in theory been informed by the broadly nationalistic and cultural conception of literature which had descended from Herder, Friedrich Schlegel, and other romantics. Once this scholarship became institutionalized in academic fields, specialties, and courses, however, it became increasingly difficult to discern the evolutionary unity of culture that supposedly gave coherence to the whole.

In the group dynamics of the academic humanities, it seems that once a methodological innovation has been institutionalized in the form of an uncorrelated set of fields, programs, and courses, not only is the particular theory that initially inspired the innovation forgotten, but so eventually is the fact that any theory has been involved at all. During the full century in which literary studies have been centered in the university, this process of stagnation has become so chronic that some observers now see it as an unavoidable result of bureaucratic institutionalization. Such a diagnosis seems overly fatalistic, but it points up a problem that needs to be addressed in any consideration of the future of literary theory: on the one hand, the cycle of stagnation explains why the cry for theory has been perennial; on the other hand, as each new theoretical reaction has been institutionalized, it has itself become caught up in the cycle of stagnation, thus generating a further outbreak of theoretical reflection which in its turn is assimilated and routinized. We will have to come back later to the question of how this unfortunate pattern might be broken.

2

If the theoretical impulse in academic literary studies is perennial, the form that impulse has recently taken is certainly unprecedented. Before

254 • The Teaching of Literature

around 1970, virtually no academic literary theorizing presented itself as a counter-discourse aimed at putting into question the premises of traditional humanism. Insofar as the word "theory" has become synonymous with post-structuralist, feminist, or neo-Marxist theory (a usage which these schools have not discouraged), the antagonism between theory and traditional humanism is obviously profound. Recent theory contests concepts of literary-critical discourse that were formerly taken for granted—concepts such as "literature," "text," "author," "meaning," "reader," "interpretation," "history," "rhetoric," "evidence," and "story." These and other standard concepts have been shown to be far from natural or self-evident, along with the boundaries which formerly kept domains such as the intrinsic and extrinsic, the literary and the political, the linguistic and the erotic, in place. The very term "theory" can be defined as a discourse that is generated when assumptions and concepts which once went without saying have become objects of discussion and dispute.

There is little point, then, in trying to claim that the discourses of traditional humanism and of current theory are the same. Yet to deny any commonality between these discourses would be unfortunate for the interests of current theory itself. For one thing, it would permit traditional humanists to go on acting as if Arnoldian humanism is not itself a form of theory. For another, it would obscure the fact that, in the very process of assaulting that humanism, recent theory has revived a number of eminently Arnoldian questions which "traditional" academic literary studies have neglected.

This last point is hard to see because recent theory does often repudiate the public discourse of Arnoldian criticism and retreat into esoteric vocabularies and coteries. One sympathizes with the beleaguered instructor who finds literature already an abstruse enough subject to teach to resistant students without plunging them into a morass of theoretical abstractions. But if recent theory is often inaccessible to laymen, we need to remember that so is most professional literary research and criticism of whatever kind, whether humanist or anti-humanist. From the lay viewpoint, the difference between the critical modes of Jacques Derrida and Walter Jackson Bate would probably seem less wide than the difference between both and that of the journalistic criticism with which the layman is familiar. Intrinsically, recent theory is only marginally more obscure than the New Criticism seemed to many observers to be before it was naturalized.

It is easy to forget that in its early phases the New Criticism was derided in terms very similar to those in which theory is derided today: New Critics, it was charged, turned literary works into abstract mathematical puzzles; they made literary study seem esoteric, pseudo-scientific, and inhumane; they came between literature and students; they elevated the interests of an elite coterie over those of common readers, and so forth. If current theory requires knowledge of Nietzsche, Heidegger, and Marx, the New Criticism had its abstruse sources in Kant, Coleridge, and Croce. Like other academic vocabularies, current theory needs to be popularized before it can become generally accessible. Though a special problem is posed by those deconstructive forms of theory whose inspiration lies in resistance to being appropriated, even there the issues are of potentially general interest, many of them, as I have suggested, being versions of older issues stated in new forms or pushed in new directions: what is literature, and is the term susceptible of a unitary definition? What is reading? What is literary value and how is it related to other kinds of value? What is entailed in such concepts as meaning, genre, authorship, intention, influence, historical period, character, plot, and so forth? How has the literary been implicated in political, philosophical, psychological, and scientific experience?

The attractions of belonging to a closed coterie can explain some but hardly all of the appeal of recent theory, which could hardly have been so seductive if it did not speak to the wider social and moral concerns of literary study as more orthodox forms of literary study have failed to do. Again, recent theory has revived the traditional cultural questions which "traditional" literary studies have neglected. It has reinstated the Arnoldian questions while rejecting the Arnoldian answers to them.

This point has been forcefully made by Terry Eagleton, who argues that orthodox academic criticism, by promoting "an isolated concern with the 'literary text,'" has only helped widen the gap effected by advanced industrial capitalism between criticism and "the classical public sphere." Eagleton speaks of the need "to recall criticism to its traditional role, not to invent some fashionable new function for it." He argues that much current theory represents not a rupture with tradition so much as a return to a pre-bourgeois rhetorical and social conception of literature which re-connects "the symbolic to the political" spheres of life.[7] If Eagleton is right, as I think he is, then the proper antithesis to tradition and humanism is not literary theory, but the kind of conventional literary study that asks no theoretical questions and assumes that as long as students are exposed to the major texts and periods, the larger theoretical and cultural issues will take care of themselves.

3

If all teachers of literature are necessarily literary theorists, then the *collective* enterprise of teaching literature is also a kind of theoretical statement. That the teaching of literature is a collective enterprise may seem too obvious a point to need stating, but it is easily overlooked.

The teaching of literature has always been conceived as an almost idyll-ically individualistic activity. Its rewards, for those who gravitate to it, are often associated with a degree of freedom from bureaucratic super-vision and management afforded by few other vocations. As the ico-nography of the college catalog suggests, the literature (or other humanities) class is typically pictured as an intimate semicircle made up of a lone teacher and a small cluster of students, sprawled beneath a leafy tree on the campus lawn or cozily grouped in a seminar room or in the professor's book-lined study. It is this image of the pastoral in-timacy of the literature course, seen as a personal bond between teacher and flock, that makes attempts to "theorize" the teaching of literature seem vaguely sacrilegious, a cold reduction of an organic process to mechanically abstract and institutional terms.

Like all versions of pastoral, however, this image of the literature class gains its seductiveness by making an otherwise bewildering institutional situation seem more intelligible than it is. The image lends a certain apparent identity to an institution which has always been notoriously prone to corporate identity-crisis. Academic literary study has never possessed an agreed-upon theory of what it stands for, a fact that helps account for its difficulties in establishing a visible, recognizable image in the lay world. Other fields of the humanities such as history and philosophy have had similar visibility problems, but these disciplines have been able to take for granted a degree of public comprehension of their enterprise which departments of literature have lacked. It is still a common professional inside joke that, in the eyes of most laymen the primary social function of English professors is to correct mistakes in grammar.

People need a sense of what an institution as a corporate body stands for in order to be able to enter—or to want to enter—into its issues, methods, and modes of talking and thinking. The low corporate visibility of literary studies prevents students from internalizing the institution's rituals or from seeing why it might be in their interests to do so. To put it in the theoretical idiom, the legibility of the texts we teach depends on the legibility of the institutions in which we teach them. Illegibility in the "institutional text" reproduces itself in the illegibility of the written texts which are the object of study. If the institutional text is opaque, so are the texts mediated by the institution.

To be more specific, literature teachers expect students to be able to "thematize" literary texts, to apply to them a "rule of significance" by which narratives exemplify general patterns of experience. The pri-mary convention of classroom reading is the "rule of significance" (I borrow Jonathan Culler's formulation), which dictates that when we read a text as literature, we read it "as expressing a significant attitude to some problem concerning man and/or his relation to the universe."[8] A problem arises when this process of thematization is to be mastered in an institutional setting which itself is largely unthematized. The very words "theme" and "thematize" are part of a discourse unfamiliar to most laymen—a kind of Litspeak subdivision of the larger discourse of Culturespeak. A symptom of the collective invisibility of the academic humanities is the gulf between Litspeak/Culturespeak and lay discourses.

The gulf expresses itself in the literature student's time-honored complaint about being forever expected to look for "hidden meanings" (or "symbolism") in texts. It also underlies the student's frequent need to ask what it is the literature instructor "wants." The mystery about what literature teachers want is ultimately a function of the low corporate visibility of the institution which regulates their exchanges. The literature teacher stands before the class not as a member of an identifiable collective engaged in modes of thought that most students might see themselves as internalizing, but as a representative of alien requirements which tend to be seen as obstacles to be circumvented with as little damage to the students' career ambitions as possible.

None of this is the fault of individual teachers and students. The effects I am describing are independent of whether courses are taught well or badly at the individual level—though individual effort can significantly alleviate these effects or make them worse. The habit of evaluating teaching on a purely individual basis is another symptom of the tendency to overlook the collective identity of literary studies, or to assume that that collective identity will somehow form itself for the student out of an accumulation of disconnected experiences.

The disconnected nature of the students' experience helps greatly to deepen the mystery about what literature instructors want, for a feeling is encouraged that the demands of each literature course are not generalizable or transferable beyond the confines of that course. The student's task presents itself as one of determining the unique demands of each course, conforming to them for the duration of the semester, and then setting them aside when it is time to move on to the new demands of the next course. The uncertainty resulting from this discontinuity increases both teachers' and students' dependence on writing models which, though mechanical and dreary, at least provide understood conventions to fall back on: the "research paper" which distinguishes itself from plagiarism only by a scrupulous deployment of footnotes; the contextless explication of poetic images or themes which contains no hint of why these images or themes were felt to be worth explicating. When these models fail to give sufficient direction, there are the *Cliffs* or *Monarch Notes*, a study of which would be most useful for theorizing the problem of studying literature from the students' point of view. Given the commercial constraints under which they operate, the producers of these cribs have a more urgent stake than college educators do in finding out what studying literature entails from the student's side.

The research paper, the contextless explication, and the *Cliffs* and *Monarch Notes* help to keep alive the institutional fiction that the rationale for studying literature is tacitly understood, so that student papers can afford to be technical exercises which do not need to be placed in a larger context. That is, the fiction can prevail that because literature is being contextualized effectively in individual courses—and this may often be the case—the question of how the sum total of the various different contextualizations may be assimilated and synthesized by the student can be left to take care of itself.

4

So far, I have spoken of the failure of departments of literature to form a visible, identifiable community, and I have connected that failure of community with the lack of a common theoretical rationale. But such a diagnosis raises the question of whether teachers of literature really *do* comprise a community in any useful sense, and whether they could realistically be expected to possess a common theoretical rationale. Complaints about the fragmentation, incoherence, and "cafeteria counter" quality of the curriculum have become so common in critiques of literary studies (and of the humanities in general) that they have now achieved virtually official status in numerous reports and position papers.[9] Yet these complaints have been commonplace at least as far back as the polemics in the thirties of Robert Maynard Hutchins, to which recent educational critics have added little.

It is easy to deplore fragmentation and incoherence, but the question is, unless it is to be imposed by force, what kind of coherence can be realistically expected in an institution harboring so democratic a diversity of conflicting subjects, methods, interests, ideologies, and values. It was just this question, in fact, which the educational critics of the thirties (most notably, John Dewey and Harry Gideonse) accused Hutchins of evading, and it is still evaded by today's conservatives, who criticize the academic humanities for being overspecialized and chaotic, for failing to transmit a common ground of humanistic values and cultural traditions, and for debasing intellectual standards. It is easier to produce righteous oratory about intellectual incoherence and deteriorating standards than it is to propose a practical alternative in an institution where there is no agreed-upon principle of coherence and no consensus about whose standards ought to be enforced—not even a consensus that greater coherence and consensus would be desirable.

If conservative critics of the university beg important questions, however, when they lament the breakdown of humanistic coherence, so do those radical critics of the university who propose mobilizing literary studies behind semiotics, discourse studies, and the analysis of ideology in the service of a critique of capitalist society. Eagleton's recommendation in *Literary Theory: An Introduction* that literature programs move in the direction of cultural studies seems a democratic conception, but his further plea that they place themselves in the service of "the socialist transformation of society"[10] is calculated to attract only those whose politics run in that direction. I count myself one of those, but cannot help wondering what is to be done with those who do not share the aim of demystifying the text of social power.

Like the Right, in other words, the Left neglects to consider the role which is to be played by those substantial segments of the university not already committed to its particular solution. Both Left and Right assume a hypothetical university in which the parties opposed to their particular programs will quietly go away or allow themselves to be outflanked—neither of which is a probable outcome—unless, that is, we imagine there is to be an ideological resorting of the educational landscape into Universities of the Left, of the Right, and of the Center. Though such a rearrangement might have advantages—it would give cultural and political conflicts a dramatic visibility they have lacked—it does not seem a practical possibility.

Justifiable though the reproach may be, then, that literature departments (and universities) have evaded matters of theoretical principle, it does not take us very far. For whenever attempts to confront matters of theoretical principle have been made, they have led to a deadlock of competing theories: the claims of skills vs. those of content, values, or cultural literacy; the pedagogy of the oppressed vs. the pedagogy of back-to-basics; textual/sexual/politics, radical theory, and the opening up of the canon vs. core curricula and the shoring up of the cultural heritage. Departments naturally feel justified in retreating from questions of theory when they find it impossible to get agreement on them, or when getting agreement requires watering proposals down to such diluted and innocuous form that little is left of their original thrust.

The major conflict today pits those who conceive the goal of literary study to be the promotion of literate appreciation of the traditional monuments of high culture against those who want to subject that culture and what they see as its repressive effects to a radical critique—if not to liberate students from it wholly. The radicals' goals actually tend to be more and less subversive than their traditionalist opponents recognize: most of them wish not to drop Shakespeare and other classic writers from the canon, as is often charged, but to subject these writers to ideological critique. Traditionalists might actually find it in their interests to urge that the traditional canon *not* be taught—something which would at least protect it from the political interrogation it is increasingly likely to be in for if recent critical trends persist.

Of course if my earlier point is correct, recent theory is closer to certain genuinely traditional practices than is orthodox criticism and scholarship, but recognition of this fact is unlikely to calm tempers on either side or produce a new consensus. On the fundamental matters of dispute there is little room for compromise: whereas some believe in the validity of separating literature and criticism from their political determinants and effects, others argue that such an outlook is itself a patently political strategy aimed at repressing political concerns and keeping established interests in control. There is not even any agreement on how the existing state of affairs should be described: one side sees a situation in which traditional humanism has become pathetically weak, while the other sees one in which traditional humanism remains oppressively powerful. One sees a situation in which consensus has been fragmented, while the other sees one in which apparent fragmentation masks a deeper consensus that excludes genuinely oppositional points of view.

Elementary group-dynamics suggest three possible models of resolution for such an intra-institutional conflict: (1) one party wins, either by driving the other out by force or converting it; (2) a compromise is reached in which the parties halve their differences; (3) stability is achieved through a condition of hostile coexistence in which each party consolidates its territory and erects barriers protecting it from having to deal with the enemy. In models (1) and (2) resolution is achieved by reaching a consensus through force, persuasion, or compromise; in (3) resolution is achieved by "patterned isolation" based on mutual nonrecognition.[11]

Clearly, in the present circumstances models (1) and (2) are not realistic options. Given the existing balance of power, neither side is likely to drive out the other nor, given the depth and bitterness of polarization, can either convert the other. (The radicals, being younger, can better afford to wait out a stalemate and win by attrition, but this will take time.) For the same reasons, a compromise seems out of the question. The dynamics of the situation consequently favor model (3) by default: traditionalists circle the wagons around what is left of their turf and plot retrenchment strategies, while radical theorists consolidate their gains and await the opportunity for the next advance. The result is an armed truce which satisfies neither party but appeases each with a partial share of the departmental and curricular terrain.

The literature curriculum thus becomes an aggregate of political trade-offs that ends up lacking the visibility of either a consensus or a dramatic conflict. In a game of "let's make a deal," courses taught from feminist, Marxist, and deconstructionist viewpoints coexist in uneasy isolation with courses taught from conventional period, genre, and thematic perspectives. Since there is no means of foregrounding the relations between orthodox and adversarial courses, the perspectives of comparison and contrast are lost. By unspoken agreement, no course is obliged to acknowledge the challenge posed by courses based on rival methods, theories, and ideologies. Instead, the aggregate is laid before the students in the hope that *they* will somehow make better sense of it than their educators have been able to do—as, remarkably, a minority actually manages to do.

The reluctance to help students make correlations is powerfully reinforced by the unspoken fear that they will become confused or demoralized if allowed to discover that there are conflicts among the authorities. It is felt to be unwise to expose students to the possibility that the body of knowledge and the cultural heritage represented by the disciplines are, and always have been, contested. But if those who complain about educational incoherence mean seriously to do something about it, they must confront the possibility that incoherence is a function of conflicts which have no institutional means of being negotiated rationally and democratically. Healing the fragmentation of the university means taking the risk of exposing conflicts to public view.

Such a situation demands a hypothetical fourth model of conflict resolution, in which the aim is not necessarily to bring conflicts to a consensual resolution, but to exploit the conflicts themselves as an organizing principle. In theory, such a conflict-model is what democratic pluralism claims to have stood for all along, but in fact such a model has never found institutional expression. Though many literature departments are now pluralistically diverse, few of them make use of this diversity beyond presenting students with a rich array of choices. A more functional pluralism would mean not just agreeing to differ, but to stage differences openly.

A conflict-model of education, in other words, would oblige us to rethink the consensus philosophy which still implicitly governs discussions of educational organization and reform. This philosophy says that educators need to get *agreement* on first principles before they can be expected to work together, that in order to have educational *coherence*, there must be theoretical *consensus*. One sees this philosophy at work in most of the official commission reports, white papers, and symposia on the state of the humanities, where the standard procedure is to convene a panel of distinguished humanists who are asked to abstract from the great monuments of the humanities some conceptual core which can be put forth as "the knowledge most worth having." This core knowledge will then supposedly represent the values behind which, now that they have been spelled out, humanists can come together in order to propagate their interests more effectively.

Invariably it is discovered that no consensus on the core values exists. Even worse, the consensus on the core values is defined in such vague terms that the consensus is meaningless. Worst of all, a consensus is reached only by excluding important groups from the discussion at the outset, which intensifies resentment all around. Whichever the outcome, the effect is to deepen the sense of paralysis and encourage a reversion to managed isolation and armed truce. In such a situation, it would seem wise to recognize that there is no longer, if there ever were, any interesting set of concepts or values which link all the disparate and mutually conflicting activities which have gone under the name of "humanities" (or "the literary tradition").

The assumption of the conflict-model, however, is that it is not, after all, necessary to resolve cultural and theoretical conflicts in order to exploit them educationally. If corporate visibility cannot be achieved through consensus, whether humanist or anti-humanist, there seems little choice but to ground it on whatever may be instructive in the conflicts themselves. But so far, academic literary studies have hardly begun to exploit the potential educational value of their conflicts, whether they be intraprofessional ones or the external cultural conflicts which have traditionally opposed literature to the scientific and practical spheres.

Take the issue I touched on a moment ago in my observation that the literature curriculum has been determined by political negotiation rather than rational deliberation. Some current theorists have argued that this political process is not only the way curricula have always been determined, but that in principle no other way is possible. For what counts as "rational deliberation," according to this theory, depends solely on matters of institutional power and authority within a given culture—on who gets to decide what counts as "rational." No appeal to disinterested principle is possible, since what passes for disinterestedness will already have been determined by community ideology and self-interest.[12]

Whatever side one takes, the point here is that such a dispute must continue to be disabling as long as our feeling is that it has to be resolved before it can become productive in humanities education. A wiser course would be to proceed on the premise that the question of whether the curriculum is determined by principle or by power figures to continue to be a disputed question—so that we would do well to let students in on whatever may be instructive in the dispute itself instead of keeping it hidden from them. Once consensus has broken down and the question of political interests has been posed, educators have little choice but to confront such questions and try to make the debate over them part of what education is about.

What has proved disabling is not the failure of humanists to *agree* on objectives, but their failure to *disagree* on them in ways that might become recognizable and intelligible to outsiders. The recent contentions over the place of theory and the politics of literature and criticism represent probably the most fundamental clash of principles in the history of the humanities, yet few students and fewer laymen know of the existence of these contentions, much less see what might be at stake for themselves in them. The low level at which the issues are described when a well-meaning journalist in *The New York Times Magazine* or elsewhere tries to report on them is an indication of how pathetically little of our most hard-fought professional conflicts leaks out.[13] It is doubtless in the nature of the subject matter that professional disputes like those over the status of theory will be fought out mostly behind the public and educational scenes in the technical vocabularies of specialized field journals, conferences, and other semi-private arenas. But these disputes are not so intrinsically untranslatable that they cannot be edifying to laymen.

Here, it seems to me, is where theory can come in, "theory" conceived not as a specialized idiolect (though it will and should remain that at some level), but as the generalized language for staging conflicts in ways that increase rather than lessen institutional visibility. Theory is potentially the medium in which the literary, cultural, and educational conflicts which underlie professional differences can be worked through and made part of the informing context of literary education. Again, it is important to insist on the broad sense of "theory," whereby a Matthew Arnold, an F.R. Leavis, a George Orwell, or an Edmund Wilson is just as much a theorist as any deconstructionist or post-structural feminist. The disparate vocabularies may prove incommensurable, but then something useful can always be learned from that.

5

As I am conceiving it here, then, theory can be a means of making ideological conflict into part of what literary study is about instead of something that has to paralyze the institution and rob it of public visibility. But the mere determination by literature departments to offer more theory courses and encourage more open discussion of theoretical issues is likely to be no more effective than will pious resolutions to become more humanistic. Good intentions can do little without an alteration in the institutional conditions which, in the past, have always defeated them. The future of theory in literary education, then—whether or not theory can be an agent of constructive transformation—depends on how theory is institutionalized.

Here it becomes important to reflect on the historical precedents I mentioned at the start of this essay, and ask how the theory-revolution can be prevented from succumbing to the dispiriting cycle which has overtaken previous methodological innovations and paradigm-shifts in the history of academic literary studies. As long as the habitual group dynamics are left to take their course, one can predict that theory will be assimilated as one more field added to the aggregate, with the general issues it raises remaining optional concerns.

I come back to the problem I deferred earlier, which is why, throughout the history of literary studies, promising innovations in methods and practices have repeatedly tended to become detached from the theories that initially gave them meaning, with the effect of deepening the student alienation which it was hoped the innovations would lessen. If my analysis is correct, this stagnation is not an inevitable result of academic institutionalization, but a consequence of the institutionalized evasion of conflict which I have been describing. To reduce the point to a maxim, stagnation sets in whenever the theoretical presuppositions of any innovation are forgotten. And theoretical presuppositions tend to be forgotten when that innovation reaches the stage at which it ceases to be uncontroversial. In other words, stagnation, or the separation of theory from practice, is the product of a structure that discourages open controversy.

One could hardly find a better example of such a structure than the array of uncorrelated fields that has typically ordered the staffing and curriculum of the literature department. This field-coverage structure, which first arose in America at the time of the departmentalization of the university just before the turn of the century, could never have taken so powerful a hold if it had not had great practical advantages. The most notable of these was to make departments and curricula virtually self-regulating. By assigning each instructor the role of "covering" a pre-defined field of inquiry, the field-coverage model created a system in which research and instruction could proceed in seemingly automatic fashion, without the need for collective debate over methods and aims. Instructors could be left on their own to fulfill their duties with little need for elaborate supervision and management. A professional literature department could essentially run itself—rather like a baseball game, where the players' roles are so stereotyped by position that the game can be readily played without managers or umpires.

A second benefit of the field-coverage model was to make departments and universities enormously flexible in assimilating new ideas, subjects, and methods, all of which could be painlessly added to the already established fields without forcing them to alter their ways. Previously, when colleges had been dominated by a narrow religious and social outlook, innovation had been largely excluded or suppressed. By contrast, the new university thrived on innovation, partly because attitudes had become more secular, but also because the new principle of bureaucratic accretion permitted universities to assimilate innovation without incurring the ideological friction that innovation would earlier have occasioned. New and avant-garde interests could now be added without asking tradition-bound sectors of the campus to modify their outlook. Modern literature scholars could be added to antiquarians, analytic critics added to positivistic research scholars and armchair men of letters, Americanists, comparativists, and modernists added to Anglophiles, without the clashes of principle which were now latent in the mix as departments expanded and colonized more and more subjects. Not everyone remained compartmentalized, for both controversy and cross-fertilization occurred, but they occurred so unobtrusively that they went largely unnoticed by outsiders.

Obviously, the benefits of such a system were paid for at a severe price. By making the teaching staff and the curriculum self-regulating, the field-coverage model freed instructors to get on with the job of teaching and research in an efficient and untroubled way. But it also relieved them of the need to rationalize their behavior to themselves or in discussions with their own or other departments. The specialization of the system resulted in critical progress of an undeniable and often impressive kind, but at the expense of the relationships which might have put specializations in some context.

In effect, administrative organization took the place of context, and of theoretical controversy. As long as the designated fields were staffed and taught, no one had to have a theory of individual or collective goals in order for the department to proceed on its way. The grid of literary periods and genres in the catalog was a sufficiently clear expression of what the department stood for, which is to say that the official fiction of a shared humanistic goal did not have to be theorized or tested. Teachers of period and genre courses did not need to ask what "period" and "genre" meant, how periods and genres connected or contrasted, or what the implications were of approaching literature in a historical or generic way. This is not to blame specializations, fields, or even curricular coverage, but the absence of correlation within these divisions. The point is that no methodological model, including a theoretical one, can be effective as long as it operates in an uncorrelated structure.

But if this is the case, then the worst thing which we could do would be to institutionalize theory in the traditional additive fashion as one more field among others. Such a step would not only permit the challenges posed by theory to be ignored, but would encourage theory itself to become just the sort of esoteric in-group conversation that its detractors say it cannot help being. For this reason, theory at the moment may be threatened less by outright opponents who are willing to argue with it than by those who are cheerfully willing to add it to the scheme of departmental coverage so that they can forget about it. The various fields will assimilate theoretical perspectives, as they are now assiduously doing with valuable results, but without increasing the theoretical consciousness, and therefore the corporate visibility, of literary studies as a whole. In short, literary theory will not make a major difference in the institutional pattern of literary studies unless some means is found to correlate different discourses.

The most promising steps toward an alternative seem to me represented by the numerous programs now being planned and implemented which integrate literary theory and history in an interdisciplinary framework, often under such rubrics as "cultural studies" and "cultural history." These programs follow the blueprints outlined in recent work such as Eagleton's *Literary Theory: An Introduction*, Raymond Williams's *Writing in Society*, William E. Cain's *The Crisis in English Studies*, and Robert Scholes's *Textual Power*, and more or less implicit in much feminist criticism.[14] Most of the current programs consist of a few required "core" courses with a series of electives, but they conceive the core not a fixed canon of major authors and masterpieces but as a group of debatable theories and contexts. This shift of emphasis assumes not that there are no major authors or masterpieces—though what constitutes an "author" or "masterpiece" and why is taken not as a given but a question to be debated. It is assumed that students will more intelligently grasp what it means for a work to be called canonical when the problem of canonicity is foregrounded as the controversial issue it has become.

Such programs risk two opposite dangers. On the one hand, there is the danger I pointed to earlier in connection with proposals like that of Eagleton which at times seems aimed at turning literary studies into an arm of the political Left. The danger of a new dogmatism of "cultural studies" replacing the older forms of dogmatism has already raised its head in some institutions. But probably the more common danger is that of replacing older kinds of incoherence with newer ones. Merely provoking interdisciplinary conjunctions and confrontations in the hope that something productive will come out of them no more assuredly results in educational coherence than covering standard periods and genres assuredly results in humanism. Nor is opening up the literary canon immune to false hopes. One can all too easily imagine those students who have not mastered the academic modes of thematic reading to which I referred earlier (or the ones who have mastered it too glibly) reacting to a revised, radical canon with the same passive docility with which they have reacted to the traditional one.

Institutionalizing theory within cultural studies or other interdisciplinary programs, then, will not ensure it against dogmatism, incoherence, and the malaise occasioned by the gulf between academic Culturespeak and lay discourse. What causes me to hope that the new programs will succeed where previous innovations have failed is not that the new programs are problem-proof, but that they are designed to exploit their problems rather than to hide them. Their guiding principle is that the way to bring educational and cultural problems under control is to make their causes and consequences part of the context of study.

If we are to gain a measure of control over the problems of the academic humanities, it seems to me we are more likely to do so not by waiting for a consensus to emerge on how best to address those problems, but by seeking to build our diverse views of the problems themselves into the subject matter of education, where they can be worked through openly—whether to a consensus or not. Once again, we do not have to agree on the question of new vs. old canons, or of literature or humanism vs. theory, in order to teach literature more effectively than we now do. An institutional identity-crisis does not have to be cured in order to be made educationally and culturally productive. It does, however, have to be staged, and theory is the language for staging the one we are going through at the moment.

15

Paul de Man's Contribution to Literary Criticism and Theory

Jonathan Culler

Paul de Man has been one of the most influential figures in American criticism and theory since the 1960s. His death in 1983 left us an array of difficult texts, many of them still unpublished. One of the major tasks of American criticism in the future will be to interpret these essays, exploring the implications of de Man's critical and theoretical writing. This will not only entail understanding what these texts say and why— a daunting assignment in itself—but especially working out their possible relationships to other contemporary critical discourses, such as psychoanalysis, feminism, and revisionist Marxisms, which have frequently engaged those versed in deconstruction but did not interest de Man.

The discovery in 1987 that at age 21 and 22, at the beginning of the German occupation of Belgium, de Man had written a regular literary column for the leading Belgium newspaper, *Le Soir*, which had been taken over by collaborationists, and that one of these 169 columns, in March 1941, adopted the language of anti-Semitism to argue that European literature had not been corrupted by the Jews, both shocked those who had known de Man and found him exceptionally just and upright in his dealings with students and colleagues, and dismayed those who had been interested in his work. This discovery imposes a number of tasks. First there is that of elucidating what de Man actually did, investigating the circumstances of his collaboration and the arguments of his wartime juvenilia. Whatever account emerges, the fact that he could have written an anti-Semitic text will block an inclination to idealize the man and will prevent him from being cited simply as an authority— will force any authority to be earned by argument from and about his writings.

A second project this discovery encourages is a more careful thinking about such phenomena of recent European history as fascism and Nazism, which for so many American critics exist in a something of a comic-book version—a story of villainy emerging out of nowhere and unconnected to other trends in Western thought or politics—and the exploration of how intellectuals might have made themselves complicitous with these movements. It is a striking feature of European history between the Wars that so many intellectuals were drawn to political and theoretical programs whose actual instantiations—fascism in Germany, Italy and Spain; communism in Russia and elsewhere—proved totalitarian. For Marxist theory, thinking through the implications of the occurrence of fascism as a mass movement has been a major task since the thirties; and this crucial work in political theory becomes increasingly pertinent as literary theory seeks to transform itself into cultural theory, and as the fascist tinge of the religious right in America becomes more ominously apparent.

Third, de Man's wartime juvenilia pose the question of their relation to the critical and theoretical writings of his academic career. The criticism of his Belgian years is for the most part book reviews, highly evaluative, with all the callowness of brash youth enjoying the role of cultural arbiter. It combines a desire to map European literature, a conviction that one can grasp the immutable laws of literary history, with diverse critical impulses that make him appear, not surprisingly, a young man experimenting with various *idées recues*.[1] It bears little resemblance to the sort of analytical criticism, focused on imagery, that he was to develop in the 1950s, and still less to the style of rhetorical readings that he was to develop in the 1970s in contact with Jacques Derrida and deconstruction.

These writings do, however, give aspects of his mature writings a different resonance. For instance, emphasis in the book reviews of 1941 and 1942 on implacable laws of literary evolution, by which forms grow like organisms, makes more striking de Man's critique, in his later writings, of these organicist and narrative figures generated through a misreading of romanticism, whose greatest works provide the instruments for their undoing. The serious academic study of literature after 1950 brought de Man to see the power of literary language to undo the historical schemes through which he had sought to master literature for journalistic purposes. "Generic terms such as 'lyric,' " he later wrote, "as well as pseudo-historical period terms such as 'romanticism' or 'classicism,' are always terms of resistance and nostalgia, at the furthest remove from the materiality of actual history."[2]

De Man's talk in his wartime reviews of the "destiny" of a people and his use of figures promoting an organicist conception of history give a new sharpness and pertinence to the critique of Martin Heidegger that animates articles he wrote in the 1950s, when he took up literary criticism once again. "La Tentation de la permanence" and "Heidegger's Exegeses of Hölderlin" identify the mystifications in the temptation to take poetic language, with its supposed fusion of the material and the spiritual, as the model for an organic, authentic relation to Being, for a recovery of the primordial destiny that civilization has obscured. Heidegger takes Friedrich Hölderlin as the one poet whose work overcomes the forgetting of Being to articulate its absolute presence. "Since Being has founded itself in language in the work of the poet [Hölderlin], by 'thinking-of' [*an-denken*] this work as we do in commentary, we ready ourselves to live in the presence of Being, to 'dwell poetically on earth.' "[3] Taking up the passages Heidegger interprets, de Man argues that Heidegger gets Hölderlin precisely backwards: "the poet does not say Being but rather the impossibility of naming anything but an order that, in its essence, is distinct from immediate Being" (BI, 261). Poetic language, far from serving as the "common ground" on which "poetically man dwells," is a site of division and struggle, "always constitutive, able to posit regardless of presence, but, by the same token, unable to give a foundation to what it posits except as an intent of consciousness" (RR, 6).

Heidegger's insight into the importance of the question of Being in Hölderlin is accompanied, even made possible, by his blindness to the workings of his own rhetoric which mystifies the nature of poetic language as it links it with the organicism of natural processes. Heidegger's commentaries, de Man writes, "were thought out just before and during World War II and are directly linked to an anguished meditation upon the historical destiny of Germany, a meditation that finds an echo in the 'national' poems of Hölderlin" (BI, 254). Critical reading of Hölderlin is a way of undoing the mystification that draws from poetry a supposed reconciliation which repairs the divisions of human experience and offers this as an organic model for human destiny. The connection in de Man's wartime journalism between organic models and the conception of the destiny of a German people which had discovered its identity gives a political resonance to his essays of the 1950s that has hitherto been ignored.

Above all, his wartime writings help one understand more clearly what is implied by de Man's continuing critique of the aesthetic ideology and his linking of it to violence, as in late essays on Kleist and on Kant and Schiller. "Since fascism can be characterized formally as an entry of aesthetic criteria into the political and economic realms,"[4] de Man's critique of the aesthetic ideology resonates also as a critique of the fascist tendencies he had known. In her study of fascism in French literary and intellectual life, Alice Kaplan stresses fascism's revolt against alienation and the fascist conception of the state as an organism: "Against the distance between the state and the people, they hoped for immediacy; against alienation and fragmentation, they hoped for unity of experience . . . Their fascism involved a new poetic language, an immediate vocal presence, an entirely new way of writing and speaking about the state and the world."[5] This political context gives a new dimension to de Man's attempt—from the early critiques of Heidegger to his late critiques of phenomenality—to undo totalizing metaphors, myths of immediacy, organic unity, and presence and combat their fascinations. In his essay, "Aesthetic Formalization in Kleist," de Man makes clear the stakes of his critique of aesthetic ideology: "The aesthetic, as is clear from Schiller's formulation, is primarily a social and political model . . . The 'state' that is being advocated is not just a state of mind or of soul, but a principle of political value and authority that has its own claims on the shape and limit of our freedom. It would lose all interest if this were not the case, for it is as a political force that the aesthetic still concerns us as one of the most powerful ideological drives to act upon the reality of history" (RR, 264). The critique of aesthetic ideology in his later writings finds in literary and philosophical texts powerful tools for combating the ideology with which he had earlier been complicitous.

How, then, might one estimate de Man's contributions? Which of his arguments should literary criticism particularly attend to or pursue? I isolate, somewhat artificially, five contributions that seem to me important for the future of criticism and theory.[6]

1. First, there is de Man's revaluation of allegory, which our post-Coleridgean criticism has treated as an undesirable and unsuccessful type of figuration, a product of the operations of fancy rather than imagination. An assumed superiority of the symbol came to underlie literary taste, critical analysis, and conceptions of literary history. In "The Rhetoric of Temporality," looking at the supposed shift from allegorical to symbolical imagery in late eighteenth-century poetry, de Man challenges the view that romantic literature produces through the symbol a reconciliation of man and nature and instead identifies the allegorical structures at work in its most intense and lucid passages. Allegorizing tendencies "appear at the most original and profound moments . . ., when an authentic voice becomes audible," in works of European literature between 1760 and 1800. "The prevalence of allegory," he writes,

> always corresponds to the unveiling of an authentically temporal destiny. This unveiling takes place in a subject that has sought refuge from the impact of time in a natural world to which, in truth, it bears no resemblance. . . . Whereas symbol postulates the possibility of an identity or identification, allegory designates primarily a distance in relation to its own origin, and, renouncing the nostalgia and the desire to coincide, it establishes its language in the void of this temporal difference. In so doing, it prevents the self from an illusory identification with the non-self, which is now fully, though painfully, recognized as a non-self. It is this painful knowledge that we perceive at the moments when early romantic literature finds its true voice. (BI, 206–7)

Allegory and irony are thus linked in their discovery of discontinuity, disjunction, non-identity. They are also linked in their common de-mystification of an organic world postulated in a symbolic mode of analogical correspondence or in a mimetic mode of representation in which fiction and reality could coincide. The tension between symbol and allegory, as Minae Mizumura writes, "is already another name for the tension between a temptation of assuming the readability of a text, that is, of reconciling sign and meaning, and a renunciation of this temptation."[7] It brings together this linguistic problematic with that of the self: literature comes into being in the tension between the temptation of reconciling an empirical self and a self that exists only in language, and the renunciation of that temptation—or in the exposure of the dis-continuity between a self that will die and a self that knows this but cannot change it.

"The Rhetoric of Temporality," describing the symbol as a mystification and associating allegory with an "authentic" understanding of language and temporality, hints at a reversal that makes symbol a special case of figural language, for which allegory, with its explicit discrepancy be-tween signifier and signified, seemed a better model. *Allegories of Reading* then uses the same term for texts' implicit commentary on modes of signification, implied second- or third-order narratives about reading and intelligibility. Foregrounding the way texts function as allegorical statements about language, literature, and reading, it poses a question about the relation of figuration to interpretation that needs to be pursued.

2. As his critique of an organicist aesthetics of the symbol indicates, one of de Man's achievements has been the revaluation of romanticism. With his Yale colleagues Geoffrey Hartman and Harold Bloom, who formed a "school" only in this respect, he successfully challenged the New Criticism's notion of romanticism as deluded or sentimental. His studies of Rousseau, Hölderlin, Wordsworth, Shelley, Keats, and Baude-laire work to show it to be the boldest, most self-conscious writing of the Western tradition.

Beginning in 1960 with "Structure intentionelle de l'image roman-tique," which takes issue with the nostalgia for the natural object in romantic and post-romantic literature and discussions of it, de Man suggests that we look to the first romantics, Rousseau, Wordsworth and Hölderlin, who will consistently remain his examples of undeluded ro-mantics, "the first modern writers to have put into question, in the language of poetry, the ontological priority of the sensory object" (RR, 16). Poetic language, de Man writes, "seems to originate in the desire to approximate the condition of the natural object," but "this movement is essentially paradoxical and condemned in advance to failure" (RR, 7). Romanticism should be seen not to center on a dialectic of subject and object, mind and nature, but rather to explore a conflict between spatial and temporal schemes, and the articulation of a temporal perspective "not as a memory of a unity that never existed but as the awareness, the remembrance of a precarious condition of falling that has never ceased to prevail."[8]

De Man insists that the question of romanticism is not just one of characterizing a period or a style. Discussion of romanticism is particularly difficult, he suggests, because it requires a coming to terms with a past from which we are not yet separated, a past whose most intense questioning involves precisely this interpretive relation to experiences become memories—that is, the very structure on which our relation to it depends. Descriptions of romanticism always miss the mark, for reasons which are structural rather than due to failures of intelligence. A further complication is introduced by the fact the genetic categories on which literary history depends—the models of birth, development, death—are most decisively promoted but also undercut by the romantic works that they would be used to discuss: "one may well wonder what kind of historiography could do justice to the phenomenon of romanticism, since romanticism (itself a period concept) would then be the movement that challenges the genetic principle which necessarily underlies all historical narrative."[9] As a result, "the interpretation of romanticism remains for us the most difficult and at the same time the most necessary of tasks" (RR, 50).

3. Third, there is de Man's identification of the relationship between blindness and insight. His book of that title argues that critics "owe their best insights to assumptions these insights disprove," a fact which "shows blindness to be a necessary correlative of the rhetorical nature of literary language" (BI, 141). The New Critics' concentration on language (rather than on authors, for example) was made possible by their conception of the work as organic form but led to insights into the role of irony that undermine the conception of literary works as harmonious, organic wholes. For them, as for other critics, an

> insight could only be gained because the critics were in the grip of this peculiar blindness: their language could grope towards a certain degree of insight only because their method remained oblivious to the perception of this insight. The insight exists only for a reader in the privileged position of being able to observe the blindness as a phenomenon in its own right—the question of his own blindness being one which he is by definition incompetent to ask—and so being able to distinguish between statement and meaning. He has to undo the explicit results of a vision that is able to move toward the light only because, being already blind, it does not have to fear the power of this light. But the vision is unable to report correctly what it has perceived

in the course of its journey. To write critically about critics thus becomes a way to reflect on the paradoxical effectiveness of a blinded
vision that has to be rectified by means of insights that it unwittingly
provides. (BI, 105–6)

One result of the arguments of *Blindness and Insight* has been a new
interest in reading critical discourses with the kind of attention given
literary works. The argument, however, is a more general one about the
dependency of truth upon error. Edmund Husserl in his 1935 lectures
on "The Crisis in European Philosophy" promotes the conception of
philosophy as a self-reflective critique of philosophy, "of man himself
and all the values by which he is consciously or preconsciously governed," but in so doing Husserl relies on precisely a privileging of what
he identifies as the European values of disinterested inquiry, rationality,
and self-reflexiveness, which are the culmination of European culture.
Noting "the pathos of such a claim at a moment when Europe was about
to destroy itself as center in the name of its unwarranted claim to be the
center" (BI, 16), de Man pursues as relentlessly as possible a critique of
the Husserlian sort, while emphasizing that it must be blind to the light
which it affords and which others can turn back on the critique itself.

One might note that, far from excusing his own youthful blindness,
as some have suggested, de Man's account would rather indict it: it is
scarcely the case that, in his wartime juvenilia, blindness makes possible
some insight. One might conjecture that his subsequent discovery of his
wartime blindness produced insight, but that is quite different, quite
explicitly not the structure that de Man discovers in other critics, where
insights are made possible by a blindness that those insights expose.

This relation is structural, not psychological, for de Man; his account
of the character and functioning of the relationship invalidates psychoanalytical criticism in the traditional sense. However, it engages in
the same activity as a post-structuralist psychoanalytic criticism which
attends to conflicts in texts' rhetorics and in psyches and explores how
texts are structured by the psychic and rhetorical operations they theorize. The attempt to work out the relationship between de Man's non-
psychoanalytic accounts and an analytical discourse inspired by Sigmund
Freud and Jacques Lacan is a challenging task for criticism and theory.

4. The insight developed in a phenomenological vocabulary of consciousness in *Blindness and Insight* and which depends on a certain enabling blindness of that vocabulary, is transformed with de Man's move
to a rhetorical terminology and a focus on operations of language. What
was first described as the division at the heart of Being, and then as the
complex relation between blindness and insight that prevents self-pos-
session or self-presence, is in his later work analyzed as a "linguistic
predicament" (RR, 81), the figural structure of language that insures a

division variously described as a gap between sign and meaning, between meaning and intent, between the performative and constative functions of language, and between rhetoric as persuasion and rhetoric as trope.

Literary theory has to a considerable extent assimilated the demonstration that reading should focus on the discrepancies between the performative and constative dimensions of texts, between their explicit statement and the implications of their modes of utterance; but criticism has not yet fully explicated or worked with the more difficult and unsettling aspects of de Man's writing on language and their relation to questions of history. In emphasizing certain non-semantic aspects of language, from the indeterminate significative status of the letter, as in Ferdinand de Saussure's work on anagrams, to the referential moment of deixis, as in Hegel's *"this piece of paper,"* he shows that language is not coextensive with meaning; rhetorical reading becomes in part an exposure of the ideological imposition of meaning as a defense we build against language—specifically against the inhuman, mechanical aspects of language, the structures or rhetorical possibilities that are independent of any intent or desire we might have, yet which are neither natural nor phenomenal either. There are, in de Man's accounts, two levels of imposition. First there is the positing by language, which does not reflect but constitutes, which simply occurs. De Man speaks of "the absolute randomness of language prior to any figuration or meaning" (AR, 299). "The positing power of language is entirely arbitrary, in having a strength that cannot be reduced to necessity, and entirely inexorable in that there is no alternative to it" (RR, 126). Then there is the conferring of sense or meaning on this positing, through figuration. Positing does not belong to any sequence or have any status; these are imposed retrospectively. "How can a positional act, which relates to nothing that comes before or after, become inscribed in a sequential narrative? . . . it can only be because we impose, in our turn, on the senseless power of positional language the authority of sense and meaning" (RR, 117). We transform language into historical and aesthetic objects, or embed discursive occurrences in narratives that provide continuities, in a process of troping that de Man calls "the endless prosopopoeia by which the dead are made to have a face and a voice which tells in turn the allegory of their own demise and allows us to apostrophize them in their turn" (RR, 122). "We cannot ask why it is that we, as subjects, choose to impose meaning, since we are ourselves defined by this very question" (RR, 118).

Among other things, this raises questions about the status of narrative and of history. De Man suggests that history is the product of the combination of freedom and determinacy that characterizes a generalized textuality. The disparate, mutually disjunctive modes of determination that are specific to linguistic structures, to texts, are determining of historical reality. For instance, "the divergence which prevails, within the State, in the relationship between the citizen and the executive is in fact an unavoidable estrangement between political rights and laws on the one hand, and political action and history on the other. The grounds for this alienation are best understood in terms of the rhetorical structure that separates one domain from the other" (AR, 266). That rhetorical structure is the discrepancy between language conceived as grammar and language as reference or intentional action, and the ineluctability and indeterminacy of this structural relationship is what de Man calls "text." "The structure of the entity with which we are concerned," writes de Man in his exposition of *The Social Contract*, "(be it as property, as national State, or as any other political institution) is most clearly revealed when it is considered as the general form that subsumes all these particular versions, namely as legal *text*" (AR, 267). The problematical relationship between the generality of law, system, grammar, and its particularity of application, event, or reference is the textual structure Rousseau expounds in the relationship between the general will and the particular individual, or between the state as system and the sovereign as active principle. The tension between grammar and reference

> is duplicated in the differentiation between the state as a defined entity and the state as principle of action or, in linguistic terms, between the constative and performative function of language. A text is defined by the necessity of considering a statement, at the same time, as performative and constative, and the logical tension between figure and grammar is repeated in the impossibility of distinguishing between two linguistic functions which are not necessarily compatible. (AR, 270)

The pertinence of the aporia between performative and constative emerges clearly in Rousseau's question of whether "the body politic possesses an organ with which it can *énoncer* [articulate] the will of the people." The constative function of stating a preexisting will and the performative positing or shaping of a will are at odds, and while the system requires that the organ only announce what the general will determines, the action of the state or "lawgiver" will in particular instances declare or posit a general will, especially in the founding of the state, where the authority of the postulated will depends on its claim to correspond to a will that it posits. The structural tension between performative and constative here in what de Man calls the text is determinative of history, with the violence of its positings, its tropological substitutions, and their "eventual denunciation, in the future undoing of any State or any political institution" (AR, 274–75).

5. Finally, de Man's late essays, collected in *Aesthetic Ideology*, undertake a critique of an aesthetic ideology which imposes, even violently,

continuity between perception and cognition, form and idea, and which literature, properly read, is always undoing. Retrospectively, we can now see this project in his writings of the 1950s as well, in his critique of the "salvational poetics" which sees poetic imagination as a way of overcoming contradictions, and of the "naive poetics" which "rests on the belief that poetry is capable of effecting reconciliation because it provides an immediate contact with substance through its own sensible form" (BI, 244), as well as in his discussion of Heidegger. Much of his career is staked on the premise that close reading attentive to the working of poetic language will expose the totalizations undertaken in the name of meaning and unity.

The late essays find in Kant's work on "the aesthetic" a critique of the ideology of the aesthetic developed, for instance, by Schiller and applied, or misapplied, both in humanistic conceptions of aesthetic education and in fascist conceptions of politics as an aesthetic project. Traditionally, the aesthetic is the name of the attempt to find a bridge between the phenomenal and the intelligible, the sensuous and the conceptual. Aesthetic objects, with their union of sensuous form and spiritual content, serve as guarantors of the general possibility of articulating the material and the spiritual, a world of forces and magnitudes with a world of value. Literature, conceived here as the rhetorical character of language revealed by close reading, "involves the voiding rather than the affirmation of aesthetic categories."[10] Thus the convergence of sound and meaning in literature is an effect which language can achieve

> but which bears no relationship by analogy or by ontologically grounded imitation, to anything beyond that particular effect. It is . . . an identifiable trope that operates on the level of the signifier and contains no responsible pronouncement on the nature of the world—despite its powerful potential to create the opposite illusion. (RT, 10)

Literary theory, in its attention to the functioning of language, thus "raises the question whether aesthetic values can be compatible with the linguistic structures from which these values are derived" (RT, 25). Literature itself raises this question in various ways, offering evidence of the autonomous potential of language, of the uncontrollable figural basis of forms, which cannot therefore serve as the basis of reliable cognition, or as de Man argues in the essay on Kleist in *The Rhetoric of Romanticism*, allegorically exposing the violence that lies hidden behind the aesthetic and makes aesthetic education possible.

De Man's essay "Kant and Schiller" concludes with a quotation from a novel by Joseph Goebbels, which casts the leader as an artist working creatively on his material:

> The statesman is an artist too. The leader and the led ["Führer und Masse"] presents no more of a problem than, say, painter and color.

> Politics are the plastic art of the state, just as painting is the plastic art
> of color. This is why politics without the people, or even against the
> people, is sheer nonsense. To shape a People out of the masses and a
> State out of the People, this has always been the deepest intention of
> politics in the true sense.

This aestheticization of politics, which seeks the fusion of form and idea,
is, de Man writes, "a grievous misreading of Schiller's aesthetic state,"
but Schiller's conception is itself also a misreading, which must be undone by an analysis that takes us back to Kant. Kant had "disarticulated
the project of the aesthetic which he had undertaken and which he
found, by the rigor of his own discourse, to break down under the power
of his own critical epistemological discourse."[11] The fact that de Man's
wartime juvenilia had themselves on occasion exhibited an inclination
to idealize the rebirth of the German nation in aesthetic terms gave him
a special reason for demonstrating how the most insightful literary and
philosophical texts of the tradition expose the unwarranted violence
required to fuse form and idea, cognition and performance.

More generally, it seems pertinent to emphasize the relevance of deconstruction to this critical project. What makes Nazism the worst excess
of Western civilization is the fact that it took to a horrendous extreme
the process of constituting a group by opposing it to something else and
attempting to exterminate what it falsely defined as a corrupting element.
Nazism sought to construct a "pure," Aryan German nation by imagining
Jews as its opposite and then slaughtering the Jews within. Never has
there been so clear a case of the horrendous functioning of a culturally
constructed binary opposition. Deconstruction seeks to undo all oppositions that, in the name of unity, purity, order and hierarchy, try to
eliminate difference.

De Man's writing grants great authority to texts—a power of illumination which is a power of disruption—but little authority to meaning.
This highly original combination of respect for texts and suspicion of
meaning will give his writing a continuing power in years to come. His
works respect great literary and philosophical texts for their insightful
undoings of the meanings that usually pass for their value. His cum-
bersome writing, with its tone of authority and elusive yet resonant key
terms, effectively teaches suspicion of meaning, and "the danger of
unwarranted hopeful solutions" that provide excuses for violent
imposition.

His insistence that we not give in to the desire for meaning, that reading
follow suspensions of meaning and resistance to meaning, encourages
a rigorous questioning of any stopping place, any moment that might
convince us that we have attained a demystified knowledge. "More than

any other mode of inquiry, including economics," he writes, "the linguistics of literariness is a powerful and indispensable tool in the unmasking of ideological aberrations, as well as a determining factor in accounting for their occurrence" (RT, 11). Such conceptions will, I believe, prove productive for criticism as it explores the resources of de Man's writing and its possible links with other contemporary theoretical discourses—of psychoanalysis, feminism, and Marxism.

16

The Future of an Illusion

Rosalind Krauss

1.

Everyone knows Jacques Lacan's story of the tin can, the one he tells his seminar on the way to explaining "What Is a Picture." He is in a boat with a group of fishermen. It is sunny and they are waiting to pull in their nets. One of the fishermen points to a sardine can glinting at them in the waves. "You see that can?" the man asks Lacan. "Do you see it? Well, it doesn't see you." This, Lacan tells us, is followed by much laughter.

Drawing the moral, Lacan reflects, "I am not simply that punctiform being located at the geometral point from which the perspective is grasped. No doubt, in the depths of my eye, the picture is painted. The picture, certainly, is in my eye. But I, I am in the picture."[1] This moral, the second punch line, the one that occurs at the level of theory is also, presumably greeted by laughter, the laughter of recognition, of getting the point.

But there are certain readers, no doubt, who are not amused. Many art historians are among this class.

2.

Norman Bryson's book *Tradition and Desire: From David to Delacroix,* subtitled with a reference (sly? respectful? ironic?) addressed to every art historian who recognizes there the appropriation of another famous work (Walter Friedlaender's *From David to Delacroix*), carries as its epigraph a verse from Louis Aragon:

> Je suis ce malheruex comparable aux miroirs
> Qui peuvent réfléchir mais ne peuvent pas voir
> Comme eux mon oeil est vide et comme eux habité
> De l'absence de toi qui fait sa cécité

For James Ackerman

No fuller reference is given for this citation, nor is it translated. This was no doubt considered unnecessary.

But Lacan quotes this verse twice in the course of his *Four Fundamental Concepts of Psycho-Analysis,* once in the context of that same series of seminars on the subject of the gaze, within which the tin can story takes its maddening place. Lacan explains that he is quoting "Contrechant" from Aragon's *Fou d'Elsa* and the English version of the seminars provides a translation.[2]

From the threshold of *Tradition and Desire,* this epigraph seems to function in a way that is parallel to the "David to Delacroix" part of Bryson's title. Just as that had suggested a play with tradition within the art-historical line, so the verse seems to be an avowal of intellectual filiation within the lineage of psychoanalytical paternity. For Lacan has indeed fathered many of Bryson's concepts. David's major defense against the overpowering weight of tradition is, for example, given by Bryson as "The Gaze of the Other." And Ingres's individuality or subjecthood is mapped in its very self-evacuated abjectness as a function of desire operating in the register of lack.

Art historians, however, are bound to be as irritated by this as they are annoyed at the seeming pointlessness of the tin can story. Lorenz Eitner ends his review of Bryson's work by saying "For all its dark intricacy of argument and language, this is a frivolous book."[3]

Sons are perfectly happy to be chastised as rebels. But how disconsolating it is merely to be called a fop.

3.

Art historians are shy of theory, rarely enunciating the ones they must undoubtedly have in order to be able to work at all. Theories of historical change. Theories of continuity. Theories of representation. Theories of the role of form. Theories of referentiality. Theories of function. And most important, theories of verification. For art history is proud of its roots in the German soil of *Wissenschaft,* even before that of *Geschichte.*

Perhaps the most theoretically self-conscious of major living art historians is Ernst Gombrich, who has consistently approached the subject from the same broad, sweeping point of view as the founders of the discipline, searching as they had for a single, unifying, encompassing principle of explanation that would account for the fact that art has a history at all, that would, that is, account for change. Gombrich's theory is the one that Bryson, himself, has consistently been eager to contest, anxious to show how Gombrich's "perceptualism" is the enemy not the friend of either the critic or the historian of art.

At the core of Gombrich's theory is the little picture on the retina, projected there from the world outside—the tiny retinal image that the artist supposedly attempts, faithfully, to transcribe onto his canvas. Modern optics, physiology, neural science, have all complicated the simplicity of those early perspective diagrams within which the original picture, formed amidst the array of the landscape, was seen to gather itself together and, along the geometrical lines of the perspective, to focus on a point at the back of the observer's eye. Gombrich has fed these complications into his model (now called the "eyewitness principle"), and although they make it more sophisticated they do not change what is an essentially mimetic account of art's ambitions, of the artist's enduring struggle to replicate for others the optically registered panorama of what he sees. Gombrich's history, the one he constructs around this model, arises, as everyone knows, from the long set of interferences between eye and brush, the rigidifying baffles of convention and method, the distractions of conceptual reorganization. The history he has written could be called "Empiricism and Its Vicissitudes."[4]

It is the theoretical, explanatory prestige of the little picture on the retina, thrown there from the contents of the world, that is Bryson's enemy. In his earlier *Vision and Painting* he had called it the perceptualist model; in *Tradition and Desire* he simply terms it vision. He wants, he says, to show its inadequacy to account for . . . well, not just painting, although in its character as a signifying practice painting can be shown to exceed vision; but the little retinal excitation is also inadequate in the very first place to model the connection, in vision, of humans to their world. Vision, Bryson argues, is not adequately drawn by the eyewitness principle; vision must be subsumed by that more complicated connection, which for distinction's sake he calls "visuality."

4.

Lacan refers the auditors in his seminar to Diderot's *Letter on the Blind*, in which the sighted are pictured as merely doing at a distance what the blind, as they move their fingers over objects, are doing close up. But the model of the optic rays as an extension of the blindman's cane will only give us a picture, Lacan objects (along with Maurice Merleau-Ponty as with many others), of vision as an essentially tactile procedure. And through this manipulation, though it may grasp the object, what is fundamental to sight will escape.

The web of perspectives in which the sighted blind grasp the object, tying it as it were into a palpable bundle, this web is called (after Leibniz) the geometral. What they cannot tie into that same sort of bundle is space—space as an ether, an atmosphere, a surround. If space is modeled through the geometral, then it remains dissociated from the viewer, the space of a stage he looks onto from his own preserve in another dimension: that of audience. The space that is actually lived by the sighted, however, is lived visually not tactilely; it is an emanation, an irradiation, an ether, not a thing. As such it is not only out there, on the stage, but next to the viewer, and behind him. This is to say that a viewer can only really see space insofar as he gets in its way, interrupting it, and blocking it off from his own view. So that what is most crucial to vision is the paradox of an essential invisibility. The viewer is only really seeing space insofar as his own presence functions as the guarantor of a blind spot, a limit case in the visually possible.

5.

What could be called "getting vision right," within those disciplines that want to analyze visual culture, historically, critically, theoretically, is the basis for certain current revisionary practice; it is the fulcrum by which to get leverage on what is now experienced as inadequate presupposition. The phenomenological model, for example, has informed the work of Michael Fried in building his historical category of "absorption" and in reconsidering the issue of realism in the work of Courbet.[5] The distinction between vision as the function of a constituting consciousness and the consequences of empiricism as that operated in the practice of Dutch painting is the foundation of recent work by Svetlana Alpers.[6] But Bryson is of course further from his contemporaries in the field of art history and closer to those in film studies in his interest in a specifically Lacanian model of vision. His language, with its references to alterity and *Spaltung* and the Gaze of the Other, is thus more available to the readers of Christian Metz and *Screen* than it is to subscribers to the *Art Bulletin*.[7]

6.

Bryson plays the model of the Gaze of the Other in two registers simultaneously. The first is the register of space. The second is the register of tradition.

It could be thought that Gombrich had thoroughly prepared art historians for Bryson's story of tradition's dispossession or expropriation of the artist's vision; of tradition's always having gotten there first so that nothing I see is seen by "me"—"I" am always rehearsing the visual scenarios that have been written by others. Gombrich's famous vectors of "making before matching" or "schema and correction" have impressed many fields of cultural history with an array of evidence underlining the degree to which convention precedes and deadens a supposed originary connection between viewer and world.

The difference is, of course, that Gombrich is focusing for his readers the effort required to break the grip of convention and to make direct contact with the world, thereby gaining access to an undistorted version of the little picture, a version that is for Empiricism always possible. Bryson is a lot less sure that breaking the grip is ever an option. If subjectivity is always, structurally, a blind spot, if it is always what is elided in vision, then it is always a vacancy that can only be filled by others.

From a structural argument that this is always the case, Bryson goes on to the historically specific occasion of Neo-Classicist painting, where the conditions are ripe for an artist's becoming unusually conscious of this situation. For obeissance to tradition, to a long canon of predecessors, is the norm for practice under the rule of the Academy. And this constant demand that vision in the present be legitimated by reference to Classical precedent, produces in its acutest possible form the feelings of belatedness, of everything's having been both seen and said already, before one; of tradition's always having gotten there first, so that one's own vision is merely a function of another's.[8]

In what is perhaps Bryson's most convincing critical moment, we see this applied to a reading of David's *Oath of the Horatii*. The most visually arresting aspect of this painting is doubtlessly the triplicated image of the sons of Horace, the echo of their profiles piled one against the other, the underlining, the insistence, the repetition of their gesture. This emphasis is designed into the work by exploiting the formal clarity of Classical sculptural relief, as in the Parthenon frieze, in preference to recording the physically possible. This is why one of David's contemporaries greeted his work with the sneer, "Well, Monsieur. In the *Horatii* you have managed to get three figures on the same plane: something never before achieved in painting."

Bryson wants to set forth the reason why one would feel the impossibility of this arrangement so powerfully. And this, he argues, is because the model of space used in the rest of the painting contradicts the effect of the frieze, for it is one that diagrams a possible circumnavigation of the forms, projecting what the stage set would look like from all its sides. The result of "this *irrational* placing of a planar design in a cubic space" is that we cannot miss the lithic nature of this father and his sons, we cannot but stub our toes on the fact that in a world perceived of flesh and blood this frieze is conceived in stone.

The point of this model is then as follows: In the *Oath of the Horatii* David throws off the weight of precedent enough to see with a high degree of naturalism, a startling directness of detail. This is the pressure of originality that one recognizes in this work. And yet, in this moment unburdened by the direct intervention of tradition in the forms of Nicolas Poussin, Jean-François-Pierre Peyron, Joseph-Marie Vien . . . David encounters not the little picture but the absoluteness of his own lateness. And so he paints the real as petrified, he paints it in the general form of what has always been already seen, he paints it under the sign of the Antique, which is to say, as sculpture. The real is thus experienced as having already been seized by death, and it comes to us in the form of the uncanny. This, Bryson argues, is the source of David's brilliance and his affect; this is a real encounter with the implacableness of tradition.

7.

Lacan is trying to net for his seminar the psychoanalytic consequences of the blind spot. In the model of the geometral, of the perspective diagram, of the eyewitness of the little picture, in these models the eye onto which the image is cast cannot itself be in the image. "But I," Lacan had insisted, "I am in the picture."

So another model is built, one that tries to account for the evanescent, unlocatability of light, for its condition as an ungovernable expansion, for its supercession of the geometral. As it shines from everywhere onto the subject, light exposes him simply as the opacity (the blind spot, the stain, the screen) that gets in its way. So it is precisely as blind spot, as limit in the visually possible, that he becomes total visibility (to light). He becomes what Merleau-Ponty had called *speculum mundi*. This condition as seen surface Lacan wants to understand in its ontological sense, that is, as a state of pure access to visibility, existing below or apart from a system of intersubjective vision—of my being visible for or by someone else. It is a condition of pure monstrance which Lacan calls *voyure*. Referring throughout the seminars to Roger Caillois's work on animal mimicry, Lacan asks his listeners to consider the example of the insect that makes itself indistinguishable from the branch on which it sits or the flowers that it eats, that makes itself, through an act of self-effacement, part of the world's picture. If this is done, for example, to hide from a predator, then it follows the pattern of the intersubjective model. But evidence shows that this does not appear to be the case. Instead it would seem that the animal simply opens itself to a visibility behind which there is no subject. And in the strength of this connection the insect turns itself into a function of light, a mark on the field of the light's picture. Pure monstrance. Pure drive "to show." Pure elision of the subject.

The visual as a system of pre-intersubjective otherness, of an outsideness that is not peopled, is the atmosphere of *voyure* that subtends intersubjectivity. It comes before, forever destabilizing that ground of connection, through which the subject looks towards others for those exchanges of glance that are so many reassurances of his own being. That bouncing, caroming light will always insure that the gaze slides away from the spot at which I try to catch it, so that "You never look at me from the place from which I see you."[9] The price, then, for being in the picture is that I am there as function, not as subject.

8.

The art historian, carefully distinguishing himself from what he distainfully views as the critic, assumes that he is not in the picture. His is the objective vision of the geometral.

Yet this outsideness to the historical field has not always been the case. There is the famous example of Aloïs Riegl, empowered by his own, contemporary experience of Impressionism to erect the category of the *optical* as a legitimate alternative, in the realm of the Beautiful, to volumetric form; and on this foundation to mount his intellectual rescue mission which would concern the whole of Early Christian art. There are the other examples of similar revivals made possible for eyes newly opened by contemporary practice: of Piero della Francesca, rendered accessible by Léger; of El Greco's availability to early 20th-century sight guaranteed through Expressionism.[10]

Bryson is writing about the capture by tradition of an evacuated subject, an artist whose vision (his possession *for himself* of the little picture) has been expropriated in advance. Art histoy thinks that he's doing something intolerably fancy, making something up, projecting. Eitner complains about Bryson's model, his "complicated apparatus of analysis," saying that it "constantly occupies the centre of the stage, blocking the view of its ostensible subjects."

But there is something indeed in the present that both blocks the way and makes a new aspect of the past available. We could call it the crisis of modernism, if the term postmodernism is distasteful. How could it have been possible for an age that thought that the limit of invention would never be reached, that there were always new forms, new structures for art to discover, how could this sensibility experience the burden of tradition and the strict discipline of the copy? It is only now, it could be argued, now that we feel ourselves slammed up against the limit, so that every image comes to us already in a nest of quotation, so that artists everywhere are operating through the terms of reproduction, that this historical recovery is possible. It is only from the vantage of the hyper-real, the simulacrum, that we can really *see* Academic practice in the light of its own system, that we can experience not just the price but the cost of the formulaic. Would it ever be possible to do that such that we were not ourselves the limit of its conditions of visibility?

9.

Gombrich's synthetic, overarching glance at the whole of Western art both occupies the position of objective observer, based on the geometral, and organizes his historical account through the geometral's perceptual model. Following Riegl who follows Heinrich Wölfflin who, indeed, follows Kant in essentializing the analytical tools of art history around the terms through which objects are given to consciousness, Gombrich is focused on vision.

But André Malraux, looking back over that same perspective, has a different story to tell. Interested less in what paintings or sculptures represent than in the representations formed by means of them, Malraux shifts the grounds of art history from the model of vision to the model of language. Or rather, he is interested in the moment of that shift inaugurated around the development of the museum, the institution created to gather together trophies of the beautiful (Classicism in its various forms), but which proceeded by transposing form into the register of meaning.

Malraux demonstrates how the 19th-century museum became a great field of comparison, but not in the old way, with Classicism at the center and everything else seen as marginal to it: barbaric or demotic deviations from a norm. Rather, the museum's comparisons began to operate within a space neutralized by efforts to range and to classify: all objects of type A in one place, those of type B in another. This collectivization—the work of the museum and its eventual partner, the art historian—began to create unities with what could be seen as their own internal coherence. These were then understood not as fallings away from a master center, but as inventions of so many epicenters, so many variants within the field of meaning. Meaning, indeed, became a function of the comparisons set up between type A with *its* center, and type B with its own. And this establishment of meaning as a function of comparison—classical versus baroque; south versus north; line versus color—organized the understanding of art within the model of language: oppositive, negative, relative. Each artistic form had something to say and its own language/dialect/idiom with which to say it. Within art historical practice, these linguistic branches then became what is known as *style*.

With meaning now the master model—having supplanted beauty— all the arts—high and low, east and west, court and folk—begin to find a place in the museum. It is their presence in turn, Malraux goes on to argue, that would hasten the rupture with the entire past of the western tradition and would usher into being, by mid-20th century, the *musée imaginaire*.

Malraux's *musée imaginaire* is more than just that impossibly huge collection of works that can be gathered between the pages of an art book. It is instead a medium within which to grasp the collective language spoken by all of style's separate voices at once: the single, universal language called Art. A now self-consciously textual space, it belongs more to fiction than it does to history. For Art's story now depends on the freedom to fragment, to reorganize and to rearrange what is available only through the photographic reproduction. Malraux describes this form of writing the story of art:

> Indeed reproduction (like the art of fiction, which subdues reality to the imagination) has created what might be called "fictitious" arts, by systematically falsifying the scale of objects; by presenting oriental seals the same size as the decorative reliefs on pillars, and amulets like statues. As a result, the imperfect finish of the smaller work, due to its limited dimensions, produces in enlargement the effect of a bold style in the modern idiom. Romanesque goldsmiths' work links up with the sculpture of the period, and reveals its true significance in sequences of photographs in which reliquaries and statues are given equal dimensions. True, these photographs figure solely in specialist reviews. But these reviews are made by artists, for fellow artists—and do not fail to take effect. Sometimes the reproductions of minor works suggest to us great styles which have passed away—or which "might have been." . . . In the realm of what I have called fictitious arts, the fragment is king.[11]

What strikes us as quaint in this passage is the idea of a decorum of reproduction, the notion that reproduction could be confined within specifiable limits, contained "in specialist reviews." Malraux is writing just after the war, and thus before the photograph of the work of art had quit the domain of the specialist journal to join the vast overproduction of images which now constructs our simulated landscape. In 1949 Malraux's fictions could continue to find their place within his linguistic model of art as the production of meaning.

The Museum without Walls suggests a periodization scheme for the modern (19th and 20th century) reception of art built first on the museum and then on the photographic reproduction or substitute. One could view this scheme as mapping two phases in the production of those sets of representations through which art is consumed, the first projected in the field of the symbolic and the second, in the domain of the imaginary. This would move Malraux's final stage, his "fictions," out of the realm of the linguistic and into that of the visual.

10.

The desiring subject has a horror of seriality, of replication, of substitution, of the copy. If the object of his desire can be replaced, then in this logic, so can he; he ceases to be the unique object of desire. The seriality of the object provokes in its most acute condition the contingency of the subject: the thought that there is no necessity for his being, that he might have been another.

Lacan collects the four seminars on visuality under the master title "The Gaze as *objet a*." The Lacanian *objet a* would, in another descriptive system be called a deixic marker, an indication of the specific place—in all its temporary, shifting, non-necessity—from which a speaker enters the transpersonal system of signs that form a language. Or in psychoanalytic terms it marks the point from which a subject attempts to insert his unique story into the impersonal system that Lacan terms the Other. For the subject takes the *objet a* as something or someone addressed to him, and through this address, affirming him as the object of its desire. And his desire, the price of his very being, is to be this object. But the *objet a* is not the marker of contingency for nothing. For this thing on which the subject himself depends appears to him under constant threat of withdrawal, replacement, substitution.

In speaking of the gaze as one of the avatars of the *objet a*, Lacan evokes it as a kind of fascinating glitter on the horizon towards which the subject looks to see himself reflected. The forms of this glitter, however, are those in which substitution is already at work. And in this guise the gaze is described as the castrated sex of the mother, as the Medusa, the jewel, the fetish. In this guise the gaze that welcomes the subject simultaneously multiplies into the undifferentiated sign of contingency, drops into the condition of seriality.

Seriality, Bryson points out, is the very form of Ingres's art. For we must add to Ingres's extraordinary pillaging of the art of the past, his compulsion to repeat his own. Ingres was his own copyist, the industrious maker of replicas of his own works. His auto-plagarism was one of the grounds for the contempt in which his contemporaries held him, as in Théophile Silvestre's, "M. Ingres has passed his life as much in repeating the same forms as in insidiously combining the most famous traditional types with the living models." Even Ingres admitted that perhaps, "I reproduce my own compositions too often."[12]

There are many examples. One of the most arresting is that of the *Valpinçon Bather*, the placidly beautiful image of the back of a seated nude, her head swathed in a striped silk turban, her arms holding a sheet up to the breasts we are never to see. Ingres painted the first version of this work in 1808, the last in 1865. Between these two dates he executed her image more than twenty times, sometimes alone, sometimes in groups, sometimes in oil, sometimes in gouache, always turbaned, always seen from behind.

The serialization of the *Valpinçon Bather* takes on a certain resonance within the logic of the *objet a*. For this figure glitters in a very special way on the horizon of Ingres's experience. She is, in Bryson's reading as in that of other scholars, Raphael's *La Fornarina*, Raphael's mistress as he had pictured her: nude, her head swathed in a striped silk turban, her hands holding a sheet up to her breasts; she is the Fornarina, only now turned away.[13] In this, her seriality, her condition as substitution compulsively multiplied, is mirrored the abjectness of Ingres's dependency, his displacement even as a desiring subject onto Raphael and Raphael's desire.

11.

Fetishism begins in the realm of the scopic and, through a denial of sexual difference, opens onto the pure play of substitution. The power of this spectacle of systematicity, the fascination it exercises, both derives from and re-ignites what Jean Baudrillard has called our "passion for the code."[14] This vanishing point, this moment of passage between the visual and the coded, this sense of the gaze as *objet a*, places us in an analytic space that is as far as possible from that of *Art and Illusion*.

Operating on the hinge between the visual and the textual, this gaze as *objet a*, this model of the fetish in formation, opens simultaneously onto many fields of analysis, of which art history is only one. It is probably clear by now that in this domain Bryson's explorations, both interesting and tentative, are conducted in almost total isolation.[15] Practically no one, at least no one in art history, is looking.

17

The Future of Genre Theory: Functions and Constructional Types

Alastair Fowler

Now that criticism is beginning to recuperate from the fevers of structuralism and deconstruction, genre theory is likely to come into new prominence. For it offers a way forward. The study of genre offers a way round several of the issues that divide deconstructionists and traditionalists.

Genre in Hermeneutics

In attempting to cross the historical gaps that shut off the texts of other periods from our own, the reader has often to puzzle over difficult meanings that depend on earlier meanings, even less accessible. These may belong, however, to enabling or constraining semantic types, by reference to which they can be recovered. Genre theory, especially, has much to say about the ways in which types are modified (without being obliterated) in the course of successive literary communications. As experience shows, such modifications can succeed in prompting an appropriate uptake, without their codes ever having been defined, let alone authorized.

The deconstructionists' notion of *différance*—of the impossibility of determinate communication—depends partly on confusion between definition and communication, partly on exaggeration of the role of codes in the latter. When Jacques Derrida says "There is not a single signified that escapes . . . the play of signifying references that constitute language,"[1] he appears to have forgotten how much, in communication, we share a manifest cognitive environment—how much we can infer from experience, how quick we are to notice ostensive departures from the ordinary. When a waitress asks "Coffee?," the speech is really quite a determinate one; and the same would be true even if, for once, she asked "Hogwash?" Uptake depends not on authoritative definition but on many experiences of language and of life, which have established language as a far more dependable medium of communication than Derrida would have us believe.

Derrida often focuses on potential ambiguities in single words or phrases; suggesting that with more words that slipperiness would be even greater. But in fact longer strings have more knots to fix the meaning with, more error-obviating structures, more "redundancies." In literature these commonly operate across wide historical gaps; although we usually only become aware of them in cases of imperfect communication. For, of course, tradition is so frail that literary communication sometimes does break down, even with a critic as great as Dr. Johnson.

In the famous Rambler 168, Johnson faults Macbeth's speech "Come thick night!/ And pall thee in the dunnest smoke of hell":

> What can be more dreadful than to implore the presence of night, invested not in common obscurity, but in the smoke of hell? Yet the efficacy of this invocation is destroyed by the insertion of an epithet now seldom heard but in the stable, and *dun* night may come or go without any other notice than contempt.[2]

It certainly exposes the frailty of dramatic tradition, that a great passage—in which, as Johnson recognizes, "is excited all the force of poetry"—should come to be misunderstood so strikingly. But, from a more positive point of view, this failure also illustrates the obstinate resistance of literature's interlocking structures. For one can see that the good critic Johnson sensed a contradiction between two distinct bases for inference: between tragic decorum on the one hand (the requirements of a particular high style, with all its subsidiary codes), and, on the other hand, the register of "dun" (a word basely associated with stables and farriary). One code called for "high" diction; the other placed "dun" low in the scale. Johnson was unable to resolve this contradiction. But now that we have historical dictionaries (thanks in no small part to the Harmless Drudge himself), we know that "dun" had changed its meaning in the interval between Shakespeare and Johnson. *OED*, sense 1, "dingy brown colour, as of horse," had survived, albeit with a more limited social register; but not sense 2, "dark, dusky . . . murky, gloomy," as in Milton's "dun air sublime"—later to be quoted by Johnson himself in his great Dictionary.

It is a matter of common experience among critics habituated to the use of dictionaries that familiarity with old literature brings a sense of which words to look up in them. In such ways scholarship amplifies error-correction redundancies, and otherwise augments the ordinary processes of inference, so as to restore communication. Just as linguistics and philology offer routes round some of the problems of the herme-neutic gap, so genre theory offers others. Often a hermeneutic gap will open up in the lexical coding, only to be closed, as in the *Macbeth* example, by the generic.

Indeed, it is genre history as much as any branch of the literary dis-cipline that makes it possible to retrace more or less stable series of intended meanings across the centuries. Genre is when we speak of the sun "rising," long after our ancestors rejected the Ptolemaic planetary system. Because of the continuity of experience, ordinary language is seldom unintelligible. And in literature the tape of change can often be partly rewound through genre study.

New Genres

At the same time, in approaching these persistent old genres, theorists will have to find new ways of understanding them, in accordance with the ever-changing perspectives of our own time. And they must also keep up with literature's mimetic reflection of life by recognizing when distinctively modern genres have emerged. Criticism ought to be much more concerned than it is, indeed, with identifying new genres. Such descriptions as are attempted tend to be rather loosely conducted, and overfree with novelties of labeling. There are advantages in retaining traditional nomenclature so far as possible, to keep etiological links with the past.

What, then, are the new genres? In poetry criticism, much recent attention has been given to poems about pictures. But many other ex-tremely common new or revived genres have gone largely unmentioned: among them the essayistic epigram and the familiar elegy (which may even be replacing the epigram as the dominant form).[3] An enormous amount of work remains to be done in the way of identifying contem-porary poetic subgenres.

In fiction, there have been many studies of "metafiction," or writing which makes its own artefactual status thematic and self-consciously explicit. Such are Patricia Waugh's *Metafiction* (1984) and Linda Hutch-eon's *Narcissistic Narrative: The Metafictional Paradox* (1981). Metafiction has now to be regarded as a well-established contemporary genre; al-though in some ways it hardly constitutes a very satisfactory one, being almost more of a grouping by period manner than a genre. Another new kind is mosaic fiction (exemplified most notably by Thomas Pynchon's *The Crying of Lot 49* and *Gravity's Rainbow*). This multi-perspective form presumably reflects social changes characterized by increased flows of information and decreased attention span. Also a modern favorite (but by no means a new invention) is the epicyclic or elaborative work, which directly depends on the imaginative world of a familiar classic—as Michael Moorcock's *Gloriana* (1978) depends on Spenser's *The Faerie Queene* and Sidney's *Arcadia* for subtexts, or John Seelye's *The True Adventures of Huckleberry Finn* on Twain's novel of more or less the same name. Work needs to be done on the special nature of intertextuality in this area.

But the most outstanding fictional genre of recent decades has surely been the poioumenon, or work-in-progress novel—the narrative of the making of a work of art.[4] In this genre fiction and reality, characters and their creator, mingle problematically; so that it is sometimes treated within the broader grouping of metafiction. Although its beginnings have been traced back to Sterne's *Tristram Shandy*, as a prominent genre it is distinctively modern. Recently, indeed, the poioumenon has been so dominant that it has exerted a strong influence on the epicyclic genre. This has in consequence moved in what may be called a psychobiographical direction. The epicyclic work of the eighties tends to treat its subtext by restoring it to a putative psychoanalytic matrix. This it does by melding the subtext world with a speculatively reconstructed emotional biography of its author. This possibility was already half-realized in Jean Rhys's fine novel *Wide Sargasso Sea* (1966), as well as in Frederick Busch's *Mutual Friend* (1978). More recently, it has been realized most often in drama. I am thinking of the Salieri biography in Peter Shaffer's *Amadeus* (especially the Miloš Forman film version); the Bram Stoker in Liz Lochhead's *Dracula;* and the Kafka in Alan Bennett's television play *The Insurance Man.* Each of these implicitly traces the genesis of a classic work.

All sorts of poioumenon have been well received critically. But it is possible to see the genre as representing something of a critical juncture for mimesis. For its existence points to the difficulty of maintaining traditional authorial roles—as regards character analysis, say, or moral commentary—in the face of psychoanalysis and relativistic ethics.

It is sometimes asked whether new kinds of kinds may be emerging—genres not produced by the usual assemblage, abstraction, modulation, and the like, but instead by novel processes of development. And indeed something of the sort might conceivably be found in the forms arrived at by radical subtractions from earlier generic repertoires, as in the *nouveau roman*, in poetic minimalism, and in the work of Samuel Beckett. Or again, in John Ashbery's poetry, where abandonment of stable mimetic contexts seems almost to react directly to contemporary literary theory. In fact, one might think in terms of "theoretic genres," motivated at least in part by a wish to illustrate (and perhaps validate) some particular theory. Obvious examples would be the novels of Alain Robbe-Grillet, B. S. Johnson, and Umberto Eco. But in the long run such works are not worth attention unless they transcend their programs. And in any case, are they really generated in a novel way? Are they very different, in their theoretic purposiveness, from Ben Jonson's comical satires?

Others may detect a new sort of modal play in the rhapsodic sketches of Richard Brautigan, or the camp gothic of Joyce Carol Oates and Angela Carter. But are these effects arrived at by generic processes radically different from those that led to nineteenth-century retrospective forms? Future genre criticism should certainly be much concerned with identifying new genres (together with genres neglected since the eighteenth century). But they will probably be genres that originated through familiar processes of development. In this sense, at least, there is nothing new under the generic sun.

Differentiated Functions

A marked tendency of the last decade or two, potentially important for genre theory, is the interest in how literary works function—in the means of their communication. There have been several fine studies of specific elements in literature. Among these are a number of narratological inquiries, whether concentrating on narrator roles, point-of-view, and structure, like F. K. Stanzel's *A Theory of Narrative* (originally 1979) and Gérard Genette's *Figures III* (1972), or on plot, like Peter Brooks's *Reading for the Plot* (1984), or on character, like Thomas Docherty's *Reading (Absent) Character* (1983) and J. W. Smeed's *The Theophrastan 'Character'* (1985). Other studies of functioning include Barbara Herrnstein Smith's *Poetic Closure* (1968); Thomas Greene's *The Light in Troy* (1982), on imitation; Jean H. Hagstrum's *The Sister Arts* (1958) and Michael Irwin's *Picturing: Description and Illusion in the Nineteenth-Century Novel* (1979), on description; and Francis Berry's *The Shakespeare Inset* (1965) and Mary Ann Caws's *Reading Frames in Modern Fiction* (1985), on framing—the last influenced by Erving Goffman's *Frame Analysis* (1974). Then, there are recent or forthcoming treatments of such other functions as naming (Anne Barton), digression (Arden Reed), numerology (John MacQueen), listing, catalogues, and the like. And we can doubtless expect further work on dialogue to follow Goffman's pioneering *Frames of Talk* (1981). Throughout this phase, critics have aimed at determining exactly how literature works, as regards the specific operation under their scrutiny. It has been an impressive program of inquiry, and it has led at times to gains in understanding and appreciation.

Nevertheless most of this criticism has the same great deficiency: an almost total neglect of generic implications. Barbara Smith, to be sure, shows a good appreciation of how closure is subject to generic differentiation. But in general most of the critics mentioned leave genre out of their inquiry altogether. Sometimes this loss of proportion seems to be bound up with a kind of formal monism; as when Mary Ann Caws's engaging book enlarges framing imperialistically, until it overruns other functions (like digression) and absorbs them into itself. Of "The Turn of the Screw" Caws says that it "is distinct from the other framing and framed tales discussed" (p. 146). She nowhere considers whether this different framing effect might have a generic aspect. But James's ghost stories hardly function like novels; indeed, in their perspectival narration they have more kinship with the romances. Any full study of "architectural borders" in James would surely have to return to the gothic window from which Clifford and Phoebe survey the modern world in *The House of the Seven Gables,* and perhaps beyond Hawthorne's innovative work to frames in even earlier fiction. (Such a line of inquiry might be very fruitful; since it would stand a chance of supporting or undermining the formal continuity between medieval and Victorian romance that is commonly assumed by contemporary theorists.) In fact, the manner of framing varies from genre to genre in a sensitive way; resembling in this the other elements of literature. To put it bluntly, most recent work on functions needs to be done again, with more cognizance of genre.

It might be no bad thing, in fact, for literary theory as a whole to be reformulated in terms of genre, rather as mathematics was in large part reformulated, earlier this century, in terms of set theory.

However that may be, the implications of the recent studies of functions are immense so far as genre is concerned. Until now, genre theory has largely consisted of empirical listing of generic repertoires, or (more superficially still) of structuralism's aprioristic dichotomies. These preliminaries behind, it should now be possible to investigate how the features of generic repertoires are related functionally. Accepting that genres exist as cultural objects, we can go on to ask how they work. How, for example, does the diction of seventeenth-century georgic, with its metaphorical generality ("finny drove"; "scaly flocks"), relate to the kind's impulse of descriptive specificity? How is conceptual generality reconciled with particularity of attention? Is the apparent contradiction the result of a scientific impulse to classify, and so to order, particulars that are inadequately understood? Has georgic description any functional coherence, beyond that of being a convenient indicator of genre? How does georgic description relate in terms of function to the absence of description in pastoral? If particulars are excluded from pastoral along with knowledge, how far is georgic description a necessary function of making the natural world an object of knowledge rather than of innocence? How far, in a word, is the interaction of georgic and pastoral systemic?

With modern genres, questions about function are naturally harder to formulate. However, as a hypothetical illustration in miniature, one might consider the multiplication of references to writing in the poioumenon or work-in-progress fiction. How do these references work? In view of the fact that so many poioumena containing such references appeared in the 1970s, the question arises whether they may not reflect contemporary structuralist ideas—particularly the notion of ubiquitous codes, of codes intertextually "inscribed" in everything. But then one recalls that such references to writing go back to Sterne. Even the multitudinous loose papers, which we think of now as distinctively postmodern, were as early as Carlyle's *Sartor Resartus* a feature of the kind, and so may be suspected to have a function integral to it. Perhaps they serve to confess the speculative provisionality of the poioumenon? Or the author's difficulty in binding his ideas together? Do they work to diminish the reader's expectation of strong closure? Or to specify the area of concern: namely, the nature of writing itself? Sterne and Carlyle agree at least in their conception of writing as a means not of delivering known truths (the Book of Nature) but of arriving at new ones (the natural sketchbook).

Constructional Types

What I have just called functions are referred to in more structural terms by Thomas Greene, where he speaks of "episodes, descriptions, speeches, similes, characters" as "minor forms" of the *Aeneid*.[5] And it is true that each function must be embodied in a rhetorical structure (or perhaps in several; as describing may take the form of ekphrasis, or topothesia, or chronographia). In *Kinds of Literature* (p. 128), I termed such structures "constructional types," and emphasized their purely formal character. They form a vast and neglected generic category; including as it does not only literary devices such as theme and variation, sequence, catalogue, inset, allusion, and digression, but also extraliterary importations such as game, testament, and matrix.[6] Investigation of this category warrants an important place in the program for future genre criticism. For one thing, constructional types may be easier to respond to, initially, than the historical kinds of traditional theory. (Who can see tragedy freshly, without Aristotelian colorations?) For another, constructional types seem to have a fundamental status as an inescapable element in composition. A work may relate to historical genres only very loosely;

but it must deploy at least one constructional type with precision, in order to be taken as literature. The author may have had no conscious generic intention. But the implied author—"Author X" of Michael Baxandall's *Patterns of Intention*—must have thought in terms of a constructional type. Unless, that is, he fell back on the default type of direct expression.

Constructional types are unlike historical kinds in their elasticity of scale. Allegory, for example, can be a brief *allegoria* within a phrase ("steering the ship of state"); it can be the structural armature of a paragraph (as in the account of Time's operations that opens *Dombey and Son*); it can order a whole episode within a non-allegorical work (the Logostilla allegory in the *Orlando Furioso*); or it can be a full-length form in its own right (*Piers Plowman*). (Since the death of the medieval kind, full-length allegory has tended to operate as a mode: thus *Animal Farm* is labeled "allegorical fable" rather than "allegory.") Such flexibility and overlap will not dismay the theorist who thinks in terms of family resemblances rather than classes. Nevertheless the relation of type to kind remains somewhat problematic. We may like to think of the constructional type as purely formal. But it seems to be able to exert pressure on substantive elements, sometimes to such an extent that a new subgenre eventuates.[7] In these instances it is almost as if the constructional type were an incomplete or aspiring genre. A promising line of inquiry would be to investigate how far such a type may represent the nucleus of an emergent genre.

A case in point might be Edwin Morgan's brilliant application of the matrix constructional type. In mathematics, a matrix is a rectangular array of symbols which in certain operations may be selected in turn. Something like this happens (although in a way anything but regular) in Geoffrey Hill's ordering of associations in *Mercian Hymns*. And a generic history could be contrived, by tracing the origin to medieval and Renaissance *versus rapportati*, and emphasizing schematized instances like that in a poem possibly by Raleigh:

Hir face,	Hir tong,	Hir wit,
So faire,	So sweete,	So sharpe
First bent,	Then drew,	Then hit,
Mine eie,	Mine eare,	My hart. . . .[8]

But with Morgan's "Bees' Nest" (1968), it may be nearer the truth to speak in terms of constructional type—of an innovatory formal "device":

> busybykeobloodybizzinbees
> bloodybusybykeobizzinbees
> bizzinbloodybykeobusybees
> busybloodybykeobizzinbees . . .[9]

Here the first five elements ("busy," "byke," "o," "bloody," and "biz-zen") are combined in turn with "bees"—almost as one multiplies matrices—according to a permutation rule. The type could have been introduced directly from mathematics; but more probably it came to Morgan via concrete poetry, where similar procedures were fairly common in the 1960s.[10] His characteristically witty applications of the matrix, here and elsewhere, adumbrate an emergent subgenre; particularly when, as in "The Computer's First Christmas Card,"[11] he diversifies the permutation rule with irregularities of association:

> jollymerry
> hollyberry
> jollyberry
> merryholly
> happyjolly
> jollyjelly
> jellybelly
> bellymerry
> hollyheppy
> jollyMolly . . .

The type certainly seems to be severely formal. Yet its effect is to press the content away from rational meaning, towards a lightly humorous unpredictability.

When constructional types have been studied in the past, a philological method has generally predominated; series of imitations being traced back to a creative *fons et origo*. This is not a ridiculous practice. In approaching Anne Stevenson's "A Legacy: On my Fiftieth Birthday" it would be very rewarding to follow up the implications of the subtitle "After François Villon."[12] And there is no doubt that many poets, since Villon, have added their codicils to his *Grand Testament* of 1461, in direct or indirect knowledge of his seminal example. Others, however, stand in a more distant relation to the Villonesque grouping, and prompt the speculation whether there may not be polygenetic fresh starts, leading to works that share nothing more than a fundamental testamentary constructional type. How much, for example, has Isabella Whitney's "Wyll and Testament" (1573), addressed to London, in common with Villon's poem?[13] Certainly on turning to the much-imitated "Adrian Henri's Last Will and Testament"[14] one senses a quite distinct impulse. It is hard to believe that genre exerted much pressure in this case. Far from the personal gravity of Villon and Stevenson, Henri strikes jaunty but impersonal political postures. And he not only declines to draw on the resources of genre, but even short-circuits the forms of verse: "2. I leave the entire East Lancs Road with all its landscapes to the British people."

Yet however determinedly Henri rejects the fully generic forms of literature, he seems to find those of the constructional type inescapable. The testamentary idea is all, and Henri plays it for all it is worth.

Some of the most widely disseminated constructional types are accumulative—additive structural patterns such as one finds in children's rhymes, like "Seven little rabbits."[15] And poets have often taken up these nursery rhyme devices and used them with very different, adult registers. A striking example is the accumulative rhyme *The House that Jack Built*. Since William Hone's *The Political House that Jack Built* (1819), this has been the subtext for many political poems. These may be said to have something of a generic relationship, although one attenuated by the dominance of the subtext. It is a different matter with Elizabeth Bishop's "Visits to St. Elizabeths" (1950), where the accumulative repetitions are delicatedly varied:[16]

> . . . This is the soldier home from the war.
> These are the years and the walls and the door
> that shut on a boy that pats the floor
> to see if the world is round or flat.
> This is a Jew in a newspaper hat
> that dances carefully down the ward,
> walking the plank of a coffin board
> with the crazy sailor
> that shows his watch
> that tells the time
> of the wretched man
> that lies in the house of Bedlam.

The symbolism, like the decisive change of substantive content, points to a secondary or even tertiary rendering of genre, rather than mere parody. But what relation has any of these with the accumulative Hebrew folksong *Had Gadya?*—

> And the Holy One, blessed be He,
> came and smote the Angel of Death
> Who took the butcher
> That slew the ox
> That drank the water
> That quenched the fire
> That burnt the stick
> That beat the dog
> That bit the cat
> That ate up the goat
> That Papa bought for two zuzim.[17]

It is not even certain that there is any causal link at all between the folksong and the much-parodied nursery rhyme. Nevertheless they share a particular accumulative content, with a proliferating syntactic pattern and a correspondingly inexorable logic of consequences. It seems almost as if this structural (and rhythmic) pattern has a life of its own.

Larger Prospects

This organic metaphor has, of course, its dangers. When so much foolish animism is talked about texts writing texts, it becomes imperative to treat biological analogies with some circumspection. All the same, there are ways in which the development of organisms can usefully be compared to that of genres. In each case, after all, one is probably dealing with the generation of structures by codes (DNA codes, genre rules). Does the concept of organic growth assume continuities uncharacteristic of the actual course of literary history? In a developing system (such as I described in *Kinds of Literature*) is "revolution" or complete discontinuity impossible? To suppose so is to underestimate the biological analogy, which is perfectly capable of application to interrupted development and to change *per saltum*. Biologists know a good deal now about the part played in sudden change by mutation. But of course, mutations are rare. And a literary "revolution" would not be noticed unless it took existing generic forms as its point of departure.

Literary critics of every school tend to use metaphors of energy—as when we speak of genre's "pressures." Then why not metaphors of organic energy? Perhaps if the biological analogy were explored cautiously, it might provide a useful language in which to describe developmental processes. Are not our "inertias," against which writers struggle to be original, as much biological and psychological as physical? Literature everywhere bears the impress of personality, of individual and communal experience. It would be interesting, therefore, to explore how far genres contain communal energies and aspirations. In such inquiries the biological analogy has at least the advantage of avoiding unrealistic notions of genre as predictable. For some systems are tighter than others, and genre, if it is a system at all, surely resembles a physical one less than a loose system in biology or ecology. Eventually we might even progress to models of psychological development. And then we would begin to understand something of the real unpredictability of literature, which has little to do with local indeterminacy.

Any successful genre theory of the future will have to be a good deal less remote than those of the past, less couched in terms of neat but undemonstrable classes. In actual literature, such categories as historical kinds, modes, and constructional types seem to overlap, change, and change places in more fluid ways than most theorists have cared to admit. In striving for generality and clarity—as strive we must—it may be that we have lost flexibility, and with it a just proportion between abstraction and description. There is even a tendency towards "theoreticism—towards an excess of metatheory. This has shown itself in increasingly stereotyped or else silly theorizing, more and more concerned with the internal relations of doctrinaire schools. On any optimistic view, the next phase of genre theory is likely to be less "pure," more subject to confirmation by the evidence of examples.

We need to pay more attention to what is really the case in literature. It will not do to deal with genres "in terms of *fixed form*," as Fredric Jameson proposes in a justly admired article:[18]

> . . . romance is that form in which the *world-ness* of *world* reveals itself.
> . . . for romance as a literary form is that event in which *world* in the technical sense of the transcendental horizon of my experience becomes precisely visible as something like an innerworldly object in its own right, taking on the shape of *world* in the popular sense of nature, landscape, and so forth. (p. 142)

Interesting as this formulation is, it fails to describe Chaucer's The Knight's Tale, *Aucassin and Nicolette*, *La Fille du Comte de Pontieu*, and many other works which are often thought of as romances, but which have none of them much in the way of nature or landscape. Does that disable Jameson's theory fatally? I am not at all sure that many will feel this to be the case, so absolute is the "autonomy" currently conceded to literary theorists.

Somehow we must escape from theoreticism's manipulation of aprioristic ideas about ever narrower ranges of convenient examples. In the last resort, literary theory is only as comprehensive and as penetrating as the reading it is based on.

But is the evidence of *reading* still the essential criterion?—reading in the sense of responsive uptake of a structure of words? For such increasingly prominent forms as radio and TV drama, science fiction, and other popular genres in deliberately unstructured styles now raise a pressing taxonomic problem. True, if one were to follow Northrop Frye's approach in *The Secular Scripture*, science fiction could be seen as a successor of medieval popular romance. It would take its place as a new sub-literature, with a few exceptional instances like *Canticle for Leibowitz* and *The Torturer's Apprentice* claiming individual consideration, and most being of interest only collectively. There is something in this—and perhaps even in the more extreme view that this constitutes the "normal" state of affairs—that literature in the traditional text-based sense is a Renaissance departure. But not enough, surely, to make us try to turn the clock back. Nor will it quite do merely to alter the hierarchy of kinds in favor of science fiction and other popular genres, as some of their proponents would like. Such paradigms of rank were always far too crudely schematic, too oblivious to variations in the temperament of readers and the genius of writers.

A more radical taxonomic shift seems called for: one that will take cognizance of literature's new role in a culture using artistic media in which written language is no longer the sole substrate. In literature, organization focuses primarily on the text as a form of words; but this is not true of all contemporary writing with a claim to attention. For example, I have enjoyed science fiction avidly for some forty years; yet I have no certainty that its pleasures were literary ones. Of what sort were they, then? Or, to pose the problem in a different way: certain genres seem to span the divide between literature and other arts such as film. Should these amphibious genres now be regarded as the center of an emergent canon? Or are they not rather to be thought of as peripheral, or even separate?

As always, future theorists will continue to rewrite generic histories; supplying new pedigrees of descent in accordance with new standards of respectability, of aesthetic pleasure, or of spiritual depth. And their retrospective inventions of our genres will not always be merely aberrant or evanescent. Doubtless some of their rearrangements of our generic ideas will be irrevocable, as expressing permanent and legitimate changes of interest. Nevertheless good literary historians will try, as always, to escape intoxication by the effervescent new groupings, and to penetrate, through what is merely said to have happened, to an actual course of generic development that includes the genres as we see them. For groupings are merely frivolous if they fail to come to terms with the filiations of the past—if only to terms of unconditional rejection. Cyrano de Bergerac's *Histoire comique des états et empires de la Lune* cannot simply be treated as science fiction, *tout court*, without any consideration of its original very different affiliations. A radical rewriting of genre history can only be achieved through acknowledging continuities, not by ignoring them and inventing ruptures. This profound paradox of historicity, however, is not one that we can expect even the next phase of genre theory to resolve.

18

Mystory: The Law of Idiom in Applied Grammatology

Gregory L. Ulmer

The emergence of a regionalized epistemology, the dysfunctioning of the grand explicating metanarratives, and the effectiveness of feminist appeals to personal experience are among the trends encouraging the development of *mystory*—a term designating the nexus of history, politics, language, thought, and technology in the last decade of this millenium.[1] The mystorical approach to a topic such as "the future of theory" involves a reworking of certain ancient problems—the relation of the particular and the general, the reality of change, the invention of the "subject," to name a few. Whether ancient or modern, it is not always easy to recognize the peculiar configuration of possibility in one's own moment, hence the use of a neologism to name this movement, or this "mythical concept" (to use Roland Barthes's term for that historical, unstable dimension of myth).

> The concept is a constituting element of myth: if I want to decipher myths, I must somehow be able to name concepts. The dictionary supplies me with a few: Goodness, Kindness, Wholeness, Humaneness, etc. But by definition, since it is the dictionary which gives them to me, these particular concepts are not historical. Now what I need most often is ephemeral concepts, in connection with limited contingencies: neologism is then inevitable. (Barthes, 1972: 121)

The peculiar mixture of bells, rickshaws, and opium dens that constitute "China" for a Frenchman Barthes dubs "Sininess," noting that the ugliness of the term is compensated for by the fact "that conceptual neologisms are never arbitrary: they are built according to a highly sensible proportional rule."

As a conceptual neologism, mystory is the title for a collection or set of elements gathered together temporarily in order to represent my comprehension of the scene of writing. It is an idea of sorts, if nothing like a platonic *eidos,* whose name alludes to several constituent features:

1) *History.* In her contribution to the authoritative (for an earlier generation) *Relations of Literary Study,* the late Rosalie L. Colie explained the difference between history and mystory:

> I have often been forced, by myself and by kind friends, to give up some beautiful theory which depended on material I happened to unearth. The words are important: that *I* happened to unearth, and that I *happened* to unearth. Though it is demonstrably true that chance favors the prepared mind, and serendipity is rarely arbitrary, one should not bank on the reliability of Pasteur's axiom in relation to one's self. After all, as medieval allegorists and Renaissance mythographers amply demonstrate, anything can be made to connect with anything: the trick is to distinguish the real from the illusory connection. (Colie, 1967: 20)

Dr. Colie made a valiant effort, in her dissertation seminar at Brown, to do me the favor of forcing me to give up a beautiful theory I happened to unearth, but that was before any of us knew about semiotics, intertextuality, the return of allegory, the aleatory research pun. Still, this distinction between history and mystory might have made her last spring more pleasant.

2) *Herstory.* The progress from history to mystory is a classic example of the growth of language, of word formation by a certain mimesis. Feminism, in any case, makes mystory possible, although race, class, region, nation are given as much attention in it as are gender and sex. Still, the pun on *maistrie,* from *The Wife of Bath's Tale* ("And whan that I hadde geten unto me, / By maistrie, al the soveraynetee"), suggests the problem, shared with feminism, of finding an alternative to "mastery" and assertion as they are practiced in conventional scholarship.

3) *Mystery.* The function of narrative in historiography is a major question for mystory, which seeks an alternative to the manipulation of enigma and delay, and the exploitation of identification and recognition, that inform realistic narrative in fiction and history alike. Mystory continues to rely upon narrative knowledge, but prefers to work with forms such as the anecdote in order to expose the way the grand metanarratives position the subject in a particular ideology. The anecdote is a more appropriate form in which to investigate the future of theory, about which there can be no authoritative account (mystory is not a science). To write a mystory about the future of theory is not to create an expectation of resolution, the illusion of an explanation; not to predict, assert, or attack, neither in the tone of science nor manifesto. Rather, the mystorical voice may be that of the analysand—perhaps this attitude is the one practical lesson from Jacques Lacan—who wonders about the process or trajectory of my knowledge, my syllabi, my research projects,

as if they were symptoms or clues. Mystified by those colleagues who view poststructuralism as a cultural disease, as nihilism or anarchy, the mystorian attempts self-reference, to see myself positioned in the line of glances Lacan described in the seminar on "The Purloined Letter," an ostrich, an embarrassed avowal of that set of elements I happened to find convincing. My own knowledge is the mystery to me. Or is this way of putting it still too semiotic?

4) *My Story*. The mystorian relates to the materials of a discipline in a way that Jean-François Lyotard describes as "pagan."

> What is very important is that among the pagans, these gods, even when they have the position of first speaker, are themselves narrated in narratives that tell what they are telling. This relation—an intradiegetic relation—means that the one who speaks is at the same time the hero of a story in which he is narrated himself; and these embeddings can be multiplied without end. It is, mutatis mutandis, the same situation as that of the Cashinahua narrator in relation to the story he tells since he narrates the story, I repeat, from a position where he is himself narrated. (Lyotard and Thébaud, 1985: 39)

The teacher, the researcher, is the tenor of the explanation, the analysis, the information or knowledge set forth as scholarship or instruction. When Nietzsche suggested that every theory is an autobiography it was never a question of psychological determinism. Rather, if applied grammatology is my story it is because poststructuralism befell me as an experience. Roland Barthes's novelesque of the intellect will be recognizable in the conceptual neologism being elaborated here, with "concepts that come to constitute allegories, a second language, whose abstraction is diverted to fictive ends" (Barthes, 1977: 124). The embedding of the narrator within the narrative, such that the sender always speaks from the position of the receiver of the story for which one serves as a relay, may be recognized as the "scene of writing" described by Derrida in terms of the *envois*.

These then are some of the properties of mystory—history, herstory, *maistrie*, mystery, my story, the novelesque of the intellect, paganism, *envois* or pragrammatology. And one more: paradigm shift. Thomas S. Kuhn's *The Structure of Scientific Revolutions* marks the incommensurability of competing paradigms: "That is why a law that cannot even be demonstrated to one group of scientists may occasionally seem intuitively obvious to another" (Kuhn, 1970: 150). Poststructuralists, for example, hold fundamentally different assumptions about the world of culture from those held by Marxists or traditional humanists, for reasons that might not even count as reasons, or that are temperamental rather than logical. The mystorian is not proving a case, nor persuading an opponent (as if such an event were possible), but avowing the history of my own conversion or turn, of that which for me has counted as proof and pudding. "Let me tell the theory of applied grammatology and how it happened."

The World Picture

Why do I think that mystory is a reasonable response to change? One way to answer that question is to review Martin Heidegger's critique of science in "The Age of the World Picture." Heidegger pointed out that one of the essential phenomena of the *modern* age is its science. Indeed, one way to understand what is at stake in the move to postmodernism is to observe the textualist attempt to displace and resituate science in the discourse of the humanities disciplines.

The science Heidegger described is the one we all recognize, whose essence is research, including: 1) A procedure projecting within the realm of nature or history "a fixed ground plan of events." 2) A methodology "through which a sphere of objects comes into representation," clarified by explanation. Explanation, bringing the known and the unknown into relation, takes place by means of investigation and experiment, controlled in advance by a program of calculation which guides the researcher. 3) Ongoing activity, the third feature of research, is the process by which the methodology adapts to its own results over time, which is to say that to be a science a procedure must be capable of being institutionalized (Heidegger, 1977: 118–24). The primary examples noted were physics and historiography, the latter's demand for rigor bringing it closer to physics than to the humanities, which were still clinging, Heidegger said, to mere erudition and the empty Romanticism of scholarship.

One of the interesting implications of "ongoing activity" is that the scientific way of knowing and the institution of the university are interdependent, if not synonymous. The university as we know it is the institutional manifestation of science as ongoing activity. When we review Heidegger's description of exactly what the scientific way of knowing entails, we realize why there is so much controversy over whether or not poststructuralist or postmodernist procedures should or even can be institutionalized.

> Knowing, as research, calls whatever is to account with regard to the way in which and the extent to which it lets itself be put at the disposal of representation. Research has disposal over anything that is when it can either calculate it in its future course in advance or verify a calculation about it as past. Nature, in being calculated in advance, and history, in being historiographically verified as past, become, as it were, "set in place" [gestellt] . . . Only that which becomes object in this way *is*— is considered to be in being. (126–27)

The object of knowledge implies a subject, Heidegger's point being that in the modern age the essence of man changed, becoming *subiectum:* "Man becomes that being upon which all that is, is grounded as regards the manner of its Being and its Truth. Man becomes the relational center of that which is as such" (128)—an event made possible by the reframing of what is in terms of a "picture." In the age of the world picture (so named because only the modern age grasps the real as picture) thought is organized by the subject/object relation known as Cartesian dualism, a characterization first formulated in Plato's *eidos* ("idea" as the aspect or view of a form). Modern representing, Heidegger says, "means to bring what is present at hand before oneself as something standing over against, to relate it to oneself, to the one representing it, and to force it back into this relationship to oneself as the normative realm. Wherever this happens, man 'gets into the picture' in precedence over whatever is" (131).

Here we have the crucial issue for mystory, for we might say that mystory amounts to a reframing of the relation between subject and object. That this question is the one informing all of poststructuralism may be seen when Heidegger adds that, "Now for the first time is there any such thing as a 'position' of man. . . . There begins that way of being human which mans the realm of human capability as a domain given over to measuring and executing, for the purpose of gaining mastery over that which is as a whole" (132). Mystory figures the positioning of the subject of science in the postmodern discourse.

Heidegger's account of science as the essence of the modern age places in a useful perspective all the critiques of modern culture, from the situationist complaint about "spectacle" to the feminist analysis of narrative as structured for the masculine voyeur. We may understand now that knowing—in the realm of the doxa as much as in that of the episteme—is, in the modern paradigm, scopophilic. Regardless of the gender, sex, class, race, or nationality of the knower, the one who knows in the mode of science is in the position of voyeur, so to speak. But if science is the dominant mode of knowledge in the age of the world picture, it is not the only knowledge possible.

Feminism, as I mentioned before, opens the way for mystory, and for all postmodern attempts to refunction representation in the discourses of knowledge. A good expression of this general import of the feminist project is "For the Etruscans," by Rachel DuPlessis. DuPlessis's essay takes note of the two issues of most importance for mystory—the function of personal experience in a discourse of knowledge (which I will return to in the next section), and the value of formal experimentation as a strategy with political as well as epistemological goals.

To take up first the question of formal experimentation in academic writing, it is important to note that for DuPlessis the feminine aesthetic is not an essentialist project: "We are making a creation, not a discovery" (DuPlessis, 1985: 281). In an essay that shows this creation as much as it tells it, DuPlessis states the assumption that is also central to mystory:

> If it's really the forms, the language, which dominate us, then disrupting them as radically as possible can give us hope and possibilities. What I'd like to try to understand and explain to other people (*you yourselves are the riddle*) is how the form of women's writing is, if ambiguously (*of double, sometimes duplicitious* [sic] *needs*) nonetheless profoundly revolutionary (as are, in their confusing ways, modernism and postmodernism, also written from positions of marginality to the dominant culture). (287)

The interesting point for now is to note that groups and movements with the widest possible divergence of political views have nonetheless agreed in practice on one thing—the use of formal experimentation as a means to challenge the age of the world picture.

The next event was Theodor Adorno. No matter that Adorno and Heidegger were contemptuous of one another's politics, for they agreed on the necessity of a certain mode of composition discouraged by the academy, one capable of competing with the treatise (the conventional form of representation still used for disciplining most graduate programs). The text in question is Adorno's "The Essay as Form," which may be read as a response to "The Age of the World Picture" in at least two ways (mystorically). The first way I will only mention—that both establish Descartes and Cartesian method as the essence of that which is to be overcome. The second concerns the kind of writing both recommend as the alternative to methodology as representation (understood in Heidegger's terms as "an objectifying that goes forward and masters"). Heidegger exemplifies in his own style the new genre but he makes little effort to define it. Rather, with a gesture towards poetry (Hölderlin), he alludes to its nonrepresentational character:

> This becoming incalculable remains the invisible shadow that is cast around all things everywhere when man has been transformed into *subiectum* and the world into picture. (Heidegger, 1977: 135–36)

The name Adorno gives to the discursive formation that functions against the paradigm of calculation is "essay." "The Essay as Form" may be read as a set of instructions for a writing that thinks in "the shadow cast around all things" noted by Heidegger. The feature that distinguishes the essay from the treatise, distributed through a long list of contrasting qualities, is the element of art, the aesthetic dimension. Against the treatise with its positivistic presuppositions favoring method and universal categories to the exclusion of luck, play, and the particular, Adorno identifies the specific way in which art may intervene in a discourse of knowledge.

What does it mean to work theoretically in the mode of art? For one thing, we are given a hint about how to write in the shadow cast by calculation: "The essay must let the totality light up in one of its chosen or haphazard features but without asserting that the whole is present" (164) (even if, with Derrida, we must also later question the complicity of this metaphor of light and shadow with the sight of *eidos*). I must skip over the list of techniques by which the essay achieves such effects (and which reads like an *organum* for the feminist-postmodern text) in order to attend to the treatment of concepts in the essay. Concepts are not to be defined and classified, but are brought into relation with one another, in a "mosaic-like relation" or the "weave of a textile," creating an interactive configuration. Here we have a formula for "text" to which I will return in a later section.

For now, let me just call attention to the profound implications of the essay for academic writing, and especially for the writing produced within the academy by students. No matter how many theorists demonstrate that clarity and distinctness are ideologically loaded values, the humanities discourse still clings to something like *The Elements of Style* (Strunk and White) as the standard for student writing.

But Adorno has a different view. Anticipating, perhaps, the students' taste for postmodernist critical theory, Adorno notes: "The naiveté of the student, to whom the difficult and formidable seems good enough, is wiser than the adult pedantry that admonishes thought with a threatening finger to understand the simple before risking that complexity which alone entices it. Such a postponement of knowledge only prevents knowledge" (162). With respect to the strategy of the essay as "the immanent criticism of cultural artifacts" (it confronts artifacts with their own concept), Adorno offers an insight into the fundamental inappropriateness of the treatise for writing in the humanities.

> Science, as cultural science, negates what it promises to culture: to open up its artifacts from within. The young writer who wants to learn at college what an art-work is, what linguistic form, aesthetic quality, even aesthetic technique are, will only haphazardly learn anything at all about the matter; at best he will pick up information ready culled from whatever modish philosophy and more or less arbitrarily slapped on to the content of works currently under discussion. (157)

What kind of writing can replace the treatise which held the subject apart from the object of study? This new writing specifically refuses, Adorno says, to glorify the "primal" over the mediated; neither "primal words of historical concepts extracted from historical languages" nor "instruction in 'creative writing' " are to be privileged in place of the treatise. But this is as far as I could go with Adorno.

The Conjectural Paradigm

I turn now to the second issue of importance to mystory manifested in the feminist project—the function of personal experience in a discourse of knowledge. Adorno had already promoted the dimension of experience and reminiscence as a kind of experimentation, exemplified in a "man of letters" such as Proust, treating acts of knowledge inaccessible to the "net of science." "The relation to experience—and from it the essay takes as much substance as does traditional theory from its categories—is a relation to all of history; merely individual experience, in which consciousness begins with what is nearest to it, is itself mediated by the all-encompassing experience of historical humanity" (158). The essay, that is, against the traditional notions of truth and method, attempts to integrate the "transitory" and the "eternal," the fact and the concept, in a new way.

Adorno's concern is taken up again in the contemporary debate about the relation of individual to collective history, with the insistence by feminists on the value of oral history and popular autobiography.

> In one domain, the modern Women's Movement well understands the process of silencing and is raising the "hidden" history of women's feelings, thoughts and actions more clearly to view. Feminist history challenges the very distinction "public"/"private" that silences or marginalizes women's lived sense of the past. But similar processes of domination operate in relation to specifically working-class experiences, for most working-class people are also robbed of access to the means of publicity and are equally unused to the male, middle-class habit of giving universal or "historic" significance to an extremely partial experience. (Popular Memory Group, 1982: 210)

Although it frequently takes the form of stories and autobiography, herstory is still representative and true "for women in a particular historical phase," according to the Popular Memory Group, "because of the personal character of women's oppressions" (238).

An alternative to method, then, is experience. Indeed, it is possible to see in this context that the shadow surrounding the paradigm of calculation initiated by Plato and codified by Descartes is nothing vague or hypothetical, but a specific, alternative paradigm identified by Carlo Ginzburg as "conjecture." The conjectural, interpretive, or semiotic mode of knowledge (relying on the judgment of signs) has shadowed the calculative mode to which it has been subordinated throughout the long evolution of the scientific method.

The conjectural mode of knowledge has its own procedures, of course, as practiced in hunting, divination, medicine, and most recently in psychoanalysis. As Ginzburg explains, "the hunter could have been the first 'to tell a story' " due to the particular kind of knowledge involved: "Its characteristic feature was that it permitted the leap from apparently insignificant facts, which could be observed, to a complex reality which—directly at least—could not. And these facts would be ordered by the observer in such a way as to provide a narrative sequence—at its simplest, 'someone passed this way'. Perhaps indeed the idea of a narrative, as opposed to spell or exorcism or invocation, originated in a hunting society, from the experience of interpreting tracks" (Ginzburg, 1983: 89).

Ginzburg adds that the disciplines practicing conjecture could never "meet the criteria of scientific inference essential to the Galilean approach," being concerned, as they were, "with the qualitative, the individual case or situation or document *as individual.*" Such disciplines, including history, must make room for the element of chance while attending to the concrete, particular case, which is known through "signs and scraps of evidence" (92–93). Conjectural thinking, based on experience, is learned not from books but from "listening, from doing, from watching; their subtleties could scarcely be given formal expression and they might not even be reducible to words" (100). Against the classifications of types that one might find in a treatise on physiognomy Ginzburg invokes the practice of horse dealers, card players, and lovers. The key term to identify the kind of knowledge that defies all rules, that enables a lover to differentiate the beloved from everyone else, is "intuition," which has its "high" forms, as in Arabic *firasa* ("the capacity to leap from the known to the unknown by inference on the basis of clues"), and its "low" forms (rooted in the senses) (98). "It exists everywhere in the world, without geographic, historical, ethnic, gender, or class exception," and has been the heritage of Bengalis, hunters, mariners, and women.

Ginzburg's article was included in the volume *The Sign of Three* collecting essays relating detective fiction to C. S. Peirce's theory of semiotics. The mode of detection ("the making of retrospective predictions"—"When causes cannot be repeated, there is no alternative but to infer them from their effects" (103]) dramatized in the characters of Sherlock Holmes and Auguste Dupin, manifests the abductive guesswork defined by Peirce. When read at this level, Jacques Lacan's seminar on "The Purloined Letter" constitutes an emblematic promotion of the conjectural paradigm (represented by Dupin's psychology) over the calculative (the reliance of the police on an empirical grid) paradigm. Freud's borrowing of the Oedipus story from Sophocles, in this context, may be seen less as the privileging of a particular content and more as an affirmation of the mode of knowledge that psychoanalysis would reactivate against Platonic-Cartesian methodology.

And yet the mystorian hesitates to embrace this alternative. It is tempting to say that the humanities have been conjectural all along, that even if, as Ginzburg notes, linguistics managed (alone among the cultural disciplines) to cross over into calculation, the others were wrong to try to follow (structuralism). Why should we not now explicitly and without apology explore the experiential dimension of particular cases? There is some reason for caution, in the first place, because of what Ginzburg shows us about the use to which conjectural knowledge has been put in society. The same semiotic skills that enable the historian to recognize the hand of the master in the stylistic peculiarities of a painting also allow the state to register the singular identity of its citizens (which suggests a point of entry into the question of the politics of style).

We encounter here the problematic of the signature, and of grammatology in general. Ginzburg reminds us of the "Chinese tradition explaining the origins of writing, according to which it was invented by a high official who had remarked the footprints of a bird in a sandy riverbank" (89). For graphology the way one shaped the "characters" of a script revealed the "character" or personality of the writer (96), a fact that again situates Lacan, with his interest in "the insistence of the letter in the unconscious," in the conjectural tradition. Conjecture is precisely the knowledge of identity, distinguishing copies from originals, including the whole metaphysics of property that goes with this capacity. In fact, the analysis of style in art history "coincided with the emergence of an increasingly clear tendency for state power to impose a close-meshed net of control on society, and once again the method that was used involved attributing identity through characteristics which were trivial and beyond conscious control" (104). The "hand of the master" has a double meaning, then, and the mastery made possible through fingerprinting ("every last inhabitant of the meanest hamlet of Europe or Asia thus became, thanks to fingerprints, possible to identify and check" [109]) duplicates in culture the position of mastery over nature developed through calculation.

Still, mystory has at least two important lessons to learn from the conjectural style as it is applied in psychoanalysis. The first lesson has to do with the very fact that Lacan uses a story ("The Purloined Letter") to represent the concept of the subject, thus reversing the normal direction of explanation in the treatise. Literature here serves as a "creditor" discourse, no longer an object of study but a ground or cognitive field whose inventions are brought to bear on a conceptual problem in order to achieve an explanatory effect. The problem, however, is that Lacan is still working in terms of "representation" (the practice of the university in the age of the world picture). Derrida's critique of Lacan, of course, addresses the assumptions of adequacy and referentiality that inform Lacan's seminar with the project to expose "what Freud really said." Mystory attempts to extricate the cognitive function of artistic or literary devices from the constraints of classic representation and from the referential bias of conventional pedagogy.

The second lesson has to do with the way the subject/object differentiation is treated in psychoanalysis. Psychoanalysis offers a provocative model for the feminist project noted by DuPlessis: "I think we haven't even grasped the most radical implications of feminism for a theory which mediates back to practice: that we have a vision which men have barely glimpsed of what dialectical thought is really about—about a total, specific, feeling and thinking subject, present in her interaction with 'objective' materials, overcoming in the division between thought and action" (DuPlessis, 288). The conjunction in psychoanalytic discourse of the patient's particular case with a general theory of the subject is still the most extensive attempt yet to integrate peculiarities of everyday life with the generalizations of a conceptual framework.

But the mystorian does not share the anxiety of psychoanalytic commentators about the irreducible disparity between the actual life experience and the narrative conventions, about the way in which the narrativizing of the analysand's scraps and signs imposes on the life a coherence that may not be "true." For mystory it is never a question of a theory representing an autobiography, or vice versa. Rather, mystory, which is not committed to Freud's metastory, proposes to conjoin the personal anecdote with the narrativizing of any and all metastories, but in a way that puts the narrative structure and the historical document, the narrative document and the historical structure, into an alternative arrangement, perhaps to tell a personal anecdote by means of the materials of theory. The best examples of this post-conjectural composition go by the name of *text*.

Post-Conjectural Text

Having in mind that the example Ginzburg gave for intuitive conjectural experience was a lover's knowledge of the beloved, I then could read Barthes's *A Lover's Discourse: Fragments* as a critique of the conjectural, semiotic, interpretive paradigm. And *Fragments* told me exactly where to look for an alternative, how to go on after conjecture, by contrasting the lover with the modern text. The text abolishes the image-repertoire within which the lover is positioned.

> In the text, the fade-out of voices is a good thing; the voices of the narrative come, go, disappear, overlap; we do not know who is speaking; the text speaks, that is all: no more image, nothing but language.

> But the other is not a text, the other is an image, single and coalescent;
> if the voice is lost, it is the entire image which vanishes (love is mon-
> ologic, maniacal; the text is heterologic, perverse). (Barthes, 1978: 112)

What attitude is being recommended here? In the register of the doxa
the lover performs what the psychoanalyst reenacts in the register of
the episteme—for both of them everything is meaningful, everything is
a sign to be interpreted. Not so for the text, which does without deci-
pherment or concept, leaving the object of study (the beloved) as an
affirmation: "I love, not what he is, but *that he is*"; "And what would
best resemble the loved being *as he is, thus and so,* would be the Text,
to which I can add no adjective: which I delight in without having to
decipher it" (222).

With this attitude goes a refunctioning of narrative. The mystorian
most needs to understand what happens to narrative in the post-conjectural text, and *Fragments* shows one answer. When Barthes wrote the
opening section of *Fragments*—'How this book is constructed"—he did
not intend to found a genre, anymore than he intended to fix the codes
of narrative when he wrote *S/Z*. Nonetheless, the five codes proved to
be readily generalizable and have enjoyed a career of their own in a
variety of new contexts. The future of mystory is similarly based on a
generalization of the strategy in *Fragments* as a model for theorizing a
new academic writing.

The first feature of this genre—the mystory—has to be inferred from
the fact that *Fragments* opens with a set of instructions for making the
fragments of a discourse—for any discourse whose purpose it is to put
narrative in a textual frame. Here we have an answer to the puzzle that
has prevented many a willing experimenter from taking up the project
of theory. If one was not to undertake close formal analyses as in the
mode of calculation, nor to decipher signs as in the conjectural paradigm,
then what else was there to do? The mystorical answer is, to make a
text. The mystorian reads any and all works as a set of instructions for
making something (not necessarily something of the same kind).

Next we may examine the specific instructions Barthes provides, which
are divided into three parts—figure, order, and references. I begin with
references, for here is the crucial matter for mystory. This text, that is,
draws equally upon four levels of cultural experience: 1) "ordinary reading"—here Goethe's *Werther,* but generalizable as the primary works of
the language and literature disciplines; 2) "insistent reading"—Barthes
mentions Plato's *Symposium,* Zen, psychoanalysis, etc., generalizable as
the learned, epistemic background of the author's context; 3) "occasional
readings"—understood to mean popular culture, newspapers, maga-
zines, and the like; 4) lived experience, including conversations with
friends as well as personal events.

The first point to make with respect to this list of materials is that it excludes nothing; it makes no distinction between the realms of knowledge and opinion, general and particular, specialized discourse and commonsense experience. The second point is to note the instructions Barthes adds regarding how to use these materials, how to select from what is obviously an extensive collection of possibilities: the references "are not authoritative but amical: I am not invoking guarantees, merely recalling, by a kind of salute given in passing, what has seduced, convinced, or what has momentarily given the delight of understanding (of being understood?). Therefore, these reminders of reading, of listening, have been left in the frequently uncertain, incompleted state suitable to a discourse whose occasion is indeed the memory of the sites (books, encounters) where such and such a thing has been read, spoken, heard" (9). In place of the authoritative citations of the treatise, the mystory offers "site-tations"—telling what I happened to find convincing in terms of the *punctum* (from *Camera Lucida*), the anecdotal memory I have of my experience with learning the theory I am telling: the site, place, location of the general in association with my particular encounter with it.

The section on figures offers a more detailed outline of how to generate the site-tations. The text will actually consist of a series of figures or poses that are typical or characteristic of a discursive practice (we are asked to compose or compile the rhetoric, the commonplace book, for a given practice). The general figures are called poses to suggest the way in which when I use a specialized language I am constrained to take up certain positions, as in a choreographed production. The text will consist of as many of these topoi as I care to provide, all of which are to be identified and produced according to the following procedure: the "heading" of each figure refers to something the subject of that discourse *says* (not to something I am) upon encountering that pose, figure, or stereotypical situation. Underneath the figure, that is, there lies a sentence, or perhaps, Barthes adds, merely an "articulation" that is more affective than syntactic, although it always has a verbal dimension.

> A figure is established if at least someone can say: "that's so true! I recognize that scene of language." For certain operations of their art, linguists make use of a vague entity which they call linguistic feeling; in order to constitute figures, we require neither more nor less than this guide: amorous feeling. (4)

Amorous feeling for the lover's discourse, but the figure evokes an affect in any discourse (in academic writing the feeling of polemic, of refutation, of insight). The exclamation—"that's so true!"—will be recognized for its similarity to the emotional sentence that identifies ideology (that-which-goes-without-saying), the stereotypes of a discursive formation being the vehicles of ideology in a specific practice: the effect of truth includes a certain feeling that must be used to sort out and name the figures.

What are these instructions asking us to do? Mystory approaches a discourse formation, a knowledge practice, from an unusual angle, admittedly—in terms of a personal experience in which a general science functions as a stereotype and as an idiom. At the level of practice these two dimensions cross and exchange properties. To reiterate, the figure is a stereotype of a collective practice for which the reader (and the writer of a mystory is in the position of the reader) is asked to supply the unique instances of enactment. "Each of us can fill in this code according to his own history; rich or poor, the figure must be there, the site (the compartment) must be reserved for it. . . . Now the property of a Topic is to be somewhat empty: a Topic is statutorily half coded, half projective" (5). "Ideally,' Barthes adds, "the book would be a cooperative." The text is literally a fragment, not only because it is composed in a discontinuous manner, but because half of it, the instances of the figures, are to be provided during the reading process. The numbered sections under each title and heading, meanwhile, are Barthes's own instances of the types.

The other unusual aspect of such a composition is that it enters a practice at the oral level. The figures' headings being something said when the pose is encountered (the position struck) suggests that a literature practice always carries with it an oral accompaniment. Certainly this is true of academic writing. A tension then is created between the ordinary language of the speaking academic and the specialized discourse of the written argument, a point of crossing and interchange between oral and literate genres, to the point that the mystorian tells anecdotes about concepts.

Which brings me to the last part of the instructions—order—which reveals the peculiar existence of narrative in textual mystory. The text as a whole, we readily observe, is not given a narrative structure. The figures collectively constitute an "encyclopedia" or a "thesaurus" organized alphabetically out of which could be generated any number of individual accounts. The paradigmatic axis of language, the axis of selection, we might say, is given predominance over the syntagmatic axis of combination in the construction of the text. The structuralist critics worried about the way in which the paradigm—the set of possible meanings or terms—influenced the specific term selected in a sentence. Hence they directed their attention to what a work did not say but could have (and this "unsaid" part of the linguistic process became confused with

the more romantic notion of the "unthought," even the "unthinkable,"
in ideological criticism). The basic unit of meaning in mystory, that is,
is not the specific selection from the paradigmatic set (that is left up to
the reader) but the whole paradigm (in this linguistic sense). In the case
of *Fragments,* we are not offered any particular lover's story, but all such
stories in a way that reorganizes the traditional opposition between the
particular and the general.

The instructions suggest that two different operations are involved.
The text explicitly provides, in numbered sections following each heading, a series of asides or soliloquies. These are the composer's comments
on the narrative that is itself never told (although indirectly a certain
scene tends to emerge dramatically from the anecdotes of instances
provided by the reading writer). At the same time, there is also an implied
narrative. Here is Barthes's description of the "love story," which I will
want to generalize for mystory:

> Every amorous episode can be, of course, endowed with a meaning: it
> is generated, develops, and dies; it follows a path which it is always
> possible to interpret according to a causality or a finality—even if need
> be which can be moralized ("I was out of my mind, I'm over it now,"
> "Love is a trap which must be avoided from now on," etc.): this is the
> *love story,* subjugated to the great narrative Other, to that general opinion
> which disparages any excessive force and wants the subject himself to
> reduce the great imaginary current, the orderless, endless stream which
> is passing through him, to a painful, morbid crisis of which he must
> be cured. . . . the love story is the tribute the lover must pay to the
> world in order to be reconciled with it. (7)

The great narrative Other in mystory—the new genre of academic
writing—is the metastory, or stories, of the verified and institutionalized
disciplines, to which the mystorian must accede if my text is to be credited
at all, received and counted. This story may be glimpsed, overheard, in
what is said about "deconstruction" these days (it is only literary criticism;
it is irreducible to any pedagogy; it is without an effective politics).

But before I advocate the genre extrapolated from Barthes's *Fragments*
as a possible direction for the future of theory let me use it to gather a
collection of examples, to give us some idea of what has already been
accomplished along these lines.

Toward Teletheory

I can now tell about the texts that instill in me the desire to write and
teach, and which I count among the examples of mystory. Because it
matches so well with the themes of Barthes's *Fragments,* the text I will

mention first is *Post-Partum Document* by Mary Kelly. The *Document* could have been subtitled "A Mother's Discourse: Fragments" (Kelly actually began her project before Barthes), its intertitles, like Barthes's headings, being something the mother says ("What have I done wrong?" "Why don't I understand?"). Each of these intertitles or headings organizes a multi-level set of documents relevant to a period in the mother-child relationship.

> The work, begun in 1973 with the birth of her child, covers the first six years of the child's development and is divided into six sections including, in all, approximately 135 pieces. Each section examines a stage in the constitution of a woman's identity in and through significant moments in her child's development: for instance, weaning from the breast, weaning from the holophrase (learning to speak), weaning from the dyad (periodic separation from the mother), the first questions about sexuality and the collection of cathected objects which represent loss, not only of the child but of the maternal body, and finally the child's entry into the law of the father—learning to write, starting school (Kelly, 1983: 203).

Both Kelly and Barthes feature the mother-son relationship, albeit from different positions in the dyad, including the theme of mourning rehearsing the castration-complex—the adjustment to separation and loss experienced in the formation of individuality; both use Lacan to direct and displace the strong emotional tone of the experience, testing the theoretical discourse against the lived dimension.

The *Document* interests me for several reasons, not least of which is that it demonstrates an overcoming of the impasse of representation produced during the age of the world picture, and an alternative to the opposition between the paradigms of calculation and conjecture. Kelly weds the methodologies of science with the narratives of conjecture in a hybrid procedure that draws equally on the resources of personal experience and the specialized disciplines. Acknowledging that mothering is lived in the particular but understood in general, the *Document* subordinates the narrative of the mother-child relationship to a scientific taxonomy, refracted through the presentational devices appropriate to the institution of the museum as a medium of culture.

Being the "fragments of an academic's discourse," mystory more or less takes up where the *Document* leaves off (with the child entering school). The second important lesson for mystory, then, concerns the functioning of narrative in the *Document*. Within the documentary taxonomy the narrative exists in the form of anecdotes and brief dramatic scenes buried in the notes of Kelly's commentary. In general the couching of a personal narrative in terms of psychoanalytic theory and ethnographic, museum display tends to transform the scientific systems into narrative vehicles. The nature of the displays, the effect of insistence created by mounting as documents the mother's memorabilia (diapers, casts of the child's hand, scrawls, verbal utterances, gifts to the mother such as insects and shells), reinforced by the supporting commentaries juxtaposing personal anecdotes and diary notations with theoretical commentaries, lends to the *Document* the status of allegory. The child's entry into ordinary language becomes an allegory for the student's entry into a specialized discourse, for the academic's acquisition of theory. The process of constructing a text in this way—disseminating a personal event through the categories of knowledge and representation dominant in the culture—suggests the political potential of mystory as an action within a specific institution.

As just one illustration of the mix of modes relating narrative to theory consider the way the *Document* treats the theme of the world picture. The heading linking the documentation to the commentary in Part Five is the question "What am I?" (a man or a woman?). The gifts the child brought his mother (insects, shells, flowers) are mounted as specimens and labeled with all their scientific specifications. During this period the child had been asking questions about sexuality. The reader recalls Freud's argument in his study of Leonardo that curiosity, the desire for knowledge, begins with the attempt by the infant to understand the mystery of birth. On the progress of these early researches rests the child's intellectual future. The infant's research is doomed, Freud said, because the information needed to solve the problem—knowledge of anatomy—is unavailable to the child. In this context the record of one of Kelly's conversations with her son is significant, for she supplies her son with the missing data (supported in the documentation by medical drawings of the stages of pregnancy): "Age 3;10, July 13, 1977. (8:00 P.M. coming into the bathroom). K [the boy's first name is "Kelly"]. Do babies come from your bottom? M [Mary Kelly]. No, . . . from vaginas. Girls have three holes; one for poohs, one for wees, and one where babies come out—that's the vagina" (148). By exhibiting the origins of scientific will-to-know during the moment of the formation of sexual identity, Mary Kelly dramatizes a critique of the fetishism of truth ("classification, in this document, is used to construct a metaphorical space in which the mother's body is *named* through the researches of her child" [113]; "The child's spontaneous scopophilia provokes the mother's sense of 'shame' " [161]).

Kelly found herself in the course of family relations in the position of the Queen in Lacan's model story, seeing herself seen without the ability to act. The lesson or moral of Poe's story, in any case, according to Lacan, is repetition automatism: "It is not only the subject, but the subjects, grasped in their intersubjectivity, who line up, in other words our ostriches, to whom we here return, and who, more docile than sheep, model their very being on the moment of the signifying chain which traverses them" (Lacan, 1972: 60). Mystory has been following the lead of feminist research until now, but Kelly's astonishing insight into the phenomenon of feminine fetishism (a contradiction in terms?) indicates how difficult it will be to get out of line (the series of glances, each finally not seeing itself being seen), how difficult to know the world other than as picture. The fetishism that motivates masculine interest in pornography, Kelly suggests, finds its feminine equivalent in the mother's memorabilia which serve as *"emblems* of desire" (xvi). The juxtaposition of a bronzed baby shoe and a girlie magazine, reflecting the gender difference in our psychic economies, is a part of Kelly's general critique of representation as fetish.

I only mention this one item from *Post-Partum Document* to suggest the potential of Kelly's composition for creating powerful critical effects. Indeed, in this article I make no attempt to demonstrate the theoretical capacities of the genre in question, but only to establish the fact that such a genre exists. Another text of the same sort, for example, is "Mushroom Book" by John Cage. Again, what appeals to me is the collage character of the composition, as indicated in this prospectus included in the text: "handwritten mushroom book including mushroom stories, excerpts from (mushroom) books, remarks about (mushroom) hunting, excerpts from Thoreau's *Journal* (fungi), excerpts from Thoreau's *Journal* (entire), remarks about: Life/Art, Art/Life, Life/Life, Art/Art, Zen, Current reading, Cooking (shopping, recipes), Games, Music mss., Maps, Friends, Invention, Projects,—Writing without syntax, Mesostics (on mushroom names)" (Cage, 1974: 133–34).

Having discussed this text elsewhere,[2] I will only note the generic features relevant to mystory. Cage uses mycology—the science of mushrooms—in the same way that Barthes and Kelly use Lacan's psychoanalysis. In such cases the disciplinary or specialized knowledge has a double-function at least, operating directly on its own terms as information, and indirectly as a figure, symbolically or allegorically, in the personal narrative. Participating in a general trend affecting the postmodern humanities, in which the devices of art are being put to work as primary resources of cognition and conceptualization, Cage remotivates science as image. He extends as well his theory and practice of music into a system for theorizing political and social conditions (which is to say that he deserves a chapter to himself in applied grammatology).

The other feature of Cage's composition that is of special value to mystory is the major role played in it (not only in "Mushroom Book") by anecdotes. In fact, during a significant period of Cage's career, the anecdote served as the basic unit of composition in all his scores, lectures, and books. He began collecting stories, he notes, any that stuck in his mind, in a way that replicates Barthes's commonplace organization of the *Fragments:* "Others I read in books and remembered—those, for instance, from Sri Ramakrishna and the literature surrounding Zen. Still others have been told me by friends—Merce Cunningham, Virgil Thomson, Betty Isaacs, and many more" (Cage, 1966: 260). The stories could stand alone (an entire lecture consisting of nothing but anecdotes), be combined with other media—dance numbers by Merce Cunningham or piano pieces by David Tudor—or be disseminated through collage texts such as "Mushroom Book." "My intention in putting the stories together in an unplanned way was to suggest that all things—stories, incidental sounds from the environment, and, by extension, beings—are related, and that this complexity is more evident when it is not oversimplified by an idea of relationship in one person's mind" (260).

But I must confine myself for now to treating Cage again as a symptom, noting that his experimentation with the anecdote is another instance of the arts preparing a device that is just the one theory needs. A glance at Spalding Gray's *Swimming to Cambodia,* composed entirely of anecdotes, conforms the critical, political, and aesthetic range of this form (performance art in general could be characterized as the theater of the anecdote). I say that the anecdote is just the form theory needs by way of remarking the way Derrida in recent years has been framing his lectures in an anecdotal strategy, mixing the oral form with the analytical letter. In "Ulysses Gramophone: Hear say yes in Joyce," for example, Derrida works his way toward the puncept *"oui"* through recurring references to a trip to Tokyo: "I decided to date it like this—and dating is signing—on the morning of 11 May when I was looking for postcards in a sort of news agency in the basement of the Okura Hotel. I was looking for postcards which would show Japanese lakes, or let's call them inland seas. It had crossed my mind to follow the edges of lakes in *Ulysses.*"[3] This strategy will be recognized as the one used in the "Envois" section of *La Carte Postale,* except that there the travelogue is not distributed through the theoretical study that follows it (on Freud's *Beyond the Pleasure Principle*). Favoring the chance encounters also advocated by Cage, Derrida has been telling anecdotes about experiences that happen to verify his meetings with remarkable words—the incident with the wrapping "bound to take off" on his copy of Francis Ponge, or the incident with the umbrella recounted in *Spurs.* Grammatology, deconstruction, happen to people, who live to tell the tale, or rather, the theory.

Reserving for another occasion a fuller invention of the theoretical function of anecdotes in poststructuralism, I can only assert for now that the contemporary mushrooming of anecdotal material in postmodern texts has to do with a peculiarity of the video medium. As Andrew Tolson argues, "an anecdotal effect might, to some extent, be built into the structure of TV's discursive regime: both within particular program formats and in terms of the way many TV narratives are organized. Finally, this possibility, that television's *regime* is anecdotal, might account for some of its problematic pleasures" (Tolson: 1985, 24). The point is both that the anecdotal form organizes many television programs, and that television as such creates anecdotal effects. Pursuing his thesis that the anecdotal structure is specific to television, Tolson finds that news shows, and by extension all uses of interviewing and the like in documentaries—the format of truth—fall within the anecdotal framing. Michel de Certeau made a similar case, collapsing the distinction between scholarship and popularization and thus clearing the way for a mystorical reorganization of history.

> Scholarly discourse is no longer distinguishable from that prolix and fundamental narrativity that is our everyday historiography. Scholarship is an integral part of the system that organizes by means of "histories" all social communication and everything that makes the present habitable. The book or the professional article, on the one hand, and the magazine or the television news, on the other, are distinguishable from one another only within the same historiographical field which is constituted by the innumerable narratives that recount and interpret events. (de Certeau: 1986, 205).

I linger over this topic because the central project of applied grammatology is to put critical theory on television, and to set the academy to writing with video. Mystory is theory performed in the dimension of anecdotes, which is to say in a word, a word of fundamental significance for the future of theory, that through mystory theory fits television.

19

Authority, (White) Power, and the (Black) Critic; or, it's all Greek to me

Henry Louis Gates, Jr.

> For a language acts in divers ways, upon the spirit of a people; even as the spirit of a people acts with a creative and spiritualizing force upon a language.
> —Alexander Crummell, 1860

> Slowly but steadily, in the following years, a new vision began gradually to replace the dream of political power—a powerful movement, the rise of another ideal to guide the unguided, another pillar of fire by night after a clouded day. It was the ideal of "book-learning"; the curiosity, born of compulsory ignorance, to know and test the power of the cabalistic letters of the white man, the longing to know. Here at last seemed to have been discovered the mountain path to Canaan; longer than the highway of Emancipation and law, steep and rugged, but straight, leading to heights high enough to overlook life.
> —W. E. B. Du Bois, 1903

> . . . the knowledge which would teach the white world was Greek to his own flesh and blood. . . . and he could not articulate the message of another people.
> —W. E. B. Du Bois, 1903

I

Alexander Crummell, a pioneering nineteenth-century Pan-Africanist, statesman, and missionary who spent the bulk of his creative years as an Anglican minister in Liberia, was also a pioneering intellectual and philosopher of language, founding the American Negro Academy in 1897 and serving as the intellectual godfather of W. E. B. Du Bois.[1] In his first annual address as President of the Academy, delivered on December 28, 1898, Crummell selected as his topic "The Attitude of the American Mind Toward the Negro Intellect."[2] Given the occasion of the first annual meeting of the great intellectuals of the race, he could not have chosen a more timely or appropriate topic.

Crummell wished to attack, he said, "the denial of intellectuality in the Negro; the assertion that he was not a human being, that he did not belong to the human race," assertions, he continued, which set out "to prove that the Negro was of a different species from the white man" (p. 10). Crummel argues that the desire "to becloud and stamp out the intellect of the Negro" led to the enactment of "laws and statutes, closing the pages of every book printed to the eyes of Negroes; barring the doors of every school-room against them!" This, he concludes, "was the systematized method of the intellect of the South, to stamp out the brains of the Negro!," a program which created an "almost Egyptian darkness [which] fell upon the mind of the race, throughout the whole land" (p. 10).

Crummell next shared with his audience a conversation which he had overheard in 1833 or 1834, when he was "an errand boy in the Antislavery office in New York City":

> A distinguished illustration of this ignoble sentiment can be given. In the year 1833 or 4 the speaker was an errand boy in the Anti-slavery office in New York City.
>
> On a certain occasion he heard a conversation between the Secretary and two eminent lawyers from Boston,—Samuel E. Sewell and David Lee Child. They had been to Washington on some legal business. While at the Capitol they happened to dine in the company of the great John C. Calhoun, then senator from South Carolina. It was a period of great ferment upon the question of Slavery, States' Rights, and Nullification; and consequently the Negro was the topic of conversation at the table. One of the utterances of Mr. Calhoun was to this effect—"That if he could find a Negro who knew the Greek syntax, he would then believe that the Negro was a human being and should be treated as a man." (pp. 10–11)

"Just think of the crude asininity," Crummel concluded rather generously, "of even a great man" (p. 11).

For John C. Calhoun, then—who held during his lifetime the offices of U.S. Congressman, Secretary of War, Vice President, Senator, and Secretary of State, and who stood firmly to his dying day a staunch advocate of states' rights and as a symbol of an unreconstructed South— the person of African descent would never be a full member of the human community, fit to be anything but a slave, until one individual black person—just one—demonstrated mastery of the subtleties of Greek syntax, of all things! Perhaps fearing that this goal would be too easily achieved, Calhoun later added mastery of the binomial theorem to his list of black herculean tasks.

The salient sign of the black person's humanity—indeed, the only sign for Calhoun—would be the mastering of the very essence of Western civilization, of the very foundation of the complex fiction upon which white Western culture had been constructed, which for John C. Calhoun turned out to have been Greek syntax. It is highly likely that "Greek syntax," for John C. Calhoun, was merely a hyperbolic figure of speech, a trope of virtual impossibility, the first to leap to mind during an impassioned debate over states' rights and the abolition of slavery. Calhoun, perhaps felt driven to the hyperbolic mode because of the long racist tradition, in Western letters, of demanding that black people *prove* their full humanity, a tradition to which Calhoun was heir. We know this tradition all too well, dotted as it is with the names of great intellectual Western racialists, such as Francis Bacon, David Hume, Immanuel Kant, Thomas Jefferson, and G. W. F. Hegel, to list only a few. Whereas each of these figures demanded that blacks write *poetry* to prove their humanity, Calhoun—writing in a post-Phillis Wheatley era—took refuge in, yes, Greek syntax.

And, just as Phillis Wheatley's mistress and master had urged her to write poetry to refute racialists such as Hume and Kant, Calhoun's outrageous demand would not fall upon the deaf ears of the inarticulate intellectual inferior. In typical African-American fashion, a brilliant black intellectual accepted Calhoun's challenge, just as Wheatley had done almost a century before. The anecdote that Crummell shared with his fellow black academicians, it turns out, was his shaping scene of instruction. For Crummell, Calhoun's challenge was his reason for jumping on a boat, sailing to England, and matriculating at Queens' College, at the University of Cambridge, where he mastered (of all things) the intricacies of Greek syntax in a broader field of study in theology. Calhoun, we suspect, was not impressed.

But even after both John C. Calhoun and racial slavery had been long dead, Alexander Crummell never escaped the lesson he had learned as an errand boy at the Anti-slavery office. Crummell never stopped believing that mastering the master's tongue was the *sole* path to civilization and to intellectual freedom and social equality for the black person. It was the acquisition of Western "culture," he argued, which the black person "must claim as his rightful heritage, as a man: not stinted training, not a caste education, not," he concludes prophetically, "a Negro curriculum" (p. 16). As he argues so passionately in his well-known speech of 1860, entitled "The English Language in Liberia,"[3] the acquisition of the English Language, along with the simultaneous acquisition of Christianity, is the wonderful sign of God's providence encoded in the nightmare of African enslavement in the racist wilderness of the New World:

> The acquisition of [the English language] is elevation. It places the native man above his ignorant fellow, and gives him some of the dignity of civilization. New ideas are caught up, new habits formed, and superior and elevating wants are daily increases. (p. 35)

Crummell accepted fully an argument central to the Enlightenment, that written and spoken language-use was the tangible sign of reason, and it was the possession of reason which, as Francis Bacon put it in *The New Organon*, was "that which made man a god to man." Crummell's first anonymous epigraph states this relation clearly:

> Language, in connection with reason, to which it gives its proper activity, use, and ornament, raises man above the lower orders of animals, and in proportion as it is polished and refined, contributes greatly . . . to exalt one nation above another, in the scale of civilization and intellectual dignity. (p. 8)

English, for Crummell, was "in proportion . . . polished and refined" in an *inverse* ratio as the African vernacular languages were tarnished and unrefined. And, while the fact that black people spoke English as a first language was "indicative of sorrowful history," a sign of "subjection and conquest," it was also "one of those ordinances of Providence, designed as a means for the introduction of new ideas into the language of a people; or to serve as a transitional step from low degradation to a higher and nobler civilization" (p. 18).

English, for Crummell, was "the speech of Chaucer and Shakespeare, of Milton and Wordsworth, of Bacon and Burke, of Franklin and Webster," and its potential mastery was "this one item of compensation" which "the Almighty has bestowed upon us" in exchange for "the exile of our fathers from their African homes to America . . ." (p. 10). English was "a transforming agency, which is gradually subverting the native languages of our tribes," he maintains with great approval, as the imperialistic forces of Great Britain "introduce trade and civilization, pioneer letters and culture, and prepare the way for the *English Language* and Religion" (pp. 34, 32; Crummell's emphasis). It is "this noble language," he concludes on the unmistakable air of triumph, which is "gradually lifting up and enlightening our heathen neighbors" (p. 32). In the English language are embodied "the noblest theories of liberty" and "the grandest ideas of humanity" (p. 51). By mastering the master's tongue, these great and grand ideas will become African ideas, because "ideas conserve men, and keep alive the vitality of nations. . . . With the noble tongue which Providence has given us, it will be difficult for us to be divorced from the spirit, which for centuries has been speaking through it" (p. 52).[4] "And this," Crummell proclaims, "is our language," and it is "upon the many treasures of this English tongue" that he was "dwell[ed] with delight" (p. 29).

In direct and dark contrast to the splendor and wonders of the English language, Crummell pits the African vernacular languages.[5] ". . . The refined and cultivated English language" is "alien alike from the speech of [our] sires and the soil from whence they sprung . . ." (p. 11). Let us, he continues, inquire "into the respective values of our native and acquired tongue. . . . The worth of our fathers' language, will, in this way, stand out in distinct comparison with the Anglo-Saxon, our acquired speech" (p. 19). Black vernacular languages, for Crummell, embody "definite marks of inferiority connected with them all, which place them at the widest distances from civilized languages." Crummell then lists these shared "marks of inferiority" of the black vernacular:

> Of this whole class of languages, it may be said, in the aggregate that (a) "They are," to use the words of Dr. Leighton Wilson, "harsh, abrupt, energetic, indistinct in enunciation, meagre in point of words, abound with inarticulate nasal and gutteral sounds, possess but few inflections and grammatical forms, and are withal exceedingly difficult of acquisition." This is his description of the Grebo; but it may be taken, I think, as, on the whole, a correct description of the whole class of dialects which are entitled "Negro." (b) These languages, moreover, are characterized by lowness of ideas. As the speech of rude barbarians, they are marked by brutal and vindictive sentiments, and those principles which show a predominance of the animal propensities. (c) Again, they lack those ideas of virtue, of moral truth, and those distinctions of right and wrong with which we, all our life long, have been familiar. (d) Another marked feature of these languages is the absence of clear ideas of Justice, Law, Human Rights, and Governmental Order, which are so prominent and manifest in civilized countries. And (e) lastly—Those supernal truths of a personal, present Deity, of the moral government of God, of man's Immortality, of the Judgment, and of Everlasting Blessedness, which regulate the lives of Christians, are either entirely absent, or else exist, and are expressed in an obscure and distorted manner. (pp. 19–20)

So much for the black vernacular!

Any attempt even to render the master's discourse in our own black discourse is an egregious error, Crummell continues, because to do so is merely to translate sublime utterances "in broken English—a miserable caricature of their noble tongue" (p. 50). Such was the case when the English, in the West Indies, translated the Bible from the rich cadences of King James into the "crude, mongrel, discordant jargon" of the black vernacular. No, translation just won't do, because "a language without its characteristic features, stamp, and spirit, is a lifeless and unmeaning thing. . . ." The attempt to translate from English to the black vernacular is "so great a blunder." We must abandon forever both indigenous African vernacular languages as well as the neo-African vernacular languages that our people have produced in the New World. We must do so, concludes Crummell, because:

> All low, inferior, and barbarous tongues are, doubtless, but the lees and dregs of noble languages, which have gradually, as the soul of a nation has died out, sunk down to degradation and ruin. We must not suffer this decay on these shores, in this nation. We have been made, providentially, the deposit of a noble trust; and we should be proud to show our appreciation of it. Having come to the heritage of this language we must cherish its spirit, as well as retain its letter. We must cultivate it among ourselves; we must strive to infuse its spirit among our re-claimed and aspiring natives. (p. 50)

I cite the examples of John C. Calhoun and Alexander Crummell as metaphors of the relation between the critic of black literature and the broader, larger institution of literature. (However, lest anyone believe that the arguments of Calhoun, Kant, Jefferson, Hume, or Hegel have been relegated to their proper places in the garbage can of history, she or he need only recall the words of Japanese Premier Nakasone a few months ago, when he remarked that America will *never* be the intellectual equal of Japan because of the presence of Chicanos, Puerto Ricans, and blacks whose presence lowers the country's collective IQ!—to which Ronald Reagan responded, when queried, that before responding he needed to see Nakasone's remarks "in context!")

Calhoun and Crummell are my metaphors for acts of empowerment. Learning the master's tongue, for our generation of critics, has been an act of empowerment, whether that critical language be New Criticism, So-Called Humanism, Structuralism, Marxism, Poststructuralism, Feminism, New Historicism, or any other "ism" that I have forgotten. Each of these critical discourses arises from a specific set of texts within the Western tradition. At least for the past decade, many of us have busied ourselves with the necessary task of learning about these movements in criticism, drawing upon their modes of reading to explicate the texts in our tradition.

This has been an exciting time for critics of Afro-American literature, producing perhaps not as much energy as did, say, the Harlem Renaissance or the Black Arts movement, but certainly producing as many critical essays, and books, about black literature, and yes, even jobs and courses in white English departments. Even with the institutionalization of the racism inherent in "Reagonomics" and with the death of Black Power, there have never been more jobs available in Afro-American literature in white colleges and universities than there are today, as even a cursory glance at the MLA Job List will attest. (Last year alone, thirty-seven such positions were advertised.) In a few years, we shall at last have our very own Norton Anthology, a sure sign that the teaching of Afro-American literature already has been institutionalized and will continue to be so, as only the existence of a well-marketed, affordable anthology can do. Our pressing question now becomes this: in what languages shall we choose to speak, and write, our own criticisms? What are we now to do with the enabling masks of empowerment which we have donned as we have practiced one mode of white criticism or another?

II

Before considering these questions, it is useful to consider the resistance to (white) theory in the (black) tradition.[6] Unlike almost every other literary tradition, the Afro-American literary tradition was generated as a response to allegations that its authors did not, and *could not*, create "literature." Philosophers and literary critics, such as Hume, Kant, Jefferson, and Hegel, seemed to decide that the presence of a written literature was the signal measure of the potential, innate "humanity" of a race. The African living in Europe or in the New World, seems to have felt compelled to create a literature both to demonstrate, implicitly, that blacks did indeed possess the intellectual ability to create a written art, but also to indict the several social and economic institutions that delimited the "humanity" of all black people in Western cultures.

So insistent did these racist allegations prove to be, at least from the eighteenth to the early twentieth centuries, that it is fair to describe the sub-text of the history of black letters as this urge to refute the claim that because blacks had no written traditions, they were bearers of an "inferior" culture. The relation between European and American critical theory, then, and the development of the African and Afro-American literary traditions, can readily be seen to have been ironic, indeed. Even as late as 1911, when J. E. Casely-Hayford published *Ethiopia Unbound* (the "first" African novel), that pioneering author felt compelled to address this matter in the first two paragraphs of his text. "At the dawn of the twentieth century," the novel opens, "men of light and leading both in Europe and in America had not yet made up their minds as to what place to assign to the spiritual aspirations of the black man; . . . Before this time," the narrative continues, "it had been discovered that the black man was not necessarily the missing link between man and ape. It has even been granted that for intellectual endowments he had nothing to be ashamed of in an *open* competition with the Aryan or any other type."[7] *Ethiopia Unbound*, it seems obvious, was concerned to "settle" the matter of black mental equality, which had remained something of an open question in European discourse for two hundred years. Concluding this curiously polemical exposition of three paragraphs, which precedes the introduction of the novel's protagonist, Casely-Hayford points to "the names of men like [W.E.B.] Du Bois, [Booker T.] Washington, [Wilmot E.] Blyden, [Paul Laurence] Dunbar, [Samuel] Coleridge-Taylor, and others" as *prima facie* evidence of the sheer saliency of what Carter G. Woodson once termed "the public [Negro] mind."[8] These were men, the narrative concludes, "who had distinguished themselves in the fields of activity and intellectuality," men who had demonstrated conclusively that the African's first cousin was indeed the European, rather than the ape.

That the presence of a written literature could assume such large proportions in several Western cultures from the Enlightenment to this century is even more curious than is the fact that blacks themselves, as late as 1911, felt moved to respond to this stimulus, indeed felt the need to speak the matter silent, to end the argument by producing literature. Few literary traditions have begun or been "sustained" by such a complex and curious relation to its criticism: allegations of an absence led directly to a presence, a literature often inextricably bound in a dialogue with its potentially harshest critics.[9]

Black literature, and its criticism, then, have been put to uses that were not primarily aesthetic; rather, they have formed part of a larger discourse on the nature of the black, and his or her role in the order of things. The integral relation between theory and a literary text, therefore, which so very often in other traditions has been a sustaining relation, in our tradition has been an extraordinarily problematical one. The relation among theory, tradition, and integrity within the black literary tradition has not been, and perhaps cannot be, a straightforward matter.

Let us consider the etymology of the word *integrity*, which I take to be the keyword implied in this matter. *Integrity* is a curious keyword to address in a period of bold and sometimes exhilarating speculation and experimentation, two other words which aptly characterize literary criticism, generally, and Afro-American criticism, specifically, at the present time. The Latin origin of the English word, *integritas*, connotes wholeness, entireness, completeness, chastity, and purity; most of which are descriptive terms that made their way frequently into the writings of the American "New Critics," critics who seem not to have cared particularly for, or about, the literature of Afro-Americans. Two of the most common definitions of "integrity" elaborate upon the sense of "whole-ness" derived from the Latin original. Let me cite these here, as taken from the *Oxford English Dictionary*:

1. The condition of having no part or element taken away or wanting; undivided or unbroken state; material wholeness, completeness, en-tirety; something undivided; an integral whole.
2. The condition of not being marred or violated; unimpaired or un-corrupted condition; original perfect state; soundness.

It is the second definition of "integrity"—that is to say, connoting the absence of violation and corruption, the preservation of an initial whole-ness or soundness—which I would like to consider in this deliberation upon "Theory and Integrity," or more precisely upon that relationship which ideally should obtain between African or Afro-American literature and the theories we borrow, revise, or fabricate to account for the precise nature and shape of our literature and its "being" in the world.

Despite the fact that Houston Baker and I are often attacked for using theory and that some black readers respond to our theories by remarking that "It's all Greek to me," it is probably true that critics of Afro-American literature (which, by the way, I employ as a less ethnocentric designation than "the Black Critic") are more concerned with the complex relation between literature and literary theory than we have ever been before. There are many reasons for this, not the least of which is our increasingly central role in "the profession," precisely when our colleagues in other literatures are engulfed in their own extensive debates about the intel-lectual merit of so very much theorizing. Theory, as a second-order reflection upon a primary gesture such as "literature," has *always* been viewed with deep mistrust and suspicion by those scholars who find it presumptuous and perhaps even decadent when criticism claims the right to stand, as discourse, on its own, as a parallel textual universe to literature. Theoretical texts breed other, equally "decadent," theoretical responses in a creative process that can be remarkably far removed from a poem or a novel.

For the critic of Afro-American literature, this process is even more perilous precisely because the largest part of contempoary literary "the-ory" derives from critics of Western European languages and literatures. Is the use of "theory" to write about Afro-American literature, we might ask rhetorically, merely another form of intellectual indenture, a form of servitude of the mind as pernicious in its intellectual implications as any other form of enslavement? This is the issue raised, for me at least, by the implied presence of the word "integrity" in this discussion. Does the propensity to theorize about a text or a literary tradition "mar," "violate," "impair," or "corrupt," the "soundness" of an "original perfect state" of a black text or of the black tradition? To argue the affirmative is to align one's position with the New Critical position that texts are "wholes" in the first place.

To be sure, this matter of criticism and integrity has a long and rather tortured history in black letters. It was David Hume, after all, who called the Jamaican poet of Latin verse, Francis Williams, "a parrot who merely speaks a few words plainly";[10] and Phillis Wheatley has for far too long suffered from the spurious attacks of black and white critics alike for being the original *rara avis* of a school of so-called "mockingbird poets," whose use and imitation of received European and American literary conventions has been regarded, simply put, as a corruption itself of a "purer" black expression, privileged somehow in black artistic forms such as the blues, signifying, the spirituals, and the Afro-American dance. Can we, as critics, escape a "mockingbird" relation to "theory," one destined to be derivative, often to the point of parody? Can we, moreover, escape the racism of so many critical theorists, from Hume and Kant through the Southern Agrarians and the Frankfurt School?

As I have argued elsewhere, there are complex historical reasons for the resistance to theory among critics of comparative black literature, which stem in part from healthy reactions against the marriage of logocentrism and ethnocentrism in much of post-Renaissance Western aesthetic discourse. Although there have been a few notable exceptions, theory as a subject of inquiry has only in the past decade begun to sneak into the discourse of Afro-American literature. The implicit racism of some of the Southern Agrarians who became the "New Critics" and Theodor Adorno's bizarre thoughts about something he calls "jazz," did not serve to speed this process along at all. Sterling A. Brown has summed up the relation of the black tradition to the Western critical tradition; in response to Robert Penn Warren's line, from "Pondy Woods" (1945): "Nigger, your breed ain't metaphysical." Brown replies, "Cracker, your breed ain't exegetical."[11] No tradition is "naturally" metaphysical or exegetical, of course. Only recently have some scholars attempted to convince critics of black literature that the racism of the Western critical tradition was not a sufficient reason for us to fail to theorize about our own endeavor, or even to make use of contemporary theoretical innovations when this seemed either useful or appropriate. Perhaps predictably, a number of these attempts share a concern with that which, in the received tradition of Afro-American criticism, has been most repressed: that is, with close readings of the text itself. This return of the repressed—the very language of the black text—has generated a new interest among our critics in theory. My charged advocacy of the relevance of contempoary theory to reading Afro-American and African literature closely has been designed as the prelude to the definition of principles of literary criticism peculiar to the black literary traditions themselves, related to and compatible with contempoary critical theory generally, yet "indelibly black," as Robert Farris Thompson puts it.[12] All theory is text-specific, and ours must be as well. Lest I be misunderstood, I have tried to work through contemporary theories of literature *not* to "apply" them to black texts, rather to *transform* by *translating* them into a new rhetorical realm. These attempts have been successful in varying degrees; nevertheless, I have tried to make them at all times interesting episodes in one critic's reflection on the black "text-milieu," which he means by "the tradition," and from which he extracts his "canon."

It is only through this critical activity that the profession, in a world of dramatically fluid relations of knowledge and power, and of the re-emerging presence of the tongues of Babel, can redefine itself away from a Eurocentric notion of a hierarchial "canon" of texts, mostly white, Western, and male, and encourage and sustain a truly comparative and pluralistic notion of the institution of literature. What all students of literature share in common is the art of interpretation, even where we do not share in common the same texts. The hegemony implicit in the phrase, "the Western tradition," reflects material relationships primarily, and not so-called universal, transcendant, normative judgments. Judgment is specific, both culturally and temporally. The sometimes vulgar nationalism implicit in would-be literary categories such as "American Literature," or the not-so-latent imperialism implied by the vulgar phrase "Commonwealth Literature," are extra-literary designations of control, symbolic of material and concomitant political relations, rather than literary ones. We, the scholars of our profession, must eschew these categories of domination and ideology and insist upon the fundamental redefinition of what it is to speak of "the canon."

Whether we realize it or not, each of us brings to a text an *implicit* theory of literature, or even an unwitting hybrid of theories, a critical gumbo as it were. To become aware of contemporary theory is to become aware of one's own presuppositions, those ideological and aesthetic assumptions which we bring to a text unwittingly. It is incumbent upon us, those of us who respect the sheer integrity of the black tradition, to turn to this very tradition to create self-generated theories about the *black* literary endeavor. We must, above all, respect the integrity of the separate traditions embodied in the black work of art, by bringing to bear upon the explication of its meanings all of the attention to language that we may learn from several developments in contemporary theory. By the very process of "application," as it were, we recreate, through revision, the critical theory at hand. As our familiarity with the black tradition and with literary theory expands, we shall invent our own theories, as some of us have begun to do—black, text-specific theories. We must learn to read a black text within a black formal cultural matrix.

I have tried to utilize contemporary theory to *defamiliarize* the texts of the black tradition, to create a distance between this black reader and our black texts, so that I may more readily *see* the formal workings of those texts. Wilhelm von Humboldt describes this phenomenon in the following way:

> Man lives with things mainly, even exclusively—since sentiment and action in him depend upon his mental representations—as they are conveyed to him by language. Through the same act by which he spins language out of himself he weaves himself into it, and every language draws a circle around the people to which it belongs, a circle that can only be transcended in so far as one at the same time enters another one.

I have turned to literary theory as a "second circle." I have done this to preserve the integrity of these texts, by trying to avoid confusing my experience as an Afro-American with the black act of language which defines a text. On the other hand, by learning to read a black text within a black formal cultural matrix, and explicating it with the principles of criticism at work in *both* the Euro-American and African-American traditions, I believe that we critics can produce richer structures of meaning than are possible otherwise.

This is the challenge of the critic of black literature in the 1980s: not to shy away from white power—that is, literary theory; rather, to translate it into the black idiom, *renaming* principles of criticism where appropriate, but especially *naming* indigenous black principles of criticism and applying these to explicate our own texts. It is incumbent upon us to protect the integrity of our tradition by bringing to bear upon its criticism any tool of sensitivity to language that is appropriate. And what do I mean by "appropriate"? Simply this: *any* tool that enables the critic to explain the complex workings of the language of a text is an "appropriate" tool. For it is language, the black language of black texts, which expresses the distinctive quality of our literary tradition. A literary tradition, like an individual, is to a large extent defined by its past, its received traditions. We critics in the 1980s have the especial privilege of explicating the black tradition in ever closer detail. We shall not meet this challenge by remaining afraid of, or naive about, literary theory; rather, we will only inflict upon our literary tradition the violation of the uninformed reading. We are the keepers of the black literary tradition. No matter what theories we seem to embrace, we have more in common with each other than we do with any other critic of any other literature.

We write for each other, and for our own contemporary writers. This relation is a critical trust.

It is also a *political* trust. How can the demonstration that our texts sustain ever closer and sophisticated readings *not* be political at a time in the academy when all sorts of so-called canonical critics mediate their racism through calls for "purity" of "the tradition," demands as implicitly racist as anything the Southern Agrarians said? How can the deconstruction, as it were, of the forms of racism itself (as carried out, for example, in a recent issue of *Critical Inquiry* by black and non-black poststructuralists) not be political?[13] How can the use of literary analysis to explicate the racist social text in which we still find ourselves be anything *but* political? To be political, however, does not mean that I have to write at the level of diction of a Marvel comic book. No, my task—as I see it—is to help to guarantee that black and so-called Third World literature is taught to black and Third World (and white) students by black and Third World and white professors in heretofore white mainstream departments of literature and to train university graduate and undergraduate students to think, to read, and even to *write* clearly, helping them to expose false uses of language, fraudulent claims, and muddled arguments, propaganda, and vicious lies—from all of which our people have suffered just as surely as we have from an economic order in which we were zeroes and a metaphysical order in which we were absences. These are the "values" which should betransmitted through black critical theory.

And, if only for the record, let me state clearly here that only a black person alienated from black language-use could fail to understand that we have been deconstructing white people's languages and discourses since that dreadful day in 1619 when we were marched off the boat in Virginia. Jacques Derrida did not invent deconstruction; *we* did! That is what the blues and signifying are all about. Ours must be a signifying, vernacular criticism, related to other critical theories, yet indelibly black, a critical theory of our own.

III

In the December 9, 1986, issue of the *Voice Literary Supplement*, in an essay entitled "Cult-Nats Meet Freaky-Deke," Greg Tate argues cogently and compellingly that "black aestheticians need to develop a coherent criticism to communicate the complexities of our culture. There's no periodical on black cultural phenomena equivalent to *The Village Voice* or *Artforum*, no publication that provides journalism on black visual art, philosophy, economics, media, literature, linguistics, psychology, sexuality, spirituality, and pop culture. Though there are certainly black editors, journalists, and academics capable of producing such a journal, the disintegration of the black cultural nationalist movement and the brain-drain of black intellectuals to white institutions have destroyed the vociferous public dialogue that used to exist between them" (p. 5). While I would argue that *Sage, Calaloo,* and *BALF are* indeed fulfilling that function for academic critics, I am afraid that the truth of Tate's claim is irresistible. But Tate's real and very important contribution to the future of black criticism is to be found in his most damning allegation. "What's unfortunate," he writes, "is that while black artists have opened up the entire "text of blackness" for fun and games, not many black critics have produced writing as fecund, eclectic, and freaky-deke as the art, let alone the culture, itself . . . For those who prefer exegesis with a polemical bend, just imagine how critics as fluent in black and Western culture as the postliberated artists could strike terror into that bastion of white supremacist thinking, the Western art [and literary] worlds" (p. 5). To which I can only say, echoing Shug in Alice Walker's *The Color Purple,* "Amen. Amen." Only by reshaping the critical canon with our own voices in our own images can we meet Tate's challenge head-on.

Tate's challenge is a serious one because neither ideology nor criticism, nor blackness can exist as an entity of itself, outside of its forms, or its texts. This is the central theme of Ralph Ellison's *Invisible Man* and Ishmael Reed's *Mumbo Jumbo,* for example. But how can we write or read the text of "Black Theory"? What language(s) do black people use to represent or to contain their critical or ideological positions? In what forms of language do we speak, or write, or *rewrite?* These are the issues at the heart of my essay.

Can we derive a valid, *integral* "black" text of criticism or ideology from borrowed or appropriated forms? That is, can an authentic black text emerge in the forms of language inherited from the master's class, whether that be, for instance, the realistic novel or poststructuralist theory? Can a black woman's text emerge authentically as borrowed, or "liberated," or revised, from the patriarchial forms of the slave narratives, on one hand, or from the white matriarchial forms of the sentimental novel, on the other, as Harriet Jacobs and Harriet Wilson attempted to do in *Incidents in the Life of a Slave Girl* (1861) and *Our Nig* (1859)?

How much space is there between these two forms through which to maneuver, to maneuver without a certain preordained confinement or "garreting," such as that to which Valerie Smith alludes so pregnantly in her superb poststructural reading of Jacobs's *Incidents in the Life of a Slave Girl?*[14] Is to revise, in this sense, to exist within the confines of the garret, to extend the metaphor, only to learn to manipulate the representation of black structures of feeling between the cracks, the dark spaces, provided for us by the white masters? Can we write true texts of our ideological selves by the appropriation of received forms of the oppressor—be that oppressor patriarchy or racism—forms in which we see no reflection of our own faces, and through which we hear no true resonances of our own voices? Where lies the liberation in revision, where lies the ideological integrity of defining freedom in the modes and forms of difference charted so cogently by so many poststructural critics of black literature?

It is in these spaces, or garrets, of difference that black literature has dwelled. And while it is crucial to read closely these patterns of formal difference, it is incumbent upon us as well to understand that the quest was lost, in a major sense, before it had even begun, simply because the terms of our own self-representation have been provided by the master. Are our choices only to dwell in the quicksand or the garret of refutation, or negation, or revision? The ideological critique of revision must follow, for us as critics, our detailed and ever closer readings of these very modes of revision. It is not enough for us to show that these exist, and to define these as satisfactory gestures of ideological independence. In this sense, our next set of concerns must be to address the black political signified, that is, the cultural vision and the black critical language which underpin the search through literature and art for a profound reordering and humanizing of everyday existence. We must urge for our writers and critics the fullest and most ironic exploration of manner and matter, of content and form, of structure and sensibility so familiar and poignant to us in our most sublime forms of art, verbal and nonverbal black music, where ideology and art are one, whether we listen to Bessie Smith or to postmodern and poststructural John Coltrane.

But what of the ideology of the black critical text? And what of our own critical discourse? In whose voices do we speak? Have we merely renamed terms received from the White Other? Just as we must urge of our writers the meeting of this challenge, we as critics must turn to our own peculiarly black structures of thought and feeling to develop our own language of criticism. We must do so by turning to the black vernacular, the language we use to speak to each other, when no white people are around. My central argument is this: *black people theorize about their art and their lives in the black vernacular*. Unless we turn to the vernacular to ground our theories and modes of reading, we will surely sink in the mire of Nella Larsen's quicksand, remain alienated in the isolation of Harriet Jacobs's garret, or masked in the received stereotype of the Black Other helping Huck Honey to return to the Raft again, singing "China Gate" with Nat King Cole under the Da Nang moon, standing with the Incredible Hulk as the monstrous split doubled selves of mild-mannered, yet implicitly racist white people, or reflecting our balded heads in the shining flash of Mr. T's signifying gold chains.

IV

Before I return to John C. Calhoun and Alexander Crummell, those metaphors of progress, elevation, and intellectual equality with which I began my talk, let us consider another example of the black artist at the peculiar crossroads where the black world of letters meets the white. If mastering the forms of Western poetry to refute the racist logocentrism epitomized by John C. Calhoun motivated Phillis Wheatley to break forever the silence of the black voice in the court of Western letters, and motivated Crummell to sail to Cambridge to master Greek syntax, how did Wole Soyinka respond to becoming the first black recipient, in 1986, of the Nobel Prize in Literature, that sacred icon of Western intellectual and artistic attainment which many of us thought would be withheld from us for still another century, and which many of us take to be another nuclear warhead dropped upon the last bastion of white racism—that is, their theories of our intellectual inferiority? Soyinka, born in Abeokuta, Nigeria, which Crummell had predicted to be one of the places in West Africa at which the English language would reach perfection as spoken by black people (p. 36), responded not as Crummell did to the racism which led him to Cambridge by extolling the virtues of the English language over the African vernacular languages, which he thought to reflect the animal propensities of an inferior, barely human intellect, but by recalling the irony that this single event in the history of black literature occurred while Nelson Mandella languishes in prison and while Western capitalism guarantees the survival and indeed the growth of the prison-house of apartheid. Dedicating his Laureate Speech to Nelson Mandella, Soyinka proceeded to attack the existence of apartheid and the complicity of the West in its continuation, as a nervous Swedish Academy shifted its weight uneasily.[15]

Soyinka was most concerned to analyze the implications of African artistry and intellect being acknowledged before the white world, at long last, through this curious ritual called the Nobel Prize, endowed by the West's King of Dynamite, and weaponry. Soyinka refused to address his black audience; rather, he addressed his white auditors and indeed the racist intellectual tradition of Europe as exemplified by Hegel, Hume, Locke, Voltaire, Frobenius, Kant, and others, who "were unabashed theorists of racial superiority and denigrators of the African history and being" (p. 10).

The blacks of course are locked into an unambiguous condition: on this occasion I do not need to address *us*. We know, and we embrace our mission. It is the *other* that this precedent seizes the opportunity to address, and not merely those who live outside, on the fringes of conscience . . .

Some atavistic bug is at work here which defies all scientific explanation, an arrest in time within the evolutionary mandate of nature, which puts all human experience of learning to serious question! We have to ask ourselves then, what event can speak to such a breed of people? How do we reactivate that petrified cell which houses historic apprehension and development? Is it possible perhaps that events, gatherings such as this [the Nobel Prize] might help? Dare we skirt the edge of hubris and say to them: Take a good look. Provide your response. In your anxiety to prove that this moment is not possible, you have killed, maimed, silenced, tortured, exiled, debased and dehumanized hundreds of thousands encased in this very skin, crowned with such hair, proudly content with their very being. (pp. 8–9)

Soyinka's brilliant rhetorical gesture was to bring together an uncompromising renunciation of apartheid and a considered indictment of the racist tradition in Western letters which equates the possession of reason with the reflection of the voice and the face of the master, a tradition which overwhelmed Alexander Crummell standing as he did at a point of liminality between Western culture and African culture. Citing the work of Hume, Hegel, Montesquieu, and a host of others as "Dangerous for your racial self-esteem!" (p. 19), Soyinka marshalled a most impressive array of citations to chart the racist tradition in Western letters which would deny to the black world the particularity of its discourse, as typified for Soyinka by the following sentiment of the expressionist, Johannes Becher: "Negro tribes, fever, tuberculosis, veneral epidemics, intellectual psychic defects—I'll vanquish them" (p. 16). To underscore the failure of the Western intellectual to escape his or her own myopic racism in even the most sublime encounters with the Black Other, Soyinka compares Becher's exhortation with the commentary of Leo Frobenius upon encountering the most sacred, and most brilliantly rendered, bronze of the Yoruba people:

And was it by coincidence that contemporaneously with this stirring manifesto, yet another German enthusiast, Leo Frobenius—with no claims whatever to being part of, or indeed having the least interest in the Expressionist movement, was able to visit Ile-Ife, the heartland and cradle of the Yoruba race and be profoundly stirred by an object of beauty, the product of the Yoruba mind and hand, a classic expression of that serene portion of the world resolution of that race. In his own words: "Before us stood a head of marvellous beauty, wonderfully cast in antique bronze, true to the life, incrusted with a patina of glorious dark green. This was, in very deed, the Olokun, Atlantic Africa's Poseidon." Yet listen to what he had to write about the very people whose handiwork had lifted him into these realms of universal sublimity: "Profoundly stirred, I stood for many minutes before the remnant of the erstwhile Lord and Ruler of the Empire of Atlantis. My companions were no less astounded. As though we had agreed to do so, we held our peace. Then I looked around and saw—the blacks—the circle of the sons of the 'venerable priest,' his Holiness the Oni's friends, and his intelligent officials. I was moved to silent melancholy at the thought that this assembly of degenerate and feeble-minded posterity should be the legitimate guardians of so much loveliness." A direct invitation to a free-for-all race for dispossession, justified on the grounds of the keeper's unworthiness, it recalls other schizophrenic conditions which are mother to, for instance, the far more lethal, dark mythopoeia of [the Nazis]. (pp. 16–17)

"He is breaking an open door," one member of the Swedish Academy said to me, while Soyinka spoke. "Why would he choose to indict apartheid at an historic moment such as this?" Soyinka chose to do so to remind the world that no black person can be truly free until we all are freed from even the *possibility* of racial oppression, and that even Nobel Prizes in Literature are only useful when its first black recipient reminds the world of that fact, and of the history of the use of race and reason as tropes of oppression in Western letters. As critics and artists, Soyinka argues, we must utilize the creative and critical tools at hand to stomp racism out. This is our first great task.

But what else contributes to the relation, then, between (white) power and the (black) critic? Soyinka's terms, and my title, might suggest that ours is the fate of perpetual negation, that we are doomed merely to "oppose," to serve within the academy as black signs of opposition to a political order in which we are the subjugated. We must oppose, of course, when opposition is called for. But our task is so very much more complex. Again, to define this task, I can do no better than to cite Soyinka: "And when we borrow an alien language to sculpt or paint in, we must begin by co-opting the entire properties of that language as correspondences to properties in our matrix of thought and expression."[16] Soyinka's own brilliant achievement in the drama is to have done just this, to have redefined the very concept of "tragedy" by producing a synthesis of African and European tragic forms. At all points, his "English" is Yoruba-informed, Yoruba-based. To assume that we can wear the masks, and speak the languages, of Western literary theory without accepting Soyinka's challenge is to accept, willingly, the intellectual equivalent of neo-colonialism, placing ourselves in a relationship of discursive indenture.

It is the challenge of the black tradition to critique this relation of indenture, an indenture that obtains for our writers and for our critics. We must master, as even Jacques Derrida understands, how "to speak the other's language without renouncing [our] own."[17] When we attempt to appropriate, by inversion, "race" as a term for an essence—as did the negritude movement, for example ("We feel, therefore we are," as Leopold Senghor argued of the African)—we yield too much: in this case, *reason* as the basis of a shared humanity. Such gestures, as Anthony Appiah observes, are futile and dangerous because of their further inscription of new and bizarre stereotypes. How do we meet Soyinka's challenge in the discourse of criticism? The Western critical tradition has a canon, as the Western literary tradition does. I once thought it our most important gesture to *master* the canon of criticism, to *imitate* and *apply* it, but I now believe that we must turn to the black tradition itself to develop theories of criticism indigenous to our literatures. Alice Walker's revision of Rebecca Cox Jackson's parable of white interpretation (written in 1836) makes this point most tellingly. Jackson, a Shaker eldress and black visionary, claimed like John Jea to have been taught to read by the Lord. She writes in her autobiography that she dreamed a white man came to her house to teach her how to *interpret* and understand the word of God, now that God had taught her to read:

> A white man took me by my right hand and led me on the north side of the room, where sat a square table. On it lay a book open. And he said to me. "Thou shall be instructed in this book, from Genesis to Revelations." And then he took me on the west side, where stood a table. And it looked like the first. And said, "Yea, thou shall be instructed from the beginning of creation to the end of time." And then he took me on the east side of the room also, where stood a table and book like the two first, and said, "I will instruct thee—yea, thou shall be instructed from the beginning of all things to the end of all things. Yea, thou shall be well instructed. I will instruct."
>
> And then I awoke, and I saw him as plain as I did in my dream. And after that he taught me daily. And when I would be reading and come to a hard word, I would see him standing by my side and he would teach me the word right. And often, when I would be in meditation and looking into things which was hard to understand, I would find him by me, teaching and giving me understanding. And oh, his labor and care which he had with me often caused me to weep bitterly, when I would see my great ignorance and the great trouble he had to make me understand eternal things. For I was so buried in the depth of the tradition of my forefathers, that it did seem as if I never could be dug up.[18]

In response to Jackson's relation of interpretive indenture to "a white man," Walker, in *The Color Purple*, records an exchange between Celie and Shug about turning away from "the old white man" which soon turns into a conversation about the elimination of "man" as a mediator between a woman and "everything":

> You have to git man off your eyeball, before you can see anything a'tall.
> Man corrupt everything, say Shug. He on your box of grits, in your head, and all over the radio. He try to make you think he everywhere. Soon as you think he everywhere, you think he God. But he ain't. Whenever you trying to pray, and man plop himself on the other end of it, tell him to git lost, say Shug.[19]

Celie and Shug's omnipresent "man," of course, echoes the black tradition's synechdoche for the white power structure, "the man."

For non-Western, so-called noncanonical critics, getting the "man off your eyeball" means using the most sophisticated critical theories and methods available to reappropriate and redefine our own "colonial" discourses. We must use these theories and methods insofar as they are relevant to the study of our own literatures. The danger in doing so, however, is best put by Anthony Appiah in his definition of what he calls "the Naipaul fallacy":

> It is not necessary to show that African literature is fundamentally the same as European literature in order to show that it can be treated with the same tools; . . . nor should we endorse a more sinister line . . . : the post-colonial legacy which requires us to show that African literature is worthy of study precisely (but only) because it is fundamentally the same as European literature.[20]

We *must* not, Appiah concludes, ask "the reader to understand Africa by embedding it in European culture" ("S," p. 146).

We must, I believe, analyze the ways in which writing relates to race, how attitudes toward racial differences generate and structure literary texts by us *and* about us. We must determine how critical methods can effectively disclose the traces of ethnic differences in literature. But we must also understand how certain forms of difference and the *languages* we employ to define those supposed differences not only reinforce each other but tend to create and maintain each other. Similarly, and as importantly, we must analyze the language of contemporary criticism itself, recognizing especially that hermeneutic systems are not universal, color-blind, apolitical, or neutral. Whereas some critics wonder aloud, as Appiah notes, about such matters as whether or not "a structuralist poetics is inapplicable in Africa because structuralism is European" ("S," p. 145), the concern of the Third World critic should properly be to understand the ideological subtext which any critical theory reflects and embodies, and the relation which this subtext bears to the production of meaning. No critical theory—be it Marxist, feminist, poststructuralist,

Kwame Nkrumah's "consciencism," or whatever—escapes the specificity of value and ideology, no matter how mediated these may be. To attempt to appropriate our own discourses by using Western critical theory uncritically is to substitute one mode of neocolonialism for another. To begin to do this in my own tradition, theorists have turned to the black vernacular tradition—to paraphrase Jackson, they have begun to dig into the depths of the tradition of our foreparents—to isolate the signifying black difference through which to theorize about the so-called discourse of the Other.

Even Crummell recognized that Western economic and political subjugation has inflicted upon us a desire to imitate, to please, to refashion our public discursive images of our black selves after that of the colonizer: "he will part," Crummell with great satisfaction concludes of the colonized African, "at any moment, with the crude uncouth utterances of his native tongue, for that other higher language, which brings with its utterance, wealth and gratification" (pp. 34—35). This, it seems to me, is the trap, the tragic lure, to which those who believe that critical theory is a color-blind, universal discourse, or a culturally neutral tool like a hammer or a screwdriver, have unwittingly succumbed. And by succumbing to this mistake, these critics fail to accept the wonderful opportunity offered to our generation of critics as heirs to the Black Arts movement, the great achievement of which, as Greg Tate correctly concludes, was to define a "black cultural *difference*" and "produce a post-liberated black aesthetic [which is] responsible for the degree to which contemporary black artists and intellectuals feel themselves heirs to a culture every bit as def [sic] as classical Western civilization. This cultural confidence," he concludes, "has freed up more black artists to do work as wonderfully absurdist as black life itself" (p. 5). As Tate concludes, where is the black critical theory as great as this greatest black art? Our criticism is destined merely to be derivative, to be a pale shadow, of the white master's critical discourse, until we become confident enough to speak in our own black languages as we theorize about the black critical endeavor.

We must redefine "theory" itself from within our own black cultures, refusing to grant the racist premise that theory is something that white people do, so that we are doomed to imitate our white colleagues, like reverse black minstrel critics done up in white face. We are all heirs to critical theory, but we black critics are heir to the black vernacular critical tradition as well. Our task now is to invent and employ our own critical theory, to assume our own propositions, and to stand within the academy as politically responsible and responsive parts of a social and cultural African-American whole. Again, Soyinka's words about our relation to the black tradition are relevant here:

That world which is so conveniently traduced by Apartheid thought is of course that which I so wholeheartedly embrace—and this is my choice—among several options—of the significance of my presence here. It is a world that nourishes my being, one which is so self-sufficient, so replete in all aspects of its productivity, so confident in itself and in its destiny that it experiences no fear in reaching out to others and in responding to the reach of others. It is the heartstone of our creative existence. It constitutes the prism of our world perception and this means that our sight need not be and has never been permanently turned inwards. If it were, we could not so easily understand the enemy on our doorstep, nor understand how to obtain the means to disarm it. When this society which is Apartheid South Africa indulges from time to time in appeals to the outside world that it represents the last bastion of civilization against the hordes of barbarism from its North, we can even afford an indulgent smile. It is sufficient, imagines this state, to raise the spectre of a few renegade African leaders, psychopaths and robber barons who we ourselves are victims of—whom we denounce before the world and overthrow when we are able—this Apartheid society insists to the world that its picture of the future is the reality which only its policies can erase. This is a continent which only destroys, it proclaims, it is peopled by a race which has never contributed anything positive to the world's pool of knowledge. A vacuum, that will suck into its insatiable maw the entire fruits of centuries of European civilization, then spew out the resulting mush with contempt. How strange that a society which claims to represent this endangered face of progress should itself be locked in centuries-old fantasies, blithely unaware of, or indifferent to the fact that it is the last, institutionally functioning product of archaic articles of faith in Euro-Judaic thought. (pp. 11–12)

As deconstruction and other poststructuralisms or even an a-racial Marxism, and other "articles of faith in Euro-Judaic thought" exhaust themselves in a self-willed racial never-never land in which we see no true reflections of our black faces and hear no echoes of our black voices, let us—at long last—Master the critical traditions and languages of Africa and Afro-America. Even as we continue to reach out to others in the critical canon, let us be confident in our own black tradition and in their compelling strength to sustain systems of critical thought as yet dormant and unexplicated. We must, in the truest sense, turn inwards even as we turn outwards to redefine every institution in this profession—the English Institute, the MLA, the School of Criticism, what have you—in our own images. We must not succumb, as did Alexander Crummell, to the tragic lure of white power, the mistake of accepting the empowering language of white critical theory as "universal" or as our own language, the mistake of confusing the enabling mask of theory with our own black faces. Each of us has, in some literal or figurative manner, boarded a ship and sailed to a metaphorical Cambridge, seeking to master the master's tools, and to outwit this racist master by compensating for a presupposed lack. In my own instance, being quite literal-minded, I booked passage some fourteen years ago on the QE2! And much of my early work reflects this desire to outwit the master by trying to speak his language as fluently as he. Now, we must, at last, don the empowering mask of blackness and talk *that* talk, the language of black difference. While it is true that we must, as Du Bois said so long ago, "know and test the power of the cabalistic letters of the white man," we must also know and test the dark secrets of a black and hermetic discursive universe that awaits its disclosure through the black arts of interpretation. For the future of theory, in the remainder of this century, is black, indeed.

20

A Criticism of Our Own: Autonomy and Assimilation in Afro-American and Feminist Literary Theory

Elaine Showalter

The Other Woman

In the summer of 1985, I was one of the speakers at the annual conference on literary theory at Georgetown University. On the first morning, a distinguished Marxist theorist was introduced, and as he began to read his paper, there appeared from the other side of the stage a slender young woman in a leotard and long skirt who looked like a ballet dancer. Positioning herself a few feet from the speaker, she whirled into motion, waving her fingers and hands, wordlessly moving her lips, alternating smiles and frowns. There were murmurs in the audience; what could this mean? Was it a protest against academic conferences? A Feifferesque prayer to the muse of criticism? A celebratory performance of the Althusserian two-step? Of course, as we soon realized, it was nothing so dramatic or strange. Georgetown had hired this young woman from an organization called Deaf Pride to translate all the papers into sign language for the hearing-impaired.

Yet from the perspective of the audience, this performance soon began to look like a guerilla theatre of sexual difference which had been staged especially for our benefit. After the first ten minutes, it became impossible simply to *listen* to the famous man, immobilized behind the podium. Our eyes were drawn instead to the nameless woman, and to the eloquent body language into which she mutely translated his words. In this context, her signs seemed uncannily feminine and Other, as if we were watching a Kristevan ambassador from the semiotic, or the ghost

Thanks for helpful suggestions on drafts of this paper to members of the School for Criticism and Theory at Dartmouth College, and also to Skip Gates, Houston Baker, Brenda Silver, Marianne Hirsch, Evelyn Fox Keller, Valerie Smith, Daryl Dance, and English Showalter.

of a Freudian hysteric back from the beyond. Anna O. is alive and well in Georgetown!

The feminist implications of this arrangement were increasingly emphasized, moreover, throughout the first day of the conference, because, although the young woman reached ever more dazzling heights of ingenuity, mobility, and grace, not one of the three white male theorists who addressed us took any notice of her presence. No one introduced her; no one alluded to her. It was as if they could not see her. She had become transparent, like the female medium of the symbolists who, according to Mary Ann Caws, "served up the sign, conveying it with fidelity, patience, and absolute personal silence. She herself was patiently ruled out."[1]

Sitting in the audience that first morning, I wondered what would happen when *I* was introduced as the fourth speaker. I had wild fantasies that Georgetown would provide a bearded male interpreter who would translate my paper into the rhetoric of deconstruction. (It turned out that there were two young women who alternated the task of interpretation. This does not seem to be a man's job.) I wondered too how I should speak from the position of power as the "theorist" when I also identified with the silent, transparent woman? The presence of the other woman was a return of the repressed paradox of female authority, the paradox Jane Gallop describes as fraudulence: "A woman theoretician is already an exile; expatriated from her *langue maternelle*, she speaks a paternal language; she presumes to a fraudulent power."[2] The translator seemed to represent not only the *langue maternelle*, the feminine other side of discourse, but also the Other Woman of feminist discourse, the woman outside of academia in the "real world," or the Third World, to whom a Feminist critic is responsible, just as she is responsible to the standards and conventions of criticism.[3] Gayatri Chakravorty Spivak has reminded us that she must always be acknowledged in our work: "Who is the other woman? How am I naming her? How does she name me?"[4]

At the Georgetown conference, my awareness of the Other Woman was shared by the other women on the program; all of us, in our presentations, introduced the interpreter, and changed our lectures in order to work with her presence. Yet the only male speaker who took notice of the interpreter was Houston Baker. By the time he spoke on the second day, Baker had learned enough sign language to produce a virtuoso translation of the beginning of his own talk, and to work with the translator in a playful duet.

The Georgetown conference was not the first time that Afro-American and feminist critics have found ourselves on the same side of otherness, but it was certainly one of the most dramatic. For those of us who work within "oppositional" or cultural criticisms—black, socialist, feminist, or gay—questions of the critic's double consciousness, double audience, and double role come with the territory and arise every day. They are not just the sort of global questions Terry Eagleton poses in *Literary Theory*, as to whether an analysis of the Lacanian imaginary can help welfare mothers, but more mundane problems of ethnicity and ethics: how we will answer the mail, how we will conduct ourselves in the classroom or on the podium, and how we will act not only in symbolic relationships but also in real encounters with constituencies inside and outside of academia.

In this essay, I briefly sketch out the parallel histories of Afro-American and feminist literary criticism and theory over the past twenty-five years, in order to learn from our mutual experience in relation to the dominant culture. This may seem like a strange moment for such a project. In both feminist and Afro-American criticism, the Other Woman, the silenced partner, has been the black woman, and the role played by black feminist critics in bridging the two schools is controversial. While black and white feminists have objected to the sexism of black literary history, black women have also challenged the racism of feminist literary history. Black male writers have protested against the representation of black men in the fiction of Afro-American women novelists, and Ishmael Reed's latest novel, *Reckless Eyeballing* (1986), imagines a violent vengeance on feminists in general and black feminist writers in particular.

Yet this record of misunderstanding obscures what I think are the strong and important connections between the two kinds of cultural criticism; we have much to gain by a dialogue.[5] Both feminist and Afro-American criticism have brought together personal, intellectual, and political issues in our confrontations with the Western literary tradition. We have both followed traditional patterns in the institutionalization of critical movements, from our beginnings in a separatist cultural aesthetics, born out of participation in a protest movement; to a middle stage of professionalized focus on a specific text-milieu in an alliance with academic literary theory; to an expanded and pluralistic critical field of expertise on sexual or racial difference. Along with gay and post-Colonial critics, we share many critical metaphors, theories, and dilemmas, such as the notion of a double-voiced discourse, the imagery of the veil, the mask, or the closet; and the problem of autonomy versus mimicry and civil disobedience.

In abandoning marginal territories of our own for places in the post-structuralist critical wilderness, do black and feminist critics also risk exchanging authenticity for imitation, and self-generated critical models for what Lisa Jardine calls Designer Theory? If we oppose the idea that women should have the exclusive franchise on "gender" or blacks the franchise on "race," what can be the distinguishing idiom or role of the black of feminist critic, and how do we identify the place from which we speak? Can we make the compromises necessary for acceptance by the mainstream, and still work for a criticism of our own? Or is the dream of an alternative criticism which is "simultaneously subversive and self-authenticating" the most utopian of all sub-cultural fantasies?[6]

The Black Critical Revolution

In a splendidly argued essay called "Generational Shifts and the Recent Criticism of Afro-American Literature," Houston Baker has drawn on the work of Thomas Kuhn and Lewis Feuer to account for the transformations within Afro-American criticism from the 1950s to the early 1980s. He suggests that intergenerational conflict and the pressures of ascendant class interests can explain the movement towards alliance with the mainstream.[7] While Baker's essay is the most important and coherent account we have of the black critical revolution, his concept of the "generational shift" still raises a number of problems. First of all, critics cannot be assigned to generations with any precision, since, as David Riesman reminds us, people "are not born in batches, as are pancakes, but are born continuously."[8] The shifts within the critical fields, moreover, cannot be seen simply in generational terms, since in the humanities, intelligent people often transform and revise their theoretical positions in the light of new ideas, rather than stubbornly clinging to their original paradigms unto death. Within feminist criticism, indeed, the tendency of such writers as Toril Moi to construct rigid binary oppositions of feminist thought without regard for the complex permutations and exchanges within feminist discourse today, ignores the historical contexts in which ideas began, and the process of self-criticism and revision which has kept them sharp.[9]

A second problem with Baker's essay, and with Afro-American critical history in general, is that it does not take sufficient account of gender, and of the role of black women in shaping both literary and criticial discourse. In using a number of his categories, then, I have tried to rethink them as well in the light of black feminist writing.

Before the Civil Rights Movement, criticism of Afro-American literature was dominated by "integrationist poetics"—skepticism about a unified black consciousness, and the ambition to have black writers merge with the mainstream of the American literary tradition. This view was articulated in the 1940s and 1950s by such male writers and scholars as Richard Wright, Arthur P. David, and Sterling Brown, who denied any specificity to "Negro writing" and insisted that black literature should measure up to and be judged by the standards of the dominant critical community. As Davis wrote in an introduction to *The Negro Caravan* in 1941, "the Negro writes in the forms evolved in English and American literature. . . . The editors considered Negro writing to be American writing, and literature by American Negroes to be a segment of American literature."[10] Since black Americans were promised equal rights under such legislation as the 1954 Supreme Court decision, so too, integrationist critics hoped, "Negro writing" would win an equal place in American literary culture. Meanwhile, they argued, black writers "must demand a single standard of criticism," and reject any special consideration on the basis of race. The occasional success of a writer like Ralph Ellison was taken to prove that a serious black artist would be recognized.

Yet integrationist poetics rested on the optimistic and deluded belief that a "single standard of criticism" could respond equitably and intelligently to Afro-American writing, that the "single" standard could be universal, rather than a cultural straitjacket based on the limited and exclusive literary values of an elite.[11] In practice, black writing was often viewed by white critics using the excuse of integrationist poetics as inferior or flawed. Moreover, even when black male writers won recognition, novels by black women such as Ann Petry's *The Street* (1946) and Gwendolyn Brooks's *Maud Martha* (1953) were marginalized by the black and white male literary communities. As Mary Helen Washington has argued, the "real 'invisible man' of the 1950s was the black woman."[12]

Integrationist poetics, however, was challenged in the 1960s by the new political ideology which Stokely Carmichael christened "Black Power." Calling for racial leadership and identity, and for a rejection of the racist standards masked as equality offered by white society, Black Power generated the cultural forms of the Black Arts movement, led by Afro-American writers, artists, and intellectuals such as Amiri Baraka (LeRoi Jones), Larry Neal, Addison Gayle, Jr., and Stephen Henderson. These leaders of the black male intelligentsia insisted on the uniqueness and authenticity of black expression, especially in folk forms and music, and rejected the idea that a uniform standard of criticism derived from white culture could be adequate to the interpretation and evaluation of Black Art. Indeed, Black Art proposed "a radical reordering of the Western cultural aesthetic . . . a separate symbolism, mythology, critique, and iconology."[13] The term "negritude," originating in Paris, the Caribbean, and Francophone Africa, celebrated the existence of a unique black artistic consciousness transcending nationality. Via the concept of negritude, as Melvin Dixon has explained, a "generation of blacks dispersed through the world reclaimed a part of their identity as members of the African diaspora."[14]

In the United States, the Black Aesthetic attempted to produce "a distinctive code for the creation and evaluation of black art."[15] "Blackness" itself became an ontological and critical category for assessing Afro-American literature. Stephen Henderson, one of the major theorists of the Black Aesthetic, argued that the black poem must not be considered in isolation, as the New Critics had maintained, but as a verbal performance in the fullest contexts of the "Black Experience," the "complex galaxy of personal, social, institutional, historical, religious, and mythical meanings that affect everything we say or do as Black people sharing a common heritage."[16] Its value could be determined only by the black interpretive community which shared the "Soul Field" of Afro-American culture.

Thus the Black Aesthetic offered the possibility of an autonomous and coherent black literary-critical discourse, not merely imitative of or parasitic on the white tradition, but in possession of its own roots, themes, structures, terms, and symbols from Afro-American culture. Moreover, the theoretical privileging of the black interpretive community gave the individual black critic a kind of cultural authority that enabled him or her to rise within the profession. As Baker notes, the predication of blackness as a "distinct and positive category of existence . . . was not only a radical political act designed to effect the liberation struggles of Afro-America, but also a bold critical act designed to break the interpretive monopoly on Afro-American expressive culture that had been held from time immemorial by a white liberal-critical establishment that set 'a single standard of criticism.' "[17]

The importance of the Black Aesthetic in the establishment of Afro-American literature cannot be overestimated. But to many black intellectuals, the Black Aesthetic also appeared narrow, chauvinistic, mystical, and theoretically weak. If only black critics were qualified by virture of their racial experience to interpret black literature, they feared, it would remain ghettoized forever.

In practice, too, the theoretical privileging of the revolutionary black artist and the black critical imagination was open to charges of sexism; the major texts of the Black Aesthetic ignored or patronized women's imaginative and critical writing, just as the Black Power movement, in Stokely Carmichael's other notorious phrase, defined the position of women as "prone."[18] By 1970, beginning with the publication of Toni Morrison's The Bluest Eye, black feminist writers and critics began to make their voices heard within the literary community. Alice Walker was teaching courses on black women writers at Wellesley and the University of Massachusetts in the early 1970s, and leading others such as Toni Cade Bambara in "looking for Zora"—carrying out the quest for

Zora Neale Hurston, who had been ignored by male critics of the Black Aesthetic, as the literary and critical foremother of the black female literary tradition. Black feminist critics such as Barbara Smith, Mary Helen Washington, Gloria Hull, and Barbara Christian raised important questions about the place of women within the Afro-American literary canon, and within the decade, some male theorists of the Black Aesthetic, including Stephen Henderson and Amiri Baraka, reconsidered their earlier positions. "When Black women discovered a political context that involved both race and gender," Henderson wrote in the introduction to Mari Evans's *Black Women Writers* (1983), "Our history in this country took a special turn, and our literature made a quantum leap toward maturity and honesty."

Yet even when the question of sexism was addressed, there were blatant theoretical weaknesses in the Black Aesthetic. Their concept of "race" was romantic and ideological; they ignored new developments within literary criticism. As Houston Baker concludes:

> The defensive inwardness of the Black Aesthetic—its manifest appeal to a racially-conditioned, revolutionary, and intuitive standard of critical judgment—made the new paradigm an ideal instrument of vision for those who wished to usher into the world new and *sui generis* Afro-American objects of investigation. Ultimately, though, such introspection could not answer the kinds of theoretical questions occasioned by the entry of these objects into the world. In a sense, the Afro-American literary-critical investigator had been given—through a bold act of the critical imagination—a unique literary tradition but no distinctive theoretical vocabulary with which to discuss this tradition.[19]

The political collapse of the Black Power movement, the advent of women's liberation, and the impact of European literary theory in the United States, all led to the demise of the Black Aesthetic. It was succeeded in the late 1970s by a new wave of young black intellectuals, benefitting from the academic prestige the Black Aesthetic had won for black writing, yet skeptical of the cultural claims of the Black Arts Movement, and opposed to its separatist policies and poetics. Trained in such deconstructionist centers as Cornell and Yale, these critics sought to establish a "sound theoretical framework for the study of Afro-American literature," by situating it within the discourse of poststructuralist literary theory. Instead of seeing themselves primarily as spokesmen for art in the black community, with the mission of helping to create a revolutionary black literary consciousness in American society, they defined themselves as Afro-American specialists in the theoretical community, with the goal of rendering "major contributions to contemporary theory's quest to 'save the text.' "[20]

Among the central critical texts of the generation Houston Baker calls the "reconstructionists" are two major anthologies, *Afro-American Literature: The Reconstruction of Instruction* (1979), edited by Robert B. Stepto and Dexter Fisher; and *Black Literature and Literary Theory* (1984), edited by Henry Louis Gates, Jr. Stepto's "Introduction" to *Afro-American Literature* argues for a mixture of formal and cultural approaches to the black literary text, which is still seen as the object of a black critical practice, and as the primary subject of a sophisticated and formalized Afro-American pedagogy. *Afro-American Literature,* published by the Modern Language Association, represented the intersection of Afro-American studies and the English department. It suggested ways that black or white teachers of American literature could learn to be competent readers of Afro-American writing.

Gates's anthology goes considerably further, and could easily be subtitled "the reconstruction of deconstruction." Dedicated to the memories of Charles Davis and Paul de Man, *Black Literature and Literary Theory* presents itself in its structure, themes, and rhetoric, as a "two-toned" critical discourse, poised between black studies and the Yale School. Gates defines his textual territory as African, Caribbean, and Afro-American literatures, and his purpose as the application of contemporary literary theory to black literature. The anthology begins with Gates's own dazzling manifesto of black deconstruction, "Criticism in the Jungle." Like Ishmael Reed's *Mumbo Jumbo* (1972) a central novel in Gates's canon of black literature, which provides the epigraph to the essay, the title itself is double-voiced. Gates parodies or signifies upon Geoffrey Hartman's manifesto of rhetorical criticism, *Criticism in the Wilderness,* published in 1980; he alludes ironically to a stereotyped image of primitive and exotic African origins (cf. Vachel Lindsay's "The Congo") and thus literalizes the "sacred jungle" of Hartman's text; and he slyly suggests that black theory must make its way not only in the indeterminate heart of darkness and in the pan-African cultural jungle (the home of the "signifying monkey" and the Tar Baby), but also in the far more dangerous blackboard jungle of professional critical debate.

Gates sees his mission as one of saving the black text from the political and ideological contexts which have repressed its signifying systems, in treating it more as sociology, anthropology, or a document of the black experience, than as art. If the black tradition is to move "into the mainstream of critical debate in the profession," it must free itself from polemic and apply the lessons of formalism, structuralism, and poststructuralism. Gates is a bold and confident spokesman for this new program:

> The black literary tradition now demands, for sustenance and for growth, the sorts of reading which it is the especial province of the literary critic to render; and these sorts of reading will all share a fundamental concern

with the nature and functions of figurative language as manifested in specific texts. No matter to what ends we put our readings, we can never lose sight of the fact that a text is not a fixed "thing" but a rhetorical structure which functions in response to a complex set of rules. It can never be related satisfactorily to a reality outside itself merely in a one-to-one relation.[21]

Two major problems came to the fore, however, in the reconstructionist project. First, who is qualified to be a critic of black literature? Second, can black criticism appropriate white or Western literary theory without sacrificing its hard-won independence and individuality? In the earlier phases of black criticism, black critics were first the reluctant or de facto partisans of "Negro writing" and then the passionate advocates of "black literature." During the phase of the Black Aesthetic, black artists and intellectuals who had become frustrated by the condescension or indifference of the white literary establishment toward Afro-American writing staked their own claim to a privileged critical authority within the black cultural tradition. With the early reconstructionist phase, however, the emphasis on the blackness of the ideal critic was abandoned in the interests of establishing black literature in the canon, and replaced by a focus on professional expertise. For Stepto and Fisher in 1979, the teacher of Afro-American literature need no longer be black, and blackness is no guarantee of authority in deciphering the text. Rather, the teacher must be trained to read the "ingrained cultural metaphors," "coded structures," and "poetic rhetoric" of the Afro-American text.[22]

By 1984, as Gates asserts, the "critic of black literature" no longer needs to have a special relationship to Afro-American culture, or a commitment to social change, obligations which saddle the critical project of reading black literature well with an impossible sociological burden. Instead the critic of black literature is an intellectual specialist who writes "primarily for other critics of literature."[23] Moreover, the critic of black literature can no longer be a mere amateur, either an ordinary reader, a practicing artist, or an untheoretical teacher, but must come from the professional community of poststructuralist literary critics, trained in the difficult new methodologies and theories of reading, and fluent in their terms.

The retreat from the populism of the Black Aesthetic could scarcely be more emphatic. Houston Baker, himself a critic who has tried to mediate between the cultural anthropology of the Black Aesthetic and poststructuralism, and whose essay on Ralph Ellison is included in *Black Literature and Literary Theory*, links the rise of black poststructuralism to the rise of black professionals in academia "whose class status . . . and privileges are . . . contingent upon their adherence to accepted (i.e., white) standards . . ." With the decline of a mass black audience for critical or political discourse in the aftermath of the 1960s, Baker argues, a "class-oriented professionalism among Afro-American literary critics" has led to a "sometimes uncritical imposition upon Afro-American culture of literary theories borrowed from prominent white scholars."[24] While Baker maintains that reconstructionist critics impose such theories without a rigorous analysis of their enthnocentrism, Gates, as we have seen, believes that the black literary tradition itself "demands" to be read in these sophisticated theoretical ways, for "sustenance and growth"— that is, in order to maintain a critical growth curve within academia that gives it parity with the dominant tradition of Dante, Milton, Hölderlin, and Rousseau.

In a more telling critique than these sociological objections, however, Baker further protests that Gates simplifies and distorts the theories of the Black Aestheticians, and that he creates a semiotic circle around literature that cuts literary language off from the verbal behavior of Afro-American culture and that isolates the black text from the complex cultural systems that give meaning to its words. Gates's response is to challenge the idea of a unified black subject in terms taken from post-structuralism. Both in his introduction and in his own essay on Ellison and Reed, Gates emphasizes this critique of the "transcendent black subject, integral and whole, self-sufficient and plentiful, the 'always already' black signified, available for literary representation in received Western forms as would be the water dipped from a deep and dark well."[25]

Yet despite his critical rhetoric, Gates is not completely prepared to abandon either the politics of black presence or a vividly particularized sense of Afro-American culture and the black vernacular; and there are a number of contradictions and tensions in his essay pointing towards a different, if repressed, desire. He refers frequently to a "signifying black difference" produced by the process of applying literary theory to the black text, as if the black text were so powerful a catalyst that its combination with deconstruction explosively "changes both the received theory and received ideas about the text."[26] Moreover, his anonymous expert, the "critic of black literature," sometimes merges with a more personal and specific black critic struggling to represent a "black self" in ethnocentric Western languages that makes blackness a figure of absence and negation. This black critic speaks in the Afro-American idiom "which makes the black tradition our very own," as well as in the professional idiom of Ithaca or New Haven.[27]

These conflicts between academic centrality and a black tradition and "criticism of our own" became even more pronounced with the newest critical wave. Most recently, the black critic and the critic of black literature have been joined by the Third World critic and the critic of Third

World literature, whose subject is "the curious dialectic between formal language use and the inscription of metaphorical racial differences."[28] Metaphorical? Yes, according to the leading figure and theorist in this group, once again Henry Louis Gates, Jr., who edited a special issue of the journal *Critical Inquiry* called " 'Race,' Writing, and Difference" in Autumn 1985: "Race, as a meaningful criterion within the biological sciences, has long been recognized to be a fiction. When we speak of 'the white race' or 'the black race,' 'the Jewish race' or 'the Aryan race,' we speak in biological misnomers, and more generally, in metaphors."[29] As Anthony Appiah points out, "apart from the visible morphological characteristics of skin, hair, and bone, by which we are inclined to assign people to the broadest racial categories—black, white, yellow—," current genetic research proves that there are few biological characteristics of "race."[30] Apart from these unimportant "gross differences," the kind of positive black racial identity advocated by W. E. B. Du Bois, involving a common language, history, and tradition, is thus wholly unscientific, and "must go" (p. 27). At the mitochondrial or cellular level, according to Appiah, race has little to do with biological differences between people. What we are talking about, then, is a linguistic construct.

While some black critics, like Houston Baker, might observe that "the shift to the common ground of subtle academic discourse is . . . ultimately unhelpful in a world where New York taxi drivers scarcely ever think of mitochondria before refusing to pick me up,"[31] the move to "race" as a fundamental rhetorical category in the study of writing and the shaping of critical theory would seem to be the manifest destiny of black criticism, giving it an unlimited access to Third World, colonial, and Western literature, and granting it a primary term like class in Marxist criticsm. One of the major advantages of the category of "race" is that it problematizes the dominant as well as the Other, and provides a way of talking about "Western" or "white" genres and forms. Moreover, the emphasis on "race" is a brilliant solution to the problem of establishment indifference to the black literary tradition. If black criticism requires expertise in the black text, there will be a lot of important "other critics of literature" who will never qualify. There is no way to compel Jacques Derrida to read Toni Morrison or Ishmael Reed. But when the subject is the rhetorical inscription of "race," Derrida can legitimately be brought inside the hermeneutic circle of Third World criticism, with a political essay on South Africa, while it would be very hard to include him in the reconstructionist project except as a mentor.

From another perspective, however, the shift to "race" also marks an obvious swerve away from Afro-American criticism. The quotation marks around "race" signal not only the questioning of racial essentialism, but also the effacement of black identity and an Afro-American literary canon.

The very small number of Afro-American literary critics in the volume itself is striking. In a follow-up issue, which became part of the book version published by the University of Chicago Press, there were additional pieces by Jane Tompkins, Christopher Miller, and Tzvetan Todorov, and a debate between two South African critical activists and Derrida. Most of these essays are extremely good, and several are even brilliant; what is disturbing about the issue is not the quality of the criticism, but the implications of the fact that the first issue of *Critical Inquiry* edited by a black critic and devoted to the question of race and writing has a list of contributors virtually indistinguishable from any other issue of *Critical Inquiry*. The most unusual part of the issue is the ad section at the back, where books by Trudier Harris, Sunday Anozie, and Hortense Spillers, among others, are featured. The reader of the volume must wonder whether the installation of "race" will displace the study of black literature, and reinstitute a familiar canon, now seen from the perspective of the racial trope. It's troubling, too that while gender is given some rhetorical attention as a fundamental category of critical analysis in Gates's introduction, and has been a central concern of both his and Houston Baker's recent work, in this volume the responsibility for dealing with gender is almost entirely delegated to the female contributors.[32] And finally, it's revealing that after a vigorous critique and rebuttal of Tzvetan Todorov's contribution to the debate, Gates still believes that the counter-cultural critic must use the language of the dominant since it is the only one Todorov will even pay mild attention to: "Todorov can't even hear us, Houston, when we talk his academic talk; how he gonna hear us if we 'talk *that* talk,' the talk of the black idiom?"[33] In the female vernacular of my own past, or as my mother used to say, why talk to the wall? Why does it still matter so much to be heard by the tone-deaf masters of European theory when other and larger audiences want to listen?

These aspects of the volume are particularly disturbing since in his introductory essay, Gates announces a significant shift in his own thinking, away from his defiant reconstructionist stance to a recognition of the dangers of assimilation, and a renewed emphasis on the cultural grounding of black literature: "I once thought it our most important gesture to *master* the canon of criticism, to *imitate* and *apply* it, but I now believe that we must turn to the black tradition itself to develop theories of criticism indigenous to our literatures." Gates now warns of the dangers in black poststructuralism and the need for Third World critics to "analyze the language of contemporary criticism itself, recognizing especially that hermeneutic systems are not universal, color-blind, apolitical, or neutral. . . . To attempt to appropriate our own discourses by

using Western theory uncritically is to substitute one mode of neocolonialism for another."[34]

The Feminist Critical Revolution

The debates within Afro-American criticism and theory have many
parallels within the feminist critical community, and indeed the genealogies of black and feminist criticism are strikingly similar in many
respects. For the sake of emphasizing these parallels, and for convenience
of reference, I have given names to the various phases and modes which
make up the complex totality of feminist literary criticism; but it should
be understood that none of these approaches has the exact historical
and political specificity that may be claimed by some of the stages of
Afro-American criticism. None of these overlapping phases has been
superseded or discredited, and in general each has undergone considerable change through a vigorous internal debate.

Before the Women's Liberation Movement, criticism of women's writing took the form of an *androgynist poetics*, denying the uniqueness of a
female literary consciousness, and advocating a single or universal standard of critical judgment which women writers had to meet. The wom-
en's movement of the late 1960s initiated both a *feminist critique* of male
culture and a *Female Aesthetic* celebrating women's culture. By the mid-
1970s, academic feminist criticism, in league with interdisciplinary work
in women's studies, entered a new phase of *gynocritics*, or the study of
women's writing. With the impact of European literary and feminist
theory in the late 1970s, *gynesic* or poststructuralist feminist criticism,
dealing with "the feminine" in philosophy, language, and psychoanalysis, became an important influence on the field as a whole. And in the
late 1980s, we are seeing the rise of *gender theory*, the comparative study
of sexual difference.

In contrast to black criticism, where integrationist poetics is at least
currently unacceptable, androgynist poetics continues to have many
partisans among women writers, creating an apparent conflict between
writers and critics that the media have relished. It disturbed many feminist critics, including myself, when Gail Godwin and Cynthia Ozick
attacked the *Norton Anthology of Literature by Women* on the grounds that
the creative imagination is sexless and that the concept of a female literary
tradition was insulting to women who (like Godwin) regard themselves
as disciples of Joseph Conrad. I think it unlikely that black writers will
raise similar objections to the forthcoming *Norton Anthology of Black Literature*, edited by the indefatigable and phenomenal Skip Gates.

Nevertheless, androgynist poetics, which can be an unexamined misogyny that demands a spurious "universality" from women's writing,
as integrationist poetics did from black writers, as well as a form of
feminine self-hatred, also speaks for genuinely serious and permanent
concerns within feminist criticism. The androgynist position was articulated early on by Mary Ellmann in *Thinking About Women* (1969), which
wittily deconstructed the pernicious effects of thinking by sexual analogy;
and by Carolyn Heilbrun in *Toward a Recognition of Androgyny* (1973),
which argued that "our future salvation lies in a movement away from
sexual polarization and the prison of gender."[35] Among contemporary
American writers, Joyce Carol Oates is probably the most persuasive
representative of this position. In an essay entitled "(Woman) Writer:
Theory and Practice" (1986), Oates protests the category of "woman" or
"gender" in art: "Subject-matter is culture-determined, not gender-de-
termined. And the imagination, in itself genderless, allows us all things."

Since the 1970s, however, while acknowledging the writer's need to
feel free of labels, most feminist critics have rejected the concept of the
genderless "imagination," and have argued from a variety of perspectives
that the imagination cannot escape from the unconscious structures and
strictures of gender identity. These arguments may emphasize the impossibility of separating the imagination from a socially, sexually, and
historically positioned self, as in Sandra Gilbert's sensible insistence that
"what is finally written is, whether consciously or not, written by the
whole person. . . . If the writer is a woman who has been raised as a
woman—and I daresay only a very few biologically anomalous human
females have *not* been raised as women—how can her sexual identity
be split off from her literary energy? Even a denial of her femininity . . .
would surely be significant to understanding of the dynamics of her
aesthetic creativity."[36] A more systematic feminist critique of the woman
writer's unified and sexless "imagination" comes from Lacanian psychoanalysis, which describes the split in the female subject within language. In a psycholinguistic world structured by father-son resemblance
and by the primacy of male logic, woman is a gap or a silence, the
invisible and unheard sex. In contrast to the "writer only" problems of
androgynist poetics, therefore, most feminist critics insist that the way
to contend with patriarchal bias against women is not to deny sexual
difference but to dismantle gender hierarchies. Not sexual difference
itself, but rather its meaning within patriarchal ideology—'division,
oppression, inequality, interiorized inferiority for women"—must be
attacked.[37]

The first break with androgynist poetics was the affirmation of wom-
anhood as a positive factor in literary experience. As in the development
of a Black Aesthetic, the Female Aesthetic evolved during the early years

of the women's liberation movement as a racial response to a past in which the assumed goal for women's literature had been a smooth passage into a neuter and "universal" aesthetic realm. Instead the Female Aesthetic maintained that women's writing expressed a distinct female consciousness, that it constituted a unique and coherent literary tradition, and that the woman writer who denied her female identity restricted or even crippled her art. At the same time, a feminist critique of androcentric literature and criticism examined the "misogyny of literary practice: the stereotyped images of women in literature as angels or monsters, the . . . textual harassment of women in classic and popular male literature, and the exclusion of women from literary history."[38]

Virtually all of the romantic and invigorating images of independence that characterized the Black Aesthetic have their counterpart in the Female Aesthetic as well. In contrast to the hegemony of what it characterized as the arid and elitist "methodolatry" of patriarchal criticism, the Female Aesthetic proposed the empowerment of the common woman reader (indeed we could also see here a conjunction of Women's Liberation with what Terry Eagleton has called the Reader's Liberation Movement), and the celebration of an intuitive female critical consciousness in the interpretation of women's texts. In striking parallels to the Black Aesthetic, the Female Aesthetic also spoke of a vanished nation, a lost motherland; of the female vernacular or Mother Tongue; and of a powerful but neglected women's culture. In her introduction to an anthology of international women's poetry, for example, Adrienne Rich put forth the compelling hypothesis of a female diaspora:

> The idea of a common female culture—splintered and diasporized among the male cultures under and within which women have survived—has been a haunting though tentative theme of feminist thought over the past few years. Divided from each other through our dependencies on men—domestically, tribally, and in the world of patronage and institutions—our first need has been to recognize and reject these divisions, the second to begin exploring all that we share in common as women on this planet.[39]

This phase of intellectual rebellion, gynocentrism, and critical separatism was a crucial period in the experience of women who had always played subordinate roles as dutiful academic daughters, research assistants, second readers, and faculty wives. Via the Female Aesthetic, women experimented with efforts to inscribe a female idiom in critical discourse and to define a feminist critical stylistics based on women's experience. In "Toward a Feminist Aesthetic" (1978), Julia Penelope Stanley and Susan J. Wolfe (Robbins) proposed that "the unique perceptions and interpretations of women require a literary style that reflects, captures, and embodies the quality of our thought," a "discursive, conjunctive style instead of the complex, subordinating, linear style of classification and distinction."[40]

French feminist writing of the same period, although it came out of radically different intellectual sources, also produced the concept of *écriture féminine*, analyzing women's style as a writing-effect of rupture and subversion in avant-garde literature, available to both men and women, but connected or analogous to female sexual morphology. The French feminist project of "writing the body" is a particularly strong and revolutionary effort to provide women's writing with an authority based in women's genital and libidinal difference from men. While the French critique of phallocentrism takes very different paths in the work of Hélène Cixous, Luce Irigaray, and Julia Kristeva, all explore the possibility of a concentric feminine discourse. Whether clitoral, vulval, vaginal, or uterine; whether centered on semiotic pulsions, childbearing, or jouissance, the feminist theorization of female sexuality/textuality, and its funky audacity in violating patriarchal taboos by unveiling the Medusa, is an exhilarating challenge to phallic discourse.

Yet the Female Aesthetic also had serious weaknesses. As many feminist critics sharply noted, its emphasis on the importance of female biological experience came dangerously close to sexist essentialism. Its efforts to establish a specificity of female writing through the hypothesis of a women's language, a lost motherland, or a cultural enclave, could not be supported by scholarship. The initial identification with the Amazon as a figure of female autonomy and creativity (in the work of Monique Wittig and Ti-Grace Atkinson, among others), and with lesbian separatism as the correct political form for feminist commitment, was both too radical and too narrow for a broadly based critical movement. The concepts of female style or *écriture féminine* described only one avant-garde mode of women's writing, and many feminists felt excluded by a prescriptive stylistics that seemed to privilege the non-linear, experimental, and surreal. Insofar as the Female Aesthetic suggested that only women were qualified to read women's texts, feminist criticism ran the risk of ghettoization. Finally, the essentialism of the universal female subject and the female imagination, was open to charges of racism, especially since black women's texts were rarely cited as examples. As black women and others within the women's movement protested against the inattention to racial and class differences between women, the idea of a common women's culture had to be re-examined.

Gynocritics, which developed alongside the Female Aesthetic in the 1970s, has been an effort to resolve some of these problems. It identified women's writing as a central subject of feminist criticism, but rejected the concept of an essential female identity and style. In an essay called

"Feminist Criticism in the Wilderness" (1981), a response to Geoffrey Hartman whose title now seems feeble compared to the brilliant riposte of Skip Gates, I argued against feminist fantasies of a wild zone of female consciousness or culture outside of patriarchy, declaring instead that "there can be no writing or criticism outside of the dominant culture." Thus both women's writing and feminist criticism were of necessity "a double-voiced discourse embodying both the muted and the dominant, speaking inside of both feminism and criticism."[41]

Instead gynocriticism has focused on the multiple signifying systems of female literary traditions and intertextualities. In studying women's writing, feminist critics have challenged and revised the prevailing styles of critical discourse, and asked whether theories of female creativity could be developed instead from within the female literary tradition itself. Influenced by the interdisciplinary field of women's studies, they have brought to their reading of women's texts theories and terms generated by the work of such feminist scholars as the historian Carroll Smith-Rosenberg, the psychologist Carol Gilligan, and the sociologist Nancy Chodorow, whose enormously influential study, *The Reproduction of Mothering* (1978), revised Freudian psychoanalysis and British object-relations psychology to emphasize the pre-Oedipal phase as the key factor in the construction of gender identity.

The work of Smith-Rosenberg, Chodorow, and Gilligan has led to a wide range of studies in philosophy, social history, and religion endorsing what are called "matriarchal values" of nurturance, caring, non-violence, and connectedness, and urging their adoption by society as a whole. Feminist critics have used metaphors of this idealized maternity both in the quest for a strong literary matrilineage, and in the rejection of the adversary method in critical discourse. In a famous and moving essay, Alice Walker has described black women writers' "search for our mother's gardens," tracing the suppressed creativity of black women under slavery and poverty to non-verbal art forms.[42] In sharp contrast to the Oedipal poetics of aggression, competition, and defense put forth by Harold Bloom, some American feminist critics have postulated a pre-Oedipal "female poetics of affiliation," dependent on the daughter's bond with the mother, in which intergenerational conflict is replaced by female literary intimacy, generosity, and continuity. Joan Lidoff, Judith Kegan Gardiner, and Elizabeth Abel are among the feminist critics who see women's fluid ego boundaries affecting plot and genre conventions, blurring the lines between lyric and narrative, between realism and romance. Here the Female Aesthetic and postmodernism join in a celebration of heterogeneity, dissolving boundaries, and *différance*.

Although I can hardly claim to be an innocent bystander on the subject of gynocriticism, I would argue that over the past decade it has been sufficiently large, undogmatic, and flexible to have accommodated many theoretical revisions and criticisms, and it has been enormously productive. In a relatively short period of time, gynocritics has generated a vast critical literature on individual women writers, persuasive studies of the female literary tradition from the Middle Ages to the present in virtually every national literature, and important books on what is called "gender and genre": the significance of gender in shaping generic conventions in forms ranging from the hymn to the Bildüngsroman. Nevertheless, many of the original gynocritical theories of women's writing were based primarily on nineteenth-century English women's texts, so that a black feminist critic such as Hortense Spillers sees "the gynocritical themes of recent feminist inquiry" as separate from a "black women's writing community."[43] Only in recent years has attention to black women's writing begun to address and redress this issue.

A pivotal text of gynocritics is Sandra Gilbert and Susan Gubar's monumental study, *The Madwoman in the Attic* (1979). Gilbert and Gubar offer a detailed revisionist reading of Harold Bloom's theory of the anxiety of influence, transforming his Freudian paradigm of Oedipal struggle between literary fathers and sons into a feminist theory of influence which describes the nineteenth-century woman writer's anxieties within a patriarchal literary culture. Strongly influenced by the work of Gilbert and Gubar, the theoretical program of gynocritics by the 1980s has been marked by increasing attention to "the analysis of female talent grappling with a male tradition," both in literature and criticism, a project that defined both the female literary text and the feminist critical text as the sum of its "acts of revision, appropriation, and subversion," and its differences of "genre, structure, voice, and plot."[44] Gynocritics had derived much of its strength from its self-reflexive properties as a double-voiced mode of women's writing; the anxieties of the nineteenth-century woman writer were much like those of the modern Feminist critic attempting to penetrate literary theory, the most defended bastion of patriarchal prose. Now, as Feminist critics began to profit from their labors and to enjoy some prestige and authority within the profession of literary studies, questions of the complicity between the feminist critical talent and the male critical tradition became acute, and the acts of theoretical revision, appropriation, and subversion in gynocritics itself became the source of a troubling, sometimes obsessive and guilty, self-consciousness.

About this time, too, as reports on the French feminists began to appear in women's studies journals, and as their work became available to American readers through translation, a new group of feminist critics entered the field, primarily through departments of French and Comparative Literature. They saw post-Saussurean linguistics, psychoanalysis, semiotics, and deconstruction as the most powerful means to understanding the production of sexual difference in language, reading, and writing, and they wrote in a language accessible chiefly to other literary critics, rather than to a wider audience. Following the work of Jacques Derrida, Jacques Lacan, Hélène Cixous, Luce Irigaray, and Julia Kristeva, Franco-American feminist critics focused on what Alice Jardine calls "gynesis": the exploration of the textual consequences and representations of "the feminine" in Western thought. Deconstruction has paid little attention to women writers individually or as a group; "for Derrida and his disciples," Jardine notes, "the question of how women might accede to subjecthood, write texts or acquire their own signatures, are *phallogocentric* questions."[45] Some poststructuralist feminist critics thus maintain that "feminist criticism should avoid 'the women's literature ghetto' . . . and return to confrontation with 'the' canon."[46] While gynocritics looks at the patrilineage and matrilineage of the female literary *work*, poststructuralist feminist criticism views the literary *text* as fatherless and motherless; its feminist subjectivity is a product of the reading process. From a gynesic perspective, moreover, disruptions in discourse constitute disruptions of the patriarchal system.

Gynesic criticism has been a major intellectual force within feminist discourse, but the gynesic project has also raised a number of problems. First of all, as black poststructuralism has questioned the transcendent black self, however, so poststructuralist feminist criticism has had to wrestle with the parodox of fundamental theoretical affiliations that undermine the very notion of female subjectivity. Other modes of feminist criticism have had the empowerment of the female subject as a specific goal. Within the Female Aesthetic, female consciousness was celebrated as an interpretive guide; within gynocritics, the woman critic could use her own confrontation with the male critical tradition and her own experience of writing as a guide to understanding the situation of the woman writer. But if women are the silenced and repressed Other of Western discourse, how can a Feminist theorist speak *as* a woman about women or anything else? As Shoshana Felman asks "If 'the woman' is precisely the Other of any conceivable Western theoretical focus of speech, how can the woman as such be speaking in this book? Who is speaking here, and who is asserting the otherness of the woman?"[47] Kaja Silverman also admits that "the relationship of the female subject to semiotic theory is . . . necessarily an ambivalent one. The theory offers her a sophisticated understanding of her present cultural condition, but it also seems to confine her forever to the status of one who is to be seen, spoken, and analyzed."[48] The rhetorical problems of expressing a black male self to which Gates briefly alludes in "Criticism in the Jungle" are much less disabling than the burden, inherent in a gynesic feminist criticism heavily and necessarily dependent on psychoanalytic theory, of speaking from the feminine position of absence, silence, and lack.

Furthermore, while poststructuralist feminists have played a significant role within poststructuralism as translators and advocates, as well
as critics, of the European male theorists, the male feminists who have
participated in gynesis, with some outstanding exceptions (such as Neil
Hertz, Stephen Heath, and Andrew Ross) have tended to present themselves as metacritical masters of the feminine rather than as students of
women's writing, or critics of masculinity. When the Australian critic
Ken Ruthven (sometimes called the Crocodile Dundee of male feminism)
observes in his book *Feminist Literary Studies: An Introduction*, that "the
female 'problematic' is too important to be left in the hands of anti-
intellectual feminists," and could be subjected to much more rigorous
metacritical inspection by impartial men like himself, it's difficult not to
be suspicious. Since, when you come right down to it, Ruthven argues,
feminist criticism is "just another way of talking about books," and he
is a guy who "makes a living talking about books," it would be churlish
(or girlish) to try to keep him out of the conversation.[49] In other cases,
as I have learned from sad experience, "male feminists" do not even
bother to read the feminist critical texts they are allegedly responding
to, since they always already know what women think. Poststructuralism
and feminism are a familiar and almost obligatory critical couple in the
1980s, but they are still having to work at their relationship.

Finally, some recent discussions of what they call "Anglo-American"
feminist criticism by poststructuralist feminists have been startlingly *ad
feminam* and harsh, introducing a tone of acrimony into what we had
hoped was a mutual, if pluralistic, enterprise, and eliciting equally in-
temperate attacks on "theory" in defensive response. Certainly there are
real issues at stake in the theoretical debates, as well as struggles for
what Evelyn Fox Keller has called epistemic power in the feminist critical
arena. But the polarization of feminist discourse along dualistic lines
seems particularly unfortunate at a moment when there is such a lively
exchange of ideas. While *The Madwoman in the Attic* has yet to be translated into French, gynesic criticism has been widely read by American
feminist critics; it has modified American work in gynocritics, and vice-
versa. It's not exceptional that Sandra Gilbert, for example, should have
edited the first English translation of Cixous and Catherine Clément's
La Jeune Née, or on the other hand, that Barbara Johnson is currently
working on black women writers. The complex heterogeneities of contemporary feminist discourse cannot be reduced to hierarchal oppositions.

The latest and most rapidly growing mode of feminist criticism is
gender theory, corresponding to the Third World critic's focus on "race."
Within American feminist scholarship, the term "gender" is used to mean
the social, cultural, and psychological constructs imposed upon biologica^{l}
sexual difference. Like "race" or "class," "gender" is a fundamental o$_{\text{l}}$

organic social variable in all human experience. Within gender theory, the object of feminist criticism undergoes another transformation; unlike the emphasis on women's writing that informs gynocritics, or on the signification of "the feminine" within gynesis, gender theory explores ideological inscription and the literary effects of the sex/gender system: "that set of arrangements by which the biological raw material of human sex and procreation is shaped by human social intervention."[50]

The interest in gender theory is not confined to feminist criticism, but has also appeared in feminist thought in the fields of history, anthropology, philosophy, psychology, and science. In "Anthropology and the Study of Gender," Judith Shapiro argues that the goal of feminist research is not to focus on "women," and thus to reify female marginalization, but rather "to integrate the study of gender differences into the central pursuits of the social sciences."[51] In the natural sciences, the path-breaking work of Evelyn Fox Keller, Ruth Bleier, and Donna Haraway has analyzed "the critical role of gender ideology in mediating between science and social forms."[52] The most searching analysis of gender as a historical concept has been carried out by Joan W. Scott; in an essay called "Gender: A Useful Category of Historical Analysis," Scott outlines three goals of gender theory: to substitute the analysis of social constructs for biological determinism in the discussion of sexual difference; to introduce comparative studies of women and men into the specific disciplinary field; and to transform disciplinary paradigms by adding gender as an analytic category.[53]

What are the advantages of gender theory for feminist criticism? Most significantly, gender theory insists that all writing, not just writing by women, is gendered. To define the objective of feminist criticism as an analysis of gender in literary discourse completely opens the textual field. It also provides a way of uncovering the implicit assumptions about gender in literary theory that pretends to be neutral or gender-free. Secondly, the term "gender," like race, problematizes the dominant. Gender theory promises to introduce the subject of masculinity into feminist criticism, and to bring men into the field as students, scholars, theorists, and critics. It has already opened feminist criticism to include the consideration of male homosexuality, both through the pioneering work of Eve Kosofsky Sedgwick and through writing by gay men. Third, the addition of gender as a fundamental analytic category within literary criticism moves feminist criticism from the margin to the center, and has revolutionary transformative potential for the ways that we read, think, and write. Thinking in terms of gender is a constant reminder of the other categories of difference that structure our lives and texts, just as theorizing gender emphazies the connections between feminist criticism and other minority critical revolutions.

As with Third World criticism, however, it is too soon to be certain how these possibilities will work out. One danger is that men will continue to read "gender" as a synonym for "femininity," and pontificate about the representation of women without accepting the risks and opportunities of investigating masculinity, or analyzing the gender subtexts of their own critical practice. Another danger, seemingly paradoxical but actually related, is that gender will become a postfeminist term that declares the study of women, and women's writing, obsolete, or what Ruthven denounces as "separatist." The most troubling risk is that gender studies will depoliticize feminist criticism, that men will declare an interest in what one of my colleagues recently called "gender and power," while refusing to call themselves feminists. Even Ronald Reagan and Sylvester Stallone, after all, are interested in gender and power; in some respects, as Joan Scott acknowledges, the term "gender" seems to transcend the politics of feminism, and to promise a "more neutral and objective" scholarly perspective, certainly one more acceptable to men, than the focus on "women."[54] Despite the risks, however, none of these outcomes is inevitable. Gender can be an important expansion of our work, rather than a displacement or depoliticization, if it is defined within a feminist framework that remains committed to the continuing struggle against sexism, racism, and homophobia.

Repetition and Difference

Where do we go from here? The parallels between Afro-American and feminist criticism show how problematic the idea of a unified "black" or "female" self has become. Whether it is the linguistic skepticism of poststructuralism, or our acknowledgment of the differences between women that stops us, Feminist critics today can no longer speak as and about women with the unselfconscious authority of the past. The female subject, we are told, is dead, a position instead of a person. Our dilemma has even reached the pages of the *New Yorker;* in Tama Janowitz's short story "Engagements," a graduate student in feminist criticism at Yale takes notes as her distraught professor tells of being severely attacked for trying to talk about "women" and "female identity" at a Poetics of Gender conference.[55] Without a claim to subjectivity or group identity, how can we have a feminist criticism of our own?

Black and Third World critics haunted by the messages of poststructuralism are now facing the same dilemma. Is there a critic-position as well as a subject-position? Gates asks whether "the critic of black literature acquires his or her identity parodically, as it were, in the manner of the parrot," but hopefully concludes that "we are able to achieve difference through repetition" by looking at a different critical object.[56]

Homi Bhabha addresses the issue in the contexts of colonialist discourse, citing "mimicry" as a form of "civil disobedience within the discipline of civility: signs of spectacular resistance."[57] In *Ce sexe qui n'en est pas un,* Luce Irigaray too locates the subversive force of Feminist discourse in a playful mimesis, a mimicry both of phallocentric discourse which exceeds its logic, and of the feminine position within that system. Yet playing with mimesis cannot offer us authority except in individual star turns, especially if the dominant culture wants to play with your mesis too. And in mimicking the language of the dominant, how can we guarantee that mimicry is *understood* as ironic—as civil disobedience, camp, or feminist difference rather than as merely derivative?

Feminist criticism can't afford to settle for mimicry, or to give up the idea of female subjectivity, even if we accept it as a constructed or metaphysical one. To paraphrase Baker, men's clubs hardly ever think of metaphysics before they keep women out; we need what Gayatri Spivak calls a "strategic essentialism" to combat patriarchy.[58] Neither can we abandon our investigation of women's literary history, or give up the belief that through careful reading of women's texts we will develop a criticism of our own that is both theoretical and feminist. This is a task worth pursuing for its intellectual challenge and for its contribution to a truly inclusive theory of literature, rather than for its "defense" of women's creative gifts. The goal Virginia Woolf envisioned for feminist writers and critics in 1928, to labor in poverty and obscurity for the coming of Shakespeare's sister, no longer seems meaningful or necessary. Our enterprise does not stand or fall by proving some kind of parity with male literary or critical "genius"; even assuming that a female Shakespeare or a female Derrida would be recognized, to question the very idea of "genius" is part of Woolf's legacy to us.

Despite our awareness of diversity and deconstruction, feminist critics cannot depend on gynesic ruptures in discourse to bring about social change. During a period when many of the meager gains of the civil rights and women's movements are being threatened or undone by Reaganism and the New Right, when, indeed, there is a backlash against what the Bennetts and Blooms see as too *much* black and female power in the university, there is an urgent necessity to affirm the importance of black and female thinkers, speakers, readers, and writers. The Other Woman may be transparent or invisible to some; but she is still very vivid, important, and necessary to us.

21

Beautiful Science and the Future of Criticism

Arthur C. Danto

On 11 April, 1986, the prestigious journal, *Science*, published two papers by the same team of microbiologists—Jeremy Nathans and his associates at Stanford University—a remarkable event considering the extreme recognition conferred by acceptance even of a single article by the official organ of The American Association for the Advancement of Science. Beyond this, the papers were deemed of sufficient moment that the editors printed an explanatory piece—a "Perspective"—by the distinguished geneticist, David Botstein. The papers themselves were on the microbiology of color vision, to which they make a clear contribution. But more than that, they take us, Botstein observes, from discovery to understanding, they exemplify "beautiful science," and constitute a "treat" for those who appreciate the "aesthetics" of this procedure. I want to cite Botstein's description of beautiful science in full:

> First, the confrontation of the human mind with a natural phenomenon, then its investigation through observations and experiments, the continual proposal of theories, the testing of predictions, and finally, in the best case, the convincing demonstration of the validity of one of the theories through confirmation of its specific predictions. The process can take only a few years and involve only a few scientists or it can span centuries and involve many. The practical consequences may be revolutionary and change the course of history (for example special relativity) or it may have little or no use. In either case, a full scientific story, especially one that has been unfolding over historic times, can be a lovely thing, like a classical symphony or a gothic cathedral. (p. 142)

I think it beyond controversy that there is, today, no settled philosophical analysis of the main terms of this elegant characterization: "confirmation," "confrontation," "validity," "experiment," "observation," even "theory," let alone "the human mind," "the proposal of theories," "the testing of predictions," remain fiercely contested high ground in the philosophical wars. But much as philosophers will largely agree that something like "justified true belief" will serve as an analytical definition of propositional knowledge for most purposes, while at the same time disagreeing bitterly and minutely over the analysis of its constituent terms, "truth," "justification," and even "belief," so there are few in the philosophy of science who would find Botstein's characterization terrifically wrong or, at its level of generality, uselessly inexact. This is what beautiful science is—it is what science is, which is beautiful when it succeeds. Its elements, Botstein says, are familiar and they are indeed familiar. Aristotle would have found such expressions as "gothic cathedral" or "classical symphony" incomprehensible (not to mention "special relativity"), but the operative vocabulary of the account would have been largely accessible to him, and the general picture of science it depicts would have been intelligible, and convincing, to the earliest students of *The Posterior Analytics.*

It is on the other hand difficult for me to suppose Aristotle could have made anything much out of Jeremy Nathans's two reports. Even the concept of color blindness, which they explain through the idiom of modern molecular genetics, would not have been accessible to him. Any native speaker is equipped with a rich vocabulary of color terms—and when they are lacking one has recourse to "the color of . . ."—and there are always enough secondary cues that the color-blind can answer correctly questions about the colors of culturally familiar objects. There would have been no occupation in Aristotle's time which would make urgent the disqualification of color-blind candidates, as signal-light indiscrimination mandates their elimination as railroad engineers or ship navigators, or air traffic controllers—though they might have been slow hands in harvest time for raspberries, having difficulty in red-green discrimination. And beyond that, it is difficult to know what the concept could have meant without the apparatus of spectral colors. The first reference to color blindness is said to be in the Transactions of the Royal Society of 1684. The chemist John Dalton diagnosed himself as dichromate in 1798, observing that whereas others required three primary colors to describe their chromatic array, he required but two. The misleading term "color blindness"—misleading because dichromates are not blind to the colors in question—replaced the more appropriate term "Daltonism" by which the relevant defect was long known (*it* may have been misleading if a description of dichromates by J. Scott preceded that of Dalton by twenty years).

I am anxious to make something of the contrast between the extreme familiarity of the description of Beautiful Science down the ages, by contrast with the unfamiliarity and even inaccessibility of Nathans's results to early scientists among those who worked at the problem of color vision over two centuries, from 1672, when Newton's account of light and color was presented to the Royal Society on February 8, until the appearance of Nathans's paper in *Science* on April 11, 1986. To all the earlier investigators in this history, beginning with Isaac Newton, John Dalton, Thomas Young, and later H. L. F. von Helmholz and James Clark Maxwell, some components in Nathans's work would have been incomprehensible in terms of the science of their day: they lacked the theoretical matrices for understanding various of its central terms. All of them, on the other hand, would have understood and most if not all of them would have accepted the general picture of Beautiful Science which Nathans's work, like their own, very adequately exemplifies.

I am anxious to make something of this because there are two ways in which we can think of the future of science. If we think of it as an activity truly described by Botstein, then we really know what there is to know about the science of the future. It will be as much like it is today two centuries hence as it was two centuries ago. Nothing can be science which greatly differs from what science is today. But if we mean the future exemplars of Beautiful Science, well, we can have as dim an idea of what they will be in time to come as Newton or Dalton would have had two centuries ago—or which J. W. S. Rayleigh would have had a hundred years ago when he discovered that persons with evidently normal color vision required different amounts of red or green in making color matches—of the Stanford results in 1986. Since I am later to be interested in the future of criticism, it might be interesting to question whether we have any widely accepted characterization of Beautiful Criticism to place alongside that of Beautiful Science—and there are views of criticism that would insist there can be no such paradigm. Neither, I think, is there consensus that there are or can be sustained histories culminating, as in the case in science of the work of Nathans and his associates, in final critical validations. But it would be dangerous at this point to press for disanalogies that would in any case perhaps misspeak the relationship between science and criticism I aim to defend. Let me instead describe very briefly Nathans's discoveries in the historical context of the problem they solve.

Normal color vision is trichromatic, not in the sense that we really see ("really see") only three colors—we in fact see all the colors we are capable of discriminating, the seven spectral colors, say, (red, orange, yellow, green, blue, indigo, and violet) and countless—well almost countless, other colors not in the spectrum—fleshtones, browns, pure purple, the metallic colors and others. It means, rather, that all we require in order to do this is three centers for receiving color information, with the primary colors being those, the effect of which on the eye cannot be achieved by combination. These are at either end of the spectrum— red and violet—and roughly at its midpoint, green, which when combined with the other primaries gives the sensation of white. The process is rather like color printing which, in the form in which we know it today, was invented in 1740 by Le Blom, who produced mezzotint reproductions of paintings by analyzing them into their primary colors, using a separate plate for each, and achieving the remaining colors by superimposition. I forebear moralizing the extension to human vision of the technological processes of color reproduction, widely practiced by craftsmen in Europe well before Thomas Young got the idea that the eye functions something like a chromograph, though my sense is that it furnishes a fine example of how our understanding of ourselves is in hostage to prevailing technologies. In any case, Young had a theory of three primary receptors in 1802, each of which is excited by homogenous light, but with different intensities as a function of wavelength: long, medium, and short waves exciting the postulated centers sensitive, respectively, to red, green, and violet. Neither Young nor Helmholz knew enough of retinal physiology to know what these centers were or how they worked, but that there had to be three, strongly suggested by color printing technology, defined a program of research. Imagine reproducing, say, Titian's *Rape of Europa*, with two primary colors and you will get a pretty fair idea of the world of the dichromate, and if we systematically make the effort using red-green red-violet, and green-violet as primary pairs, we will get a gallery of the world as it appears to the three main classes of dichromates postulated by Helmholz: the red-blind, the green-blind, and the violet-blind.

I now cut the story short. What Nathans *et al.* did was isolate the genes that specify the protein moieties, or "opsins," of the postulated three color-sensitive pigments of the human eye. They used DNA probes to analyze the defects in the DNA of the various categories of dichromates. It is quite striking how much science had to be in place before this was possible. Evolutionary theory, for example, suggests homology between the gene for human rhodopsin and its bovine counterpart. Genetic theory suggests that dichromatism is X-linked: roughly four percent of males against 0.4 percent of females is afflicted; and since females have two X-chromosomes and are usually heterozygous for the recessive defect, they pass it on to their sons who, having only one X-chromosome, show the symptom. Nathans—I here follow Botstein very closely—located two of the three opsin genes on the X-chromosome, and when the DNA of the red-blind were analyzed, "loss or alteration of one of the genes was observed." This then licensed the inference that the gene in question specified the red opsin ("specified" is the philosophically crucial term). And the corresponding predictions for the other forms of dichromaticism were able, precisely, to identify gene with function. It may be said that Nathans's work magnificently confirms the Young-Helmholz theory (it even accounts for the anomalous class of trichromates who nonetheless see differently from the normal by finding a hybrid gene and postulating a hybrid opsin)—but it confirms it with the help of theories of evolution, of genetics, of the topology of DNA which permits the possibility of gene cross-over—which were largely unthinkable in 1802, or even in 1866 when Helmholz's *Physiological Optics* was completed. The first actors in the history lacked the concepts, let alone the language, for framing the predictions that specify the confirmation of the theories. In a way it is not their theories so much as related theories in a different scientific vocabulary that are confirmed, which is perhaps the germ of certain radical critiques of continuity in science that have been so fashionable. But that is not my concern in this essay.

Rather, what I want to say is that we are in even darker waters when it comes to predicting the microbiology of Beautiful Science than Young and Helmolz would have been in predicting the microbiology of color vision, except that we are all, I think, reasonably convinced that, sometime in the future, pages of *Science* will report such a discovery and preface it with a perspective by a leading scientist putting it in a historical light that we cannot easily even guess at, not even knowing if we are at or over or nowhere close to the history he or she will take for granted. With regard to familiar Beautiful Science we are very much in the pre-Helmholz, even pre-Dalton stage, and the present disarray to which I referred in the philosophy of science for the analysis of truth, confirmation, confrontation, observation, and the like may symptomize the darkness: we do not even yet know how, so to speak, the field of beautiful science is to be structured. There may be deep analogies between color theory and what we might term "science theory." When the formal deductive system recommended itself as *the* form of scientific representation to students of the subject, it would have been wholly natural to sense an analogy between primary colors and primitive terms—or between axioms, on the one hand, and theorems on the other arrived at by logical admixture of the axioms construed as primitive. There could then be dicognates and tricognates. The discovery that the choice of primitives may be arbitrary might correspond to the fact that any color sensation may be reasonably matched with three selected wavelengths, varying their intensities. The normal scientist might then be tricognate, and it should then be possible to identify the dicognates genetically, to the immense enhancement of curriculum and of human happiness. (Color blindness is incurable, and so might science blindness be.) If the mind works at all the way science does, *something* like this mode of organization is called for. Introspection is of little help: even the eye is incapable of deciding whether a color is simple or compound (they are all homogenous, phenomenologically speaking). This takes me far ahead of anything I want to say for the moment, though it also forecasts what I shall want to say, namely that it would be with reference to a certain ordered structure of propositions—or sentences, if you prefer—that we would want to represent Beautiful Science if we are to imagine its microbiology achieved. Whether it will have the structure of formal deductive systems is for the Youngs and Daltons of the science of Beautiful Science to say. It is they who in effect will begin the history that will culminate in the Nathanses of the science of Beautiful Science, who will locate the appropriate genes.

Now the microbiology of Beautiful Science will itself be an example of Beautiful Science, and it will be a great achievement of Beautiful Science in that it will have arrived at the microbiology of itself. What can we now say about that future piece of science? We cannot say, of course, what the observations, the theories, let alone the experiments and tests will be: to *that* future we are as blind as Helmholz was to the future of the science that vindicated his and Young's theory. But then we would not expect the microbiology of Beautiful Science to be a microbiology of these. We do not expect that Nathans's theory is itself encoded in the DNA. We do not expect that when the human genome is fully sequenced (at an estimated cost of 30,000 person years of effort and $2 billion), it will reveal the microbiology of itself somewhere in the twists and catenaries of the 3 billion nucleotides that compose the human genome. The microbiology of Beautiful Science will indeed be the microbiology of those who do Beautiful Science, but that would include the scientists at either end of the relevant history—the DNA of Dalton and Young would not be relevently different from the DNA of Nathans and Botstein. The content of Nathans's theory would not refer us to some genes that specify exactly it. The sciences of the future, then, are not encoded in the genes of present scientists, or past scientists for that matter, so there would be no point in a visionary shift in the strategies of Beautiful Science namely to give over experimenting with the different sectors of the universe and instead learn to read the human genome where the science of everything is inscribed. My hunch is that such a possibility would be like having some god hand us a text in which the whole of knowledge is inscribed, so that had he possessed it, Aristotle would have gazed upon the special theory of relativity, the theory of evolution, the kinetic theory of heat, the atomic theory of matter, the theory of fractals and the microbiology of Beautiful Science—the key to the key that unlocks itself—but he would have been unable to read it. In effect, we would still require the future history of Beautiful Science to read our own DNA; and microbiology would be a historically limited subject, requiring the future history of science, like a revelation, to render intelligible the god's pointless gift. The present would be dark for the very reason that the future is dark.

No: the structure of history imposes deep limits on a microbiology of science if we extravagantly imagined that microbiology were to take us from genes to the content of theories: from the microbiological gene, say, to the theories of microbiology itself. So I shall suppose—who can do otherwise?—that our human genetic endowment, cognitively speaking, is invariant from Aristotle and before to Nathans and after: it is, relative to the contents of theories, a kind of tabula rasa. Any scientist—anyone with the right kind of DNA if there is anything to that—could enter the history at any point and carry it forward, or be carried forward by it. To be sure, it would be difficult to imagine Thomas Young himself entering the history he began, but at some later point, just because it would not have been that history had he not instead have been there at the appropriate earlier point. But the thought is perhaps clear enough. There may be—no, I am certain there will be discovered—a microbiology of linguistic competence, which accounts for the fact that any child can learn any natural language. But that is not the same as saying that in every child every language—including languages for possible worlds that never are to become actual—are stored as DNA sequences: that there are Russian, French, and Yiddish genes. So except at a very abstract level, we must suppose the content of Beautiful Science's microbiology will not be among the things of which it is the microbiology. So of what *will* it be a microbiology?

The answer, of course, is plain, and in a way it is contained already in the familiar description of Beautiful Science given by David Botstein: it is the microbiology of what scientists do when they confront nature, propose theories, perform experiments, make observations. Now these are things we all do, at a certain level, when we perceive something, form a belief about it, infer certain propositions that must be true if our beliefs are sound, and perform certain actions to see if they are sound. I hear a certain rapatapatapa on the roof, form the belief that it is raining, infer that if it is, the ground will be wet, and look out the window to see if it is wet. It will, then, be a microbiology of perceiving, believing, inferring, and acting. Small wonder then that the picture of Beautiful Science is so familiar, small wonder that it would have been familiar to Aristotle, small wonder, we may assume, that it will be familiar to those microbiologists of these very ordinary cognitive dimensions of very ordinary human beings (and doubtless of some very ordinary animals). In addition to these basic operations, two further sets of things required by Botstein's account might need to be reckoned in. There is, first, the very notion of aesthetic satisfaction carried by the concept of *Beautiful Science*, which renders consistent Aristotle's conception of us as rational animals with the theory of human beings as driven by pleasure. And beside this we must place another feeling, namely caring about there being answers to questions, wanting to know. There is as little philosophical consensus today on aesthetics, and on care, desire, and cognitive appetite, as there is on confirmation, justification, and truth. But they clearly belong to the picture in which such controversy is represented, if only because the philosophers who moot these matters exemplify them, caring for the truth and having some antecedent sense of what it means for a philosophical problem to be solved.

Now, just these components of Beautiful Science—belief, perception, action, inference, desire, and feeling—have lately been conjectured to belong to a science of Beautiful Science very different from microbiology: they belong collectively instead to a theory somewhat abusively designated Folk Psychology, a theory as old as our consciousness of ourselves as human. They answer as terms that have pivotal roles to play in an explanatory scheme we acquire with our language, much as we acquire our color vocabularies; and I suppose, further, that it must be their explanatory role in everyday social and human life that in the first place recommends the striking thought that this portion of our language is, as it were, a piece of science embedded in the wider framework of natural languages; and then the further thought that it is to be judged the way we do judge scientific theories. The familiar picture of Beautiful Science is in fact an explanation of what scientists do, and it is a theory which, as we say, also very adequately fits what a lot of humans and animals do a lot of the time. There is a view abroad that Folk Psychology is sclerotic and in need of replacement, and the best candidate for replacing it is some form of neurophysiology. Of this we can know, today, perhaps as little as we can of the microbiology of Beautiful Science. Except that now, on this view of the latter's replaceability, we can say that there after all will be no microbiology of Beautiful Science, mainly because the familiar description of Beautiful Science will be inapplicable, employing and presupposing, as it does the challenged vocabularies of Folk Psychology. But Folk Psychology is destined for replacement, and will finally prove as little resistant to this as phlogiston or entelechies or animal spirits or black humors or astral influences or gods have shown when they crumbled, as explanatory concepts, under more enlightened views.

The problem with this jaunty proposal has already been displayed: in wiping out Folk Psychology, it wipes out Beautiful Science, which is after all only Folk Psychology as applied to the characteristic conduct of scientists: they confront, infer, act, observe. To imagine that Beautiful Science will succeed in wiping out Beautiful Science is to raise the question of how it is to do this. And surely the answer is to refer to the proposal of theories, the inferring of predictions, the performance of experiments, the checking out of theory against reality—and these are precisely what was to have been eliminated. So the elimination is strictly unthinkable, just because the moment we try to think about doing it, we are enmeshed in the repudiated categories of Folk Psychology. Since we require science to get rid of Folk Psychology, it is plain that we cannot get rid of Folk Psychology by science, for we have no way of representing science save through the categories of Folk Psychology. It is exhilarating to encounter a genuine deconstruction as we approach the point at which we want to take up the question of the future of criticism, for we have settled the question of the future of science by a kind of transcendental argument. No one can say for certain that there will be science in the future. All we can say is that if there is science in the future, it will be familiar. Dalton would have no difficulty in recognizing that what Nathans and his associates achieved is science. He would have a lot of catching up to do, on the other hand, to recognize what they have achieved. If you like, Beautiful Science can have a genuine history—a future unintelligible to its past—only if it does not itself have a history: only if it is intelligibly the same at all stages of itself as the same thing, Beautiful Science, with a remarkable potential for cognitive adventure. Those things that can have histories in some sense lie outside history, like platonic forms. Or like souls or selves. So we may assume that Folk Psychology is not really part of history, certainly not part of the history of psychology. It was there with the first cross-overs, the first duplications and divergences that account for the emergence of human DNA. It will be with us for as long as our species endures, like trichromate vision. The microbiology of Beautiful Science will in effect be the microbiology of Folk Psychology.

There is an instant problem generated by the thought that there might thinkably be a microbiology of Beautiful Science though not thinkably a beautiful science of microbiology itself—no gene that specifies the concept of gene. It is due to the fact that each component of Beautiful Science refers to what, following Bertrand Russell, philosophers designate "propositional attitudes:" "perceiving that . . .," "observing that . . . ,'" "believing that . . . ," "doing x in order that . . .," "feeling that . . . ," "caring that . . . ," and the like. The "that" requires completion by a proposition. Socrates was aware that we cannot believe just as such—we have to believe something—and went on to elaborate a theory of doxastic objects which we recognize as a component in platonic metaphysics. If propositional attitudes were in the genome but propositional objects not, it must be clear that Beautiful Science could never have come about by genetic process alone. There may, to be sure, be some innate beliefs, as Leibniz supposed all our beliefs were and Descartes supposed some of them are, and these may indeed be genetically coded (I tend to think that all the beliefs that are philosophically crucial are of this sort), but Leibniz's thesis seems to me genetically impossible: the propositions have to come from somewhere outside the genome, and the best explanation of where they do come from is through interaction with the genetic product—us—and the world. One might ponder the human brain at this juncture, which contains 10^{14} synapses. But there are not enough genes to account for this, and, as Pasko Rakic recently argued, "Even if we knew all the genes and what they were coded for, we still could not predict in detail what kind of brain you would have."[1] If we think of the brain as bearing the inscribed record of experience, with neuronal circuitry the product of interchange with the world, you would have a good analogy to what I am getting at. What I am getting at is underscored by the scientific project of studying neuronal circuitry by depriving animals of one or another mode of sensory input.

The world in which Dalton lived could not have been, as such, remarkably different from the world we live in, so it will not be mere interchanges with the world that accounts for the differences between Dalton's views and Nathans's views at either end of a history: we have to add something about the historical transformation of the world. Dalton and Young stand too early in a history to have been able to understand what could be meant, by their successors, by such an expression as "the primary receivers of color information." That expression could of course have been formed in English before Newton, but it required Newton to give it the sense "primary" came to have in the history, and it required a lot of science that came after Young and Dalton for the remaining expressions to mean what they do to Nathans and Botstein and our contemporaries. It has been widely subscribed to by philosophers of mind that the propositions which are objects of propositional attitudes form holistic systems—that we are not, in understanding the mind, to consider propositions one at a time but only in the systematic *Zusammenhang* of a whole complex of propositions, and that history must account for the difference, or some of the differences, between thinkers like Dalton and Young at the beginning, Helmholz and Clerk Maxwell in the middle, and Jeremy Nathans at the term of a process. It is this that makes a synchronic approach to the human sciences so finally unsatisfactory. It is as though the embedding system constitutes a text, and as the text changes, the sentences in it themselves undergo a change in meaning. And with this we begin to approach the topic of criticism, understood now as the theory of texts.

The term *Zusammenhang* is a *Gastarbeiter* in English, which lacks an honest word to do the work *Zusammenhang* does, and whose absence from our tongue may explain the fact that English philosophers balk at certain forms of thought with which Continental theorists garb themselves easily and naturally. It is meant to sound an allusion, in my text, to a famous and familiar claim by Gottlob Frege that a word has meaning only in the *Zusammenhang* of a sentence (*ein Satzes*). One might partially gloss this as implying that to understand a word is to know how to use it in a sentence (which leads the philosopher Peter Geach to say that the blind of course know the meaning of "red").[2] My dog Emilio understands the words "walk" and "breakfast," and displays an expression of acute interested awareness whenever these are uttered. But he understands them as he understands my picking up a leash or handling a can of Alpo—as signals which happen to be irrelevantly vocal. To understand them as *words* would demand sentential competence, and Frege is given credit for having made the sentence—or proposition—central in logic, overthrowing the term as the unit of philosophical intelligibility (the history of the concept of understanding massively confirms this assessment). In any case, philosophers since Frege have been more or less arrested at the analysis of sentences, when what I am anxious should happen is that we press past this boundary to the thought that a sentence has meaning only in the *Zusammenhang* of a text. And a parallel to the limitations of Emilio may be found in the case of those who may not be said to understand a sentence for want of possessing the *Zusammenhang* in which, as Frege might put it, the sentence *meint etwas*. That is to say, there can be no such thing as understanding just two words (as in the case of Emilio), not even if the two words form a grammatical sentence, for there can be no such thing as understanding just one sentence. The least unit of sentential comprehension is the discourse, which of course has exceedingly fluid boundaries.

Consider an example meant to tell decisively against a sentential theory of the mind. Steven Stich invokes an old family retainer, long gone senile, who is said nevertheless to remember the assassination of President McKinley. At least she says "Yes" when asked if she remembers that. But it may be she says this because she is rewarded, as Emilio is rewarded for complying with "Sit." In any case she is unable to answer questions presupposed by understanding "McKinley was assassinated." Let's say she does not remember that McKinley was President, does not understand what it means to kill, and so on. Briefly, if a certain surrounding body of propositions is erased, leaving but one sentence, it is not really a sentence at all unless we can imagine a constructable text in which it has a meaning. It is a sentence only if we can construe it as a textual fragment, as a word is a sentential fragment only if truly a *word*. The fragment-whole relationship gives us a model for the holistic concept introduced above, even if something should meet the standard grammatical and logical tests of well-formedness to be a sentence.[3] Stich's argument, that the retainer does not understand the sentence if it is the only sentence she "understands," strongly resembles arguments used by John Searle and by Hubert Dreyfus, among others, against certain claims made on behalf of artificial intelligence. There is a famous script, designed by R. P. Abelson and Roger Schank, meant to demonstrate that a computer understands narratives since it is able to furnish answers to questions it was not explicitly programed to know. The script is somewhat simple minded, dealing with a man going into a restaurant and ordering and paying for a hamburger. I have seen Searle and Dreyfus make quite merry at the number of things the machine does not understand—does the man eat the hamburger with his ear? Does he sit on the hamburger?—which any child experienced in the milieu of McDonald's would know the answers to. Stich argues from his interesting example to the reckless conclusion that Folk Psychology must be wrong and hence replaced with another model of cognition altogether— when the reverse seems to me to be the case, namely that a textual theory of the mind is entailed by the fact that someone really does understand a single sentence when she or he understands all that has been erased from the brain or mind of that ancient retainer. And my point is that Dalton and Nathans have to understand the same sentences—say "Normal color vision is trichromate"—in different if centrally overlapping ways, because of what Nathans, but not Dalton, can be supposed as understanding about photochemistry, genetics, statistics, and the like. That sentence cannot have meant in 1798 quite what it altogether means in 1986, if my augmentation of the Fregean unit to the text is justified. "Normal color vision is trichromate" is, then, a fragment that generates different texts in these two widely separated years, and would have been unintelligible or false before 1672, when Newton's work was laid before the Royal Society.

I want now to characterize criticism as the theory of texts, and to consider the future of criticism as the future of that. Here is the thought I want to advance: if the Folk Psychological premises of Beautiful Science cannot be thought away; if the propositional objects entailed by the truth of Folk Psychology themselves imply that we are structured propositionally; if the propositional attitudes true of us if we are propositionally structured imply that we are structured as texts, then criticism is preemptive psychology and even now the strategies evolved for addressing literary texts have application to us: they apply to us if the deep premises of Beautiful Science themselves apply. But then criticism defines the future of Beautiful Science if there ever is to be Beautiful Science of

Beautiful Science. Something like the reductions of color vision must be worked out for the textual psychology entailed by Folk Psychology if there is to be a microbiology of Beautiful Science (you could not deduce from the microbiology of color vision the interior decoration of our rooms). The two cultures meet at this point. They are not like two circles without a tangent point. They are like two halves of a single circle that join at the theory of texts.

I have just been striding along in my fourteen-league boots, and the gaps between each step are sufficiently wide that, as Charles Sanders Peirce once said, a coach and four could be driven through. That matters not in the least, for any demonstration of some logical unbridgability between the steps would have to be immensely illuminating in regard to criticism, texts, science, and the architecture of the human mind. I now draw off those boots, and replacing them with my seven-league clodhoppers, mince my way to the conclusion of this reflection.

If the mind—by which I mean that dimension of our beings specified by Folk Psychology—hangs together in the manner in which texts hang together—if we are, so to speak, a text made flesh—then a beginning might be made in addressing certain problems concerning the identity and unity of a person against the model of the unity and identity of a text. There is a very famous passage in Hume's *Treatise*, in which he disclaims having any idea of his self, since his theory requires that ideas be caused by impressions and there is no *impression* of the self.

> For my part, when I enter most intimately into what I call myself, I always stumble on some particular perception or other, of heat or cold, light or shade, love or hatred, pain or pleasure. I never catch *myself* at any time without a perception, and never can observe anything but the perception.

And, after a passage of characteristic irony directed at metaphysicians who pretend to find, contrary to himself and the rest of mankind, something "simple and continued which he calls himself," Hume concludes in his characterization of what we are:

> A bundle or collection of different perceptions which succeed one another with an inconceivable rapidity, and are in perpetual flux and movement.[4]

Now what constitutes the identity of a text? It would certainly be peculiar, though parallel to Hume's straw opponents, to postulate some underlying textual substance that runs through the poem and constitutes the unity of the poem, when in truth, tracking Hume's analysis, "we can never enter most intimately into what we call" the poem, and encounter anything but words, or lines, or whatever, and were someone then to say that the poem is but a bundle of different words or lines which succeed one another, he would certainly be right. That, in a certain sense, is what a poem is. If experience inscribes my history on the tabula rasa of the self, someone who was to peer into me would see the inscriptions succeeding one another and might wonder where *I* was. It would be laughable were one to say he had overlooked the tabula rasa itself, for that would be like trying to establish the unity of a poem with reference to the unity or identity of the paper it was printed on. No doubt the self has at times been regarded, primitively, as a sort of meta-physical parchment which carries the taint of original sin as a moral watermark and which bore the inscription, as so many stains, of misdeeds and transgressions unless and until erased by confession, penance, or absolution.

But a poem is not a list of words or a mere concatenation of sentences, even though it is true that each of them is separate in the way Hume supposes, correctly enough, that our "particular perceptions" are. "All these are different, and distinguishable, and separable from each other, and may be separately considered, and may exist separately, and have no need of anything to support their existence," he writes. They are, to use his typical expression "altogether loose and separate." I mean you can count the words, and there is no reason why, in a line of print and considered as printed, "mice" requires the existence of "three" or "blind." "Three," "blind," and "mice" are different, distinguishable, separable, may be separately considered, and certainly "need not one another in order to exist." In second thoughts on this subject, Hume is adamant on the looseness and separateness of perceptions—"all our perceptions are distinct existences"—and he doubtless entertained as a target just what his fellow resident at La Flèche tendered, in the Synopsis of his *Meditations*, was the criterion of the mind in contrast with matter: its unity and indivisibility. Hume pretended to find no connection among these distinct existences, as indeed there are no tiny ligatures, barely visible, binding "three" and "blind" and "mice" into a single striking expression. The spaces between them are empty, as are the spaces between the words of Hume's own history of England. What prevents that history from disintegrating into a collection of separate existences? That it refers to a single entity, England? That it is written by a single individual, Hume? The text would not lose its unity were it discovered that it was written by a team of Scotsmen, nor is its unity shaken by the consideration that England itself got to be a unity well after the events with which the narrative begins. And what of the unity of the texts about Oz?

My sense is that Hume's psychology, constructed on the model of simple terms—"love, hatred, pain, pleasure, light shade"—would have been impossible had the proposition emerged in his time as the psychologically central unit. Hume's theory of belief as a certain intense feeling accompanying an impression, while it got right the fact that belief

384 • *Beautiful Science*

is something that accompanies something and does not occur on its own, got the object wrong because he lacked the grammatical insight that beliefs require propositional objects; and then, in propositionalizing the contents of the mind—in recognizing that a term has meaning only in the *Zusammenhang* of a proposition—he would have been in a position to see that the kind of connections needed were the kind that kept his books from disintegrating into staccatos of unconnected words. What binds the self into a unity is of a piece with what binds histories and essays into unities—and Hume as psychologist and man of letters would similarly have found a unity that parallels what he found lacking between Hume as skeptic and Hume as man of the world. If Beautiful Science is an extension and refinement of the fundamental practices covered by Folk Psychology, texts, as literary artifacts, are projections and extensions of the unifying structures of a self or of a life. The principles, whatever they are, that enable us to tell and follow stories, to construct and read poetry, are the principles that bind lives into unities, that give us the sense of chapters ending and of new ones beginning. The future of criticism lies in making these principles explicit.

In recent years a number of audacious theorists in Paris have achieved something so remarkable that I am certain we will some day look back upon Paris during the thirty years after World War II as we look back on Amsterdam in the three decades in which Dutch painting achieved its supremacy, or to Florence in the somewhat more protracted period of the Florentine high renaissance. The writings were dark, self-indulgent, portentous, agonizingly frivolous, and silly, infuriating, and absurd. But collectively they expanded upon the concept of the text to integrate history, culture, psychology, as well as to revolutionize the reading of literature narrowly considered. Six decades of analytical philosophy had devoted itself to the exploration of the proposition as the unit of meaning and bearer of truth, culminating in the truth-conditional analysis of meaning and the thought that "S is true if and only if S." But when we seek to widen our horizons beyond "Snow is white if and only if snow is white," this analysis helps us very little. Logic takes up some of the slack, language game, or speech-act theory takes it up in a different way, but these leave us with the thesis that the larger encompassing contexts are calculi or *Lebensformen*. Even when Jerry Fodor advanced the singular thesis that there is a language of thought, he continued to construe it as formulating T-rules for propositions, raising the particulate theory of Hume to a higher level, treating propositions one at a time as though each was a tiny vessel of meaning. If the mind *zusammenhangs* as Jacques Lacan insists, if cultures *zusammenhang* as Claude Lévi-Strauss proposes, if history *zusammenhangs* as conceived by Michel Foucault or Fernand Braudel, then even if texts do not hold together the way Jacques Derrida supposes they do, Hume really was a victim of the metaphysics of presence, which is another name for atomist, and the scope of textual theory is collectively widened and a redistribution of the map of learning is in order. Criticism is then the paradigm human science, and I find it surprising, even exhilarating, that the matrix for understanding the physiology and ultimately the molecular biology of human cognition should be those strategies applied to analyzing the poems of Donne and the plays of Shakespeare; and that the humanists, with all their touching inadequacies, should be in the forefront of science. We had always been taught that the last shall be first, but whoever would have suspected metaphysics of becoming once more queen of the sciences?

22

Computers, Literary Theory, and Theory of Meaning

Gregory G. Colomb and *Mark Turner*

Computing has become a form of life, like using toasters or TVs, making phone calls, driving cars. It is for so many of us a practical necessity, part of the technological background that enables our intellectual and professional activity. Soon, scholars for whom computing is as necessary—and as interesting—as driving a car will be the norm, and those unacquainted with computing will be as those for whom the automobile remains a mystery. It is already clear that computing will greatly change those literary studies that depend on information storage and retrieval. Computing will bring within the powers of any adept undergraduate a body of information—and an appearance of learning—that would make Erasmus look down from high heaven and weep for envy.[1]

Envy aside, this change ought to make us rejoice. It will free our profession from one of its burdens: rightly employed, computers can free us to use our minds more than our index cards. The kind of learnedness that comes chiefly from diligence will be a cheaper virtue, more easily and more widely had. Anyone will be able to do what once took a lifetime of reading. More importantly, we will be able to ask questions that were once unthinkable. Of course, the trick will be to know which questions are worth asking, and what to make of the answers.

It would be fascinating to spin out the implications for literary studies of the oncoming revolution in information storage and retrieval or to discuss ways to improve and implement available technology.[2] But questions of storage and retrieval hold little direct interest for theory of literature. Although few questions of literary theory make us want to run to a computer for answers, there is emerging an area of convergence between computer science and literary theory. It concerns meaning. All theories of literature either presuppose or explicitly ponder some theory of meaning, and especially, some theory of textual understanding. Such questions have been asked for some time now in the branch of computer science known as artificial intelligence. And computer science's answers, especially those concerning *representation of knowledge* and *natural language processing*, have begun to raise important questions about key theoretical assumptions about meaning and understanding, assumptions that govern literary theory as much as artificial intelligence.

At first blush, introducing artificial intelligence into the discourse of literary theory ought to create at least surprise, if not bewilderment. How can anyone have thought that a computer could be made to understand language at all, much less understand it in a way pertinent to the aesthetic powers of literature? At first, no one did. Computer science did not set out to make computers an experimental tool in the study of meaning and the human mind. Researchers in artificial intelligence (AI) had practical reasons for investigating meaning. Anyone who has learned to use an artificial computer language (especially the earliest ones) knows why it would be important to teach a computer to understand natural languages. How much better it would be if computers could be given artificial intelligence so that humans need not waste their natural intelligence learning artificial computer languages. In the history of AI, these practical concerns immediately led to theoretical speculation. What would it mean for a computer to understand English? By Turing's criterion—and in keeping with the early practical goals—, it would mean that a computer imitates and responds appropriately to the human use of English. So the branch of AI that concerned natural language came to be known as Natural Language Processing (NLP). Programs were written that could hold question-and-answer dialogues, paraphrase text, summarize text, move objects in response to commands, explain obedience to commands, discuss psychological matters, fill in the obvious missing parts of stories, tell simple stories, and narrate a story from the differing perspectives of differing characters.[3] This may seem a long way from literary understanding, but we can recognize in such projects many questions important to recent literary theory, and we must marvel at their technical and conceptual achievement.

Since AI's goal was to imitate human language use, AI naturally looked to model its mechanical procedures on the natural, working object—the human mind. Thus AI attempted to model cognitive processes, imitating existing models in linguistics and psychology and, when there were no models or existing ones didn't work, creating models for themselves. And always AI's criterion for a linguistic-psychological model was, Does it work? From the first, theorists such a MIT's Marvin Minsky insisted that a successful psychological model must do more than say what happened in the mind. It must also say how—and then AI would test it on a machine. In this way research in AI has created an impressive body of knowledge of linguistics and psychology, knowledge with something very much like an experimental groundwork. When AI *was* able to implement a particular model and that model did not work, we learned a great deal about the actual complexity of artificial, much less natural intelligence, and we learned even more about the usefulness of particular models.

AI has become a discipline centrally concerned with the nature of meaning, of meaningful objects, and of the means by which we produce and understand them. These days, AI researchers often write articles not about computers but about human meaning or human representation of knowledge, as a way of exploring the issues to be resolved before better programs can be written. In such studies, AI's contributions are indispensable—as, for instance, AI's demonstration that meaning and knowledge are interrelated. One purpose of this essay is to introduce literary scholars to the pertinence of research in artificial intelligence and in those areas of linguistics and cognitive psychology closely related to AI. But just as literary theory has largely ignored AI and related studies of meaning, so AI has worked in relative isolation. Therefore we will also evaluate AI research from the perspective of theory of meaning as understood in literary theory and its related discipline[4]—in a sense, introducing the two disciplines to each other.

Our overriding goal, however, is to offer an extended critique of what we take to be the central feature both of AI approaches to meaning and of many, perhaps most, literary approaches to meaning: the assumption that meaning is compositional, that meaning is a product of some aspect of a (broadly conceived) grammar. This view is not universal, and some theorists have successfully overcome it. But many more, who have seriously confronted the pitfalls of a simple compositional theory, have mistakenly come to believe that they have purged their work of compositional assumptions. Among the accomplishments of research in artificial intelligence is that it has brought that discipline (as it can bring literary studies) to a point where we can recognize how deeply entrenched are our assumptions about the compositional nature of meaning and how widespread are the difficulties they cause. We will show how AI, textlinguistics, cognitive psychology, *and* literary theory unknowingly share a body of questions and answers about the nature of meaning and understanding. We believe that AI, which has tried to conceive meaning too narrowly, will find that what literary theorists know about meaning is crucial to the agenda for future AI research. We believe that literary theory, which has tried to find value in "literary" meaning by marginalizing it, can learn from AI (and related inquiries) not only information essential for any study of meaning but also a new—and far more accurate—sense of the place of theory of literature in the general arena of textual studies.

The Nature of AI

The compositional foundations of artificial intelligences

The foundation of AI theories of meaning is compositionality, which comes in many varieties. Simple, Fregean compositionality claims that the meaning of the whole is a function of the meaning of the components and their interaction (Frege 1892). We see this simple Fregean compositionality in traditional semantics as formulated by Katz and Fodor (1963). They argue that there exists a set of primitive semantic features (such as *young, male,* and *human*) and that every meaning of a word is a bundle of grammatical and semantic features (so that "boy" is [+ noun, + count, etc., + young, + male, + human, etc.]). The meaning of a sentence is the composition of the features belonging to the words it contains. In this view, we understand by composing atomic, bottom-level primitives into larger and more complex structures.

Katz and Fodor's semantics attempted to extend to meaning a Saussurean account of phonology. Saussure showed that a phoneme is constituted by differential contrasts within the sound system. We cannot determine whether a phonological instance constitutes a phoneme simply by looking at the instance itself—we have to look at the regularities and contrasts of all instances possible within the system. Thus the phoneme is determined by the relational structure between elements in the system. Extended to lexemes (for the most part, words), this kind of analysis makes meaning a function of a relational structure. For Katz and Fodor, as for many others, the meaning of a lexeme is not a matter of all the information we associate with that lexeme, but is purely a matter of its contrasts with the meanings of all other lexemes. Meaning, in this account, is immanent in the system of language and is entirely a matter of structure.

The compositional analysis most familiar to literary scholars is that of French structuralism and related kinds of semiotics. The notion that meaning resides in systems of differential contrasts was extended to structuralist analyses not only of myths and other verbal texts, but also of kinship, fashions in dress, table manners, the whole gamut of cultural systems. Of course the French movement had been anticipated in East European linguistic and literary theories associated with Roman Jakobson and the Prague School, with Louis Hjelmslev, Vladimir Propp, and others. This compositional view even underlies the efforts of those who would explode Saussurean notions of meaning. The thrill of deconstructing Saussurean grammars (see Derrida 1966, 1967) depends upon the observation that, if meaning is a matter of differential contrasts within a system, then nothing in the relational system can prevent indefinite slippage of meaning. The mistake in this reasoning lies in the premise, not the conclusion. Only a simple compositional view of meaning can bring us deconstruction's "vertiginous possibilities of referential aberration" (de Man 1979).

In AI, simple Fregean compositionality guides the first efforts in representation of knowledge and natural language processing, projects such as theories of semantic networks.[5] A semantic network is founded on the observation that, in making sense of language, we seem to use standard connections between concepts and that members of a linguistic community share these standard connections. If these standard connections could be modeled, the logic goes, then natural language processors could use these connections to process language in natural ways. A semantic network links concepts to other concepts. For example, the concept MARY is linked to the concept WOMAN with the link IS-A. DOG is linked to TAIL with the link HAS-A, or maybe HAS-AS-PART (see Findler 1979). But even the most sophisticated AI approaches are still guided by simple compositionality in their first-pass attempts at understanding a sentence. As Yorik Wilks writes, "primitives are to be found in all natural language understanding systems—even those . . . that argue most vigorously against them" (Wilks 1977; also see Jakendoff 1975). We might show this compositionality by looking at any number of sophisticated approaches—KRL, Preference Semantics, or SHRDLU[6]— but we will look instead at Roger Schank's Conceptual Dependence system.

In Schank's (1975) Conceptual Dependency theory, the computer maps an input sentence onto a language-free representation of its meaning.[7] This language-free representation combines primitive conceptual roles and conceptual categories.[8] There are seven roles (Actor, Object, Direction, etc.) and six conceptual categories (ACTS, nominals called PPs, locations in space coordinates called LOCs, object-attributes called PAs, etc.). Conceptual categories combine in exactly fifteen ways (certain PPs can ACT, ACTs have objects, etc.), and there are exactly eleven primitive actions (PROPEL, MOVE, INGEST, etc.) with ten conceptual tenses (past, future, negation, start of a transition, etc.). There are nine numerically scaled states (e.g., HUNGER), some states with more absolute measures (e.g., COLOR), and some non-scaled states (e.g., CONTROL, PART, etc.). Given this apparatus, Schanks's system would understand "Mary cried" by calling up its representation of "cry." It would ultimately determine that MARY is a PP who ACT (past tense), that the primitive ACT is EXPEL, that the object of EXPEL is TEARS, and that the direction of the ACT was from Mary's EYES to outside MARY.

Meaning and knowledge

Simple compositional accounts of meaning survive almost nowhere. No matter the discipline, it quickly becomes apparent that a simple compositional model cannot handle a sentence as ordinary as "The police officer raised his hand and stopped the car." In understanding that sentence, we call into play knowledge that is not explicitly a part of the semantic representation of any word in the sentence. We know, for example, that a raised hand can be a stop sign, that police officers use such signs in directing traffic, and that directing traffic is a common activity for police officers. Theories of meaning in most disciplines recognized that understanding language requires knowledge, not just of language but of the world represented in the language, and so they tried to build knowledge into their models. They became knowledge-based.

Traditional linguistics attempted to allow for the seemingly unlimited range of knowledge involved in understanding by arguing that there are two levels of meaning. The first level consists of simples and bundles, and formal operations upon them. This is *linguistic* meaning in the sense that it is independent of general psychological processes of understanding. This first level of meaning is named *semantics*. Semantics supposedly concerns meaning immanent in the system of language independent of contexts of use. In practice, semantics is usually taken to be a bottom-up affair: words have meanings composed of primitives, and we process these meanings to construct the meaning of a sentence, building up from word to sentence.

The second level of meaning consists of pretty much everything else we know, especially about contexts of language use: meaning depends on contexts of use and large knowledge bases. This subordinate second level, called *pragmatics*, comes to the rescue when semantics is not enough. Sometimes, when we use semantics to construct the meaning of a sentence, we find that it is incoherent. For example, "you" is [+ person], "cream" is [− person], and the literal semantic meaning of "You are the cream in my coffee" is incoherent. In such cases of incoherence, we step outside semantics into the world of pragmatics, to apply some familiar context of use, or imagine a possible context of use, such that we can see the sentence as coherent in that context.[9]

To their credit, AI researchers very quickly abandoned as untenable the distinction between semantics and pragmatics and between skills and knowledge, just as they had in the very early days shown that a natural language processing model based on a Chomskian syntax-driven parse would not work. AI researchers attempted to overcome the grave inadequacies of simple Fregean compositionality by developing inference and prediction capabilities for their systems and by building knowledge into the system in the form of frames, which do not distinguish so-called semantic and pragmatic knowledge.

For example, Schank's system uses information it has already parsed to set up expectations about what it will encounter next: particular words, particular concepts, or more general conceptual structures. Thus, one sense of "hit" would come with the expectation of an instrument of hitting. If the system provisionally selects that sense of "hit," then the system expects to find some mention of the instrument. The system also sets conditions on including that instrument in the conceptual dependency diagram or "understanding" of the text. One very simple condition would be that the system encounter, after the word "hit," the word "with" followed by a noun group whose head noun is in the computer dictionary as an instrument of hitting (e.g., "bat"). A more complex condition would be that the system recognize that the AGENT of "hit" is represented in the computer dictionary as holding an object listed as an instrument of hitting. Another part of the system works not on these simple expectations about the language of a text but on larger features of the conceptual dependency diagram itself. This part has information about topics (e.g. hunting, contests) or environments of comprehension events (e.g., a joke, a lecture), and tries to make inferences and corrections based on that information. In both cases, expectations set up gaps in the conceptual structure, and the system attaches predictions and requests to the gaps. Predictions and requests are removed as the system fills the gaps to which they are attached. Thus, filling gaps drives the processing.[10]

For more sophisticated analyses, a system must have more than this knowledge of linguistic expectations. It must also have the kind of knowledge of the world that is embodied in frames. A frame is something like a schematized scenario.[11] An early example was Marvin Minsky's (1975) frame for a birthday party. It included the default knowledge that appropriate dress is Sunday best, that there should be a present to please the host, that the present should be bought and gift-wrapped, that appropriate games include hide and seek, etc. In addition to such items of knowledge, frames can include other frames. For example, the frame for birthday party would itself fill a slot in the larger frame for birthday. Using these frames, a computer can handle texts like "John bought a present for Joe's birthday. He walked to the party with the present under his arm." The computer "handles" it in the sense that it can respond appropriately to a range of questions. If asked, "Why did John carry a present to the party?," the computer can print on its screen, "To give to Joe for his birthday."

Thus frames such as the birthday party frame defined mini-worlds, well-defined conceptual spaces that represent interrelated facts about the world.[12] Of course, we see right off that such mini-worlds do not approximate our world very well. So the knowledge supposedly represented in frames is *default* knowledge, to be used only if we have no indications to the contrary. Although limited, frames did give computers more specific knowledge about mini-worlds and moved them closer to natural language capabilities.

Some of the most elaborate means for representing knowledge were devised by Schank's Yale group, who used frame-like structures called scripts. Their classic example was the restaurant script. This script included the knowledge that a restaurant has patrons, cooks, waiters, etc.; that the patrons eat, the cooks cook, the waiters take orders, serve, and collect the payment for the bills; that the events have a sequence (the patron sits down, the waiter approaches and takes the order, and so on). So when the computer receives the sentence "John entered the restaurant and ordered the chef's salad," the computer would know that John sat down, and that he ordered the chef's salad from somebody waiting on him, that he expected to eat the salad, etc. And the computer could flesh out restaurant stories in paraphrase, and answer questions about what it had been told.[13]

Here, too, the scenario defined by the restaurant script proved too rigid. So the Yale group added two kinds of flexibility. They made scripts more flexible by building in alternative tracks, so that, e.g., the restaurant script might have tracks for sit-down vs. fast-food, which share some components but differ on others. But the Yale group also observed that people understand stories for which they lack the kind of generalized, prepackaged knowledge represented in the machine's script. The group proposed that this happens because people understand goal-based planning behavior. (See also Bower 1982 and Fikes and Nilsson 1971.) So they built PAM—Plan Applier Mechanism. PAM knew, for instance, that people have eating as a goal; that goals have sub-goals; that in order to use (e.g., eat) something, you have to have it; that if you don't have it, you have to get it or have it brought; that to get it, you have to know where it is, and have a way to get there. PAM's more flexible approach tried to process narrative text in terms of both scripts and of plans leading to a goal.[14] In the obvious way, scripts and plans could be turned around to generate stories as well as understand them.[15]

The Current State of AI

AI has helped to break down the illusory distinction between semantic and pragmatic knowledge and between reasoning and facts. Doing so, it has discovered many things about the kinds of knowledge we bring to understanding texts. AI has shown that, even with the simplest sentences, knowledge (as in scripts) and general psychological process (as in planning) must be part of the analysis from the first because such knowledge and processes cannot be distinguished from the apparatus associated traditionally with semantics. AI has exploded the vain hope that linguistic knowledge and competence can be compartmentalized and studied apart from the rest of our knowledge and competences.

AI has also kept its game honest by attempting to implement its theories. This is a very important point. Unlike other investigations of meaning, AI does not allow itself the luxury of "black boxes"—places in the theory where the analyst's intelligence intervenes to supply what the mechanism of the model cannot. When an AI system analyzes a text, the system is left to do the whole of the work on its own. Whenever a human intelligence must intervene in the process, that intervention is rightly regarded as a failure or a trick. Other forms of text analysis are less rigorous. When, for example, a cognitive psychologist or a textlinguist begins by saying that the relationship between the text in question and the first step in the analysis (its propositional representation in a "text base") runs "in the normal way," that researcher is taking out a "loan of intelligence" (Dennett 1978: 3–38). That is, the researcher creates a black box in which *our* intelligence operates on the text (and who can say how and with what anticipation?) to produce the text base that the model needs to work. Researchers in AI *know* there is nothing obvious or easy about "the normal way" of understanding a text to generate a propositional representation of it. They know this because they insist that their models actually perform the tasks they model, that they work. Similarly, we can find talk of scripts and frames in cognitive psychology, in textlinguistics, even in literary theory.[16] But in these disciplines, talk of scripts and frames is at best a trope: it only locates the place in the analysis where we see that knowledge is somehow involved and names the place in a way that seems to obviate the need for further analysis. When, for example, Teun van Dijk builds a "cognitive set" into his "Construction Rule," explicitly referring to AI research (1980: 83, 203–213), he does what AI refused to allow itself: he leaves the content and the operation of this script/frame/plan entirely opaque.[17] AI researchers know the enormous difficulties of the script/frame approach because they have tried to implement it, and have seen the difficulties that arise. By being in this way tough-minded about its own (and others') models, AI has shown how little we do know and how difficult it is to know more.

Grammars vs. meaning

In making its advances, AI has adopted a theory of meaning—one it shares with most linguistics, cognitive psychology, textlinguistics, *and* literary theory—that can only fail under the properly stringent tests which AI demands. Our first issue is a general one. It concerns AI's claims that what it studies is meaning. We do not agree that to devise a model that allows a machine to act as if it could move blocks or answer questions about stories or even construct rudimentary stories is to study meaning. The AI view, we think, confuses *meaning* with *grammars* of meaning. To devise models that can "understand" is to study grammars, where a grammar is an account both of the systematic or codified aspects of meaningful objects and of the relation between those codified aspects and meaning. That study is not directly a study of meaning. To be sure, grammars are indispensable to studying meaning. And something on the order of the mental equivalent of a grammar probably exists to help us organize, access, search, select from, and process meanings. But grammars are useful (and understandable) *only* if we already know meanings, and the working of a grammar does not itself produce meaning.

Implicit in most AI is the claim that a mechanism with a good grammar can produce meaning by shuffling word-like symbols, especially if that mechanism can do lots and lots of shuffling. This mistake is easy to make. When we see a good grammar—a feature bundle of semantic markers, a semantic net, or a script or frame for a familiar concept—we feel that we are looking at meaning. Good grammars make eminent sense to us, since good grammars give us a perspicuous display of what we know. The feature bundle for *boy* and the script for *restaurant* look as if they capture (at least some of) the meaning of *boy* and *restaurant*. And they do indeed capture meaning—for persons who have/know/recognize/process meanings for *human, young, eat, sit,* and so on. The bundle or the script only translates (meaningful) terms into (meaningful) paraphrases, hence deferring the question of how they are meaningful. They are meaningful because we provide meaning for the feature bundle or the script. The most elaborate array of word-like descriptors for a concept catches none of its meaning, though it may characterize a lot of the grammar that concerns that concept. We persons, who know meanings, provide for grammars, bundles, or scripts a functional level of mind—the level where we deal not with symbols but with concepts already integrally meaningful, and where those concepts interact, not only with our knowledge, but also with our beliefs, desires, hopes, and fears.

We do much the same for the language spoken or written by any person. We fill in their arrays of words with meanings we know, using grammatical hints and guidance as they become relevant. We project in the words a functional level of mind—only in the case of other persons this projection seems natural, unproblematic. This is why the Turing Test for intelligence is misconceived. Suppose an artificial intelligence team produces a computer program that holds conversations with me so that I simply cannot distinguish between its talk and the talk of a person. Does that computer have the intelligence to understand my language?—or, better, does it know meanings? I am still the one who finds meaning in that talk. I am the one who projects a functional level of mind in that talk. It would seem to me, once I knew the facts about my situation, that the computer has only managed to mimic grammars of various sorts.[18] In order to know whether the computer could understand natural language, I would want to know whether it knew meanings, whether it projected a functional level of mind in my talk.[19]

This is not to say that, in principle, computers will never understand language. We now believe that, at the neurobiological level, the brain pushes around electro-chemical bits that look as if they may be symbols. Computers are very good at pushing around symbols. So it is at least reasonable to think of the neurobiological level of the brain as something very much like a computer. What we do not at present know is how these neurobiological events (the symbol-shuffling) relate to the functional level of mind (meanings). Perhaps someday we will. If we do, then computer hardware and software may be able to replicate not only neurobiological events, but also their cohesion into mental functionality and so meaning. That day is not yet upon us.

By confusing the neurobiological and functional level of the mind, we put ourselves in thrall to a metaphor. The mind, or at least the brain, is, under some descriptions, so much like a computer and the mind-as-computer is such a useful trope that we come to forget its analogical base. Moreover, the modern trope has its roots in an ancient tradition of seeing the mind as a symbol-processing device. The positivist tradition of seeing thought as abstract and disembodied gives us ample provenance for the idea of non-human thought. If thinking is logical symbol-processing, then it is accidental that the device processing the symbols happens to be situated in a human body. Any other equivalently powerful computer can do the job just as well. The problem is, concepts like *chair* exist for us along with cerebellar routines for integration of motion. We know the meaning of "chair" partly by connection with these interactional routines. The meaning of "Sally pulled the chair as John sat down, and he fell to the floor" somehow includes the feel of the interactional routine for sitting. While the frame for SIT might include, associated with CHAIR, the strings "GRASPABLE" and "WEIGHT-BEARING," knowing the meaning of these concepts involves the interactional routines for grabbing and for resting one's weight. The meaning cannot be captured simply by including strings in a frame. The problem of meaning is not so much a problem of creating artificial intelligence as a problem of creating artificial persons.

AI grammars of meaning

We raise the challenge to AI's claims to be engaged in the production of meaning and understanding right at the start because, while fundamental, that issue is also peripheral to the day-to-day business of AI research. In one sense, it would not matter whether one thought that in constructing a natural language processor one was only teaching a machine to mimic grammars or was teaching a machine to understand. The task at hand would still be to devise or borrow a good grammar and to find the hardware and software to implement that grammar. So we can, for the most part, bracket the question of meaning and concentrate on the question of grammar—especially since good grammars are likely to offer helpful evidence in our struggles with the question of meaning. We turn, then, to consider how current models in AI (and in related disciplines) stand up, not as producers of meaning, but as grammars of meaning.

Grammars of meaning according to objectivist philosophy. AI grammars of meaning concern only the kind of meaning allowed in standard objectivist philosophies of language, what can be called *propositional meaning*. These philosophies assume that objective reality consists of logically related objects and features. Any object (for example, a chair) is a composition of primitive elements. Any feature (for example, purple) is a composition of primitive features. Any relation (for example, class inclusion) is a composition of primitive logical relations. Reality, then, consists of states of affairs which are compositions of logically related objects and features. Correspondingly, thought consists of a compositional array of concepts and conceptual features which are logically related. Thus true thoughts accurately represent reality, the conceptual array corresponding, item-for-item, to the objective state of affairs. Such knowledge is called *propositional*.

Propositional knowledge produces propositional meaning. In this view, a true statement stands in place of a true thought, its words presenting an array of semantic primitives that corresponds, item-for-item, to the objective state of affairs represented in the statement. Thus a theory of propositional meaning restricts the kind of language that can occur in a true statement: a true statement's language is literal, either names that correspond to primitives (or compositions of primitives) that exist in objective reality, or words that correspond to features or relations in the objective states of affairs. To understand a sentence is to understand the correspondence between its elements and the elements of states of affairs.

A theory of propositional meaning does acknowledge other kinds of sentences and other uses of language. Sometimes, literal language is misused, when words are used to mean something other than the states of affairs to which they correspond. Some misuses are simply false. Others are figural and decorative. Since figural uses violate the correspondence between literal meaning and objective reality, figural meanings are false, and play no role in truth. They are also peripheral, and parasitic upon the proper literal core of language. Consequently, in this view—as in the view of much contemporary literary theory—these figural processes of meaning and other processes we think of as centrally literary are marginal and subversive of the literal.

AI grammars suffer under most of these misconceptions. AI's tools for representing meaning—semantic networks, frames, conceptual dependency graphs, preference semantics templates, KRL, and so on—mainly borrow their notions from propositional accounts in philosophy. However, this propositional approach excludes important aspects of meaning, many of which might be called "literary" processes of meaning. The problem is, as we shall see, these literary processes underlie so-called everyday language. It cannot be that these processes are marginal to or parasitic upon *everyday* language, however we see its relation to the literary. Thus, as a way of studying how persons understand language, a propositional account of meaning is impoverished from the start.

In a propositional account, a bachelor is an unmarried adult male, and a lie is a false statement. If we raise counterexamples, a propositionalist will handle them by adding features to the definition. But as Fillmore (1982) has shown, something can be a bachelor only with respect to a large model "of a human society in which certain expectations about marriage and marriageable age obtain." There is no set of features the possession of which makes someone objectively a bachelor, and in fact some failures of features for bachelor may not correspond to failures in meaning for uses of *bachelor*. The concept exists not as a composition of features, but only as a situation with respect to some elaborate cognitive model. In a critique of recent attempts to salvage propositional accounts by using weighted feature bundles (see Coleman and Kay's [1981] analysis of *lie*), Sweetser (1987) shows how that analysis, too, makes sense only as situated with respect to a larger cognitive model. AI researchers themselves have sometimes noted the inadequacy of defining a concept in terms of features and have suggested that sometimes concepts are defined only relative to a frame (see Bobrow and Winograd 1977).

A propositional theory of meaning also creates problems in categorization. Propositional traditions assume that items (both concepts and things) belong to a category because they share the criterial attributes that define the category (see Smith and Medin 1981). Organized along classical lines, categories which share attributes are grouped into a supercategory defined by the shared attributes. This familiar model gives us categories as tree-structures whose branching nodes represent bundles of attributes. But this classical model of categorization has been seriously challenged on at least two counts. The first question concerns the role of attributes. As the later Wittgenstein showed, members of a category often share no property common to all. For example, there is no criterial attribute common to all members of the category *game*. Rather, games seem to fall into a category because of family resemblance: each member shares some attributes with some other members. (Family resemblance is just one non-classical principle of categorization; for others see Lakoff 1987.) The second question concerns the structure of vertical and horizontal connections between concepts. The tradition of research associated with Eleanor Rosch has pointed out that there is one vertical level around which we organize most information. This basic level of categorization is the level at which we find medium-sized categories (e.g., dog) for which we have easily imagined prototypes (contrast imagining a dog with imagining a mammal). There is generally very little overlap between contrasting categories at or above the basic level, but high overlap between contrasting categories below the basic level. This structure of relations between our categories influences both the meanings of concepts, and the way we construe natural language.[20] To the extent that classical categorization is untrue to the way we organize concepts and to the way that organization underlies natural language, propositional theories of meaning, and AI theories based on them, must fail.

Nearly all AI construes concepts as compositions of primitives. In math and physics, systems may be reduced to primitive elements and primitive relations defined upon them. The results have been compelling, and we therefore feel that the approach has been justified. No such justification exists for doing the same to natural language. Assuming that meanings consist of semantic primitives standing in primitive relations has no justification other than that such an assumption permits one to apply set-theory and propositional calculus and other mathematical logical machinery to the analysis of meaning. (Indeed, most of what we find lacking in AI, in traditional semantics, and in philosophy of language derives from this attempt to impose mathematics on natural language.) People understand concepts in terms of other concepts in circular fashion, and what counts as basic concepts may vary from context to context.

Often, one conceptual domain is understood in terms of other conceptual domains. (See Nagy 1972; Reddy 1979; Lakoff and Johnson 1980; Turner 1987; Lakoff and Turner 1989.) For example, we understand communication in terms of the conduit metaphor: meanings are objects that are placed into containers; these containers are sent to others, who open the containers and take out the objects. Such metaphoric understanding is ubiquitous. It is fundamental to human knowledge and meaning. But no AI theory captures the metaphoric nature of knowledge. At its best, AI allows an abstract and reductive rendering of metaphoric meaning. Wilk's system, for example, understands "My car drinks gasoline" by abstracting *drink* to *use*. AI's attempts to model metaphor try to match attributes that are already in the representation of the concept, independent of the metaphor. This misses the point: the metaphor *creates* meaning. It imposes meaning on the target domain. AI in no case allows for understanding one conceptual domain *in terms of* another.

There are many other supposedly "figural" kinds of statements, statements involving metonymies, images, and any number of tropological constructs. Propositional semantics has tried to do without any of them. Resting meaning in the accurate mirroring found in a literal core of language, it has sought a knowledge untainted by the unreliable fancies of human imagination. These matters are left to a second realm of statement, either decorative or false, which is parasitic on the literal and which occurs only at the level of linguistic manifestation. Propositional semantics allows the figural no analogue in cognition. The facts are otherwise. These supposedly "literary" processes of meaning are fundamental, at the cognitive as much as the linguistic level. They are not marginal. They are not secondary. An approach to meaning that attempts to situate them at the derivative periphery is mistaken from the outset.

The frame selection problem. AI has been very good at showing that to understand sentences, we must bring to bear a great deal of knowledge, of all sorts. So it makes sense to look to AI—as cognitive psychology, textlinguistics, and literary theory have done—to tell us something about the grammar of bringing knowledge to bear on texts. How does an AI system know what knowledge base to bring to bear? The answers so far have been unsatisfying, and the difficulties that crop up are known as the "frame selection problem" (see Bobrow and Winograd 1977). Consider the following naturally occurring paragraph, written by a lawyer, in a letter warning its reader about minor but frequent weights and measures violations charged against a company:

> At the outset, this sum may not appear to be particularly onerous. However, the troublesome provision is not the $500 fine, but the "six months in county jail." Even though no jail sentences have been rendered against Abco so far, the fact that the violations are criminal in nature causes serious concern. Our concern over the criminal aspects

of the violations is only deepened by California's emphasis on consumerism and the growing hostility toward large, international corporations. In view of these factors, we should reevaluate the way these alleged violations are dealt with.

The first question we want to ask the grammar of frame-use is, what frames or scripts must we bring to bear on the text, and how do we know? One might, for instance, try to construct a business-decision script. Or, since that seems too tall an order, a legal-fine script. Such a script would be needed, and it would be immensely richer than Schank's restaurant script. But this paragraph calls for more than a simple business decision about a legal fine. It would also require other knowledge that stretches the very idea of a script: a letter-from-the-lawyer script, a dealing-with-problems-in-California script, a business-law script, perhaps a business-ethics script, and a public-relations script—not to mention a general plan mechanism for balancing business costs, legal risks (including personal risks), public image, and ethical considerations.[21] The frame selection problem, then, is threefold. Can we build frames rich enough to deal with naturally occurring texts but general enough not simply to translate the object language? Can we devise procedures for selecting the right frames? And can we devise mechanisms for balancing among competing frames?

The frame selection problem also turns us back on the question of frames themselves. Even if we can imagine formulating immensely rich scripts and delicate mechanisms for coordinating them, there remain instances of understanding for which scripts do not appear to be the best answer. As originally conceived, frames and scripts were meant to be expressions of recurrent structures of knowledge that are, in a sense, pre-packaged—bodies of cultural knowledge that we learn as a body. It would be impossible to suggest that all our knowledge belongs to scripts. Even to suggest that any substantial portion of our knowledge is scripted creates enormous memory demands, a difficulty which would disqualify scripts as viable psychological models. And yet it seems that any part of our knowledge might be necessary to understand a text. AI has no explanations for how knowledge not belonging to scripts or frames can be used in understanding.

Notice, for example, the penultimate sentence of the jail paragraph, "Our concern over the criminal aspects of the violations is only deepened by California's emphasis on consumerism and the growing hostility toward large, international corporations." In order to understand the relevance of this sentence, the reader must make a series of inferences that, as they are made, feel simple and obvious. The information about consumerism and hostility is relevant because it increases the sense of Abco's vulnerability. When this text was produced, in the early Reagan years, competent executives knew that in the social domain of consumer rights, when the public is down on big companies, small violations can bring severe and inconvenient penalties as a sort of object lesson. Even if we can imagine a processor with an "early Reagan years" script, an "object lesson" script, and most importantly a way to call up these scripts from this text, it seems doubtful that this inference can be made on the basis of those (or any) scripts. One wants to say that these matters are the sorts of thing we "just know" or "simply understand"—different from having a script—if to say that did not feel so much like begging the question. The question is, however, unavoidable. Are there forms of understanding that engage so much of our knowledge of life in so fine-grained a way that they cannot be modeled by such formal mechanisms as scripts and frames? Is the whole of our knowledge formalizable? Though some will want to say yes, both the question and that answer should strike us as odd. And it is up to those who say yes to show that it can be done and how we might do it.

Grammars of meaning as a series of propositions. AI grammars treat text meaning as a composition of logical propositions. That is, they "read" a text one proposition at a time, constructing from the text a network of interrelated propositions. Doing so, AI participates in the dominant tradition for thinking about text meaning. In their classic analysis, Halliday and Hasan formulated the principle that, while texts may have "texture," they can have no text structure because they have no constituent structure (1976: 1–3). In response to this challenge, researchers in a variety of disciplines have posed non-constituent models of text structure that see texts as collections of propositions configured into a conceptual hierarchy which the producer/receiver constructs proposition by proposition. Since AI routines deal only with very limited narrative texts, their hierarchies are constructed around simple scripts and plans.[22] In disciplines that deal with more complex texts, the hierarchies are constructed by more generalized logical procedures, the best know of which are Teun van Dijk's (1980) "macrorules."[23] In all cases, a compositional/propositional account of text meaning misses crucial aspects of understanding. On the one hand, such accounts prejudge the question of what can be important, structuring information in a given text. On the other, they ignore discourse-level grammatical features that signal the very structure they seek to describe.

The problem of prejudging importance is something like the frame selection problem writ large. When text meaning is composed proposition-by-proposition, then the nature of that meaning will be determined by the principles that govern the composition. Insofar as those principles are determined in advance of understanding the text, then the structure of the understanding will be a function not so much of the text as of the principles. Every text that activates Schank's restaurant script, for example, will be given a structure predefined by the script (though of course different texts will activate different aspects of the script). Given a story about Jane's trip to the restaurant with her Michelin guide, the routine will "understand" Jane's trip as an effort to eat, but never as a chance to drive her new car, or to get away from it all, or to visit a new place, or to see beautiful cutlery. Thus, even when (as in this case) the frame selected is the right one, the frame cannot know what *in* the frame is important to the text at hand. The problem is the same for the looser procedures of textlinguistics.[24] Whenever a model understands text meaning as a proposition-by-proposition composition, the resulting text structure will always have already built into it the text meanings privileged/required by the method of composition.

The problem of ignoring discourse-level grammatical features arises because as proposition-by-proposition processing strategy must limit itself to the grammatical information of sentence syntax. Even such low-level features of discourse grammar as topic, focus, and thematization are lost to proposition-based analysis. The sentence parsing procedures of present AI routines cannot recognize thematization effect (even though knowing themes would somewhat mitigate the frame selection problem.[25] And in textlinguistics, the situation is even worse. Textlinguistic models begin by constructing a "propositional text base," in which all supra-propositional information is necessarily lost.[26] Thus, for example, a macroanalysis of the jail paragraph of the last section would lose one of the most important elements of its text structure, the thematized concept JAIL (because, under van Dijk's "Generalization Rule" it is subsumed within the macroproposition "violations are criminal"). It would lose this information because, based on the propositional text base alone, the analysis cannot know that JAIL is given special emphasis by the discourse level-grammar.[27]

Above the level of thematization are yet more elaborate discourse structures entirely unrecognizable by AI sentence parsers and lost in any propositional analysis. Texts of the kind of the jail paragraph do have a constituent structure of the sort shared by all texts that make points (see Colomb and Williams 1987). One aspect of the constituent structure of *pointed* texts marks the end of the second sentence in the jail paragraph ("six months in county jail") as especially significant for establishing the discourse topic.[28] The key to this grammar is the point of a given discourse unit. Discourse grammar involves (1) the relation between the point and the constituent structure through which it is realized, (2) the relations among any given unit of discourse and those it dominates and is dominated by, and (3) the relations between discourse-level structure and lower levels of text structure (such as syntactic and thematic structures). No propositional text base can be sufficiently complicated even to approach this level of text grammar and meaning.

Compositionality, Knowledge Bases, and the Top-Down/Bottom-Up Distinction. Like other textual disciplines, AI has included knowledge bases as a way to avoid the limitations of simple Fregean compositionality. But the question of compositionality is complex, and must be addressed along two axes. The first axis concerns the relationship between the text and understanding. Does the understander gather meaning from the text—is understanding "text-based"? Or does the understander bring meaning to the text—is understanding "reader-" or "knowledge-based"? Most researchers hold relatively reader-based models,[29] and knowledge-based AI routines easily escape the simple compositionality of text-based models. The second axis is, however, for our purposes the more important. This axis concerns the "direction" assigned to understanding, whether a model proceeds "top-down," understanding smaller units in terms of the larger units that dominate them, or "bottom-up," understanding larger units as compositions of smaller units.[30] In some quarters, knowledge-based models have also been called "top-down," suggesting that knowledge-based models escape compositionality altogether (see Spiro 1980:262 and Barr and Feigenbaum 1981:334). But it is a mistake simply to equate knowledge-based with top-down and text-based with bottom-up. A knowledge-based model can still be compositional and so bottom-up. A case in point is Schank's script analysis. As they are presently constructed and deployed, scripts are only especially large and complicated feature bundles. Conceptual Dependency analysis may call upon the knowledge represented in its scripts and plans to process texts, but it nevertheless processes proposition-by-proposition, building meaning by constucting upward from minimal units. It is complex, flexible, and knowledge-based. It is also compositional and bottom up.

The distinction between top-down and bottom-up rests on how a model handles global structure and its relation to meaning. A top-down grammar has as its primary unit of representation the largest, most encompassing structure in question; it assumes that meaning resides at the top-level structure; and it then proceeds to represent that structure and its meaning by a process of decomposition into constituents. Thus, a top-down model of text meaning takes the text as the primary unit and subordinates lower levels of grammar (sentence meaning, word meaning) to the text grammar.[31] It would also, however, subordinate text grammar to a yet more general theory of meaning, one that encompassed the whole of the situation that makes a text meaningful. A bottom-up model, on the other hand, has as its primary unit of representation some unit smaller than the structure in question, usually a minimal unit (e.g., a primitive act or a proposition). A bottom-up model assumes that meaning resides in the smaller, primary unit; and it then proceeds to represent the structure in question by constructing increasingly complex combinations of the primary unit.[32]

The question whether a model is top-down or bottom-up is wholly different from the question whether and to what degree a model assumes that readers bring information to the text (knowledge-based) or take information from the text (text-based). It is true that any top-down model of discourse structure will necessarily be knowledge-based in that any top-down model must assume as its starting point a reader's understanding. But top-down models can vary in this respect. It is perfectly possible to construct a fully top-down model which emphasizes the information that readers take from a text, that is, which is relatively text-based. (Aristotle constructed such a model.) That model would be false, but nevertheless coherent. A knowledge-based, bottom-up model is equally possible. Nothing precludes a model which assumes the reader must supply vast amounts of information in order to begin processing the primitives that constitute the base-line of a proposition-by-proposition compositional process. Schank has constructed such a model. State of the art AI models are at the moment knowledge-based, but bottom-up because they propose to process texts proposition-by-proposition.

Grammar as a Model for Processing. Closely related to the question of top-down or bottom-up models is the question of the role of grammars in understanding. Underlying all AI, most cognitive psychology, and most textlinguistics is a common assumption—that grammars provide a model for the processes by which we understand. And so long as we are guided by the metaphor of the mind as a computer, no other view seems possible. If the mind can only push around electro-chemical bits of information and if grammars describe the structure of that information, then grammars must describe the structure of understanding. If the mind is now just a symbol-processor, then a different view is necessary. While it seems inevitable that grammatical structures must somehow guide our accounts of the process of understanding (since what we are understanding is a grammatical object), that grammar need not be the same as the process. There are two difficulties in taking grammars as models of processing, one concerns how we understand and the other concerns the nature of the objects that occasion our understanding.

The first difficulty is that understanders come to texts with any number of purposes, and those purposes guide their understanding. Consider again the jail paragraph. If its reader is new to the company, new to the job, and hearing about these weights and measures violations for the first time, then the reader may well process each sentence carefully and thoroughly, using all or (since grammar is highly redundant) a substantial portion of its grammatical information. If, however, the same reader receives the letter to confirm a long telephone call with the writer (an altogether probable situation), the reader can achieve what we would have to take as the same understanding by processing much less grammatical information (although we can predict that the information processed will be relatively high in the text structure). We can, of course, suppose many other things—a reader who is warned yearly about weights and measures violations, a reader who had already taken care of the problem, a reader who never pays attention to lawyers. Each of these readers can reach an understanding of the text by processing different aspects of the grammatical information in the text, and none of these readers is likely to attend consciously to its grammar—unless, that is, something about the reading makes the grammar matter. But of course knowing when grammar matters is the whole ballgame.

The second difficulty in supposing that grammar models processing is that for most texts, grammatical information is strikingly redundant. Though we may want to take the grammar of the text as a template for the possible paths by which a given understanding might be reached, that grammar is so richly overdetermined (and often sufficiently inconsistent) that the template defines a very large number of paths through the text. Are we then to posit some one, central, "complete" understanding against which the others are to be measured as deviations? Which is it? That of the ignorant reader, who attends carefully word by word? or that of the informed reader, who knows what the letter says without much bothering to read it? or perhaps that of the grammarian?

The difficulty of multiple processing is insurmountable for bottom-up grammars, since they can describe only one path through a text—proposition by proposition construction. The reader can reach the highest and most important levels of meaning only by working through all the lower levels. A genuinely top-down grammar finds less difficulty on two counts. First, because a top-down grammar locates meaning in the whole of the text, it recognizes that a text is not only overdetermined, but downwardly overdetermined. It allows readers to understand higher and more important levels of meaning without necessarily working through all lower levels, and so it describes multiple paths for working down the textual hierarchy. Second, a top-down grammar can acknowledge that readers come to texts with any number of purposes. Since such a grammar describes multiple paths through a text, it allows a variety of readings. Since it recognizes hierarchically related components of meaning, each of which contributes to higher-level meanings, readers can intelligibly jump into the text at any level, attending only to that information relevant to the situation. A grammar must be as flexible and as supple as the persons who use it.

Non-Compositional Theories of Meaning

What AI and other grammar-based studies of language must have is a non-compositional account of meaning that is compatible with the enterprise of writing and implementing grammars. Non-compositional theories of meaning are not now unknown. Most areas of language study have produced at least one prominent rejection of the compositional principle. But where these non-compositional positions do not simply reject grammatical study, the best instances are concerned with philosophical issues several removes from the enterprise of writing grammars. We have here sketched a few instances of non-compositional grammars. Our final question is how such grammars can be integrated into a theory of meaning.

A non-compositional theory of meaning must begin with the assumption that meaning is not composed of parts. At first puzzling, this claim is less counter-intuitive than it might seem. To say that meaning is not composed of parts is not to say that meaningful objects are not composite. They are. Our grammars are ample testimony to the composite nature of all signs. Nor is it to say that meaning is unitary. It clearly is not. I can know what your utterance means "in itself"; what you intended your utterance to mean; what you mean by uttering it; what it "really means"; what its words mean; and so on. And I can have a sense of knowing only a part of your meaning—what your words mean but not what you mean by them; what you mean to say but not what your words mean; the words but not(as we say) the tune.

By saying that meaning is not composed of parts, we do not claim that compositional grammars are necessarily incorrect as grammars. Both Turner and Colomb are engaged in the study of grammar, and both of us have produced grammars that treat texts as composite. Moreover, texts are constructed and understood in accord with a grammar. We all use our knowledge of grammar (both intuitive and conscious) to guide our behavior with respect to constructing and understanding texts— when, that is, our behavior needs guidance. What we do claim is simply that grammars do not construct meaning. We do not substitute a theory whereby meaning flows down a grammatical model in a way that a compositional model has it flow upward. Meaning exists from the bottom up as much as from the top down, because meaning is to be found at all levels, in all structure.[33]

Meaning does not have parts so much as aspects. Compare, for instance, Wittgenstein's account of perception. Wittgenstein's duck-rabbit

(1953:II.xi), like meaning, is composite but not compositional. We all see that it is both duck and rabbit—in Wittgenstein's useful vocabulary, we all see both its duck aspect and its rabbit aspect. But we do not see the duck part and the rabbit part. Meaning, too, has aspects. Given an utterance that is for us meaningful, we can attend to its intentional aspect, its unconscious aspect, its semantic aspect, its syntactic aspect, its thematic aspect, and so on. Each aspect will have a structure, and for some aspects we have fully described grammars. But that does not require that meaning somehow be a composite of all of these aspects. In fact, like the aspects of the duck-rabbit, aspects of meaning are hard to attend to simultaneously: some aspects can seem to compete for our attention, and focusing on one aspect can seem to overwhelm our ability to attend to others. Nor is meaning a function of any one aspect of the speech act—or, since "speech act" is now associated with a theory of a single aspect of meaning, we might call it a rhetorical act. As is evidenced by the variety and the unhappy fate of attempts to make meaning a function of particular aspects, the meaning of a rhetorical act is not equivalent to intention, thought, truth value, sentence structure, text structure, semantic primitives, or any other aspect.

What makes meaning in this sense an all or nothing affair is its ties to life—or, using a now familiar language, its ties to what Wittgenstein calls forms of life. Even the Wittgenstein of the superbly compositional *Tractatus* recognized the enormous complexity of the "tacit conventions on which the understanding of everyday language depends," a complexity that comes about because "Everyday language is a part of the human organism and is no less complicated than it" (§4.002). To understand the meaning of an utterance is to understand it in terms of the action of an embodied creature whom we recognize as human—that is, recognize as one with ourselves. Now we might sometimes make such ascriptions to entities that do not fit the bill—as, for example, when we think of our car as having a mind of its own, or of a society as malignant, or of a computer terminal as smart or dumb, or of a natural language processor as understanding. But every ascription of meaning must be made under a description that has the *form* of description of meaningful human actions: "Even if writing appeared on a wall as at Belshazzar's feast, or a house rose up not made by men, they would be identified as writing or a house because of their visible likeness to what we produce—writing and houses" (Anscombe 1963:84). One cannot so much as recognize a meaning without the context of the forms of life that make meaning possible (which forms of life would be explicated in terms of conventions, habitual actions, beliefs, knowledge, needs, etc.).[34] None of us knows what it would be to attribute meaning to something other than a person, to attribute meaning apart from such forms of life.

Meaning is the primitive unit of analysis. We can know its aspects only in virtue of knowing meaning. That is not to say that we somehow just know meaning and then notice its aspects. Knowing a meaning is noticing some of its aspects and knowing some of its grammars.

Does such a theory of meaning rule AI out of court? Does it make us, in Hilary Putnam's apt phrase, "oxygen-hydrogen chauvinists"? Not necessarily. It does put us in a position that our standards for understanding cannot be approached by any currently conceivable technology. Were we confronted by a perfected Turing machine that can type on its screen perfectly appropriate responses to any and all kinds of stories, questions, or complaints but that is otherwise a wholly self-contained computing machine, we would not be tempted to ascribe understanding to it except in the sense that we ascribe intentional attributes to dogs and automobiles. But if we were someday confronted by a perfected automaton, one that not only imitated our use of grammar but imitated the forms of life in which grammar finds meaning, then our situation would be quite different. We would be perfectly happy to attribute *understanding* to the automaton. Our problem would lie elsewhere. The question of meaning would be wholly subsumed by the question of personhood, which would seem to us perplexingly open. Once we were in such a position, wondering whether the other who seems to require us to treat it as a person is indeed a person, the interesting and difficult questions are no longer questions about mechanism and material realization (see Cavell 1979: 329–407). This is more than enough opening for AI to make its claims to speak about the nature of our grammars and so to speak for the nature of meaning.

Does such a non-compositional theory similarly reshape literary studies? Most literary criticism would be relatively unaffected, although criticism of the formal, semiotic variety may have to reconsider its talk of grammars. Literary theory, on the other hand, would feel the effects at almost every turn. Again, the most direct effects would be in formal theories: current ones are highly compositional and would face major overhauls. The effects would also be felt in the old debates that equate meaning with one or another aspect of meaning—as, for example, when Knapp and Michaels (1982) recently raised a small tempest by reviving that old chestnut, intention, as a stand-in for meaning. But most important and widespread would be the effects on how we understand the place of literature among texts. It is a rare literary theory that does not in one way or another marginalize literature. We like to understand literature as what stands against the norm, as what is not literal, not referential, not mere representation, not really said, and so on. Though strange to say, AI and related studies of understanding language have brought an essential insight to the study of literature because they have brought the study of the non-literary face-to-face with the insuperable difficulties of our attempts to conceive the literal, the referential, the mere representation, the really said. If those conceptions cannot hold in the face of our efforts to find the truth in them, then neither can our conception of a literature on the margins of discourse, science, philosophy. If we have misunderstood literature, it is because we have caricatured and so misunderstood its other. An adequate theory of meaning must, inevitably, make us rethink our theories of literature.

Notes

2. "Figuring the nature of the times deceased": Literary Theory and Historical Writing

1. Jacques Barzun, "The Critic, the Public, the Past," *Salmagundi*, 68–69 (Fall, 1985–Winter, 1986), 206.

2. Paul Veyne writes: "There is no method of history because history makes no demands; so long as one relates true things, it is satisfied. It seeks only truth, in which it is not science, which seeks exactness. It imposes no norms; no rule of the game subtends it, nothing is unacceptable to it. That is the most original characteristic of the historical genre." *Writing History: Essay on Epistemology*, trans. Mina Moore-Rinvolucri (Middletown, 1984), 12.

3. Benedetto Croce, *Primi saggi*, 3rd ed. (Bari, 1951), 38. I have surveyed the debate over the status of narrative in historiography in "The Question of Narrative in Contemporary Historical Theory," *History and Theory*, XXIII, 1 (1984), 1–33. Most of my own work in historiographical theory addresses this question: *Metahistory: The Historical Imagination in the Nineteenth Century* (Baltimore, 1973); *The Tropics of Discourse: Essays in Cultural Criticism* (Baltimore, 1978); and *The Content of the Form: Narrative Discourse and Historical Representation* (Baltimore, 1987). These works constitute the background of this essay, so I will not cite them repeatedly.

4. Cfr. Christopher Norris, "Narrative Theory or Theory-as-Narrative: the Politics of 'Post-Modern' Reason," in *The Contest of Faculties: Philosophy and Theory after Deconstruction* (London and New York, 1985), Ch. 1.

5. I tried to deal with this issue in an essay,, "The Problem of Style in Realistic Representation: Marx and Flaubert," in *The Concept of Style*, ed. Berel Lang (Philadelphia, 1979), 213–29. But see now Stephen Bann's brilliant *The Clothing of Clio: A Study of the Representation of History in Nineteenth-Century Britain and France* (Cambridge, 1984), and Linda Orr's superb review of it in *History and Theory*, XXIV, 3 (1985), 307–25.

6. The best summary of the importance of the work of these philosophers for theory of the historical text is F. R. Ankersmit's "The Dilemma of Contemporary Anglo-Saxon Philosophy of History," which serves as an introduction to *History and Theory*, Beiheft 23 (1986). Professor Ankersmit kindly sent me a copy of the manuscript of his article, which should be in print by the time my essay appears. Meanwhile, readers can profit from study of Ankersmit's *Narrative Logic: A Semantic Analysis of the Historian's Language* (The Hague, Boston, London, 1983), which places the discussion of historical narrative on a ground quite new and different from all previous discussions.

7. Prior to the early nineteenth century, historiography was regarded as a branch of oratorical discourse and a proper subject of the theory of rhetoric. It was, however, disengaged from rhetoric in the course of the nineteenth century as a result of the movement to render historical studies more scientific. The twofold attack on rhetoric, from Romantic poetics, on the one side, and Positivist philosophy, on the other, led to the general disparagement of rhetoric throughout Western high culture. "Literature" supplanted oratorical discourse as the practice of "writing" and "philology" supplanted rhetoric as the general science of language. The theoretical problem of historical writing then became the specification of history's relation to "literature," but since literature was commonly thought to be a mysterious product of "poetic creativity," no solution of the problem was possible. As for history's relation to philology, it was generally acknowledged that philology was simply "the historical method" applied to the study of linguistic phenomena. But since "the historical method" was in turn regarded as simply "the philological method" applied to the study of the historical (documentary) record, the problem of method remained locked within a tautological circle from which there was no exit. See my essay, "Rhetoric

and History," in Hayden White and Frank E. Manuel, *Theories of History: Clark Memorial Library Papers* (Los Angeles, 1978); and Lionel Gossman, "History and Literature: Reproduction or Signification," in *The Writing of History: Literary Form and Historical Understanding*, eds. Robert H. Canary and Henry Kozicki (Madison, 1978). For an exposé of "philology" as pseudo-science, see Hans Aarsleff, *From Locke to Saussure: Essays on the Study of Language and Intellectual History* (Minneapolis, 1982), 278–92. For a typical example of the way historiography was dealt with in eighteenth century rhetoric, see the shrewd observations of the unfairly maligned Hugh Blair, *Lectures in Rhetoric and Belles-Lettres* [1783] (Carbondale and Edwardsville, 1965), II, 246–89.

8. F. R. Ankersmit, "The Dilemma of Contemporary Anglo-Saxon Philosophy of History," in *Knowing and Telling History: The Anglo-Saxon Debate*, ed. F. R. Ankersmit, Beiheft 25: *History and Theory* (Middletown, 1986), 19.

9. E. H. Gombrich, *Art and Illusion: A Study in the Psychology of Pictorial Representation* (London and New York, 1960), *passim*. Cfr. my essay, "The Culture of Criticism," in *Liberations: New Essays on the Humanities in Revolution*, ed. Ihab Hassan (Middletown, 1971), Ch. 4.

10. I discuss Ricoeur's theories in "The Metaphysics of Narrativity: Time and Symbol in Ricoeur's Philosophy of History," in my book, *The Content of the Form*. This is a revision and expansion of a review of Ricoeur's *Time and Narrative*, originally published as "The Rule of Narrativity: Symbolic Discourse and the Experiences of Time in Ricoeur's Thought," in *À la recherche du sens/In Search of Meaning*, ed. Theodore-F. Geraets (Ottawa, 1985), 287–99.

11. Ankersmit, "Dilemma of Contemporary Anglo-Saxon Philosophy of History," 20.

12. Ankersmit, "Dilemma of Contemporary Anglo-Saxon Philosophy of History," 25.

13. Roland Barthes, *The Fashion System*, trans. Matthew Ward and Richard Howard (New York, 1983), 230–32.

14. Paul Ricoeur, *Time and Narrative*, trans. Kathleen McLaughlin and David Pellauer (Chicago, 1984), II, 208–25.

15. I follow Valesio's lead in trying to establish the usage of "rhetorics" as indicating the theoretical study of discourse, by analogy with "poetics" as indicating the theoretical study of poetry. See Paolo Valesio, *Novantiqua: Rhetorics as a Contemporary Theory* (Bloomington, 1980), Ch. 1.

16. But our tropology is useful for the analysis, not only of non-formalized discourses, but of formalized ones as well. Formalized discourses are simply those in which lexicons, grammars, and syntaxes have been openly and *systematically*, rather than covertly and unsystematically, tropologized. This is why formalized discourses do not require the same kind of analysis as non-formalized ones. But see the work of the Iowa University group for the study of the rhetoric of the sciences, social and natural. The proceedings of the group's conference on "The Rhetoric of the Human Sciences," March 28-31, 1984, is gradually being published by The University of Wisconsin Press.

17. Some years ago, David Hackett Fischer published a work entitled *Historians' Fallacies: Toward a Logic of Historical Thought* (New York, 1970), which catalogued all the various kinds of fallacies that could be found in historians' discourses, from the most technical to the most speculative. Fischer's aim was to make historians more aware of the technical aspects of argumentation. What he demonstrated was the virtual impossibility of writing a historical discourse without committing a host of logical fallacies. Did that mean that historians' works containing a large number of logical fallacies should be thrown out? Obviously not, what was needed was a rhetorical analysis of such work. The "logic" of historical discourse is "rhetoric."

18. Tropology is the unfinished business of modern, and especially semiotic linguistics. For some theorists, it is a secondary, for others a primary problem of discourse analysis. For Roman Jakobson, Emile Benveniste, Kenneth Burke, Heinrich Lausberg, Harold Bloom, Paul de Man, Jacques Derrida, the *Mu* group of the University of Liège, Chaim Perelman,

Tzvetan Todorov, Roland Barthes, and so on, it was a primary problem. I began with Vico, went on to Nietzsche ("Geschichte der griechischen Beredsamkeit," in *Nietzsche's Werke*, Bd. XVIII, Dritte Abteilung. Bd. II. *Philologica*, herausgegeben von Otto Crusius. [Leipzig, 1912], 201–67), thence to Kenneth Burke (especially *The Grammar of Motives* [Berkeley and Los Angeles, 1969], Appendix D, "Four Master Tropes," 503–19), and from there to the authors mentioned in the preceding sentence. Traditional rhetorical theory deriving from the classical period tends to view tropology as the theory of figures of speech and thought, whereas the authors I cite view it as the basis for a theory of discourse. Crucial to anyone interested in the psychological basis of tropology is Sigmund Freud's essay on primary process thought in "The Dreamwork," Chapter VI of *The Interpretation of Dreams*. Here Freud reinvents the tropes in the form of the four mechanisms he identifies as operative in the transformation of the dream thoughts into the contents of the dream: condensation, displacement, symbolization, and secondary revision.

19.   This is argued at length in my *Metahistory* and *Tropics of Discourse*. Many critics do not like this argument. Cfr. Ricoeur, *Time and Narrative*, I, 161–68; and Sande Cohen, *Historical Culture: On the Recoding of an Academic Discipline* (Berkeley and Los Angeles, 1986), 81.

20.   Arnaldo Momigliano, "La retorica della storia e la storia della retorica," *Sui fondamenti della storia antica* (Torino, 1984), 466. This is a critique of my work, basically hostile but fair. I forebear analyzing the rhetoric of Momigliano's own discourse, but if I were to do so I might begin with the title of this essay.

21.   Momigliano, "La retorica della storia."

22.   Gene H. Bell-Villada, "Criticism and the State (Political and Otherwise) of the Americas," in *Criticism in the University: Triquarterly Series on Criticism and Culture*, no. 1 (Evanston, 1985), 143.

23.   See note 3 above.

24.   On the functions of the speech situation, see Roman Jakobson, "Closing Statement: Linguistics and Poetics," in *Style in Language*, ed. Thomas A. Sebeok (Cambridge, 1978), 350–58.

25.   Roland Barthes, "Le discours de l'histoire" and "L'effet de réel," in *Le bruissement de la langue* (Paris, 1984), 153–74.

26.   This debate has been fully surveyed by Ricoeur, *Time and Narrative*, I, Ch. 4, but see Ankersmit, "Dilemma of Contemporary Anglo-Saxon Philosophy of History."

27.   See Barthes, "Le discours de l'histoire" and "L'effet de réel"; Julia Kristeva, "The Novel as Polylogue," in *Desire in Language: A Semiotic Approach to Literature and Art*, trans. Thomas Gora, Alice Jardine, and Leon S. Roudiez (New York, 1980), Ch. 7; Jean-François Lyotard, *The Postmodern Condition: A Report on Knowledge*, trans. Geoff Bennington and Brian Massumi (Minneapolis, 1984); Jacques Derrida, "The Law of Genre," *Critical Inquiry*, 7, 1 (Autumn, 1980), pp. 55–82; Cohen, *Historical Culture*, Intro., Ch. 1, Conclusion. The whole question of narrative in historical writing is discussed in Pietro Rossi, ed., *La teoria della storiografia oggi* (Milano, 1983), with contributions by Arthur C. Danto, Mommsen, Furet, Kosseleck, Dray, Winch, *et alia*. See also the provocative study by Jean Pierre Faye, *Theorie du récit: Introduction aux "langages totalitaires"* (Paris, 1972).

28.   Laurence Stone, "The Revival of Narrative: Reflections on the Old New History," *Past and Present*, 5 (November, 1979), 3–24; James Henretta, "Social History as Lived and Written," *American Historical Review*, 84 (1979), 1293–1322; Bernard Bailyn, "The Challenge of Modern Historiography," *American Historical Review*, 87 (1982), 1–24; Emmanuel Leroy Ladurie, *The Territory of the Historian*, trans. Ben and Sian Reynolds (Chicago, 1979), 111ff.; and Dominick LaCapra, *History and Criticism* (Ithaca and London, 1985), Ch. 1. It should be said that LaCapra's book is more of a defense of rhetorical historiography than of narrative historiography per se.

29.   See Fredric Jameson, "Foreword" to Lyotard, *The Postmodern Condition*, xi. Jameson's *The Political Unconscious: Narrative as a Socially Symbolic Act* (Ithaca, 1981), is an extended, sustained, and powerful defense of this view.

414 • *Notes*

30. See Christopher Norris, "Philosophy as a Kind of Narrative: Rorty on Postmodern Liberal Culture, in *The Contest of Faculties*.

31. "I take temporality to be that structure of existence that reaches language in narrativity and narrativity to be the language structure that has temporality as its ultimate referent. Their relationship is therefore reciprocal." Paul Ricoeur, "Narrative Time," *Critical Inquiry*, 7, 1 (Autumn, 1980), 169.

32. I regret not being able to develop this notion at greater length on this occasion. If I had the space, I would argue something like the following: it is generally agreed that historical narrative produces knowledge-as-understanding by what W.H. Walsh, as early as 1951, called "colligation." See his *Philosophy of History: An Introduction* (Harper: New York, 1960), 59–66. The late Louis O. Mink picked up this notion and developed it in his conception of the "configurational" mode of thinking which he identifies with historical understanding (in contrast to the "theoretical" and "categoreal" modes). See especially Mink's "History and Fiction as Modes of Comprehension," *New Literary History*, 1, 3 (Spring 1970), 541–58. Ricoeur uses the notion of "configuration" as the centerpiece of his argument about narrative as "emplotment" in both historiography and fictional writing. See *Time and Narrative*, 1, Ch. 2; and Volume II of this work, subtitled "The Configuration of Time in Fictional Narrative." As analyzed by these theorists, the operations of "colligation" and "configuration" (and Ricoeur's "emplotment") appear to be exactly what is involved in "synecdoche," i.e., the tropological act of "grasping together." Of course, the relation of synecdoche to symbolization is manifest: you can only "grasp together" what has already been "thrown together." On the figure of synecdoche, see Heinrich Lausberg, *Handbuch der literarischen Rhetorik* (Munich, 1960), Sections 572–77.

33. The classic formulation is by Erich Auerbach, *Mimesis: The Representation of Reality in Western Literature*, trans. Willard R. Trask (Princeton, 1968), Chs. 17–18. All of Georg Lukács's work on realism in nineteenth-century literature carries the same theme, but for a brief handling in connection with narrative, see his "Narrate or Describe?" in *Writer and Critic and Other Essays*, trans. Arthur D. Kahn (New York, 1971), 110–48. Fredric Jameson develops further the Lukácsian indictment in *The Political Unconscious*, wherein modernism is interpreted as a phase in the development of realism in which "history" is repressed. On the topic of realism in modern criticism, cfr. René Wellek, "The Concept of Realism in Literary Scholarship," in *Concepts of Criticism* (New Haven and London, 1967), 222–55.

34. This is the explicit theme in Fredric Jameson's *Fables of Aggression: Wyndham Lewis, the Modernist as Fascist* (Berkeley, Los Angeles, London, 1979).

35. There is a massive literature on the subject, but the whole development both of historicism and the debate over it are surveyed authoritatively by Georg Iggers, *The German Conception of History: The National Tradition of Historical Thought from Herder to the Present* (Middletown, 1968).

36. Roland Barthes, "Jeunes chercheurs," *Communications*, 19 (1972), 1–5.

37. Barthes, "Le discours de l'histoire," 166.

3. Historical Worlds, Literary History

1. For a review of the issues, see Harold Berman, *Law and Revolution: The Formation of the Western Legal Tradition* (Cambridge, Mass., 1983).

2. E.R. Curtius, "The Medieval Bases of Western Thought," a lecture delivered on 3 July 1949 in Aspen, Colorado, reprinted in *European Literature and the Latin Middle Ages*, trans. W.R. Trask (New York and Evanston, 1953), 585ff. This statement is on p. 587.

3. On this question, see Günther Roth and Wolfgang Schluchter, *Max Weber's Vision of History: Ethics and Methods* (Berkeley, Los Angeles, and London, 1979), ch. V: "Duration and Rationalization: Fernand Braudel and Max Weber," pp. 166ff.

4. Hugh of St. Victor, *Didascalicon de Studio Legendi*, lib. II, cap. XXX, ed. C.H. Buttimer (Washington, D.C., 1939), 46–47.

5. On this question, see the highly suggestive remarks of Judson Allen, *The Ethical Poetic of the Later Middle Ages* (Toronto, Buffalo, and London, 1982), 3–66.

6. Huizinga's title literally means something like autumntide harvest, not "waning." The *Ergänzungsband* to Kantorowicz was published in Berlin in 1931. Only volume one was translated into English: *Frederick the Second 1194–1250*, trans. E.O. Lorimer (London: Constable, 1931).

7. Sir Richard Southern, "Aspects of the European Tradition of Historical Writing . . .," *Transactions of the Royal Historical Society*, 5th Series 20 (1970), 175.

8. See, in general, Paul A. Kolers, "Three Stages of Reading," in H. Levin and J.P. Williams, eds., *Basic Studies on Reading* (New York, 1970). For recent statements of research trends in a large literature, see two papers from Rand J. Spiro, Bertram C. Bruce, and William F. Brewer, eds., *Theoretical Issues in Reading Comprehension* (Hillsdale, N.J., 1980): Rand J. Spiro, "Constructive Processes in Prose Comprehension and Recall," 245–77, and David E. Rumelhart, "Schemata: the Building Blocks of Cognition," 33–58, dealing respectively with the minimal and maximal elements of text comprehension.

9. I review them briefly; for a more extensive discussion, see my study, *The Implications of Literacy* (Princeton, 1983), chs. 2 and 3.

10. For a recent review of the issues, see Giles Constable, "Forgery and Plagiarism in the Middle Ages," *Archiv für Diplomatik Schriftgeschichte Siegel-und Wappenkunde* 29 (1983), 1–41.

11. See Nelson Goodman, *Ways of Worldmaking* (Indianapolis and Cambridge, Mass., 1978) and *Of Mind and Other Matters* (Cambridge, Mass., 1986).

12. For a statement of similar views without historical considerations, see Donald Davidson, "On the Very Idea of a Conceptual Scheme," in *Inquiries into Truth and Interpretation* (Oxford, 1984), 183–98.

13. Alfred Tarski, "The Semantic Conception of Truth," in L. Linsky, ed., *Semantics and the Philosophy of Language* (Urbana, 1952), 341ff.

14. For a review of major issues, see Paul Saenger, "Silent Reading: Its Impact on Late Medieval Script and Society," *Viator* 13 (1982), 367–414.

15. On these distinctions, see Endel Tulving, "Episodic and Semantic Memory," in E. Tulving and W. Donaldson, eds., *Organization of Memory* (New York, 1972), ch. 10, as well as Tulving's reconsideration of his position in his "Memory and Consciousness," *Canadian Psychology* 26 (1985), 1–12.

16. See Haijo Jan Westra, "Jauss and Adorno: Beyond the Negative Aesthetic," *Vanguard* (October, 1985), 19–20.

17. For an analysis of this problem, see George A. Lindbeck, *The Nature of Doctrine: Religion and Theology in a Postliberal Age* (Philadelphia, 1984).

18. See, for instance, Jürgen Habermas, *The Theory of Communicative Action*, vol. 1, trans. T. McCarthy (Boston, 1984), 143–271.

19. For a review of the issues, see Werner Kelber, *The Oral and Written Gospel: The Hermeneutics of Speaking and Writing in the Synoptic Tradition, Mark, Paul, and Q.* (Philadelphia, 1983); and, on the Hebrew Bible, see now Jacob Neusner, *The Oral Torah, The Sacred Books of Judaism: An Introduction* (New York, 1986).

4. Perceptive Equilibrium: Literary Theory and Ethical Theory

1. All page references to *The Ambassadors* are to the Everyman's Library edition (London and New York, 1971). The epigraph is from p. 29.

2. Throughout this paper, I tend to use the term "ethical theory" rather than "moral theory," since the former does not imply a division of human values into two distinct groups, the moral and the non-moral. On this division and some reasons for rejecting it,

see Bernard Williams, *Ethics and the Limits of Philosophy* (Cambridge, MA, 1985), and my *The Fragility of Goodness: Luck and Ethics in Greek Tragedy and Philosophy* (Cambridge, 1986), chs. 1 and 2. I use the term "moral philosophy" here simply because no corresponding term "ethical philosophy" is in use (as both "ethical theory" and "moral theory" are). My use of the distinction between "ethical theory" and "moral philosophy" is closely related to Rawls's use of the distinction between "moral theory" and "moral philosophy" (in John Rawls, *A Theory of Justice* (Cambridge, MA, 1971), 46 ff.: "moral philosophy" is a general and inclusive rubric covering, in principle, many different types of ethical investigations, of which one sort will be the theoretical study of substantive ethical positions, or ethical (moral) theory. A consequence of this distinction for my project is that an ethical investigation that is not systematic and theoretical, and therefore not "ethical theory," might still lie within "moral philosophy." It was with this broad understanding of "moral philosophy" that I argued (in "Flawed Crystals: James's *The Golden Bowl* and Literature as Moral Philosophy," NLH 15 [1983], 24–50) that certain works of literature are part of moral philosophy.

3. This view is effectively criticized in Arthur Danto, "Philosophy As/And/Of Literature," *Proceedings and Addresses of the American Philosophical Association* 58 (1984), 5–20, and in Anthony Cascardi, ed., *Literature and the Question of Philosophy* (Baltimore, 1987).

4. Jacques Derrida, *Spurs: Nietzsche's Styles*, trans. Barbara Harlow (Chicago, 1979).

5. Friedrich Nietzsche, *Thus Spoke Zarathustra*, trans. Walter Kaufmann (New York, 1966), Part I, "On Reading and Writing."

6. Feminist criticism and Marxist criticism are major exceptions, clearly. But they are, in their difference from and frequent opposition to what surrounds them, exceptions that prove the rule. For a recent example of Marxist criticism dealing subtly with Henry James, among others, see E. Ahearn, *Anatomies of Civil Society: Marx and Modern Fiction* (New Haven, 1989 forthcoming).

7. Cf. Danto, "Philosophy As" (above n. 3).

8. See Nussbaum, *The Fragility of Goodness* (above n. 2), Interlude 2; also Hilary Putnam, "Literature, Science, and Reflection," in Putnam, *Meaning and the Moral Sciences* (London, 1979), 83–96.

9. On this see Nussbaum, "The Discernment of Perception: An Aristotelian Conception of Private and Public Rationality," *Proceedings of the Boston Area Colloquium in Ancient Philosophy* 1 (1985), 151–201.

10. I think first of F. R. Leavis and Lionel Trilling. More recently, one might think, for example, of Peter Brooks, *Reading for the Plot* (New York, 1984); of Martin Price, *Forms of Life* (New Haven, 1983).

11. Compare my sketch of a moral inquiry in "Flawed Crystals" (above n. 2), and also in *Fragility*, chs. 1 and 8. See also Cora Diamond, "Having a Rough Story about What Moral Philosophy is," *NLH* 15 (1983), 155–70.

12. On this question and its relation to the moral/non-moral distinction, see Williams, *Ethics* (above n. 2), and Nussbaum, *Fragility*, ch. 1.

13. Henry James, Preface to *The Princess Casamassima*.

14. I discuss this further in "Therapeutic Arguments: Epicurus and Aristotle," in *The Norms of Nature*, ed. M. Schofield and G. Striker (Cambridge, 1986), 31–74, and also in *The Therapy of Desire: Theory and Practice in Hellenistic Ethics*, The Martin Classical Lectures, forthcoming.

15. Rawls, *A Theory*, pp. 46 ff. (Rawls's discussion refers both to Aristotle and to Sidgwick's *The Methods of Ethics* [1907].)

16. Cf. Nussbaum, *Fragility*, ch. 8, and "The Discernment of Perception"; also Rawls, *A Theory*, pp. 46 ff.

17. Cf. Rawls, *A Theory*, pp. 46 ff; also the excellent discussion of Rawls's method in Henry Richardson, *Deliberation is of Ends*, Harvard Ph.D. Thesis 1986, ch. 4 ("Aristotelian Reflective Equilibrium").

18.   Rawls, *A Theory*, pp. 46–53, 130–35; see also Rawls's Dewey Lectures, "Kantian Constructivism in Ethical Theory," *Journal of Philosophy* 77 (September 1980).

19.   This is not explicitly stated by Rawls, but is implied in his discussion; it is argued convincingly by Richardson, in a way that seems to have met with Rawls's agreement.

20.   Rawls, *A Theory*, p. 47.

21.   Rawls, *A Theory*, pp. 47–48.

22.   Rawls, *A Theory*, p. 135. Since this discussion is not part of the discussion of reflective equilibrium, there is some unclarity as to whether it is supposed to be a part of the general method that we use to consider all theories, or whether it is to be understood as a part of the specific account of the moral point of view that is contained in the (Kantian) original position. But since its restrictions are said to "hold for the choice of all ethical principles and not only for those of justice" (130), and since they govern the choice of the theories that the parties are even permitted to consider, it seems likely that Rawls regards them as reasonable moral constraints to impose upon all practical reasoning, not only the reasoning of the specifically Kantian conception. (There is in any case some difficulty in disentangling these two levels of Rawls's project, since even the account of "considered judgments" that is explicitly made a part of the general method that we use to consider all alternative conceptions—and which should therefore be fair not only to the Kantian conception but to its rivals as well—has strong affinities with Kantianism. This problem is further discussed in the Dewey Lectures.

23.   Aristotle, *Nicomachean Ethics* 1109b18–23, 1126b2–4; see also Nussbaum, "The Discernment of Perception."

24.   The figure in the dream is actually identified as Sarah Pocock; but she figures, here, as Mrs. Newsome's ambassador.

25.   See Nussbaum, " 'Finely Aware and Richly Responsible': Moral Attention and the Moral Task of Literature," *Journal of Philosophy* 82 (1985, 516–29, in a longer version in Anthony Cascardi, ed., *Literature and the Question of Philosophy* (Baltimore: Johns Hopkins University Press, 1987). At the original American Philosophical Association symposium where I presented this paper, I had the benefit of excellent comments by Cora Diamond, entitled "Missing the Adventure," which have shaped my views on these questions.

26.   The charge that the view has no standards was forcefully made (against the Jamesian view in my "Flawed Crystals") by Hilary Putnam, in his "Taking Rules Seriously: a Response to Martha Nussbaum," *NLH* 15 (1983), 193–200. I try to answer it in "Reply to Gardiner, Wollheim, and Putnam," *NLH* 15 (1983), 201–8, and at greater length in my " 'Finely Aware' " and in "The Discernment of Perception."

27.   Cf. Nussbaum, "The Discernment," " 'Finely Aware.' "

28.   Richardson, *Deliberation* (above n. 17). I am very grateful to Richardson for discussion of these issues.

29.   Cf. Nussbaum, "The Discernment."

30.   Cf. James, *The Ambassadors*, pp. 118, 126, 147.

31.   Cf. *Ambassadors*, also p. 124: "Our poor friend, conscious and passive . . ."

32.   *Ambassadors*, p. 4; the description of Strether that follows is the result of this vision.

33.   The negative reference to dramatic writing encourages, clearly, our connection of Strether with Henry James himself.

34.   There is a fine account of the novel's style by Ian Watt, "The First Paragraph of *The Ambassadors*: an Explication," *Essays in Criticism* 10 (1960), 254–68; a revised version appears in *The Ambassadors*, Norton Critical Edition, ed. S. P. Rosenbaum, 468–81, and in *Twentieth Century Interpretations of The Ambassadors*, ed. A. E. Stone, Jr. (Englewood Cliffs, N.J., 1969), 75–87.

35.   The phrase is used by James in the Preface to *Portrait of a Lady*—see Henry James, *The Art of the Novel* (New York, 1934), 45.

36. For some elements in that contrast, see Nussbaum, "The Discernment," and also Nussbaum, "Plato on Commensurability and Desire" (*Proceedings of the Aristotelian Society, Supplementary Volume* 58 [1984], 55–80).

37. On this, see Nussbaum, "Therapeutic Arguments."

38. These aspects of the novel are well discussed by Philip Weinstein in *Henry James and the Requirements of the Imagination* (Cambridge, MA, 1971), 121–64.

39. This passage, and others using the word "life," are well discussed in Joan Bennett, "The Art of Henry James: *The Ambassadors*," *Chicago Review* 9 (1956), 16–26, reprinted in Stone, ed., *Twentieth Century Interpretations*.

40. From a letter quoted in Leon Edel, *Henry James: The Untried Years* (New York, 1953), 49.

41. I am thinking particularly of the essay "The Moral Philosopher and the Moral Life," in William James, *Essays on Faith and Morals* (New York, 1962), 184–215.

42. F.R. Leavis, *The Great Tradition* (New York, 1973), 154–72.

43. Lionel Trilling, *The Liberal Imagination: Essays on Literature and Society* (New York, 1940), especially the essays "The Princess Casamassima" and "Manners, Morals, and the Novel," and "The Meaning of a Literary Idea."

44. James, *The Art of the Novel*, 223–24.

45. This paper was first read at the conference on Virtue and Agency at Santa Clara University, February 1987. I am grateful to the members of the Philosophy Department there for the invitation, to David Fisher for stimulating written comments, and to the audience for questions. I am also very grateful to Paul Seabright and Amartya Sen, whose questions and comments led to numerous revisions, as did questions from audiences at York University, Oxford University, Yale University, and the Rhode Island Humanities Forum.

5. The State of the Art of Criticism

1. For some reflections on the rise and impact of propaganda, see my "From Common to Uncommon Reader: Theory and Critical Style," in *Révue Internationale de Philosophie: Philosophical Aspects of Literary Criticism*, 41, pp. 398–413.

2. The paragraph from I. A. Richards's *Coleridge on Imagination* continues as follows: "It guides us in our metaphorical, allegorical, symbolical modes of interpretation. The hierarchy of these modes is elaborate and variable; and to read aright we need to shift with an at present indescribable adroitness and celerity from one mode to another. Our sixteenth- and seventeenth-century literature, supported by practice in listening to sermons and by conventions in speech and letter-writing which made 'direct' statement rare to a point which seems to us unnatural, gave an extraordinary training in this skill. But it was skill merely; it was not followed up by theory. . . ."

3. Richards quotes Coleridge's praise of "Shakespeare's time, when the English Court was still foster-mother of the State and the Muses; and when, in consequence, the courtiers and men of rank and fashion affected a display of wit, point and sententious observation, that would be deemed intolerable at present—but which a hundred years of controversy, involving every great political, and every dear domestic interest had trained all but the lowest classes to participate. Add to this the very style of the sermons of the time, and the eagerness of the Protestants to distinguish themselves by long and frequent preaching, and it will be found that, from the reign of Henry VIII to the abdication of James II, no country ever received such a national education as England." See *Coleridge on Imagination*.

4. See my "Tea and Totality" in *After Strange Texts: The Role of Theory in the Study of Literature*, eds. G. S. Jay and D. L. Miller for a fuller account. Stanley Cavell prefaces his *Themes out of School* (subtitled "Effects and Causes") with a defense of the causerie that modifies "causes" by the idea of the casual (topical) conversation and even the ungenteel

shmooz. He reinstitutes a tension between origin and occasion, between the formal or scientific discourse on origins (causes) and the idling power of the occasional essay. Richard Rorty, in a similar revolt against the truth claims of his profession, also prefers the idea of philosophy as a conversation. The rediscovery that there is a question of style in philosophy brings about a conversational anti-style (with a Jamesian formality in Cavell), and shows that philosophy and literary studies, as professions, are running parallel yet out of sync with each other.

5. "Sexless" is puzzling. It describes more, surely, than the cry's indeterminate gender. Does the indeterminacy suggest a dehumanizing erosion of gender difference? Or does "sexless" imply (despite Woolf's dislike of D. H. Lawrence) a Lawrentian critique? Lawrence's till recently unpublished *Mr. Noon*, written in the 1920s, uses authorial intrusions to mock the "Gentle reader, gentille lecteuse" tradition and its desexualized "dummy" values. Indeed, Lawrence prefers to address the woman reader as more capable of removing false sublimations. "The sterner sex either sucks away at its dummy with such perfect innocent complacency, or else howls with such perfectly pitiful abandon after the lost dummy, that I won't really address the darling any more." Woolf's "usual terrible sexless . . . cry" evokes the world of the prostitute, curiously if powerfully intruding on virginal and majestic Sasha. One is made to feel that both worlds are sexless, but that, if anything, the dutiful chatter which Sasha tolerates and even abets is more sadly empty.

6. The Function of Literary Theory at the Present Time

1. Paul de Man, *Allegories of Reading* (New Haven and London: Yale University Press, 1979), pp. 16–17, henceforth AR. This essay was written before the discovery of the wartime writings of Paul de Man, and the subsequent flood of essays in the mass media and elsewhere, about them. I have written elsewhere about de Man's early writings, but will say here that I remain as convinced as when I wrote this essay that de Man's later writings are indispensable to present-day study of literature.

2. See Walter Jackson Bate, "The Crisis in English Studies," *Harvard Magazine*, 85, No. 12 (1982), 46–53. For a forceful response see Paul de Man, "The Return to Philology," *The Times Literary Supplement*, No. 4,158 (Friday, December 10, 1982), 1355–56. This essay is now collected in de Man's *The Resistance to Theory* (Minneapolis: University of Minnesota Press, 1986).

3. Paul de Man, "The Resistance to Theory." First published in *Yale French Studies*, 63 (1982), 3–20, henceforth RT. Now available as the title essay of the book by de Man listed in footnote two above.

4. Jacques Derrida, "Deconstruction in America," *Critical Exchange*, no. 17 (Winter, 1985), 1–33.

5. This is discussed in de Man's "The Return to Philology." See footnote two above.

6. Though Jonathan Culler and I might conceivably disagree a bit about exactly what it means to teach good reading, I take heart from his substantial agreement with what I am saying here. Here are some sentences from a forthcoming essay by him entitled "The Future of Criticism," which I have just encountered as I have been typing up my own essay:

> But when one thinks about the future of our multi-lingual, multi-racial society, one finds it hard seriously to imagine the establishment of a common culture based on the Greeks or other classics. Such common culture as we have will inevitably be based on the mass media—especially films and television. Schools will not counter this culture effectively by requiring the study of particular historical artifacts, seeking to impose a canon. The struggle against the debilitating effects of mass culture must take place on a different front: by teaching critical thinking, perhaps by analyzing the ideological stakes and structures of mass media productions and exposing the interests at work in their functioning. Argument about what literary works and what historical knowledge to require will only distract attention from the pressing problem of how to insure that schools

encourage intellectual activity, teach critical thinking, close reading, analysis of narrative structures and semiotic mechanisms.

Framing the Sign: Criticism and Its Institutions (Norman, Oklahoma: University of Oklahoma Press, 1988.

8. Woolf's Room, Our Project: The Building of Feminist Criticism

1. Virginia Woolf, *A Room of One's Own* (New York: Harcourt, Brace and World, Harbinger Book, 1929, 1957). Hereafter cited in the text by page number. The best account of Woolf's influence on feminist critics is Jane Marcus, "Still Practice, A/Wrested Alphabet: Toward A Feminist Aesthetic," *Tulsa Studies in Women's Literature*, 3, 1/2 (Spring/Fall 1984), 79–97. For other citations that reveal the range of Woolf's appeal, see Lillian S. Robinson, "Who's Afraid of *A Room of One's Own*?," *The Politics of Literature: Dissenting Essays on the Teaching of English*, ed. Louis Kampf and Paul Lauter (New York: Pantheon, 1972; Vintage, 1973), pp. 354–411; Sheila Delaney, "A city, a room: the scene of writing in Christine de Pisan and Virginia Woolf," *Writing Woman* (New York: Schocken Books, 1983), pp. 181–97; Teresa de Lauretis, *Alice Doesn't: Feminism, Semiotics, Cinema* (Bloomington, Indiana: Indiana University Press, 1984), p. 158; Mary Jacobus, *Reading Woman: Essays in Feminist Criticism* (New York: Columbia University Press, 1986), pp. 27–40; Elizabeth Abel, *Virginia Woolf and the Fictions of Psychoanalysis* (Chicago: University of Chicago Press, forthcoming), Chap. 5.

Making A Difference: Feminist Literary Criticism, ed. Gayle Greene and Coppélia Kahn (London and New York: Methuen, 1985), and *The New Feminist Criticism*, ed. Elaine Showalter (New York: Pantheon, 1985) survey current feminist criticism, especially in the West.

2. Virginia Woolf, *The Diary of Virginia Woolf*, Vol. III, 1925–1930, ed. Anne Olivier Bell (New York: Harcourt Brace Jovanovich, 1980), p. 200. Hereafter cited in the text by page number.

3. See Martha Vicinus, *Independent Women: Work and Community for Single Women 1850–1920* (Chicago: University of Chicago Press, 1985), pp. 247–80.

4. This is the move Myra Jehlen advocates in the influential "Archimedes and the Paradox of Feminist Criticism," first published in *Signs: Journal of Women in Culture and Society*, 6, 4 (Summer 1981), 575–601. Ellen Messer-Davidow advances a similar argument in "The Philosophical Bases of Feminist Literary Criticism," a superb survey in *New Literary History* XIX (1987–88) pp. 63–103. Cora Kaplan, "Pandora's box: subjectivity, class and sexuality in socialist feminist criticism," *Making A Difference*, pp. 146–76, reconciles two strains of seeing/acting within feminist criticism: socialist feminist theory, concerned with social and economic processes, and liberal humanist theory, concerned with the "self," with psychological autonomy, desires, feelings. Kaplan has shaped my comments on Mary Wollstonecraft and Virginia Woolf.

5. I quote and paraphrase Rosalind E. Krauss, "Poststructuralism and the Paraliterary," *The Originality of the Avant-Garde and Other Modernist Myths* (Cambridge: MIT Press, 1985), pp. 292–93.

6. Isobel Grundy, " 'Words Without Meaning—Wonderful Words': Virginia Woolf's Choice of Names," *Virginia Woolf: New Critical Essays*, ed. Patricia Clements and Isobel Grundy (London: Vision Press and Barnes and Noble Books, 1983), 215–16, discusses the importance of these names. She points out that Woolf leaves unmentioned the fourth Mary of the ballad, the narrator herself, Mary Hamilton, about to be hung for the murder of the baby "who resulted from her seduction by the king." This absent, but present, Mary is, like Judith Shakespeare, a figure of female suffering. See, too, Susan Gubar, "The Birth of the Artist as Heroine," *The Representation of Women in Fiction: Selected Papers from The English Institute*, ed. Carolyn G. Heilbrun and Margaret R. Higonnet (Baltimore: Johns Hopkins University Press, 1983), pp. 20–21.

7. Woolf anticipates Judith Fetterley's formulation of the "resisting reader" and Jonathan Culler's question, "How does one read as a woman?" For Culler, this is a theoretical

vantage point; a biological fact that experience has privileged; and a reminder of the construction of identity, including that of the reader (*On Deconstruction: Theory and Criticism after Structuralism* [Ithaca, New York: Cornell University Press, 1982, paper 1983], pp. 43–64). *Gender and Reading: Essays on Readers, Texts, and Contexts*, ed. Elizabeth A. Flynn and Patrocinio P. Schweickart (Baltimore: Johns Hopkins University Press, 1986), is the best inquiry into the theory and practice of women readers.

8. I have discussed this in my essay, "Feminism and Feminist Criticism," *Massachusetts Review*, 24, 2 (Summer 1983), 272–88.

9. I adapt the term from Alice A. Jardine, *Gynesis: Configurations of Woman and Modernity* (Cornell: Cornell University Press, 1985), one of the most brilliant examples of the newer study of representations of women.

10. Sandra M. Gilbert and Susan Gubar, *The Norton Anthology of Literature by Women* (New York: W.W. Norton and Co., 1985).

11. For a succinct analysis of some of the difficulties of the Norton anthology, see Marjorie Perloff, "Alternate Feminisms," *Sulfur 14*, V, 2 (1985), 132, 134.

12. Hortense J. Spillers, "Afterword," *Conjuring: Black Women, Fiction, and Literary Tradition*, ed. Marjorie Pryse and Hortense J. Spillers (Bloomington: Indiana University Press, 1985), p. 258. Among the many recent studies are Paula Gunn Allen, *The Sacred Hoop: Recovering the Feminine in American Indian Traditions* (Boston: Beacon Press, 1986); Mary V. Dearborn, *Pocahontas's Daughters: Gender and Ethnicity in American Culture* (New York: Oxford University Press, 1986); Dexter Fisher, ed., *The Third Woman: Minority Women Writers in the United States* (Boston: Houghton Mifflin, 1980); Dianne F. Sadoff, "Black Matrilineage: The Case of Alice Walker and Zora Neale Hurston," *Signs*, 11, 1 (Autumn 1985), 4–26; Marta Ester Sánchez, *Contemporary Chicana Poetry: A Critical Approach to an Emerging Literature* (Berkeley: University of California Press, 1985).

13. Judith Rodriguez, "Nu-Plastik Fanfare Red," *Penguin Book of Australian Verse* (Sydney: Penguin Books, 1972), pp. 428–29.

14. Toril Moi, in *Sexual/Textual Politics* (London and New York: Methuen and Co., 1985), celebrates this Virginia Woolf.

15. An argument for this, which includes but is not limited to feminist criticism, is R. Radhakrishnan, "The Post-Modern Event and the End of Logocentrism," *boundary 2*, 12, 1 (Fall 1983), 33–60. My essay, "Nancy Reagan Wears A Hat," takes up these issues in more detail. Reprinted in my *Where the Meanings Are: Feminism and Cultural Spaces* (New York: Routledge, 1988).

16. Nancy K. Miller, a major feminist critic, fully aware of structuralist and post-structuralist theory, speaks of the need for such resistance. She traces the woman writer staging the drama of subjectivity. However, Miller shows how that drama can take place outside of older, false universals without leading to new universals. In *Feminist Studies/Critical Studies*, ed. Teresa de Lauretis (Bloomington, Indiana: University of Indiana Press, 1986), p. 107.

17. Teresa de Lauretis, ed., *Feminist Studies*, p. 10. Elizabeth A. Meese, *Crossing the Double-Cross: The Practice of Feminist Criticism* (Chapel Hill, North Carolina: University of North Carolina Press, 1986), also seeks connections among post-modern criticism, feminist criticism, and political acts.

18. Rachel Blau DuPlessis, *Writing Beyond the Ending* (Bloomington, Indiana: Indiana University Press, 1985), p. 33.

19. Margaret Homans, *Bearing the Word* (Chicago: University of Chicago Press, 1986). Susan Rubin Suleiman, "Writing and Motherhood," *The (M)other Tongue: Essays in Feminist Psychoanalytic Interpretation*, ed. Shirley Nelson Garner, Claire Kahane, Madelon Sprengnether (Ithaca: Cornell University Press, 1985), pp. 352–77, lucidly surveys the connections among psychoanalysis, the figure of the mother, and writing.

20. I stress Woolf's androgyny more than a clever article that reads *A Room* as a covered

422 • Notes

"... manifesto for female difference." Frances L. Restuccia, " 'Untying the Mother Tongue': Female Difference in Virginia Woolf's *A Room of One"s Own*," *Tulsa Studies in Women's Literature*, 4, 2 (Fall 1985), 253–64.

21. Gayatri Chakravorty Spivak, "Three Women's Texts and a Critique of Imperialism," *Critical Inquiry*, 12, 1 (Autumn 1985), special issue on " 'Race,' Writing, and Difference," ed. Henry Louis Gates, Jr., 243–61. See, too, Chikwenye Okonjo Ogunyemi, "Womanism: The Dynamics of the Contemporary Black Female Novel in English," *Signs*, 11, 1 (Autumn 1985), 63–80. Gilbert and Gubar's Norton anthology reprints three novels: *The Awakening, The Bluest Eye*, and *Jane Eyre*.

22. In his essay, "Freedom of Interpretation: Bakhtin and the Challenge of Feminist Criticism," *Critical Inquiry*, 9, 1 (September 1982), 45–76, Wayne C. Booth connects theories of textual differences with feminist inquiry. Bringing Bakhtin and feminist theory together is more and more common. See, for example, Myriam Diaz-Diocaretz, "Sieving the Matri-heritage of the Sociotext," paper at the conference, *The Differences Within: Feminism and Critical Theory*, University of Alabama, October, 1986. Professors Elizabeth Meese and Alice Parker are editing the event's proceedings.

9. The Mirror and the Vamp: Reflections on Feminist Criticism

1. Christine de Pizan, *The Book of the City of Ladies*, trans. Earl Jeffrey Richards, foreword by Marina Warner (New York: Persea Books, 1982); Mary Astell, *A Serious Proposal to the Ladies*, excerpted in *The Norton Anthology of Literature by Women: The Tradition in English*, ed. Sandra M. Gilbert and Susan Gubar (New York: W.W. Norton, 1985), pp. 113–17; and Virginia Woolf, *Three Guineas* (New York: Harcourt, Brace, Jovanovich, 1938).

2. M.H. Abrams, *The Mirror and the Lamp: Romantic Theory and the Critical Tradition* (1953; New York: W.W. Norton, 1958), pp. 90–91; to be sure, Abrams includes a brief discussion of Mme. de Stael in the book, in which he notes that "Hers is a cloudy and sentimentalized version of the doctrines she had learned from August Schlegel and other early romantic theorists. . . ."

3. Abrams, *The Mirror and the Lamp*, p. 34.

4. Elaine Showalter, "Towards a Feminist Poetics," *Women Writing and Writing About Women*, ed. Mary Jacobus (London: Croom Helm, 1979), p. 25. Showalter has extended this argument in her more recent "Feminist Criticism in the Wilderness," reprinted in *The New Feminist Criticism: Essays on Women, Literature, and Theory*, ed. Elaine Showalter (New York: Pantheon Books, 1985), pp. 243–70.

5. Showalter, "Towards a Feminist Poetics," p. 25.

6. Katherine Rogers, *The Troublesome Helpmate: A History of Misogyny in Literature* (Seattle: University of Washington Press, 1966).

7. Judith Fetterley, *The Resisting Reader: A Feminist Approach to American Literature* (Bloomington: Indiana University Press, 1978), p. xi; Susan Shibanoff, "Taking the Gold Out of Egypt: The Art of Reading as a Woman," *Gender and Reading: Essays on Readers, Texts, and Contexts*, ed. Elizabeth A. Flynn and Patrocinio P. Schweickart (Baltimore and London: The Johns Hopkins University Press, 1986), p. 83–106.

8. See Marilyn French, *Shakespeare's Division of Experience* (New York: Summit Books, 1981); Linda Bamber, *Comic Women, Tragic Men: A Study of Gender and Genre in Shakespeare* (Stanford: Stanford University Press, 1982); Lee Edwards, "Women, Energy and *Middlemarch*," *The Massachusetts Review* 13 (Winter/Spring 1972), 223–54; Suzanne Juhasz, *Naked and Fiery Forms, Modern American Poetry by Women: A New Tradition* (New York: Harper Colophon Books, 1976); and Denise Levertov, *Light Up the Cave* (New York: New Directions, 1981).

9. Carolyn Heilbrun, *Toward a Recognition of Androgyny* (New York: Knopf, 1973); Nina Auerbach, *Communities of Women* (Cambridge, Mass.: Harvard University Press, 1978) and *Woman and the Demon* (Cambridge, Mass.: Harvard University Press, 1982); Suzette Henke,

ed., *Women in Joyce* (Urbana: University of Illinois Press, 1982); and Bonnie Kime Scott, *Joyce and Feminism* (Bloomington: Indiana University Press, 1984).

10. Showalter, "Towards a Feminist Poetics," p. 26.

11. Ellen Moers, *Literary Women* (New York: Doubleday, 1976); Patricia Meyer Spacks, *The Female Imagination* (New York: Alfred A. Knopf, 1975); Elaine Showalter, *A Literature of Their Own* (Princeton: Princeton University Press, 1977); Sandra M. Gilbert and Susan Gubar, *The Madwoman in the Attic* (New Haven: Yale University Press, 1979).

12. Barbara Christian, *Black Women Novelists: The Development of a Tradition, 1892–1976* (Westport, Conn.: Greenwood Press, 1980); and Rachel Blau DuPlessis, *Writing beyond the Ending* (Bloomington: Indiana University Press, 1985).

13. Cheri Register, "American Feminist Literary Criticism: A Bibliographical Introduction," *Feminist Literary Criticism*, ed. Josephine Donovan (Lexington: The University Press of Kentucky), 1975, pp. 18–19.

14. Lillian Faderman, *Surpassing the Love of Men: Romantic Friendship and Love between Women from the Renaissance to the Present* (New York: William Morrow, 1981), p. 321–23.

15. Lillian Robinson, "Treason Our Text," in *The New Feminist Criticism*, p. 110.

16. Nina Baym, *Woman's Fiction: A Guide to Novels by and about Women in America, 1820–1870* (Ithaca: Cornell University Press, 1978), p. 14–15.

17. Jane P. Tompkins, "Sentimental Power: *Uncle Tom's Cabin* and the Politics of Literary History," in *The New Feminist Criticism*, p. 83–84.

18. Nina Baym, "Melodramas of Beset Manhood," in *The New Feminist Criticism*, pp. 63–80.

19. Ann Douglas, *The Feminization of American Culture* (New York: Alfred A. Knopf, 1977). The debate over sentimental fiction is summarized by Mary Kelley in "The Sentimentalists: Promise and Betrayal in the Home," *Signs* 4 (Spring 1979), 434–46.

20. Mary Jacobus, "The Difference of View," in *Women Writing and Writing About Women*, p. 12.

21. Julia Kristeva, *Revolution in Poetic Language*, trans. Margaret Waller, intro. Leon S. Roudiez (New York: Columbia University Press, 1984), p. 29.

22. Luce Irigaray, *This Sex Which Is Not One*, trans. Catherine Porter with Carolyn Burke (Ithaca: Cornell University Press, 1985), p. 29.

23. Toril Moi, *Sexual/Textual Politics: Feminist Literary Theory* (Methuen: London and New York, 1985), p. 126; Peggy Kamuf, "Writing Like A Woman," *Women and Language in Literature and Society*, ed. Sally McConnell-Ginet, Ruth Borker, and Nelly Furman (New York: Praeger Special Studies, 1980), p. 285.

24. Hélène Cixous and Catherine Clément, *The Newly Born Woman*, trans. Betsy Wing, intro. Sandra M. Gilbert (Minneapolis: University of Minnesota Press, 1975), p. 136.

25. Cixous, *The Newly Born Woman*, p. 95.

26. Moi, *Sexual/Textual Politics*, p. 62.

27. Jonathan Culler, *On Deconstruction* (Ithaca: Cornell University Press, 1982), p. 92.

28. Luce Irigaray, *Speculum of the Other Woman*, trans. Gillian C. Gill (Ithaca: Cornell University Press, 1985); Clément, *The Newly Born Woman*, pp. 3–40; Cixous, *The Newly Born Woman*, pp. 68–69; the quote, spoken by Cixous, appears in *The Newly Born Woman*, p. 160.

29. Moi, *Sexual/Textual Politics*, p. 78.

30. For Chinese women, see Julia Kristeva, *About Chinese Women*, trans. Anita Barrows (New York: Urizen Books, 1977); for Shakespeare's Cleopatra, see Cixous, *The Newly Born Woman*, pp. 122–30; for Lewis Carroll's Alice, see Irigaray, "The Looking Glass, from the Other Side," in *This Sex Which Is Not One*; and for Bernini's madonnas, see Kristeva's *Desire*

in Language, trans. Thomas Gora, Alice Jardine, and Leon S. Roudiez (New York: Columbia University Press, 1980).

31. See, for instance, Kristeva, *Revolution in Poetic Language*, pp. 82–83.

32. See Gilbert and Gubar, *The Madwoman in the Attic*, chapters on Austen and Eliot; and Gilbert and Gubar, chapters three and five, "Tradition and the Female Talent," and "Sexual Linguistics," in *No Man's Land: The Place of the Woman Writer in the Twentieth Century*, volume 1, *The War of the Words* (New Haven: Yale University Press, 1987); see also Susan Suleiman, "Pornography, Transgression, and the Avant-Garde: Bataille's 'Story of the Eye'," in *The Poetics of Gender*, ed. Nancy K. Miller (New York: Columbia University Press, 1986), pp. 183–207.

33. Moi, *Sexual/Textual Politics*, p. 126.

34. Moi, *Sexual/Textual Politics*, pp. 172 and 62.

35. Nelly Furman, "The Politics of Language: Beyond the Gender Principle?," *Making a Difference: Feminist Literary Criticism*, ed. Gayle Greene and Coppélia Kahn (London and New York: Methuen, 1985), p. 69.

36. Kamuf, in *Women and Language in Literature and Society*, p. 297.

37. Adrienne Rich, "When We Dead Awaken: Writing as Re-Vision," *Adrienne Rich's Poetry*, ed. Barbara Charlesworth Gelpi and Albert Gelpi (New York: W.W. Norton, 1975), p. 94.

38. Kristeva, *Revolution in Poetic Language*, p. 79; Irigaray, *This Sex Which Is Not One*, p. 29; Roland Barthes, "The Death of the Author," *Image Music Text*, ed. Stephen Heath (New York: Hill and Wang, 1977), p. 147.

39. Leon S. Roudiez, "Introduction," in Kristeva, *Revolution in Poetic Language*, p. 8.

40. See Hayden White, *Metahistory* (Baltimore: The Johns Hopkins University Press, 1973), p. x: "The historian performs an essentially *poetic* act, in which he *pre*figures the historical field and constitutes it as a domain upon which to bring to bear the specific theories he will use to explain what was '*really* happening.' " See also pages 3–4: "Continental European thinkers . . . have cast serious doubts on the value of a specifically 'historical' consciousness, stressed the fictive character of historical reconstructions, and challenged history's claims to a place among the sciences. At the same time, Anglo-American philosophers have produced a massive body of literature on the epistemological status and cultural function of historical thinking, a literature which, taken as a whole, justifies serious doubts about history's status as either a rigorous science or a genuine art."

41. Luce Irigaray, "And the One Doesn't Stir without the Other," tr. Hélène Vivienne Wenzel, in *Signs* 7, no. 1 (Autumn 1981), 60–67.

42. Sigmund Freud, "The 'Uncanny' " (1919), in *Studies in Parapsychology*, ed. and intro. Philip Rieff (New York: Collier Books, 1963), p. 51.

43. Freud, "The 'Uncanny,' " p. 55–56.

44. Irigaray, *Speculum*, footnote pp. 47–48.

45. Virginia Woolf, *A Room of One's Own* (New York and London: Harcourt, Brace, Jovanovich, 1929), pp. 35–36.

46. Mary Elizabeth Coleridge, "The Other Side of a Mirror," in *The Norton Anthology of Literature by Women*, pp. 1162–63.

47. Judith Wright, "Naked Girl and Mirror" in *The Norton Anthology of Literature by Women*, pp. 1835–36.

48. See footnote 6 to "Kubla Khan" in *The Norton Anthology of English Literature*, 4th edition, Vol. 2, General Editor M. H. Abrams (New York: W.W. Norton, 1962), p. 355. We should note here that our reading of the poem differs significantly from such classic interpretations as those of Humphrey House (1953) and Harold Bloom (1962), both of whom emphasize the power of the speaker's imagination and read "Could I revive within

me" as implying "I *can* revive within me." " 'Kubla Khan,' " says House, "is a vision of the ideal human life *as the poetic imagination can create it*"; and Bloom adds that " 'Kubla Khan' is a poem of self-recognition, in which the figure of the youth as virile poet is finally identified with the poem's speaker." See Humphrey House, "*Kubla Khan, Christabel,* and *Dejection,*" reprinted in *Romanticism and Consciousness,* ed. Harold Bloom (New York: W.W. Norton, 1970); and Harold Bloom, " 'Kubla Khan' " in *The Visionary Company* (New York: Doubleday, 1962). We are arguing that, if one historicizes Coleridge's dream-vision, such optimistic interpretations of "Could I revive within me" and "I would build that dome in air" are by no means inevitable.

49. William Shakespeare, *The Tempest,* Act IV, scene 1, lines 152, 150.

50. Freud, "The 'Uncanny,' " p. 51.

51. Freud, "The 'Uncanny,' " p. 51.

52. Abrams, *The Mirror and the Lamp,* p. 170. In a fine meditation on "Kubla Khan," Theodore Weiss comments that the text's "juxtapositions seem precursive of the often feverishly ranging, rearranging mind of a Pound. Had 'Kubla Khan' continued, it might have consisted of an extended series of such interruptions and couplings, fragments yoked to fragments, a veritable imagist poem." See Theodore Weiss, *The Man from Porlock: Engagements 1944–1981* (Princeton: Princeton University Press, 1982), pp. 4–5.

53. Harold Bloom, *The Anxiety of Influence* (New York: Oxford University Press, 1973); and also, of course, Walter Jackson Bate, *The Burden of the Past and the English Poet* (New York: W.W. Norton, 1972).

54. See Margaret Homans, *Women Writers and Poetic Identity* (Princeton: Princeton University Press, 1980); and Irene Tayler and Gina Luria, "Gender and Genre: Women in British Romantic Literature," in *What Manner of Woman,* ed. Marlene Springer (New York: New York University Press, 1977), pp. 98–123.

55. Joan Kelly [Kelly-Gadol] has explored the problems of historical periodization in her classic essay "Did Women Have a Renaissance?" in Renate Bridenthal and Claudia Koonz, ed., *Becoming Visible: Women in European History* (Boston: Houghton-Mifflin, 1977), pp. 137–64.

56. Tayler and Luria, "Gender and Genre," *What Manner of Woman,* p. 115.

57. Matthew Arnold, *Letters of Matthew Arnold,* ed. George W.E. Russell (New York and London: Macmillan, 1896), 1: 34. See our discussion of these figures in *The Madwoman in the Attic.*

58. Gerald Graff, *Criticism in the University,* ed. Gerald Graff and Reginald Gibbons (Chicago: TriQuarterly Series on Criticism and Culture, No. 1; Northwestern University Press, 1985), p. 56.

59. See Woolf, *Three Guineas,* pp. 62–74.

60. Freud, "The 'Uncanny,' " p. 50.

61. Abrams, *The Mirror and the Lamp,* title page.

11. The Sense of an Answer: Ambiguities of Interpretation in Clinical and Applied Psychoanalysis

1. See, e.g., Melanie Klein, *Contributions to Psycho-Analysis 1921–1945* (New York: McGraw Hill, 1964). For an up-to-date, comparative analytic review and critique of object relations theory, see Jay R. Greenberg and Stephen A. Mitchell, *Object Relations in Psychoanalytic Theory* (Cambridge, Mass. and London: Harvard University Press, 1983).

2. Heinz Kohut, *The Restoration of the Self* (New York: International Universities Press, 1977). See also his *How Does Analysis Cure?* (New York: International Universities Press, 1984).

3. See my *The Analytic Attitude* (New York: Basic Books, 1983); *Narrative Actions in Psychoanalysis: Heinz Werner Lecture Series 14* (Worcester, Mass.: Clark University Press, 1981); and "Wild Analysis," *Journal of the American Psychoanalytic Association* 33 (1985), 275–300. In these, I review and extend my earlier work on action language in psychoanalysis, set forth my conception of psychoanalysis as a narrative undertaking, and begin to situate these presentations in a comparative psychoanalytic context.

4. Sigmund Freud, "Constructions in Analysis" (1937), in *The Standard Edition of the Complete Psychological Works of Sigmund Freud*, Vol. 23 (London: Hogarth Press, 1964), pp. 255–70.

5. David Willbern, "Freud and the Inter-Penetration of Dreams," *Diacritics* 9 (1979), 98–110.

6. See my "Problems in Freud's Psychology of Women," *Journal of the American Psychoanalytic Association* 22 (1974), 459–85; also my "Impotence, Frigidity, and Sexism," in *Language and Insight: The Sigmund Freud Memorial Lectures 1975–1976 University College London* (New Haven and London: Yale University Press, 1978) pp. 139–71.

7. Anna Freud discussed some of the special problems of child analysis taking place outside the standard verbal free-association situation, in *The Ego and the Mechanisms of Defense* (London: Hogarth Press, 1942), pp. 40–42.

8. For Heinz Kohut on defense and resistance analysis, see especially Ch. 7 of his *How Does Analysis Cure?*.

9. Sigmund Freud, "Analysis Terminable and Interminable" (1937), in *The Standard Edition of the Complete Psychological Works of Sigmund Freud*, Vol. 23, pp. 216–53. See also Edward Glover (1931) "The Therapeutic Effect of Inexact Interpretation: A Contribution to the Theory of Suggestion," in E. Glover, *The Technique of Psychoanalysis* (New York: International Universities Press, 1955), pp. 353–66.

10. See my "The Psychoanalytic Vision of Reality" in *A New Language for Psychoanalysis* (New Haven and London: Yale University Press, 1976), pp. 22–56.

11. Reference is made here to Jonathan Culler's *Structuralist Poetics: Structuralism, Linguistics, and the Study of Literature* (Ithaca: Cornell University Press, 1975); Stanley Fish's *Is There a Text in This Class? The Authority of Interpretive Communities* (Cambridge, Mass. and London: Harvard University Press, 1980); and my "The Imprisoned Analysand," in *The Analytic Attitude*, pp. 257–80.

12. Towards a Literary Anthropology

1. Cf. Edmund Burke, *A Philosophical Inquiry into the Origin of our Ideas of the Sublime and the Beautiful, The Works* I (London: 1899), pp. 110, 130, 140, 164, 192, 218 and 233.

2. Cf. *Betham's Theory of Fictions*, ed. C. K. Ogden (Paterson: 1959), pp. 30, 49ff, and 154.

3. Cf. Hans Vaihinger, *Die Philosophie des Als-Ob* (Leipzig: 1922), pp. xii and 194–219.

4. Vaihinger, *Philosophie des Als-Ob*, p. iv.

5. Frank Kermode has advanced this concept in his important book, *The Sense of an Ending: Studies in the Theory of Fiction* (New York: 1967) and has also given a very illuminating account of its history.

6. Francis Bacon, *The Advancement of Learning and New Atlantis*, ed. Thomas Case (London: 1974), p. 96.

7. Kermode, *Sense of An Ending*, p. 64.

8. Cf. Vaihinger, *Philosophie des Als-Ob*, pp. 219–30.

9. Compare for instance the essays devoted to the study of fiction in issues 1 and 2 of *Poetics* 8 (1979).

10. For details see Nelson Goodman, *Ways of Worldmaking* (Hassocks: 1978), esp. pp. 10–17 and 101ff.

11. Maurice Merleau-Ponty, *Das Auge und der Geist: Philosophische Essays*, German trans. H. W. Arndt (Reinbek: 1967), p. 84, considered this a basic criterion for an art work.

12. David Hume, *A Treatise of Human Nature*, ed. L. A. Selby-Bigge (Oxford: 1968), p. 24.

13. P. F. Strawson, "Imagination and Perception," in *Experience and Theory*, ed. Lawrence Foster and J. W. Swanson (Amherst, MA: 1970), p. 43.

14. Mary Warnock, *Imagination* (Berkeley and Los Angeles: 1978), p. 192.

15. Cf. Jean-Paul Sartre, *Das Imaginäre: Phänomenologische Psychologie der Einbildungskraft*, German trans. by Hans Schöneberg (Hamburg: 1971), pp. 263ff.

16. Cf. Wolfgang Iser, "Feigning in Fiction," in *Identity of the Literary Text*, ed. by Mario J. Valdés and Owen Miller (Toronto: 1985), pp. 204–28.

17. I have dealt with that issue in my essay "Changing Functions in Literature," in *London Germanic Studies* III, ed. J. P. Stern (London: 1986), pp. 162–79.

18. See Iser, "Changing Functions," pp. 171ff.

19. Cf. Theodor W. Adorno, *Negative Dialektik* (Frankfurt: 1966), p. 389.

20. Helmuth Plessner, "Die anthropologische Dimensions der Geschichtlichkeit," in *Sozialer Wandel: Zivilisation und Fortschritt als Kategorien der soziologischen Theorie*, ed. H. P. Dreitzel (Neuwied: 1972), p. 160.

21. This idea has been given very strong support by the Czech Marxist Karel Kosík, *Die Dialektik des Konkreten: Eine Studie zur Problematik des Menschen und der Welt*, German trans. by Marianne Hoffman (Frankfurt: 1967), see especially pp. 123ff.

13. The Future of Theory: Saving the Reader

1. I am particularly indebted here to Kate Soper, *Humanism and Anti-Humanism* (London: 1986).

2. Cf. Soper, *Humanism*; and Ernst Fischer, *Art Against Ideology* (London: 1969), 77ff.

3. Catherine Belsey, *Critical Practice* (London 1980), 131.

4. Cf. Rosalind Coward and John Ellis, *Language and Materialism* (London: 1977); Fredric Jameson, *The Political Unconscious* (London: 1981), esp. ch. 3; and the discussion of Jameson's use of Lacan in Dominick LaCapra, *Rethinking Intellectual History* (Ithaca: Cornell UP, 1983), 245ff.

5. Terry Eagleton, *Literary Theory* (Oxford: Basil Blackwell, 1985), 199, 207, 210. This last remark could only be made by one who is unaware of the liberal tradition of political philosophy, e.g., that stemming from John Rawls's *A Theory of Justice* (Oxford: 1971).

6. Soper, *Humanism*, p. 102.

7. The recognition which may be hardest to reconcile with the traditional view of autonomous action may well be the psychoanalytical one; cf. e.g., Ernst Gellner, *The Psychoanalytic Movement* (London: 1985), esp. ch. 1.

8. Soper, *Humanism*, p. 114.

9. Cf. Alasdair MacIntyre, *After Virtue* (London: 1981), 243; and B. Kamenka, *Marxism and Ethics* (London: 1969).

10. Compare Hamlet as bearer of all his symbolic archetypal baggage according to Northrop Frye (*Anatomy of Criticism* [Princeton: 1957], 140) so that when he leaps into the grave after Laertes, he reenacts the trip to the underworld. I choose this as a relatively uncontroversial example of the removal of original intention by a preferred historical interpretation. For surely Hamlet didn't think he was doing this? Cf. also LaCapra, *Rethinking*, p. 256.

11. Soper, *Humanism*, p. 128.

12. John Berger, *G* (London: 1970). Further references are given in the text.

13. John Bayley, *The Characters of Love* (London: 1960), 5.

14. Cf. John Berger, *Ways of Seeing* (Harmondsworth: 1972), 45ff.

15. Cf. e.g., Simone de Beauvoir, *The Second Sex* (Harmondsworth: 1972), 29. One has of course to remember that Leonie is implicated in the novelistic discourse of a male here.

16. Donald Barthelme, *Unspeakable Practices, Unnatural Acts* (New York: 1976), 122–31. Further references in the text.

17. Toril Moi, *Sexual/Textual Politics* (London: 1985), 101.

18. Umberto Eco, *The Role of the Reader* (London: 1981), 5, 60.

19. Cf. e.g., the last chapter of Lévi-Strauss's *The Savage Mind* (London: 1966), cit. Soper, *Humanism*, p. 98.

20. Soper, *Humanism*, p. 6.

21. Jean-Paul Sartre, *What is Literature?* (London: 1950), 14. Cf. 32–57 and 264ff.

22. This to some degree modifies Sartre's strict reflection theory for prose; but I think it can be defended. Cf. my *Interpretation Deconstruction and Ideology* (Oxford: 1984), ch. 4.

23. Cf. MacIntyre, *After Virtue*, p. 30, who also argues that it is typical of that loss of earlier virtuous practices in "modernity" that the self is dissolved into its social roles, as in the work of Erving Goffman.

24. Roland Barthes, *The Pleasure of the Text*, trans. Richard Miller (New York: Hill and Wang, 1975), 34ff.

25. Cf. Gabriele Schwab, "Genesis of the Subject, Imaginary Functions and Poetic Language," in *New Literary History*, vol. 15, no. 3 (Spring 1984), 453ff.

26. MacIntyre, *After Virtue*, p. 21.

27. MacIntyre, *After Virtue*, pp. 22, 31.

28. MacIntyre, *After Virtue*, pp. 193, 199, 203.

29. Richard Rorty, "The Contingency of Language," *London Review of Books* (17 April 1986), p. 3.

30. Rorty, "The Contingency of Language," p. 3.

31. Leo Bersani, *A Future for Astyanax* (London 1978), 6, 7. Further references in the text.

32. Cf. Andreas Huyssen, "Mapping the Postmodern," *New German Critique* no. 33 (Fall 1984), 41ff.

33. Cf. Jameson, *Political Unconscious*; and LaCapra's discussion, *Rethinking*, 238ff.

14. The Future of Theory in the Teaching of Literature

1. See, for example, my "Interpretation on Tlön: A Response to Stanley Fish," *New Literary History*, XVIII (1985–86), pp. 109–17, and Fish's reply to my critique ("Resistance and Independence: A Reply to Gerald Graff") in the same issue, pp. 119–27.

2. See my *Professing Literature: An Institutional History* (Chicago: University of Chicago Press, 1987); see also my essay, "Taking Cover in Coverage," *Profession 86* (Modern Language Association, 1986), pp. 41–45.

3. Irving Babbitt, *Literature and the American College: Essays in Defense of the Humanities* (New York: Houghton Mifflin & Co., 1908), p. 181.

4. John Crowe Ransom, *The World's Body* (Baton Rouge: Louisiana State University Press, 1938), p. 173.

5. René Wellek and Austin Warren, *Theory of Literature*, Third ed. (New York: Harcourt, Brace and Co., 1977), p. 19.

6. I have developed this point in *Literature Against Itself* (Chicago: University of Chicago Press, 1979), and again, from a different angle, in *Professing Literature*.

7. Terry Eagleton, *The Function of Criticism: From the Spectator to Post-Structuralism* (London: Verso Editions, 1984), pp. 123–24.

8. Jonathan Culler, *Structuralist Poetics: Structuralism, Linguistics, and the Study of Literature* (Ithaca: Cornell University Press, 1975), p. 115.

9. The most widely discussed of these reports is William Bennett's "To Reclaim a Legacy," in *The Chronicle of Higher Education*, XXIX, no. 14 (November 28, 1984), pp. 16–21.

10. Terry Eagleton, *Literary Theory: An Introduction* (Minneapolis: University of Minnesota Press, 1983), p. 211.

11. I borrow the phrase "patterned isolation" from Laurence R. Veysey, *The Emergence of the American University* (Chicago: University of Chicago Press, 1965), p. 338.

12. See my discussion of this issue in "Interpretation on Tlön: A Response to Stanley Fish," and "Humanism and the Hermeneutics of Power: Reflections on the Post-structuralist Two-Step, *boundary 2*, XII, No. 3/ XIII, No. 1 (Spring/Fall, 1984), pp. 495–505.

13. See, for example, the article by Clarence Campbell, "The Tyranny of the Yale Critics," *New York Times Magazine* (February 9, 1986), pp. 20–26.

14. See Eagleton, *Literary Theory: An Introduction*; Raymond Williams, *Writing in Society* (London: Verso Editions, not dated), pp. 177–226; William E. Cain, *The Crisis in Criticism: Theory, Literature, and Reform in English Studies* (Baltimore: Johns Hopkins University Press, 1984); Robert Scholes, *Textual Power* (New Haven: Yale University Press, 1985).

15. Paul de Man's Contribution to Literary Criticism and Theory

1. For the texts from a pre-occupation journal, *Les Cahiers du libre examen*, and those from *Le Soir* and *Het Vlaamsche Land*, see Paul de Man, *Wartime Journalism, 1939–1943* (Lincoln: University of Nebraska Press, 1988).

2. Paul de Man, *The Rhetoric of Romanticism* (New York: Columbia University Press, 1984), p. 262. Henceforth cited as RR.

3. Paul de Man, "Heidegger's Exegeses of Hölderlin," *Blindness and Insight*, enlarged edition (Minneapolis: University of Minnesota Press, 1983), p. 254. Henceforth cited as BI. For further discussion of de Man's rereading of Heidegger, see Christopher Norris, "Paul de Man's Past," *London Review of Books* (4 February 1988).

4. Alice Jaeger Kaplan, *Reproductions of Banality: Fascism, Literature, and French Intellectual Life* (Minneapolis: University of Minnesota Press, 1986), p. 26.

5. Kaplan, *Reproductions of Banality*, p. 3.

6. For fuller discussion of the entire range of de Man's writings, see the chapter "De Man's Rhetoric" in my *Framing the Sign* (Oxford: Basil Blackwell, and Norman: University of Oklahoma Press, 1988).

7. Minae Mizumura, "Renunciation," *Yale French Studies* 69 (1985), p. 91.

8. Paul de Man, "Time and History in Wordsworth," *Diacritics* 17 (Winter 1987), p. 13.

9. Paul de Man, *Allegories of Reading* (New Haven: Yale University Press, 1979), p. 82. Henceforth cited as AR.

10. Paul de Man, *The Resistance to Theory* (Minneapolis: University of Minnesota Press, 1986), p. 10. Henceforth cited as RT.

11. Paul de Man, "Kant and Schiller," *Aesthetic Ideology*, ed. Andrzej Warminski (Minneapolis: University of Minnesota Press, forthcoming).

16. The Future of an Illusion

1. Jacques Lacan, *The Four Fundamental Concepts of Psycho-Analysis*, trans. Alan Sheridan (New York: Norton, 1978), p. 96. Sheridan gives the last sentence as, "But I am not in the picture." In the French, however, it reads, "Mais moi, je suis dans le tableau." *Les quatre concepts fondamentaux de la psychanalyse* (Paris,: Seuil, 1973), p. 89.

2. Lacan, *Four Fundamental Concepts*, p. 17:
> I am that wretch comparable with mirrors
> That can reflect but cannot see
> Like them my eye is empty and like them inhabited
> By your absence which makes it blind.

3. Lorenz Eitner, "Foregrounding the trope," *Times Literary Supplement* (April 12, 1985), 413.

4. There is an exchange, both amusing and painful, between Murray Krieger and Ernst Gombrich, in which Professor Krieger wonders what has happened to Gombrich's earlier, staunch conventionalism, and Gombrich answers that he was never a conventionalist. (See Murray Krieger, "The Ambiguities of Representation and Illusion—A Gombrich Retrospective," and E. H. Gombrich, "Representation and Misrepresentation," both in *Critical Inquiry*, vol. 11, no. 2 [1984].) For a discussion of Gombrich's relation to the idea of the "natural sign" as opposed to convention, see W. J. T. Mitchell, *Iconology* (Chicago: University of Chicago Press, 1986), pp. 74–94. See also my review of Gombrich's *The Image and the Eye* (London: Phaidon, 1981), in "Seeing as Believing," *Raritan Review*, II (Fall 1982).

5. Michael Fried, "The Beholder of Courbet," *Glyph*, no. 4 (1978); "The Structure of Beholding in Courbet's *Burial at Ornans*," *Critical Inquiry*, vol. 9, no. 4 (1983); and *Absorption and Theatricality: Painting and Beholder in the Age of Diderot* (Berkeley: University of California Press, 1980).

6. Svetlana Alpers, *The Art of Describing: Dutch Art in the Seventeenth Century* (Chicago: University of Chicago Press, 1983).

7. See, for example, Christian Metz, *The Imaginary Signifier: Psychoanalysis and Cinema*, trans. Celia Brittan, Annwyl Williams, Ben Brewster, Alfred Guzzetti (Bloomington: Indiana University Press, 1982); Stephen Heath, *Questions of Cinema* (Bloomington: Indiana University Press, 1981); and Teresa de Lauretis and Stephen Heath, eds., *The Cinematic Apparatus* (London: Macmillan Press, 1980).

8. Bryson acknowledges the debt his analysis of belatedness owes to the Bloomian psychologizing of influence, and follows Bloom in describing as "tropes" the defenses he sees the Neo-Classical artist erecting against the influence of the precursor-figure. But Bloom's mapping of the Freudian defense mechanisms onto the standard figures of classical rhetoric derived its logic from the way rhetoric itself can be seen as a conventionalized naming of those figurative deviations from the literal that are essential to language. In transferring the field of relationship from verbal to visual space, Bryson pulls his tropes, or figures of misprision, from the entirely disparate domains of the psychological (the trope of desire), the tropological (the trope of irony), the visual (the trope of counter-presence), and the political (the trope of aegis). The arbitrariness of this procedure does much to sabotage Bryson's ambitions to construct an analytic system. See, Harold Bloom, *The Anxiety of Influence* (New York: Oxford University Press, 1973); and Harold Bloom *A Map of Misreading* (New York: Oxford University Press, 1975).

9. Lacan, *Four Fundamental Concepts*, p. 103.

10. Svetlana Alpers, in "Is Art History?" (*Daedalus* [Summer 1977], 1–13), addresses the question of subjectivity shaping the contemporary art historian's enterprise.

11. André Malraux, *The Voices of Silence*, trans. Stuart Gilbert (New York: Doubleday, 1953), p. 24.

12. The basic material on Ingres' practice of the copy is collected in Patricia Condon, *In Pursuit of Perfection: The Art of J.-A.-D. Ingres* (Louisville: J. B. Speed Art Museum, 1983).

13. See, Elson van Liere, "Ingres' 'Raphael and the Fornarina': Reverence and Testimony," *Arts*, LVI (December 1981), 108–15.

14. Jean Baudrillard, *For a Critique of the Political Economy of the Sign*, trans. Charles Levin (St. Louis: Telos Press, 1972).

15. See my "Corpus Delicti," *October*, no. 33 (Summer 1985); and "Anti-Vision," *October*, no. 37 (Summer 1986); also, Kate Linker, ed., *Difference: On Representation and Sexuality* (New York: The New Museum, 1984).

17. The Future of Genre Theory: Functions and Constructional Types

1. Jacques Derrida, *Of Grammatology*, trans. Gayatri Chakravorty Spivak (Baltimore: Johns Hopkins Univ. Press, 1976), 7.

2. Samuel Johnson, *The Rambler*, ed. Walter Jackson Bate and A. B. Strauss, 3 vols. (New Haven and London: Yale Univ. Press 1968), iii, 127.

3. On the poem about a picture, see Alastair Fowler, *Kinds of Literature* (Cambridge, Mass.: Harvard Univ. Press, and Oxford: Clarendon Press, 1982); "Poems on Pictures," *Word and Image* vol. 2, no. 1 (Jan.–Mar., 1986). There are several examples of the essayistic poem in Dannie Abse, *The Bloody Horse* (London: Hutchinson, 1985).

4. See Fowler, *Kinds of Literature*, pp. 122–26; Patricia Waugh, *Metafiction: The Theory and Practice of Self-Conscious Fiction* (London and New York: Methuen, 1984); and Steven G. Kellman, *The Self-Begetting Novel* (New York; Columbia Univ. Press, 1980).

5. Thomas Greene, *The Light in Troy* (New Haven and London: Yale Univ. Press, 1982), 66.

6. On games as a model for literary structure, see Peter Hutchinson, *Games Authors Play* (London and New York: Methuen, 1988). There are many Renaissance examples of works based on games, such as the Penelope game that provides the numerological basis of Sir Philip Sidney's *Astrophel and Stella*; the barley break game used by Sir John Suckling and by Sidney in "Other Poems," 4, discussed in Alastair Fowler, *Conceitful Thought* (Edinburgh Univ. Press, 1975), ch 3; and the seasonal games in Shakespeare's *Twelfth Night*. One of the few critics to write about constructional types is Robin Skelton, in *The Practice of Poetry* (London: Heinemann, 1971).

7. Cf. Fowler, *Kinds of Literature*, p. 128.

8. *The Poems of Sir Walter Ralegh*, ed. A. Latham (London: Routledge & Kegan Paul, 1951), 80. See Ernst Curtius, *European Literature and the Latin Middle Ages*, trans. Willard R. Trask (London: Routledge & Kegan Paul, 1953), 286–87, with different examples.

9. Edwin Morgan, *The Second Life* (Edinburgh Univ. Press, 1968), 141.

10. Cf., e.g., Bohumila Grögerova's "Mutterbeere beerenbutter butterbeere berlenleere" (1965), in *Edition Hansjörg Mayer* (The Hague: Gemmentemuseum, 1968), 28.

11. Morgan, *The Second Life*, p. 159.

12. Anne Stevenson, *The Fiction-Makers* (Oxford and New York: Oxford Univ. Press, 1985) 59–64.

13. Isabella Whitney, "Wyll and Testament," ed. Betty Travitsky, in *ELR*, vol. x, no. 1 (1981), 83–94.

14. Adrian Henri, "Adrian Henri's Last Will and Testament," *Penguin Modern Poets*, vol. 10 (Harmondsworth, Middlesex: Penguin, 1967), 13–14.

15. John Becker, *New Feathers for the Old Goose* (New York: Pantheon, 1956), 54–63.

16. Elizabeth Bishop, *The Complete Poems* (London: Chatto & Windus, 1969), 155–67.

17. This version of the *Had Gayda* is by El Lissitzky.

18. Fredric Jameson, "Magical Narratives: Romance as Genre," *NLH* vol vii, no. 1 (1975), 137.

18. Mystory: The Law of Idiom in Applied Grammatology

1. See also my "Teletheory: A Mystory," in *The Current in Criticism*, eds. Clayton Koelb and Virgil Lokke, (West Lafayette: Purdue University Press, 1987). Thanks to the students in my seminar on modern theory for their help with this project. They and their peers, of course, will decide the issue raised in this collection.

2. See my "The Object of Post-Criticism," in *The Anti-Aesthetic: Essays on Post-Modern Culture*, ed. Hal Foster (Port Townsend: Bay Press, 1983), pp. 83–110.

3. "Ulysses Gramophone," Jacques Derrida, lecture delivered at the University of Florida, Gainesville (September 19–20, 1985)

18. Works Cited

Adorno, T. W. "The Essay as Form." *New German Critique* 11 (1984).

Barthes, Roland. *Mythologies*. Trans. Annette Lavers. New York: Hill and Wang. 1972.

———*Roland Barthes*. Trans. Richard Howard. New York: Hill and Wang. 1977.

———*A Lover's Discourse: Fragments*. Trans. Richard Howard. New York: Hill and Wang. 1978.

Cage, John. *Silence*. Cambridge: The M.I.T. Press. 1966.

———*M: Writings '67–'72*. Middletown: Wesleyan University Press. 1974.

Colie, Rosalie L. "Literature and History." In *Relations of Literary Study: Essays on Interdisciplinary Contributions*. Ed. James Thorpe. New York: Modern Language Association. 1967.

De Certeau, Michel. *Heterologies: Discourse on the Other*. Trans. Brian Massumi. Minneapolis: University of Minnesota. 1986.

DuPlessis, Rachel Blau. "For the Etruscans." In *The New Feminist Criticism: Essays on Women, Literature, and Theory*. Ed. Elaine Showalter. New York: Pantheon Books. 1985.

Ginzburg, Carlo. "Morelli, Freud, and Sherlock Holmes: Clues and Scientific Method." In *The Sign of Three: Dupin, Holmes, Peirce*. Eds. Umberto Eco and Thomas A. Sebeok. Bloomington: Indiana University. 1983.

Heidegger, Martin. "The Age of the World Picture." In *The Question Concerning Technology*. Trans. William Lovitt. New York: Harper and Row. 1977.

Kelly, Mary. *Post-Partum Document*. London: Routledge and Kegan Paul. 1983.

Kuhn, Thomas S. *The Structure of Scientific Revolutions*. 2nd Ed. Chicago: University of Chicago. 1970.

Lacan, Jacques. "Seminar on 'The Purloined Letter.' " *Yale French Studies* 48 (1972).

Lyotard, Jean-François, and Jean-Loup Thébaud. *Just Gaming*. Trans. Wlad Godzich. Minneapolis: University of Minnesota. 1985.

Popular Memory Group. "Popular memory: theory, politics, method." In *Making Histories: Studies in history-writing and politics*. Eds. Richard Johnson et. al. London: Hutchinson. 1982.

Tolson, Andrew. "Anecdotal Television." *Screen* 26 (1985).

19. Authority, (White) Power and the (Black) Critic; or, it's all Greek to me

1. W. E. B. Du Bois acknowledges Crummell's influence in a moving essay in *The Souls of Black Folk* (1903). See Chapter XII, "Of Alexander Crummell."

2. Alexander Crummell, "The Attitude of the American Mind Toward the Negro Intellect," *The American Negro Academy, Occasional Papers, No. 3* (Washington, DC: The Academy, 1898), pp. 8–19. Subsequent citations will be given parenthetically.

3. Alexander Crummell, "The English Language in Liberia," in *The Future of Africa* (New York: Charles Scribner, 1862), pp. 7–54. All subsequent citations will be given parenthetically.

4. Crummell is here echoing Emerson's diction about the necessity of black people producing written "ideas" because "ideas only save races." See Emerson's speech, "Emancipation in the West Indies," 1844.

5. Despite his sustained and energetic effort in "The English Language in Liberia" to utilize the acquisition of English as the saving grace of African enslavement, it is only fair to note that Crummell is not unaware of the terrible irony in his argument. As he admits,

> . . . I would not have you to suppose that I forget the *loss* which has accompanied all this *gain*. . . . No! I do not forget that to give our small fraction of the race the advantages I have alluded to, a whole continent has been brought to ruin; the ocean has been peopled with victims; whole tribes of men have been destroyed; nations on the threshold of civilization reduced to barbarism; and generation upon generation of our sires brutalized! No, my remarks, at best, are discordant; and I avoid collateral themes in order to preserve as much unity as possible, while endeavoring to set forth the worth and value of the English language. (p. 30)

6. See Paul de Man, "The Resistance to Theory," *Yale French Studies*, No. 63 (1982), pp. 3–20. Fuller versions of this section of my essay appear in my "Criticism in the Jungle," in *Black Literature and Literary Theory*, ed. Henry Louis Gates, Jr. (New York, 1985), pp. 1–24, and "Writing 'Race' and the Difference It Makes," *Critical Inquiry*, 12, No. 1 (Autumn 1985), pp. 1–20.

7. J. E. Casely-Hayford, *Ethiopia Unbound: Studies in Race Emancipation* (London, 1911), pp. 1–2; hereafter cited in text.

8. Carter G. Woodson, "Introduction," *The Mind of the Negro as Reflected in Letters Written During the Crisis, 1800–1860* (New York 1969), p. v.

9. I have traced the history and theory of this critical debate in my *Black Letters and the Enlightenment*, forthcoming from Oxford University Press.

10. David Hume, "Of National Characters," in *The Philosophical Works*, ed. Thomas Hill Green and Thomas Hodge Grose (Darmstadt, 1964), III, 252 n. 1.

11. Sterling A. Brown, Lecture, Yale University, 17 April 1979.

12. Robert Farris Thompson, *Indelibly Black: Essays on African and Afro-American Art* (forthcoming).

13. See *Critical Inquiry*, 12, No. 1 (Autumn 1985).

14. Valerie Smith, " 'Loopholes of Retreat': Architecture and Ideology in Harriet Jacobs's *Incidents in the Life of a Slave Girl*," paper presented at the 1985 American Studies Association meeting, San Diego.

15. Wole Soyinka, "Nobel Lecture, 1986: This Past Must Address Its Present" (December 10, 1986). All subsequent citations will be given parenthetically.

16. Wole Soyinka, cited in "Nigeria: The New Culture," *New York Post* (February 17, 1987), Supplement, p. 1.

17. Jacques Derrida, "The Last Word in Racism," in Henry Louis Gates, Jr., ed., *"Race," Writing, and Difference* (Chicago, 1986), p. 333.

18. Rebecca Cox Jackson, "A Dream of Three Books and a Holy One," *Gifts of Power: The Writings of Rebecca Jackson, Black Visionary, Shaker Eldress*, ed. Jean McMahon Humex (Amherst, Mass., 1981), pp. 146, 147.

19. Alice Walker, *The Color Purple* (New York, 1982), p. 179.

.

20. Anthony Appiah, "Strictures on Structures: The Prospects for a Structuralist Poetics of African Fiction," in *Black Literature and Literary Theory*, ed. Gates, pp. 146, 145; all further references to this work, abbreviated "S," will be included in the text.

20. A Criticism of Our Own: Autonomy and Assimilation in Afro-American and Feminist Literary Theory

1. Mary Ann Caws, "The Conception of Engendering, the Erotics of Editing," in *The Poetics of Gender*, ed. Nancy K. Miller (New York: Columbia U. P., 1986), pp. 42–63. This episode is all the more ironic in the light of the successful protest in Spring 1988 by deaf students of Gallaudet College in Washington.

2. Jane Gallop, *The Daughter's Seduction: Feminism and Psychoanalysis* (Ithaca: Cornell U. P., 1982), pp. 126–27.

3. In this paper I need to make distinctions between a generic feminist criticism, practiced by a feminist critic of either sex; "Feminist" criticism practiced by women; and male feminist criticism, practiced by men.

4. Gayatri Chakravorty Spivak, "French Feminism in an International Frame," *Yale French Studies* 62 (1981): 184. See also Jane Gallop, "Annie Leclerc Writing a Letter, with Vermeer," *The Poetics of Gender*, p. 154.

5. For a stimulating example of how such critical cross-fertilization might take place, see Craig Werner, "New Democratic Vistas: Toward a Pluralistic Genealogy," in *Studies in Black American Literature*, II, ed. Joe Weixlmann and Chester Fontenot (Florida: Penkevill Press, 1986), pp. 47–83.

6. See Jonathan Dollimore, "Shakespeare, Cultural Materialism and the New Historicism," *Political Shakespeare: New Essays in Cultural Materialism*, ed. Jonathan Dollimore and Alan Sinfield (Ithaca: Cornell U. P., 1985), p. 15.

7. Houston A. Baker, Jr., "Generational Shifts and the Recent Criticism of Afro-American Literature," *Black American Literature Forum* 15 (Spring 1981): 3–21. My discussion of Afro-American literary theory is profoundly indebted to Baker's essay, and to my discussions with him about parallels to feminist criticism.

8. Quoted in Werner Sollers, *Beyond Ethnicity* (Cambridge: Harvard U. P., 1986), p. 209.

9. See Toril Moi, *Sexual/Textual Politics* (London and New York: Methuen, 1985).

10. Arthur P. Davis, Ulysses Lee, and Sterling Brown, eds., *The Negro Caravan* (New York: Dryden Press, 1941). Through the 1950s, Davis and other Afro-American critics envisioned the eventual disappearance of the social conditions that produced identifiably "Negro" literature.

11. See Baker, "Generational Shifts," pp. 3–4. The term "integrationist poetics" comes from his essay.

12. Mary Helen Washington, "Rage and Silence in *Maud Martha*," in *Black Literature and Literary Theory*, ed. Henry Louis Gates, Jr. (New York and London: Methuen, 1984), p. 258.

13. Larry Neal, "The Black Arts Movement," in *The Black Aesthetic*, ed. Addison Gayle, Jr. (New York: Doubleday, 1971), p. 272.

14. Melvin Dixon, "Rivers Remembering Their Source," in *The Reconstruction of Instruction*, ed. Robert Stepto and Dexter Fisher (New York: MLA, 1979), pp. 25–26.

15. Baker, "Generational Shifts," p. 6.

16. Stephen Henderson, "The Forms of Things Unknown," in his book *Understanding the New Black Poetry* (New York: Morrow, 1973), p. 41.

17. Baker, "Generational Shifts," p. 9.

18. See Barbara Smith, "Towards a Black Feminist Criticism," in *The New Feminist Criticism*, ed. Elaine Showalter (New York: Pantheon, 1985), pp. 168–87; Deborah Mc-Dowell, "New Directions for Black Feminist Criticism," in *The New Feminist Criticism*, pp. 186–99; and Mary Helen Washington, "New Lives and New Letters: Black Women Writers at the End of the Seventies," *College English* 43 (Jan. 1981): 1–11.

19. Baker, "Generational Shifts," p. 10.

20. Baker, "Generational Shifts," p. 12; and Henry Louis Gates, Jr., "Criticism in the Jungle," *Black Literature and Literary Theory*, p. 9.

21. Gates, "Jungle," pp. 5, 8.

22. Robert B. Stepto, quoted in Baker, "Generational Shifts," p. 12.

23. Gates, "Jungle," p. 8. By 1987, Gates had drastically changed this formulation: "No matter what theories we seem to embrace, we have more in common with each other than we do with any other critic of any other literature. We write for each other and for our own contemporary writers." (*Figures in Black*, New York: Oxford U. P., 1987, xxii).

24. Baker, "Generational Shifts," p. 11.

25. Henry Louis Gates, Jr., "The Blackness of Blackness: A Critique of the Sign and the Signifying Monkey," *Black Literature and Literary Theory*, p. 297.

26. Gates, "Jungle," p. 9.

27. Gates, "Jungle," p. 8.

28. Gates, "Introduction," *Critical Inquiry*, vol. 12, no. 1 (Autumn 1985): 6.

29. Gates, "Writing, 'Race,' and the Difference It Makes," *Critical Inquiry* vol. 12, no. 1 (Autumn 1985): 5, 6.

30. Anthony Appiah, "The Uncompleted Argument: Du Bois and the Illusion of Race," *Critical Inquiry* vol. 12, no. 1 (Autumn 1985): 21–22.

31. Houston A. Baker, Jr., "Caliban's Triple Play," *Critical Inquiry*, vol. 13, no. 1 (Autumn 1986): 186.

32. The exception is Sander L. Gilman, who contributed a controversial essay on race and female sexuality.

33. Henry Louis Gates, Jr., "Talkin' That Talk," *Critical Inquiry*, vol. 13, no. 1 (Autumn 1986): 210.

34. Gates, "Introduction," pp. 13, 15.

35. Carolyn G. Heilbrun, *Toward a Recognition of Androgyny* (New York: Harper Colophon Books, 1973), p. ix.

36. Sandra Gilbert, "Feminist Criticism in the University," in *Criticism in the University*, ed. Gerald Graff and Reginald Gibbons (Evanston: Northwestern U. P., 1985), p. 117.

37. Michèle Barrett, *Women's Oppression Today: Problems in Marxist Feminist Analysis* (London: Villiers, 1980), pp. 112–13.

38. Elaine Showalter, "The Feminist Critical Revolution," in *The New Feminist Criticism*, p. 5.

39. *The Other Voice* (New York: Morrow, 1975), p. xvii.

40. Adrienne Rich, "Toward a Feminist Aesthetic," *Chrysalis* 6 (1978): 59, 67.

41. Showalter, "Feminist Criticism in the Wilderness," in *The New Feminist Criticism*.

42. Alice Walker, *In Search of Our Mothers' Gardens* (New York, 1983).

43. Hortense Spillers, *Conjuring*, ed. Spillers and Marjorie Pryse (Bloomington: Indiana U. P., 1985), p. 261.

44. Elizabeth Abel, "Introduction," *Writing and Sexual Difference* (Chicago: U. of Chicago Press. 1982), p. 2.

45. Alice Jardine, "Pre-Texts for the Transatlantic Feminist," *Yale French Studies* 62 (1981): 225; and *Gynesis: Configurations of Women and Modernity* (Ithaca: Cornell U. P., 1985), pp. 61–63.

46. Gayle Greene and Coppélia Kahn, "Feminist Scholarship and the Social Construction of Woman," in Green and Kahn, eds., *Making a Difference: Feminist Literary Criticism* (London: Methuen, 1985), pp. 24–27.

47. Shoshana Felman, "Woman and Madness: The Critical Phallacy," *Diacritics* 5 (1975): 10.

48. Kaja Silverman, *The Subject of Semiotics* (New York: Oxford U. P., 1983), p. viii.

49. Ken Ruthven, *Feminist Literary Studies: An Introduction* (Cambridge: Cambridge U. P., 1985), p. 6.

50. Gayle Rubin, "The Traffic in Women," in Rayna Rapp Reiter, ed., *Toward an Anthropology of Women* (New York: Monthly Review Press, 1975), p. 165.

51. Judith Shapiro, "Anthropology and the Study of Gender," in *A Feminist Perspective in the Academy*, ed. Elizabeth Langland and Walter Gove (Chicago: U. of Chicago Press, 1983), p. 112.

52. Evelyn Fox Keller, *Reflections on Gender and Science* (New Haven: Yale U. P., 1985), p. 3.

53. Joan W. Scott, "Gender: A Useful Category of Historical Analysis," *American Historical Review* 5 (November, 1986).

54. Scott, "Gender," p. 1065.

55. Reprinted in Tama Janowitz, *Slaves of New York* (New York: Crown, 1986).

56. Gates, "Jungle," p. 10.

57. Homi Bhabha, "Signs Taken for Words," *Critical Inquiry*, vol. 12, no. 1 (Autumn 1985): 162.

58. See Gayatri Chakravorty Spivak, *In Other Worlds: Essays in Cultural Politics* (London and New York: Routledge, 1987).

21. Beautiful Science and the Future of Criticism

1. Cited in Deborah Barnes, "Brain Architecture: Beyond Genes," in *Science*, 11 July, 1986, p. 155.

2. Peter Geach, *Mental Acts: Their Content and Objects* (London; Routledge & Kegan Paul, N.D.), p. 35 ff.

3. Steven Stich, *From Folk Psychology to Cognitive Science.* (Cambridge, Massachusetts, MIT Press, Bradford Books, 1986), p. 176.

4. David Hume, *A Treatise of Human Nature.* Book 1, Part IV, "Of Personal Identity." (London; Everyman Books), I, 239.

22. Computers, Literary Theory, and Theory of Meaning

1. We, in our own small way, already feel such envy. One of us spent years randomly perusing books of all sorts for certain types of semantic structures; the other, as long tracing the rhetoric of medical controversy in seventeenth-century England. With the appropriate texts available in machine-readable form (an eminently foreseeable possibility), these searches could be completed more accurately and extensively on a computer— overnight. On our current PCs (1985 vintage and so obsolete), it might take two weeks.

2. For a range of such discussions, see *Literary and Linguistic Computing: Journal of the Association for Literary and Linguistic Computing*, which began publishing in 1986. Two state of the art literary storage and retrieval systems are TLG (Thesaurus Linguae Graecae),

which was first developed by Theodore Brunner at the University of California, Irvine, and which now runs on the Ibycus system or on a Unix-based system developed at Harvard University, and ARTFL (Project for American and French Research on the Treasury of the French Language), which was developed at the University of Chicago. ARTFL participates in an interdisciplinary research group called TIRA (Textual Information Retrieval and Analysis), which seeks to devise more efficient storage and retrieval procedures. We both have served on TIRA's advisory committee.

3. For a survey, see Barr and Feigenbaum (1981), vol. 1.

4. From the perspective of literary theory, many developments considered innovative in AI seem less so. For example, researchers in AI thought they were standing the Chomskian tradition of linguistic inquiry on its head when they asked computers to use meaning to understand sentences. But similar inversions of Chomsky's position were commonplace in humanistic studies. For another example, our emphasis on the "tropological" nature of language, new to AI, is now old hat in literary theory.

5. We skip over NLP syntactic parsers, and early NLP semantic models that failed, or that succeeded through uninteresting forms of trickery. See Barr and Feigenbaum (1981).

6. For KRL see Bobrow and Winograd (1977); for Preference Semantics see Wilks (1975, 1978); for SHRDLU see Winograd (1972) and Boden (1977).

7. See Schank's "basic axiom": "For any two sentences that are identical in meaning, regardless of language, there should be only one representation of that meaning in CD" (Schank and Abelson 1977:11). Such calls for an *interlingua* (a language-free "language") associate Schank not only with Wilks's defense of semantic primitives, but also with early calls for "machinese" (Weaver 1949) and with Wilkins's (1668) universal language scheme.

8. Schank's Conceptual Dependency theory resembles many programs based on the idea of deep case grammar, as proposed by Fillmore (1968). For a survey see Bruce (1975).

9. Pragmatics can be conceived more narrowly, as involving specific knowledge about specific contexts of use. The distinction is not crucial to our discussion.

10. Schank's ELI (English Language Interpreter) builds conceptual dependency diagrams from sentences. A second program, MEMORY, stores and makes inferences with evaluated plausibility about the representation supplied by ELI. A third program, BABEL uses an Augmented Transition Network grammar to generate natural language sentences from conceptual dependency representations. Also see Davis and de Jong (1979).

11. See Metzing (1979) for a survey of uses of frames. For the relation between case systems and frames, see Charniak (1981). For the use of frames (called schemata) in cognitive psychology, see Bartlett (1932) and Rumelhart (1975). See also Abelson (1975), Bobrow et al. (1977), Charniak (1978).

12. Mini-worlds had their origin in the "blocks world" of Terry Winograd's SHRDLU, which could hold conversations about a mini-world of geometric blocks.

13. The software that understood in these terms was called SAM—Script Applier Mechanism; see Cullingford (1981).

14. Give PAM "Jane was hungry. She pulled out the Michelin guide and got in her car." PAM will use hunger to establish the goal of eating and will try to understand subsequent text in terms of goal-based behavior. If you are hungry, you try to get food.

15. See Meehan (1981) and Dehn (1981).

16. See, for example, Kintsch (1974), van Dijk (1980), Iser (1978), Eco (1979).

17. We do not suggest that the proliferation of black boxes in such studies is necessarily a defect. One consequence of AI's insistence on implementation is that AI can study only the most rudimentary texts. For a wider range of texts, black boxes are at present unavoidable.

18. Searle's (1980) well-known Chinese box argument follows similar lines. Also see Searle (1984).

19. There is, of course, a puzzle in such a question, since a well-designed artificial intelligence might answer my question affirmatively, and I would then not know what other kind of evidence I might seek. This is in part a puzzle about the grammar of our concept to knowing ("in order to know whether the computer could understand . . ."). It cannot be that I want to find something more than a computer program *behind* the behavior that mimics grammars. My problem, once I know the facts about my situation, would be that I want to find something more *in* the behavior that mimics grammars. There is a way to come to terms with this dilemma, which we discuss in section III, below.

20. See Rosch 1975a, 1975b, 1977, 1978, 1981; Dahlgren 1985. Lakoff (1987) includes a useful survey and a bibliography.

21. Schank and Abelson (1977) have suggested that we might deal with some of these features as *themes*, which include such matters as occupations, relationships with others, and general aims. These themes are, however, just the kind of extended script we propose and so are subject to the same questions.

22. Each script has its built-in conceptual hierarchy. It selects as relevant to text meaning elements anticipated by the script, and it gives those elements the hierarchical level they hold in the script itself. Thus, for a script-based system, the script selection procedure is the chief determinant of text structure. For a plan-based system, the textual hierarchy is a function of the structure built into the routine that creates the goal stack.

23. Also see Petofi and Reiser (1973), Kintsch (1974), Grimes (1975), Meyer (1975b), and Kintsch and van Dijk (1978). For a survey of the field, see de Beaugrande and Dressler (1981).

24. Van Dijk's macroanalysis, for example, always structures texts in terms of predetermined forms of understanding. It subjects the text's propositions to the operations known as macrorules, which produce *macropropositions*. Macropropositions represent increasingly dominant levels of text structure, the higher levels composed of macropropositions which result from applying the macrorules to macropropositions at lower levels.

Each macrorule generalizes the information in texts, and macroanalysis equates textual importance with generality (1980:85). All propositional textlinguistics in one way or another makes the same equation. They must: once a text has been decomposed into propositions, the only principled means of reconstructing a meaning from those propositions are logical. All major models end up constructing the conceptual hierarchy of texts so that textual importance is equated with generality.

25. Like all other areas of linguistics, AI research strives to work up to ever-higher levels of grammatical structure, but is hampered by a syntax-based understanding of language.

26. There are various proposals for constructing text bases, all of which decompose the text into minimal propositions. See Kintsch 1974; Kintsch and van Dijk 1978; van Dijk and Kintsch 1983; Grimes 1975; and Meyer 1975a, 1975b.

27. Explanations come easily when we are not cut off from higher grammatical structures. JAIL is one of a series of related concepts thematized as sentence topics: sum, troublesome provisions, jail sentences, violations, criminal aspects of the violations. Because they are consistently thematized and because they form a coherent conceptual group, they stand as a single master-concept thematized at the level of the paragraph, a *discourse topic* for the paragraph.

Discourse-level features escape sentence parsers and propositional text bases. It would be possible to complicate a parser or a text base to incorporate some features of sentence topic (e.g., by recording position in a sentence). But such an analysis could not recognize, for example, that here the thematized concepts form a natural group for the target audience. Thematization is more than simple position. (For an account of thematization in narrative texts, see Uspenskij 1970.)

28. A discourse unit in a pointed text is composed of two major constituents: an *Issue* segment (somewhat akin to sentence Topic), which among other things establishes discourse topics and the lexical fields that are the basis for lexical cohesion; and a *Discussion* segment, which among other things develops the topics and lexical fields established in the Issue. The position at the end of the Issue is marked as having the first claim on the discourse topic of the Unit as a whole. That position and the position at the end of the Discussion are the two possible locations for the point of the discourse unit. Akin to the traditional "thesis," the point is that stretch of text that stands as the most explicit expression of the controlling intention (i.e., principle of selection) for that discourse unit. An easy way to think of the point is as that stretch of text one might send as a telegram.

29. In textlinguistics Dillon

assumes the correctness of the view of reading that developed in literary criticism and psycholinguistics in the 1970's, namely that reading involves the construction (or re-construction) of the text read. The meaning of the text is not on the page to be extracted by readers; rather, it is what results when they engage (e.g., scan, study, reread) texts for whatever purposes they may have and with whatever knowledge, values, and preoccupations they bring to it. Thus the written marks on the page more resemble a musical score than a computer program; they are marks cuing or prompting an enactment or realization by the reader rather than a code requiring deciphering. (1981:xi)

Compare the survey of empirical reading research in Spiro:

Meaning does not reside in words, sentences, paragraphs, or even entire passages considered in isolation. . . . What language provides is a skeleton, a blueprint for the creation of meaning. Such skeletal representations must then be enriched and embellished so that they conform with the understander's preexisting world views and the operative purposes of understanding at a given time. This process of knowledge-based, contextually influenced, and purposeful enrichment in comprehending language is what is referred to as "construction." (1980:245).

30. AI sometimes equates *bottom-up* with *forward reasoning*, that is, with working from the problem state to the goal, and equates *top-down* with *backward reasoning*, that is, with working backward from the goal to the problem state (Barr and Feigenbaum 1981:24). Though related to ours, this use is different and is more pertinent to game-playing rather than to text-understanding tasks.

31. To insist on top-down grammars is not to deny the relevance or the relative independence of lower-level grammars. A complete grammar will build into lower-level grammars an account of possible relations to higher-levels and will have a general account of subordination of lower-levels to higher levels (including an account of how usually subordinate, lower-level considerations can themselves become dominant).

32. Kintsch (1974) makes some claims not to offer a bottom-up model, but with respect to text meaning, Kintsch's decision to begin with unanalyzed "word concepts" rather than "semantic primitives" is only an analytical convenience. It would make no difference if the word concepts were represented not by words but by feature bundles.

33. The point here is exactly analogous to that reached by Michel Foucault in his top-down analysis of the role of power in the workings of social codes: "Power is everywhere; not because it embraces everything, but because it comes from everywhere. And 'Power' . . . is simply the over-all effect that emerges from all these mobilities, the concatenation that rests on each of them and seeks in turn to arrest their movement. One needs to be nominalistic, no doubt: power . . . is the name that one attributes to a complex strategical situation in a particular society" (1976:93).

34. Among literary theorists, this position is now perhaps most closely associated with Stanley Fish, though on this score he is something of a latecomer. (Fish [1980] gives a personal record of how he flirted with compositionality and then rejected it.) The now widely repeated argument about the importance of beliefs, knowledge, etc., only restates the well-established philosophical argument without confronting the question of grammar.

440 • Notes

Even an account as elaborate as Iser's (1978) takes as unproblematic the relation between meaning and "the structures of the [non-literary] text," which he too explains in terms of conventions, beliefs, knowledge, etc.

22. Works Cited

Abelson, R. P. Concepts for Representing Mundane Reality in Plans. In Bobrow and Collins, 1975.

Anscombe, G. E. M. *Intention*. 2nd edition. Ithaca: Cornell University Press, 1963.

Bach, E. and Harms, R., eds. *Universals in Linguistic Theory*. New York: Holt, Rinehart & Winston, 1968.

Barr, A. and Feigenbaum, E. A., eds. *The Handbook of Artificial Intelligence*. 2 vols. Los Altos, CA: William Kaufmann, 1981–82.

Bartlett, F. C. *Remembering: A Study in Experimental and Social Psychology*. Cambridge: Cambridge University Press, 1932.

Bates, Madeleine. The Theory and Practice of Augmented Transition Grammars. in Bolc, 1978.

Bobrow, Daniel G. and Collins, A. M. *Representation and Understanding: Studies in Cognitive Science*. New York: Academic Press, 1975.

Bobrow, Daniel G., Kaplan, R. et al. GUS: A Frame-driven Dialog System. *Artificial Intelligence*, 8, 155–173, (1977).

Bobrow, Daniel G. and Winograd, Terry. An Overview of KRL: A Knowledge Representation Language. *Cognitive Science*, 1, 3–46, (1977).

Boden, Margaret. *Artificial Intelligence and Natural Man*. New York: Basic Books, 1977.

Bolc, Leonard, ed. *Lecture Notes in Computer Science: Natural Language Communication with Computers*. Vol. 63. New York: Springer-Verlag, 1978.

Bower, Gordon H. Plans and Goals in Understanding Episodes. In Flammer and Kintsch, 1982.

Braddock, R. The Frequency and Placement of Topic Sentences in Expository Prose. *Research in the Teaching of English*, 8, 287–302, (1974).

Bruce, B. C. Case Systems for Natural Language. *Artificial Intelligence*, 6, 327–360, (1975).

Cavell, Stanley. *The Claim of Reason: Wittgenstein, Skepticism, Morality, and Tragedy*. Oxford: Clarendon Press, 1979.

Charniak, Eugene. The Case-Slot Identity Theory, *Cognitive Science*, 5, 285–292, (1981).

——On the Use of Framed Knowledge in Language Comprehension. *Artificial Intelligence*, 11, 225–266, (1978).

Coleman, Linda and Kay, Paul. Prototype Semantics: The English Word "lie." *Language*, 57, 26–44, (1981).

Colomb, Gregory G. and Williams, Joseph M. *Discourse Structures*. Research Report #3. Writing Programs of the University of Chicago, 1987.

——Perceiving Structure in Professional Prose. In Odell and Goswami, 1986.

Cullingford, Richard E. SAM. In Schank and Riesbeck, 1981.

Dahlgren, Kathleen. The Cognitive Structure of Social Categories. *Cognitive Science*, 9, 379–398, (1985).

Davis, R. and de Jong, Gerald. Prediction and Substantiation: Two Processes that Comprise Understanding. *Proc International Joint Conference on Artificial Intelligence*. Tokyo, Japan, 1979.

de Beaugrande, Robert and Dressler, W. U. *Introduction to Text Linguistics*. London: Longmans, 1981.

Dehn, Natalie. Story generation after TALE-SPIN. *Proceedings of the Seventh IJCAI*, 16–18, (1981).

de Man, Paul. *Allegories of Reading: Figural Language in Rousseau, Nietzsche, Rilke, and Proust*. New Haven: Yale University Press, 1979.

Dennett, Daniel. *Brainstorms: Philosophical Essays on Mind and Psychology*. Cambridge, MA: Bradford Books/MIT Press, 1978.

Derrida, Jacques. Structure Sign and Play in the Discourse of the Human Sciences. In Derrida, 1978.

———*Of Grammatology*. Trans. G. C. Spivak, 1974. Baltimore: Johns Hopkins University Press, 1967.

———*Writing and Difference*. Trans. A. Bates. Chicago: University of Chicago Press, 1978.

Dillon, G. *Constructing Texts: Elements of a Theory of Composition and Style*. Bloomington: Indiana University Press, 1981.

Eco, Umberto. *The Role of the Reader: Explorations in the Semiotics of Texts*. Advances in Semiotics. Bloomington: Indiana University Press, 1979.

Eisner, Elliot ed. *Learning and Teaching the Ways of Knowing*. Chicago: National Society for the Study of Education. Distributed by the University of Chicago Press, 1985.

Fikes, Richard and Nilsson, Nils. STRIPS: A New Approach to the Application of Theorem Proving to Problem Solving. *Artificial Intelligence*, 189–208, (1971).

Fillmore, Charles J. Frame semantics. In *Linguistics in the Morning Calm*. Linguistic Society of Korea. Seoul: Hanshin, 1982.

———The Case for Case. In Bach and Harms, 1968.

Findler, N. V., ed. *Associative Networks: Representation and Use of Knowledge by Computers*. New York: Academic Press, 1979.

Fish, Stanley. *Is There a Text in this Class? The Authority of Interpretive Communities*. Cambridge, MA: Harvard University Press, 1980.

Flammer, August and Kintsch, Walter, eds. *Discourse Processing*. Amsterdam: North-Holland, 1982.

Foucault, Michel. *The History of Sexuality: Volume I: An Introduction*. Trans. R. Hurley, 1978. New York: Random House, 1976.

Frege, Gottlob. *Translations from the Philosophical Writings of Gottlob Frege*. P. Geach and M. Black, eds. Oxford: Basil Blackwell, 1966.

———On Sense and Meaning. In Frege, 1966.

Glaser, Robert. Education and Thinking: The Role of Knowlege. *American Psychologist*, 39, 93–104, (1984).

Grimes, J. E. *The Thread of Discourse*. The Hague: Mouton, 1975.

Halliday, M. A. K. and Hasan, R. *Cohesion in English*. London: Longman, 1976.

Holland, Dorothy and Quinn, Naomi. *Cultural Models of Language and Thinking*. Cambridge: Cambridge University Press, 1987.

Iser, Wolfgang. *The Act of Reading: A Theory of Aesthetic Response*. Baltimore: Johns Hopkins University Press, 1978.

Jackendoff, Ray. A System of Semantic Primitives. In Schank, 1975.

Katz, J. J. and Fodor, J. A. The Structure of a Semantic Theory. *Language*, 39, 170–210, (1963).

Keenan, Edward L., ed. *Formal Semantics of Natural Language*. Cambridge: Cambridge University Press, 1975.

Kintsch, Walter. *The Representation of Meaning in Memory*. Hillsdale, NJ: Lawrence Erlbaum Associates, 1974.

Kintsch, Walter and van Dijk, Teun. Toward a Model of Text Comprehension and Production. *Psychological Review*, 85, 363–394, (1978).

Knapp, Stephen and Michaels, Walter Benn. Against Theory. *Critical Inquiry*, 8, 1982.

Lakoff, George. *Women, Fire, and Dangerous Things: What Categories Reveal About the Mind.* Chicago: University of Chicago Press, 1987.

Lakoff, George and Johnson, Mark. *Metaphors We Live By.* Chicago: University of Chicago Press, 1980.

Lakoff, George and Turner, Mark. *More Than Cool Reason: A Field Guide to Poetic Metaphor.* Chicago: University of Chicago Press, 1989.

Locke, W. N. and Booth, A. D. eds. *Machine Translation of Languages.* New York: Technology Press of MIT and Wiley, 1955.

Mandl, H., Stein, N. L., and Trabasso, T., eds. *Learning and Composition of Text.* Hillsdale, NJ: Lawrence Erlbaum Associates, 1984.

Meehan, James. Tale-Spin. In Schank and Riesbeck, 1981, pp. 197–226, (1981).

Metzing, D., ed. *Frame Conceptions and Text Understanding.* Berlin: de Gruyter, 1979.

Meyer, B. J. F. Identification of the Structure of Prose and its Implications for the Study of Reading and Memory. *Journal of Reading Behavior*, 7, 7–47, 1975a.

——*The Organization of Prose and Its Effects on Memory.* Amsterdam: North-Holland, 1975b.

——Text Dimensions and Cognitive Processing. In Mandl, Stein, and Trabasso, 1984.

Minsky, Marvin. *A Framework for Representing Knowledge.* In Winston, 1975.

Mitchell, W. J. T., ed. *Against Theory.* Chicago: University of Chicago Press, 1985.

Nagy, William. Figurative Patterns and Redundancy in the Lexicon. Ph.D. dissertation, University of California at San Diego, 1974.

Newell, A. and Simon, H. A. *Human Problem Solving.* Englewood Cliffs, NJ: Prentice-Hall, 1972.

Odell, Lee and Goswami, Dixie. *Writing in Non-Academic Settings.* New York: Guilford Press, 1986.

Ortony, Andrew, ed. *Metaphor and Thought.* Cambridge: Cambridge University Press, 1979.

Petofi, J. S. and Reiser, H., eds. *Studies in Text Grammar.* Dordrecht: Reidel, 1973.

Reddy, Michael. *The Conduit Metaphor.* In Ortony, ed., 1979.

Rosch, Eleanor. Categorization of Natural Objects. *Annual Review of Psychology*, 32, 89–115, (1981).

——Principles of Categorization. In Rosch and Lloyd, 1978, pp. 27–48.

——Human Categorization. In *Advances in Cross-Cultural Psychology.* New York: Academic Press, 1977.

——Cognitive Reference Points. *Cognitive Psychology*, 7, 532–547, (1975a).

——Cognitive Representations of Semantic Categories. *Journal of Experimental Psychology: General*, 104, 192–233, (1975b).

Rosch, Eleanor and Lloyd, B. B., eds. *Cognition and Categorization.* Hillsdale, NJ: Lawrence Erlbaum Associates, 1978.

Rumelhart, David. Notes on a Schema for Stories. In Bobrow and Collins, 1975.

Schank, Roger C. *Conceptual Information Processing.* North-Holland, 1975.

Schank, Rogert C., ed. *Theoretical Issues in Natural Language Processing.* Cambridge, MA: MIT Press, 1975.

Schank, Roger C. and Abelson, R. P. *Scripts, Plans, Goals, and Understanding.* Hillsdale, NJ: Lawrence Erlbaum Associates, 1977.

Schank, Roger C. and Riesbeck, Christopher K., eds. *Inside Computer Understanding: Five Programs Plus Miniatures.* Hillsdale, NJ: Lawrence Erlbaum Associates, 1981.

Searle, John. *Minds, Brains and Science.* Cambridge, MA: Harvard University Press, 1984.

———Minds, Brains, and Programs. *The Behavioral and Brain Sciences,* 3, 417–424, (1980).

Smith, E. E. and Medin, D. L. *Categories and Concepts.* Cambridge, MA: Harvard University Press, 1981.

Spiro, R. J. Constructive Processes in Prose Comprehension and Recall. In Spiro, Bruce, and Brewer, 1980.

Spiro, R. J., Bruce, B. C., and Brewer, W. F., eds. *Theoretical Issues in Reading Comprehension.* Hillsdale, NJ: Lawrence Erlbaum Associates, 1980.

Sweetser, Eve Eliot. *Semantic Structure and Semantic Change.* Ph.D. diss., University of California, Berkeley. To be published by Cambridge University Press, 1984.

———The Definition of Lie: An Examination of the Folk Models Underlying a Semantic Prototype. In Holland and Quinn, 1987, pp. 43–60.

Turner, Mark. *Death is the Mother of Beauty.* Chicago: University of Chicago Press, 1987.

Uspenskij, Boris. *A Poetics of Composition: The Structure of the Artistic Text and Typology of a Compositional Form.* Trans. V. Zavarin and S. Wittig, 1973. Berkeley: University of California Press, 1970.

van Dijk, Teun. *Macrostructures.* Hillsdale, NJ: Lawrence Erlbaum Associates, 1980.

van Dijk, Teun, and Kintsch, Walter. *Strategies of Discourse Comprehension.* New York: Academic Press, 1983.

Weaver, W. Translation. In Locke and Booth, 1955. pp. 15–23.

Weizenbaum, J. ELIZA—A Computer Program for the Study of Natural Language Communication between Man and Machine. *Communications of the Association for Computing Machinery,* 9, 36–45, (1966).

Wilkins, John. *Essay towards a Real Character, and a Philosophical Language,* London, 1668.

Wilks, Yorick. Making Preferences More Active. *Artificial Intelligence,* 11, 197–223, (1978).

———Methodological Questions about Artificial Intelligence: Approaches to Understanding Natural Language. *Journal of Pragmatics,* 1, 69–84, (1977).

———Preference Semantics. In Keenan, 1975.

Winograd, Terry. *Understanding Natural Language.* New York: Academic Press, 1972.

Winston, P., ed. *The Psychology of Computer Vision.* New York: McGraw-Hill, 1975.

Wittgenstein, Ludwig. *Philosophical Investigations.* New York: Macmillan, 1953.

———*Tractatus Logico-Philosophicus.* Trans. D. F. Pears and B. F. McGuiness, London: Routledge and Kegan Paul, 1961.

List of Contributors

Christopher Butler is a Fellow and Tutor in English at Christ Church, Oxford.

Ralph Cohen, Kenan Professor of English and Director of the Commonwealth Center for the Study of Literary Change, University of Virginia, is also editor of *New Literary History*.

Gregory G. Colomb is Associate Professor of English and Director of Writing Programs at the Georgia Institute of Technology.

Hélène Cixous is head of the Centre d'Etudes Feminines and Professor at the University of Paris VIII-Vincennes at Saint-Denis.

Jonathan Culler is Professor of English and Comparative Literature and Director of the Society for the Humanities at Cornell University.

Arthur C. Danto is Johnsonian Professor of Philosophy at Columbia University and the art critic for *The Nation*.

Alastair Fowler is a Visiting Commonwealth Professor at the University of Virginia, and Regius Professor Emeritus of Rhetoric and English Literature at the University of Edinburgh.

Henry Louis Gates, Jr. is Professor of English, Comparative Literature, and Africana Studies at Cornell. He is the General Editor of *The Norton Anthology of Afro-American Literature*.

Sandra M. Gilbert is Professor of English at Princeton University.

Gerald Graff is Professor of English at Northwestern University and codirector of Northwestern University Press.

Susan Gubar is Professor of English at Indiana University, Bloomington.

Geoffrey H. Hartman is Karl Young Professor of English and Comparative Literature at Yale University.

Wolfgang Iser, Professor of English and Comparative Literatures at the University of Konstanz and the University of California, Irvine, is founder and coeditor of *Poetik and Hermeneutik*.

444

Hans Robert Jauss is Professor of Literary Criticism and Romance Philology Emeritus, University of Konstanz. He is the founder of *Poetik und Hermeneutik*.

Rosalind Krauss is Professor of Art History at Hunter College and the Graduate Center, City University of New York. She is co-editor of *October Magazine.*

J. Hillis Miller is Distinguished Professor of English and Comparative Literature at the University of California, Irvine.

Martha Nussbaum is Professor of Philosophy and Classics and an affiliate of the Department of Comparative Literature at Brown University.

Jean-Marie Schaeffer is working at the Centre National de la Recherche Scientifique, Paris, and is a member of the Centre de Recherches sur les Arts et le Langage at the École des Hautes Études en Sciences Socials.

Roy Schafer practices psychoanalysis in New York City.

Elaine Showalter is Professor of English at Princeton University.

Catharine R. Stimpson is Professor of English and Dean of the Graduate School at Rutgers University.

Brian Stock is a Fellow of the Institute of Mediaeval Studies, Toronto.

Mark Turner is an Assistant Professor of English at the University of Chicago and was a founding member of the Berkeley Cognitive Science Group.

Gregory L. Ulmer is Professor of English at the University of Florida.

Hayden White is Presidential Professor of Historical Studies at the University of California, Santa Cruz.